W9-BAH-492

The Developing Child

Understanding Children and Parenting

Eighth Edition

Holly E. Brisbane

Glencoe McGraw-Hill

New York, New York   Columbus, Ohio   Woodland Hills, California   Peoria, Illinois

Glencoe/McGraw-Hill

*A Division of The **McGraw·Hill** Companies*

Send all inquiries to:
Glencoe/McGraw-Hill
3008 West Willow Knolls Drive
Peoria, Illinois 61614-1083

ISBN 0-02-642708-7 (Student Edition)
ISBN 0-02-642709-5 (Teacher's Wraparound Edition)

Printed in the United States of America

6 7 8 9 10 11   071/043   04 03 02

CONTENTS IN BRIEF

CONTENTS

UNIT 4   THE CHILD FROM ONE TO THREE 344

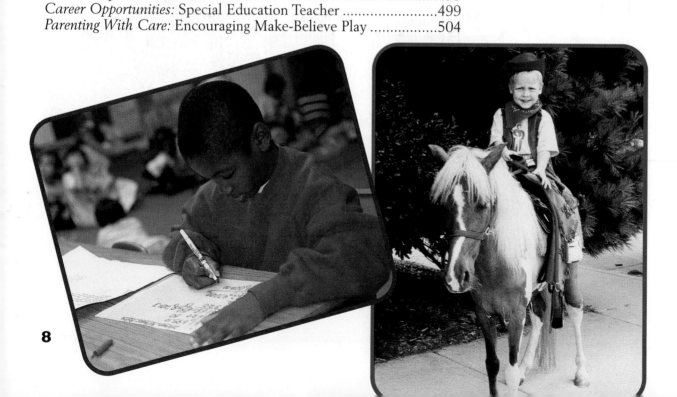

FEATURES

Parenting With Care

CAREER OPPORTUNITIES

Practicing Parenting

The World's Children

Ask the Experts

Pat Brodeen
Teen Parent Coordinator

Pat Brodeen received her bachelor and master of science degrees from Texas Tech University, where she specialized in child development and family studies. She has taught at Theodore Roosevelt High School in San Antonio, Texas, for more than 25 years. Twelve years ago, Ms. Brodeen began teaching a class for teen parents. She finds her greatest reward in watching a teen develop into a responsible parent. She advises teen parents to "stay in school if you want to provide a good life for yourself and your baby."

Dr. Van D. Stone
Pediatrician

Dr. Stone is practicing pediatrician in Tupelo, Mississippi. He received his medical degree at the University of Mississippi Medical Center at Jackson, Mississippi, and his pediatric training at Arkansas Children's Hospital. Over the last twenty years he has seen a substantial change in the area of children's nutrition and is pleased that "parents of all ages are open to new ideas and methods of quality care." Many of his patients' mothers are teens whose mothers participate in raising their grandchildren. He finds that these younger grandmothers are familiar with current trends in child care, and he values the wisdom of their experience.

Jacqueline Mault
Director of Special Services

Jacqueline Mault, who received her doctorate from the University of Oregon, has worked in early childhood education administration, in a state Department of Education, in a public school, and as a consultant. As Director of Special Services in Toppenish, Washington, she develops and manages programs for children from birth through high school. Dr. Mault urges people to "continue to meet the demands of changing families and work within communities for quality, comprehensive care and education."

Rachel Thompson Perkins
College Instructor of Child Development Technology

Rachel Thompson Perkins is a Child Development Technology Instructor at Hinds Community College in Utica, Mississippi. She received her master of science degree in Home Economics from Mississippi College, specializing in Child Development. She has worked in the public school system for more than 21 years teaching family and consumer sciences and occupational child care and guidance. She was very instrumental in beginning a school-to-work program and an after-school program for the lab school. Her main goal in teaching is to ensure that students "reach their potential while helping them develop a marketable skill."

Jean Illsley Clarke
Author and Parenting Workshop Facilitator

Jean Illsley Clarke is the director of J.I. Consultants in Minneapolis, where she designs and directs workshops in self-esteem, parenting, and group dynamics. She has written several books, magazine articles, and journal articles; appeared in videotapes and hosted a local television show; and received an honorary doctorate from Sierra University in Costa Mesa, California. Much of her background comes from teaching and conducting research abroad. These experiences have convinced her that "all human needs are the same, and children are best cared for by adults whose needs are met."

Children, Parenting, and You

CHILDREN LEARN WHAT THEY LIVE

If children live with criticism, They learn to condemn.

If children live with hostility, They learn to fight.

If children live with ridicule, They learn to be shy.

If children live with shame, They learn to feel guilty.

If children live with tolerance, They learn to be patient.

If children live with encouragement, They learn confidence.

If children live with praise, They learn to appreciate.

If children live with firmness, They learn justice.

If children live with security, They learn to like themselves.

If children live with acceptance and friendship, They learn to find love in the world.

—*Dorothy Law Nolte*

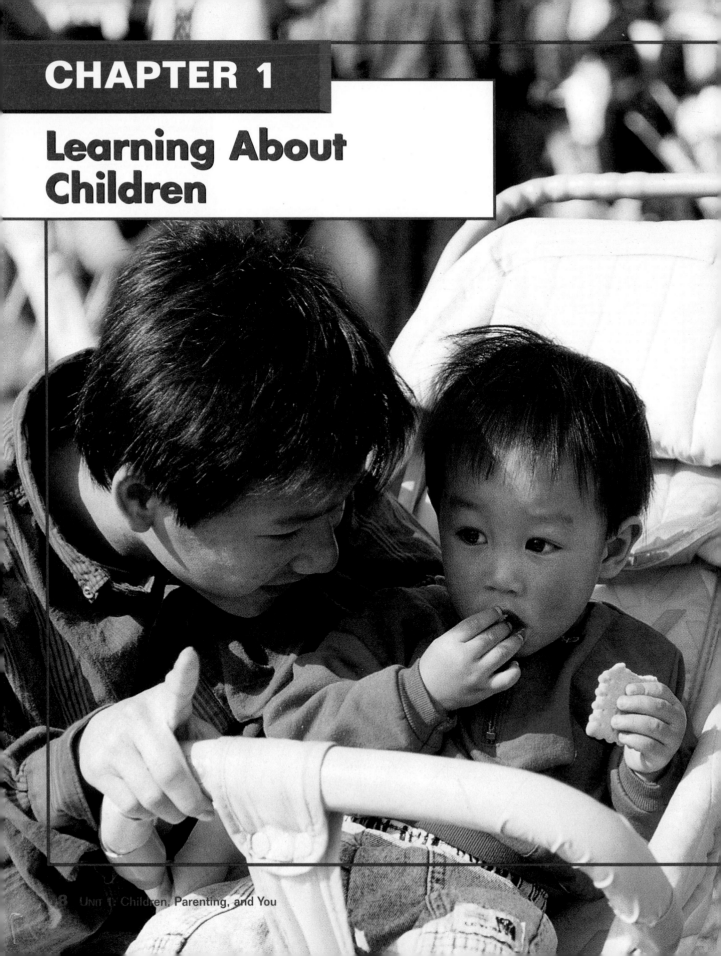

CHAPTER 1
Learning About Children

Seven-month-old Chen is lucky, although he does not know it. Chen's parents talk to him constantly as they move about the house. They talk to him while they are changing his diaper and getting his food ready. They talk to him while they are bathing him and feeding him. His mother talks to him while running errands as Chen sits in his car seat. Everyone in the family talks to him when they go rollerblading after dinner while he rides in the stroller. His parents take turns singing to him when they put him to sleep at night. The next morning, when Chen wakes up, the talking starts all over again.

The constant talking is amazing because Chen—only seven months old—cannot answer back. Chen is lucky because all this talking is one of the best influences on his growing brain.

"Talking to a young child is one of the best influences on brain development."

Beginning Your Study of Children

Have you ever seen a baby's delight as he plays peekaboo? Have you ever seen the look of triumph on a five-year-old's face as she ties her shoes? If so, you may have felt a surge of pleasure yourself. Children's mastery of new tasks reminds older people of just how far they themselves have come.

KEY TERMS

behaviors
caregivers
child development

OBJECTIVES:

- Explain why childhood is an important time of development.
- Identify ways that play benefits children.
- Describe reasons for studying children.

Why Is Childhood Crucial?

Childhood is a time of preparation. Scientists are finding that early childhood may be the most important stage of life for a person. They have learned that in the first few years of life, the brain develops connections between nerve cells that allow it to think and control the body in certain ways.

These connections do not simply happen on their own. They can be encouraged when caregivers give a child lots of stimulation—especially by talking to him or her often. The links that develop in the child's brain promote mental and physical skills. They also have an impact on the social and emotional characteristics of that person as an adult.

Another way children form these links is through play. Researchers have learned a great deal about **child development**, the study of how children master new skills. They have found, for instance, that children benefit from play in many ways:

- **Physically.** Activities such as running, climbing, jumping rope, and riding a bicycle help the large muscles of the back, arms, and legs develop. Making jigsaw puzzles, finger painting, and stringing beads all help a child learn to control the small muscles of the hands.
- **Socially.** At first children play alone. Gradually, they learn to play together. From this play, they learn how to take turns, work together toward a common goal, lead, and follow.
- **Emotionally.** Play can help children work through life's challenges and problems. For example, acting out the role of a parent, firefighter, or jungle explorer can lessen the frustrations of being a small person in a big world.
- **Morally.** Play teaches valuable lessons about right and wrong. Through play, children learn to follow rules and act fairly toward others. They learn to share and to encourage the efforts of others.

Giving children a loving, caring environment does more than help them have a healthy childhood. It helps them prepare for the future. *What responsibilities do you think parents have toward children?*

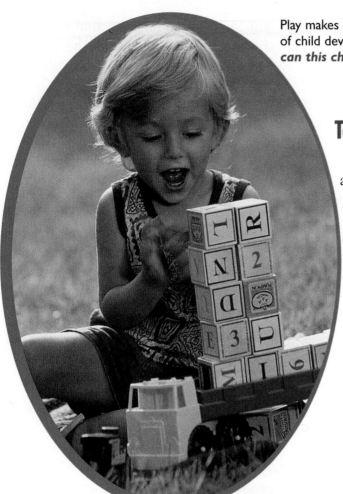

Play makes an essential contribution to all five areas of child development. *How many different things can this child learn from playing with blocks?*

To Understand Children

In studying children, you will read about them, observe them, talk with them, play with them, and help them. In the process, your understanding of children will grow:

- **You will better understand why children act, feel, and think as they do.** It can be difficult to understand children, especially before they learn how to talk. Yet there is a set of typical **behaviors**—ways of acting or responding—for each stage of childhood. For example, Denise was puzzled that her two-year-old brother never played with a two-year-old neighbor boy, even when they were in the same room. Then Denise learned in her child development class that it's normal for two-year-olds to play alongside each other but not with each other.

- **You will understand the importance of caregivers.** Parents and others who take care of children are called **caregivers.** As you learn how children develop, you will see why they depend on others for such a long time. You will also learn why they need affection to grow emotionally and why they need the guidance and support of older people.

Finally, by learning about children, you'll come to see that children are fun. The more time you spend with children, the more you can appreciate how delightful they are. In their innocence, humor, generous affection, and curious minds, they are fascinating—and rewarding—to be with.

- **Intellectually.** A toy or game doesn't have to be "educational" to promote mental development. Simple activities such as singing nursery rhymes, stacking blocks, and sorting through a box of buttons help a child learn language, balance, and how to organize objects.

Why Study Children?

You can benefit from studying children in many ways. You can improve your understanding of how children grow and change. Studying children can also improve your understanding of yourself—and help you think about your future.

To Gain Skills

As you learn about children, you will also gain many skills. You'll learn what children need at each stage of development and how to meet those needs.

You will have opportunities to apply your growing knowledge whether in a child care center, as a babysitter, or in your own family. The practice that you gain as a caregiver will make you a more effective one, too. Knowing how to bathe a baby, prepare a nutritious meal for a toddler, or encourage a three-year-old to settle down for a nap will give you confidence. Children feel more comfortable with people who care for them with confidence.

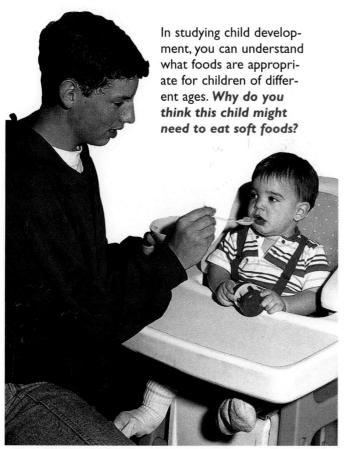

In studying child development, you can understand what foods are appropriate for children of different ages. *Why do you think this child might need to eat soft foods?*

To Understand Yourself

As you learn to understand children better, you will also come to know yourself better. You will learn more about what makes you the person you are.

You may think of yourself as a different person from the child you once were. It's true that you have grown and changed in many ways. No one changes completely, however. Who you are right now has developed from the child you once were and will continue to develop into your adult self. Experience, education, and life's situations help you mature. Still, the self you have already developed will always be part of you.

Ask family members or older friends what you were like as a young child. They may describe you as quiet, amazingly independent, or constantly active. Do those descriptions match how you are today?

To Build for the Future

Your increased understanding of children will be valuable not only now, but also throughout your life. Today, it may help you become a better babysitter, teacher's aide, or playground supervisor. In the future, your understanding of children may help you as a parent or in a career related to children.

Studying children can also help you make decisions about your future career. One high school student was planning on being a nurse until he took a child development course. By the end of the course, he wanted to be a teacher. "Now that I understand them better," he explained, "I like kids more than I used to."

Ask the E?perts

Rachel Perkins
Child Development Technology
Instructor
Hinds Community College
Utica, Mississippi

MAKING *a Difference in a Child's Life*

What can I do to make a difference in a child's life?

You're off to a good start in making a positive difference to children—you are interested, and you are concerned about learning to help children. Even your attitude in itself is a contribution to a child with whom you spend time.

I think what you need now is a chance to watch others work with children; you also need many comfortable experiences with children that will help you develop your own abilities and confidence.

Probably the best way to learn about interacting with children is to watch parents and teachers who work successfully with young children. Take time to observe these experienced people carefully. How do they talk to children? How do they listen? How do they use words, facial expressions, and physical contact to encourage and support children? How do they use positive reinforcement to guide children's behavior?

After your observation, think about how each teacher or parent approached the children. Which of these approaches will you feel comfortable using when you interact with children?

Remember when you observe successful parents and teachers, you are looking at models. As you learn more and more about children and about successful approaches and attitudes, you will develop your own personal style of interacting successfully with young children.

It's also important to remember that, just as teachers and parents serve as your models, you serve as a model for young children. Young children will observe—and try out for themselves—the words, attitudes, and actions that you demonstrate.

Thinking It Through

1. How do children learn from you when you are a caregiver? Give a specific example.
2. Think of someone whom you admire. How can you model your behavior on that person?

Finally, learning about children can help you think about parenthood and prepare for its responsibilities. One student in a parenting course said, "I never realized that being a parent was so much work!"

Children and You

You are in an excellent position to study children—close to adulthood and able to think and reason but young enough that you can still remember what it was like to be a child. As you learn, you'll find some of your opinions reinforced and others challenged. You'll discover answers to questions that puzzled you—and find new questions that have no answers yet. Perhaps someday you will help answer them.

English poet William Wordsworth revealed a truth when he wrote, "The child is the father to the man." Childhood is a vital and significant time. In this period, the foundations are laid for the person who will be an adult. Knowing about childhood can help you help children build a strong foundation. It can also give you insight into the foundation you built for yourself.

SECTION 1-1 REVIEW

✔ Check Your Understanding

1. Why is childhood an important time of life?
2. What is one way parents and other caregivers stimulate the development of connections in a child's brain?
3. Name the five areas in which children benefit from play. Give an example of how children benefit from a particular kind of play.
4. Identify four reasons to study children.
5. Why is it helpful if caregivers are confident?
6. Would you assume two-year-olds and four-year-olds act the same when frustrated? Why or why not?

Putting Knowledge Into Practice

1. **Comparing.** Think of two younger children you know who are two different ages. Compare how they play. What kinds of play activities do they prefer? How do they act when they play?
2. **Applying.** Make a poster that expresses how you are a unique person.
3. **Observing and Participating.** Look at all the different people in your class. Write a paragraph explaining the range of different talents and abilities your classmates possess.

Understanding Childhood

Think back to when you were a child. How did it feel when you could not do something that you wanted to do, such as tie your shoes? How did it feel when you *did* manage to tie them? What makes children different from adults?

KEY TERMS

adolescence
developmental tasks
environment
heredity
neurons
self-esteem
sequence

OBJECTIVES:

- Compare childhood in the past and present.
- Outline the leading ideas about how children develop.
- Describe five principles of development.
- Explain influences on development.
- Explain the role of self-esteem in development.

What Is Childhood?

Childhood is a period of life separate from adulthood. During this period, development occurs very rapidly. Babies are almost completely dependent on adults for every need. When childhood ends, people begin to prepare to be independent.

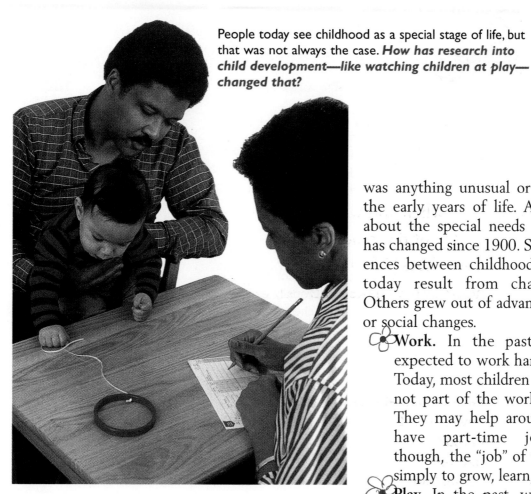

People today see childhood as a special stage of life, but that was not always the case. *How has research into child development—like watching children at play—changed that?*

Many people have made a special study of this period. They have looked at how children develop, what their needs are, and how those needs can best be met. Perhaps their most important finding is that childhood has a profound influence on later life.

Childhood has not always been considered a separate, important stage of life, however. In fact, childhood—as we know it—is a fairly recent "discovery."

Childhood Past and Present

Until the twentieth century, few people in Western civilization believed that there was anything unusual or important about the early years of life. Adults knew little about the special needs of children. That has changed since 1900. Some of the differences between childhood in the past and today result from changing attitudes. Others grew out of advances in technology or social changes.

Work. In the past, children were expected to work hard at an early age. Today, most children in our society are not part of the world of adult work. They may help around the house or have part-time jobs. Nowadays, though, the "job" of young children is simply to grow, learn, and play.

Play. In the past, when children did play, they had fewer toys than today's children. Until the 1800s, toys were often homemade, carved out of wood or made from other natural materials. Even common games like baseball, football, and basketball didn't develop until the middle or late 1800s. Video games became available only in the 1970s.

Education. Public education for all children did not become widespread in the United States until the early 1800s. Even then, schools were small and often included children of different ages and abilities. Today, schools are larger than the one-room schools of the past. Students now use modern technology such as computers to learn.

The World's Children

Children at Work

*T*he fact that most American children don't work today reflects more than changing attitudes toward childhood. It also results from the general economic well-being of Americans.

In many societies throughout the world, people struggle to grow enough food to feed their families. For these people, having every person possible helping to grow food can make the difference for survival. Among the Kipsigis people of Kenya, children are traditionally expected to work, not to play. Children as young as two are given household chores. By age six, Kipsigis children spend about half their time working. Another factor influences this practice as well. Kipsigis parents believe that by giving children tasks to do, they are promoting the children's intelligence.

——— SHARE YOUR THOUGHTS ———

1. Why do Kipsigis parents give their children work to do?

2. How are parents in our society helped if children do chores around the house? What kinds of chores do you think children are capable of doing at ages five, ten, and fifteen?

• **Health.** Before the twentieth century, parents could not hope to raise every child born to them. Diseases caused the deaths of children in almost every family. In developed countries today, deadly diseases have been controlled. Better nutrition has helped children grow and thrive as never before.

• **Dress.** Until the seventeenth century, children were dressed as small adults. Around that time, children's clothing became more common, although these styles didn't permit much activity or play. Today, many boys and girls wear clothing that is similar in style and color. Practical, washable, lightweight clothing allows them comfort and freedom of movement.

• **Parental love.** Although childhood in the past was different in many ways from today, one thing hasn't changed—parents' love for their children. Parents have always worked hard to build lives for their children and to raise them as moral, responsible people.

Children's lives have changed in many ways from the past to the present. They are less likely to work and spend more time in school. *How have advances in health care changed children's lives?*

The Study of Children

This century, many researchers have studied children closely. They have developed theories about development. Not everyone agrees on how parents and educators should apply their findings. Still, taken together, these scientists have made great strides in understanding how children develop. The chart on pages 30-31 summarizes the work of some major researchers. You will learn more about theories of child development throughout this book.

Brain Research

One of the most important areas of recent research has been about the work-ings of the brain. What scientists have learned has great significance for caregivers.

At birth, the brain has billions of nerve cells called **neurons** (NER-ons). In the first year of life, babies begin to develop pathways that link their neurons. These links "wire," or program the brain so that it can control different functions of the body or thinking processes. The wiring of the brain takes place very quickly. Babies just four days old respond more to their parents' language than to another language. Over time, the higher, thinking areas of the brain are "wired," giving the growing baby greater control over his or her body and understanding of the world. A two-year-old has almost as many of these pathways as an adult.

Major Theorists of Child Development

These are just a few of the researchers and thinkers who have added to our understanding of child development in the twentieth century.

Theorist	Findings or Ideas	Significance
Sigmund Freud (1856-1939)	Freud believed that personality develops through a series of stages. Emotional experiences in childhood have profound effects on a person as an adult.	The idea that early experiences affect adult life has profound importance for anyone caring for a child.
Maria Montessori (1870-1952)	Montessori stressed that children learn by using their senses and that they learn best by pursuing their interests.	Children need to be given objects to manipulate so they can exercise their sensory learning.
Arnold Gesell (1880-1961)	Gesell developed basic information about the order in which children master various skills and the typical rate of this development.	Parents and other caregivers need to be aware of the standard course of development.
Jean Piaget (1896-1980)	Piaget, the first to study children in a scientific way, focused on how children learned. He said that children go through four stages of thinking that shape how they see and learn about the world.	Children should be given learning tasks that are suitable for their stage of thinking.
Lev Vygotsky (1898-1934)	Vygotsky believed that both biological development and cultural experience influenced children's ability to think and learn. He said social contact was essential for intellectual development.	Children should have many opportunities for social interaction to develop intellectually.
Erik Erikson (1902-1994)	Erikson, like Freud, said personality develops through stages. He thought that each stage includes a unique psychological crisis. If that crisis is met in a positive way, the individual develops normally.	Parents and other caregivers must be aware of a child's needs at a particular stage and be sensitive to the child's needs at that stage.

How fast children developed.

Theorist	Findings or Ideas	Significance
B. F. Skinner (1904-1990)	Skinner argued that when a child's action repeatedly brings positive effects, it will be repeated and learned. When negative results repeatedly occur, the child will eventually stop the action.	Parents and other caregivers can use rewards and punishments to try to influence a child's behavior.
Albert Bandura (1925-)	Bandura said that children learn by modeling. He disagreed with Skinner. He pointed out that although the environment shapes behavior, behavior also affects the environment.	Since children learn by modeling, parents and caregivers must provide good examples.
Robert Coles (1929-)	Coles has studied children's moral development. He stresses the important role that parents and other caregivers play by the examples they set.	For children to adopt moral learning, parents must show moral behavior.

The areas of the brain that control different kinds of learning reach their peak at different times. The illustration on pages 32-33 shows the differences.

What Researchers Have Found

None of these researchers has provided all the answers to questions about how children develop. Taken together, though, their findings and ideas have revealed much.

Characteristics of Development

As you have read, children develop through certain stages. Researchers have found that this development follows five patterns:

- **Development is similar for everyone.** Children go through the same stages in about the same order. For example, all babies lift their head before they lift their body and stand before they can walk.

When the brain is ready to learn

The brain is most ready to learn different tasks at different times. The area of the brain that controls vision is active by the second month of life. The part that relates to reasoning becomes active as early as six months. How can parents use these research findings?

Math/logic: Starting at age one

Vision: Starting in the first year

Vocabulary: Starting in the first year

Acquiring a second language: Starting at age one

Emotional control: Starting in the first year

Motor development: Starting before birth

Music: Starting at age three

Social attachment: Starting in the first year

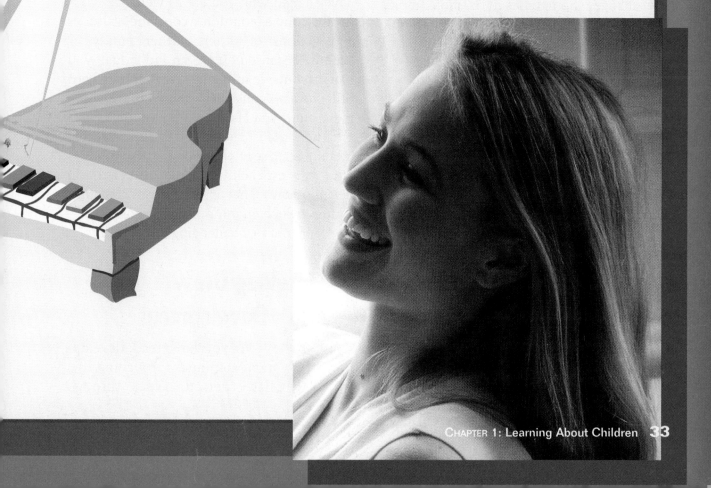

- **Development builds on earlier learning.** Development follows a step-by-step pattern, a **sequence**. The skills a child learns at one stage build directly on those mastered earlier. Before learning to run, a child must learn to walk. Before learning to speak in sentences, a child must learn to say single words.
- **Development proceeds at an individual rate.** Although all children follow a similar pattern of development, each child is an individual. The rate of growth differs from one child to another.
- **The different areas of development are interrelated.** Researchers find it easier to focus on one area of development at a time. In fact, however, changes in many areas are taking place at the same time.
- **Development is continuous throughout life.** The rate of development changes. Sometimes it is more rapid and sometimes less so. Still, development never stops.

Influences on Development

Each child develops as an individual because of the unique combination of factors that he or she experiences. Those factors can be placed in two categories:
- **Heredity.** One important influence is **heredity** (huh-RED-uht-ee), the passing on of certain characteristics from earlier generations. Blood type, eye color, and hair color are some characteristics set by heredity.
- **Environment.** Another major influence is the **environment,** the people, places, and things that surround and influence a

person. Your family, home, friends, and community are part of your environment.

Scientists and philosophers have debated for many decades about which factor has the stronger influence. Some have said heredity, often called *nature*, whereas others say environment, called *nurture*. Most now agree that the two work together. Psychiatrist Stanley Greenspan summarized this view: "Nature affects nurture affects nature and back and forth."

Consider how heredity and environment have worked together to make you you. From your parents and past generations, you inherited certain physical characteristics. From your family, you also learned certain attitudes and ways of doing things. You have also been influenced by the world around you. What you read, what you see on television, the type of community you live in—all these and countless other factors have shaped who you are as well.

Of course, you don't copy the attitudes and actions of others, either family or friends. Because you are an individual, you react to outside influences in your own way. Still, you are constantly shaped by the people around you and by your experiences.

The same is true for every child. During infancy and early childhood, outside forces have an especially strong influence on development. That is why caring for children is such an important responsibility—and such a challenging opportunity.

Lifelong Growth and Development

As you have read, development continues throughout life. Each person passes through various stages *after* childhood. This is sometimes called the human life cycle. As with the stages of childhood, people follow typical patterns of development through these stages. Of course, people differ in how each individual experiences this pattern.

Development After Childhood

Each stage of life has particular challenges called **developmental tasks**. Meeting those challenges—mastering those tasks—prepares a person for the next stage.

You are now in the middle of **adolescence**, the stage of life between childhood and adulthood. In this important time of growth and change, you have three developmental tasks to achieve:

- Finding your identity.
- Becoming independent.
- Planning for your life's work.

After adolescence comes young adulthood, when a person is in his or her twenties. The young adult finishes preparing for a career and begins working in it. Many people marry in this period.

In middle life, from the thirties to the fifties, a person typically meets these tasks:

- Establishing roots, during the thirties, often means forming a family and settling down to live in a particular place.
- Reevaluating life leads many people in their forties to question the choices that they have made.
- Finding stability and peace, in the fifties, is a matter of.readjusting. Very often the children who were born in earlier stages have moved out to make homes of their own. People in their fifties often have a new sense of freedom as a result. They may travel or spend time with friends.

The final stage of adulthood is late life, which covers the years from the sixties on. The main developmental task for a person in this period is to come to terms with life.

Development does not end in childhood—it continues throughout life. *What are the developmental tasks of adolescents?*

The Role of Self-Esteem in Development

One resource that can help you meet these developmental tasks—both those of childhood and of adulthood—is something you carry within you. Your **self-esteem** is how you value yourself. If you think of yourself as a worthwhile person, your self-esteem is high. If you think you are not important, you have low self-esteem.

High self-esteem is more than just a good feeling about yourself. It is a tool that you can use to push yourself to achieve new goals. Look at the developmental tasks of adolescence. It may sound simple to say that one task is to plan your future. Making those plans isn't easy, though. You may feel confused trying to sort out what kind of a person you are and what kind of a job you want. Many people do. You may stumble on the road to a career. Many people do. High self-esteem can give you the energy to pick yourself up and the confidence to start moving down that road again.

Perhaps your self-esteem is low. It doesn't have to stay that way. Learning about child development will help you appreciate the tough challenges you have already met. Feel proud of what you have done, and remember that you have the resources within you to do even more.

SECTION 1-2 REVIEW

✔ Check Your Understanding

1. In what five areas does childhood today differ from childhood in the past?
2. Describe the importance of the work of Freud and Erikson in the understanding of young children.
3. What work do the pathways in the brain perform?
4. Identify the five principles of development and explain one.
5. What two factors influence development? Give an example of each.
6. What are the stages of life after childhood?
7. How can self-esteem affect development?

Putting Knowledge Into Practice

1. **Applying.** Give an example of how findings about brain development can be utilized by parents.
2. **Analyzing.** Suppose you heard someone say to a child "Do as I say, not as I do." In light of the ideas of Bandura and Coles, is this an effective way of guiding children's behavior? Why or why not?
3. **Observing and Participating.** Think of an activity that you are able to perform well—perhaps a hobby, a sport, or a subject in school. Create a chart showing how the skills you have or the facts you know now built on skills or facts that you learned earlier.

CAREER OPPORTUNITIES

Parent

A CONVERSATON WITH CATHY REYNOLDS

How did you become interested in being a parent? I always wanted to have children. My husband and I simply waited until we were ready for the responsibility.

What are the tasks and responsibilities of being a parent? You name it! You have to teach children and encourage them. You have to help them learn right and wrong, how to tie their shoes, what foods are good for them, and what their name and address is.

What is the work environment like? The work environment is your home. I try to make ours as safe and comfortable and interesting as I can.

What are the working hours like? All day, every day. With the baby, I feed and change her, play with her, then start over again. Just when I have a moment to sit, she wakes up again! Older children need interaction and supervision, too.

What aptitudes are needed to be a parent? The first thing is patience. The second is cheerfulness. You can get very tired with children, but you can't let it show. You have to be curious about things because as they get older, children always ask "why?" Finally, you need to let go. Children have to learn to live their own lives. All you can do is give them the best start you can.

Career Facts

PARENT

Education and Training. Most parents learn on the job, although they can get help and information from classes and from books and other sources.

Career Outlook. Parents will always be in demand.

CONNECTING SCHOOL TO CAREER

1. **Basic Skills.** Write a letter to the editor explaining why you think parents should or should not be paid for their work.
2. **Information.** If you were creating a course for future parents, what information and skills would you teach?

Observing Young Children

Child development comes to life when you can observe young children in action. Learning how to observe young children is an important skill for parents, teachers, and others who take care of children. With this skill, they constantly learn from what they see. In this course you will have the opportunity to observe children both formally and informally.

KEY TERMS

anecdotal record
baseline
confidentiality
developmental checklist
frequency count
interpret
objective
running record
subjective

OBJECTIVES:

- Explain the importance of observing young children.
- Evaluate four methods of observation.
- Discuss guidelines for observing young children.
- Explain why confidentiality is essential when observing and interpreting the behavior of children.

Why Is Observing Children Important?

One of the most important reasons for observing children is to better understand their development. For instance, infants pass through a sequence of stages in learning to walk. Observing infants at various stages of this sequence makes it easy to see how each skill leads to the next. When you understand the sequence, you can provide experiences that will promote each skill.

Reading about child development gives valuable information about children. Observing children makes what has been read come alive. *What can caregivers learn about themselves through observing children?*

Observation also helps you learn about individual children. Each child moves through developmental stages at his or her own rate. By observing a particular child's development, you can identify activities to meet his or her particular needs.

Observing children can also help you identify children who have special needs or disabilities. Once they have been identified, they can receive the special care and learning opportunities they need.

Finally, observing children gives you important feedback about your own approach to parenting or teaching. By observing how children respond to your attempts at rewarding behavior, for instance, you can judge how effective your methods have been.

How to Observe Young Children

Observing children goes far beyond just watching what children do. Knowing how to observe effectively will make your observations more valuable.

Objective Versus Subjective Observations

One of the most difficult parts of becoming a good observer is learning to separate facts from opinions. Study these two observations of the same event:

- **Example 1.** Robbie is feeling selfish. He won't let anyone play with the toys in the sandbox. He gets mad at Eric a lot.

- **Example 2.** Robbie is sitting in the sandbox. He reaches out and takes a truck away from Eric. Eric grabs for the truck, but Robbie pulls it away. "It's my turn now," says Robbie, looking Eric straight in the face.

Example 1 is a **subjective** observation, one that uses personal opinions and feelings, rather than facts, to judge or describe things. Notice that, from reading this observation, you can't tell what really happened between Robbie and Eric. The observer in Example 1 is not recording facts, but writing down his or her opinions about Robbie's feelings.

Example 2 is an **objective** observation, It uses facts, not personal feelings or prejudices, to describe things. The observation describes what the observer saw and heard—and nothing more.

Objective observations are much more valuable than subjective ones. Subjective observations are based on the false assumption that the observer knows what is going on in the child's mind. They can also be misleading. Robbie might not have been acting selfishly. He might have had an earlier agreement with Eric about taking turns.

Finally, because subjective observations don't record facts, they are hard for others to use. A teacher who knew that Robbie was generally shy at school would want the full facts presented in Example 2. She might interpret Robbie's behavior as a sign of growing self-assertion.

It takes practice and discipline to write objective observations. Remember to record only what you see and hear, avoiding such words as *happy* or *sad*, *good* or *bad*. You can record that a child smiled or laughed, but avoid saying that the smiling or laughing child is happy. Such a comment is an interpretation, and interpretation takes place later. Stick to the facts.

Types of Observation Records

Four methods of recording observations are particularly useful. You will learn more about these later.

Observations can be written up subjectively or objectively. *Why are objective reports more useful to other child care workers?*

- **Running record.** The **running record** involves writing down for a set period of time everything observed about a particular child, group, or teacher. This method is useful if you are just getting to know a child or a group. A running record is also useful for analyzing a certain area of development, such as social interaction or motor skills.

- **Anecdotal record.** The **anecdotal** (AN-ek-DOE-tuhl) **record** is similar to a running record, but the behavior recorded all has to do with the same issue. (In a running record, *all* behaviors are recorded.) For example, suppose that you want to see how a child is adjusting to a new child care center. In that case, you could use an anecdotal record to write down how the child behaved at arrival time each day for several days.

- **Frequency count.** The **frequency count** is a tally of how often a certain behavior occurs. You can simply use a tally mark on a record sheet to note how often a particular child takes the action under study. This kind of record is useful when you are trying to change an undesirable behavior. First you find a **baseline,** which is a count taken before any methods are made to change the behavior. As you work with the child to change the behavior, you can make other frequency counts to see how well the efforts to change the behavior are succeeding.

- **Developmental checklist.** The **developmental checklist** identifies a series of specific skills or behaviors that a child of a certain age should master. To use the checklist as a record, simply check off the skills or behaviors you observe in a particular child.

When making observations, it is important to write down what you see as you see it. Otherwise, important information may be forgotten. Each record should include basic information: the date and time of the observation, the number of children present, their names and ages, and the number of adults working with them. The record should also mention the setting where you made the observation (school or home) and exactly where it occurred (for example, on the playground or in the science area).

How to Act While Observing

While observing young children, you don't want to be noticed. Your presence can affect their behavior and make it difficult for you to gather objective information. There is also the possibility that you might disrupt an adult who is with the child you are observing.

When observing, then, you should blend into the background. Choose a spot outside the area where the children are. Sit or stand off to one side with notepad and pen or pencil ready. Be sure to read the observation assignment completely before beginning to observe.

At first, the children may come over to ask who you are and what you are doing. Answer politely, but briefly. Avoid asking them any questions, which will only encourage more talking. If the children need to be persuaded to return to their

Do you think this worker is positioned appropriately to make an observation? Why?

activities, you might say "I am writing a story about how children play. If you go back to playing, I can write about you in my story."

At times, you may need to stop being just an observer and take action. If, for instance, you see that a child is hurt and no adult knows about it, you should step in.

Sometimes an observer who is doing a developmental checklist does need to interact with the child. For instance, to find out how well a child can catch and throw a ball, you may take part in the activity.

Using Observations

Once you have the information, the next step is to use it. To **interpret** is to find meaning in, explain, or make sense of something. When recording, you made every effort to be objective. Now, however, it is time to express your ideas and opinions about what you observed. An hour's run-

ning record of a child's behavior is of little use unless you analyze and interpret it.

Anyone who observes children and interprets information about them should follow the basic rule of **confidentiality** (CON-fuh-den-shee-AL-uht-ee), or privacy. This means sharing the information only with the child's main caregivers or your child development teacher.

Remember that you observe the child only for a brief time. How you interpret that child's behavior may not be accurate because you do not have all the relevant facts. For this reason, it's important to avoid saying things about a child to someone else. Comments such as "Devon is spoiled" or "Kendra's child is a slow learner" might lead to rumors that could hurt the child or family.

You may, of course, have questions or concerns about a child you observe or a child care setting that you visit. You can discuss these questions with your child development teacher—and no one else.

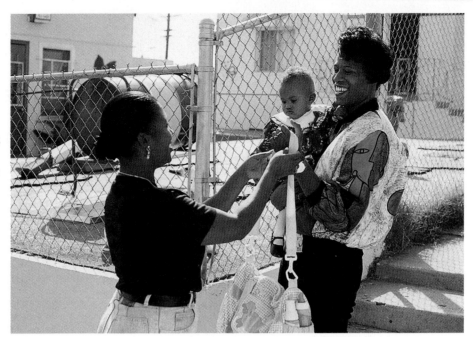

Child care workers must be sure that they maintain confidentiality about their observations. *Why is this so important?*

SECTION 1-3 REVIEW

✔ Check Your Understanding

1. List four reasons for observing children.
2. What is the difference between a subjective and objective observation?
3. Describe the four types of observation records.
4. What basic facts should an observation record include?
5. List three things an observer can do to avoid disrupting children he or she is observing.
6. In what two situations is it acceptable to participate?
7. What does it mean to interpret an observation?

Putting Knowledge Into Practice

1. **Analyzing.** Why is confidentiality important in observations of children?
2. **Applying.** Clip a photo showing at least two children from a magazine or newspaper. Imagine you are viewing the scene. Write an observation of it. Share the photo and your observation with the class.
3. **Observing and Participating.** With a partner, observe a child for at least ten minutes. Each of you should write a running record. Then compare records with your partner to identify which notes are objective.

Working with Children

Juan wanted a career working with children, but he didn't know how to find out more about his options. You may be looking for more information about careers but be unsure of how to find it. A good place to start is with an understanding of the working world.

KEY TERMS

aptitudes
entry-level job
lifelong learner
paraprofessional
professional
service learning
systems
work environment
work-based learning

OBJECTIVES:

- Name three different levels of jobs.
- Describe different methods of researching jobs.
- Identify factors that can be used to analyze careers.
- Describe skills needed to prepare for jobs of the future.

Levels of Jobs

Jobs are often categorized on the basis of the amount of education and training needed. There are three general levels of jobs:

A dance teacher is a professional. Workers can also be classified as paraprofessionals and entry-level workers. *What level would a dental assistant be?*

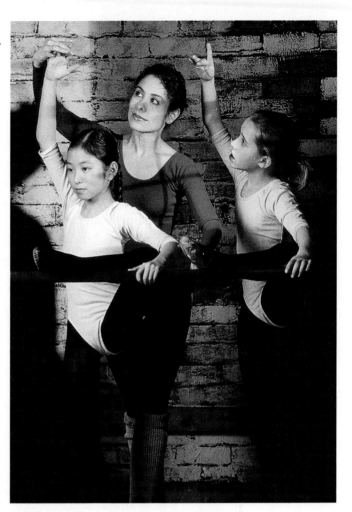

- An **entry-level job** is for beginners in a field—people with limited education and training. This is the kind of job that many people take when they enter a career area. A sales clerk in a children's store has an entry-level job. Most people, however, don't stay at this level. With more experience and perhaps more education, many move up to more responsible jobs.

- A **paraprofessional** (pare-uh-pro-FESH-uhn-uhl) has education beyond high school that trains him or her for a certain field. Many paraprofessional jobs require a related degree from a two-year college. An assistant teacher in a child care center, for instance, is a paraprofessional.

- A **professional** has a position that requires at least a degree from a four-year college or technical school in a particular area. Many professionals have more advanced degrees and years of experience. Professionals may be in charge of programs or supervise entry-level workers and paraprofessionals. Teachers are professionals.

Entry-level jobs can be used to test your interest in a career field—and how suitable you are for that field. Linette worked one summer as a camp counselor. She wanted to see if she really liked working with children. By the end of the summer, she knew that she loved it.

Finding Career Information

Linette found out about this career area through work experience. There are many other ways of learning about careers. One source is this textbook. Each chapter has a "Career Opportunities" feature that gives you information about a job related to children.

Gathering Information

The search for career information can lead you in many directions. On-line sources, libraries, and people can all be helpful.

The Internet, particularly the World Wide Web, can help put you in touch with trade and professional organizations, government resources, job listings, and people working in various careers. Many Web sites have links to related sites. You can also start your search by entering key terms to indicate what you are looking for.

Don't overlook your school or public library as a resource. The librarian can help you with your search. Most libraries have three key books published by the United States government that offer job information. These may also be available on-line.

- *The Guide for Occupational Exploration* describes many careers.
- *The Occupational Outlook Handbook*, which is revised every two years, gives detailed information on hundreds of jobs.

- *The Occupational Outlook Quarterly*, published every three months, updates information on trends in careers.

You can also talk to people about their work. Ask your school counselor, teachers, relatives, and friends about possible contacts. Most people are happy to share information on their career with others. Remember, though, that these people are doing you a favor. Find a time to meet that is convenient for them. Show up on time and with a list of questions. Be sure to thank the person—and send a thank-you note afterward, too.

Work Experience

As Linette discovered, you can learn a great deal about a career—and yourself—by working. Summer work and part-time jobs are good ways to get started.

The library has many sources of career information. *How could a librarian help you use these sources?*

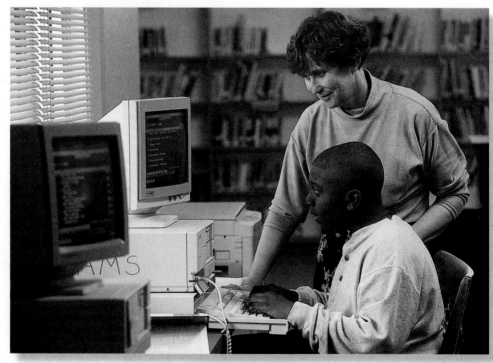

You can also learn a great deal by being a volunteer. Although volunteers don't get paid for their work, it offers great experience. Sometimes it even leads to a paying job. Tran volunteered to work in his city's children's museum. After volunteering one summer, he was given a full-time job the following summer.

Some school or community programs offer direct work experience. Some communities have programs called **service learning**, in which doing some form of community service is part of schoolwork. Some school systems offer special **work-based learning** programs in which students combine in-school and on-the-job learning.

Work experience gives you another benefit besides a real taste for a job. You meet people who might be able to put you in touch with others in the career area which interests you. Coworkers may also be willing to serve as a reference that a prospective employer can contact for information about your skills and character.

- **Work with people, information, or technology.** Each career tends to emphasize one area over another. A teacher works mainly with people. An editor of children's books works mainly with information. A designer of children's clothing works mainly with technology.
- **Work environment.** The **work environment** is the physical and social surroundings at the workplace. Camp counselors work outdoors; nurses work indoors. Some people work alone, but others work in teams. Which kind of environment is most appealing to you?
- **Working hours.** Many people work from 9:00 in the morning to 5:00 at night, but many other workers have different hours.
- **Aptitude.** Your **aptitudes** are your special talents or abilities. These talents can lead you to a particular career.

Analyzing Careers

Now you know where to look for career information, but what should you try to find out? You can use eight factors to analyze careers:

- **Tasks and responsibilities.** What does a worker in this career do? Is the work the same every day or varied? Is the pace fast or slow? How much control does a worker have over the work?

What talents does this career require?

- **Education and training.** Though many people gain experience on the job, they need the right education to land that job in the first place. Start planning now for the education you need. Your school counselor, libraries and the Internet have information about opportunities for schooling and how to fund it.
- **Salary and benefits.** Income goes up with training and education. Income also tends to rise with experience—a first-year paraprofessional earns less than a coworker with five years in the same job.
- **Career outlook.** What do experts think will happen to this job in the future? Will the demand for the job grow or shrink? Answers to these questions affect how easy it will be for you to find a job. Many sources estimate future trends for a variety of jobs.

Preparing for Your Future

Preparing for your career involves more than learning about careers. You also have to prepare yourself for the working world of today—and the future. In the past, people often stayed with the same career all their lives. Now, people tend to change careers several times. To succeed in this working world, people need to be flexible.

People can build that flexibility by developing their skills in certain areas:

- **Basic skills.** To succeed at work, workers need skills in reading, writing, math, speaking, and listening.
- **Thinking skills.** Workers need to be able to learn, reason, think creatively, make decisions, and solve problems.
- **Personal qualities.** Workers need to show responsibility and have the ability to organize and manage themselves.
- **Resources.** Workers must know how to use time, money, materials, space, and people to get work done efficiently.
- **Interpersonal skills.** Workers need to be able to get along with coworkers and customers. They must work well in teams and with people from different cultures.

More and more jobs in the future will require computer skills. Becoming computer literate will help prepare you for those jobs. *How can using computers add to your ability to use resources?*

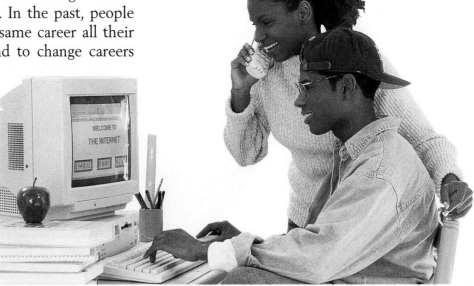

- **Information.** Workers must know how to find, organize, and use information.
- **Systems.** Some systems are made up of things, like phone or computer systems. Others—like work teams—are made up of people. All **systems** are complex networks of people or objects that interact with each other. Families, schools, and communities are all examples of systems.
- **Technology.** Workers need to be able to use technology effectively.

Career counselors also stress another feature of the new world of work. Workers need to be prepared to be **lifelong learners**—to spend their whole lives learning new information and new skills. With technology changing so rapidly, the tools you use in your first job are likely to be replaced in just a few years—and those new tools, too, will be replaced. By keeping up-to-date with these changes, you can make yourself a more effective worker.

SECTION 1-4 REVIEW

✔ Check Your Understanding

1. Differentiate between the three levels of jobs.
2. What kinds of information about careers can you find in libraries?
3. What is the difference between service learning and cooperative education programs?
4. Where can you learn about the education you need so you can prepare for different jobs?
5. Which of the skills workers need in the future do you think is the hardest to gain? Why?
6. Why is lifelong learning important?

Putting Knowledge Into Practice

1. **Comparing.** Write a paragraph comparing the kind of information you can learn about a job from sources of published information, such as libraries, to what you can learn from interviewing someone who has the job.
2. **Prioritizing.** Write the list of factors you can use to analyze careers. Then rank them in order of most to least important, as you see them.
3. **Observing and Participating.** Choose one of the skills needed for a worker to be successful. If you have a job, explain how that job requires the skill. If you don't, explain how that skill is used by someone whose work you observed in your everyday life.

Parenting With Care

Helping Children Play

Play is children's most important activity.

It is how they learn and how they experience their world. Among the most important things that parents can do, then, are to encourage children to play and to provide them opportunities to play.

Psychologist Bruno Bettelheim added another important role. Parents, he says, need to take an interest in children's play. "All too often," he warned, "parents look on play as a 'childish' pastime." He reminded parents, though, that they must "give play not just respect and tolerance but also their personal interest" for the child to truly benefit. Children's play changes as they grow. Here's a brief look at typical kinds of play enjoyed by children of different ages:

- **From birth to age one.** Mobiles, rattles, mirrors, games with sounds, peekaboo, and hide-and-seek.
- **From ages one to two.** Blocks, stacking toys, music boxes, pail and shovel, shape sorters, play clay, pots and pans, push-and-pull toys.

- **From ages two to three.** Wheeled vehicles, clothes for dressing up, easy climbing games, crayons and fingerpaints, puzzles, large beads for stringing.
- **From ages three to four.** Balls, books, interlocking blocks, bubbles for blowing, climbing equipment, hand puppets, paper and scissors, sandbox, tricycle.
- **From ages four to five.** Simple board games, toy camera, magnets, musical instruments, paints and paintbrushes, playground equipment.
- **From ages five to seven.** Ball games, craft materials, dolls, bicycle, gardening tools, paints and paintbrushes.
- **From ages seven to twelve.** Board games, card games, models, complex imaginary play, magic, sports.

This is not a complete list, of course. Children at each stage enjoy a huge range of play, some involving running and jumping and others that call for sitting still. The important thing for parents is to give them a chance to play what they enjoy—and what they will learn from.

Following Up

1. Choose any one of the age groups listed. What kind of play could a child that age enjoy that doesn't involve any toys?

2. **Management.** Name three activities that involve no expenditure of money.

3. **Thinking Skills.** Why does Bettelheim say that parents must show an interest in children's play?

Summary

✔ Studying children helps you learn about children and yourself and prepare for the future. (Section 1-1)

✔ Research has revealed how children learn and develop. (Section 1-2)

✔ Development follows a predictable set of steps, but each person develops at his or her own rate. (Section 1-2)

✔ There are several methods used to record observations of children. (Section 1-3)

✔ Observations should be objective, private, and interpreted carefully. (Section 1-3)

✔ Some sources of career information involve direct experience. (Section 1-4)

✔ Workers need to develop key skills to prepare for a changing workplace. (Section 1-4)

9. How does learning about careers through work experience benefit you? (Section 1-4)

Thinking Critically

1. **Synthesizing.** Think of a play activity you enjoyed when you were younger. Make a list of ways you benefited from that activity.

2. **Analyzing.** "Only students who are parents, who plan to become parents, or who want careers in a child-related field should learn about children." Do you agree or disagree? Why?

3. **Distinguishing Fact and Opinion.** Identify the facts and the opinions in this observation: "Sarah was happy when she arrived today. She was smiling and singing a song. When her mother left, she began to play. She did not like the way Ron played with the blocks, so she hit him."

Reviewing the Facts

1. Why is childhood an important time? (Section 1-1)

2. What four benefits do you get from studying children? (Section 1-1)

3. What is the significance of the work of Bandura and Coles? (Section 1-2)

4. What is the significance of recent research on the brain? (Section 1-2)

5. Babies in Florida and Sri Lanka both begin to speak at the same time. What principle of development does this reveal? (Section 1-2)

6. Why is an objective observation more useful than a subjective one? (Section 1-3)

7. With whom should you discuss any questions or concerns you have about a child you observe? (Section 1-3)

8. Name three sources of information about a career. (Section 1-4)

Taking Action

1. **Looking at Theorists.** Research the work of one of the child development theorists profiled in the chapter. Make an oral presentation describing what you learned. *(Communication)*

2. **Writing Objectively.** Think of something that happened in one of your classes today. Write an observation, remembering to keep it objective. *(Communication)*

CONNECTIONS

 Cross-Curricular Connections

1. **Language Arts.** Write a poem or story that reflects the idea that childhood is an important time of life.

2. **Health.** Research any of the following diseases: smallpox, measles, polio, diphtheria, malaria. What impact did the disease have on children in the past? What can health care workers do now prevent and treat the disease? Make a poster displaying your findings.

 Workplace Connections

1. **Systems.** Compare and contrast the purpose, organization, and flexibility to change in a school system and a locally owned child care center.

2. **Basic Skills.** Suppose you learned that a certain job paid $400 per week. How much would a person in that job earn in a year? If the worker received a 3 percent salary increase the next year, what would be his or her new weekly and yearly income?

 Family and Community Connections

1. **Making a Time Line.** Create a time line showing your own or someone else's personal growth. Identify at least six developmental stages that you want to chart—when you first spoke or walked or climbed the stairs. Talk to others in your family to find out when you reached the early stages. Use the information to create your time line.

2. **Childhood.** Interview two family members or friends who have a child. Ask what one topic or problem they wish they had known more about. Discuss your findings with the class.

3. **Schools.** Find out if there is a Montessori school in your community. If there is, talk to a teacher or administrator at the school. Ask him or her to describe the methods and materials used. Report your findings to the class.

 Technology Connections

1. **Internet.** Conduct an Internet search to find the latest information about research on the brain. Report your findings to the class.

2. **Computer.** Use a computer program to create a table showing the factors you would want to analyze when considering a career for yourself. Expand on the factors listed in the textbook. Compare your table to those of classmates.

CHAPTER 2

Learning About Families

As far back as Michael can remember, his family was there to help him. He can recall when he was small, and his father would take him on walks and carry him on his shoulders. He can remember riding in the shopping cart while his mother was at the supermarket. He laughs whenever he thinks about the time he and his brother built the huge sand castle at the beach or when they used to shoot baskets at the playground.

All these memories are flooding over him now as he waits for the picture to be taken. Michael and Stephanie are about to have their first picture taken with Michael's parents and their baby. As he waits for the photographer, Michael makes a silent promise to the new baby—a promise that he'll do everything he can to give his daughter as many good memories as he has had.

"Parents build memories for their children."

Understanding Families

In every society, people gather into families. In some societies, family includes only parents and children. In others, aunts and uncles are important parts of the family. No matter how it is defined, though, the family is the foundation on which every human society is built.

KEY TERMS

adoption
blended family
extended family
family life cycle
foster children
guardians
nuclear family
single-parent family
values

OBJECTIVES:

- Explain the functions that families fulfill.

- Describe types of family structures and special issues related to each type.

- Identify stages that families with children go through.

- Analyze trends that affect families today.

The Functions of Family

Each day when she finishes school, Marisa picks up her little brother at the child care center. When they arrive home, she makes him a snack. Then they read, play, or watch television together until their mother gets home from work. Marisa's schedule sounds routine, but underlying these actions is the secret to the importance of family. The members of a family help meet each other's basic needs. Families also prepare children to live in society.

Families take many different forms and include different numbers of people—even different generations. Still, all societies are built on families. *What do you think of when you think about the word family?*

Meeting Basic Needs

All people need food, clothing, and shelter. Families make sure that these basic needs are met.

Can you remember a time when an adult put a bandage on a cut or gave you some medicine when you were ill? Families also make sure that members' basic needs for safety and health are met.

Families meet their members' intellectual needs as well. The family is a child's first teacher, from whom he or she learns language, numbers, colors, and other concepts. In some families, children learn how to do the work they will perform as adults. Later, by encouraging children to do homework, parents contribute to a child's schooling.

Finally, families meet social and emotional needs. Each family member has the opportunity to love and to be loved, to care and to be cared for, to help others and to

A strong family foundation is one of the best gifts to give a child. The family is the child's first connection to the world, and it provides each individual with the chance to love—and be loved. *How can simply spending time with children meet those emotional needs?*

57

receive help. By living in families, we learn how to get along with others—how to share and take turns, how to work together toward a common goal.

The Developing Brain

Children need an environment with low stress. When a person feels stress, the body releases a chemical meant to prepare it for a physical response. If there is too much stress over time, though, that chemical can damage the brain's ability to learn and remember.

Preparing Children to Live in Society

Some years ago, Robert Fulghum wrote a book called *All I Really Need to Know I Learned in Kindergarten*. His point was that kindergarten teaches basic rules of life: "share everything," "play fair," "don't hit people," and several more. He might have said the same thing about family. By learning how to live with others in the family, we prepare to live with others in society.

Adults teach children what is important to people in their society. They pass on these **values** in three ways:

- **Through example.** In how they treat children and each other, adults show children how to behave.
- **Through talking.** When a parent tells a toddler not to hit or talks to a teen about respecting people's differences, he or she is passing on values by talking.
- **Through religious training.** In houses of worship, of whatever faith, children learn how to act in a moral way.

Each society has its own culture—its own way of life. Culture is revealed through art and music, through cooking and clothing styles, through how people greet one another and how they view work and play. The family introduces a child to the society's culture.

Adults also teach children about the traditions of society. Do you remember being told why people celebrate Thanksgiving? Adults also explain how to behave. What kind of language is appropriate? How should a child speak to adults? These and similar questions are first answered in the family.

Family Structure

Families come in many shapes and sizes. These variations can be grouped into a few common types.

Nuclear Families

A **nuclear family** includes a mother and father and at least one child. An advantage of the nuclear family is that there are two parents who can both help with raising the children. These families differ depending on how many children there are and how many parents work outside the home.

The Wongs have three children and both parents work outside the home. The Hendersons have one child, who the mother cares for while the father works outside the home. In the Martinez family, both parents work, but at different times so there is always one parent home with their toddler. With the Kojoyians, the mother works outside the home while the father works in a home office and looks after the twins.

The World's Children

Brothers and Sisters

*I*n some societies, the key relationship between females and males is not the one between wife and husband. It is the bond between brothers and sisters.

These societies often trace membership in a family through the mother. A man works to help his sister and her children because it is she—the woman—who continues his family's line. The Ashanti people of Ghana follow this pattern. To Ashanti males, it is more important that their sister has children than that they have children of their own.

Ashanti sisters and brothers remain close throughout their lives. They trust each other and are confident that a sibling will never betray a secret. Many brothers and sisters discuss important matters—such as those involving property or their own children—with each other rather than with their own husbands or wives.

SHARE YOUR THOUGHTS

1. What is the sister-brother relationship like in your culture? How does it differ from the Ashanti way?
2. What kinds of problems might arise in marriages in societies with such strong brother and sister bonds?

Single-Parent Families

A **single-parent family** includes either a mother or father and at least one child. The parent may be unmarried, or the other parent might be gone due to divorce or death.

Raising a child alone puts many demands on the parent. He or she has little free time and has no spouse who can share the work or help solve problems. Single parents often have less income than two-parent families, which makes the burdens of parenting harder.

Many single parents receive help from friends or relatives. They may provide child care while the single parent works. They may help simply by giving the parent a sounding board—someone he or she can talk to in the search for solutions to problems.

Blended Families

A **blended family** is formed when a single parent marries another person, who may or may not be a parent as well. To the child, the parent's new spouse is a stepparent. To the new spouse, each child of the husband or wife is a stepchild. If both spouses have children when they marry, the children become stepbrothers or stepsisters.

At first, the members of a blended family may have problems in establishing the new family unit. Parents and children need time to adjust to one another. Each has to

Ask the E**X**perts

Pat Brodeen
Teacher and Teen Parent Coordinator
at Theodore Roosevelt High School in
San Antonio, Texas

ADJUSTING *to a Blended Family*

Q What special adjustments are needed to live in a blended family?

A You're right to think that blended families provide special challenges to people. Many factors are at work to create problems. Blended families bring together two different sets of habits, customs, or ways of thinking. Often, too, one family moves into the other family's home. The members of one family may still feel pain or regret over the breakup of that family unit.

All these factors can produce friction. Problems can be met, however. It simply requires patience, understanding, hard work, and desire for the new family to succeed.

Here are some tips for building a healthy blended family:

- *Recognize that a new family is being created and that each member can—and should—contribute to it. Be open to new ideas.*

- *Communicate openly, honestly, and with respect and consideration.*

- *Help the new parents build their relationship. A successful marriage will be the foundation for the new family.*

- *Give a chance to stepparents and their children.*

- *Respect relationships with parents outside the household.*

- *Incorporate traditions from both of the former families.*

- *If the new family moves into your home, help them feel at home. If you are moving into theirs, show respect for their things.*

Forming a blended family is like starting in a new school. There are new rules, routines, and people to adapt to. Over time, they will all become familiar. Just be willing to give it time—and to do your part to help.

Thinking It Through

1. Do you think it is easier to form a blended family when children are of similar ages or widely different ages? Explain your answer.

2. Suppose you were a man who married a woman with two children aged six and eight. What would you do to establish a relationship with the children?

learn about and adapt to a new person's habits, likes, and dislikes. Being in a blended family creates challenges.

Extended Families

An **extended family** includes relatives other than a parent or child who live with them. A grandparent may live with a nuclear family or an aunt or uncle with a single-parent family. Another example is an adult child who lives in his or her parent's house.

Sometimes, the term *extended family* is used to refer to people who do not live with the core family but play important roles in the child's life. Among some Native American people, for instance, uncles help instruct boys in the group's traditional religion.

Entering a Family

Most families include the parents' biological children. Some include children who have joined the family in other ways, though. If both parents die, other relatives may take the children into their homes. These **guardians** take all financial and legal responsibility for raising the children.

Practicing Parenting

Telling the Truth About Adoption

*A*t some time or other, adopted children will probably ask why their biological parents "gave me away." They may feel rejected—and they need reassurance. Parents should avoid saying that the biological parents did not want the child. A hug and the comment "I don't know, but I'm glad it worked out this way" can give the child the comfort he or she needs. Showing adopted children that they are loved and wanted helps them realize that they truly belong in the family—and will not be given up again.

Parents also should avoid saying anything against the child's biological parents. Children need to know that putting a child up for adoption is difficult but can be necessary.

APPLY YOUR KNOWLEDGE

1. The adoption of older children can present special challenges to parents and other family members. How many can you identify? How could adoptive parents deal with those problems?

2. How would you tell a child he or she had been adopted? At what age would you tell?

Adoption is a legal process in which children enter a family they were not born into. The adopted child has the same rights as any biological children those parents have.

In the past, children were always matched closely with the families adopting them. Adoption agencies looked carefully at the child's and parents' race, ethnic and religious background, and physical characteristics. The emphasis now is more on finding a good home rather than a home with parents who match the child in some outward ways.

Some children enter a family as **foster children.** Usually, foster children come from troubled families. They need a temporary home until their parents can solve their problems or until the children can find a permanent adoptive home. Foster parents care for the child until then. Adults must apply to the state government to become foster parents. They receive training and a license. They also get some money to help meet the expenses of caring for the child.

The Family Life Cycle

There are many differences between families, but there are many similarities, too. Families go through a series of stages called the **family life cycle.** The chart on pages 64-65 shows these different stages.

Of course, families differ in how they experience this pattern. Families spend different amounts of time in the same stage. Some may return to a stage after they had left it. The Desais, for instance, adopted a baby after their last child moved out of the home. This started them in the expanding stage all over again. Changes like divorce or remarriage have an effect on the pattern too.

Trends Affecting Families

Families of all types are affected by trends in the society around them. These trends may put pressure on families.

Mobility

A hundred years ago, it was not unusual for an adult to die in the same home where he or she had been born. Today, most adults do not even live in the same community where they were born.

As a result, families often lack close, supportive connections with relatives. Family groups need to rely more on their own members and on close friends. They have to work to maintain relationships with grandparents, aunts and uncles, or cousins who live in other areas.

Many adults now are caring not only for their own children but for their elderly parents. *What factors have contributed to this trend?*

Many families now are headed by single parents who work outside the home or by two parents who work. *What can teens who live in these families do to help their parents?*

Aging Population

People now live longer than they used to. Advances in medical practice and better nutrition have contributed to this trend. As a result, more people find themselves caring not only for children, but also for their aging parents. Many elderly people now live in the homes of their adult children, who can better care for them in that way.

This trend has many benefits. It gives children more time to get to know their grandparents. The retired adults can watch the grandchildren to give parents a chance to have some time for themselves.

There may be problems as well. Sometimes elderly parents create financial burdens for the family. When older adults move into the home, the whole family has to adjust to new circumstances. When Carl's sister graduated from college, his parents said that he could have her room and would no longer have to share with his brother. Then they decided his elderly grandmother needed to move in with them.

She was put into his sister's room, and Carl had to continue sharing.

Economic Changes

Many families struggle to make ends meet. This is one of the reasons many mothers work outside the home.

When both parents work outside the home, there is an impact on the children. Families are generally smaller now than they used to be. Couples sometimes delay having children until later in life, and many, to reduce costs, limit the number of children they have. The rise in two-worker families has also added to the growing demand for child care.

The Family Life Cycle

As you study the chart, think about the special challenges and rewards that may be associated with each stage in this life cycle.

BEGINNING STAGE:
A couple works to establish a home and a marriage relationship.

PARENTAL STAGE 1:
Expanding: The couple prepares for and adjusts to parenthood.

PARENTAL STAGE 2:
Developing: As children grow, parents work to meet children's changing needs and help them develop independence.

RETIREMENT:
The couple retires and adjusts to their new lives.

MIDDLE AGE:
The couple renews their relationship and prepares for retirement. If they had children who have left home, this is called the "empty nest" stage.

PARENTAL STAGE 3:
Launching: Children gradually leave home to support themselves. Parents help their children adapt to life on their own.

Workplace Changes

The working world is changing rapidly. Old manufacturing industries are declining. Many companies decide to employ fewer workers. As a result of these changes, people have lost their jobs. While they look for new jobs, families must adjust to reduced income.

Another change is the growing demand for more education and new skills. This has convinced many workers to invest time and money on additional education. These workers are building for the future, but the decision has an impact today. Markeeta's mother decided to take a course in computer programming. Markeeta was happy for her mother, but she also missed having her at home.

Another trend is the growing number of people who work at home. Whether working in the house for an employer or running their own business, more and more people are making the home a place of business. Such an arrangement puts new demands on children, who have to be quiet during work hours and who might be asked to help out.

Technology

The spread of computers and fax machines has contributed to the rise in home offices. Other changes in technology are affecting the family as well. Cable and satellite television and computer games offer people many ways to entertain themselves. The rising popularity of the Internet allows people to obtain information from all over the world. Some critics say that these forms of entertainment tend to isolate people from one another. They say that people are losing the ability to talk to one another.

Some of the new technology also helps family members stay in touch. When Joe Silvestri was caught on an empty road with a car trouble, he used his cell phone to call for help. E-mail gives family members living far apart a chance to communicate.

Coping with Pressures on the Family

All these trends have made profound changes in how people live. Some experts talk about the growing problem of the "frantic family." Parents have to juggle their time to do their work, run the household, and help children with school and after-school activities. As adults and children rush around, they have too little time for each other.

There are some steps you can take to avoid the "frantic family syndrome":

- **Avoid scheduling too many activities.** Allow some free time in every week. This will give each family member a chance to do something for himself or herself—and for the whole family to be together.
- **Watch for clues that family members need a break.** If people are always tired or grumpy, they may need some rest.

- **Focus on responsibilities and on activities that people enjoy.** There isn't enough time to do everything, so concentrate on activities that people must do and those they really like.
- **Schedule family meals.** Meals are excellent opportunities for family members to gather together and share their thoughts and feelings.
- **Organize your life.** Take time each night to prepare school lunches or take out the next day's clothes. Plan trips to consolidate errands. By thinking ahead, you can cut down on trips rushing around and on wasted effort.
- **Maintain your sense of humor.** Having a good laugh—even at yourself—can help relieve the pressure.

SECTION 2-1 REVIEW

✔ Check Your Understanding

1. Give an example of each of the basic needs—physical, intellectual, social, and emotional—that families meet.
2. How do parents pass along values?
3. Describe four different family structures.
4. What is the difference between an adopted child and a foster child?
5. What stage of the life cycle do you think causes the greatest adjustment for a couple: the beginning stage, the first parental stage, or the retirement stage. Explain your answer.
6. How does increased mobility affect families?
7. How have workplace changes affected the family?

Putting Knowledge Into Practice

1. **Applying.** Think about what your culture has to offer and what you have learned from others about your culture. What unique qualities would you like to pass on to future generations?
2. **Drawing Conclusions.** On balance, do you think recent advances in technology are generally a help or a hindrance to family life? Explain why.
3. **Observing and Participating.** Watch a young child and an adult in a public place like a store or a park. How does the child imitate the adult's behavior? What implications does this have for setting an example for children?

CAREER OPPORTUNITIES

Family Counselor

A CONVERSATION WITH PAT WILKINS

How did you become interested in becoming a family counselor? My parents had a great marriage, but many of my friends were not so fortunate. When the parents of my closest friend divorced, he took the blow very hard. I tried to listen and help him. Later, I thought about a career in counseling.

What are the tasks and responsibilities of a family counselor? My main job is to meet and talk with married couples or with parents and children. At these sessions, I try to help them find solutions to their problems.

What is the work environment like? I work in an office in a busy clinic. Some colleagues have their own practices as counselors. They work out of small offices or their homes.

What are the working hours like? I work weekdays plus two nights a week and one Saturday a month. The extra hours make time for clients' work schedules.

What aptitudes are needed to be a family counselor? You have to be a good listener first of all. You also have to be able to hear more than what people say. Sometimes words don't convey people's full meaning. You have to be patient with people who aren't ready to open up, and you have to build up their confidence and trust so that they will. Most of all, you have to treat what people tell you in strictest confidence.

FAMILY COUNSELOR

Education and Training. Family counselors must have a bachelor's degree (sociology, psychology, or social work). Some have master's degrees or doctorate degrees.

Career Outlook. The demand for family counselors is expected to grow moderately.

CONNECTING SCHOOL TO CAREER

1. **Thinking Skills.** What kinds of problems do you think a family counselor would help people with?
2. **Interpersonal Skills.** How would you rate your ability to listen, your patience, your ability to build trust, and your ability to hold information in confidence? In which of these areas do you think you need to improve? Why?

What Parenthood Means

When a baby is born, parents can feel great joy. Some also feel that a great burden has been placed on their shoulders. The decision to become a parent is a serious one. Being a parent radically changes a person's life and creates new responsibilities.

KEY TERMS

emotional maturity
parenthood

OBJECTIVES:

- Describe the changes that parenthood brings.
- List considerations couples should look at before deciding to become parents.
- Use a process to build management skills.

Parenthood Brings Changes

When April was born, Dominique and Ross were more excited than they had ever been. Life with April seemed easy at first. Dominique's parents stayed with them for a week to help. Everyone was smiling all the time, and they were happy.

CHAPTER 2: Learning About Families **69**

however. Having a child brings dramatic and long-lasting changes. Some involve great joy, but others can be difficult to deal with.

New Responsibilities

Raising a child is more than just a day-to-day assignment. It is a lifelong commitment. A child needs physical care, financial support, love, and guidance into adulthood. Once they become parents, people can no longer think of their own needs first. They first have to consider what their child needs.

First-time parents can feel overwhelmed by these new responsibilities. They need to remember that they are not alone. Family and friends can help in many ways, from watching a child while the parent goes shopping to just listening. The community has many resources as well, from religious leaders to government agencies to private groups.

Changes in Lifestyle

New parents have to adjust to major changes in their daily lives. Caring for a child—especially a newborn—takes a huge amount of time and energy. A newborn needs to be fed every few hours, both day and night. In addition, babies must be diapered, played with, and comforted.

With children of any age, parents have limits placed on their personal freedom. They may not be able to go out with friends because they have to stay home to watch the children. Instead of relaxing right after a hard day's work, they have to fix dinner.

Couples are better able to adjust to these changes in life if they prepare for them. They can read books and articles on parenting and child development, talk to

A big part of being a parent is accepting responsibility for a child's welfare—not just for days or weeks, but for many years. *How might this responsibility affect this parent's career?*

After her parents left, though, things changed. The baby cried every night and hardly slept. Dominique and Ross didn't get much sleep, either. Ross dragged himself off to work each day feeling exhausted. Meanwhile, Dominique was alone with the baby—feeling abandoned. Having a baby didn't seem like much fun anymore.

Parenthood begins with having a child by birth or adoption. It doesn't end there,

Practicing Parenting

What Every Child Needs

*P*arents are responsible for meeting ten key needs that each child has:

- ❤ The loving reassurance that comes in hugs.
- ❤ An environment that is safe and healthy.
- ❤ A relationship with caregivers that lasts.
- ❤ Communication by talking and gestures.
- ❤ A chance to see and hear other people.
- ❤ A place where they are safe to explore and learn.
- ❤ Praise, to build their self-esteem.
- ❤ Opportunities to play so they can learn.
- ❤ Music and rhythm.
- ❤ Being read to.

APPLY YOUR KNOWLEDGE

1. Why is it important for children to have lasting relationships with caregivers?
2. Why do you think reading is more important for children than watching television?

Some new mothers, who care for their babies full time, feel that they never have a break. Some new fathers, who work outside the home, may feel that they miss their baby's growth. *How can talking help couples handle these feelings?*

family members or friends who are parents, and take parenting classes. These steps can make the demands of parenthood less surprising and unsettling.

Emotional Adjustments

Parenthood requires many emotional adjustments. Going through so many changes is stressful in itself. On top of that, many parents feel conflicting—and sometimes difficult—emotions, such as:

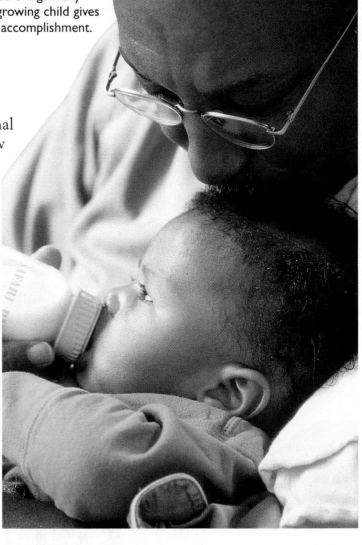

Raising a child brings a parent carries heavy responsibilities—but it also brings many rewards. Seeing a happy, growing child gives a parent a deep sense of accomplishment.

- Fear of not being a good parent.
- Frustration at the loss of personal freedom and the addition of new responsibilities.
- Worry over money matters.
- Jealousy of the baby and the attention he or she gets.
- Depression due to exhaustion or to the physical changes of pregnancy and birth.

Parents can feel confused and troubled by these negative emotions, but these feelings are normal. With time, most parents get over these rough spots. They learn to accept that they will have negative feelings from time to time, and they learn how to handle them.

Changes in Relationships

When people have a child, they are likely to notice changes in how they interact with each other and with other family members. This is especially true for first-time parents.

The birth of a baby is a wonderful time. Some parents, though, feel overwhelmed by negative emotions and begin to bicker or fight with one another. Having patience and being understanding can reduce the danger of frustration boiling over into anger. The key to getting past trouble spots is for the couple to have good communication.

A birth changes the relationship between the child's parents and their parents. Grandparents feel love and joy of their own and want to spend time with the baby.

Many want to help with the baby or with chores around the house. Sometimes, offers of help cause friction. New parents may feel that the grandparents' advice is really a criticism and resent it. At the same time, the grandparents feel hurt if their suggestions are rejected.

Many new parents feel that having a baby brings them closer to their own parents. Understanding what it is to be a parent, they now appreciate their own parents more.

Changes at Work

Having children has an impact on careers. Working women may quit work or cut back on their hours to care for their child. Workers who often worked overtime or weekends before a child may be less willing to put in extra hours once they become parents.

At the same time, a growing number of companies have policies to help working parents. Some have child care facilities at the workplace. Others offer flexible hours or part-time work, which allows a parent to be there when children arrive home from school.

The Rewards of Parenthood

Parenthood brings many joys as well. Nothing is quite like a baby's first smile or hearing a three-year-old say "I love you, Mommy." Parents feel happiness, pride, and love that they never felt before.

By helping children discover the world, parents can see it with new eyes themselves. Having children can enrich an already strong marriage. Finally, raising children can give parents a great sense of accomplishment.

Making Decisions About Parenthood

People who are thinking about parenthood should have a clear picture of what parenthood is. They also need to take a realistic look at themselves to see if they are ready for parenthood.

Emotional Maturity

To handle the changes that parenthood brings, a person needs **emotional maturity.** That means being responsible enough to consistently put someone else's needs before your own. It means being secure enough to devote your full attention to an infant without receiving any attention in return. It means being able to hold your temper when a toddler breaks something you treasure.

Prospective parents should take an honest look at their maturity. Are they equipped to handle the challenges of parenthood? If they have any doubts, it may be best to postpone becoming a parent.

Desire for Parenthood

Some prospective parents hope that having a child will solve some other problem. Not all the reasons for wanting children indicate real readiness for parenthood. Think about the reasons shown on the chart on page 74.

Health Considerations

It is best for both prospective parents to see a doctor for a checkup. If either has a medical problem, it could affect the health of the baby or the person's ability to care for the child. The age of the prospective mother should also be considered. If she is under seventeen or over thirty-five, pregnancy is riskier for both her and the baby.

Reasons for Parenthood

UNSOUND REASONS	SOUND REASONS
• Our marriage is in trouble. Maybe having a baby will solve our problems.	• Having children will add depth to our relationship, which is already strong.
• A baby is someone who will love me and belong to me.	• I want to give a baby my care and love.
• I feel like I'm nobody. Being a parent will make me somebody.	• I feel good about myself and believe that parenthood will be a rewarding experience.
• I want someone who will take care of me when I'm old.	• I want to experience the special bond between parent and child, which lasts a lifetime.
• Our parents want grandchildren.	• I love children, and I want to be a parent.

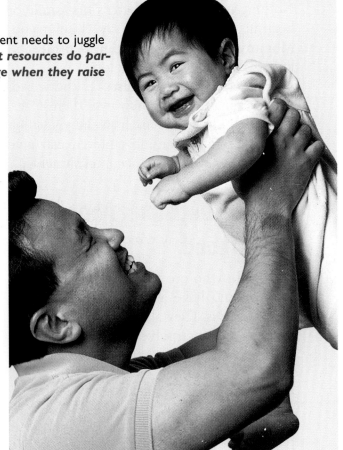

To raise a child, a parent needs to juggle many demands. *What resources do parents have to manage when they raise children?*

Financial Concerns

Raising a child is expensive. Before deciding on parenthood, couples should take a careful look at the costs involved over the years ahead. They may need to change their way of life to prepare for these expenses.

If both prospective parents work, they need to think about what they will do after the baby arrives. Will one leave his or her job to care for the baby? If so, the family's income will drop. Will they both continue working? If so, they will need additional money to pay for child care for the baby.

Management Skills

Whatever the decision, parents will need good money management skills. In fact, they will need to effectively manage their other resources—such as time and energy—as well. Becoming a good manager is a matter of following five steps:

- **Set goals.** Decide what is important to you and then make them into objectives for you to achieve.
- **Identify resources.** Figure out your resources for achieving your goal.
- **Make a plan.** Decide how you will use your resources to meet that goal.
- **Put the plan in action.** Once you have a plan, start working toward your goal.
- **Reevaluate from time to time.** Step back and take stock of your progress. Do you need more resources or different ones? Did you achieve your goal more easily than you expected? What new goals do you now have?

SECTION 2-2 REVIEW

✔ Check Your Understanding

1. Which of the changes caused by parenting do you think is the biggest? Explain your answer.
2. How can parents-to-be prepare for the changes brought on by parenthood?
3. Why are the negative emotions of parenthood hard to accept?
4. What impact can having a child have on a working parent?
5. Use your own words to define *emotional maturity.*
6. Why is "Our parents want grandchildren" an *unsound* reason for having a baby?
7. List the five steps of being a good manager.

Putting Knowledge Into Practice

1. **Drawing Conclusions.** Suppose that people had to earn a license before becoming parents, as they must earn a driver's license. What skills do you think they would need to possess to qualify for the license?
2. **Applying.** With a group of classmates, take turns acting out various situations in which people express their feelings about having a new child. Identify the specific emotions being expressed, and discuss the probable reasons for those emotions.
3. **Observing and Participating.** Observe a new parent caring for a young baby for a period of two hours or more. Briefly describe the demands made by the baby. Then explain how the parent responded to those demands. Did the parent try to accomplish anything else while with the baby, such as studying, working, or doing chores around the house? If so, was he or she successful? If not, why do you think he or she didn't try to do anything else?

Parenting With Care

Building a Healthy Family

A strong family requires everyone working together.

Because families serve such important functions, they should be supported and encouraged.

What does it take for a family to function well? Every member must take responsibility for making the family work. Here are some ways:

- **Feeling Committed.** In a healthy family, each member feels committed to the family as a whole and to each other member. Each person can show this commitment through respect, support, and consideration.

- **Making Time Together.** By spending time together, family members build strong bonds. A family with young children might go to the park. A family with teens might take a hike or biking trip. Even shopping for clothes, cooking meals, or cleaning the home can help build bonds if people share the work together.

- **Communicating.** Families need open and honest communication. Members need to tell each other what they think and feel—and they need to be considerate of other members' thoughts and feelings. Of course, family members will not always agree with each other. If they respect each other, though, they can disagree without hurting feelings.

- **Appreciation.** People in healthy families like each other—and say so. They speak and act affectionately and in a caring way.

- **Shared Beliefs.** Healthy families build their strong relations on a foundation of shared beliefs. These beliefs form a basis for making decisions—they reflect what is important to family members.

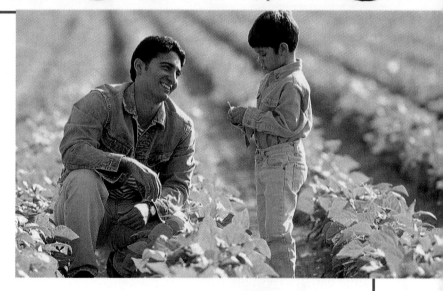

- **Coping Skills.** Every family has to deal with problems. Having good coping skills helps them get past these problems. Two important coping skills are the ability to recognize a problem and the willingness to admit to it. Admitting to a problem is not a sign of weakness but of strength.

Following Up

1. Make a list of local sites, events, or outings that would be appropriate for a family with children aged one to three, with children aged four to six, with children aged seven to twelve, or with teens.

2. **Communication.** Why does open and honest communication help build strong families?

3. **Thinking Skills.** How is admitting to a problem a sign of strength?

Summary

✔ Families meet members' basic needs and prepare them to live in society. (Section 2-1)

✔ Family structure, stages of life, and changes in society all have an impact on families. (Section 2-1)

✔ Parenthood causes many changes, especially for first-time parents. (Section 2-2)

✔ Before deciding to become parents, couples should seriously consider their readiness for parenthood. (Section 2-2)

✔ Learning management skills helps parents cope with the demands on their time, energy, and money. (Section 2-2)

Reviewing the Facts

1. What kinds of basic needs do families meet? (Section 2-1)

2. What two difficulties do single parents face that are not present in two-parent families? (Section 2-1)

3. What skills are especially useful in blended families? Why? (Section 2-1)

4. Give examples of two different variations on the family life cycle. (Section 2-1)

5. Families eat more and more meals outside the home. Which social trends described in the chapter do you think this is related to? Explain why. (Section 2-1)

6. Give an example of a change in lifestyle caused by parenthood. (Section 2-2)

7. How do parents and grandparents of a new baby have to adjust? (Section 2-2)

8. Describe a situation in which a parent shows emotional maturity. (Section 2-2)

9. Why are financial issues significant for parents? (Section 2-2)

10. How can management skills help a parent? (Section 2-2)

Thinking Critically

1. **Analyzing.** Marty's father died. Two years later, his mother married a man who had a daughter. Because there were only two bedrooms available for children, Marty was asked to give up his room for his stepsister and share a room with his brother. Do you think that was fair? Why or why not?

2. **Synthesizing.** Adults who care for both their own children and their aged parents are sometimes called members of the "sandwich generation." Why is that an appropriate name?

3. **Ranking.** Which of the issues about parenthood do you think is the most important? Why?

Taking Action

1. **Sending a Message.** Write a public-service announcement that informs young couples about the responsibilities of having children. *(Leadership)*

CONNECTIONS

2. In the News. Scan the newspaper or a magazine for articles that you think describe a social trend that has an impact on the family. Bring one article to class and explain how the trend affects the family. *(Communication)*

3. Making a List. Write down a list of ten questions that you think a person should ask himself or herself before deciding to become a parent. Share your list with the class. *(Thinking Skills)*

Cross-Curricular Connections

1. Math. Searching in the library or online, find the number of households headed by two parents and one parent in both of the last two censuses. Calculate the percentage of change for both types of family structures.

2. Language Arts. Write a scene in which a young couple discusses whether or not to have children. You can end the scene with either decision, but be sure to have both characters show good communication skills as they talk about the issue.

Workplace Connections

1. Personal Qualities. List the personal qualities you think would be needed by someone who worked with families wanting to adopt a child.

2. Thinking Skills. Suppose you were a business owner. What policies could you devise for your business that would be helpful for your employees who had children?

Family and Community Connections

1. Foster Children. Find out from local agencies what a person needs to do to qualify as a foster parent. Present your findings to the class and discuss them.

2. Community Resources. Identify a local agency or group that offers child care classes to prospective or new parents. Prepare a fact sheet that tells where and when the class are held, how many sessions are included, how long each session lasts, and what material is covered.

Technology Connections

1. Internet. Search for Web sites that offer help for people in single-parent or blended families.

2. Video or Audiotape. Tape an interview with an adult who describes the changes experienced when he or she had a first child. If tape equipment is not available, write down the interviewee's comments and share them with the class.

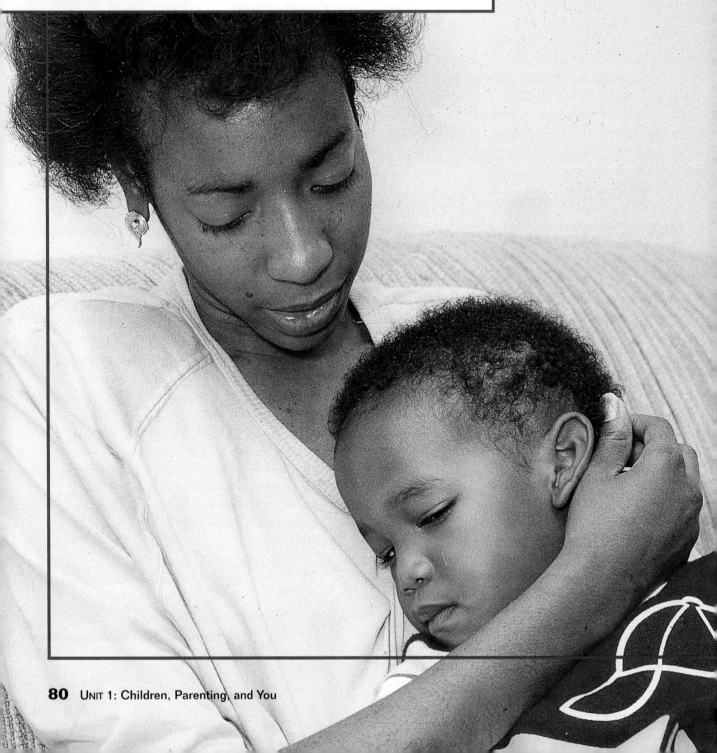

CHAPTER 3

Effective Parenting Skills

As the thunder rolled and the lightning cracked during the night, two-year-old Ian cried out. His mother awoke from her own sleep with a start and quickly ran to his room. She took Ian out of the crib. Holding him close, she carried him to the rocking chair. She sat down and began rocking, singing softly to comfort him. The storm passed and so did his fears. Soon Ian was asleep again. Once his mother was sure he was sound asleep, she put him back in his crib.

The next morning, Ian awoke as though nothing had happened. He was cheerful and ready to take on the world. His mother gave him a reassuring hug, and he ran off to play.

> "She sat down and began rocking, singing softly to comfort him. The storm passed and so did his fears."

What Is Parenting?

Parenting is a strange kind of job. If you do the job right, you work yourself out of it! By the time you are done parenting, the child has grown to adulthood and is ready to start an independent life.

KEY TERMS

authoritarian style
democratic style
deprivation
nurturing
parenting
permissive style

OBJECTIVES:

- Explain how knowledge of child development is linked to reasonable expectations.

- Distinguish among different parenting styles.

- Identify ways to improve parenting skills.

- Describe how to nurture children.

Parenting: A Learning Process

Parenting—caring for children and helping them develop—is complicated. It requires understanding a child's needs and meeting those needs. It also demands good judgment in three ways:

- Parenting requires knowing when to help and when to back off so that a child can do a task himself or herself.

- Parents need to avoid pushing children to try activities they are not yet ready for. On the other hand, they have to avoid holding children back out of fear that they might fail. Children have to learn how to bounce back and try again.
- The skills that parents need change as children grow up. Parents must adapt their parenting skills at each stage of a child's development.

It's not just parents who need parenting skills. They are essential for anyone who works with children.

Having Reasonable Expectations

Have you ever heard an adult tell a child, "Act your age." Children usually *do* act their age, but adults don't always know what to expect. That's why understanding child development is so important. Having reasonable expectations for children is an essential first step in effective parenting. Kristin grew increasingly frustrated when two-year-old Adam said "no" to everything. Then her mother told her that children usually go through a negative stage at that age. Relieved that Adam would outgrow the behavior, she was better able to handle it.

Caregivers need to be sure to match their expectations to the particular child. Some children learn to walk earlier than others. Some need more encouragement making friends. Caregivers need to respect the differences between children.

Finding a Comfortable Parenting Style

Caregivers look for a parenting style they feel comfortable with—one that matches their personality and values. There are three main styles of parenting:

- **Authoritarian style.** The **authoritarian style** is based on the idea that children should obey their parents without question. In this style, a parent tells a child what to do, and the child's responsibility is to do it. When rules are broken, the authoritarian parent usually acts quickly and firmly.
- **Democratic style.** In the **democratic style,** children have more input into rules and limits. Children are given a certain amount of independence and freedom of choice within those rules.
- **Permissive style.** In the **permissive style,** parents give children a wide range of freedom. In this style, children may set their own rules.

Of course, few parents follow any one style exclusively. A parent may use a more authoritarian style on some issues—say, where health or safety are involved—and be more democratic on, say, clothing. Parents may change their style as children age, too. They may feel that before, say, age eight, children need firm rules, but after that age they can have more freedom.

Getting Help

How do people learn parenting? High school classes in child development and parenting are good sources of information and help. Hospitals, schools, community groups, and private instructors also offer courses or workshops in parenting. These courses can be very helpful. Instructors know the subject and have experience in how to pass their information to others.

Even if you don't take a course, there are many ways to build parenting skills:

- Reading books and magazine articles about parenting.

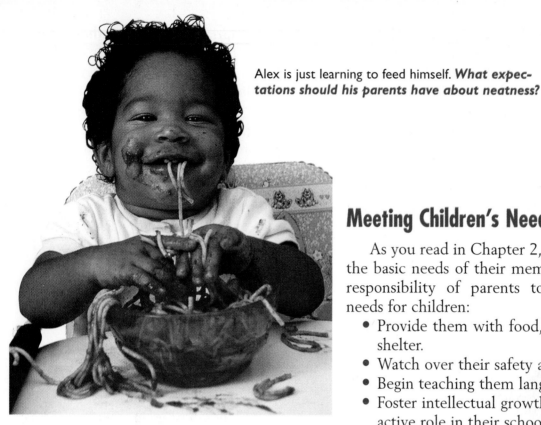
Alex is just learning to feed himself. *What expectations should his parents have about neatness?*

- Gaining experience with children.
- Asking the advice of family members and friends.
- Observing other parents and children.

Whatever the method used, try to give yourself as many options as possible. Each child is different, and ideas or techniques that work with some children do not work with others. By learning many different strategies, you are more likely to find one that will work with a particular child.

The Tasks of Parenting

Parenting has three basic tasks. The first is to meet the child's basic needs. The second is to nurture children. The third task of parenting is to guide children to show appropriate behavior. That complex task is discussed in Section 3-2.

Meeting Children's Needs

As you read in Chapter 2, families meet the basic needs of their members. It is the responsibility of parents to meet these needs for children:

- Provide them with food, clothing, and shelter.
- Watch over their safety and health.
- Begin teaching them language.
- Foster intellectual growth by taking an active role in their schooling.
- Teach them to get along with others.
- Provide opportunities for them to love and be loved.

Nurturing

Nurturing means giving a child opportunities for encouragement and enrichment. It also involves showing love, support, and concern.

Parents are children's first teachers. Children naturally learn by exploring their world, trying new things, and imitating others. Nurturing parents give children the freedom they need in order to learn.

Adults should remove as many barriers as possible that prevent children from exploring the world on their own. For an infant, this means a safe environment to explore. For a preschooler, this might mean letting the child play in the sandbox without worrying about dirty hands and clothes.

Unfortunately, some parents don't encourage their children. These children then lag behind others in their development. They suffer from **deprivation,** or the lack of an enriching environment.

Some people confuse deprivation with poverty. They are not the same. The families of deprived children may be wealthy or poor—or anywhere in between. It is not a matter of money, but of what kind of environment the child has.

 As you learned in Section 1-2, a child's brain is ready for certain types of learning at specific ages. A deprived child may have missed the "window of opportunity" for a certain type of development. After this "window", the learning process is more difficult.

Children don't really need lots of fancy toys. Everyday objects and experiences can provide great opportunities for learning.

INFOLINK

Windows of Brain Development

To learn more about *windows of brain development*, see Chapter 1, pages 29-33.

The other part of nurturing is providing love and support. Children need love just as much as they need food to eat and a bed to sleep in.

Teaching a child to ride shows parenting in action. Parents give help and guidance, but then must back off to allow children to master skills on their own. *How can failing help children learn?*

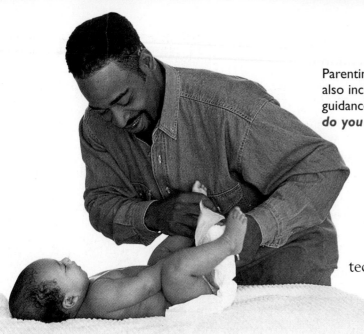

Parenting involves providing physical care but also includes giving love, encouragement, and guidance. *Which of these tasks of parenting do you think is the most important?*

Some parents become overprotective and overattentive. They shower a child with too much attention, too many toys, too many treats. They may try to shield the child from unpleasant experiences. These practices harm children, too. Children learn from trial and error. They need to make mistakes so they can learn from them.

Communicating Positively

Good communication is an important part of good parenting. Being a good listener is one way of showing children that you respect them. The way you talk to children is equally important.

Techniques for good communication include the following:

- Use words the child can understand, but avoid talking down to the child.
- Be clear. Think in terms of the child's point of view.
- Be positive and polite. Hearing a constant series of "don'ts" is discouraging. Try saying, "Please shut the door quietly."
- Give praise and love. Everyone needs to hear good things about themselves—especially young children.

The Developing Brain

Hugs do more than give a child emotional reassurance. Touching through daily massage helps premature babies gain weight faster. Massage is also linked to lower levels of stress and better motor skills.

Parents can show children love in many different ways, including hugs, kisses, and smiles. Patient listening and giving time and attention also show love and support. It can be discussing ways to get along better with a playmate or helping fix a broken toy.

Some parents have difficulty showing affection for their children. They may be embarrassed or feel that affection will make their children "too soft." Without a loving parent's recognition of their accomplishments, however, children may feel insecure and worthless. They may have a difficult time forming healthy relationships because they never learned how to give and receive love.

- Children often tune out adults who only give commands or directions. Limit the directions to those that are essential.
- Talk about what's meaningful to the child. Comments about the picture he drew or the tower she built says you care about what he or she does.

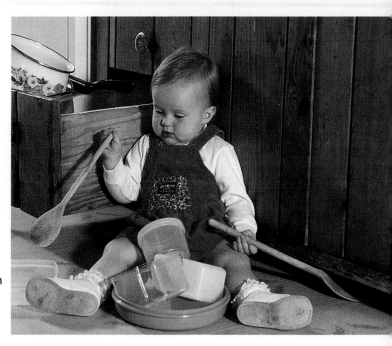

Everyday objects like these wooden spoons and plastic containers can become opportunities for young children to explore, learn, and have fun. *What skills can children develop by playing with these things?*

SECTION 3-1 REVIEW

✔ Check Your Understanding

1. Why must parents learn to adapt their parenting skills over time?
2. Why is it important to understand child development?
3. Describe the three styles of parenting.
4. What do you think is an advantage of taking a course in parenting?
5. Why is providing enrichment part of nurturing?
6. Why should caregivers avoid talking down to a child?

Putting Knowledge Into Practice

1. **Predicting Consequences.** What will probably happen to a child if parents consistently give him or her tasks for which he or she is not developmentally ready?
2. **Drawing Conclusions.** Thirteen-year-old Danette wants a bicycle, but her parents can't afford a new one. They say that if she uses some of her money from babysitting they will match the sum to buy her a used bike. Is this an example of deprivation? Why or why not?
3. **Observing and Participating.** Observe the teachers in your classes. Without naming names, describe an incident you saw in which a teacher encouraged a student to try something new or to recover from a mistake.

Guiding Children's Behavior

Amy was frustrated because four-year-old Jenny never put her toys away. She tried reminding Jenny, scolding her, and even banning television until the toys were picked up. Nothing seemed to work. She didn't know what to do.

KEY TERMS

conscience
guidance
negative reinforcement
positive reinforcement
self-discipline
time-out

OBJECTIVES:

- Explain the importance of consistency in guiding children.
- Apply effective techniques for encouraging appropriate behavior.
- Explain how and why to set limits.
- Identify effective ways of dealing with misbehavior.

Understanding Guidance

Some people think of guiding behavior as disciplining children when they do something wrong. Punishment *is* part of guidance, but just a small part. It should be used only when necessary and only in specific

Being positive and encouraging is an important principle of good communication. *Does it only apply to communication between parents and children? Why or why not?*

ways, as you will learn. Guidance doesn't mean "making children behave" either. **Guidance** means using firmness and understanding to help children learn to control their own behavior. As a result of effective guidance, children achieve **self-discipline.** They have the ability to control their own behavior.

This learning is important to emotional and social development. Effective guidance helps children learn to get along with others and to handle their own feelings in acceptable ways. It promotes security and a positive feeling about self.

Guidance also helps children in their moral development. Very young children understand right and wrong only in terms of being praised or scolded. Gradually, children develop a **conscience** (KON-shuns), or an inner sense of what is right. As they mature, they use this conscience to act morally when facing new situations.

Consistency

Being consistent is the key to guiding children's behavior. Consistency is a matter of clearly making rules and applying them in the same way in all situations. Consistency helps children know what is expected of them and what responses they can expect from parents.

Children lose trust and confidence in a caregiver who constantly changes rules or fails to enforce them in a consistent way. If a parent permits a behavior one day and punishes the child for the same behavior the next, the child will feel confused and insecure. He or she will pay little attention to the next limits that are set.

Consistency becomes an important issue when more than one person cares for a child. These people need to agree in advance on rules and ways to enforce them. Each one also needs to be careful not to undercut the other's decisions. If caregivers don't agree, children can use the inconsistency to their advantage, playing one adult against the other.

There are three ways that adults can guide children to behave appropriately:

- Encouraging appropriate behavior.
- Setting and enforcing limits.
- Dealing with inappropriate behavior in effective ways.

"Time-out" is an effective way of giving a child a chance to calm down. *Do you think this method would work with an infant? Why or why not?*

Encouraging Appropriate Behavior

Suppose you are a young child. No one ever explains to you what kind of behavior is expected or praises you for doing the right thing. Every so often, you are punished for something. Perhaps it is for spilling juice or pulling someone's hair. In this situation, you can't understand how you are supposed to behave. Guidance that is applied only after a child has done something wrong has little chance of success.

You can encourage appropriate behavior by setting a good example, explaining what is desired, praising correct behavior, and offering choices.

Setting a Good Example

Children are great imitators. Children learn best by being shown what to do rather than by just being told. For instance, parents who want their child to talk politely to others get good results when they themselves consistently are polite.

The desire to imitate applies to all the examples—not just good ones. Five-year-old Mark sees his older brothers yell at each other when they disagree. It's little wonder, then, that Mark yells at his friends when he is upset with them.

Telling What Is Expected

Children need to be told what is expected of them in ways they can understand. At first, it isn't necessary to explain the reasons for expected behavior. For a one-year-old, the instruction "Pat the doggy" combined with a demonstration of gentle handling is enough.

When a child is in danger, the appropriate response is to act immediatelly to protect the child. *In other situations, how can a parent respond to a child's inappropriate behavior?*

Around age three, children begin to understand simple reasoning. Then they can understand a direction that includes the reason for it: "It hurts the dog when you pull his tail. If you want to play with him, you will have to be gentle."

Praising Appropriate Behavior

Giving a child attention when his or her actions are appropriate is an example of **positive reinforcement,** a response that encourages a particular behavior. When children learn that an action wins attention and approval from adults, they are likely to repeat that action.

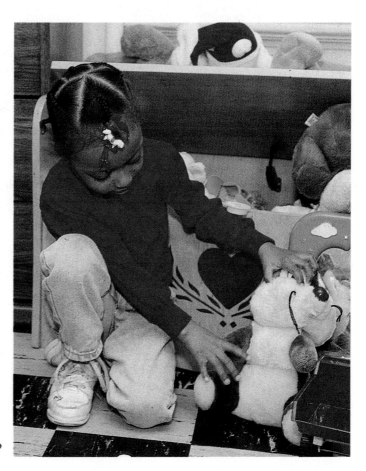

Learning to put toys away after playing with them is just one example of how children learn self-discipline. *Can you name another?*

Practicing Parenting

How to Talk to Children

*P*arents and other caregivers are often called on to tell children what to do. These suggestions can help you give those directions in a way that makes it easier for children to follow them:

❤ **First, be sure that you have the child's attention.** Try to make eye contact—you may need to stoop down or sit beside the child to do so.

❤ **Use a pleasant voice.** Speak normally, not in a harsh way.

❤ **Use positive statements.** A child will respond better if told "Dry the dishes thoroughly" rather than "Don't put wet dishes in the cabinet."

❤ **Use specific words.** Say "Be sure to paint on the paper," not "Don't paint sloppily."

❤ **Begin with an action verb.** Beginning this way helps keep directions simple.

❤ **Give only one direction at a time.** Limit directions to make them easier to understand, remember, and follow.

APPLY YOUR KNOWLEDGE

1. Read the following direction: "Don't track mud into the house." Why is it an ineffective one? How would you word it to be effective?
2. How would you tell a four-year-old playing with modeling dough to be sure not to get any dough on the floor?
3. What would you do if you wanted to give a child several directions?

The following guidelines will help you encourage appropriate behavior:

• **Be specific.** Clearly comment on the behavior you are acknowledging: "You did a good job brushing your teeth."

• **Notice the behavior as soon as possible.** Recognize the behavior right away to help the child link the action and the praise.

• **Recognize small steps.** Encourage steps in the right direction—don't wait for perfect behavior. If a child usually spends story time trying to distract others, acknowledge even a short moment of "being a good listener."

• **Help the child take pride in his or her actions.** Saying "That was hard work to pick up your toys, but you did it!" helps a child feel competent. Saying "I'm so happy you picked up your toys!" encourages a child to behave only to gain your approval.

- **Tailor the encouragement to the needs of the child.** Praise behaviors that are difficult for that child. The child who usually forgets to put away toys should be rewarded with approval for remembering to do so.

Offering Choices

As children become more mature, they can be allowed to make some decisions for themselves. This helps them learn that they are responsible for their actions.

For example, three-year-old Gavin sometimes hits his younger sister. To encourage appropriate behavior, his parents might say, "Sonya looks up to you. That's why she wants to play with the same toy you do. I know that it makes you angry when she grabs your toy, but I can't allow you to hurt her. Either choose one of your toys that she can play with, or play in your room alone for a little while so you have privacy."

Of course, the choices offered have to reflect acceptable behavior. Gavin is given choices that respect his right to have some control over his toys and his play. At the same time, he must respect Sonya's right not to be hurt.

Setting Limits

Setting limits is another way to guide children toward appropriate, safe behavior. Limits include physical restrictions, such as preventing a child from crossing the street.

Enforcing rules in a consistent way helps children feel more comfortable and secure. **Why?**

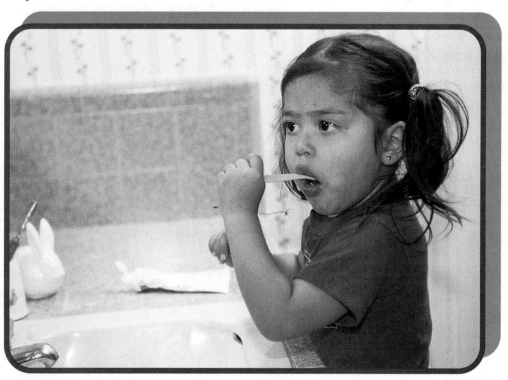

Another kind of limit is a rule of behavior: "We don't hit other people."

What Should Limits Be?

In setting limits, parents and other caregivers often follow this general guideline: Limits should keep children from hurting themselves, other people, or property. Children will respect and follow limits if they are few and reasonable.

When setting limits, keep these questions in mind:

- Does the limit allow the child to learn, explore, and grow? Too much restriction hinders development.
- Is the limit fair and appropriate for the child's age? A toddler might be restricted to a fenced-in yard. A school-age child might be permitted to visit a friend living down the street.
- Does the limit benefit the child, or is it merely for the adult's convenience? Restrictions should be for the child's good, not because they fit a routine.

Making Limits Clear

State limits simply and briefly—for example, "We walk inside the house. Running is done outside." You will probably need to restate the limit each time the situation arises. Children, especially young ones, don't always remember limits from one day to the next. They may not realize that limits stated one day still apply another day.

If you think the child remembers the limit, ask. Doing so gives the child a chance to show that he or she is learning—and gives the parent an occasion to praise the child. Keith's mother asks, "What do we do before rollerblading?" Keith quickly answers, "Put a helmet and pads on!" His mother then says, "That's right! That's the way to take care of yourself!"

Limits must be clear. Telling three-year-old Julie that she can have "a small snack" is not a useful limit. She can't know what makes a snack "small." A better limit would be "You can have an apple or a banana and a glass of milk."

Use a calm, direct tone of voice when setting limits. This indicates the limit is real and should be respected.

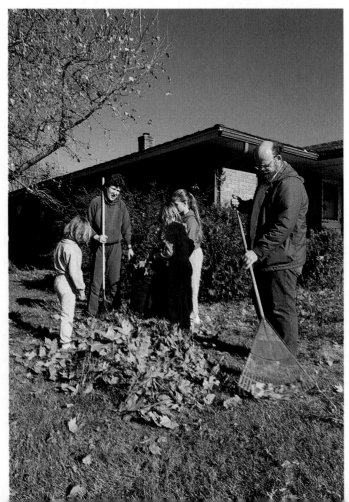

Setting a good example is one way of encouraging appropriate behavior. **What are three other ways?**

Children can be given praise for many different activities, such as helping around the house.

Setting limits includes four steps:

- **Show understanding of the child's desires.** "I know you think it is fun to draw on the wall."
- **Set the limit and explain it.** "You may not draw on the wall. It is hard to clean crayon marks off the wall."
- **Acknowledge the child's feelings.** "I know you may not be happy with this, but some things are not acceptable."
- **Give alternatives.** If possible, give the child a chance to continue the same activity but in an acceptable way. "If you want to draw, you may draw on this paper. Or, you can do something else, like playing with your blocks. Which would you like?"

Once established and explained, limits should be firmly and consistently enforced. Parents who give in teach their children that they don't mean what they say. Children take rules more seriously if they remain in force at all times.

Dealing with Inappropriate Behavior

No matter how much adults do to encourage appropriate behavior, children—*all* children—misbehave from time to time. When this happens, adults must deal with the situation appropriately and effectively.

The child's age should shape the response. A one-year-old who bites another child can be told, "No! Don't bite," but the child can't be expected to understand the meaning of his or her action. A four-year-old can understand that biting is unacceptable. With a child this age, a punishment may be in order.

A caregiver should ask these questions when responding to a child's misbehavior:

- Is the expected behavior appropriate, given the child's development?
- Does the child understand that the behavior is wrong?

- Was the behavior done knowingly and deliberately, or was it beyond the child's control?

Unintentional Misbehavior

With children of any age, misbehavior is sometimes unintentional. A young child may drop a glass of milk that is too heavy or accidentally break something that should have been out of reach. These unintentional actions shouldn't be punished.

Misbehavior is also unintentional if the child had no way of knowing it was wrong. For example, Brittany picked a flower in the park and brought it to her father. People shouldn't pick the flowers in parks, but Brittany had never been told that. Rather than scolding, Brittany's father simply explained that she shouldn't have done it.

Using Punishment Effectively

When children deliberately do something that they know is wrong, some form of punishment may be necessary. Punishment is **negative reinforcement,** a response aimed at discouraging a child from repeating a behavior. By encouraging the desired behavior and setting limits, you are more likely to teach a child to act as you wish. Still, there are times when punishment—used with good judgment—is effective. In punishing, the parent should make clear that he or she disapproves of the *behavior* but still loves the child.

The first time a child breaks a rule, many caregivers give a warning rather than a punishment. Even a child with good self-control makes an occasional mistake. A warning reminds the child of the rule and its importance. It also gives him or her a chance to regain self-control.

Parents need to tailor their explanations of limits to the age of the child. A very young child will not be able to pay attention to a long explanation. *How can this father tell this young child that it's time for a nap?*

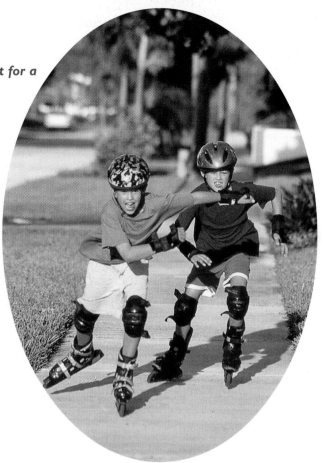

What kind of limits can parents set for a child who wishes to in-line skate?

After a rule has been broken another time, punishment is in order. The punishment given should be in proportion to the misbehavior. Forgetting to put away one set of toys before taking out another doesn't deserve severe punishment.

Here are some useful techniques for dealing with inappropriate behavior:

- **Natural consequences.** Sometimes it is punishment enough for the child to suffer the results of his or her behavior. Suppose Kwan bangs a toy on the floor and breaks it. Losing the chance to play with the toy should be enough to remind Kwan to be careful in the future.
- **Loss of privileges.** Sometimes allowing the natural consequences isn't appropriate. If a child runs into the street, the natural consequences—being hit by a car—are far too dangerous. A parent might then take away a privilege, such as playing outside, instead. This type of punishment is most effective for children five and older. It works best if the privilege taken away is related to the misbehavior. That way, the child is more likely to associate the two.
- **Giving time-out.** Another way to respond to misbehavior is to use **time-out.** This is a short period of time in which a child sits away from other peo-

ple and the center of activity. The purpose is to give the child a chance to calm down and regain self-control. One minute of time-out for each year of a child's age is a good length of time.

Poor Disciplinary Measures

Well-meaning caregivers sometimes use disciplinary methods that are less effective than others—and sometimes even harmful. Parents and caregivers who follow the positive discipline techniques already described in this chapter should find they don't need to use the following measures:

Some undesirable behavior can be prevented when the parent takes steps to avoid accidents. *Why is a plastic cup better than a glass one for a toddler?*

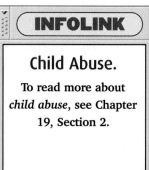

- **Bribing.** Bribing a child with a treat if he or she stops misbehaving can backfire. Instead of learning self-control, the child learns to expect rewards for ending incorrect behavior. The child may even misbehave on purpose, knowing that by stopping he or she can earn the treat again. Don't confuse bribing with rewarding desirable behavior. Giving positive reinforcement for the behavior you want is fine.
- **Making children promise to behave.** In the process of learning to control their behavior, children naturally make mistakes. When a promise has been made, the child may feel forced to lie about misbehavior rather than disappoint someone he or she loves.
- **Shouting or yelling.** When a child misbehaves, a caregiver's anger and disappointment should be expressed in a calm, reasonable voice. A loud, harsh voice can frighten a young child. Older children may learn to "tune out" yelling.
- **Shaming or belittling.** Parents and caregivers shouldn't ridicule a child's mistakes or use responses such as "If this keeps up, you'll never amount to anything." Doing so can harm the child's self-confidence.
- **Threatening to withhold love.** Using statements such as "I won't love you anymore if you don't stop hitting your brother" creates the fear of being rejected and abandoned.

Of course, there should be a clear distinction between appropriate punishment and abusing a child. A parent or other caregiver should always be in control of his or her own feelings when punishing a child.

Handling Conflict

Children may feel angry when they can't get their way. Caregivers must be prepared to deal with this anger. Avoid making the child feel guilty about his or her anger—it's a normal emotion.

INFOLINK

Child Abuse.

To read more about *child abuse*, see Chapter 19, Section 2.

By the same token, caregivers can help the child learn that there are acceptable ways of handling that anger:

- **Using words.** Rather than hitting or lashing out, children—and adults—should express feelings with words.
- **Speaking calmly.** Even when angry, people should speak calmly, not scream or yell.

- **Counting to ten.** Help the child control his or her emotions by counting to ten and taking a few deep breaths.

It may help to discuss the misbehavior and the punishment some time after the child has calmed down. Then the parent can help the child see how he or she misbehaved. The parent can also explain what the child should have done instead.

SECTION 3-2 REVIEW

✔ Check Your Understanding

1. How is guidance connected to conscience?
2. Why is consistency in guiding a child's behavior important?
3. What are the four ways of encouraging appropriate behavior?
4. What four steps are involved in setting limits?
5. When should punishment be used?
6. What is a good rule of thumb in determining how much time to give for time-out?
7. Why is bribing an ineffective form of discipline
8. What are acceptable ways of handling anger?

Putting Knowledge Into Practice

1. **Applying.** When Mike gives time-out to his five-year-old, he says "You have time-out until you can tell me why what you did was wrong and that you are ready to behave differently." Do you think this is a good idea or not? Why?
2. **Synthesizing.** Maria taught her daughter to say "please" and "thank you" whenever she asked for anything. Ever since Cristina began spending time at a child care center, she has lost this habit. What can Maria do?
3. **Observing and Participating.** Visit a child care center and watch how the workers interact with the children. What techniques described in this chapter did they use? How effective were they? Report to the class.

CAREER OPPORTUNITIES

Child Psychologist

A CONVERSATION WITH LUIS ALVAREZ

How did you become interested in becoming a child psychologist? I was always interested in psychology—how people behave and why. What brought me into child psychology was the realization that what we're like as adults is influenced by our experiences as children.

What are the tasks and responsibilities of a child psychologist? They vary. Some work in clinics and help children who have problems. Some work in schools, testing children who may have a learning disorder or some other problem. I teach at a university. My most enjoyable time, though, is when I'm at the university's child care center. My job also requires a lot of reading to keep up with new information.

What is the work environment like? I'm alone in my office at home when I do my reading and writing, and that's fairly quiet. When I'm teaching or at the child care center, I am with people constantly and the pace is quite hectic.

What are the working hours like? Teaching and work at the center occupy most of the day every day. I do my reading and writing at night, often at home.

What aptitudes are needed to be a child psychologist? You have to be a good observer with attention to detail. You need to be able to notice the subtle changes in children's behavior. You need to have an open mind so you can question your assumptions. You need empathy and good communication skills.

CHILD PSYCHOLOGIST

Education and Training. To be a counselor, people need at least a master's degree. Those who want to be a full psychologist need a doctoral degree (Ph.D.) and perhaps training in a clinic.

Career Outlook. The outlook for child psychologists is very good in the near future.

CONNECTING SCHOOL TO CAREER

1. **Technology.** What kinds of technology do you think a psychologist could use?
2. **Basic Skills.** Why do you think psychologists need good communications skills?

Child Care Options

On the way to his job each morning, Andy leaves his son Chris at a child care center. At the end of her workday, Chris's mother, Liz, comes to get him and brings him home. Liz and Andy, like millions of other parents, rely on substitute child care.

KEY TERMS

accreditation
child care center
family child care
Head Start
license
Montessori preschool
nanny
parent cooperative
play group
preschool

OBJECTIVES:

- Explain why people need substitute child care.

- Analyze the advantages and disadvantages of the types of substitute care that are available.

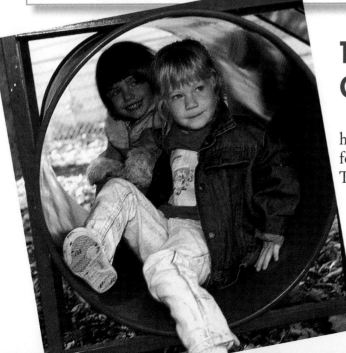

The Need for Substitute Care

In recent years, more and more parents have come to rely on other people to care for their children at least some of the time. There are several reasons for this trend:

- Many children live in two-parent families where both parents work away from home. These children usually need substitute care.

- Many more children live with a single parent who has a full-time job. Such a parent needs full-time or part-time child care.
- Some parents who care for their children at home feel that their children can benefit by being with other children. They place their child in a center for some time each week.

Types of Substitute Care

Parents who need substitute care can choose from many different types. All provide the child with physical care and a place to play. Substitute care is provided in two general settings. Some services are offered in a home. Others are provided in a child care center.

The Developing Brain
Studies show that child care outside the home *can* promote a child's brain development. What children need is a child care setting in which they get lots of verbal attention.

Home-Based Care

Many young children receive care in their own or another family's home. A home setting may be easier for a child to get used to because the surroundings are familiar. Home-based care may also be more available and convenient for parents. Some parents like this arrangement because the caregiver is a friend, relative, or neighbor—someone they know and trust.

Home-based care usually involves a smaller group of children than center-based

care. This makes it a good choice for infants or other children who need individual attention.

There are three main types of home-based care:

- **Care in the child's own home.** Many parents have their child cared for by someone who comes to their home. In-home care is convenient, but it can be costly. Also, the child may not have a chance to play with other children.

  Some families **nannies**—trained workers hired by a family to provide live-in child care. Although this arrangement is fairly expensive—including the cost of living space for the nanny—it offers reliable care at almost any time of day. Of course, a nanny's credentials and references should be checked before the person is hired.

More and more parents today use substitute care for their children. *Why does the rise in two-career families contribute to this trend?*

Some families—especially those with children with special needs—use respite care. A respite-care provider gives the family a break—a respite—during the day. Such a worker might come to the family home for a few hours, allowing the parent to do errands or other chores outside the house that may not be possible otherwise.

- **Family child care.** Some parents put their children in **family child care.** In this situation, a small number of children are cared for by someone in his or her own home. The group may include the caregiver's own children.

  Family child care provides the comfort of a home setting with opportunities for social play. Since the group size is small, there can be plenty of individual attention. Family child care usually costs less than care in the child's own home but has less extensive facilities than a child care center.

  Some states require caregivers to have **licenses,** which show that they meet health and safety standards. These licenses do not give an indication of the quality of the care provided, however.

- **Play groups.** Some parents take part in a **play group.** In this arrangement, parents take turns caring for each other's children in their own homes. A play group is similar to family child care, but it involves a number of different homes and caregivers. Most play groups involve no fees since the work is shared by many. This type of care is a good idea for parents who don't work full-time.

Quality home-based care includes both quiet and active times. Look for a good mix of planned activities and informal play. In no care setting should children be allowed to simply sit in front of the television set or be left without supervision.

One disadvantage of home-based care is the issue of backup options. If the person who runs family care becomes ill, he or she can't care for children in the usual way. Parents need to find a replacement.

The growing need for child care has revived the tradition of the nanny, a person who lives with the family and cares for its children. *What kind of training would a nanny need?*

Ask the E?perts

Pat Brodeen
Teacher and Teen Parent Coordinator
at Theodore Roosevelt High School in
San Antonio, Texas

WHAT *About Center-Based Care?*

Q Does it hurt children to put them in child care?

A This is one of the most troubling questions for many parents. They read that child development specialists consider parents a child's best source of love and learning, and that they advise parents to stay home to provide child care for as long as possible.

Yet often parents' lives do not permit them to stay home with their children. So, when they hear experts praise the benefits of home care, many parents wonder whether their child suffers by being placed in substitute care.

A recent study suggests that they need not worry so much. The study followed over 1,300 children from birth to age three. About 20 percent were cared for in the home; the rest received some form of substitute care. Researchers found that overall children with quality substitute care actually did better in some language and learning abilities than children who were cared for by a parent.

The study echoed what brain researchers have found. Children develop best in these areas when they have caregivers who provide lots of talk and interaction. Those caregivers can be parents or other people providing substitute care. The key is quality interaction between baby and caregiver.

The researchers reached one other conclusion, which should help parents set aside their worries. The most important factor to children's mental and emotional growth is not the child care arrangement but the home environment. A mother's and father's loving care still counts the most.

Thinking It Through

1. How can children benefit mentally by being in substitute care?
2. Do the results of the study convince you that children will not suffer if placed in substitute care? Why or why not?

Some parents use child care given by an adult they know—sometimes even a friend or neighbor. *What might be the advantages of this choice?*

Center-Based Care

In child care centers, several adults care for one or more groups of children. Centers vary widely in their hours, their fees, and the ages of children they accept. They also differ in the activities, equipment, and play areas provided and in the training and experience of the staff.

Some child care centers are businesses run for profit. Others charge fees to cover expenses but don't try to make a profit. Still others are funded by the city, state, or federal government. Care at these centers may be offered for free or at a reduced cost to those who qualify. Finally, some centers are run by businesses who offer child care as a benefit to their workers.

Child care centers must meet minimum health and safety requirements in order to be licensed. The license, issued by the state, also limits the number of children a center may accept, depending on space, facilities, and size of the staff.

Professionals in the field have created a system to recognize centers that meet certain standards. The National Association for the Education of Young Children (NAEYC) is a group that centers and preschools can choose to join. Members apply to the group for **accreditation.** This involves a review of the facility's staff, programs, and environment to see if they meet the association's strict standards.

These are the most common types of center-based child care:

- **Child care centers.** A **child care center** provides care for children whose parents are not available during working hours. The typical center offers children a variety of activities. Some centers emphasize specific learning activities, but others allow more time for informal play. Usually, there is a daily routine with time set aside for indoor and outdoor play, meals, and naps.

  Child care centers may offer half-day or full-day programs. Most child care centers are designed for children two years old and older. Some provide care for infants.

Practicing Parenting

NAEYC Recommendations for Child Care Centers

NAEYC—the National Association for the Education of Young Children—recommends that a child care center meet certain minimum standards:

- ❤ **Number of infant caregivers.** At least one caregiver for every three or four infants.

- ❤ **Number of toddler caregivers.** At least one caregiver for every four to six toddlers.

- ❤ **Number of preschooler caregivers.** At least one caregiver for every seven to ten children aged three to five.

- ❤ **Group size.** The total number of children in a group should be no larger than two times the ratio of staff to children. That is, there should be no more than eight infants, twelve toddlers, or twenty children aged three to five.

- ❤ **Indoor play space.** The center should have at least 35 square feet of play space indoors per child. This does not include space for other purposes.

- ❤ **Outdoor play space.** The center should have at least 75 square feet of outdoor play space per child.

- ❤ **Separating space.** The center should have indoor space divided into separate rooms, rather than being one large shared space.

APPLY YOUR KNOWLEDGE

1. A center with twenty children has 1000 square feet of indoor play space and 2000 square feet of outdoor play space. Does it meet NAEYC standards?

2. Why do you think NAEYC recommends that the indoor space be divided into separate rooms?

Some employers offer child care centers for their workers' children at the workplace. *Why would that be convenient for parents?*

- **Parent cooperatives.** In a **parent cooperative,** part of the child care is provided by the parents of the children in the program. A preschool teacher or some other qualified caregiver organizes the program and guides the work of the parents. Working at the center helps parents understand their child's development. Such a program is less expensive than a child care center. These programs are rarely suitable for parents who work full-time, however.
- **Head Start centers.** In the 1960s, the federal government began **Head Start.** This program set up locally run child care facilities designed to help lower-income and disadvantaged children become ready for school. Most Head Start centers have half-day sessions for four-year-olds.

  Head Start offers a variety of activities. It also provides children with meals, health care, and social services. Parents are expected to be active in the Head Start program.

  Critics of Head Start say that whatever benefits children enjoy from Head Start vanish after their first few years in school. Supporters point to several studies, which show that children who attend well-planned Head Start programs score better on tests and have better school readiness skills.

- **Preschools.** A **preschool** provides education programs for children aged three to five. A preschool typically offers activities that help children develop in all areas. The staff usually includes one or more teachers and a number of aides. Aides assist the person in charge. They usually have some training in child care, but not as much as a lead teacher.

  Preschools usually offer half-day sessions from two to five days a week. Some centers offer both child care for younger children and preschool programs for three- to five-year-olds.

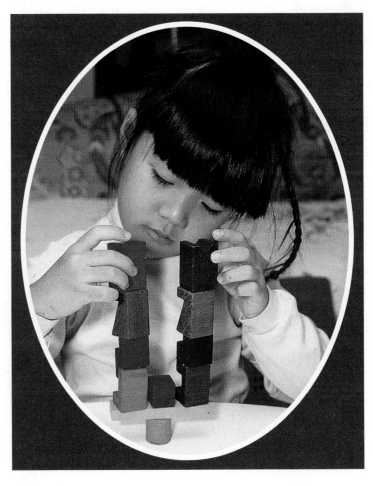

The purpose of all center-based programs should be to provide children with learning opportunities, not just care.

- **Specialized preschools.** Some preschools provide a specialized program that differs from the traditional approach. **Montessori** (mon-tuh-SORE-ee) **preschools** are one example. They use special learning materials and follow the ideas of Dr. Maria Montessori, an Italian educator. Children are encouraged to learn by exploring and experimenting with the materials provided. They are given the freedom to move from one activity to another as they wish. Another example is called Highscope. This program encourages children to be in charge of their learning.

Care for Older Children

Many school-age children need care outside the family as well. Without it, they may be left unsupervised before or after school because of parents' work schedules. In many areas, before- and after-school programs are available. Schools and community groups offer a safe place where the children can do their homework or enjoy supervised recreation.

Child care experts advise against leaving children without adult supervision before they reach their teens. Younger children, they say, are not mature enough to be alone.

Choosing Substitute Child Care

Which type of child care is best for an individual child? There are no easy answers. Parents must consider many factors. Besides quality, the types of care available in the area, the cost, the convenience, and the particular

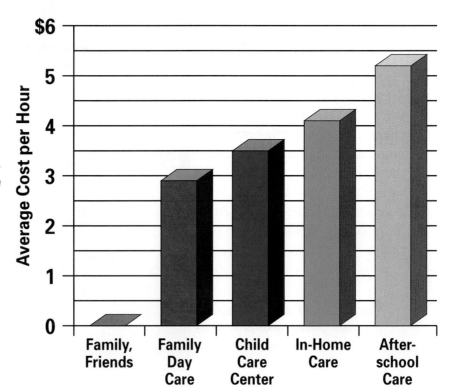

The Hourly Cost of Different Types of Substitute Care

The chart shows the national average for what parents pay each hour for different methods of substitute care. *Which type of substitute care is the least expensive? Which is most expensive?*

needs of the child all influence the decision. Whatever the type of substitute care, parents need a caregiver who enjoys the child, spends time playing with him or her, and communicates well with the parents.

Being involved in their child's care is very important for parents as well. By talking often with the caregiver, they can both discover and pass on information about the child's development. This way, too, they can keep watch on the quality of the care the child is receiving.

The Cost of Substitute Care

The costs of child care vary widely from place to place. They also change over time. The chart on page 108 gives the average cost across the nation for different types of child care. Although specific cost figures may be different in your area, the results give an idea of how the types of care compare in cost.

The cost of substitute care can add up. A working parent may need care for nine or ten hours a day, five days a week. Parents needs to plan carefully, comparing the amount they earn to what they need to spend on child care.

Sources of Information

Community groups can supply listings of sources of substitute care. Groups such as Child Care Aware and the National Association for the Education of Young Children may also have listings for your area. Many parents find substitute care by asking friends what they use—and finding out if those friends are satisfied.

It is essential that the parents visit each home or child care center they are considering before choosing one. This takes time,

Choosing the best substitute care possible is a major responsibility for parents.

but it allows parents to see the facility and the caregivers firsthand. In fact, taking the child to visit the site helps see how he or she responds to the place and the people.

When considering any substitute care option, ask for references. Any child care service—whether a center or a home-based one—should be willing to give the names and phone numbers of parents whose children attend. Ask these parents how long they have been using the service, and what strengths and weaknesses they have seen.

Child Care: Questions to Ask

These are just a few of the areas parent should look at when checking a substitute care facility. Some are questions to ask the caregiver. Others are points that the parent needs to learn by observing how the caregiver acts with children.

The Caregiver	Does the number of children per caregiver meet NAEYC standards?
	What education and experience do caregivers have?
	How long have caregivers worked at this facility? How often are new caregivers hired?
	What safety and first-aid training do caregivers have?
	How do caregivers ensure that unauthorized persons do not pick up a child?
	What arrangements are made if the caregiver is ill?
The Facilities	Does the space match NAEYC standards?
	Are both indoor and outdoor play areas safe, comfortable, and clean?
	If meals or snacks are provided, are they nutritious?
	Are sleeping areas separate from noisy areas?
	What happens if a parent must pick a child up late?
The Program	Do caregivers guide children's behavior in appropriate ways?
	Are rules reasonable for the children's age?
	Are there toys suitable for different ages?
	Are activities varied and matched the children's level?
	Do children have time for undirected play?
	Is there a regular method for the caregiver to report to parents?
	Do the children seem involved and happy?
	If you were a child, would you like to spend time there?

What to Look For

The chart on page 110 gives a checklist of questions to ask when evaluating a child care setting. It is tailored to a child care center, but the questions can be adapted to other situations as well.

Once parents have chosen a service, they should drop by unexpectedly from time to time. These visits can help confirm that the care is as promised. After two or three weeks, the parent should ask what the child thinks. The child's happiness is a good signal of the quality of the child care.

As a child grows, it may be necessary to have a new arrangement. Mary put two-year-old Todd in family child care. At four years old, she put him in a preschool. The child's behavior could signal a need to change, too. If a child suddenly begins to cause trouble at child care, it may be because he or she is bored. Perhaps the activities are no longer interesting or challenging. If the care being given a child seems to have declined in quality, it may be time to move to another setting.

SECTION 3-3 REVIEW

✔ Check Your Understanding

1. What are two reasons why people use substitute care?
2. What are the advantages of home care? Of family child care?
3. Define *license* and *accreditation*.
4. What is the difference between a play group and a parent cooperative?
5. Explain the difference between a child care center and a preschool.
6. Where can parents find after-school programs for school-age children?
7. Why should parents ask for references before deciding on substitute care?

Putting Knowledge Into Practice

1. **Drawing Conclusions.** Why aren't play groups or parent cooperatives usually suitable for parents who work full-time?
2. **Synthesizing.** The NAEYC suggests different ratios of staff to children depending on the age of the children. (See the *Practicing Parenting* feature.) Why?
3. **Observing and Participating.** Working with a partner, adapt the checklist in the chart on page 110 to be useful for evaluating family child care.

Parenting With Care

Fathers Are Caregivers, Too

Mothers and fathers bring different qualities to parenting.

There are endless opportunities for dads to get involved and stay involved with their children. The payoff is great!

Mothers often receive the most attention when parenting is being discussed because they usually take primary responsibility for children. What about fathers? They bring many skills to parenting.

Researchers have found that fathers act differently with children than do mothers. When infants begin to crawl, fathers tend to let them crawl farther than do mothers before bringing them back. Fathers usually play more physically with children—games such as wrestling or tag. When children discover something new, mothers are likely to stay nearby, offering reassurance. Fathers tend to stay back and let the children explore it. These approaches give children new chances to learn about the world. They help build independence.

Researchers have also found that when fathers take an active part in caring for infants, children are less likely to cry when a stranger nears.

Most families share care responsibilities. Some fathers raise their children alone. Here are some ideas for active involvement:

- **Mealtime.** Meals provide opportunities for talking, teaching, and showing love. Father and child can talk about many subjects: for infants, shape and color; for preschoolers, basic nutrition; for school-age children, what happened that day.
- **Baths.** Fathers can bathe babies and toddlers. In doing so, they get a chance to enjoy some close time with their child.
- **Dressing.** After a nice bath, fathers can help their children by picking out clothes and dressing them. As children get

older, fathers can teach them how to dress themselves.

- **Doctor visits.** Fathers can take a child to routine checkups and emergency care.
- **Being a role model.** Fathers can set examples for their children in many areas of life. Solving problems, calming down when angry, and caring for possessions are just a few examples.
- **Taking a walk.** A walk at the end of the day—even a short walk—can help relieve stress. In the company of a child who constantly finds new things to learn, the walk becomes a voyage of discovery.
- **Active play.** Sometimes a child needs physical activity. Then a trip to the park and an exciting ride on the swing or down the slide fits the bill.
- **Reading.** Children of all ages enjoy being read to. Sharing a book is a perfect way to end a day. All that's needed is the patience to read the same story many times— always the same way!

Following Up

1. Make a list of three ways you think a father could care for a child and explain why it would help the child.

2. **Leadership** Give an example of one specific way a father can be a role model.

REVIEW &

Summary

✔ Parents must meet children's basic needs, nurture them, and guide their behavior. (Section 3-1)

✔ Guidance includes encouraging appropriate behavior, setting limits, and dealing with inappropriate behavior. Parents should be consistent. (Section 3-2)

✔ Home-based care options provide comfortable surroundings but caregivers may not be trained. Center-based care may have better facilities but may be inflexible in hours. (Section 3-3)

✔ Parents and children should visit a substitute care facility and ask questions before choosing it. (Section 3-3)

Reviewing the Facts

1. What is the first step in effective parenting? Why? (Section 3-1)

2. Why do parents sometimes change the same parenting style they use? (Section 3-1)

3. What do you think is the best way of gaining parenting skills? Why? (Section 3-1)

4. What is *nurturing*? (Section 3-1)

5. What problems are caused by inconsistent guidance? (Section 3-2)

6. Choose one technique for encouraging appropriate behavior and describe why it is an effective technique. (Section 3-2)

7. Why is giving alternatives an important part of setting limits? (Section 3-2)

8. Why do some parents give a warning when a child first does something wrong? (Section 3-2)

9. Why do people use substitute care on a regular basis? (Section 3-3)

10. Compare home care to family child care. (Section 3-3)

Thinking Critically

1. **Comparing.** What do you think is more damaging to a child, deprivation or over-parenting? Why?

2. **Applying.** Nadine told Justin, age three, "Your room is messy. Take care of it!" How would you reword Nadine's direction?

3. **Ranking.** Which do you think are the five most important factors in evaluating a child care center? Why?

Taking Action

1. **Enriching Life.** Give an example of something parents on a tight budget could do to provide enriching experiences for a child. *(Management)*

2. **Modeling.** Write a script showing what a child will think if a caregiver tells him or her to act one way but gives examples of different ways of behaving. *(Leadership)*

CONNECTIONS

 ## Cross-Curricular Connections

1. **Language Arts.** Write a brochure describing a parenting class intended for first-time parents. In the brochure, list the topics that would be covered in the course.

2. **Math.** If a child care center costs $3.50 an hour, how much would it cost *per week* to have a child in the program for five half-day sessions of four hours each? How about five full-day sessions of nine hours each?

 ## Workplace Connections

1. **Interpersonal Skills.** Whenever two-year-old Addie becomes frustrated, she begins to hit other children. As a child care teacher, how would you talk to her parents about this problem?

2. **Information Systems.** Suppose you were providing family care for four children. What basic information would you want to keep on each child? How would you keep these records?

 ## Family and Community Connections

1. **Evaluating Resources.** Visit a library or bookstore and make a list of all the magazines that offer advice to parents. Choose one and read two or three articles. Report to the class about how good you think the advice is.

2. **Learning About Child Care.** As a class, create a fact sheet with the basic information you think is important about a child care center. Use one of those sheets to gather information about a child care center in your area. Add your sheet to a class booklet called "Community Child Care Services."

 ## Technology Connections

1. **Internet.** Use the Internet to find out more about Head Start, Montessori preschools, or Highscope preschools. What are the programs like? Who qualifies to enter each program? What role do parents play? Write a one-page summary of your findings.

2. **Computers.** Experts say that the amount of time spent watching television or playing with computer games should be limited for children in substitute care settings. Why do you think they make that recommendation? Do you agree?

The classroom was quiet. The students didn't stir. Finally, Adrienne spoke again. "You see, I was so innocent, so naïve. "It will never happen to me," I told myself. "Doug will take care of me," I thought. But I was wrong. It did happen to me, even though we only did it once. I did get pregnant, and Doug dropped me as soon as I told him. I felt so alone. I was only fifteen. I couldn't take care of the baby, but I wanted him to have a good home. I got some help from some wonderful people, and we found a great family for my baby. Every year, on his birthday, they send me a card and a picture. He's so cute, and I'm so happy for him."

Then she looked in the eyes of each student before she spoke again. "It's taken me six years to put my life back together. I'm happy now, but it was a long, hard road. Spare yourself the pain. Wait until you're married."

"'It will never happen to me,' I told myself."

The Realities of Teen Pregnancy

As you know, the teen years are filled with growth and change, new issues, new decisions. Among the most important are those related to sexual activity. What are the consequences of sexual activity? How can those results change plans for the future, and how can that be prevented? Teens are better prepared to answer these questions if they understand the meaning of sexuality and the effects of sexual activity.

KEY TERMS

abstinence
hormones
paternity
peer pressure
sexuality
sexually transmitted
  diseases (STDs)

OBJECTIVES:

- Distinguish between sexuality and sexual activity.

- Explain how values can help teens face issues of sexuality.

- Describe the negative consequences of sexual activity.

Teen Sexuality

Sexuality and sexual activity aren't the same thing. **Sexuality** refers to a person's view of himself or herself as a male or female. Sexuality involves much more than physical maturity or the ability to be sexually active. It includes a person's regard for himself or herself and that person's sense of responsibility for and understanding of other people. Thus sexuality has physical, intellectual, emotional, and social aspects.

Individuals show their sexuality in various ways. They show their maleness or femaleness in the way they walk, talk, move, dress, and laugh.

In the teen years, you develop a sense of your own sexuality. This process is influenced by a number of powerful factors. Dramatic physical changes occur as part of achieving sexual maturity. Changing **hormones,** chemicals in the body, shape these changes. They often have emotional impact as well, causing mood swings and emotional ups and downs.

Social development shifts into high gear. There are attractions to new friends. Relationships with other family members often change as you take on more personal responsibility.

In the midst of these changes, messages about sexual activity seem to be everywhere. The media—television, radio, movies, commercials, and music—often imply that sexual activity is a necessary part of sexuality. **Peer pressure,** the influence of other teens, comes with remarks like "Everyone is doing it—what's wrong with you?"

With such pressures, it's easy to lose sight of what's important. Dating—as couples or in groups—helps in learning what qualities or characteristics in another person you find attractive. You learn more about building relationships. You can have plenty of fun without the hazards of becoming sexually active.

Values and Sexuality

Who am I as a male or female? How should I treat people of the opposite sex? How can I balance old friendships and new relationships with someone of the other sex? Values help shape how each person answers those questions.

As you read in Chapter 2, one role of families is to pass on the family's and society's values. These are the principles they consider important—the rules they use to guide their lives.

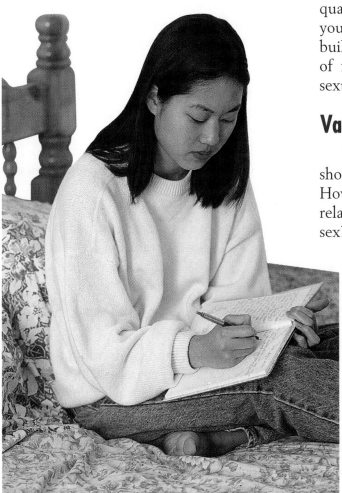

Teen years are a time of growth and change. *How can keeping a journal help you adjust to these changes?*

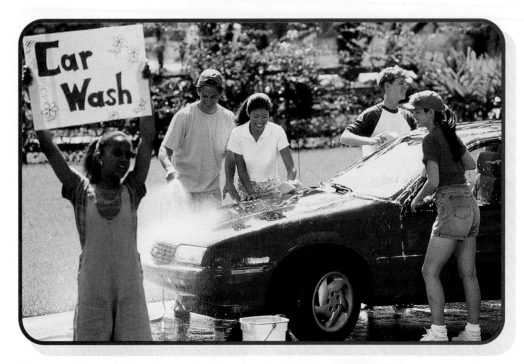

Group activities that involve both males and females give teens a chance to get to know others of the opposite sex. *How can these activities help them develop?*

Familiar examples include trust, self-respect, respect for others, commitment, and loyalty.

By drawing on your values, you can choose to build a sense of your own sexuality *without* becoming sexually active. A look at the consequences of sexual activity shows that this is a wise decision.

The Consequences of Sexual Activity

Teens who do become sexually active often regret that decision. Sexual activity can cause serious problems.

Sexually Transmitted Diseases

A **sexually transmitted disease (STD)** is an illness spread from one person to another by sexual contact. There are about 12 million cases of STDs in the United States each year. About 3 million of those cases affect teens.

All these STDs are preventable. The best way to prevent them is **abstinence**—avoiding sexual activity.

Some STDs can be treated. Others last a person's entire life. The chart on page 121 discusses the most common STDs.

AIDS

One STD has deadly results. Acquired immune deficiency syndrome (AIDS) is caused by the human immunodeficiency virus (HIV). HIV can remain in a person's blood for many years before it develops into AIDS. Although AIDS does not kill its victims, it allows other diseases to invade the body. Eventually, the AIDS patient dies. There is no known cure for AIDS at this time, although research is continuing.

Common Sexually Transmitted Diseases

Some of these symptoms may indicate other diseases or conditions as well. Anyone who experiences any of these symptoms should be tested so that his or her exact condition can be determined and treatment begun.

Disease	Symptoms	Treatment	Effects
Chlamydia (kluh-MIH-dee-uh)	Pain when urinating. Women may feel pain in the abdomen, nausea, or low fever. *Note:* Some people show *no* symptoms.	Can be cured with antibiotics.	Can cause sterility— the inability to have children.
Genital herpes (JEN-uh-tuhl HER-pees)	Open sores on sex organs, which go away in a few weeks.	There is no cure. Symptoms can be treated.	Can cause brain damage or death if passed by pregnant women to infants.
Genital warts	Small growths on the sex organs, which cause discomfort and itching.	There is no cure, but a doctor can remove them.	If left alone, they may become cancerous.
Hepatitis B (hep-uh-TY-tuhs)	Causes flulike symptoms.	There is no cure, but a vaccine is available. It can prevent the disease.	Can lead to liver disease or cancer
Gonorrhea (gon-uh-REE-uh)	Burning, itching, and the discharge of liquids from infected areas.	Can be treated with antibiotics.	Can cause sterility in females. A baby born to an infected mother can suffer eye damage.
Syphilis (SIF-uh-luhs)	In early stages: sores on the sex organs, fevers, rashes, and hair loss.	Can be cured with antibiotics.	Can cause insanity and death.
AIDS	Caused by the human immunodeficiency virus (HIV), which can remain unknown in the bloodstream for many years.	Once HIV develops into AIDS, there is no cure. Some medicines can delay the development of AIDS.	AIDS opens the door to other illnesses, which cause death.

Pregnancy

Another possible consequence of sexual activity, of course, is pregnancy. Pregnancy raises many problems—and they affect the teen father as well as the mother. When Tonya became pregnant, she and Parker married. Parker took a job, planning to finish high school after a year. Just before the year ended, the car broke down, and he needed to work extra to afford repairs. Soon after, Tonya became pregnant again. By the time their second child was a year old, Parker had been out of high school almost three years. He didn't feel like going back—although he knew if he did he could earn more money.

Teen pregnancy creates four types of problems:

- **Health risks.** Pregnancy presents special health risks for both a teen mother and her baby. A teen's body may not be ready for the extra demands pregnancy places on it. Teen mothers are more likely than those in other age groups to suffer from iron deficiency and very high blood pressure. They are also more likely to develop urinary tract infections.

   Because her own nutritional needs are high, without extra emphasis on nutrition, a teen mother may not be able to provide the nutrients her baby needs. These babies are more likely to die before their first birthday. They are more likely to be premature and to have low weight at birth. These conditions are linked to other problems, from blindness to learning deficiencies.

- **Education.** The best thing pregnant teens can do is to complete their schooling. Yet many teens drop of out school after they become pregnant or after the baby is born. Nearly half of the teen mothers who leave school—even those who planned to return—never complete their education. Without a high school diploma, these teens have a hard time finding a job and often can't support themselves and their babies.

   Pregnant teens can work with school counselors and social service agencies that help teens. Some schools have special classes for teen parents. Some provide care in school for the babies while the mothers take classes. Staying in school can help avoid life-long problems.

- **Financial problems.** Money problems begin with the pregnancy. To avoid the health risks of pregnancy, teen mothers need good medical care. That care costs money, as does childbirth. After the birth, teen parents who keep their child must bear the responsibility for providing the child with food, clothing, housing, and health care. This continues for at least eighteen years.

   Even if teen parents who keep their baby don't marry, they are legally responsible for providing financially for their child. If the father chooses not to stay involved with the child, it's especially important to establish **paternity**. This legally identifies the man as the father and his responsibilities toward the child. A medical test can prove paternity.

   For many teen couples, the financial burden becomes overwhelming. It blights hopes and often leads to bitter arguments. This tension can spill over to their relationship with other family members and even with the baby.

Ask the Experts

Pat Brodeen
Teacher and Teen Parent Coordinator
at Theodore Roosevelt High School in
San Antonio, Texas

MANAGING *the Stress of Teen Parenting*

I am a teen mom with a four-month-old son. Sometimes I just feel completely overwhelmed—can you help me help myself?

Of course you feel over-whelmed—having a child has added a lot of stress to your life. You can make your life—and your baby's life—easier by learning techniques for managing stress.

I know you feel you already have too much to do, but you'll handle stress better when you find time to take good care of yourself:

- **Exercise every day even if you are tired.** *This will help keep you physically and emotionally healthy.*

- *Eat a balanced diet. When you grab a cola and chips instead of a sandwich and fruit, you're undermining your health and making yourself more vulnerable to stress.*

- **Take time to relax.** *Learn some relaxation techniques, listen to music, take a warm bath.*

- *Develop a network of supportive friends, including other young mothers, adults, and other teens. When you feel tense, angry, or in need of support, contact someone you can count on.*

- *Keep a positive attitude to reduce stress. Ask your friends for help with this.*

- *Make plans for the future. Ask a counselor or teacher to help you explore your employment options. Find out about educational and training opportunities.*

Thinking It Through

1. How can teen fathers help teen mothers follow Pat Brodeen's suggestions?
2. Why is it important to make friends with other teen parents?
3. Why would it be helpful for a teen mother to be sure to finish high school?

- **Emotional and social stress.** Adjusting to new relationships can cause great stress. So, too, can changes to old relationships. Teen parents may miss their old friends. When they see those friends, however, they may feel that they no longer have much in common with them. Teens who enjoyed sports or other after-school activities must give them up. Teen parents realize quickly that their lives have changed in profound ways.

Why do teen parents sometimes feel isolated from their peers?

SECTION 4-1 REVIEW

✔ Check Your Understanding

1. Define *sexuality*.
2. What forces seem to push teens to choosing sexual activity?
3. What are values?
4. Why are teen mothers and their babies more likely to suffer physical problems?
5. Which sexually transmitted diseases can be fatal?
6. What four kinds of problems are associated with teen pregnancy?
7. Why do teens find that their relationships with old friends change after they become parents?

Putting Knowledge Into Practice

1. **Making Inferences.** Why are group dates a good way to reduce the pressure to become sexually active?
2. **Synthesizing.** Health care experts say that someone who becomes sexually active becomes involved not just with one partner but with all that partner's past partners. What do they mean by that?
3. **Observing and Participating.** Write down three goals you have for your future. Which of your values can help you achieve those goals?

CAREER OPPORTUNITIES

Social Worker

A CONVERSATION WITH DEANA STOLTZ

How did you become interested in becoming a social worker? My family had some problems when I was younger. A social worker helped us get through them. She really inspired me!

What are the tasks and responsibilities of a social worker? It varies a lot. We can handle twenty or so cases at a time. Some of my families need help with substance, spouse, or child abuse, and others with job issues. I find it rewarding to help teen parents—I feel like I'm helping a family get off to a good start.

What is the work environment like? We use our office for paperwork and writing reports. We meet with individuals and families, often in their homes. We also teach classes—like a class in parenting skills I teach.

What are the working hours like? Our work with clients—the people we help— is usually during the day. At night, I catch up on my reading or paperwork.

What aptitudes are needed to be a social worker? You certainly need to be a good listener. In fact, you need good communications skills of all sorts. You also need to be a problem solver. You need to be sympathetic to people who have problems—but you have to be tough, too, to help them see how to solve their own problems. You also need a positive attitude.

Career Facts

SOCIAL WORKER

Education and Training. Social workers need a bachelor's degree (psychology, sociology, social work). They also receive practical training. To practice, they must pass a licensing exam.

Career Outlook. The demand for social workers is expected to remain strong.

CONNECTING SCHOOL TO CAREER

1. **Personal Qualities.** Why would a social worker need to be well organized?
2. **Basic Skills.** Would a social worker need stronger math or language skills? Why?

Solving Problems

Think about all the choices you make. Some, such as what to eat for lunch, almost go unnoticed. Others, like which movie the group should see, take more time, but still don't have much effect on future life. Issues related to sexuality, though, are among the most profound ones you may face. They impact life in deep and lasting ways. For that reason, they deserve careful thought.

KEY TERMS

closed adoption
miscarriage
open adoption

OBJECTIVES:

- Apply the six-part process to solving problems.
- Analyze the various options a pregnant teen has.

Using the Problem-Solving Process

When making these more important decisions and solving problems, it helps to follow the problem-solving process. This process is shown in the chart on page 127. These tips can help you use that process:

- The process doesn't need to be followed in sequential order. You may need to move back and forth among the various parts.
- As you gather information, carefully evaluate the reliability of your sources.
- In identifying the consequences, or results, of an action, think not only of those that will happen right away, but also of those that will take place later.
- Remember to think about the consequences for people other than yourself. Trying out for a sports team affects more people than just you. If you make the team, and have to stay after school for practices, that will impact your family's life. If you have a job, playing on the team will affect the work schedules of other people.

- Choosing an alternative is not always a matter of choosing the one with the most good results or the fewest bad results. Use your values to look at *how important* those results are to you.
- To evaluate how you solved the problem, ask yourself some basic questions. Did the action have the results you expected? Did it have better or worse ones? Do you need to go back and reconsider other alternatives?
- Another reason to evaluate the results of the action is to improve your problem-solving skills. How did you do in identifying alternatives and weighing pros and cons? Is there something you wish you could do better next time? If so, how can you improve your performance?

THE PROBLEM-SOLVING PROCESS

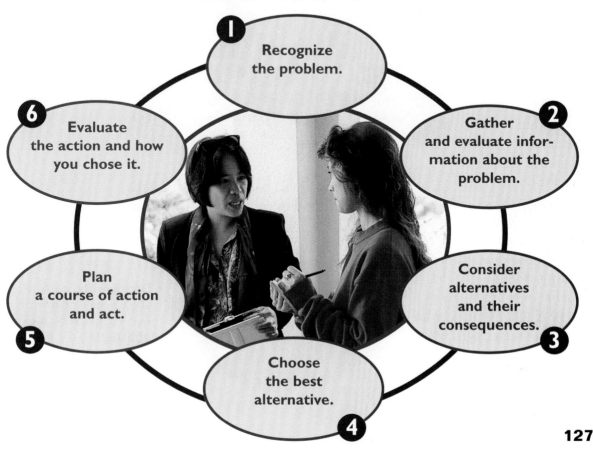

1. Recognize the problem.
2. Gather and evaluate information about the problem.
3. Consider alternatives and their consequences.
4. Choose the best alternative.
5. Plan a course of action and act.
6. Evaluate the action and how you chose it.

The problem-solving process may seem awkward or complicated at first. With everyday practice, though, you'll find it comes to you naturally. Making this process a part of your life can bring great benefits.

Making Responsible Decisions About Sexuality

The problem-solving process can help you face the difficult questions related to sexuality. These choices are too important to be made casually. They deserve careful consideration because they have serious consequences. The effects can last throughout the teen's life.

Bear in mind that choosing to be sexually active affects more than just the two teens involved. Their parents can be touched by it as well. So can their brothers and sisters. If the decision results in a pregnancy, another person—the child who will be born—has to be taken into account, too.

It can be helpful to discuss this decision with other people. Trusted adults—a parent or older family member, teacher, doctor, religious leader, or an adult friend—can be valuable resources. Peers can be good listeners who can share their own experiences.

Predicting Consequences

When you consider the consequences of sexual activity, think about the information in the previous section. The dangers of sexually transmitted diseases are real. The burdens of pregnancy are heavy. Either of these results will change your life in painful and difficult ways. These consequences can be avoided simply by abstaining from sexual activity.

You also need to think about other consequences. Sexual activity has emotional impact as well. Look inside yourself. How will you feel about yourself—and your partner—if you become sexually active? How will your partner feel about you? How will you face your parents and others?

These are difficult questions to answer. The truth lies hidden in the future. Strong emotions can cloud judgment. Still, with careful thought, you may be able to make some good predictions.

Decisions about sexuality affect people other than the teen couple. *Who else is affected?*

Reasons for Saying "No"

Sexual activity can have terrible consequences on a teen's physical and emotional health. There are many good reasons to say "no" to sexual activity:

- You don't want to be pregnant or cause someone else to be pregnant.
- You don't want to be infected by an STD.
- You would lose respect for yourself.
- Your parents would lose respect for you and trust in you.
- It goes against your values.
- It would hurt your reputation.
- You don't want a sexual relationship.
- You have big plans for your future, and being sexually active would interfere.
- You think there are better ways of showing affection.
- You want to set a good example for your younger brother or sister.
- You want to wait until marriage.

FOLLOWING UP

1. Which reason to abstain do you think is best? Why?
2. Write down a reason of your own.

It is important to be hard-headed and clear-eyed when thinking about consequences. Some teens find themselves in a troubled relationship. Some want the other person in the relationship to care for them as much as they care for him or her. These teens may feel that by becoming sexually active, they can make these wishes come true. Such thinking is giving in to wild hopes. Usually such relationships end, and the teen is left feeling hurt and alone. Hopes and wishes are not the foundation for a strong relationship. Common values, real caring, and effective communication are.

Deciding to Abstain

"It can't happen to me." Thousands of teens have thought that—and thousands were wrong. The threat of sexually transmitted diseases is very real, as is the threat of pregnancy. There is only one guaranteed way of avoiding these problems—abstaining from sexual activity.

Using the problem-solving process takes time and rational consideration. It's not reasonable to expect to reach the decision to abstain in a moment of passion. You need to take time to really think it through.

Once you have decided to abstain, stick to your decision. Talk to your partner in a setting where you can both discuss the situation calmly and without emotion. If two people cannot discuss the consequences of sexual activity in a serious way, they are not ready for that level of involvement.

Explain why you have chosen abstinence. Discuss all the negative consequences of sexual activity. Make clear to your partner that you expect him or her to respect your decision. Someone who really cares for you would show that respect and never put pressure on you to begin sexual activity.

When Pregnancy Occurs

Sometimes teens do get pregnant. Often, teens have trouble believing and acknowledging the symptoms of pregnancy. A girl who fears she might be pregnant may try to ignore the symptoms. This kind of avoidance makes it impossible for her to begin dealing with the pregnancy. It is essential for the mother's and baby's health to get good prenatal care as soon as possible.

Teens who are sexually active should be aware of the early signs of pregnancy. As difficult as this may be, a teen who suspects she might be pregnant needs to discuss her concerns with someone close—her boyfriend, a parent or other family member, a trusted friend, or a special teacher or counselor. She should also

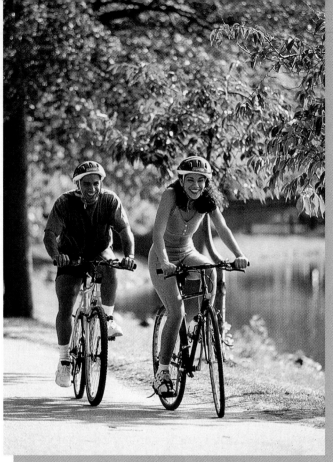

Why is abstinence the best choice for teens?

INFOLINK

Signs of Pregnancy

For more information on *signs of pregnancy,* see Chapter 6, pages 180-181.

see a physician, who can tell her definitely whether or not she is pregnant.

Once her pregnancy has been confirmed, a teen can begin to decide what to do. In order to make a responsible decision, she will have to consider her alternatives and their consequences.

The partner of a pregnant teen should take part in the decision. The father has rights and responsibilities, too. No matter what the decision is, the pregnancy will have a long-lasting effect on his life. Even if the couple does not marry, he has a responsibility to help provide for the care of the child.

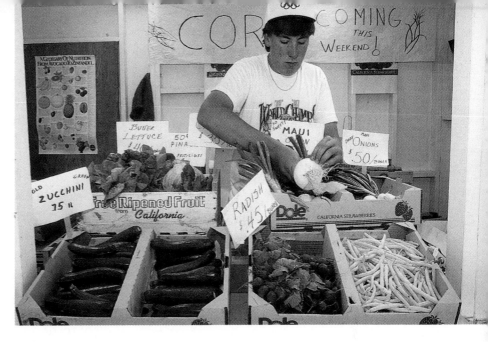

Teen fathers have rights and responsibilities toward the baby. *How can they help meet those responsibilities by working?*

Considering the Alternatives

A pregnant teen can become a single parent. She can marry and, with her husband, become a parent. She can continue the pregnancy but give the baby up for adoption. Some pregnancies end with a miscarriage or by a medical procedure.

Single Parenthood

Having a tiny baby to cuddle and love can seem very attractive. It can be rewarding to care for someone who is helpless and dependent. However, caring for a newborn is a huge responsibility, and becoming a parent is a lifetime commitment.

Single parents face special challenges because they take on—alone—complete responsibility for their child. They also have to do all household chores and meet financial obligations. All these responsibilities can be draining—especially for a teen. Not surprisingly, many teen parents suffer from burnout or depression.

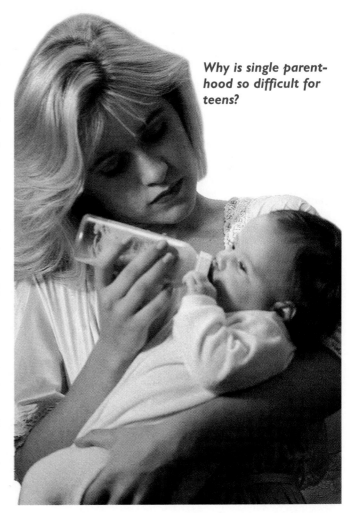

Why is single parenthood so difficult for teens?

Teens who are considering single parenthood should be as realistic as possible. How much help—emotional and financial—can the teen mother expect from the baby's father? From her own parents and other family members? A teen who is considering single parenthood must be especially careful to avoid romanticizing the situation. A teen partner who was not interested in marriage during the pregnancy is unlikely to change his or her mind once the baby is born, for example. Parents, counselors, and other adults can help teens develop realistic expectations for their own situations as single parents.

Marriage

The prospect of getting married seems exciting, but married teens face many problems. As the early excitement wears off, the strains of responsibility set in. Also, many married teens feel socially isolated. They no longer fit in with their single friends, but their interests and activities are not the same as those of older married couples. Teens who marry because of a pregnancy face an additional problem. They have to adjust to parenthood at the same time they're adjusting to being married.

At the same time, getting married has benefits. Married teens who meet these challenges can find themselves with a strong and rewarding relationship. Having two people share the load of child care lessens the work of each. Finally, married teens can build a caring home for a child—and provide the child with role models of both sexes.

Adoption

Another alternative for pregnant teens is adoption. In an adoption, the birth mother and father give up their rights and responsibilities for raising the child, which another family legally takes on.

Why do birth parents choose adoption? Many make this choice because they feel they are giving their child an opportunity for more care, guidance, and love than they can provide at this stage of their lives.

Birth parents who choose adoption should find a reputable adoption agency or program—one that will treat them fairly and try to find a good home for their child. The county department of human services or the local health department will have lists of such agencies. Birth parents can also ask a religious leader or counselor.

About 20,000 unwed teens give their babies up for adoption each year. *How does this choice help both the teen and the child?*

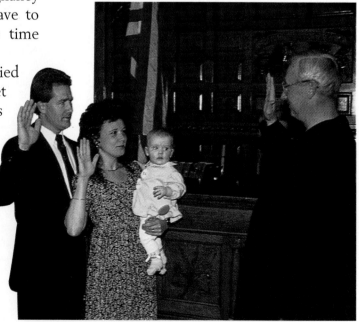

Adoption should be carried out by professionals who carefully screen prospective parents and prepare them for a new baby. Many agencies also give counseling and health care to the pregnant teen and her partner. It is important for the pregnant mother, for instance, to make sure that she and the baby are healthy during her pregnancy.

In a **closed adoption,** the birth parents don't know the names of the adoptive parents. Some adoptive parents feel more comfortable with this situation. More and more adoptions are what are called **open adoptions.** In this arrangement, birth parents are told about the adopting parents and may even get to meet them. Some agencies even let the birth parents read through the files of several possible adoptive parents and choose one for their child.

Pregnancy Termination

Sometimes difficulties develop in a pregnancy. They may produce a spontaneous abortion, commonly called a **miscarriage.** A pregnant teen who suspects she has had a miscarriage should contact a doctor immediately.

An intentional, or induced, abortion is a medical procedure. To be safe, it must be performed by a fully trained doctor. Few issues are as controversial and emotional as the question of induced abortions. Some people are strongly opposed to it.

Abortion is also deeply disturbing emotionally to the woman. Of course, this turmoil can be avoided by practicing abstinence in the first place. That prevents pregnancy from occurring.

SECTION 4-2 REVIEW

✔ Check Your Understanding

1. What are the six parts in the problem-solving process?
2. Why do you need to evaluate information you gather?
3. Name two things to remember when looking at consequences.
4. What are the drawbacks of single parenthood?
5. What pressures can affect a teen marriage?
6. Distinguish between closed and open adoption.

Putting Knowledge Into Practice

1. **Analyzing.** The text says: "If two people cannot discuss the possible consequences of sexual activity in a serious way, they are not ready for that level of involvement." Do you agree or disagree? Why?
2. **Applying.** Suppose you had a seventeen-year-old sister who told you she was pregnant. How would you respond? What advice would you give her?
3. **Observing and Participating.** Think of an example of a serious problem that teens commonly face, such as what career to choose. Make a chart showing how the problem-solving process can be used to make this decision.

Parenting With Care

Finding Help

What happens when you're a teen and the pregnancy test is positive?

Pregnancy is a life-changing event. When you are a teen, it can be hard to know where to turn.

Teens who are pregnant need help. Fortunately, that help is available from many different people:

- **The father-to-be.** The teen should certainly talk to the father. He should be involved in making decisions.
- **Parents.** Most pregnant teens are reluctant to discuss their situation with their parents. Parents are often hurt or angry when they first learn of the pregnancy. However, parents are often in the best position to help teens think through the meaning and implications of pregnancy and parenthood. The emotional support that parents offer can be valuable in helping teens deal with the problem and live with the consequences of their decisions.

- **Religious leaders.** Teens who feel uncomfortable talking with their parents right away may be able to discuss the pregnancy with a religious leader. In many cases, they can help teens discuss the matter with their own parents.
- **School personnel.** Teachers, counselors, or the school nurse can offer advice and assistance when teens feel frightened or confused. Although rules vary, discussions with these workers can usually be confidential unless a teen's life or health is in danger.
- **Family counselors.** Nonprofit and privately funded agencies have trained counselors who can help. So do many public agencies such as county departments of social services. These professionals can help teens consider their options.

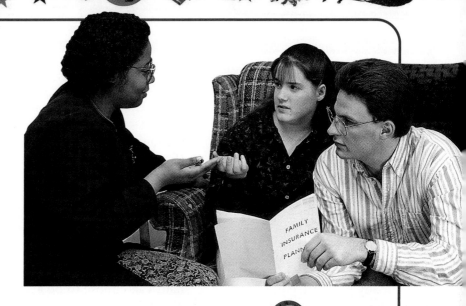

They can also help teens make contact with agencies that give financial and medical help during the pregnancy. Such groups may also provide baby clothes, food supplies, and furniture when the baby arrives.

- **National organizations.** National groups such as the National Adoption Information Clearinghouse can put teens in touch with local groups that can help.

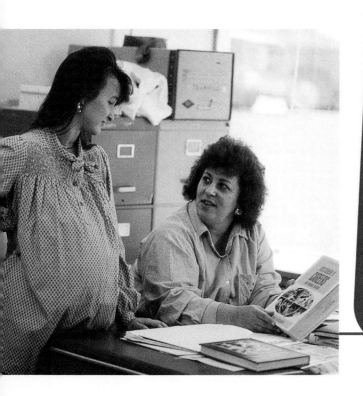

Following Up

1. Why are religious leaders and school personnel good resources?

2. **Leadership.** Write a help-wanted ad for a family counselor. What skills and qualities would such a worker need?

3. **Communication.** Suppose you worked as a school nurse. What would you tell a pregnant teen who came to you for help?

Summary

✔ Teens can use dating and other relationships with people of the opposite sex to build a sense of their sexuality. (Section 4-1)

✔ The negative consequences of sexual activity can greatly affect teens. (Section 4-1)

✔ Teen pregnancy leads to many physical, emotional, and social problems. (Section 4-1)

✔ Using the problem-solving process can help you think through important issues. (Section 4-2)

✔ The only certain way of avoiding sexually transmitted diseases and pregnancy is to abstain from sexual activity. (Section 4-2)

✔ A teen who becomes pregnant can choose to be a single parent, marry, or put the child up for adoption. (Section 4-2)

8. Why is life so hard for single teen parents? (Section 4-2)

9. What is open adoption? (Section 4-2)

Thinking Critically

1. **Analyzing.** What rights and responsibilities do you think a teen male has when his sexual partner becomes pregnant? How—if at all—does his role differ from that of the mother-to-be?

2. **Comparing.** Write a paragraph explaining why an adult would be more helpful than a peer when a teen wishes to discuss becoming sexually active.

3. **Synthesizing.** Why might having a child weaken an already weak relationship between a couple?

Reviewing the Facts

1. What is the difference between *sexuality* and *sexual activity*? (Section 4-1)

2. What values might a teen rely on to choose to avoid sexual activity? (Section 4-1)

3. What negative consequences result from sexual activity? (Section 4-1)

4. Choose one problem of teen pregnancy and explain how it affects both the father-to-be and the mother-to-be. (Section 4-1)

5. What are two kinds of consequences to consider when making choices? (Section 4-2)

6. What are two benefits you can gain from evaluating decisions? (Section 4-2)

7. What do you gain by abstaining from sexual activity? (Section 4-2)

Taking Action

1. **Identifying Alternatives.** Generate a list of activities that teens who have chosen to abstain from sexual activity can do in your community while on a date. *(Leadership)*

2. **Researching.** Investigate the legal rights and responsibilities of a father. What are the advantages of establishing paternity? *(Management)*

CONNECTIONS

 Cross-Curricular Connections

1. **Art.** Create a poster that warns teens of the dangers of sexually transmitted diseases.
2. **Language Arts.** With a partner, plan and write a skit showing a teen boy and girl discussing becoming sexually active. Have them use the problem-solving process to decide in favor of abstaining from sexual activity.

 Workplace Connections

1. **Personal Qualities.** Why is keeping information confidential important for people who work as counselors?
2. **Interpersonal Skills.** What interpersonal skills would be needed by someone who advises pregnant teens?

 Family and Community Connections

1. **Media Watch.** Some people criticize the media for showing material that promotes sexual activity. Have a class debate on whether or not television shows should be censored.
2. **Abstinence Pledge.** Students in some places write a formal pledge in which they promise not to become sexually active. Then they sign the pledge, promising to uphold it. As a class, write a pledge that contains a promise of abstinence. Discuss how you could persuade other students to sign it.

3. **First-Person Accounts.** In the library or a bookstore, find a magazine article that contains the true story of a pregnant teen who became a single parent, married and raised the child, or put the child up for adoption. Remember that the account could be written by a boy or a girl. Read the person's story and then relate it to the class.

 Technology Connections

1. **Video or Audiotape.** Create a radio or television public service announcement that calls attention to the responsibilities and realities of teen parenthood and urges teens not to become sexually active.

2. **Computer.** Using a spreadsheet program, develop a budget for a single parent or a young married couple with a child.

UNIT 2

Pregnancy and Childbirth

"SOME THINGS DON'T MAKE ANY SENSE AT ALL"

My mom says I'm her sugarplum.

My mom says I'm her lamb.

My mom says I'm completely perfect

Just the way I am.

My mom says I'm a super-special terrific little guy.

My mom just had another baby.

Why?

—Judith Viorst

CHAPTER 5

Prenatal Development

Stefan and Julia exchanged excited glances. Julia was about 20 weeks pregnant and had come to see her doctor for her monthly visit. As always, Stefan came along. This was their first child, and he wanted to know how the baby—and Julia—were doing. Besides, today was a special day. Last month, the doctor had said that they would try to hear the baby's heartbeat today.

The doctor had been asking Julia questions about how she felt in the past month. As she finished writing down Julia's answers, the mother- and father-to-be could hardly contain themselves. Then Dr. Aditya looked up from her paper with a broad smile. "Are you ready?" she asked. Stefan and Julia both nodded quickly.

Dr. Aditya listened first and said "Oh, we've got a good, strong heartbeat here." Then the nurse positioned the special stethoscope so Julia and Stefan could hear. There it was—the rapid thump, thump of their baby's heart! Smiles broke out on their faces, but they also felt a sense of awe. The reality of the new life they had created began to sink in.

"There it was—the rapid thump, thump of their baby's heart!"

The Developing Baby

During pregnancy, a single cell grows and develops into a human being capable of independent life. This amazing process, which takes about nine months, is called **prenatal development**.

KEY TERMS

amniotic fluid
conception
embryo
fetus
ovum
placenta
prenatal development
sperm
umbilical cord
uterus
zygote

OBJECTIVES:

- Distinguish among the three stages of pregnancy.
- Describe prenatal development during each stage of pregnancy.
- Explain what changes affect a woman during each stage of pregnancy.

Conception

About once each month, an **ovum** (OH-vum)—a female cell or egg—is released by one of a woman's ovaries. The egg moves through the Fallopian tube to the **uterus** (UTE-uh-rus), the organ in a woman's body in which a baby develops during pregnancy. The journey takes about two or three days.

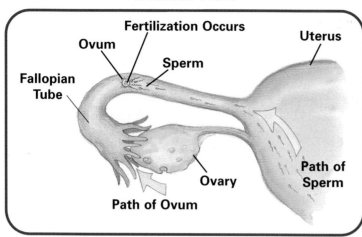

CONCEPTION

Labels: Fertilization Occurs, Ovum, Sperm, Uterus, Fallopian Tube, Path of Sperm, Ovary, Path of Ovum

The first stage in development is the period of the **zygote** (ZY-goat), or fertilized egg. It lasts about two weeks.

In this period, the zygote travels down the Fallopian tube and attaches itself to the thickened lining of the uterus. This lining provides a soft, warm bed. From the uterus, the zygote draws nourishment from the mother's body.

The zygote grows by cell division. The single, complete cell divides and becomes two. Then these two cells become four and so on, until there is a mass of cells. Despite this remarkable growth, after two weeks, the zygote is only the size of a pinhead.

When the egg reaches the uterus, it usually disintegrates and is flushed out of the body with the menstrual flow. Sometimes, however, the egg meets and is fertilized by a **sperm**, or male cell. When the ovum and a sperm unite, **conception** takes place, and pregnancy begins.

Fertilization can take place only two or three days after the ovum has been released. However, sperm can live up to seven days. So there is actually a period of about ten days each month during which a female can become pregnant.

Period of the Zygote

The baby's development is often grouped into three stages, called the periods of the zygote, the embryo, and the fetus. The charts on pages 145 to 147 show how the unborn baby and mother change during these months.

In looking at this chart, remember that growth patterns and reactions are individual. Not all babies develop at exactly the same rate. Every woman does not experience all of the effects described here.

Period of the Embryo

The second stage of pregnancy is the period of the **embryo**. The embryo is the developing baby from about the third through eighth weeks of pregnancy. During this time, the embryo grows rapidly. It is also in this period that several important and amazing changes occur.

EMBRYO ATTACHES TO UTERUS

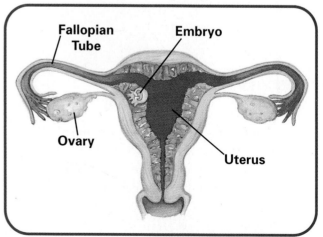

Labels: Fallopian Tube, Embryo, Ovary, Uterus

Menstruation

At the same time that an egg is released by the ovary, the woman's body releases specific hormones. These prepare the uterus in case the egg is fertilized. The inner lining of the uterus begins to grow and thicken. If the egg is not fertilized, this inner lining breaks down and passes out of the body. This is the bleeding that women experience every month as a menstrual period. Periods usually are about 28 days apart.

When fertilization takes place, though, the zygote attaches itself to this lining. In that case, the lining of the uterus cannot be shed. When fertilization takes place, then, the woman's menstrual periods stop. They will not begin again until after the baby is born.

For some women, periods may be delayed even longer. The menstrual period may not begin again while a woman is breast-feeding her baby.

FOLLOWING UP

1. What causes a woman to menstruate?
2. If a woman does not have a menstrual period, what may have taken place? What should she do?

EMBRYO AT 3 WEEKS

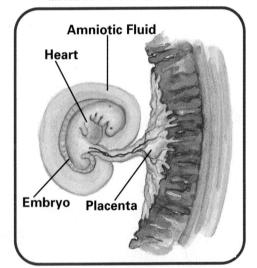

Amniotic Fluid
Heart
Embryo
Placenta

First, the mass of cells develops into all the major systems of the human body—heart and lungs, bones and muscle. These internal organs are not ready to function yet, however. They continue to develop in the rest of the pregnancy. Even this early, though, the brain begins to take control of these body systems. Because brain development can be harmed by drugs or alcohol, it is important that a pregnant woman avoid these substances.

Second, a sac filled with fluid forms around the embryo. This **amniotic** (AM-knee-AH-tik) **fluid** protects the developing baby. It cushions the embryo from any bumps or falls that the mother might have.

Third, a tissue called the **placenta** (pluh-SEN-tuh) develops. The placenta is very rich in blood vessels. The mother's bloodstream carries food and oxygen to the placenta. From there, it reaches the baby through the **umbilical** (um-BILL-uh-cuhl) **cord**—the fourth important change of this period.

Pregnancy Development
Month by Month

Month 1
- Missed menstrual period.
- Other signs of pregnancy may not yet be noticeable.

Month 2
- Breasts begin to swell.
- Pressure on bladder from enlarging uterus results in need to urinate more frequently.
- Possible nausea ("morning sickness").
- Fatigue is common.

Month 3
- Breasts become firmer and fuller, may ache.
- Nausea, fatigue, and frequent urination may continue.
- Abdomen becomes slightly larger. The uterus is about the size of an orange.
- Weight gain may total 2-4 pounds (0.9-1.8 kg).

Month 4
- Abdomen continues to grow slowly.
- Most discomforts of early pregnancy, such as morning sickness, usually gone.
- Appetite increases.

Month 5
- Enlarged abdomen becomes apparent.
- Slight fetal movements felt.
- Increased size may begin to affect posture.

Month 6
- Fetal movements sensed as strong kicks, thumps, and bumps. Some may be visible.
- Weight gain by the beginning of this month may total 10-12 pounds (4.5-5.4 kg).

Month 7
- Increased size may affect posture.

Month 8
- Discomfort may result from increased size. Backache, leg cramps, shortness of breath, and fatigue are common.
- Fetal kicks may disturb the mother's rest.
- At the beginning of this month, weight gain totals about 18-20 pounds (8.2-9.1 kg).

Month 9
- "Lightening" felt as the fetus drops into the pelvis. Breathing becomes easier.
- Other discomforts may continue.
- A total weight gain of 25-35 pounds (11.3-15.9 kg) is typical.
- False labor pains may be experienced.

Fetal Development
Month by Month

Month 1

- Size: At two weeks, the size of a pinhead.
- Egg attaches to lining of uterus.
- Internal organs and circulatory system begin to form. The heart begins to beat.
- Small bumps indicate the beginning of arms and legs.

Month 2

- Size: About ¼ inch (6 mm) long as month begins.
- Face, eyes, ears, and limbs take shape.
- Bones begin to form.

Month 3

- Size: About 1 inch (25 mm) long as month begins.
- Nostrils, mouth, lips, teeth buds, and eyelids form.
- Fingers and toes almost complete.
- All organs present, although immature.

Month 4

- Size: About 3 inches (76 mm) long, 1 ounce (28 g) as month begins.
- Can suck its thumb, swallow, hiccup, and move around.
- Facial features become clearer.

Month 5

- Size: About 6½-7 inches (16-18 cm) long, about 4-5 ounces (113-142 g) as month begins.
- Hair, eyelashes, and eyebrows appear.
- Teeth continue to develop.
- Organs are maturing.
- Becomes more active.

Month 6

- Size: About 8-10 inches (21-25 cm) long, about 8-12 ounces (227-340 g) as month begins.
- Fat deposits under skin, but fetus appears wrinkled.
- Breathing movements begin.

Month 7

- Size: About 10-12 inches long , about 1½-2 pounds (680-907 g) as month begins.
- Periods of activity followed by periods of rest and quiet.

Month 8

- Size: About 14-16 inches (36-41 cm) long, about 2½-3 pounds (1.0-1.4 kg) as month begins.
- Weight gain continues rapidly.
- May react to loud noises with a reflex jerking action.
- Moves into a head down position.

Month 9

- Size: About 17-18 inches (43-46 cm) long, 5-6 pounds (2.3-2.7 kg) as month begins.
- Weight gain continues until the week before birth.
- Skin becomes smooth as fat deposits continue.
- Movements decrease as the fetus has less room to move around.
- Acquires disease-fighting antibodies from the mother's blood.
- Descends into pelvis, ready for birth.

The umbilical cord brings nourishment to the baby and takes waste products away. It is usually stiff and firm, like a garden hose filled with water. It is generally not flexible enough to loop around the fetus, although this may occur in rare cases. Only after the baby is born does the umbilical cord become limp.

Period of the Fetus

The third and last stage of pregnancy begins about the eight or ninth week and lasts until birth. This is the period of the **fetus** (FEE-tuhs), the name for the unborn baby from about the eighth or ninth week of pregnancy until birth.

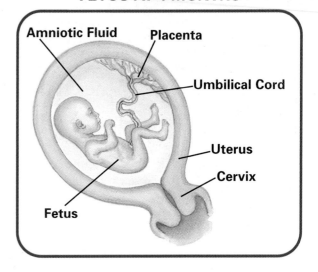

FETUS AT 4 MONTHS

Amniotic Fluid
Placenta
Umbilical Cord
Uterus
Cervix
Fetus

┌─ **The Developing Brain** ─────────

 Studies show that the fetus already learns and responds to its environment. When light is shined on the fetus, it turns away. When loud music is played, its heart rate increases, and it moves.

└────────────────────────────────

Sometime during the fourth or fifth month, the kicks and other movements of the fetus touch the wall of the uterus. These movements are faint and infrequent at first. Gloria felt her baby's movement as a kind of fluttering. Gradually, they become stronger and more frequent. These sensations, sometimes called "quickening," tell the mother that she does, indeed, carry a live child within her. Actually, the baby has been very active long before this time.

A pregnant woman's doctor usually asks her when she first felt these movements. Knowing this helps the doctor estimate the baby's age. That can be used to project a more accurate delivery date.

As the fetus grows, so does the amount of the surrounding fluid. The uterus expands, too, and the woman's abdomen grows. Just before delivery, the amount of amniotic fluid decreases. The baby is swallowing it. When the fetus grows large, it no longer has the room to stretch out. It curls up inside the uterus in what is called the fetal position.

By the seventh month, the fetus is capable of living outside the uterus, but not without a great deal of medical help. In the next few months, the fetus becomes ready to live independently. The body's major organs become ready to function without help from the mother's body. The fetus also gains weight rapidly. Fat deposits, which will help the baby maintain body heat after birth, are added under the skin. The fetus, which had been thin and wrinkled, takes on the smoother, rounder appearance of a baby. During these final weeks, the fetus also stores nutrients and builds immunity to diseases and infections.

The fetus can do a surprising number of things—suck its thumb, cough, sneeze, yawn, kick, and hiccup. A baby can even cry before birth.

Preparing for Birth

Sometime during the ninth month of pregnancy, the baby's weight seems to shift down and the mother feels more comfortable in her upper abdomen. This shift is called "lightening." It means that the baby has dropped into the birth canal. With a first baby, lightening may take place several days—or even weeks—before labor begins. If the mother has given birth before, lightening may not occur until just before labor begins.

At this point, the fetus is usually upside down, with the head nestled in the mother's pelvis. This is the easiest and safest position for birth. The baby is less active than in previous weeks, because there is little space in which to move!

The skin of the mother's abdomen appears stretched to capacity. The abdominal muscles are stretched, too. They are

FETUS AT 9 MONTHS

both capable of remarkable stretching— and contracting. The muscles of the uterus and abdomen can be stretched up to 60 times their original size during pregnancy, yet they return to nearly their original size within six weeks or so after the birth. Pregnancy brings many changes, both in the pregnant woman and the developing baby. After 37 to 42 weeks of preparation, the baby is ready to be born.

SECTION 5-1 REVIEW

✔ Check Your Understanding

1. What cells join together to cause conception?
2. What happens during the period of the zygote? How long does it last?
3. What changes might a pregnant woman feel in the period of the zygote and embryo?
4. What four changes take place in the period of the embryo?
5. What are the most important changes that take place in a fetus during the last two months of pregnancy?
6. How does a pregnant woman feel when "lightening" occurs? Why?

Putting Knowledge Into Practice

1. **Diagramming.** Draw a diagram showing the uterus, amniotic sac, placenta, umbilical cord, and fetus. Label these parts.
2. **Comparing.** In a few paragraphs, compare the three stages of prenatal development in terms of the changes that the developing baby undergoes.
3. **Observing and Participating.** Talk to a pregnant female about the physical and emotional changes she has experienced. Record her answers and share them with the class.

A Closer Look at Conception

Have you ever been at a family gathering when someone said that you looked just like a relative? Your uncle may have said "You have your mother's eyes." Perhaps your grandmother said, "Your hair is just like your father's." Why do people look like their parents?

KEY TERMS

chromosomes
dominant
genes
infertility
recessive
surrogate

OBJECTIVES:

- Describe how personal characteristics are inherited.
- Explain the causes of multiple births.
- Evaluate different possible solutions for infertility.

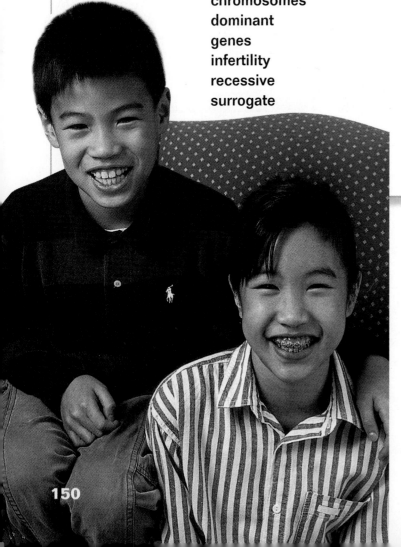

The Genetic Package

Each person inherits many characteristics from his or her parents. They include physical build; skin color; hair texture and color; the color and shape of the eyes; the shape and size of the ears, hands, and feet; and blood type. Musical ability may be passed on from parents to children. So, too, are some medical conditions. How does this happen? Scientists have learned a great deal about how heredity—the passing on of characteristics—works.

At conception, every human baby receives 46 **chromosomes** (CROW-muh-soams), tiny threadlike particles in the nucleus of every cell. These chromosomes come in 23 pairs. The father's sperm and the mother's ovum both contribute a chromosome to each pair. Each chromosome has thousands of **genes,** the units that determine the child's inherited characteristics. Genes make up chromosomes as beads make up a necklace.

For every inherited characteristic, a person receives two copies of a gene—one from the mother and one from the father. When both are the same, the child has that characteristic. Thus, two genes for blue eyes give the child blue eyes.

What happens if a person receives two different genes, such as one gene for blue eyes and one gene for brown eyes? The way the characteristic is expressed will be controlled by the **dominant,** or stronger, gene.

The **recessive,** or weaker, gene will not be expressed. In this example, they will have brown eyes because the brown eye gene is the dominant one.

Of course, the terms *dominant* and *recessive* refer only to the relationship of genes to each other. Blue eyes are not weaker than brown eyes.

Making a Unique Person

Heredity explains why brothers and sisters often resemble each other—and why they can look quite different. Each sperm or egg cell contains a different combination of genes. When they combine in a fertilized egg, they produce a unique individual. That person may have a father's brown eyes; a mother's dimples; a grandfather's tall, lean build; and a grandmother's clear, sweet singing voice. These traits—and many, many others—are determined by the particular combinations of genes brought together at conception.

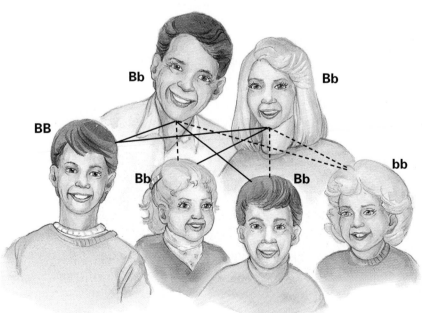

The dominant gene, for brown eyes, is shown with a capital **B.** The recessive gene, for blue eyes, is shown with a lowercase **b.** Only a child who receives the recessive gene from both parents will have blue eyes. If both parents carry the recessive gene, each child has a one in four chance of having blue eyes. *Could these parents have more than one child with blue eyes? Why do more people around the world have brown eyes than blue?*

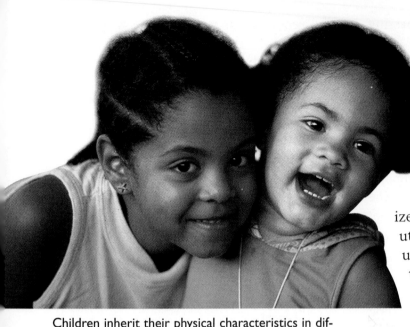

Children inherit their physical characteristics in different combinations from their parents. While they share some traits, each child has a unique genetic makeup.

to divide and grow into a separate embryo. The result is identical twins. Identical twins are always the same sex and have very similar characteristics because both began as one zygote.

Fraternal twins form when two eggs are released at the same time and each is fertilized. They grow side by side in the uterus. Because they result from the union of different eggs and sperm, fraternal twins are no more alike in terms of heredity than any other siblings. Unlike identical twins, they may even be of opposite sexes.

When more than two babies are born, they may be identical or fraternal—or a combination. As with twins, it depends on whether one fertilized egg splits or more than one egg is fertilized at the same time.

In the United States, about 2.5 percent of births are twin births. (Fraternal twins occur three times more often than identical twins.) Multiple births of more than two are rare, but are happening at a growing rate. A major reason for this increase is the treatment people receive to overcome **infertility,** or the inability to become pregnant.

The sex of a child is also set at conception. It is determined by the sex chromosomes, which come in two types, X and Y. Every egg cell contains an X chromosome. Each sperm cell contains either an X or a Y chromosome. If the sperm that fertilizes the egg carries an X chromosome, an XX combination results, and the child is a girl. If the sperm carries a Y chromosome, an XY combination results, and the child is a boy.

Multiple Births

Sometimes a pregnant woman gives birth to more than one baby. This, too, is set at conception or soon after.

As you know, a fertilized egg starts growing by dividing into two cells. These cells continue to divide. Sometimes the mass of cells splits in half soon after fertilization. Then each clump of cells continues

Infertility

Not all couples who want to have children are able to become pregnant. Infertility may have many causes.

People who have problems with fertility often feel that they aren't normal. Many feel that they are alone in facing this situation. Medical and counseling support can help them overcome these feelings.

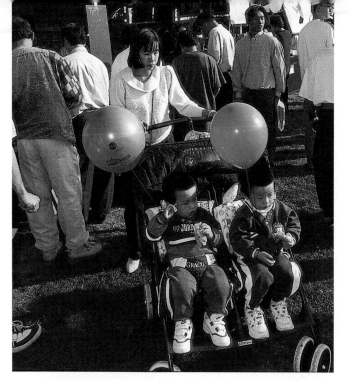

Multiple births may be identical or fraternal. *What is the difference?*

Options for Infertile Couples

Some couples can't conceive a child even after treatment for infertility. They may consider several other options.

- **Adoption.** By adopting, the couple legally takes all responsibilities and rights for raising a child already born.
- **Artificial insemination.** In this process, a doctor injects sperm into a woman's uterus with a special needle. The sperm may be the husband's. If he has a history of genetic disorders, the sperm may come from another male, who is called a donor.
- **In vitro fertilization.** This process is used when a woman has damaged Fallopian tubes that prevent pregnancy. In a small glass dish, a doctor combines a mature egg from the woman

Medical advances have helped many of these couples overcome infertility. When these couples seek medical advice, a doctor makes a detailed study of both the man's and woman's health. Often, this reveals that one or both have physical problems that prevent pregnancy. Surgery or medication may solve the problem.

If the woman's ovaries are not releasing an egg each month, the doctor may prescribe fertility drugs. These substances stimulate a woman's ovaries to release eggs. Fertility drugs have several drawbacks. Some women who take them have serious side effects, such as lung problems, abdominal pain, nausea, diarrhea, or dizziness. Also, fertility drugs increase the chances of multiple babies. The more children a pregnant woman carries, the more difficult it is for them all to survive.

People who have problems with fertility may feel alone with their problems. *How can a counselor help them?*

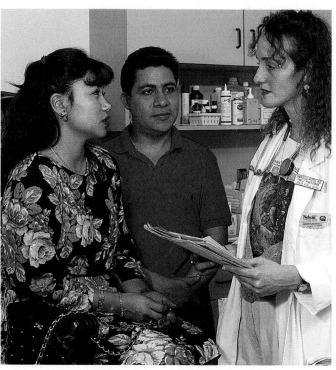

and sperm from her husband. If fertilization takes place, the doctor places the zygote in the woman's uterus. If the zygote attaches itself to the uterus, a normal pregnancy takes place.

- **Ovum transfer.** This procedure uses an egg taken from a female donor and in vitro fertilization. It may be used by women who lack working ovaries or who have inherited disorders.
- **Surrogate mother.** A **surrogate** (SIR-uh-get) or substitute, mother is a woman who becomes pregnant for another couple. She may carry a couple's fertilized egg, removed from the biological mother because she is unable to carry a pregnancy to completion. Other surrogates are artificially inseminated with sperm from the husband of an infertile woman. This process usually includes legal arrangements and must meet state laws.

Questions Raised

As technology continues to advance, other options may be available. However, not everyone thinks these alternatives are acceptable. The use of ovum transfers or surrogate mothers is especially controversial. These practices raise many ethical questions.

SECTION 5-2 REVIEW

✔ Check Your Understanding

1. List some traits that are inherited.
2. Explain how dominant and recessive genes work.
3. Why is each person unique?
4. How is the sex of a baby determined?
5. What is the difference between identical twins and fraternal twins?
6. Name some disadvantages of fertility drugs.
7. What options does an infertile couple have if fertility treatment does not work?

Putting Knowledge Into Practice

1. **Making Inferences.** Scientists are trying to identify each of the genes—up to 100,000 of them—found on human chromosomes. Why do you think they are making this effort? What benefits could this research provide?
2. **Synthesizing.** Why would having damaged Fallopian tubes prevent a woman from becoming pregnant?
3. **Observing and Participating.** Make a chart showing the generations of your family or a family you know from grandparents through parents and their brothers and sisters to the present generation—including brothers, sisters, and cousins. On the chart, show the hair color and eye color of each person. Write a paragraph describing any patterns you see.

SECTION 5-3

Problems in Prenatal Development

Will the baby be all right? This is a major concern for all parents-to-be. Fortunately, most babies develop normally and are born healthy. For a variety of reasons, however, prenatal development does not always proceed normally.

KEY TERMS

amniocentesis
birth defect
chorionic villi sampling
miscarriage
stillbirth
ultrasound

OBJECTIVES:

- Contrast miscarriage and stillbirth.

- Identify some major birth defects.

- Explain the four causes of birth defects.

- Describe how birth defects can be diagnosed and prevented.

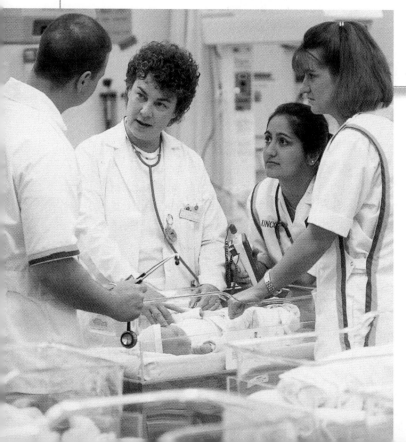

Losing a Baby

Sometimes a baby does not develop normally. In some of those cases, the developing baby dies. If this happens before 20 weeks of pregnancy, it is called a **miscarriage** (MISS-care-uj). If it occurs after 20 weeks, it is called a **stillbirth**.

A miscarriage can be difficult to accept. *How can a couple who suffered a miscarriage help each other?*

These losses can be severe shocks and bring great pain. Most couples look forward to their baby's birth. When a miscarriage or stillbirth takes place, they feel as though they lost a child who had been born. They go through the same stages of grief as does anyone who has had a family member die.

Sometimes, these parents feel terribly alone. They may blame themselves for the death. Usually, these losses happen naturally and are not the fault of either the father or the mother. Nor are these parents alone. In fact, as many as 20 percent of all pregnancies end in miscarriage.

Special services and support groups can help these couples. Most couples who suffer the death of a fetus are able to have a successful pregnancy later.

Types of Birth Defects

Some babies are born with serious problems that threaten their health or ability to live. These problems are called **birth defects**. There are hundreds of birth defects, and they vary widely in their effects. Some are mild or can be readily corrected. Others result in severe lifelong disabilities or even death. About 3 out of every 100 children born in the United States have a birth defect. Scientists and health professionals are working to decrease that rate.

Some birth defects affect the shape or size of the body or of certain parts of the body. For instance, a child may be born with a misshapen foot or an extra or a missing finger. With others, a part or system of the body does not function properly. Blindness, deafness, and mental retardation are examples.

Not all birth defects are apparent at birth. Sometimes the abnormality does not cause problems until months—or even years—have passed.

Causes of Birth Defects

Scientists don't yet understand the cause of about 60 percent of all birth defects. They are constantly researching to find the answers, though. They have found four main causes for birth defects. Some are caused by factors in the environment of the developing baby. Some result from abnormal genes or errors in chromosomes. Many result from a combination of environment and heredity.

Environmental Causes

During the first few weeks of pregnancy, a baby develops all the bodily systems needed for survival and a normal life. During this time, the developing baby depends completely on the mother's body for nourishment and oxygen.

Many choices the mother makes—as well as many conditions of which the mother may be unaware—can affect the development of her baby. They include:

- The nutritional balance of her diet.
- Any diseases or infections the mother has during pregnancy.
- Harmful substances the mother takes in, including alcohol, tobacco, and drugs.
- Some medicines that benefit the mother, but which can hurt the baby.
- Exposure to outside hazards such as radiation, especially early in pregnancy.

Many children with birth defects can still lead full, rich lives.

Taking Care of Two

*E*verything a pregnant woman takes into her body—food, coffee or tea, soda, pills, injections, tobacco smoke, and alcohol—may affect her unborn child. The placenta may act as a partial barrier, and certain substances may have difficulty crossing to the child. Most substances, however, do reach the embryo or fetus. If the concentration of any substance in the mother's blood is high enough, some of these substances can damage the baby.

Researchers have not been able to find a "safe level" for the substances that can harm a developing baby. The best course is a simple one: avoid all these substances during pregnancy. Taking this step helps more than the baby. It helps the mother be healthy, too.

Most women don't realize they are pregnant right away. If they are not careful, they could take harmful substances into their body in the crucial early weeks of the baby's development. They can avoid this problem by planning a pregnancy and by avoiding all harmful substances before they become pregnant.

FOLLOWING UP

1. Why is the developing baby affected by substances that the pregnant woman takes into her body?
2. Amira and Doug have been married two years and now want to have a baby. When should Amira stop smoking?

Hereditary Causes

Thousands of genes make up a genetic blueprint. For each person, about five or six of the recessive genes are imperfect. A single copy of these genes will have no effect on the development of that person—or the baby who inherits the gene. Sometimes, though, each parent passes on the same recessive defective gene. Sometimes, too, a defective gene is dominant. In these cases, the baby may develop a birth defect.

Some inherited conditions affect only one sex. Hemophilia, a condition that prevents the blood from clotting, and color blindness are two examples of birth defects that affect only males.

Errors in Chromosomes

A few types of birth defects are linked to a problem with the baby's chromosomes. For example, there may be too many—or too few—chromosomes in each of the

Cerebral Palsy
- **Description:** Cerebral palsy is a general term for a variety of problems of the motor system. The symptoms can include lack of coordination, stiffness, jerkiness, difficulty with speech, and paralysis.
- **Causes:** Cerebral palsy results from damage to the brain before, during, or shortly after birth. The causes of this damage vary.
- **Detection:** The symptoms usually appear during the first year of life.
- **Treatment:** The damage caused to the brain is irreversible. However, physical therapy, speech therapy, surgery, and medication can lessen the effects of this damage in many cases.

Cleft Lip and/or Cleft Palate
- **Description:** A gap in the upper lip or palate (the roof of the mouth) causes problems with eating, swallowing, speech, and appearance.
- **Causes:** Condition may be caused by hereditary or environmental factors or both.
- **Detection:** Both cleft lip and cleft palate are apparent at birth.
- **Treatment:** Surgery can correct the gap and eliminate the problems associated with it.

Cystic Fibrosis
- **Description:** Cystic fibrosis (CF) affects the respiratory and digestive systems. Many with CF die before reaching adulthood, although treatment now allows people with the condition to live longer than in the past.
- **Cause:** It is far more likely to affect whites than African or Asian Americans. CF is caused by inheriting defective recessive genes from both parents.
- **Detection:** Symptoms include very salty sweat and a cough that doesn't go away. Tests can identify carriers of the gene and can diagnose an affected child or fetus.
- **Treatment:** There is no known cure. Those with CF can be helped by special diets, lung exercises, and treatment.

Down Syndrome
- **Description:** A group of problems that may include, among other conditions, mental retardation; problems of the heart, blood, and digestive system; and poor muscle tone.
- **Cause:** Down syndrome is caused by the presence of an extra chromosome 21.
- **Detection:** It can be detected in a fetus by amniocentesis or chorionic villi sampling; can be found in a child by a blood test.
- **Treatment:** Treatment includes therapy, special schooling, and, in some cases, corrective surgery. The earlier it begins, the better for the child.

(Continued on next page)

Muscular Dystrophy
- **Description:** There are many different types of muscular dystrophy; all involve a progressive weakness and shrinking of the muscles. The most common form begins between the ages of two and six.
- **Causes:** Most types of muscular dystrophy are hereditary. The most common form is transmitted by female carriers of the gene but affects only males.
- **Detection:** The disease is recognized once symptoms appear. Genetic counseling can identify carriers.
- **Treatment:** There is no known cure. Physical therapy can minimize the disabilities.

PKU
- **Description:** PKU is a condition in which the body is unable to process and use a specific protein. Mental retardation can result.
- **Cause:** A child with PKU inherits defective recessive genes from both parents.
- **Detection:** Newborns are tested for PKU, as required by law in all states.
- **Treatment:** There is no known cure for PKU. If it is diagnosed early, a special diet can reduce or prevent brain damage.

Sickle Cell Anemia
- **Description:** Malformed red blood cells interfere with the supply of oxygen to all parts of the body. The symptoms include tiredness, lack of appetite, and pain. Sickle cell anemia can lead to early death.
- **Cause:** Sickle cell anemia is caused by inheriting defective recessive genes from both parents. African Americans are more likely to have this condition than any other group.
- **Detection:** Amniocentesis or chorionic villi sampling can identify anemia in a fetus. Genetic counseling can identify parents who carry the gene. Blood tests can show the presence of the condition after birth.
- **Treatment:** There is no known cure for sickle cell anemia. Medication can treat the symptoms.

Spina Bifida and Hydrocephalus
- **Description:** In spina bifida, an incompletely formed spinal cord may lead to stiff joints, difficulty moving the legs, partial paralysis, and problems with the kidneys and urinary tract. Seventy of every 100 children with spina bifida also have hydrocephalus, in which an excess of fluid surrounds the brain, causing brain damage.
- **Causes:** The problem seems to be caused by a combination of hereditary and environmental factors. Taking folic acid during pregnancy helps reduce incidence.

(Continued on next page)

Spina Bifida and Hydrocephalus (continued)

- **Detection:** Spina bifida is apparent at birth. Hydrocephalus is indicated by overly rapid growth of the head. Tests of the mother's blood, amniocentesis, and ultrasound can reveal suspected cases in a fetus.

- **Treatment:** Corrective surgery, physical therapy, and special schooling can minimize disabilities caused by spina bifida. Hydrocephalus can be helped by an operation that relieves the fluid that has built up.

Tay-Sachs Disease

- **Description:** Babies born with Tay-Sachs disease lack a certain chemical in their blood that makes their bodies unable to process and use fats. The condition leads to severe brain damage and to death, usually by the age of four.

- **Cause:** Tay-Sachs disease is caused by inheriting defective recessive genes from both parents. It is most common in families descended from eastern European Jews.

- **Detection:** Amniocentesis or chorionic villi sampling can identify Tay-Sachs disease in a fetus. Blood tests can identify those who carry the defective gene and can test for the condition after birth.

- **Treatment:** There is no known cure or treatment for this disease.

baby's cells. This is not a hereditary defect because the child does not inherit the condition from a parent.

The most common birth defect of this type is Down syndrome. One child in every 800 births has this condition. The risk increases if the mother is thirty-five or older. A child with Down syndrome has an extra chromosome 21. Because each chromosome carries hundreds of genes, the defect can interfere with development in many ways.

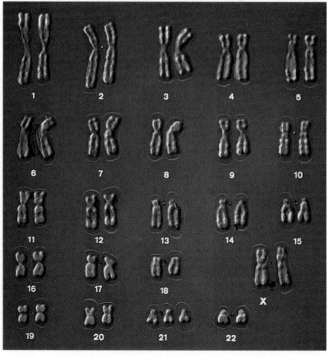

Images of chromosomes can reveal damage. *In this case, Down syndrome is shown by what unusual circumstance in chromosome 21?*

Interaction of Heredity and Environment

Some birth defects result from heredity and environment working together. For example, a baby may inherit the tendency for a heart defect. This defect appears only if some factor—such as a drug or a virus—affects the baby during his or her development. If only one of these conditions had been met, the heart would probably have been normal.

Researchers think that the interaction of heredity and the environment is probably the cause for cleft lip, cleft palate, and spina bifida. With good care, though, some of these problems may be preventable. The Public Health Service says that if pregnant women took the recommended amount of the vitamin folic acid, more than 1,000 cases of spina bifida could be prevented each year.

Parents of children born with birth defects face many challenges. One of them is to make sure that other children receive attention. *Name another.*

Prevention and Diagnosis of Birth Defects

It is difficult for a child born with a serious medical problem to lead a normal life. The rest of the child's family is affected by the emotional and financial strain the defect causes. Responsible couples do everything they can to minimize the possibility of birth defects.

Some causes of birth defects, such as infections, drugs, and alcohol, can be controlled. Parents simply need to make healthy choices to prevent a baby from being harmed by these substances. Although most birth defects cannot yet be prevented, tests can sometimes determine how probable it is that a child will develop specific defects. This can make early treatment possible.

Genetic Counseling

Some people seek genetic counseling. The patients could be a couple who wish to have a child but are concerned about their chances of having a baby with a serious birth defect. They might already have a child with a problem and want more information. Genetic counseling does not tell people what to do; it only explains the options and risks. Most people who seek genetic counseling do so because they are aware of a specific possible problem.

Ask the Experts

Jacqueline Mault
Director of Special Services for the Toppenish School District in Toppenish, Washington

Sources *of Support for Special Needs Children*

Where can the parents of young children with special needs go for help and support?

Children with special needs, such as those who have problems related to birth defects, require extra medical attention. Most also require other kinds of professional help in dealing with particular physical, social, or educational problems. In addition, parents and other family members usually benefit from support in coping with their added responsibilities in caring for a special needs child.

The first source of help usually is the child's pediatrician or the family's primary physician. Physicians are able to refer babies and young children to medical specialists. More and more, physicians are also able to refer families to other helpful resources within the community.

In many communities across the country, public schools have become an important source of assistance. Services may include center- or school-based preschool classes and home-based instruction. Speech/language therapy, physical therapy, occupational therapy, counseling, and transportation may be available as well. Many programs emphasize providing parents with the skills to help their developing child. Some public schools also provide assessment and support for children from birth to age three.

For emotional support, many parents turn to their own extended families or specific support programs, often affiliated with a local hospital; the department of social services; or the local, county, or state health department. Some parents find help on the Internet, either by using it as a source of information or by joining chat groups for support.

Thinking It Through

1. Why would transportation services help parents of children with special needs?
2. How could parents of special needs children find an Internet chat group that could provide support?

Family doctors can perform genetic counseling, but it is best provided by a specialist. Genetic counselors are trained to understand genetic disorders. They have good communication skills, so they can explain the situation to the family and help family members deal with the impact of their situation.

A genetic counselor begins by obtaining complete family medical histories from the couple. This includes information relating to diseases and causes of death of all their close relatives. If they are concerned about a baby who is already born, they are also asked about events during this pregnancy and any previous pregnancies.

The patients—and, in some cases, other family members—may be given thorough physical examinations. If necessary, special laboratory tests are also performed. The most specialized testing is done at major medical centers in large cities, but most states have regional services.

When all the questionnaires and tests are completed, the counselor can usually tell the couple whether genetic problems are present. The couple may also be told the probability that they will have a child with a serious birth defect.

Prenatal Tests

More than 100 kinds of birth defects can now be diagnosed before a baby is born. Of course, no tests will tell whether a baby will be normal. Some tests, though, can alert the physician to a condition in the baby that must be treated before or immediately after birth.

For example, the first child of a Boston woman died three months after birth. The cause of death was a hereditary problem. When she was pregnant a second time, the woman had an amniocentesis, one of the tests described here. The results showed that this child had the same condition. The

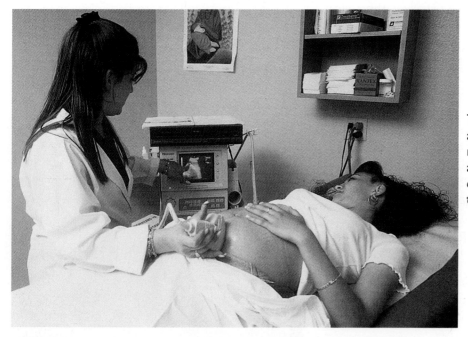

Tests like ultrasound (left) and amniocentesis (top of next page) provide valuable information. *Why aren't these tests given to all pregnant women?*

fate of the first child could be prevented, though. By giving the mother vitamins—which then reached the developing baby—doctors were able to correct the problem. The second baby was normal at birth.

Sometimes a pregnant woman or her doctor suspect that a birth defect may be likely. If so, special prenatal tests can be given to see whether specific birth defects are present.

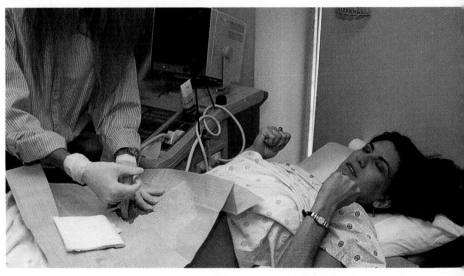

Prenatal testing can provide helpful informatioln.

Sometimes this information can be supplied through blood tests. In other cases, doctors and parents-to-be choose other methods. These tests can be risky. Although they provide valuable information, they may harm the developing baby. The doctor and the parents can use the information from blood tests to decide whether there is a good medical reason to perform one of the tests described below. The pregnant woman and her partner have the right to decide whether or not to have the tests done.

Today, doctors mainly use three procedures to make a prenatal diagnosis:

- **Ultrasound** uses sound waves to make a video image of an unborn baby to check for specific health problems. It can show whether the fetus is developing on schedule. Certain defects, such as those that involve the skeleton and other organs, can also be detected. The test can also be used to confirm the due date or that twins are present.

  This test has become common. To date, researchers have not found any risk to either the mother or the developing baby from an ultrasound.

- **Amniocentesis** (AM-knee-oh-sen-TEE-sis) is the process of withdrawing a sample of the amniotic fluid surrounding an unborn baby and testing that fluid for indications of specific birth defects or other health problems. The doctor withdraws the fluid by using a needle. An ultrasound image is used as a guide when inserting the needle. Some cells from the fetus are contained within the fluid sample. These are the cells tested for evidence of birth defects.

  Amniocentesis is most often used as a test for Down syndrome when the expectant mother is over age thirty-five. At thirty-five or older, a woman is more likely to have a baby with that condition. The procedure does involve some risks. About 1 in every 200 women who have had amniocentesis have a miscarriage. As a result of these risks, it is performed only when there is a strong medical reason.

- **Chorionic villi** (CORE-ee-ON-ik VI-lie) **sampling** tests for specific birth defects by sampling small amounts of the tissue from the membrane that encases the fetus. Guided by an ultrasound image, a doctor inserts a small tube through the vagina into the uterus. There, samples of the tissue are snipped or suctioned off for analysis.

Chorionic villi sampling is used to test for the same disorders as amniocentesis. An advantage is that this testing can be done earlier in a pregnancy than amniocentesis can. However, the risks that chorionic villi sampling will cause miscarriage or birth defects are much greater than the risks involved in amniocentesis. It is done only after careful consideration of the medical reasons and risks.

Several other methods of prenatal diagnosis are now in the experimental stages. These may someday provide more accurate information at earlier stages of development. For example, it has become possible to view the fetus directly through a special instrument, obtain samples of fetal blood and tissue, and even perform surgery on an unborn child. As yet, these tests are quite dangerous for the developing baby. Further breakthroughs may make them safe enough for widespread use.

SECTION 5-3 REVIEW

✔ Check Your Understanding

1. What is the difference between a miscarriage and a stillbirth?
2. What is the cause of Down syndrome? What is one factor that increases the risk of Down syndrome?
3. What group is most likely to have sickle cell anemia?
4. What are the four causes of birth defects?
5. How does genetic counseling help parents?
6. What are two parts of genetic counseling?
7. What can be learned from ultrasound, amniocentesis, and chorionic villi sampling? What risks are involved in each procedure?

Putting Knowledge Into Practice

1. **Analyzing Arguments.** "Genetic counseling isn't helpful because all it does is identify problems." Do you agree or disagree with this statement? Explain your answer.
2. **Making Inferences.** Why do you think some couples might wish to seek genetic counseling?
3. **Observing and Participating.** Contact a group that works to help children with birth defects such as the National Foundation/March of Dimes. Find out how they raise money for their work. Plan a fund-raising project you and your class could do.

CAREER OPPORTUNITIES

Genetic Counselor

A CONVERSATION WITH KAY TANNER

How did you become interested in becoming a genetic counselor?
When I took a biology course in high school, I became fascinated by genetics. But I really like people, too. I didn't want to spend my whole life in a lab. This career is perfect for me—it combines my interest in the science with a chance to work with people.

What are the tasks and responsibilities of a genetic counselor? We meet with couples who are concerned. First we just talk to them, then we take a family medical history and order some tests. We use statistical analysis to figure out the probability that the couple could have a baby with a problem caused by genetics.

What is the work environment like?
Well, we work in offices and labs. Sometimes meetings with parents can become very emotional especially when a couple has a high likelihood of having a baby with a birth defect. We try to comfort them and point out the options, but they face hard choices.

What are the working hours like? Our office is open 9:00 to 5:00 during the week. Some offices have evening hours.

What aptitudes are needed to be a genetic counselor? Well, like any scientist, you have to have great attention for detail. You need strong math and science skills. Because you're dealing with people so much—and in very emotional situations—you need strong people and counseling skills, too.

GENETIC COUNSELOR

Education and Training. Genetic counselors must have at least a bachelor's degree with emphasis on genetics, psychology, and counseling. Special training is needed.

Career Outlook. Job openings for genetic scientists are expected to grow faster than the average

---CONNECTING SCHOOL TO CAREER---

1. **Interpersonal Skills.** Suppose you were a genetic counselor. How would you tell a couple that they had a fairly high probability of having a child with a birth defect caused by a genetic problem?
2. **Technology.** In what ways would genetic counselors be likely to use computers in their work?

Avoiding Dangers to the Baby

In *every* pregnancy, the mother-to-be is responsible for taking the most important step in increasing the chances of having a healthy baby. She must take care of herself and keep herself safe and healthy. An essential part of good prenatal care is avoiding the harmful effects of such hazards as alcohol and other drugs, smoking, X rays, and infections.

KEY TERMS

fetal alcohol effects
fetal alcohol syndrome (FAS)

OBJECTIVES:

- Identify the hazards that alcohol and other drugs pose to prenatal development.

- Discuss other environmental hazards that pregnant women should avoid.

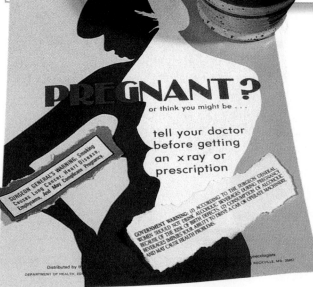

Alcohol

Alcohol is a drug—a dangerous one. The dangers of alcohol can touch a developing baby. A woman who drinks during pregnancy risks having a child with **fetal alcohol syndrome.** This condition, also called FAS, includes physical and mental problems that result from a mother drinking alcohol while she is pregnant.

One in five of the babies born with FAS dies soon after birth. Those who survive suffer from a host of problems. Almost all of them are mentally retarded. This is because alcohol interferes with tissue growth and development, and brain tissue is most easily injured by this drug. Many children born with FAS also have other problems, such as slow growth, poor coordination, heart defects, and facial disfigurement. Many also suffer from learning problems and hyperactivity. They also have difficulty controlling their behavior.

Some children suffer from **fetal alcohol effects**. This condition is less severe than FAS. Still, the baby suffers some of the damage caused by alcohol.

The degree of damage to the child is usually directly related to the amount of alcohol the mother consumed during pregnancy. It may also be affected by the stage of the pregnancy during which she drank and by the presence of other drugs in her system. There is no cure for fetal alcohol syndrome or fetal alcohol effects.

Still, both conditions can be prevented—by not drinking alcohol. Doctors don't know just how much alcohol presents a danger to the developing baby. There is no known amount of alcohol that a pregnant woman can safely drink without risking harm to her unborn child. For this reason, doctors recommend that women avoid alcohol completely when they are pregnant—and even when they plan to become pregnant.

Other Drugs

Many doctors believe that drugs taken during pregnancy are among the major causes of birth defects linked to environmental factors. Alcohol is one of those drugs. Others include:

- Medicines, including both those that doctors prescribe and over-the-counter types.
- Caffeine, found in some foods and beverages.
- Nicotine, found in tobacco.
- Illegal drugs such as heroin, LSD, marijuana, and all forms of cocaine.
- Inhalants—fumes that are inhaled into the lungs.

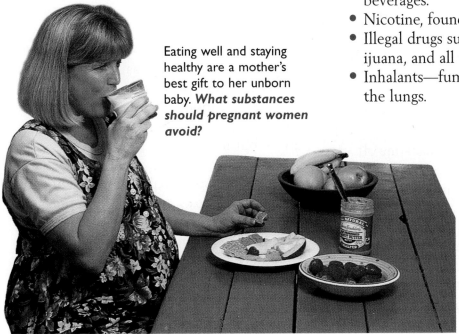

Eating well and staying healthy are a mother's best gift to her unborn baby. *What substances should pregnant women avoid?*

Even common medicines that are sold in pharmacies and supermarkets may be unsafe for an unborn baby. *How can a pregnant woman be sure that a medicine is safe?*

Prescription and Over-the-Counter Drugs

For a pregnant woman and her baby, there is no such thing as a completely safe drug. Even aspirin, cold remedies, and antihistamines can harm an unborn child. An extreme example is thalidomide, used to relieve morning sickness during the late 1950s. Before its effects were discovered, thalidomide caused more than 5,000 babies to be born with severe birth defects—including missing arms and legs.

Medicines or infections that reach the developing baby in the first three months of pregnancy have the most devastating effect. During these months, the baby's body systems are being formed. This is also a critical period of brain development, so drugs can cause mental retardation.

In the last six months of pregnancy, harmful substances that reach the fetus may cause slow growth, infections, or bleeding at birth. Drugs taken just before delivery will still be in the baby's body at birth.

Doctors say that a woman shouldn't take any medicines unless they are specifically prescribed by her physician for use while she is pregnant. Drugs needed for serious conditions, such as diabetes and high blood pressure, can be taken—but under a doctor's direction.

Caffeine

Caffeine is widely found in beverages such as coffee, tea, cocoa, and many soft drinks. It is also present in some foods and many medications. Because it is so common, caffeine is often not considered a drug—but it is.

This drug, though very common, can harm a developing baby. It is known that feeding large doses of caffeine to pregnant mice and rabbits causes birth defects in their offspring. No amount is known to be absolutely safe. Doctors advise women to be cautious about caffeine during pregnancy.

Tobacco

The nicotine in cigarettes is also a dangerous drug. The more a mother smokes, the smaller her baby is likely to be. A newborn's weight is a critical factor in survival. Heavy smoking is believed to cause premature birth as well. Finally, smoking is linked to respiratory infections and allergies among children after birth.

Smoke from others can also be harmful. Its dangerous nicotine reaches the baby just the same as if the mother had smoked herself.

Illegal Drugs

Increases in the use of cocaine, marijuana, and other illegal drugs have given doctors new problems. A mother who is addicted to a drug when pregnant usually passes her addiction on to her baby. These children suffer all their lives.

Right after birth, these addicted infants must go through a period of withdrawal. This painful condition results from the body no longer receiving the drug that it depends on. For some addicted babies, withdrawal is so severe that they die.

For the babies who survive withdrawal, the future is uncertain. Experts worry that the long-range effects of prenatal addiction may be serious. Many of these children are able to follow only very simple directions and often cannot understand school classes.

Cocaine is known to cause miscarriage, stillbirth, premature birth, and birth defects. Similar results are suggested in studies on marijuana. Other effects of drugs are still being studied. While research continues, the best advice is to avoid taking *any* drugs before or during pregnancy.

Pregnant women can enjoy many healthy alternatives to beverages with caffeine.

X Rays

X rays present another potential danger to the unborn baby. Radiation from X rays—or from other sources—can cause birth defects. A pregnant woman who is in an accident, is sick, or has dental work should inform medical personnel of her pregnancy. They can then take special precautions if X rays are necessary.

X rays are useful tools for health care workers. Still, they are also powerful and can be dangerous. It is important to avoid unneeded X rays before pregnancy. In fact, both men and women should request abdominal shields during routine X rays.

Rubella

The terrible effect of certain infections on unborn children was highlighted by the epidemic of rubella (sometimes called German measles) that swept the country several decades ago. Thousands of unborn babies were affected when their mothers came down with German measles during pregnancy. Although most of the women had few or even no symptoms of illness, the developing babies suffered. Some of these babies were born with deafness, blindness, heart disease, or mental retardation.

A vaccine for rubella is now available, and millions of children have been vaccinated. The vaccine may be dangerous, however, for women who are pregnant or who become pregnant shortly after receiving it. A woman who is unsure whether she has been vaccinated can check her health records or ask her doctor to test her. Every woman should be sure she is immune to rubella before she considers becoming pregnant.

Sexually Transmitted Diseases (STDs)

Like rubella, sexually transmitted diseases, or STDs, can do great harm to unborn babies. They include all the following:
- Syphilis
- Gonorrhea
- Hepatitis B
- Genital herpes
- AIDS
- Group B streptococcus
- Chlamydia

Many of these diseases can be passed on from the pregnant woman to the unborn baby. They can result in serious illness, deformity, or even death.

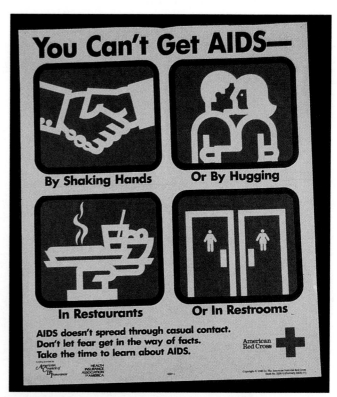

Health organizations provide a great deal of important and useful information about AIDS. *How is an unborn child affected if a pregnant woman has AIDS?*

A person can be infected with a sexually transmitted disease without realizing it. For this reason, special measures are often taken to protect babies against the effects of STDs. Most doctors routinely test pregnant women for syphilis—in fact, such tests are required by law in many states. In addition, doctors usually treat the eyes of newborns with a solution to kill gonorrhea germs that could otherwise cause blindness.

Treatment can cure syphilis and gonorrhea and can relieve the symptoms of herpes in adults. No drug can cure the damage to the newborn that results from a delay in diagnosis and treatment. Any pregnant woman who suspects she could have a sexually transmitted disease should discuss the condition frankly with her doctor.

AIDS

A developing baby can be infected with AIDS by the mother. The virus that causes AIDS may lie hidden in a person for many years before causing symptoms, so testing is essential. If a woman who has AIDS gives birth to a child, her baby also is at risk to develop AIDS and die. If a doctor knows that a pregnant woman has the virus that causes AIDS, she can be given treatment that can reduce the chances that her baby will develop AIDS. The baby can be given treatment as well. For these reasons, early testing for AIDS is very important.

SECTION 5-4 REVIEW

✔ Check Your Understanding

1. Why does alcohol harm a developing baby?
2. What kinds of drugs, other than alcohol, can harm a developing baby?
3. How much caffeine is safe for a pregnant woman to have?
4. How can smoke affect an unborn baby?
5. Why should a woman tell a dentist or orthodontist if she is pregnant?
6. Why is it a good idea for a woman to be vaccinated against rubella before becoming pregnant?
7. Why do many states require doctors to test pregnant women for syphilis?
8. How can a developing baby benefit from having the pregnant mother receive an early test for the AIDS virus?

Putting Knowledge Into Practice

1. **Applying.** Suppose a pregnant woman has a headache or a cold. What should she do to treat it?
2. **Applying.** If a pregnant woman inhales smoke from another person's cigarette, the developing baby can suffer damage. Suppose you were a pregnant woman who worked as a waitress. You often worked in the smoking section. What would you do?
3. **Observing and Participating.** Read the label on an over-the-counter medicine. Write down the type of medicine and the directions given for use by pregnant women. Bring your results to class and compare them to your classmates' findings.

Parenting With Care

Developing Healthy Habits for a Lifetime

A woman who is pregnant has a great responsibility.

How she acts can have a tremendous lifelong impact on the health of her developing baby. Expectant fathers have this impact, too. For example, a father-to-be who smokes cigarettes can be damaging his child every time the mother breathes in the smoke.

The best way to prepare for this responsibility is to develop healthy habits now. Your present health and that of any future children will benefit. Good health has three aspects:

Physical Health

An essential part of good health is taking care of yourself physically. Here are some tips about how to maintain your physical health:

- **Eat a balanced diet.** Include a variety of nutritious foods in your meals and snacks.
- **Get regular exercise.** Choose sports and other activities that you enjoy, either on your own or as part of a team or other group.
- **Get plenty of sleep.** Remember that eight hours per night is a minimum requirement for most teens.
- **Learn safety rules.** Once you know them, be sure to follow them.
- **Avoid harmful substances.** Stay away from alcohol, other drugs, and tobacco.

Emotional Health

You can build your emotional health in various ways:

- **List your accomplishments.** Your sense of worth grows from a positive feeling about yourself. You can reinforce that feeling by accomplishing things you're proud of. Make a list and look at it when you need a boost.
- **Use positive "self-talk."** Send yourself positive messages. When you think about yourself, focus on your good points. Decide how to improve the others.

- **Handle your emotions.** Learn to manage your negative emotions. Find safe ways of expressing those emotions so you can stay in control.

Social Health

The other part of your health is your social well-being. Some habits can help you build good social health:

- **Spend time with your family.** The bonds between family members are strengthened the more time the people spend together.
- **Be a good friend.** If you act as a good friend, you will have good friends.
- **Play an active part in your community.** There are many things you can do to make a difference in your community, from tutoring to cleaning up a park to spending time with older people.

Following Up

1. Give another suggestion for improving health in one of these areas.

2. **Management.** What are two effective ways of handling negative emotions?

3. **Thinking Skills.** How can adopting these habits help make a person ready to be a parent?

Summary

✔ Prenatal development begins with conception and moves through three stages. (Section 5-1)

✔ Chromosomes carry the genes that determine all the traits we inherit. (Section 5-2)

✔ Infertility problems may be treated with surgery or medication, or infertile couples can choose among other options. (Section 5-2)

✔ Birth defects have a variety of causes. Some can be predicted by tests. (Section 5-3)

✔ A pregnant woman should avoid alcohol, other drugs, and tobacco to have a healthy baby. (Section 5-4)

8. Why is it important for pregnant women to talk to the doctor as early as possible about the possibility of an STD? (Section 5-4)

Thinking Critically

1. **Analyzing.** A baby can usually survive if born in the seventh month. Why does the baby need to continue developing for two more months?

2. **Synthesizing.** If identical twins have the exact same genetic blueprint, will they have the exact same personalities? Why or why not?

3. **Evaluating.** What do you consider good reasons for having prenatal tests done? Why?

Reviewing the Facts

1. How long is each of the three stages of pregnancy? (Section 5-1)

2. What changes occur in the fetus in the ninth month of prenatal development? (Section 5-1)

3. How do genes shape the inheritance of characteristics? (Section 5-2)

4. If an infertile couple wants children, what options do they have? (Section 5-2)

5. Give an example of a birth defect caused by each of the four factors that cause birth defects. (Section 5-3)

6. Give an example of the benefits of prenatal testing. (Section 5-3)

7. What is the best advice for pregnant women regarding the use of any drugs? (Section 5-4)

Taking Action

1. **Gathering Resources.** Gather pamphlets and other resource materials on one birth defect. Use the information to create a poster to be displayed in the classroom. (Communication)

2. **Identifying Alternatives.** As a group, brainstorm a list of healthy cold drinks that a pregnant woman could enjoy in place of soda with caffeine. As a class, vote on the choice that is the most nutritious. (Management)

CONNECTIONS

Cross-Curricular Connections

1. **Language Arts.** With a partner or group, write and perform a skit showing a teen being offered alcohol. In the skit, show effective ways of saying "no" to drugs. Discuss how young adults might also feel pressured.

2. **Math.** Using the diagram in Section 5-2 on eye color, figure the odds of each child having blue eyes.

Workplace Connections

1. **Information.** Suppose you were a public health nurse. Write the text of a talk you would give mothers-to-be outlining the changes they will feel during a pregnancy.

2. **Technology.** If you ran a genetic counseling office, how could you use technology to keep genetic records private?

Family and Community Connections

1. **Multiple Births.** Search on the Internet for information from the Public Health Service on multiple births. Report to the class on the trends in the past five, ten, or twenty years in the nation as a whole and in your state. Explain why the rate is changing.

2. **Helping Others.** Search on the Internet for a group involved in helping children born with a particular birth defect. Find out what information and support the group gives to children with that birth defect and to their parents. Bring your information to class to put in a class binder called "Helping Children with Special Needs."

Technology Connections

1. **Fertility Treatments.** Research recent developments in the use of fertility drugs. How safe are they? What are the pros and cons of their use? Report your findings to the class.

2. **X Rays.** Conduct research into the discovery, use, or possible dangers of X rays. Report your findings to the class.

Elissa held her friend's hand. "Don't worry," she said. "You'll be fine. I had the same problem you did—I felt sick every morning. After the first three months, though, it went away. For the rest of the time I was pregnant, I felt great. Until the last month, of course! Then I couldn't wait for the baby to be born."

Shanta smiled weakly. "That's what my mother said, too—and so did the obstetrician. I just worry that I won't be able to eat anything until I get my appetite back. If I don't eat, then how will the baby grow?"

Elissa laughed. "Oh, you'll eat. And the baby will grow just fine. In the meantime, you can do something to help yourself feel better. Whenever you feel queasy, munch on a couple of crackers. They help settle your stomach. Now, how about doing what we said? Let me show you that crib you can use."

> **"I had morning sickness, too, but for the rest of my pregnancy, I felt great."**

SECTION 6-1

A Healthy Pregnancy

A pregnant woman carries inside her a new life. She has a huge responsibility: to get that life off to a good start. That means she has to take care of the developing baby—and of herself.

KEY TERMS

anemia
obstetrician
Rh factor

OBJECTIVES:

- List the early signs of pregnancy.

- Assess the importance of early and regular medical care during pregnancy.

- Plan a nutritious diet during pregnancy.

- Give recommendations about personal care for a pregnant woman.

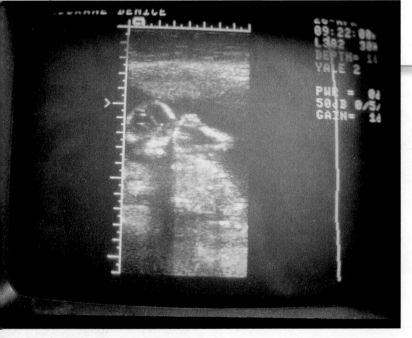

Early Signs of Pregnancy

How does a woman know that she is pregnant? Within several weeks of conception, a woman will probably feel one or more of these early signs of pregnancy:

- A missed period (usually the first indication).
- A fullness or mild ache in her lower abdomen.
- Feeling tired, drowsy, or faint.
- The need to urinate more often than usual.
- Discomfort or tenderness in her breasts.
- Periods of nausea, especially early in the day.

These symptoms may be caused by something other than pregnancy. To be sure, the woman can take a pregnancy test.

Medical Care During Pregnancy

As soon as a woman suspects she is pregnant, she should see a doctor. Some women see a general doctor. Many prefer to see an **obstetrician** (AHB-stuh-TRISH-un), a doctor who specializes in pregnancy and birth.

The pregnant woman and her doctor will have an important relationship over the next nine months. She will see the doctor many times for checkups, and the doctor will also assist when the baby is born. For these reasons, an expectant mother should choose a doctor she likes and trusts.

Many obstetricians work as part of a group. They take turns covering for each other during the night and on weekends. When the baby is born, then, one of the other doctors in the group may be present. Usually the woman sees each of the other doctors on one office visit during the pregnancy. That way, she can get to know them. Most checkups, though, are done by the woman's primary doctor.

Most obstetricians charge one lump sum for their care of a pregnant woman. This amount covers all prenatal exams, a normal birth, and a checkup after the birth. Some women think they can save money by only seeing the doctor at the end of the pregnancy. However, the doctor will charge as much then as if the woman had started care in her first month. It pays to get good prenatal care right from the start.

Women can purchase kits to test themselves for pregnancy. *Why should a follow-up visit be scheduled with a doctor?*

Ask the Experts

Pat Brodeen
Teacher and Teen Parent Coordinator at Theodore Roosevelt High School in San Antonio, Texas

THE *Myths of Pregnancy*

Q How can I unravel the myths associated with pregnancy?

A I'm glad you realize that not everything you hear about pregnancy is true. Some of the stories you hear reflect individual experiences. Others pass down cultural beliefs. Still other stories actually do give information or reliable advice.

Have you ever heard these tales?

- *If a pregnant woman is carrying high, she'll have a boy. If she's carrying low, she'll have a girl.*

- *Eating lots of hot sauce will cause the baby to have a lot of hair.*

- *A pregnant woman who sees something frightening, or rubs her belly during a full moon will have a baby with an ugly birthmark.*

All these stories are completely false. Where the baby is positioned has nothing to do with gender—only with the muscle tone of the mother's abdomen. Normal activities cannot affect the baby's safety. Nor will what the mother sees or eats affect the baby's safety or appearance—as long as the mother has a nutritious balanced diet.

Some age-old adages are at least partially true. Maybe you've heard people say this: A woman loses a tooth for every baby she has. Although this story is untrue, it does have a sound basis. A pregnant woman may lose some calcium from her teeth and bones if her diet doesn't provide enough calcium for the baby's development. Hormonal changes sometimes cause inflammation of the gums. It is especially important for a pregnant woman to keep her teeth and gums clean, and have a dental checkup regularly.

A pregnant woman has an excellent source of information—her physician. During her regular checkups, she should discuss her questions and concerns openly. Books written by doctors, dietitians, or other health professionals are also good sources of information.

Thinking It Through

1. What stories about pregnancy have you heard? Do you think they are true or a myth? Why or why not?
2. How might a librarian help a pregnant woman?

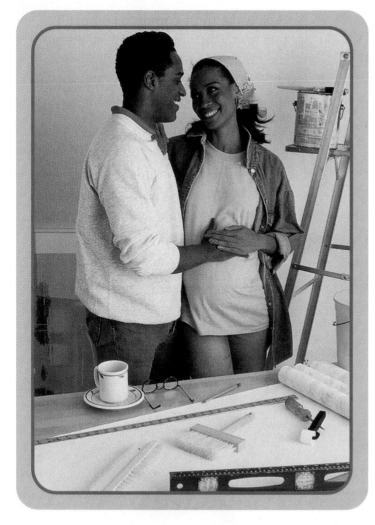

As long as no problems develop, a pregnant woman can follow her normal routine. At the initial exam—or at any of the other follow-up exams—she can ask her doctor if an activity is safe.

- The doctor analyzes her urine for the presence of infection, diabetes, or a condition called preeclampsia (high blood pressure).
- The doctor takes a blood test to see if she has **anemia** (ah-KNEE-mee-ah). This condition, caused by lack of iron, results in poor appetite, tiredness, and weakness.

The blood test is also used to check the **Rh factor** in the blood. A person's blood is either Rh positive—having a certain protein—or negative—not having that protein. Problems can arise if the mother's blood lacks that protein and the fetus's blood has it. (The fetus may inherit this blood factor from the father.) In this case, the mother's blood will produce antibodies that attack the protein in the fetus's blood, as though it were a germ invading the mother's body. By injecting a certain chemical into the mother, doctors can prevent this problem from arising.

- The doctor checks her for immunity to rubella, or German measles. This disease can seriously harm a developing baby. If the mother has not had the disease or been vaccinated for it, she has no immunity. She must then be careful to avoid coming into contact with anyone who has rubella or the baby could be in danger.

The Initial Exam

When pregnancy has been confirmed, the woman has a thorough examination:
- The doctor checks her blood pressure, pulse, respiration, and initial weight.
- The doctor asks about and records her medical history. This history may reveal conditions that require special treatment or observation.
- The doctor measures her pelvis to determine whether the birth passageway is wide enough to allow a normal-sized baby to be born.

When will the baby be born? This is one of the first questions a pregnant woman asks. The due date is nine months plus one week after the woman's last menstrual period began. Doctors usually advise that the birth could well take place any time from two weeks before or after that date.

Later Checkups

Typically, an expectant mother has a checkup once a month until the sixth or seventh month of pregnancy. Then most doctors schedule two visits a month. In the ninth month, she sees the doctor once a week. These checkups are important in monitoring the development of the baby and making sure that the woman is healthy.

Most doctors welcome an expectant father at these checkups. This gives the man a chance to meet the doctor and to be aware of the baby's growth. Both parents can use the checkups to ask any questions they might have.

Discomforts of Pregnancy

Many women go through pregnancy without any problems or complications. In fact, some women find pregnancy a time in which they feel particularly healthy.

Other women do feel some discomfort. These feelings usually do not indicate serious problems, but a woman who feels any of the following symptoms should tell her doctor:

Some women feel nausea early in the pregnancy. They can gain some relief by eating smaller, more frequent meals. Name other discomforts associated with pregnancy.

- Nausea is the most common complaint among pregnant women. It is often called morning sickness, although it doesn't only happen in the morning. Nausea rarely lasts beyond the fourth month of pregnancy. If a woman suffers severe and prolonged nausea, she should tell her doctor.
- Sleepiness—due to hormonal changes — is fairly common early in a pregnancy. Many women feel less tired in the middle months of the pregnancy, but for some, tiredness returns in the last months.
- Pregnant women often suffer from heartburn, a burning feeling in the upper stomach. (Despite the name, it has nothing to do with the heart.) A woman with heartburn should ask her doctor about the safest source of relief.

- Late in the pregnancy, a woman may feel short of breath because of pressure on the lungs from the growing baby.
- Some pregnant women develop varicose (swollen) veins in the legs from pressure on the blood vessels there. Getting regular exercise, resting with the legs and feet elevated, and using support stockings can help.
- Many pregnant women suffer muscle cramps in their legs. These cramps can be relieved by gentle stretching and rest. A diet rich in calcium may prevent these cramps.
- During the last months of pregnancy, many women feel lower back pain. Back problems can be minimized by wearing low-heeled shoes and bending the knees when lifting. Exercises can help relieve backache.

Possible Complications

A few women experience more serious complications during pregnancy. A pregnant woman who has any of the following symptoms should report them to her doctor immediately:

- Vaginal bleeding.
- Unusual weight gain.
- Excessive thirst.
- Reduced or painful urination.
- Severe abdominal pain.
- Persistent headaches.
- Severe vomiting.
- Fever.
- Swelling of the face, hands, or ankles.
- Blurred vision or dizziness.
- Prolonged backache.
- Increased vaginal mucus.

Nutrition During Pregnancy

Good nutrition is the single most important factor in prenatal care. The baby depends on the mother to grow and develop, including crucial brain development. By eating a balanced diet, a pregnant woman helps her baby and maintains her own health.

The Role of Nutrients

A healthy diet contains the five types of nutrients a body needs. Each nutrient plays a special role in promoting health:

- **Protein.** Meat, fish, poultry, eggs, milk, cheese, beans, and nuts provide this nutrient. Protein is vital for the growth of the baby and helps keep the mother's body in good repair. Because of the growing fetus, a pregnant woman needs extra protein.

Pregnant women who experience certain symptoms should call their doctor immediately.

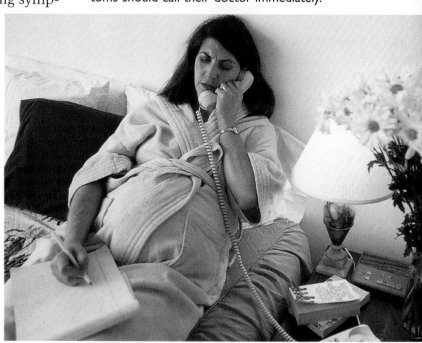

- **Vitamins.** A woman needs higher levels of vitamins during pregnancy. For instance, pregnancy doubles a woman's need for folic acid. A diet lacking in vitamins increases the risk that a baby will have birth defects. To make sure that a pregnant woman gets enough vitamins, her doctor may recommend that she take a multiple vitamin every day.

  Vitamin A ensures that the baby's eyes develop properly. B vitamins assist in the overall development of the fetus. Vitamin C helps build healthy teeth and gums and helps make the material that holds body cells together. Vitamin D aids in making bones and teeth.

  Fresh fruits and vegetables, whole-grain breads and cereal products, and fortified milk are especially rich sources of vitamins. Fortified milk will say "vitamins A and D" on the label.

- **Minerals.** These nutrients are needed for sturdy bones and teeth, healthy blood, and regular elimination of waste products. The doctor may tell the woman take a mineral supplement.

  Pregnant women have a particular need for iron, which helps prevent anemia and helps the fetus build its own blood supply. Extra iron is stored in the baby's liver to be used for several months after birth, when the baby's diet lacks iron. Meat is a good source of iron. Other sources include beans, peas, spinach, raisins, and dates.

  Calcium and phosphorous are also especially important during pregnancy. They are needed by both mother and baby to have healthy bones and teeth. Milk supplies much of the calcium and phosphorous a pregnant woman needs.

- **Carbohydrates and fats.** These nutrients are necessary for heat and energy. Good sources of carbohydrates are fruits, vegetables, whole-grain breads, and cereals. Most people get more than enough fat in their diet, so fatty foods should be avoided.

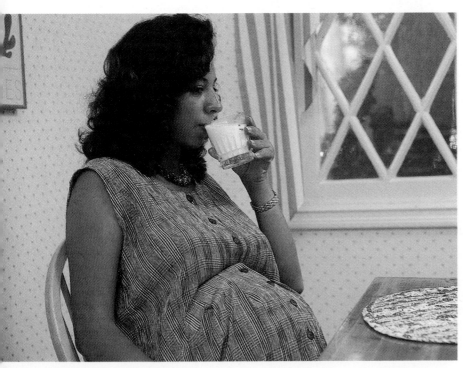

Why is milk important for pregnant women?

The Food Guide Pyramid

A Guide for Pregnant and Nursing Women

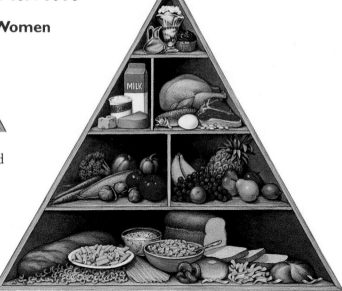

Fats, Oil, and Sweets
Use sparingly

The foods in this group, such as margarine and sugar, are generally high in calories and low in nutrition. They are not considered part of a healthy diet. Foods from other groups also include some fats and sugars.

Milk, Yogurt, and Cheese Group
3 servings (Teens 4)

The milk a pregnant woman drinks should be fortified with vitamin D and have 1 percent fat. If a woman has diffculty maintaining or gaining weight, she may drink milk with higher fat content. Cheese, yogurt, and ice cream can be substituted for some of the milk.

Meat, Poultry, Fish, Dry Beans, Eggs, and Nuts Group
2-3 servings

The foods in this group, include all types of meat, poultry, and fish and seafood, as well as eggs, nuts, dry beans and peas, and lentils.

Vegetable Group
3-5 servings

At least one of the servings from this group should be a deep yellow or dark green, leafy vegetable. A pregnant woman should also try to include vegetables high in vitamin C, such as cabbage, in her diet.

Fruit Group
2-4 servings

One or more of the servings from this group should be a fruit high in vitamin C, such as citrus fruit, berries, or melons.

Bread, Cereal, Rice, and Pasta Group
6-11 servings

Foods in this group include whole-grain or enriched breads, cereals and other grain products, such as rice, macaroni, and noodles.

These are the recommended number of servings that a pregnant or a nursing woman should eat *each day* from each of the food groups.

The Food Guide Pyramid

Everyone can eat a well-balanced diet by using the Food Guide Pyramid to choose foods. The chart on page 187 shows the pyramid for pregnant and nursing women, who also need extra nutrients.

There are other important dietary recommendations for pregnant women. They should drink six to eight glasses of water daily. They should also avoid rich and fried foods, which are usually hard to digest and have few nutrients. Of course, they should avoid eating too much sugar.

Teens' Diets

Teens have special nutritional needs because their bodies are growing and developing. For this reason, it is especially important for pregnant teens to be careful about good nutrition.

Filling up on low-nutrition snacks is never a good idea, but it is even more unwise during a pregnancy. Expectant mothers need foods rich in essential nutrients. It is especially important for pregnant teens to have enough calcium and iron. See page 186 for suggestions of good sources of these minerals.

Special Diets

Some women have a problem digesting lactose, a sugar found in milk. These women feel bloated or have stomach pain when they drink milk. How can they get the calcium they need? They can choose foods such as yogurt, cottage cheese, broccoli, kale, tuna, salmon, sardines, and tofu.

Protein is an especially important nutrient during pregnancy. Meat and poultry are high in protein, but some people are vegetarians and don't eat these foods. They can still get the protein they need from fish, eggs, and dried beans and peas eaten in combination with enriched breads, grains, and seeds.

Weight Gain During Pregnancy

	Pounds	Kilograms
Weight of average baby at birth	7-8	3.2-3.6
Placenta	1-2	0.45-0.9
Amniotic fluid	1½-2	0.7-0.9
Increased size of uterus and supporting muscles	2	0.9
Increase in breast tissue	1	0.45
Increase in blood volume	1½-3	0.7-1.4
Increase in fat stores	5	2.3
Increase in body fluids	5-7	2.3-3.2
Total	**24-30**	11.0-13.65

Weight Gain During Pregnancy

A woman usually gains about 24 to 30 pounds (11.0 to 13.65 kg) during pregnancy. The chart on page 188 shows how that weight is usually distributed.

In the first three months of a pregnancy, the woman may not gain any weight—she may even lose weight. That is nothing to worry about. Weight gain in the fourth through sixth months of pregnancy is most important for the fetus.

Doctors recommend that women gain at least 20 pounds (9.1 kg) unless they begin the pregnancy very overweight. A weight gain lower than that increases the risk of fetal death and of having a premature baby. Doctors also say that a pregnant woman should gain no more than 35 pounds (15.9 kg). However, it is not a good idea for an expectant mother to start a weight-loss diet. Pregnancy is not the time to lose weight. Moderate exercise and a diet that excludes sugary, fatty foods can help a woman have a healthy weight gain.

Some women develop diabetes while pregnant. This condition affects the body's ability to burn energy. If not controlled, it can lead to a very large size for the baby. Doctors usually give these women a special diet that controls weight gain but still supplies vital nutrients. This diet may limit the foods the women can eat from the bread, cereal, rice, and pasta group.

Personal Care and Activities

In addition to practicing good nutrition, an expectant mother should take good care of herself in other ways. She should avoid alcohol, tobacco, and all drugs or medications. She should take some other steps as well:

INFOLINK

Drugs and Tobacco

To review problems with *drugs and tobacco*. See Chapter 5, pages 158, 168-172.

- **Rest.** Women generally need more rest when they are pregnant than they did before. Taking frequent breaks during the day may revive a woman's energy.
- **Exercise.** Moderate exercise can help keep an expectant mother in good physical condition—and help make the pregnancy more comfortable. Doctors recommend walking, swimming, or biking as good exercises during pregnancy. They say that pregnancy is not a time to start any strenuous activities for the first time.
- **Hygiene.** Because the skin helps maintain correct body temperature and eliminate waste, it should be kept clean. Bathing just before bedtime also encourages relaxation and sleep.
- **Other activities.** Pregnant women can usually follow the same work routines they had before pregnancy, unless the doctor advises differently.

A woman doesn't need to change her lifestyle radically during pregnancy. Moderation may be needed in some areas, but she can continue her life as before.

Swimming is good exercise for a pregnant woman as the water relieves the feeling of added weight. *What other exercises are good?*

Maternity Clothes

By about the fourth or fifth month of pregnancy, a woman usually begins to need special clothing. Maternity clothes should be loose enough to allow for freedom of movement and circulation. Cotton knits stretch to allow room for the growing baby. Skirts and pants may include a stretch panel for comfort. Before buying any garment, a pregnant woman should consider how it will fit in the last month of pregnancy.

Comfortable, low-heeled shoes with good support are recommended. A pregnant woman should avoid wearing high heels. They throw the body out of balance and increase the risk of falling.

Emotional Health During Pregnancy

During pregnancy, expectant parents need to make emotional adjustments. It is normal for them to have concerns about the baby. Talking about these concerns with each other and with family members can be reassuring.

Pregnancy causes hormonal changes, which can produce mood swings. A pregnant woman may shift quickly from happiness to sorrow—and then back again, for no apparent reason. Even the most calm woman will feel upset and worried at times during her pregnancy. Effective techniques

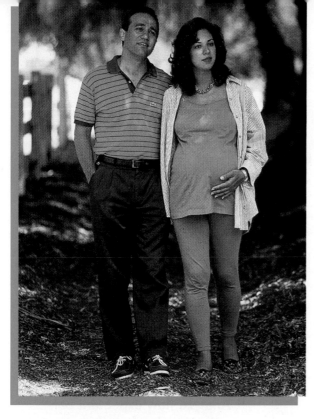

Pregnancy is an emotionally charged time. *What can couples do to prevent strong emotions from causing problems?*

for reducing stress can help the woman bounce back when she's feeling down. Exercise, as long as it is moderate, not only helps a pregnant woman feel better physically but also builds emotional health. Deep breathing can reduce stress, which promotes depression. Massage can be calming as well.

SECTION 6-1 REVIEW

✔ Check Your Understanding

1. What is usually the first sign of pregnancy?
2. Why should a pregnant woman see a doctor from the start?
3. What steps are part of the initial examination of a pregnant woman?
4. How often does a woman typically see a doctor during her pregnancy?
5. Traci is pregnant. She suffers from frequent headaches. What should she do?
6. What benefits does a pregnant woman receive from vitamins A, B, C, and D?
7. What benefits does a pregnant woman gain from iron, calcium, and phosphorus?
8. What are the minimum and maximum weight gains doctors recommend?
9. What can a pregnant woman do to reduce stress?

Putting Knowledge Into Practice

1. **Applying.** Plan a day's meals for a pregnant woman using the Food Guide Pyramid.
2. **Making Inferences.** Lucinda worries about gaining too much weight during her pregnancy. She decides to begin jogging every day. Is this a good idea? Why or why not?
3. **Observing and Participating.** Look at what you and your friends eat at lunch for the next two days, and write it down. Suppose these were the lunches of a pregnant woman. Do they reflect the recommendations found in the Food Guide Pyramid or not? If not, how would you improve the nutritional value of these meals?

Getting Ready for a Baby

The nine months of pregnancy provide expectant parents with an opportunity to learn and think about the changes to come. They can use this time to make plans and decisions as they prepare for the arrival of a new family member.

KEY TERMS

budget
fixed expenses
flexible expenses
formula
maternity leave
pediatrician

OBJECTIVES:

- Analyze how expectant parents can plan for a baby's care.

- Evaluate the preparations expectant parents should make.

- Explain how and why to make a budget.

Roles and Responsibilities

The most important question is how the parents will meet the responsibilities of child care. They need to consider many factors, such as each partner's goals, skills, schedule, and personal characteristics. Of course, they also need to take the

Some new parents ask the newborn's grandparents to care for the child so they can return to work. *What other options are available?*

Federal law requires employers with more than 50 workers to give twelve weeks of leave to workers for family reasons. This leave can be used by either parent when a baby is born. The leave is without pay, but the worker is guaranteed to have his or her job back when returning to work.

If finances allow it, a couple may decide that one parent will stay home to care for the child. Usually it is the mother, but that isn't always the case.

With the growing number of people who work in their homes, some couples plan to have one partner work in the home and also provide child care. This is possible, but very difficult. The needs of a baby can interfere with a work schedule.

Regardless of who takes primary responsibility for daily care, both parents should know the basics. This allows them to share the work—and the special joys—of caring for their baby.

In many families, neither parent stays home to care for the baby after the first few months. These parents need to make the best possible child care choices.

financial situation of the family into account. When both parents work outside the home, these decisions are especially important.

Many new mothers who work outside the home take a **maternity leave**. This time off from work allows a woman to give birth, recover, and begin to care for her new baby. An employer may offer employees from a few weeks to several months of leave. Some employers give time off to new fathers as well.

> **INFOLINK**
>
> **Child Care Options**
>
> See Section 3-3 to review *child care options*.

Preparing for Parenthood

Many expectant parents—especially if it is their first child—worry that they may not be able to care for their child well. Even the most confident mothers and fathers have these concerns.

Discussing ideas about parenting before the baby is born helps. For example, they might talk about how to give guidance, how to share in parenting, what goals they have for the children, and other issues. Of course, parents can't plan what they will do in every possible situation. Some ideas may also change as they become experienced in parenting. By agreeing ahead of time on general ideas about raising children, however, parents can reduce conflict later on.

Preparing for parenthood also involves anticipating changes in the other roles parents fill. Parents may also be spouses, family members, workers, students, volunteers, and citizens. As they begin to care for children, parents have less time and energy for these other roles and may need to make adjustments.

Parents can help themselves meet these roles by using good management skills—especially time management. Developing a schedule of activities—and then sticking to it—is a great help. So is using time wisely by, for instance, combining errands.

Other Children in the Family

Other children in the family will have to adjust to a new baby as well. How these children react to a new sibling depends in part on how well prepared they were before the newborn arrived. Of course, the age and emotional makeup of the children is a factor as well.

What can parents do to prepare other children for the coming arrival?

Practicing Parenting

Telling Children About a Baby

Parents need to help the children they already have adjust to the news that a baby is on the way.

- **Children under school age.** If the child is younger than school age, avoid saying anything too early in the pregnancy. Nine months is a long time for a small child to wait!

- **Children four and older.** If the child is at least four, be sure to tell him or her before you tell people outside the family.

- **Include in plans.** Including the child in making plans for the baby allows him or her to feel involved.

- **Changing living space.** If you are going to put the baby in the child's room and move the child to a new room, do it before the baby arrives. Allow time for the child to feel comfortable in the new room.

- **Changes in the child's life.** If you will be making changes in the child's life—such as toilet training—finish *before* the baby comes.

- **Do not create unrealistic expectations.** Do not tell the child that he or she "will have a new baby to play with." The baby won't be able to join the child in play for many, many months.

- **Sibling classes.** If the hospital offers a class for siblings, let the child take part.

- **Patience for negative behaviors.** Be patient if the child behaves like a younger child. Such behavior is often a cry for attention when the child feels pushed aside. Give some extra love. Behavior will soon return to normal.

- **Give reassurance and love.** Reassure the child that you love him or her. Whenever you have a chance, give the child a hug.

APPLY YOUR KNOWLEDGE

1. The parents of Shawn, aged four, are expecting a second child. If you were his mother or father, how would you tell Shawn the news?
2. Why is it important to tell a child before telling friends?

Parents should be prepared for a wide range of attitudes toward a new baby. It's normal for the child to feel jealousy and confusion—and excitement and love. Open communication and acceptance of a child's feelings will help foster a positive relationship between siblings. It may simply take time to adjust to all the changes.

Comparing Breast-Feeding and Bottle-Feeding

Breast-Feeding
Advantages
- Best source of nutrition for baby.
- Gives the baby some immunity against diseases.
- Creates a bond through physical closeness with the mother.
- May boost brain development.
- Reduces baby's risk of allergies.
- Causes fewer digestive upsets.
- Speeds the return of the mother's uterus to normal size.
- Reduces the mother's risk of later having breast or ovarian cancer.
- Reduces the risk that the mother will feel depressed.
- Is conveniently available at all times.
- Is free, though a nursing mother needs additional food.

Disadvantages
- Prevents father from participating in feeding.
- Baby has to be fed more often.
- In rare cases, may be medical reasons that suggest breast-feeding is not desirable.
- May be painful for some mothers.
- May be difficult because of work schedule.

Bottle-Feeding
Advantages
- Allows father to participate in feeding.
- Allows mother to have a more flexible schedule.
- Eliminates concern about mother's diet or medications she takes.
- Babies need feeding less often.

Disadvantages
- Can be expensive.
- Does not give the baby any natural immunities to disease.
- Involves a greater chance of baby developing allergies.
- Creates risk that baby may not be given close physical contact during feeding.

Choosing a Pediatrician

Before the baby is born, the parents should choose a **pediatrician**—a doctor who specializes in treating children. This doctor will be the main health care provider for the child for many years. Parents should find one who meets their needs.

The parents can ask their obstetrician to suggest names of pediatricians. They can also ask friends they know who have children. Once they have a few names, they can schedule interviews with the doctors. Pediatricians are usually willing to talk to parents before the parents make a choice.

Some considerations are practical. Where is the doctor's office, and what are the office hours? What are the fees for checkups, tests, and vaccinations? Here are some other questions parents may ask:

- When is the doctor available by phone?
- How should an emergency be handled?
- Who covers for the pediatrician if he or she is not available?
- What hospital does the doctor use?
- How often will the doctor see the child, both as a baby and later?
- What are the doctor's views on breast-feeding and bottle-feeding?
- What is the doctor's philosophy on guidance?

Some parents give their children health care through a clinic or a health maintenance organization. In these cases, they may have fewer choices about which doctor they can use.

The choice of a pediatrician should be evaluated once it is put in action. If the parents don't feel comfortable about the kind of care their child is receiving, it may be best to find a new doctor.

Decisions About Feeding

Another issue the parents should consider is whether the new baby will be breast-fed or bottle-fed. Breast milk has many benefits for the baby. For this reason, health care professionals recommend breast-feeding whenever possible, for as long as possible. The chart on page 196 shows the advantages and disadvantages of breast-feeding.

Bottle-feeding with formula is a convenient alternative to breast-feeding. **Formula**, a mixture of milk or milk substitute, water, and nutrients, provides good nutrition for babies. You can buy it as a powder or a concentrate that must be mixed with water or in ready-to-use forms. The chart on page 196 shows the advantages and disadvantages of formula.

The decision to breast-feed or bottle-feed is a personal one. Many mothers successfully breast-feed for certain feedings and use bottles at others. Whatever method parents choose, they should remember that the baby responds to the feeling and care that accompany each feeding.

Basic Baby Supplies

Diapering Needs
- A changing table or some surface to use for changing the baby
- If using disposable diapers: About 70 (a week's supply)
- If using cloth diapers: 3-4 dozen diapers; diaper pins; waterproof pants; a covered diaper pail; 8-10 disposable diapers for occasional use
- 6-10 washcloths
- Diaper rash ointment

Clothing
- 6-8 undershirts; 4-6 one-piece footed sleepers; 4-6 gowns
- 6 cotton receiving blankets; 1 warm outer wrapping blanket
- 1 dress-up outfit (optional)
- 1 sweater
- 1-2 sun hats or bonnets; warmer hat if needed for cooler weather
- Coat and mittens (optional)

Feeding Equipment
- If breast-feeding and mother works: Breast pump and pads; plastic bottles for storing breast milk
- If bottle-feeding: 6-8 large bottles (8-ounce or 237-mL); nipples and bottle caps (the same number as bottles, plus a few extra); bottle and nipple brush
- Bibs
- High chair

Bedding/Bedroom
- Crib and waterproof mattress (if the baby will sleep alone); bumper pad (fits around inside of crib just above mattress; keeps baby's arms and legs in, drafts out)
- Waterproof mattress cover; 2-4 absorbent pads

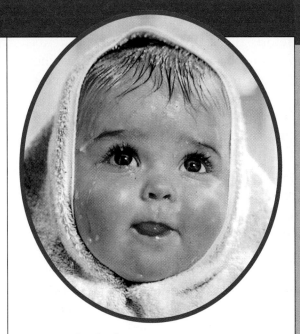

- 4 fitted crib sheets
- 2-3 lightweight blankets or spreads; heavier crib blanket
- Storage space, such as a chest of drawers
- Wastebasket

Bathing and Other Supplies
- Baby bathtub or other container
- Rubbing alcohol (for umbilical cord)
- Mild, pure soap; baby shampoo
- Several soft washcloths; 2 soft cotton bath towels
- Cotton balls
- Baby oil and baby lotion
- Blunt-tipped nail scissors; baby comb and brush set
- Thermometer

Travel Equipment
- Car seat, which meets the latest safety standards
- Tote bag for carrying supplies
- Stroller, carriage, or infant carrier (optional)

Clothing, Equipment, and Space

Basic supplies for a baby include clothing, bedding, bathing supplies, and travel equipment. Parents who choose bottle-feeding also need equipment for that.

The chart on page 198 shows basic needs. This list merely suggests possibilities. Expectant parents may get specific suggestions from a doctor or from family and friends. Advice is also given at the hospital and at classes for new parents.

Wise parents begin with only the basic items they and the baby will need at birth. They may receive some of these items—as well as those needed later—as gifts or loans. The most appreciated baby gifts are often practical ones. A box of diapers or a sleeper that can be used often may be more welcome than a fancy outfit. People who plan to buy baby gifts should ask the parents what they need.

Baby's Room

Newborns may sleep as many as 18 to 22 hours a day. During the first six months, most babies sleep for 15 to 18 hours every day. Some parents believe that babies sleep best in the parents' room. This arrangement is convenient when it is time for a middle-of-the-night feeding. Others think babies sleep best if they have a separate place, which can be kept quiet.

Of course, many families cannot provide a new baby with his or her own room. Love and pleasant conditions are more important than a spacious home. If the baby doesn't have a separate room, a quiet corner of a room can be made into the baby's special place. A room divider can be used to provide the baby—and other family members—with privacy.

The baby's first bed doesn't need to be a crib or even a bassinet. A clothes basket, long and wide enough to allow the baby to stretch out, will do nicely. With padding to protect on the sides and bottom, the basket is a good, inexpensive portable bed.

Some parents like to put a monitor in the baby's room. This listening device picks

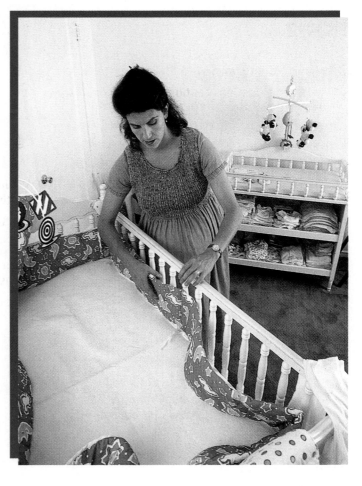

The basic needs for a baby are a crib and a dresser. A changing table with storage can be helpful as well. *Why is it helpful to have a separate room for a baby?*

up sounds from the room and sends them to a speaker. Parents put the speaker in the room where they are. This system gives the parents a chance to know if anything goes wrong while the baby sleeps.

The Diaper-Changing Area

Parents need to plan a place where the baby can be changed and dressed. Special changing tables are available, but any surface—except one used for eating—that is a convenient height and is padded can serve equally well. The top of a chest of drawers can be used as a changing table, as can a crib.

Whatever area is used, caregivers must never leave the baby unattended on it. They should pay constant attention to protect the baby from a fall and possible injury.

Making a Budget

Having a child is expensive. Prenatal care—an important expense—is costly. Equipment adds to the bills. On top of that, a growing baby seems to need new clothes every few months. Planning can help parents meet these expenses.

Do you budget your money? A **budget** is simply a spending plan used to help people set financial goals and work toward those goals. Budgets are helpful for everyone, but especially expectant parents.

The first step in making a budget is to identify income. How much money do the parents earn from work and other sources? If one parent will stop working to care for the child, the parents must remember that income will be reduced.

Next, the expectant parents should look at where their money currently goes. **Fixed expenses** are the costs of items that cannot be changed, such as payments for housing, taxes, insurance, and loans. **Flexible expenses** are costs for items over which people have some control—and which can be cut

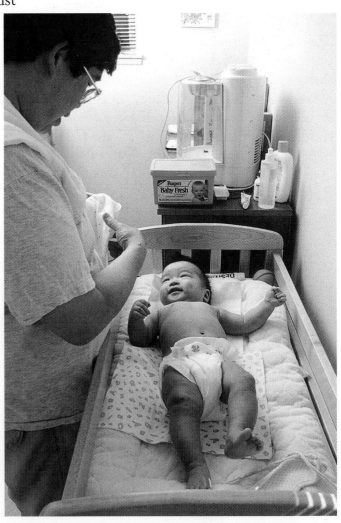

Where can a baby's diaper be changed if there's no changing table?

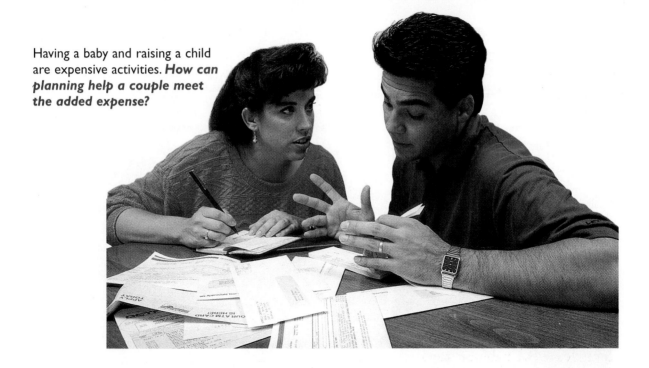

Having a baby and raising a child are expensive activities. *How can planning help a couple meet the added expense?*

back if necessary. This category includes food, household maintenance, clothing, recreation, and similar expenses.

Estimating Health Care Expenses

Medical care is a major expense. This includes the cost of health care for the mother before birth and the baby after birth. It also includes the cost of hospitalization for the birth. Hospital charges vary. They usually depend on the type of delivery, the medical needs of the baby and mother, and the length of their stay.

Health insurance can help meet these expenses. Many employers make health insurance available to their workers. These plans often cover spouses and children. A worker should find out if he or she has to pay for part of the coverage, though.

Even if there is no insurance through work, a couple can purchase health insurance on their own. Health insurance can be costly, so it pays to shop carefully. Consumers should look not only at the cost but also at what is covered.

Expectant couples should review their health insurance to see what it includes. It is also a good idea to find out whether the insurance company pays hospital bills directly or repays the parents after they have paid the hospital.

Some large hospitals have free or low-rate clinics to help people who have no insurance and can't pay the full fees. Social workers may be able to help expectant parents who have financial problems.

Estimating Other Expenses

Along with health care, expectant parents must consider other costs:
- Maternity clothes.
- The clothing, equipment, and supplies listed on page 198, as well as any other items the parents want to provide.

In most states, laws require young children to ride in a safety seat when in a car. By shopping carefully, parents can find a good quality seat that meets safety standards.

- Formula, if the baby will be bottle-fed. Some estimates put this expense at $1,200 to $1,500 per year.
- Furnishings for the baby's room.
- Child care, if needed.

Parents must also consider the costs of raising the child in the years ahead. Food, clothing, and education will all be major expenses. Parents should think about how they will manage these expenses.

Making a Plan

Once they have a clear idea of their new expenses, the parents can plan how to meet them. The money needed for the baby must be taken from another part of the budget, often by cutting back on flexible expenses.

Parents who have some money saved will find it easier to meet the early expenses of having a baby. Although it is often difficult to save money, having a budget can make this process easier. Saving even a small amount each month can help pay for the baby's future needs.

Reducing Expenses

Parents have several ways of reducing these expenses. Many parents cut costs by shopping carefully. Good quality used clothes and furniture can often be found at reasonable prices. Expectant parents have several months to comparison shop for what they need.

Many people reduce the cost of having a baby by borrowing things. Relatives and friends often share clothing or equipment among themselves. Expectant parents can find bargains at yard sales, rummage sales, and secondhand stores. If you use some-thing that is borrowed or bought second-hand, wash it thoroughly. Do so even though it may appear clean.

Special caution should be taken with equipment. Secondhand or borrowed cribs, playpens, car seats, and other items should meet current safety standards. You can find those standards by asking the pediatrician or the local health department.

SECTION 6-2 REVIEW

✔ Check Your Understanding

1. What is maternity leave?
2. How does time management help parents?
3. What steps are involved in finding a pediatrician?
4. Why are practical gifts especially good for new parents?
5. Do you think it is important for a baby to have a separate room? Why or why not?
6. What is the difference between a fixed expense and a flexible expense?
7. What factors influence the cost of hospitalization for childbirth?
8. What expenses can health insurance help with?
9. How can expectant parents save money and still get the clothing and equipment they need for a new baby?

Putting Knowledge Into Practice

1. **Making Inferences.** What factors do you think influence a mother's choice to breast-feed or bottle-feed her baby?
2. **Synthesizing.** Why might it be harder to prepare an only child for a new baby, rather than one who already has a brother or a sister?
3. **Observing and Participating.** Work in teams. Bring in ads for clothing, equipment, furniture, or supplies needed for a baby. How different are the prices? Make a list of five items and write down the prices you found. Compare those prices to the prices for the same item from different stores, as supplied by classmates. How much money can be saved by comparison shopping for these items?

CAREER OPPORTUNITIES

Nurse-Midwife

A CONVERSATION WITH ALICE QUINLAN

How did you become interested in becoming a nurse-midwife? What could be more wonderful than being part of the most miraculous event in life? I wanted to help pregnant women enjoy that experience in the most comfortable way possible.

What are the tasks and responsibilities of a nurse-midwife? We do prenatal checkups, counseling, and teaching. Of course, we help deliver babies. As long as the pregnancy is normal, we can handle everything.

What is the work environment like? Checkups take place in the office. I teach childbirth classes at the hospital and a local school. When it's time for a delivery, I work in the birthing rooms.

What are the working hours like? Checkups are usually during the day, but the classes are at night. Deliveries happen at any time—but it seems that babies always come at night!

What aptitudes are needed to be a nurse-midwife? Most important is to be calm and reassuring. Pregnancy and birth are natural processes, but people often become worried or concerned. We just try to help them get over that. You need to be a good communicator to be able to do that.

NURSE-MIDWIFE

Education and Training. Nurse-midwives need a bachelor's degree in nursing and then up to two more years of training to be a midwife.

Career Outlook. The outlook for nurse-midwives is good.

CONNECTING SCHOOL TO CAREER

1. **Thinking Skills.** Why might expectant parents want to use a nurse-midwife rather than a doctor?
2. **Technology.** What kinds of visual aids could a nurse-midwife use in teaching childbirth classes?

Childbirth Choices

When Ashley and Phil looked at the birthing room at the local hospital, they were thrilled. The room was large with comfortable furniture, lamps, and even a stereo. At the same time, they knew that the nursing staff was nearby, ready to help in an emergency. This, they agreed, was where they would have their baby.

KEY TERMS

alternative birth center
delivery
labor
lay midwife
nurse-midwife
postpartum
prepared childbirth

OBJECTIVES:

- Discuss the childbirth choices available to most parents.
- Describe how parents can prepare for childbirth.

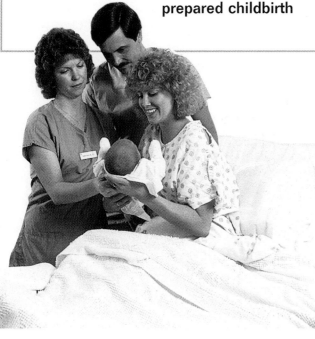

What Is Prepared Childbirth?

Prepared childbirth is a method of giving birth in which pain is reduced through the elimination of fear and the use of special conditioning exercises. Though a woman knows instinctively how to give birth, most women find childbirth education classes helpful in preparing them for this event. There are many different types of classes, including Bradley and Lamaze methods. In recent years, however, there has been a blending of these styles, so that most classes offer similar information.

In prepared childbirth, class members learn what happens during **labor**—the process by which the baby gradually moves out of the uterus and into the vagina to be born—and **delivery**—the birth itself. Class members see films of childbirth and receive reading material. Typically, they also tour the maternity area of the hospital. Much of the time is spent learning skills to cope with the discomforts of labor, such as relaxation techniques and patterned breathing.

Joining the pregnant woman in these classes is the father or someone else she chooses to serve as a partner or coach. The mother depends on the coach for emotional support and help when preparing for and going through labor and delivery.

Who Will Deliver the Baby?

Women can choose from among many different professionals to deliver the baby:

- **Obstetricians.** These doctors specialize in prenatal and postnatal care of the mother and baby. They are qualified to handle any emergencies or special situations that may arise.
- **Family doctors.** Some general-practice doctors also deliver babies and provide prenatal and postnatal care. If complications arise during pregnancy or delivery, a family doctor may need to call in an obstetrician.

- **Licensed midwives.** The are two types of licensed midwives, each with different education. A certified **nurse-midwife** is a registered nurse with advanced training in normal pregnancy and birth. Nurse-midwives must pass a special licensing exam before they can practice. A **lay midwife** has special training in the care of pregnant women and normal deliveries but does not have a nursing degree. Lay midwives must also pass a special exam.

Since most babies are delivered by doctors, that word will be used in this text. Remember, though, that parents have other options to choose from.

How do parents choose a doctor? They can get recommendations from their family doctor, the county medical society, or a local hospital. They can also ask friends to recommend the person they used. Some health insurance plans limit who the parents can use. Parents should find out if there are such limits before beginning their search.

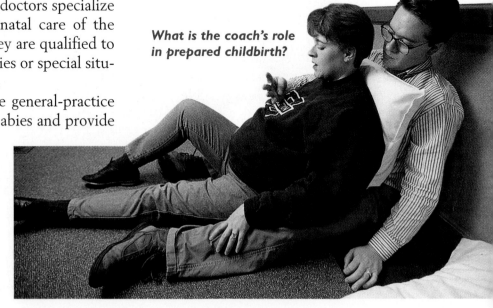

What is the coach's role in prepared childbirth?

Once the parents have a list of possible people, they should visit and talk with each one they are considering. They will want to be sure the person they choose is well qualified, makes them feel comfortable, and can answer their questions clearly.

The parents should find out how emergency calls will be handled at night and on weekends. Another consideration is which hospital or medical center the doctor is affiliated with. The parents should find out what programs and facilities that hospital has. They will also want to know whether the doctor has the same ideas about delivery procedures they do.

Although the woman should get medical care as soon as she is pregnant, she may not be ready to decide about the delivery at that time. There is no reason she cannot switch to a different doctor during pregnancy. The sooner a final decision is made, however, the better prepared both the parents and the doctor will be.

Where Will the Baby Be Born?

Until this century, almost all babies were born at home. Today, most births occur in hospitals. There, sanitary conditions, trained personnel, and special equipment make birth as safe as possible.

Hospitals now offer a variety of services to meet the needs and preferences of expectant mothers and their families. These services, often referred to as family-centered maternity care, include the following:

- Classes help the parents prepare for delivery and for caring for an infant.
- Special programs help young children get ready for having a baby brother or sister.
- Programs encourage fathers and other family members to help the mother through labor and delivery.
- Birthing rooms provide a comfortable atmosphere for labor and birth. Medical equipment is kept out of sight but is ready for use at a moment's notice.

Many hospitals offer classes that prepare expectant parents for labor and delivery. *Why would this help them?*

- Options allow women to choose the position they prefer for labor and delivery. Instead of lying flat, a woman may walk, rock in a chair, lie on her side, sit propped up, or even shower or soak in a tub. Many women find that these positions are more comfortable and make labor easier.
- Special steps may be taken to make the birth pleasant. For example, lights in the delivery room may be dimmed so the baby can open eyes without discomfort. Music can create a pleasant atmosphere.
- Plans allow the mother and her baby to stay together for all or most of the hospital stay, instead of staying in separate rooms.

Some hospitals offer what is called the LDRP concept. In this special unit, the woman labors, delivers, recovers, and spends her **postpartum** stay all in the same room.

(Postpartum is the time after the baby is born.) The baby stays with the mother; often the father can stay, too.

Expectant parents should take time to explore the various services offered by local hospitals. Many hospitals offer tours of their maternity area. After gathering information, the couple should discuss which services suit their needs.

Some couples choose not to use a hospital but go to an **alternative birth center**. This facility, separate from any hospital, has homelike rooms for giving birth. These centers emphasize prepared childbirth and usually offer the kinds of services that are part of family-centered maternity care. Usually licensed midwives handle births at these centers. Most alternative birth centers accept only mothers who have a low risk for complicated deliveries. A hospital is usually nearby, though, and mother and baby can be moved there if needed.

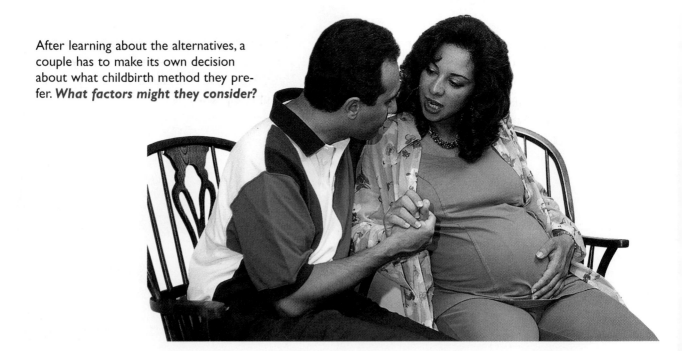

After learning about the alternatives, a couple has to make its own decision about what childbirth method they prefer. *What factors might they consider?*

Family-centered maternity care, whether at a hospital or an alternative birth center, usually costs less than traditional hospital maternity care. The time spent at the facility is usually shorter. If there are no complications, parents usually leave the hospital or birth center within 24 hours of delivery, compared with a two- to three-day stay for traditional births.

Whatever choice is made, safety for both the mother and the baby is the main concern. Couples should discuss the benefits and drawbacks of each type of delivery option with their doctor and then make their decision.

Delivery at home has gained popularity during recent years. The family that chooses this approach must carefully weigh the benefits and risks. This option is generally possible only for women with uncomplicated pregnancies. Some transportation should be available in case of an emergency.

SECTION 6-3 REVIEW

✔ Check Your Understanding

1. What is prepared childbirth?
2. Define *labor* and *delivery*?
3. What are the differences between an obstetrician and a nurse-midwife?
4. Why is it good to choose a doctor as early as possible in a pregnancy?
5. What are some of the services offered as part of family-centered maternity care?
6. What kind of health-care professional usually attends births at an alternative birth center?
7. How do family-centered maternity care and traditional childbirth compare in cost?

Putting Knowledge Into Practice

1. **Drawing Conclusions.** How can childbirth education classes reduce the fear of childbirth?
2. **Analyzing.** What are the advantages of family-centered maternity care? Of traditional childbirth?
3. **Observing and Participating.** Practice taking long, deep breaths. Does breathing in this way change the way you feel? How? Do you think this effect would help a woman in labor?

Parenting With Care

Checking Baby Equipment for Safety

Parents need a car safety seat as soon as the baby is born if they will drive the baby home from the hospital.

Some parents don't obtain a crib until several weeks or even months after the baby is born. Whether this equipment is borrowed or bought, purchased second-hand or new, it should be checked for safety.

Car Seats

Regular adult seat belts simply don't keep children securely and safely in a car's seat. Laws require that young children sit in a special seat that ensures their safety in a moving vehicle. There are two kinds of car seats:

- **Rear-facing safety seats.** These seats, also called infant seats, are meant for young babies up to 20 pounds (9.1 kg) or 26 inches (66 cm) long. The seat is placed in the center of the car's back seat, with the baby facing backwards.

- **Forward-facing safety seats.** These seats are meant for children from 20 pounds (9.1 kg) to 40 pounds (18.2 kg). Some of these seats can be turned around and used as rear-facing seats for infants.

Both types of seats use straps to keep the child securely in the seat. Both also have to be correctly connected to the car. Whatever type of seat is used, it needs to meet safety standards set by the federal government. As of the year 2000, each car seat—and each new car—must have a matching system of buckles. This system allows the child car seat to buckle into straps on both sides and on the top.

Crib

When choosing a crib, parents should consider both safety and comfort:

- **Slat width.** The government requires that the slats on the crib cannot be wider than 2⅜ inches (6.0 cm) apart.

- **Post height.** The four posts in the corners cannot be higher than ¹⁄₁₆ inch (0.16 cm) above the sides.

- **Safe decorations.** Don't use a crib with decorations cut out of the panels on either end, or a crib painted with paint that contains lead.
- **Safe edges.** The top edge of the sides should be covered with plastic because the baby might chew on them. There should be no sharp edges or rough bolts.
- **Adjustable sides.** Cribs with adjustable sides, make it easier to reach down and pick up the baby. These should be checked to make sure that they cannot slide down too easily by accident.
- **Mattress.** The mattress should fit snugly into the crib, with no space around it. The mattress and springs should be firm, not soft, to prevent suffocation.
- **Fitted sheets.** Only use fitted sheets that fit securely around the mattress. Sheets that have shrunk could pop off and become a safety hazard.

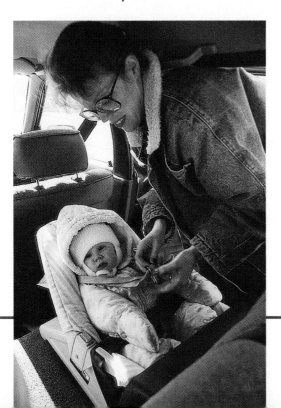

Following Up

1. **Management.** The federal government has banned cribs that have decorations cut out of the sides. Why do you think that was done?

2. **Thinking Skills.** Borrowing a used car safety seat can save money, but what possible safety problem might arise?

Summary

✔ A woman should see a doctor once she thinks she is pregnant and have regular checkups during the pregnancy. (Section 6-1)

✔ Good nutrition helps both the developing baby and the mother. (Section 6-1)

✔ Expectant parents should prepare for the birth of a child. (Section 6-2)

✔ Prepared childbirth helps expectant parents get ready for labor and delivery. (Section 6-3)

✔ Expectant parents must choose who will help deliver the baby and in what setting. (Section 6-3)

8. What three kinds of health professionals can assist at birth? (Section 6-3)

9. Are alternative birthing centers and home births available to all pregnant women? Why or why not? (Section 6-3)

Thinking Critically

1. **Analyzing.** How do you think a woman's emotional responses to pregnancy might affect how she feels physically—and the other way around?

2. **Making Inferences.** Suppose that a woman was at risk for complications in childbirth. Who would be the best health care professional to use? What setting would be best?

Taking Action

1. **Eating Well.** On a sheet of paper or an index card, write two snacks for a pregnant woman to eat, including all ingredients. Hand your paper or card to a classmate. Ask them to comment on the snacks in terms of nutrition and taste. Explain why you would or wouldn't recommend that a pregnant woman eat the snacks. *(Management)*

Reviewing the Facts

1. What should a woman do if she notices one of the early signs of pregnancy? Why? (Section 6-1)

2. What is the purpose of the Food Guide Pyramid? (Section 6-1)

3. How much weight does a woman usually gain when pregnant? (Section 6-1)

4. In what ways should expectant parents prepare for the birth of a child? (Section 6-2)

5. Do you think you would choose breastfeeding or bottle-feeding? Why? (Section 6-2)

6. What are the steps in making a budget? (Section 6-2)

7. What methods of reducing pain are taught in childbirth education classes? (Section 6-3)

2. Helping Out. A friend who moved to another town has written to say that she thinks she is pregnant but doesn't know for sure. Write a letter advising her what to do. *(Leadership)*

 ## Cross-Curricular Connections

1. Math. A new crib may cost from $150 to $500 and a mattress from $25 to $75. Sheets and blankets might add another $50 to $70. What is the range of the total cost of bedding? How much could be saved if expectant parents could buy these goods secondhand for half the cost?

2. Language Arts. Imagine the feelings of a three- to six-year-old whose mother has left home for the hospital and returns two or three days later with a new baby. Write a narrative of this from the child's perspective.

 ## Workplace Connections

1. Resources. A company offers health insurance to all its workers. This insurance adds 7 percent to payroll costs of $2 million. How much money does that represent? If the insurance cost rose to 8 percent, how much more would the employer pay for this insurance?

2. Interpersonal Skills. Suppose you are the instructor of a childbirth education class. What would you say to expectant parents on the first day of the class to ease their anxieties? Write a short talk that you would give.

 ## Family and Community Connections

1. Childbirth in the Past. Ask people in your family or others how childbirth was handled in the past. Try to talk to people from more than one generation. Were fathers allowed to participate in the birth? Who attended the woman giving birth—an obstetrician, family doctor, or midwife? Where did the birth take place? Report your findings, with approximate dates, to the class.

 ## Technology Connections

1. Blood Types. Research information on the Rh factor. What technology is used to test for the Rh factor? How are problems treated? Write a report with your findings.

2. Internet. Search the Internet to find the current safety requirements and recommendations for car seats or cribs. Report your findings to the class.

As Christine walked around the living room, she suddenly stopped. "Wow. That's a strong one," she said.

As Ed checked his stopwatch, he reminded his wife. "OK, remember your breathing. Long, deep breaths." Then he demonstrated. Christine followed his cue and did her breathing. When the contraction passed, she told him that.

"Well," said Ed, "they're 10 minutes apart and lasting about a minute."

Christine said, "This has been going on for an hour now, hasn't it?" When Ed nodded, she said "I think it's time to call the doctor and let her know. I think this is it for real!"

"I think it's time to call the doctor and let her know."

SECTION 7-1

Labor and Birth

In their ninth month, many women feel as though their pregnancy will never end. Then in just a day or so, that all changes. Giving birth is a powerful physical and emotional experience. When it is over and they are holding their babies, most women think that it is a wonderful one too.

KEY TERMS

cervix
cesarean birth
contractions
dilates
fontanels
forceps

OBJECTIVES:

- Recognize signs that labor may have begun.
- Outline the three stages of labor.
- Describe a baby's appearance at birth.

The Beginning of Labor

During the last weeks of pregnancy, women become anxious for the baby to be born. Time seems to pass slowly as they wait for labor to begin. In this time, they feel what is called "lightening." This occurs when the baby settles deep into the mother's pelvis, preparing for his or her journey into the world. When the baby moves down, the pressure on the woman's upper abdomen is reduced. With a first pregnancy, lightening may occur some days or weeks before labor. A woman who has already had a baby may experience this change just before labor begins.

Early Signs of Labor

There are some definite signals that the baby is coming. One is commonly called "show" or "bloody show"; it may also be referred to as losing the mucus plug. Throughout the pregnancy, a plug of mucus seals the **cervix** (SIR-viks), the lower part of the uterus. This mucus helps prevent bacteria from moving up the vagina into the uterus where it might cause an infection. Before birth, this mucus begins to liquefy. The woman may notice a few drops of blood or a slightly pinkish vaginal staining. This bloody show may come as early as a few days before labor begins.

In some women, the onset of labor is signaled by a trickle—or even a gush—of warm fluid from the vagina. This indicates that the membrane holding the amniotic fluid surrounding the baby has broken. In most women, this membrane does not rupture until she is at the hospital or birthing center, in active labor.

When the membrane breaks, the woman should note the time, the amount of fluid, and the color and odor of the fluid. She should call her doctor or midwife and report this information. Once the membrane has broken, the doctor may want to deliver the baby within 24 to 48 hours to protect the baby from infection.

The clear sign that labor has begun is **contractions**, the tightening and releasing of the muscle of the uterus. When the uterus contracts, it gets shorter and harder—like any other muscle. Bend an arm toward your shoulder while making a tight fist. Feel the muscle in your upper arm become thick and hard. Now, slowly relax and lower your forearm. Feel the muscle stretch and soften. The uterine muscle works the same way. With each contraction of labor, it shortens and gets harder, holds the hardness for a short time, and then relaxes and rests for a few minutes.

After the amniotic sac has broken, the doctor may want to make sure the baby is born within 24 or 48 hours. **Why?**

Are the contractions painful? Many women who have given birth say they are painful but bearable. Because there is time between each contraction, the woman can rest and recover. After the baby is born and contractions end, there is no lingering pain.

False Labor

Some women feel what is called "false labor" hours or even days before they begin real labor. They begin to feel strong contractions and believe that labor may have begun. Doctors look for three signs to see if contractions are false labor:

- They are not regular or rhythmic.
- They do not become increasingly stronger.
- They end if the woman walks around.

When contractions follow a regular pattern and grow in intensity, a woman is having real labor. The woman or her coach should time the contractions. When the woman calls the doctor to say that labor has begun, she will be asked how long the contractions are lasting, how frequently they are occurring, and how she is feeling.

At first, the doctor may advise the woman to stay home to be as comfortable as possible. The woman stays in touch by phone with the doctor, who will eventually advise when it is time to go to the hospital or birthing center.

Stages of Labor

Labor moves through three stages:
- In the first stage, contractions open the cervix.
- In the second stage, the baby is born.

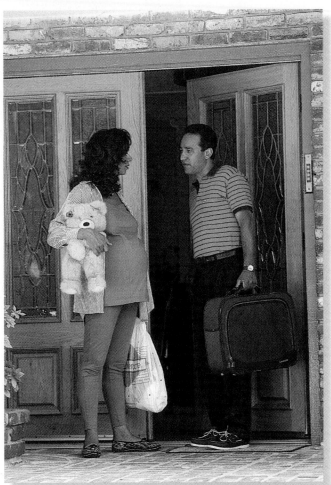

When contractions become strong, regular, and close together, it's time to leave for the hospital.

- In the third stage, the placenta is expelled.

The diagram on pages 220-221 shows what takes place during these three stages.

How long does labor last? The duration varies greatly, depending on the mother and the baby. Women often find that labor is longer the first time they give birth than with later babies. For a first birth, the first stage may last from 6 to 18 hours. It may be 2 to 5 hours for a later child. The second stage is typically 1 to 2 hours for a first child but might last 15 to 30 minutes for a later child. The third stage, the shortest, can be anywhere from 10 to 30 minutes.

The First Stage

In the first stage of labor, contractions prepare the mother's body to give birth. Each time the uterus contracts, the muscles of the uterus pull up on the cervix, slowly thinning and opening it, as shown in the illustrations.

During the first stage, contractions get stronger, longer (lasting about 60 seconds), and closer together (5 to 6 minutes apart). The woman begins to turn inward, searching for the strength to deal with the sensations of labor. She becomes more serious and focused on the labor and needs increasing support from her coach.

HEALTH TIP

Coping with Labor

*T*hroughout the first stage, the mother should try to relax as much as possible, both between and during contractions. Fear and tension cause the muscles of the body to tighten, and tight muscles can slow labor down and make it more uncomfortable.

Prepared childbirth courses teach special breathing exercises mothers can use. These exercises encourage relaxation, distract the mother from the discomfort, and help the labor progress. Fathers who attended these classes can help their wives use the techniques.

Some women change positions to become more comfortable. Most mothers may safely assume any position they find helpful. Some feel that standing or walking helps labor progress.

Some women who find the first stage very long and difficult choose to use a medication supplied by the doctor. There are several medications to choose from. Their effects vary from changing the woman's perception of pain to completing numbing the area so that no sensations are felt. All these medications have risks as well as benefits, since they have some effect on the baby. Women should talk to their doctor during prenatal checkups about the pros and cons of different medications before choosing one.

FOLLOWING UP
1. How can childbirth classes help during labor?
2. How can fathers-to-be help during labor?
3. What disadvantages do pain medications have?

The Stages of Labor

Cervix (closed)

Birth canal

Before Labor Begins

Before labor begins, the cervix is its normal size and shape.

First Stage of Labor

Contractions make the cervix **dilate**, or widen. The cervix also becomes thinner, changing from its usual thickness of about ¾ inch (19 mm) to become as thin as a sheet of paper. This thinning is called "effacement."

Cervix (beginning to open)

Birth canal

Cervix (fully dilated)

Birth canal

Transition

Transition completes the work of the first stage. The cervix becomes fully dilated to a size of 4 inches (10 cm) and the baby's head slips out of the uterus into the birth canal.

Second Stage of Labor: Crowning

First the top of the head appears at the opening of the birth canal.

Second Stage of Labor: Head Emerges

The baby's head emerges first. The head has changed its shape to ease passage through the birth canal. It will later return to normal. After the head, the shoulders follow. The rest of the baby slips out easily.

Third Stage of Labor

The woman gives birth to the placenta, no longer needed by the baby.

As the cervix opens, the baby moves down into the lower pelvis, getting ready for birth. Most of the time, the baby is head down, but some babies enter the pelvis with their feet or buttocks first. These positions are called "breech presentations." Babies in these positions may have a difficult time moving through the mother's pelvis for birth. The doctor will decide whether a vaginal delivery is possible.

The first stage ends with a period called "transition," when the cervix becomes fully dilated. The contractions become very strong, last longer (up to 90 seconds), and come more frequently (2 to 3 minutes apart) than earlier. This is usually the most difficult part of labor to cope with. A woman needs her coach's support, by touching and offering loving words, at this time.

The Second Stage

The contractions of the second stage work to move the baby down through the pelvis and out of the vagina, or birth canal. This is an exciting time, as the woman's coach and the doctor encourage her by saying, "Push! Push!" It ends with the event for which the parents have been waiting—the birth of the baby.

How could a baby ever fit through what seems to be such a narrow space? The bones of the pelvis are joined together by ligaments, which are like rubber hands. At the time of delivery, these ligaments are very stretchy, as a result of the influence of a hormone called "relaxin." As a result, the bones

of the pelvis stretch open as the baby passes through. The same hormone also makes the vagina very stretchy, so that the baby can safely pass through to be born.

The body of the unborn baby is well suited to this journey as well. The skull is soft and flexible so that the baby's head can become longer and narrower than normal. The skull consists of five separate bones. These bones can overlap each other to allow that baby's head to fit through the pelvis and vagina.

If the doctor decides that the fit between mother and baby is not adequate, he or she may widen the opening with a surgical cut called an "episiotomy." Although the procedure was done routinely in the past, many doctors and midwives now work with women to avoid it.

Women can give birth in a variety of positions. Many women use a position that is part sitting and part lying down, with

A baby's birth brings a great surge of emotion! *What specific feelings might be most common?*

their legs apart and their knees bent. Some women squat, sit in a birthing chair, lie on their side, or even kneel on their hands and knees. If a women is moved to a traditional delivery table, her legs may be supported by foot rests.

The doctor provides gentle support as the head is delivered. The head is followed by one shoulder, and then the other. Then the rest of the baby slips out into the world.

Sometimes a doctor uses **forceps.** These specialized tongs made from bands of surgical steel are modeled to fit the shape of the baby's head. The doctor can use the forceps to control the movement of the head, helping the baby emerge more quickly—or more slowly—if needed.

The Third Stage

After the baby is born, the mother often experiences a period of rest. Then she may once again feel some contractions and an urge to push. These contractions usually cause very little discomfort. They help the placenta separate from the wall of the uterus. When the mother pushes and delivers the placenta, the birth process is complete.

Although this stage of labor is usually brief, it is important. If any parts of the placenta remain, bleeding, infection, and serious illness may result.

Cesarean Birth

Not all births progress through these three stages of labor. If complications arise during the pregnancy or during labor, it may be necessary to perform a **cesarean** (si-ZARE-ee-uhn) **birth**. A cesarean is the

Some newborns have hair, but other don't. **Why are the heads of newborns somewhat lopsided?**

delivery of a baby by making a surgical incision in the mother's abdomen. With some types of medication, the mother can remain awake during cesarean surgery to see her baby's delivery. The father or coach may also be present if the doctor allows.

During the pregnancy, couples may take a special class preparing them for a cesarean if such a birth seems likely. After the surgery, the mother and baby usually stay in the hospital for about three days. Women who have had cesareans may need up to six weeks to recover from birth since they are also getting over major surgery.

The Newborn at Birth

The mother experiences amazing physical changes during labor and birth. So, too, does the baby. As a result, the baby is—for the first time—not completely dependent on the mother for life.

During its development in the uterus, the baby's lungs are collapsed. During delivery, they expand and fill with whatever amniotic fluid may have been in the baby's trachea. The pressure of being squeezed down the birth canal forces much of the fluid out. After emerging from the birth canal, the baby takes his or her first breath.

Usually, the newborn baby breathes naturally. If the baby needs help, the doctor or nurse-midwife may gently rub the baby's back to get the process started. Most of the fluid that remains in the airways or mouth is gently suctioned out.

Once the lungs have begun to take in oxygen, the baby's circulatory system changes. A valve in the heart closes and, over the next few days, becomes permanently sealed. Blood now circulates to and from the lungs, rather than bypassing the lungs as before.

The umbilical cord, through which the baby received oxygen and nourishment, is no longer needed. Within a few minutes of birth, the cord stops pulsing and begins to shrink. Health care workers clamp, tie, and cut off the cord, leaving a small stump.

How Does the Newborn Look?

What will our baby look like? When parents imagine their answers to this question, they usually picture a sturdy, smiling baby of about six months. Newborns look nothing like that.

The newborn's head is wobbly and large—about one-fourth the baby's length. The head may appear strangely lopsided or pointed because of the passage of the baby's head through the birth canal. With time, the head returns to normal.

You will recall that the bones of the skull are not yet fused together. The baby's head has two **fontanels** (FON-tuh-NELLS) open spaces where the bones have not yet joined. One of these "soft spots" is just above the baby's forehead, and the other is toward the back of the skull. These spaces allow the bones of the skull to move together during birth so that the head can fit through the birth canal. The bones come together to cover these spaces when the baby is between six and eighteen months old. In the meantime, the soft spots are protected by skin that is as tough as heavy canvas.

The face of a newborn may be swollen or puffy as a result of the birth process. The newborn typically has fat cheeks; a short, flat nose; and a receding chin. These features make the baby's face well adapted for sucking, because the nose and chin are out of the way.

At birth, a baby's eyes are nearly adult-sized. They are usually dark grayish blue at birth. The baby's permanent eye color becomes apparent within several months.

It takes time for the baby's circulatory system to adjust to life outside the uterus. As a result, fingers and toes may be slightly cooler than the rest of their body for up to 24 hours. Wrapping the baby well and covering the head with a cap helps keep him or her warm and comfortable.

Some babies, particularly those born early, have fine, downy hair called "lanugo" over their forehead, back, and shoulders. This hair disappears as the baby grows.

While in the uterus, the baby is surrounded by warm amniotic fluid. To protect their skin from constant exposure to the fluid, babies are covered with a rich, creamy substance called "vernix." After the birth, most newborns have some vernix in the folds of their skin, particularly around their ears and neck and under their arms. It can be gently removed with warm water and a washcloth.

Many babies have tiny white bumps scattered over their nose and cheeks. These bumps are called "milia," or baby acne. They are simply plugged oil ducts, caused by stimulation from the mother's hormones, which remain in the baby's system for a short time after the delivery. The milia will disappear in a week or two.

SECTION 7-1 REVIEW

✔ Check Your Understanding

1. What are contractions? How do they feel to the woman?
2. Contrast real and false labor.
3. What is the cervix? How does it change during labor?
4. How do the bone structures of both mother and baby make birth easier?
5. Why is the third stage of labor important?
6. How does cesarean birth differ from normal birth?
7. What changes take place in the baby at birth?
8. Describe the appearance of a newborn.

Putting Knowledge Into Practice

1. **Making Inferences.** Write two paragraphs about the experience of birth from the baby's perspective.
2. **Sequencing.** Describe the stages of labor in a normal delivery.
3. **Observing and Participating.** Interview a father who was present at the birth of his baby. Ask what he did to help his wife and what the experience meant to him. Find out if he had other children whose births he did not see. How were the two experiences different? Report your findings to the class and discuss the comments of different fathers.

SECTION 7-2

The Postnatal Period

The moment of birth is the end of nine months of preparation—and a beginning. Soon the newborn and parents will go home to begin their new life together. First, however, the staff at the hospital or birthing center makes sure the new family gets off to a good start.

KEY TERMS

Apgar scale
bonding
colostrum
incubator
postnatal
premature
rooming-in

OBJECTIVES:

- Explain the purpose of common hospital procedures following a birth.
- Explain the special needs of a premature baby.
- Describe a mother's needs after having given birth.

Examining the Newborn

Shortly after delivery, the newborn's physical condition is checked using the **Apgar scale**. The infant is given a rating from 0 to 2 in each of these five areas: heart rate, breathing, muscle tone, reflex to stimulation, and skin color. A total score of 6 to 10 is considered normal. A lower score is a sign that the baby needs special medical attention.

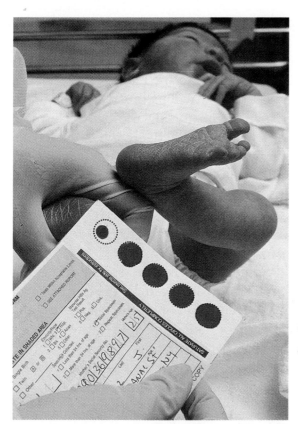

Usually, this evaluation is done one minute after birth and five minutes after birth. The baby is also given a brief examination to check for any conditions that might require special care. The baby is weighed, measured, and cleaned up.

Shortly after birth, steps are taken to identify the baby. A copy of the baby's footprint is made for public record. Two plastic bands giving the baby's family name are clamped to the baby's wrists or ankles and the mother's wrist. This prevents any confusion later.

What elements are checked in the Apgar exam?

The Apgar Scale

	SCORE		
	0	**1**	**2**
HEART RATE	Absent	Under 100	Over 100
BREATHING	Absent	Slow, irregular	Good, crying
MUSCLE TONE	Limp	Some movement of extremities	Active motion
RESPONSIVENESS (Baby's reaction when nose is irritated)	No response	Grimace	Cough or sneeze
COLOR	*Light-skinned child:* Blue or pale *Dark-skinned child:* Grayish or pale	*Light-skinned child:* Body pink, limbs blue *Dark-skinned child:* Strong body color, grayish limbs	*Light-skinned child:* Completely pink *Dark-skinned child:* Strong color with pink lips, palms, and soles

Later Tests

Newborns also have several other tests and medical procedures in their first few days of life. Within 60 minutes of delivery, drops of an antiseptic are put into the baby's eyes to protect them from infection.

When they are born, babies are low in vitamin K. This vitamin is needed to help the blood clot, which puts a stop to any bleeding. Babies are given a shot with this vitamin shortly after birth.

In a growing number of hospitals, a new test is being given to babies within a few days of birth to find if the baby has a hearing problem. The test, which measures whether the baby's ear echoes a light sound, can be done in the baby's sleep.

Health care workers also take a blood sample from the baby. This blood is studied to see if the baby has PKU, sickle cell anemia, or some other conditions.

Bonding and Attachment

In most cases, there are no problems with the newborn, and the long-awaited moment occurs: the baby is given to the mother and father to hold. Most parents feel a deep—and memorable—thrill.

In recent years, researchers have studied the emotional needs of a newborn. They have emphasized the importance of **bonding,** or forming strong emotional ties between parent and child. Most facilities have changed their policies as a result of this research. Most now delay cutting the umbilical cord, cleaning the infant, and giving eyedrops to let parents and child begin bonding right away.

The baby may be placed in the mother's arms or abdomen to feel the mother's skin and hear her familiar heartbeat and voice. The newborn instinctively focuses on the mother's face. Many mothers begin touching and talking to the baby.

If the baby will be breast-fed, the mother may begin nursing the baby. The newborn knows instinctively what to do. The mother's breasts supply the first breast milk. Called **colostrum,** this milk is easy for the newborn to digest and rich in antibodies to protect against disease. It is sometimes thick in consistency; it may be clear or yellow in color.

Some newborns have special needs that require immediate care by the hospital staff. New parents may miss the chance to bond with these children right away. Usually, though, the staff brings parents and baby together as soon as possible. Then they can begin their lifetime of love and caring.

The Hospital Stay

Birth is a momentous undertaking for both mother and baby. The newborn must adjust to a whole new world. The mother, too, needs time to adjust. In a matter of hours, her body has gone from pregnancy to labor and birth and back to being nonpregnant. Although she probably feels excited, she needs to rest and recuperate.

There are differences in the length of time mothers and babies generally stay in the hospital. In some facilities, a mother and baby who are both healthy may go home as soon as 12 hours after birth. In other hospitals, the average stay following birth is two or three days.

In the past, women and children stayed in the hospital up to four days for a normal delivery. Some critics say that insurance companies are forcing hospitals to release

Practicing Parenting

Strengthening Bonds

Bonding with a newborn is important—but this is not the only time parents can, or should, bond with their child. Bonding remains important throughout a child's life. Here are some ideas for building strong bonds between parent and child:

❤ **Infants.** Keep the baby close to you and comforted. Take time to touch the baby; infants respond to touch. Pay attention to the baby's reactions to you and continue the actions that produce the reactions you want. If the baby is soothed by rocking, use rocking when he or she is upset. Finally, remember to play with the baby. Babies crave stimulation, especially from their parents.

❤ **Toddlers and preschoolers.** Although these children are older and more independent than infants, they still need a parent's attention. Continue using touch by giving the child an occasional hug just to say "I love you." Keep playing with the child—and take interest in the games that he or she invents.

❤ **School-age children.** Talk to the child, and encourage the child to talk to you. Keep communication open. Respect the child's feelings and desires, and value his or her opinion.

APPLY YOUR KNOWLEDGE

1. For which ages are the suggestions for bonding more physical? Why?
2. Several suggestions relate to responding to the child's needs. How would this help strengthen bonds?

---

women and babies too soon. Some states have passed laws requiring insurers to pay for at least two days after a normal delivery if the woman and her doctor request it.

One condition that may delay release for a few days is newborn jaundice. Some babies have a yellow color on their skin and the whites of the eyes. This is caused by the blood having too much of a certain natural-ly occurring chemical. The newborn's liver isn't ready, just after birth, to remove that chemical from the body. If left untreated, the condition can damage to the nervous system. Treatment is only a matter of putting the child under a flourescent light for a few hours each day until the liver can do its job. The treatment may also take place at home.

Many hospitals keep the newborn in the mother's room. *What emotional needs does this practice meet?*

Grandparents and brothers and sisters can visit, hold, and get to know the new baby.

Legal Documents

All new parents should make sure their baby has a birth certificate. A birth certificate is the most important piece of personal identification anyone has. It is required for entrance into school. Getting one is simple. The parents fill out a form provided by the hospital or birthing center, at which time a temporary certificate is issued. In many states, the official birth certificate can be applied for by the family or by the hospital on behalf of the family.

The parents should also obtain a Social Security number for their new child. This number is needed to claim the child as an exemption on income taxes and to take part in many government programs.

Rooming-In

Many hospitals have a **rooming-in** program. With this arrangement, the baby stays in the mother's room day and night rather than in a hospital nursery. Hospitals with rooming-in generally allow the father to visit whenever he wishes.

Rooming-in programs have important advantages for all family members. Couples benefit by having a chance to get to know their baby and practice giving care before going home. The baby can be fed whenever hungry, rather than on a set schedule.

Caring for Premature Babies

Between 5 and 6 percent of all babies are **premature** babies. Premature babies are those born before 37 weeks of development and weighing less than 5 pounds, 8 ounces (2.5 kg).

These babies require special care. They are not really ready to live outside their mother's body. Their systems for controlling body temperature, breathing, and feeding are not yet mature. To help them, a premature baby is usually placed in an **incubator** (IN-cue-BAY-tuhr). In this special enclosed

Paraquay
(Ache)

Bonding Around the World

*T*he Ache (AH chay) people of Paraguay, in South America, quickly bring many people into the life of a newborn. When the child is born, he or she is given to a godmother. That woman cares for the child for the first few days, while the mother regains her strength. Her special bond with the child continues throughout life.

A godfather is also chosen. That person cuts the umbilical cord as a sign of his role.

Ache children have a very close relationship with their mother. In the first year of life, infants spend every minute of the night and more than 90 percent of the daytime in close contact with their mothers. One reason: mothers wish to protect their babies from the dangers of the rainforest where the Ache live.

─────── **SHARE YOUR THOUGHTS** ───────

1. What adults, other than parents, play a role in children's lives in our society? What roles do they play?

2. Do you think that Ache mothers would be more or less willing than American mothers to let their infants explore their environment? Why?

---

crib, the oxygen supply, temperature, and humidity can be closely controlled. The baby's heart and lungs can be monitored, and special steps may be taken to combat infection, breathing difficulties, and other problems. Advances in medical technology allow many premature infants—even those weighing as little as 1 pound (454 g)—to survive and become healthy.

When they become healthy enough to leave the incubator, premature babies are moved to an open bassinet. Before being allowed to leave the hospital, the baby must be able to control body temperature and gain weight at the same time.

Having a premature baby can be hard on a mother and father. They understand that the incubator is needed to save their

Premature babies suffer many physical difficulties. *How can they be helped by being placed in incubators?*

baby's life, but it also creates a barrier between them and their child. Steps can be taken to bring parent and child together, though. Some hospitals let parents reach into the incubator and touch the babies. Sometimes the baby is taken from the incubator for a while so the parents can hold him or her. This has been shown to improve the child's breathing and sleeping. Mothers can also breast-feed a premature baby by using a breast pump.

Good nutrition, healthy habits, good prenatal care, and an understanding of the warning signs of premature labor can all help prevent premature births. If premature labor is spotted soon enough, medication can be given to stop the contractions.

Postnatal Care of the Mother

In the period after birth—the **postnatal** period—it is natural for most of the attention to be focused on the baby. However, the new mother has special physical and emotional needs as well. A doctor or nurse will explain and discuss these needs before the mother and baby go home.

Physical Needs

The mother needs to recover from pregnancy and birth and to regain her fitness. She must take care of herself so that she can care for her child. The keys to meeting her needs include:

- **Rest.** During the first few days and weeks after the birth, the mother is likely to feel tired. She should try to sleep whenever the baby does. Relatives or friends can help the mother rest by doing household chores or caring for the baby for a few hours.

- **Exercise.** As soon as the mother feels able and her doctor approves, she can begin mild exercise. From just a few simple stretches, she can gradually add other exercises. Exercise helps the woman return to her normal figure and correct posture.

- **Nutrition.** Eating right is as important now as during pregnancy. As before birth, a mother who breast-feeds is supplying nutrients for the baby as well as herself. She should be sure to follow the recommendations of the Food Guide Pyramid for nursing women. She should also drink plenty of water and other liquids. Even if the mother is not breast-feeding, good nutrition is important to good health.

INFOLINK

Food Guide Pyramid.

See page 187 for the *Food Guide Pyramid for Pregnant and Nursing Women.*

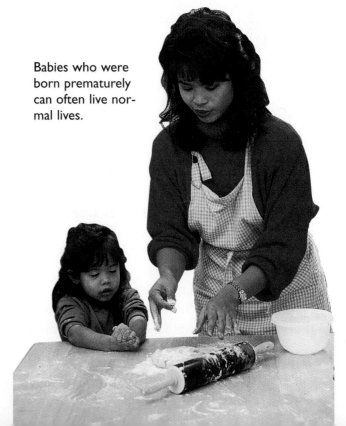

Babies who were born prematurely can often live normal lives.

Doctors recommend that after giving birth, women begin a program of mild exercise. **Why?**

It helps the woman feel good and regain energy.

- **Medical checkup.** About four to six weeks after the birth, the new mother should have a postnatal checkup. At this time, the doctor makes sure that the woman's uterus is returning to normal and that there are no unusual problems. This is also an opportunity for the mother to discuss any questions or concerns she has.

Emotional Needs

Having a baby is a joyous but stressful event. Many new mothers go through a few days of mild depression after the birth. No one knows for certain why these "baby blues" occur. New fathers may have these feelings, too.

It helps if parents talk about their feelings. Taking good care of themselves, seeking support, getting needed sleep and avoiding isolation helps parents minimize the blues. More serious or longer-lasting depression requires the care of a doctor.

SECTION 7-2 REVIEW

✔ Check Your Understanding

1. What is the Apgar scale? When is it used?
2. Why do hospitals now delay performing some tests on the newborn?
3. What is colostrum?
4. What are the advantages of rooming-in?
5. Would a baby born in week 34 who weighs 3 pounds be premature? What about one born in week 40 that weighed 5 pounds?
6. Why do premature babies need special care?
7. What issues are involved in a mother's postnatal care?

Putting Knowledge Into Practice

1. **Predicting Consequences.** Do you think parents who have cesarean births or who adopt might have trouble bonding with their babies? If so, how much of a problem do you think that would be?
2. **Synthesizing.** What could a woman do if she was having problems with breast-feeding while in the hospital?
3. **Observing and Participating.** Talk to a mother about her feelings after birth. Did she feel any "baby blues"? When or how did they go away?

CAREER OPPORTUNITIES

Intensive Care Pediatric Nurse

A CONVERSATION WITH JOHN RICHARDSON

How did you become interested in becoming an intensive care pediatric nurse? When I was in nurses training, I did a rotation in intensive care pediatrics. There was a baby born with many different problems—heart, lungs, kidneys. The staff worked and worked on her and saved her life. Her parents were there constantly. When I saw how grateful they were that she lived, I decided this would be a great career.

What are the tasks and responsibilities of an intensive care pediatric nurse? We have to watch the young children in our care all the time. We rely on machines to monitor their vital signs—pulse and blood pressure and breathing. But we also spend a lot of time with each one of them. They need holding and caring, just like any other babies.

What is the work environment like? It's very intense. A baby can have a crisis at any time, and you have to be ready to act immediately. It can be very difficult to wind down at the end of the day.

What are the working hours like? We work in shifts of eight hours, either day, evening, or night.

What aptitudes are needed to be an intensive care pediatric nurse? Intensive care nurses have to think clearly under pressure. We need a good memory to bring back everything ever studied or experienced to face each situation. Of course, a good background in science helps too. It's important to care—about babies and their parents.

Career Facts

INTENSIVE CARE PEDIATRIC NURSE

Education and Training. To become a registered nurse, a person needs to complete a four- or five-year nursing program in college and pass a licensing exam.

Career Outlook. Jobs for registered nurses are expected to grow much faster than average.

CONNECTING SCHOOL TO CAREER

1. **Personal Qualities.** Why do intensive care nurses need to think well under pressure?
2. **Technology.** How can technology help intensive care nurses do their work?

A New Family Member

For the first few months of life, every baby is considered "new." The baby's family, too, is newly expanded, with new relationships to establish. Welcoming home and getting to know this tiny person are exciting aspects of adjusting to life with a new baby.

KEY TERMS

grasp reflex
reflexes
rooting reflex
startle reflex
temperament

OBJECTIVES:

- Recognize a baby's reflexes.
- Describe babies' basic needs.
- Discuss how babies' needs can best be met.

The Amazing Newborn

Newborn babies are amazing, born with remarkable capabilities. Newborns use their senses to learn about their new world.

At birth, babies are very sensitive to strong light. Some may even cry when they encounter bright lights. Newborns are sensitive to sounds—especially the sound of the human voice. Newborns like some smells—milk, vanilla, banana, and sugar—and turn away from strong smells like vinegar. After just one week of nursing, babies turn toward nursing pads used by their own mothers, but not those used by other nursing mothers.

The newborn breathes independently. The newborn can also cry to signal a variety of needs, such as the need for food, attention, or a dry diaper.

Reflexes

Babies must be able to handle some of their needs involuntarily until they learn to do things voluntarily. **Reflexes**—instinctive, automatic responses, such as sneezing and yawning—make this possible. These coordinated patterns of behavior help the baby's body function. For example, a sneeze helps clear the baby's nose of lint. Swallowing helps the baby eat without choking.

Sneezing and swallowing continue throughout life. Other reflexes last only until the baby develops voluntary control of his or her body. Three are notable:

- **Rooting reflex.** The **rooting reflex** is a newborn's automatic response, when touched on the lips or cheek, of turning toward the touch and beginning to suck. This reflex helps the baby find food. When babies use their eyes to search for the bottle or mother's breast, around four months of age, the rooting reflex stops.

- **Grasp reflex.** The **grasp reflex** is the automatic response of a newborn's hand to close over anything that comes in contact with the palm. The grip is often so strong that it can be used to lift the newborn up. This is not a good idea, however, because the baby lets go without warning. When the baby begins to reach for objects, at about three months of age, this reflex weakens; it disappears by the time babies are one year old.

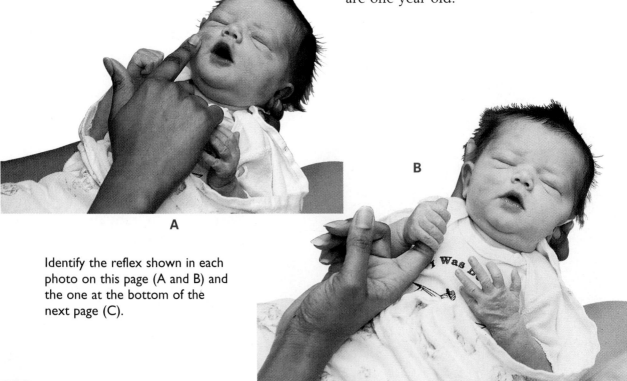

A

B

Identify the reflex shown in each photo on this page (A and B) and the one at the bottom of the next page (C).

- **Startle reflex.** The **startle reflex** is a newborn's automatic response to a loud noise or to a touch on the stomach. The legs are thrown up, fingers spread, and arms are first extended and then brought back rapidly while the fingers close in a grasping action. The startle reflex disappears when the baby is about five months old.

Learning to Care for the Newborn

At first, it may take some time for new parents to feel comfortable caring for a baby. Soon, they gain confidence and become accustomed to the baby's way of communicating. They learn how to recognize the baby's needs and adapt their responses to their baby's individual style.

c

What Do Babies Need?

Later chapters in this book present detailed information about caring for a baby. Here, however, are babies' basic needs:

- **Babies need food.** A newborn shows hunger with his or her whole body. The baby squirms about, mouth searching for the mother's breast or a bottle nipple. Hungry newborns want food immediately, and it is important to meet their need quickly. Doing so helps them learn that they can trust the world.
- **Babies need sleep.** Newborns sleep and wake throughout the day and night. A newborn sleeps an average of 15 hours a day, typically in six to eight separate sleep periods. Many sleep one long five-hour stretch during the night. However, the level of alertness or drowsiness varies from baby to baby. Every baby is different; what is normal is normal for that individual baby.
- **Babies need exercise.** In the brief times they are awake, newborns wave their arms and legs. This activity helps their muscles and nervous system develop. Before a feeding, babies usually become very active, moving all parts of their body. They may kick while their diaper is changed and splash and wiggle during a bath.
- **Babies need to be kept safe, clean, and warm.** Parents diaper and bathe babies to keep them clean. They also make sure that an adult keeps an eye on the baby at all times. Anything the baby might come in contact with—a toy, a crib, a garment—should be checked for safety, and any potentially harmful objects should be kept away.

Ask the Experts

Dr. Van Stone
Pediatrician
Tupelo, Mississippi

SUDDEN *Infant Death Syndrome*

Q What is crib death, and what can be done to prevent it?

A Crib death is known medically as Sudden Infant Death Syndrome, or SIDS. The victims are usually infants between the ages of two weeks and six months. Children who die of SIDS seemed healthy. They die in their sleep, with no warning and no evidence of pain. SIDS strikes one or two children out of every thousand.

The cause of SIDS is unknown. Research has dismissed infection, allergy to milk, and suffocation, among other causes. The most likely explanation is long pauses in breathing.

Although the causes of SIDS are unknown, research has identified some groups who are at risk. Victims are likely to be male babies who had low birthweight. Premature babies are at risk for SIDS, as are babies living in a house where a person smokes. Babies who sleep on their stomachs are a risk group as well. Finally, SIDS most often strikes in winter.

Research has also found steps that can be taken to lower the risk:

- *Most important, put babies to sleep on their backs or sides. The American Academy of Pediatrics now recommends this position for all babies but a few.*

- *Practice good prenatal care to avoid having a premature or low-birthweight baby.*

- *Avoid smoking during pregnancy and after the baby is born. A smoke free home helps a newborn in many ways, but can also help prevent SIDS.*

Parents who suffer the loss of a baby to SIDS often feel stricken by guilt as well as grief. They can benefit from counseling.

Thinking It Through

1. Is SIDS equally likely to strike any child?
2. Why might parents who lost a child to SIDS feel guilty?

Bathing is more than a time to clean the baby. It also offers the baby a chance to learn about the world. *What needs does a baby have?*

contact with warm, affectionate adults. Love is as important as food and sleep to babies. A baby who senses that he or she is loved feels at ease and secure. Each parent should express love for his or her newborn naturally, in the ways that are comfortable.

What Do Parents Need?

Parents of newborns are often so concerned about caring for their babies that they neglect their own needs. These are some of the things that parents of newborns need:

- Knowledge of how to care for an infant.
- Resources that can provide answers to their questions.
- Information about how their babies act and change and about typical emotions they might experience.
- Time to fill their many roles.
- Emotional support from family and friends.
- Financial planning.
- Reassurance and confidence that both parents are capable and needed.
- Agreement about parenting and household responsibilities.
- Personal health, rest, and nutrition.
- Privacy and time alone.

- **Babies need medical care.** In the first year, an infant will have periodic checkups to make sure he or she is healthy and developing normally, and to receive immunizations.
- **Babies need things to look at, touch, listen to, and play with.** Stimulating surroundings help babies learn. However, babies don't need expensive toys. In fact, an infant's favorite thing to look at is a human face.
- **Babies need love.** Just like everyone else, babies want to be near the people who love them. Newborns need close

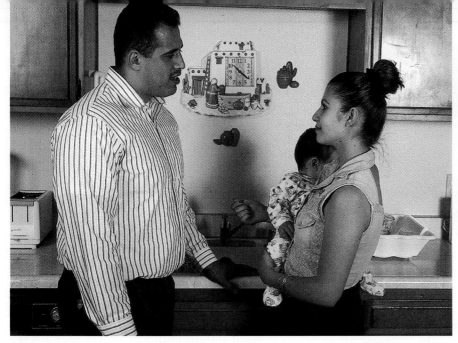

Parents and baby have to adjust to each other at first. Many first-time parents are surprised to learn that they have to keep adjusting—babies change quickly as they grow, and their needs and abilities change from week to week.

Adjusting to New Routines

During the first few weeks, both parents and babies have to adjust to new patterns of life. A newborn typically needs at least several weeks before he or she can settle into any predictable pattern of eating and sleeping. Parents must adjust their schedule to the baby's needs. That means feeding the baby whenever hunger strikes, day or night.

Some parents worry that this kind of response will spoil the child, making him or her too demanding. At this early stage of life, though, babies need to feel that they are important and their needs will receive attention. Later, when they are more mature, they can begin to learn to follow a schedule.

Of course, every newborn benefits from order in life. Daily patterns emerge to manage the baby's hunger, sleepiness, and wakefulness. It takes about a month, for example, to establish a fairly predictable feeding and sleeping routine. Meanwhile, the key to the baby's happiness is the parents' flexibility.

Understanding the Baby's Language

Babies have one way to communicate with the world—crying. Although newborns never cry for fun, their reasons may often be far less serious than worried new parents imagine. Babies cry because they are too hot or too cold, because they are lying in an uncomfortable position or because the sun is in their eyes, because their diaper is wet, or because they no longer hear their mother's voice.

The average newborn cries about one hour per day, but individual babies may cry less or much more than that. The important thing to remember is that a baby's crying seems to have nothing to do with the quality of parenting he or she is receiving. Parents soon learn to recognize their baby's different cries—one for hunger, another for discomfort, and so on.

Early Temperament

Babies differ markedly in their inborn **temperament**, or style of reacting to the world and relating to others. For example, Pete moves from sleep to wakefulness with a startled cry. Carmen awakens gradually and quietly looks around. Jake may be so easily upset that extra gentle handling and a smooth routine are necessary. Ira can be handled more playfully without objection. No two babies react in just the same way.

Parents need to be sensitive to the baby's own style. The baby, too, learns to adapt to the style of his or her parents. Studies have shown that babies as young as two weeks of age adjust their reactions, depending on how parents handle and talk to them. When parents are very gentle and soothing, the baby tends to respond with soft cooing and gentle motions. When parents are playful, the baby tends to react with excited grunts and active motions. These natural adjustments help parents and babies feel at ease with each other.

Babies reveal their own temperament soon after birth. *How do parent and newborn adjust to each other in the early weeks of the newborn's life?*

SECTION 7-3 REVIEW

✔ Check Your Understanding

1. Define *reflex* and give an example of one.
2. Describe one reflex a newborn has.
3. What do you think is the most important thing a baby needs? Why?
4. How much do newborn babies typically sleep?
5. Why is flexibility important for new parents?
6. What is temperament? Why does it matter?

Putting Knowledge Into Practice

1. **Synthesizing.** How is the way newborns respond to hunger typical of their nature?
2. **Applying.** Where can parents get the knowledge about caring for an infant that they need?
3. **Observing and Participating.** Observe parents and small infants in a public place, such as a park or a mall. Record how parents show their love for their babies. Describe how the babies respond to the parents.

Parenting With Care

Talking Promotes Development

Current research shows that talking to a child is one of the best ways of building that child's emotional and intellectual development.

Talking helps the nerves in the baby's brain become connected, which can help with later development. Babies who are talked to often know more words by age two. Talking also strengthens the bonds between caregivers and children.

What should you talk about? The answer is just about anything at almost any time. Start talking when the baby is born—and never stop. Here are some tips for infants:

- **When feeding.** Talk about which members of the family the baby looks like or why the baby was given his or her name.
- **When bathing.** Describe water and soap or talk about how much fun it will be to learn to swim.
- **When changing diapers.** Name the parts of the baby's body.
- **When dressing.** Say the names of different articles of clothing or talk about colors.

- **When driving.** Name the roads and streets or describe memories linked to particular places.
- **When walking the baby in a stroller.** Talk about the outdoors and what is seen there or about the weather and the seasons.
- **When shopping for food.** Name the fruits and vegetables and describe their shape and color. Talk about what food tastes like or particular meals.

Will the baby understand all these facts? Probably not. The baby will still benefit, though. For the baby to benefit, this talk has to come from a live person.

Sitting the child in front of the television or next to the radio to listen to that talk will not help. Babies learn most when they have an emotional attachment to the person talking. The baby will benefit more if the person talking makes eye contact while talking.

All this talking benefits another person, too. The parent who spends a long day with a demanding baby can grow tired. Talking can break the quiet and help that parent stay in good spirits.

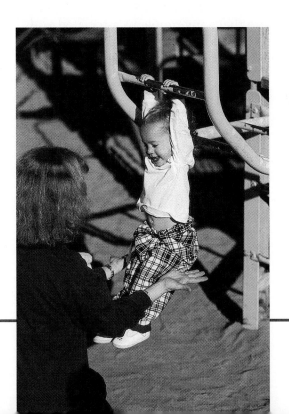

Following Up

1. **Communication.** Imagine some activity that a parent and three-year-old do and list some topics the parent could talk about.

2. **Thinking Skills.** In some families, one parent works and the other stays home with the child. Sometimes, the parent who works is faced with a torrent of words from the other parent when coming home at the end of the day. Why would that be?

REVIEW &

Summary

✔ In the three stages of labor, the baby emerges from the mother's body. (Section 7-1)

✔ Newborns have a unique appearance, unlike that of older babies. (Section 7-1)

✔ Health care workers examine a baby after birth to make sure he or she is healthy. (Section 7-2)

✔ Some babies and mothers have special needs that delay their leaving the hospital. (Section 7-2)

✔ Reflexes help a newborn's body function until the baby has more control. (Section 7-3)

✔ Newborn babies and parents of newborns have several needs that must be met. (Section 7-3)

9. How might a baby's temperament affect the way parents respond to him or her? How can a parent's temperament affect a baby? Give examples. (Section 7-3)

Thinking Critically

1. **Making Inferences.** How do you think new parents would feel when they saw their first newborn if they didn't know what newborns looked like?

2. **Analyzing.** Research how labor and delivery were handled 100 years ago. Where did childbirth generally take place? Were there any problems associated with these practices? What was done to address these problems? Report your findings.

Taking Action

1. **Being Prepared.** Make a list of things an expectant couple might want to take when they leave home to have their baby. *(Management)*

2. **Lending a Hand.** How can friends or other members of the family help someone who has just had a baby? Make a chart with the headings "Food," "Cleaning," "Errands," "Child Care." *(Communication)*

Reviewing the Facts

1. What is meant by "bloody show"? (Section 7-1)

2. What purpose do contractions serve in the first stage of labor? In the second stage? In the third stage? (Section 7-1)

3. How do a baby's lungs and heart change at birth? (Section 7-1)

4. Choose one test or procedure done to a newborn soon after birth and explain why it is performed. (Section 7-2)

5. What standards are used to determine that a baby is premature? (Section 7-2)

6. Why is good nutrition important for a mother after giving birth? (Section 7-2)

7. List three reflexes a baby is born with and describe one. (Section 7-3)

8. Why is it important to feed a hungry newborn right away? (Section 7-3)

CONNECTIONS

Cross-Curricular Connections

1. **Health.** Make a time line of a woman's labor. Use the time spans described in the text for each stage.

2. **Math.** Ten women, each having her first child, were in the first stage of labor for the following number of hours: 13, 16, 15, 20, 18, 12, 17, 14, 18, 10. What was the average length of the first stage? What was the range of times?

Workplace Connections

1. **Information Systems.** Create a system that could be used in hospitals or birth facilities to match newborn babies and their mothers. Make a poster or brochure describing it.

2. **Interpersonal Skills.** Suppose you worked in a hospital maternity area. How would you tell a couple that their new-born had to be taken away for emergency medical care?

Family and Community Connections

1. **Adapting to a New Baby.** Think of two or three guidelines for how a four-year-old sibling should behave with a new baby. Then write a song or story that communicates these guidelines.

2. **Finding Resources.** Find out what facilities there are in your community or near-by for giving premature babies the special care they need.

Technology Connections

1. **Medical Technology.** Bring in a news story about a premature or multiple birth. What health problems were involved? What medical procedures were used to confront these problems? Report to the class.

2. **Medications.** Find out what medications may be given during childbirth and what effect they have—on both the mother and the baby. Make a chart to present your findings.

UNIT 3

The Baby's First Year

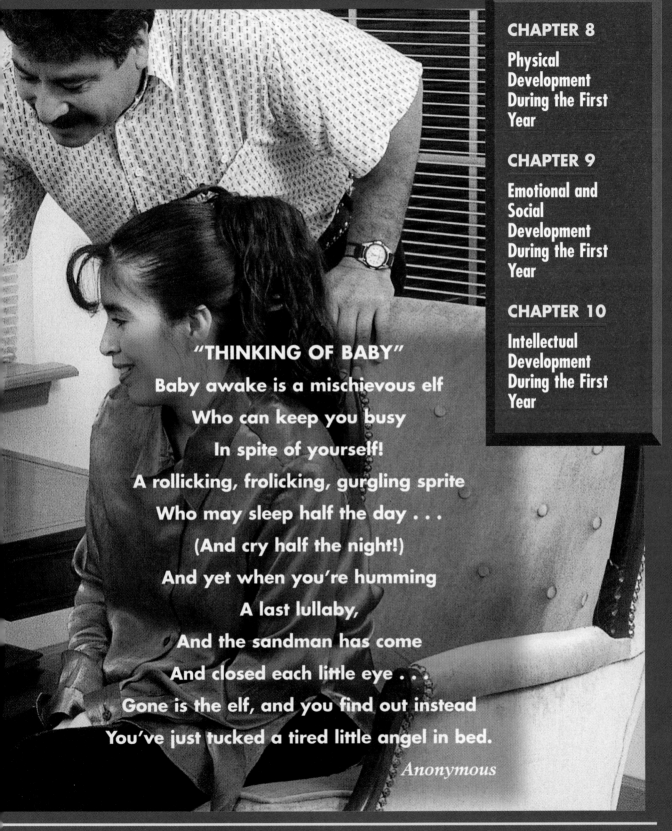

"THINKING OF BABY"

Baby awake is a mischievous elf
Who can keep you busy
In spite of yourself!
A rollicking, frolicking, gurgling sprite
Who may sleep half the day . . .
(And cry half the night!)
And yet when you're humming
A last lullaby,
And the sandman has come
And closed each little eye . . .
Gone is the elf, and you find out instead
You've just tucked a tired little angel in bed.

Anonymous

CHAPTER 8
Physical Development During the First Year

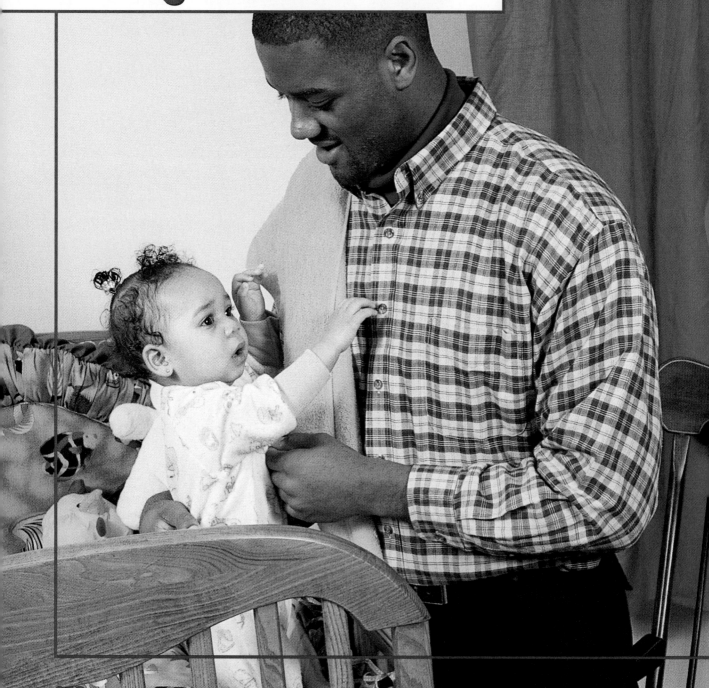

As Bret finished drying little Hayley, he asked her "Did you enjoy your bath? Don't you feel better now that you're all clean?" Hayley gurgled in response.

Bret quickly put on her diaper and then rolled the bottom of an undershirt up towards the neck. He lifted his daughter's head and slipped the opening around it. "OK, time for the arms now," he said. Then he slipped one arm followed by another into the undershirt and straightened the bottom seam over Hayley's belly.

"Hey, here's your favorite sleeper," he told Hayley as he put her feet in the covered feet of the garment. Then he rolled her onto her side and pulled the sleeper up to her shoulders and finished dressing her. Once the sleeper was on her, Bret picked Hayley up and gave her a big hug and kiss. As he raised her up, Hayley put out her arms. "No, no. No airplane now. It's bedtime," Bret said. "Let's go see Mommy and give her a good night kiss. Then I'll read you a story."

"Let's go see Mommy and give her a good night kiss. Then I'll read you a story."

Growth and Development of Infants

Growth and development during the first year are the most rapid of any time in life. In twelve months, the baby who begins as a helpless newborn triples his or her birth weight, learns to stand alone, and may even begin to walk.

KEY TERMS

depth perception
hand-eye coordination
motor skills
primary teeth
proportion

OBJECTIVES:

- Analyze children's physical development to find three patterns.

- Describe physical growth during the first year.

- Describe the development of senses and motor skills during the first year.

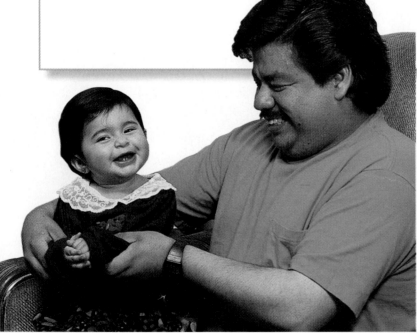

Patterns of Physical Development

As you know, all development follows a sequence, proceeding step-by-step. Physical development, which is no exception, follows three basic patterns:

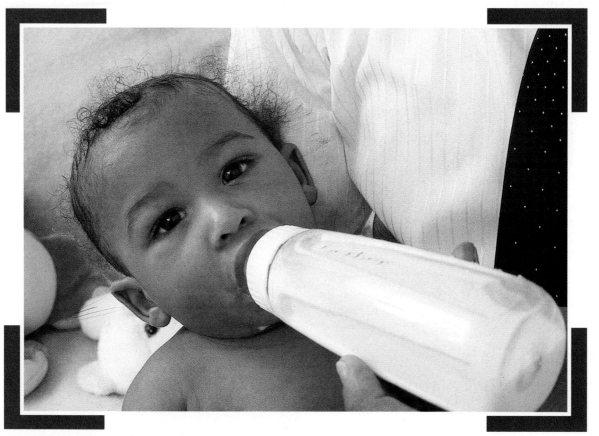

Babies first master simple tasks such as eating and sleeping and only later learn more complex tasks. *What other patterns do babies follow in their development?*

- **Head to foot.** Long before birth, the baby's head takes the lead in development. The same pattern continues after birth. First, babies lift their heads to see an object. Later, as they gain muscle control of their arms and hands, they pick that object up. Still later, they are able to walk to it.
- **Near to far.** Development starts at the trunk and moves outward. First, babies simply wave their arms when they see an object they want. Later, they grab at an object with the palm of the hand. Finally, babies learn to pick up objects with their thumb and fingers.

- **Simple to complex.** At first, babies' main activities are sleeping and eating. Gradually, they learn more complicated tasks. They eat with their fingers and later use a spoon and fork.

Growth During the First Year

Charts show the average weight, height, and abilities of children at certain ages. These charts give a general idea of growth and development, but remember that children change at individual rates.

From birth to age one year, babies grow by about 50 percent. **What role does heredity play in height?**

Weight

In babies, weight gain is one of the best signs of good health. Most babies lose a little weight after birth and then begin to gain weight rapidly. In the first six months, a healthy baby gains 1 to 2 pounds (0.45 to 0.9 kg) per month. In the last half of the first year, the average weight gain is 1 pound (0.45 kg) a month. A baby's weight usually doubles in the first few months and triples by the end of the first year.

The average weight of a one-year-old is 20 to 22 pounds (9 to 10 kg). An individual baby's weight may differ depending on heredity, feeding habits, and level of physical activity.

Height

Growth in height is steady in the first year. The average newborn is 20 inches (51 cm) long. By one year, the average infant is about 30 inches (76 cm) long.

Heredity more strongly in-fluences height than weight. A baby with tall parents is more likely to be tall than the child of short parents. Of course, tall parents can have short children. Since humans carry a mixture of genes, the results of any child's mixture can't be predicted.

Proportion

In child development, **proportion** refers to the size relationship between different parts of the body. Compared to the rest of the body, a baby's head and abdomen are larger than an adult's. The legs and arms are short and small.

The head grows rapidly during the first year to provide room for the swiftly developing brain. Over half the total growth of the head occurs at this time. The skull of a newborn has spaces called "fontanels,"

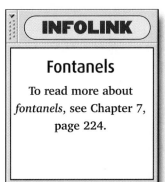

INFOLINK

Fontanels

To read more about *fontanels*, see Chapter 7, page 224.

which are gaps where bones have not yet joined. These fontanels allow the head to grow. They close around the age of eighteen months.

Development During the First Year

The terms *growth* and *development* are often used to mean the same thing, but there is a difference. Growth refers to changes in size. Development refers to an increase in physical, emotional, social, or intellectual skills. Growth and development are both rapid during the first year.

If you observed a group of teens, you could probably tell older teens from the younger ones, but it would be difficult to identify the exact age of each individual. A fifteen-year-old and a sixteen-year-old look and act much alike. In contrast, it's easy to tell a newborn from a one-year-old. A baby not only grows bigger, but also develops many skills in the first year of life.

Sight

Eyesight improves rapidly. An infant's vision is blurry at first. Within a week or so, the newborn is increasingly aware of his or her surroundings and can focus on objects that are 7 to 10 inches (17.5 to 25 cm) away. By a month, infants can focus on objects as far away as 3 feet (0.9 m). By about three and one-half months, a baby's vision is almost as good as a young adult's.

Young babies prefer patterns that show high contrast, such as alternating stripes, bull's eyes—or faces. They prefer the color red. When shown the same object in different colors, they spend a longer time looking at the red one.

In the second month, infants begin to show **depth perception**. They become able to recognize that an object is three-dimensional, not flat. By the third month, babies prefer to look at real objects rather than flat pictures of objects.

With improved vision, babies develop **hand-eye coordination**. They gain increasing ability to move their hands and fingers precisely in relation to what is seen. Around the age of three or four months, babies begin to reach for objects they see; this is an important milestone. Hand-eye coordination develops throughout childhood. It is necessary for many skills, such as eating, catching a ball, coloring, and tying shoes.

Hearing

The sense of hearing develops even before birth. In fact, babies still in the uterus often respond to sounds with altered heart rates or with changes in activity levels.

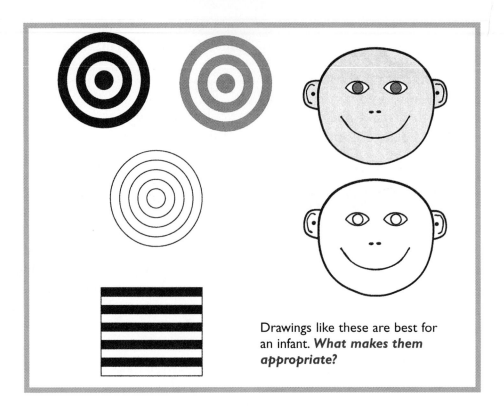

Drawings like these are best for an infant. *What makes them appropriate?*

At birth, a baby can already tell the general direction a sound comes from.

Newborns respond to the tone of a voice rather than to the words. A soothing, loving voice calms them. A loud or angry voice alarms them. Remember this when you care for a child—especially a newborn.

Smell and Taste

Since a baby is surrounded by amniotic fluid until birth, the sense of smell doesn't have much chance to develop. A study has shown, however, that even newborns respond differently to different odors. Within ten days they can distinguish by smell their mother from another person.

Babies use their mouths to explore their world. *What safety dangers does this present?*

Signs of Hearing Problems

*H*earing is essential for language development. Gradually attaching meanings to words that are heard is the baby's first step in learning to speak. Because hearing is so important, many physicians suggest that babies have a hearing test by about six months of age. This is especially important with premature babies, or if the baby has had frequent ear infections. These babies are most likely to have hearing problems.

Parents can watch for these signs of hearing problems:

- A newborn isn't startled by a sharp clap of the hands.

- A three-month-old never turns toward the source of sounds.

- A baby is not awakened by loud noises, does not respond to familiar voices, and doesn't pay attention to ordinary sounds.

A parent who notices any of these signs should discuss them with the pediatrician. If a hearing problem is found, a referral will be made to a hearing specialist.

FOLLOWING UP

1. What groups of babies are especially likely to have hearing problems?

2. Why is it important to detect hearing problems as early as possible?

The sense of taste develops rapidly. In research studies, two-week-old babies have shown, through their sucking behavior, that they can taste the differences between water, sour liquids, sugar solutions, salt solutions, and milk. Even at this early age, babies show a preference for a sweet taste.

Throughout their first year, babies learn about their world by using their mouths. They put anything and everything into their mouths. Parents need to take care that the objects they do put in their mouths are clean; not too small, which could cause choking; and without edges that could cut.

Voice

The newborn's cry, initially quite shrill, becomes softer as the baby's lungs mature. This change also results from the physical growth of the throat muscles, tongue, lips, teeth, and vocal cords. The tongue and interior of the mouth change in shape and proportion during the first months of life. This growth makes speech development possible. Babies prepare for speech by making word-related sounds. They begin babbling vowel sounds, such as "ooh" and "ah" as early as three months of age.

Babies understand many words before they are able to speak. Many are physically ready for speech by the end of the first year. However, children learn to speak at different rates, and many don't say any words until after their first birthday.

The physical changes in the mouth and throat also affect feeding. At first the infant is able only to suck liquids. After these changes, the baby can swallow solid foods.

Teeth

The development of a baby's teeth actually begins about the sixth week of pregnancy. However, the first set of teeth a baby gets, called the **primary teeth** or "baby teeth," usually doesn't begin appearing until six or seven months of age. The complete set is generally finished by about twenty months. This timing varies widely.

Teething—the appearance of these teeth—is a normal process, but may be painful. As the teeth force their way up through the baby's gums, they tear the tender gum tissues. This often causes pain and swelling. During teething, a normally happy infant may become cranky or restless. Some babies refuse food and drool a lot. Teething can also cause other symptoms, including an increased desire for liquid, coughing, and fever.

Discomfort may last from two to ten days for each tooth. If teething pain persists or other serious symptoms develop, consult a doctor. For minor teething pain, these methods may be helpful:

- Offer teething biscuits or rubber teething rings so the baby can bite down hard on something to relieve the pressure on the gums.
- Since cold is a painkiller, rub an ice cube on the baby's gums to ease the pain temporarily.

You can rub a commercial teething medication onto the swollen gums. These have limited value, though, because they soon wash out with the baby's saliva.

Motor Skills

Much of the baby's development during the first year is in the area of **motor skills**. These are abilities that depend on the use and control of muscles. Mastering motor skills requires intellectual, social, and emotional development, as well as physical. This is because development in each area affects all other areas. The chart on pages 258-259 shows motor skill accomplishments during the first year.

One of the first motor skills infants acquire is control of the head. At birth, the head is large and heavy; and the neck muscles are weak. By age one month, babies placed on their stomach can lift their head slightly. By two or three months, they can lift their chest. At this age they can keep their head steady when propped in a sitting position.

By nine months or so, the baby is crawling and beginning to explore his or her world. This is an exciting time for the baby, who has more independence than ever before. Mobility adds many new opportunities for learning.

INFOLINK

Safety

For more on *safety*, see Section 18-1.

This period also puts new demands on the parents, who have to ensure that their baby is safe while exploring. They must remove any objects that could endanger the baby, such as those made of glass. They also need to cover all exposed electrical outlets. The average home is full of things that could cause injury. Once babies start crawling, they can scoot into trouble very quickly. Parents must keep their eyes on their babies at all times.

SECTION 8-1 REVIEW

✔ Check Your Understanding

1. List the three basic patterns of physical development and give an example of one.
2. How much weight does an average healthy baby gain each month during the first year of life?
3. How do a baby's proportions compare with an adult's?
4. Describe the development of depth perception.
5. How do changes in a baby's throat muscles, tongue, lips, teeth, and vocal cords affect the ability to make sounds?
6. When do teeth generally appear?
7. List at least three motor skills that the average baby develops at seven to eight months.

Putting Knowledge Into Practice

1. **Applying.** What sensory activities could caregivers use to help stimulate hand-eye coordination in infants?
2. **Synthesizing.** Explain how speaking requires a combination of physical, emotional, social, and intellectual growth and development? Which pattern of development does it reveal?
3. **Observing and Participating.** Study the environment at an infant care center. Make a chart with headings for each of the five senses—sight, hearing, smell, taste, touch. Under each heading, list the features of the child care center that promote development of that sense in infants.

Average Motor Skills Development from Birth To Twelve Months

One to Two Months

- One month: Lifts chin when placed on stomach.
- Two months: Lifts chest well above surface when placed on stomach.

Three to Four Months

- Holds up head steadily.
- Reaches for objects, but unsteadily.
- Rolls from side to back and from back to side.

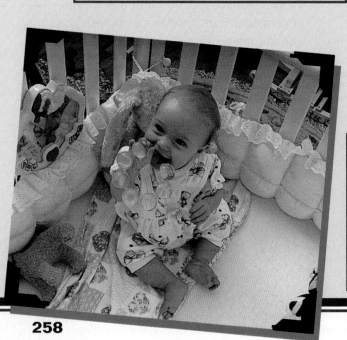

Five to Six Months

- Sits alone briefly.
- Uses hands to reach, grasp, crumble, bang, and splash.
- Turns completely over when laid on back or stomach.

Seven to Eight Months

- Sits up steadily.
- Reaches for spoon.
- Eats with fingers.
- Picks up large objects.
- Pulls self up while holding on to furniture.
- Propels self by arms, knees, or squirming motion.

Nine to Ten Months

- Is more skillful with spoon.
- Reaches for and manipulates objects, including medium-sized ones, with good control.
- Stands holding on to furniture or other supports.
- Crawls on hands and knees.
- Walks when led.

Eleven to Twelve Months

- Shows preference for one hand over the other.
- Holds and drinks from a cup.
- Fits blocks, boxes, or nesting toys inside each other.
- Picks up small objects using thumb and fore-finger.
- Stands alone.
- May walk alone.

SECTION 8-2

The Developing Brain

In their first year, babies grow and develop new skills. Hidden inside their heads—and powering the advances in development—are more amazing changes. How the brain takes shape in a baby's first year of life has profound effects on the baby's life.

KEY TERMS

axon
cortex
dendrite
myelin
neurons
synapse

OBJECTIVES:

- Explain what functions each part of the brain controls.
- Describe how brain cells work together.
- Explain how the brain becomes organized.
- Identify activities that support the development of brain pathways.

Structure of the Brain

Newborns learn about the world primarily through their senses—sight, hearing, smell, taste, and touch. The mobile moves when it is touched. Mother's heartbeat sounds familiar. Bananas give off a pleasant odor. A fist or a finger tastes different from milk. The blanket feels soft and fuzzy.

For babies, as for all of us, the information they learn through the senses is sent through the nerves to the brain. The brain is the key to intellectual development. It receives and interprets the messages from the body. The brain also develops the ability to send messages to the body, telling the muscles what to do.

In general, the responses of a newborn are physical reflexes; they don't originate in these kinds of messages from the brain. By the time the child is a year old, though, he or she has the ability to play with stacking toys, stand up, and perhaps even walk. All these skills result from the brain's growing ability to tell the body what to do.

The brain is divided into different sections, each controlling specific functions of the body. The major sections are shown in the diagram on below, along with the functions they control.

One of the most important parts of the brain is the **cortex** (CORE-teks), part of the cerebrum. Growth in this outer layer of the brain permits more complex learning. After one year of life, a baby's cortex is far better developed than it was at birth. The quality of caregiving affects brain growth.

Parts of the Brain

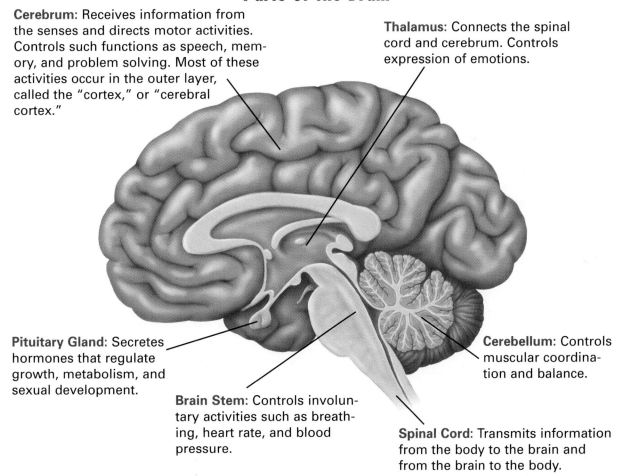

Cerebrum: Receives information from the senses and directs motor activities. Controls such functions as speech, memory, and problem solving. Most of these activities occur in the outer layer, called the "cortex," or "cerebral cortex."

Thalamus: Connects the spinal cord and cerebrum. Controls expression of emotions.

Pituitary Gland: Secretes hormones that regulate growth, metabolism, and sexual development.

Brain Stem: Controls involuntary activities such as breathing, heart rate, and blood pressure.

Cerebellum: Controls muscular coordination and balance.

Spinal Cord: Transmits information from the body to the brain and from the brain to the body.

Each area of the brain has specific functions to perform.

How the Brain Works

The brain is made up of billions of the nerve cells called neurons. An infant is born with all the neurons he or she will have—none are added during life.

Although *neurons* aren't added, dramatic changes do take place in the brain after birth. Neurons sprout arms called *dendrites* and *axons*. This process actually begins when the baby is developing in the mother's uterus. After birth, it happens more quickly. These arms can number in the hundreds or thousands for any neuron—or they can be only a few.

As the diagram below shows, these arms reach out toward the arms of other neurons. Although the arms from different neurons don't touch, they come very near. At the tiny gaps between them—the **synapses** (sin-AP-suhs)—messages are sent from one neuron to another.

The chemicals released by an axon are called *neurotransmitters*. These chemicals look for a dendrite to attach to—but they can only attach to those with the right kind

How Neurons Work

Step 1: Dendrites receive information from other neurons. Each dentrite can have many different branches.

Step 2: The dendrites pass that information to the cell body, where the information is processed.

Neurons are divided into three parts: dendrites, the cell body, and axons.

NEURON

Dendrite

Cell Body

Myelin Coating

Axon

Synapse

OTHER NEURONS

Step 3: The cell body sends an instruction to the body through **axons** (ACKS-ons) which transmit the instruction to dendrites. Axons, which are longer than dendrites, are coated with a waxy substance called **myelin** (MY-uh-lin). This substance makes for easier transmission of information.

Step 4: Chemicals called *neurotransmitters* are released by the axon and cross the gap to the dendrite of another nerve cell. That gap is called the *synapse*.

of receptors. The more times the same axon and dendrite connect, the stronger the connection grows. As a result, they can send and receive messages more quickly.

The Developing Brain

A stimulating environment promotes the development of synapses for movement, thought, and emotion.

Building the Brain

The more arms that neurons grow and the more links that develop between different neurons, the more paths the brain has. More paths give the brain more power—it can do more tasks, control more actions. Think of a road system around a city. The more roads there are, the more places a driver can go.

These increased connections also give the brain more flexibility. Again, this is like a road system. The more roads there are, the more choices a driver has. If one road is shut down, there are alternate routes.

How the Brain Becomes Organized

Each child's brain becomes organized in a unique way. The organization is unique because it grows out of the child's experiences, which are unique to that child.

Networks in the Brain

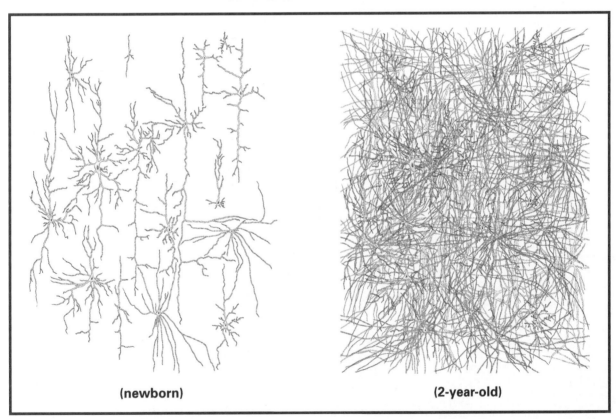

(newborn)   (2-year-old)

The image at left shows the neurons of a newborn, with few dendrites. The image at right shows the greater number of dendrites found in a two-year-old.

As connections between dendrites and axons grow stronger, a group of neurons becomes linked together. They become systems of nerve cells that control a particular action or thinking task.

For instance, one group of neurons can work together to control drinking from a cup. Each time a ten-month-old drinks from a cup, this system works together again and again. At first, the connection takes time to move the muscles. Eventually, after many repetitions, the neurons work together so well that it becomes easy for the child to drink from a cup.

These connections and systems affect all areas of behavior—not just actions. Systems of neurons work together to influence how people see and hear as well as think and remember.

The connections between neurons are not permanent. They can be broken. People lose synapses all through their lives. At the same time that some connections are being lost, new ones are added. They become part of the brain as new skills are learned or new experiences are stored as memories.

These developments have an impact on the appearance of the brain. Scientists have looked at the brains of professional violinists. These people tended to have extra large areas of the brain controlling the left hand—the one they use for their intricate fingering.

Speeding the Brain's Work

The drawing on page 262 indicates that axons have a waxy coating. This coating also plays a role in learning. Myelin makes it easier for axons to transmit signals—it speeds their work. All axons are not coated with myelin when a baby is born, however. At first, only those that control basic instincts such as nursing are.

Other axons become coated with myelin as the child grows. This process continues until about age twenty. The myelin coating is added in different areas of the brain at different times. Axons in the area of the brain that control such skills as motor abilities, vision, and hearing receive the coating the earliest. As a result, those are the areas in which babies first show development.

The addition of the myelin coat to nerve cells makes it easier for children to learn skills. *What areas of the brain first receive this coating?*

Experts say that a child can benefit by having a rich environment. They aren't referring to a family with a great deal of money. *What do they mean by this comment?*

The rate at which axons receive this waxy coating may explain why children have difficulty learning certain tasks. If the nerves handling a certain activity are not yet covered with myelin, it would be difficult for a child to learn the activity. The lack of myelin does not make it *impossible* to learn the task. The presence of myelin, however, makes learning much easier.

Rules to Build a Brain By

Parents and caregivers can use these research findings to shape the environment of children and help develop their brains:

- **Keep it simple and natural.** Cuddling and hugging a baby, talking to the baby while changing a diaper or giving a bath, and playing peekaboo are all excellent ways of encouraging the baby's brain to build paths connecting neurons. Experts urge parents to give children a rich environment—one with lots of loving interaction and talking.
- **Match experiences to the child's mental capacities.** Some parents use flash cards to try to teach their babies to read. Many people say this works, but other experts say that in the long run it doesn't help the child. Young babies need physical experiences—that is how they learn. Remember that the axons for basic physical skills are the first to have myelin. Children learn to read more easily when they are older.
- **Remember that practice makes perfect.** The more times an experience is repeated, the stronger the connections between neurons in the child's brain. When a young child asks to hear the same story every night, read it gladly.
- **Make sure the child is actively involved.** Give a child experiences in which he or she takes part. Children of all ages learn best by doing.
- **Provide variety, but avoid overloading the child.** Parents may think that by exposing their child to a many different of experiences, they can help the child become a great athlete, student, musician, *and* dancer. A more likely result is that a child would become unhappy. Give children a range of experiences engaging the senses, but avoid making them feel overwhelmed.

- **Avoid pushing the child.** Children learn better if they are emotionally involved in what they're doing. Look for clues as to whether the child is interested in the activity. If not, don't pursue it any more.

Is the Brain Organized Once Only?

During the first year of life, the brain becomes organized in the unique way that reflects the child's individuality. Is this the only time the brain can be organized? If basic groundwork is not set now, is a child locked out of certain possibilities in life?

The answer is "no." There are a number of situations which prove this isn't the case. Some children who suffered damage to the brain area that controls language have still learned to speak. Older people who suffer strokes—where neurons in an area of the brain die—can relearn skills by learning to use other areas of the brain.

The brain can be reorganized. In practical terms, that means a child doesn't have to be exposed to every possible activity in the first year—or even few years—of life. What is important is to give young children a stimulating environment. By doing so, parents and other caregivers help children's brains develop many pathways and connections.

SECTION 8-2 REVIEW

✔ Check Your Understanding

1. What activities does the cerebellum control?
2. What is the role of dendrites and axons in the brain?
3. How does the presence of myelin help axons work?
4. How do repeated experiences help organize the brain?
5. What happens to synapses throughout life?
6. What impact on learning results from the rate of the spread of myelin?
7. What is meant by giving infants a stimulating environment?

Putting Knowledge Into Practice

1. **Drawing Conclusions.** Name some activities that promote the growth of connections in the brain.
2. **Analyzing.** Would you agree with the statement "The brain can be reorganized, but it's easiest to organize it right the first time?" Why or why not?
3. **Observing and Participating.** Try writing your name with your opposite hand. Then use your normal hand. With which is it easier? Why?

CAREER OPPORTUNITIES

Nuclear Medicine Technologist

A CONVERSATION WITH AARON FORD

How did you become interested in becoming a nuclear medicine technologist? In high school, I worked as a volunteer in the local hospital, and I enjoyed it. I like computers too, and the work we do combines health care and computers, so it's perfect.

What are the tasks and responsibilities of a nuclear medicine technologist? We perform tests on patients by giving them safe doses of radioactive drugs. Then we position them carefully in a machine that can detect how those drugs are moving throughout the body. The results are displayed on a computer screen and can be used by doctors to understand a patient's condition.

What is the work environment like? We work in a hospital in an area that's like a lab. It's clean and quiet.

What are the working hours like? Usually we work forty-hours a week, but if there's an emergency we may have to work at night or on weekends.

What aptitudes are needed to be a nuclear medicine technologist? You need to be extremely careful and pay attention to detail. You have to follow strict procedures to protect the patient and yourself from radiation. You also have to carefully maintain medical records. It helps to be strong, too. For the test, patients need to be put on a table and sometimes they're too old or weak to do it themselves. It helps to be sympathetic—to put people at ease.

NUCLEAR MEDICINE TECHNOLOGIST

Education and Training. Nuclear medicine technologists need four years of training, which can include a two-year associate degree and two years in a special training program.

Career Outlook. The demand for these workers should grow much faster than average.

CONNECTING SCHOOL TO CAREER

1. **Technology.** Why is safety such an important concern for these workers?
2. **Basic Skills.** Which basic skills do you think would be more important to a nuclear medicine technologist—math or writing? Why?

Handling and Feeding Infants

An infant requires a huge amount of physical care. Learn how to lift, hold, and carry a baby gently. A baby's nutritional needs also need to be met to fuel all the physical and brain growth and development taking place.

KEY TERMS
shaken baby syndrome
weaning

OBJECTIVES:
- Explain how to hold and feed a baby.
- Identify an infant's nutritional needs.

Handling a Baby

A baby needs to be moved and held for all sorts of reasons— to have diapers changed, to be fed, to be dressed, to be bathed, to be moved. Remember that when you pick up and hold an infant, you have a chance to strengthen your bond and to help the baby feel secure and happy.

Newborns, of all babies, require the greatest care in handling because their neck muscles can't support their head. For that reason, you must keep your hand or arm under the baby's neck and head at all times. The photographs below show how to lift, hold, and put down a newborn safely.

Handling a Newborn Safely

Lifting a newborn—Slide one hand under the baby's buttocks and the other under the shoulders and head. Use your forearm to support the neck and head as you raise your hands together to lift the newborn.

Holding a newborn in your arm—Hold the baby upright, cradled in the curve of your arm. Your arm supports the baby's head and neck, and you can easily maintain eye contact with the baby.

Holding a newborn against your chest—Hold the baby against your chest, so that the baby faces—or peeks over—your shoulder. Use your hand to support the baby's neck and head.

Putting a newborn down—Continue to support both the neck and head and the body. Bend over, keeping the baby close to your body until the baby's body is resting on a surface that can support his or her body. Then remove your arms.

Whenever picking up or putting down a baby, remember to move smoothly and gently to avoid startling him or her.

By about four months, the baby can hold up his or her own head. Even then, handle the baby gently and hold the baby close to ensure a sense of security.

Gentle Handling

When you are handling a baby or young child, never—ever—shake or jiggle him or her. These actions are dangerous. Every year thousands of babies suffer serious problems due to **shaken baby syndrome**. This condition is caused when someone severely shakes the baby, usually in an effort to make the baby stop crying. It can lead to damage to the baby's brain, learning problems, mental retardation, blindness or deafness, and even death.

When babies cry a great deal, it can be very stressful to parents—especially new parents. Frustrated, they may resort to shaking. There are better—and safer—ways of handling the situation:

- Put the baby down in a safe place and go into another room to calm down before returning to the baby.
- Ask a friend or relative who is available to care for the baby.
- Take some deep breaths or look out the window to calm down.
- Call someone and talk about your problem until you are calm.

Gently rocking or playfully bouncing the baby on the knee are not dangerous. Strong shaking is.

Feeding a Baby

Mealtime provides a baby with much more than physical nourishment. The baby can also enjoy contact with other people and learn about the world. The cuddling, body contact, and nurturing that go with feeding are as important as the food.

Feeding Schedules

A newborn's schedule of eating and sleeping is unpredictable at first. Newborns need to eat as much as they want and as often as they want. In the first few weeks of life, that may be up to six to eight times—or more—in 24 hours. Frequent feedings are necessary because a newborn's stomach can hold only a small amount. Babies who are breast-fed tend to eat more often than those fed by bottle.

By the second or third month, a regular pattern generally emerges. The baby may wake for a feeding every three or four hours. Eventually, the baby will no longer need a late night feeding. By about 12 pounds (5.4 kg), a baby can usually sleep through the night. At that size, the stomach can hold more food.

As the baby grows, feeding schedules continue to change. Most one-year-olds eat three meals a day, plus snacks.

Feeding Methods

In the first year, the baby's chief food is breast milk or formula. Pediatricians recommend against cow's milk before babies are a year old. This milk is hard for babies to digest and has minerals their kidneys cannot process. Formulas based on cow's milk are acceptable—the milk has been changed to remove these problems.

A mother who breast-feeds can receive advice while still in the hospital or birthing center. Information and help are also available from La Leche League, a group that promotes breast-feeding, or the baby's pediatrician.

Whenever you feed an infant from a bottle, hold the baby close in a semi-upright position. Remember that the young baby's head and neck need to be supported, and the head should be held well above the level of the baby's stomach. Hold the bottle at an angle, so that the baby can suck comfortably. This also keeps the nipple full of milk, which prevents the baby from swallowing too much air.

Many parents prefer to give their baby a warm bottle, although this isn't really necessary. To warm formula, fill the bottle and place it in a pan of water on the stove. Then heat the water in the pan until it makes the formula lukewarm. You can also use a special bottle warmer or hold the bottle under hot running water. Check the temperature from time to time by shaking a few drops of formula onto your wrist. It should feel lukewarm, not hot.

If formula is warmed, check the temperature before feeding. *How should the formula feel?*

Never heat the formula in a microwave oven. Microwave heating can create dangerous "hot spots" in the formula that burn the baby.

If there is any formula left in the bottle, throw it away. Disease-causing bacteria can grow quickly in leftover formula and could lead to illness.

These bacteria may also stay in the bottle even after it has been emptied and cleaned. Feeding bottles should be sterilized. A pediatrician may recommend placing them in boiling water after washing, using the hot water cycle in a dishwasher, or some other method. Nipples, bottle rings, and bottle caps should be sterilized in the same way.

No matter how busy you feel, never leave a bottle propped up so that a baby can drink from it alone. The baby misses out on the important physical contact and attention. Also, the formula typically gushes from a propped bottle, which can cause digestive problems and ear infections. Finally, propping bottles can lead to tooth decay because the sugar in the formula or juice pools up around the teeth.

Whether breast-feeding or bottle-feeding, continue the feeding until the infant seems satisfied. Healthy babies usually eat the amount they need.

Burping the Baby

Whichever method of feeding is used, burp the baby at least twice—once during the feeding and once when the feeding is over. Women who breast-feed burp the baby when they

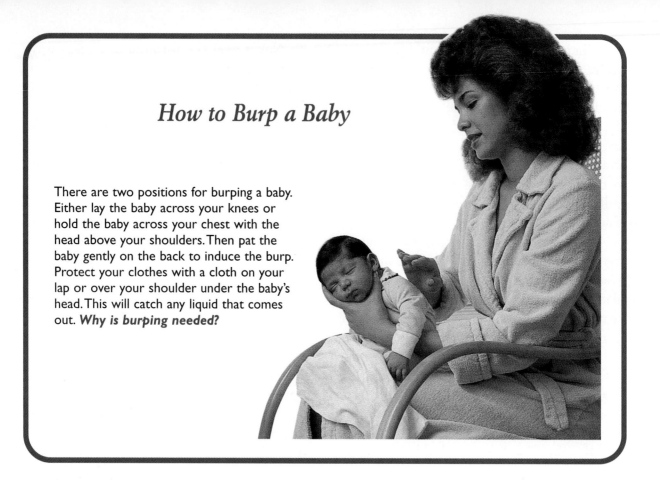

How to Burp a Baby

There are two positions for burping a baby. Either lay the baby across your knees or hold the baby across your chest with the head above your shoulders. Then pat the baby gently on the back to induce the burp. Protect your clothes with a cloth on your lap or over your shoulder under the baby's head. This will catch any liquid that comes out. *Why is burping needed?*

switch the baby from one breast to the other.

Babies often swallow air along with the liquid. Burping helps them expel this air and avoid any discomfort. Don't be surprised, though, if the baby doesn't actually burp each time.

Introducing New Foods

Around the age of six months, other foods begin to be added to the baby's diet. The pediatrician will recommend when to introduce "solids."

With most babies, there is no rush to introduce new foods. Choose a time when the baby is well, content, and happy. Don't begin solids, for example, if the infant has been sick or the family is moving. Don't worry about postponing new foods for a

while; breast milk or formula can provide all the nutrition the baby needs.

Because each new food is unfamiliar, the baby may spit back the first spoonfuls. You can reintroduce the food later, or try combining it with a favorite food to make it more acceptable. Show patience as the baby adjusts to this new experience.

Following these feeding tips will help make the experience safe and enjoyable for both the baby and you:

- For the first feedings, hold the baby comfortably in a fairly upright position.
- If the baby is used to warm formula, heat solid foods to lukewarm, too. As with formula, don't use a microwave to heat a baby's food. Check the temperature of warmed foods by placing a drop on your wrist.

Ask the Eperts

Dr. Van Stone
Pediatrician
Tupelo, Mississippi

GIVING *a Baby Solid Foods*

Q How should I introduce solid foods?

A Although offering babies solid food at a very early age is a common practice, the American Association of Pediatrics recommends waiting to introduce solids until approximately 4-6 months of age. Foods with a soft, pureed consistency should generally be introduced first.

A baby's first solid food is usually cereal—first rice, then oatmeal, barley, and wheat. Wheat is saved for last because it can cause allergic reactions in some young babies. These cereals can be bought dry and mixed with formula, breast milk, or water, or they can be served from jars.

After cereals, introduce vegetables, fruits, and meats. You can also give the baby fruit juices. Some foods pose particular problems and need to be handled carefully. Corn, eggs, and citrus juices usually aren't introduced before one year.

Avoid giving a cow's milk or milk products—including cheese—until the baby is a year old.

It is important to introduce foods slowly, bringing in a new food only about every four days. That way, if a certain food causes a skin rash or digestive trouble, you will be able to identify which food is causing the problem. You can continue to give the baby foods that he or she has already been introduced to. This gives the infant variety in his or her diet.

Most foods should be cooked, not raw. Bananas are an exception—they can simply be mashed.

You don't need to buy baby food. You can create your own by cooking vegetables, fruits, and meat. If you do, avoid putting seasonings—including salt—on the food. Once the food is cooked, put it through a blender or food processor and make it soft and easy for the baby to digest.

Thinking It Through

1. What kinds of foods are likely to be easiest to digest? Why do you say so?
2. What would be the advantages and disadvantages of purchased baby food versus home prepared?

- Be prepared for messy feedings, especially at first. Put a large bib on the baby, and be sure your own clothes are either easily washable or protected.
- When the baby starts eating cereal, make it very runny by diluting it with either breast milk or formula. Runny cereal seems more familiar to a baby—like the milk or formula he or she is used to. The cereal should be offered on a spoon, however, not in a bottle, because solid matter in the bottle may cause the baby to choke.
- If you are using baby food from a jar, take out a small portion and place it in a bowl. Then close the jar and refrigerate it immediately. Don't feed the baby directly from the jar. Bacteria from the spoon will grow rapidly in the food and cause leftovers to spoil.

Weaning

Sometimes around the first birthday, many babies are ready for **weaning**, changing from drinking from the bottle or breast to drinking from a cup. Weaning is an important sign of the baby's increasing independence.

There is no precise age at which the baby should be weaned. Nine months is common, but the age varies greatly. The baby usually shows some signs of readiness, such as playing or looking around while sucking, pushing the nipple away, or preferring to eat from a spoon. Rather than forcing weaning, wait until the baby is ready and accepts naturally. Forced weaning may result in other feeding and behavior problems for the child.

Self-Feeding

When babies can sit up steadily, usually at about eight or ten months, they start to eat with their fingers and reach for a spoon. These are signs that the infant is ready to begin self-feeding. To encourage self-feeding, provide "finger foods."

The baby's first efforts at self-feeding with a spoon will probably be fun for the baby but may not produce much actual eating. You can help by using a separate spoon and placing bits of food in the baby's mouth now and then.

It takes patience—and a sense of humor—to encourage self-feeding. You and the baby will both benefit if you allow plen-

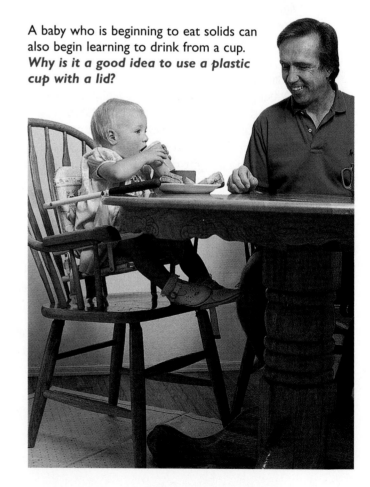

A baby who is beginning to eat solids can also begin learning to drink from a cup. *Why is it a good idea to use a plastic cup with a lid?*

ty of time for each meal. Then encourage the baby's efforts and enjoy his or her delight in new accomplishments.

Nutritional Concerns

Part of the responsibility of parents and caregivers is making sure that babies' nutritional needs are being met. This is usually not difficult if the child receives formula or breast milk until starting to eat a good variety of cereals, vegetables, fruits, and meats. However, problems can result if the baby is given too much food, too little food, or the wrong kinds of food.

Around the age of eight to ten months, infants show an interest in self-feeding. *Name one type of development needed for self-feeding to take place.*

Self-Feeding Safely

*F*inger foods—small pieces that can easily be picked up and eaten—must be chosen carefully. The baby may have no teeth at all—and even those who have teeth can't be counted on to actually chew.

- Cut the food into small pieces.

- Choose foods that are easy to break up with little or no chewing and that can't block the baby's breathing passage. Dry toast, rice cakes, cereal pieces, small pieces of chicken, or bananas are good, safe choices.

- Stay away from foods such as cut up raw vegetables, nuts, scoops of peanut butter, whole grapes, candy, chips, pretzels, or popcorn—or any other food that you think might cause choking.

- Give the baby just a few pieces of food at a time. Some babies try to stuff their mouths full of food.

FOLLOWING UP

1. Would carrot or celery pieces be good finger food for babies? Why or why not?
2. What is the main concern about finger foods for babies?

These teens enjoy active lives and eat nutritious foods. *What influence does infancy have on eating habits?*

Overfeeding

As they gain weight in the first months after birth, babies may look fat. In fact, the percentage of body fat does rise in a baby's first six months. This body fat generally is not anything to worry about—most babies slim down by age three.

Bottle-fed babies may be more likely to be overfed than those who breast-feed. Parents may urge the baby to finish all the formula left in the bottle, even if the child is full. Any parent concerned about a baby's weight should talk to a pediatrician.

INFOLINK

Food Guide Pyramid

For more on the *Food Guide Pyramid*, see Chapter 6, page 187.

Healthy eating habits are established early in life. Parents can help their babies develop those healthy habits by eating in a healthy way themselves. Using the Food Guide Pyramid is a good start. Young children need the same types of nutritious foods, but the serving sizes should be smaller. Help children learn to enjoy fresh fruits and vegetables instead of salty and fatty foods.

Inadequate Nutrition

Infants have very specific nutritional needs in order to be healthy:
- Enough calories to provide for rapid growth.
- Food that contains needed nutrients, such as protein, iron, B vitamins, vitamin C, and vitamin D.
- Food that is easy to digest.
- Adequate amounts of liquid.

Babies whose diets don't meet these needs may suffer from poor nutrition, or "under nutrition"—a lack of enough food or a lack of the proper type of food. Some parents don't have enough money to provide their babies with an adequate diet. Others don't know about babies' special food needs or they feed their children high-calorie foods that are low in nutrients. Fatty foods or foods high in sugar, for instance, should be avoided. Fat-free or diet foods are also inappropriate.

Inadequate nutrition in infancy can cause lasting physical problems. Poor nutrition at any stage of childhood is also linked to poor brain development and learning problems.

Many government and community programs try to eliminate infant and childhood malnutrition. Some of these programs provide food; others teach parents about the nutritional needs of children. The federal government's Women, Infants, and Children Program (WIC) helps meet the special food needs of new mothers and young children. Other programs in your area may be funded by state and local governments or commuting groups.

SECTION 8-3 REVIEW

✔ Check Your Understanding

1. Which part of a newborn's body do you always need to support when lifting or holding the baby? Why?
2. What damage may be caused by severely shaking a baby?
3. Why should babies not be given cow's milk in their first year?
4. Describe the position in which a baby should be held for bottle-feeding.
5. Why burp a baby?
6. What nutritional needs does a baby have?
7. If a parent is concerned that a baby is overfeeding, should the parent cut back on the baby's food? Why or why not? If not, what should the parent do?

Putting Knowledge Into Practice

1. **Sequencing.** Put the following foods in the right order for introducing solids to a baby: cereals, meat, eggs, fruit, vegetables.
2. **Analyzing.** Why not start a baby self-feeding at about six months?
3. **Observing and Participating.** Ask a parent of a small baby how often the baby feeds. Find out if the parent breast-feeds or bottle-feeds the baby. Compare your findings to those of other students in the class. What patterns, based on age and type of feeding, can you find?

Other Infant Care Skills

Caring for a baby can—and should—be fun. A caregiver who is competent and confident in carrying out basic care routines can enjoy the baby and contribute to the baby's appreciation and enjoyment of the world. These routines include bathing, dressing, and diapering. Proper sleep habits are also important for the baby's health.

KEY TERMS

cradle cap
diaper rash
sleeper

OBJECTIVES:

- Describe or demonstrate how to bathe, dress, and diaper a baby.
- Tell how to encourage good sleep habits.

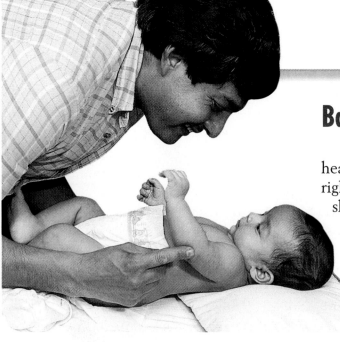

Bathing a Baby

A bath helps keep a baby clean and healthy. Any time is fine for a bath except right after feeding. Then the baby needs to sleep and digest the meal.

A newborn is given sponge baths for about two weeks, until the navel heals. After that, a tub bath may be given. Both types of baths require the parent's careful attention to ensure the baby's safety.

Until the navel heals, parents should give newborns a sponge bath. *About when does the navel usually heal?*

Sponge Baths

Many of the same basic supplies are needed for both sponge baths and tub baths. These include:

- Two soft bath towels
- A soft washcloth
- A diaper
- Mild soap
- Baby shampoo

Before bathing a baby, assemble these articles and the baby's clean diaper and clothes in a warm place with no drafts. The temperature of the room should be 70° to 80°F (20° to 26°C). Choose a room with a good work surface—usually the bathroom, kitchen, or baby's room. Place a soft bath towel over the work area for the baby's comfort and safety.

For sponge baths, it's convenient to put the bathwater in a basin on the work surface. Test the water temperature with your elbow, where the skin is more sensitive than on your hands. The water should feel lukewarm, about 98°F (37°C).

Remove the baby's clothes and place the infant on the towel. Lay another towel on top of the baby's body. Begin by washing the baby's face with clear water and a soft washcloth, while supporting the baby with your other hand. Then pat the baby's face dry. A young baby's skin is very tender, so never rub it with a towel.

Wash the rest of the body with baby soap and water, one area at a time. Rinse thoroughly. Pay particular attention to the skin creases. They should be gently separated, washed and rinsed, and thoroughly dried.

It isn't necessary to clean the inside of the baby's mouth, ears, eyes, or nose. Nature takes care of this. Never use cotton swab sticks. Babies move very suddenly and can easily be injured by them. Just wipe the outer ears, and use a clean washcloth to remove any visible mucus from the nose.

Wash the baby's scalp with tear-free baby soap or baby shampoo once or twice a week. On other days, just wipe the scalp with clear water and pat it dry.

Sometimes babies develop **cradle cap**, a skin condition in which the scalp develops patches of yellowish, crusty scales. To treat it, apply baby oil or lanolin to the scalp at night. In the morning, gently loosen the scales with a washcloth or a soft hairbrush and shampoo the hair.

You may want to apply baby powder or lotion to the baby after a bath, but neither is really necessary. If you use powder, choose one with cornstarch, not talc. First shake the powder into your own hand, and then rub it onto the baby's skin. Sprinkling the powder on the baby, puts powder in the air the baby breathes. This may cause breathing problems or even suffocation.

Tub Baths

Once the navel has healed, the baby can be bathed in a tub. At first the "tub" can be a large dishpan or special baby bathtub. By six or seven months, use the regular tub.

Before starting the bath, gather the equipment and the baby's clean clothes. Place a rubber mat or towel in the bottom of the tub to make the baby

What safety precautions should be taken with powder?

comfortable and to prevent falls. Add lukewarm water to a depth of about 2 to 3 inches (5 to 8 cm). The steps in bathing a baby are shown in the illustrations on page 282.

Most older babies enjoy baths, especially when they can sit by themselves in the tub. They love to splash and play in the water and with floating toys. Don't forget, though, that safety is the main concern when bathing a baby of any age.

Dressing a Baby

When choosing a baby's indoor clothes, consider the temperature in the home rather than the season of the year. Follow your own clothing needs—an infant doesn't need to be warmer than you.

The Newborn

A newborn's clothing needs are minimal. Many parents put their babies in a **sleeper**, a one-piece stretchy garment with feet, even when awake. Others dress the

Safety in the Tub

*T*he bathtub can be dangerous for babies, so follow these safety precautions:

- Never leave the baby alone during the bath, not even for "just a second." A baby can drown very quickly, even in very shallow water.

- Keep the baby seated in the tub. Standing or climbing can lead to falls.

- Don't count on a bathtub seat to support an infant.

- Before you put the baby in the tub, always check the water temperature. Use your wrist or elbow, not your hand, to test the water.

- Check the temperature of the hot water heater. Water should be no hotter than 120° to 130°F (49° to 54°C). If it is warmer than that, turn the hot water heater down.

- Keep babies away from faucets, which are hard and sharp and may be hot.

- Don't let the baby drink the bathwater or suck on the washcloth. If necessary, offer a drink of fresh water or a teething ring.

FOLLOWING UP
1. Which of these safety rules do you think is most important? Why?
2. Why use the wrist or elbow to check water temperature?

---

baby in a cotton undershirt and a gown. In warm or hot weather (if there is no air conditioning), the baby may wear only a diaper and a short-sleeved shirt. When taking the baby outdoors in cool weather, add warm outer garments or blankets.

Socks and booties are usually not necessary for everyday wear. They may bind or get wet or kicked off. The newborn's feet usually stay covered by a sleeper or blanket. If the feet feel cool, cover them with sleeper feet or with stretchy socks.

Older Babies

When babies begin to creep and crawl, they need different kinds of clothing—more durable, allowing for movement. Overalls, especially those with legs that snap open for easy diaper changes, are good for crawling babies. Very active crawlers may need pants with padded knees. Soft, cotton knit shirts are comfortable. A sleeper keeps the baby covered even if a blanket is kicked off.

Bathing a Baby

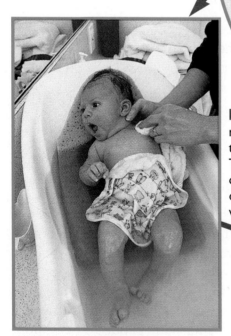

Placing the Baby in the Tub—Support the head and neck with one arm and hand and the lower body with another. Hold the baby gently but firmly. Lower the baby into the tub feet first, followed by the rest of the body. Keep one arm supporting the head and neck throughout the bath.

Washing the Face—Begin by washing the baby's face and head with clear water and patting it dry. If the baby has hair, wash it with a baby shampoo about twice a week.

Rinsing the Hair—To rinse the hair, pour water toward the sides and back. Try to keep the shampoo out of the baby's eyes. If it does get in the eyes, rinse with a clean wet washcloth.

Washing the Body—Use the free hand to wash and rinse the baby. Then lift the baby from the water with the same secure grip.

Drying the Baby—Place the infant on a clean towel and wrap the baby in it immediately to prevent chilling. Towels with hoods can prevent air from chilling the head. Then pat the baby dry.

Shoes aren't really necessary until the baby walks outdoors. Many physicians feel that the best way to learn to walk is barefoot, which leaves the toes free to grip the floor and gives the ankles flexibility. If the baby is learning to stand and walk indoors on cold floors, nonskid socks can keep the feet warm and the baby safe. Once the baby is ready for shoes, either sneakers or leather shoes are appropriate.

Dressing Tips

Dressing and undressing provide ideal opportunities for extra strokes, pats, hugs, and kisses. This is also a good time for songs, simple rhymes, or naming parts of the body or articles of clothing.

The illustrations on page 284 show how to dress a baby. As babies get older, they can help with dressing; for example, they can stretch their own arms through short sleeves. However, you may often find that even a capable baby is uncooperative. Sometimes distracting the baby with a toy or song can help make dressing easier.

Choosing Clothes

Today, most clothes for infants are simple and comfortable. Many are made of knit fabrics that contain non-irritating fibers and provide both ease of movement for the baby and ease of care for the parents.

Which characteristics are most important in choosing clothes for babies?

Baby clothes should also be flame retardant. Look for this information on clothing labels.

The size of infant wear is indicated by both weight and age of baby. Weight is the more reliable guide. It is usually best to buy nothing smaller than a six-month size for a newborn. The clothes may look large, but babies grow quickly, and the smallest sizes soon become too small. Simply fold up the hems of larger garments for a few weeks until the baby grows into them.

When choosing baby clothes, both comfort and ease in dressing are important. Since clothing is expensive, it's wise to look for clothes with generous hems and extra buttons on shoulder straps and waistbands to allow for rapid growth.

Dressing a Baby

Pullover Garments. These garments have a stretchable neck opening. If the neck is small, follow these steps. If the neck opening is larger, put the opening around the baby's face first and then pull it over the back of the head.

Step 1: Gather the garment into a loop and slip it over the back of the baby's head.

Step 2: Stretch the garment forward as you bring it down past the forehead and nose. This keeps the face and nose free so that the baby doesn't feel smothered.

Step 3: Put the baby's fist into the armhole and pull the arm through with your other hand. Repeat with the other arm. Then straighten out the bottom of the garment.

As you dress or undress a baby, work as smoothly and quickly as possible without being rough. Quick, jerking movements often frighten babies. Follow these same tips for taking each kind of garment off a baby, but reverse the order of the steps.

Open Front Shirt. For these garments, lay the baby face down to make him or her feel secure.

Step 1: Open the shirt and lay it on the baby's back.

Step 2: Gently turn the baby face up so that the shirt is underneath.

Step 3: Gently put the baby's arms through the sleeves

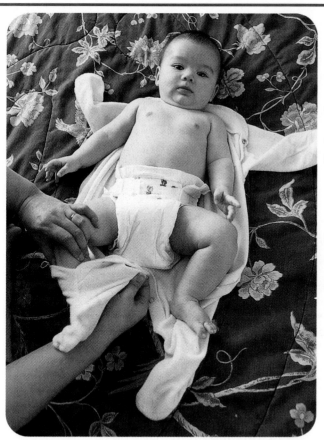

One-Piece Garment with Feet.

Putting on this type of garment is easier when the zipper or the snaps go from neck to toes.

Step 1: Start with the bottom part of the garment. Put the baby's leg on the side without the zipper or snaps into the garment leg, followed by the other leg.

Step 2: Roll the baby onto one side and pull the garment up under the baby's shoulders.

Step 3: Roll the baby back onto the garment. Then gently pull the sleeves over the baby's arms. Finish by zipping or snapping the garment closed.

Diapering a Baby

Diapers are the most essential part of a baby's wardrobe. Parents have a number of diapering options. Cloth diapers, the traditional favorite, may be the least expensive if home laundry facilities are available. Disposable diapers offer throwaway convenience, but are much more expensive than cloth diapers and add to environmental problems. Commercial diaper services, if available, are convenient and may not cost much more than using disposables. These services deliver clean cloth diapers and pick up used ones.

A very young baby probably needs a diaper change twelve to fifteen times each day. A newborn wets several times an hour, but in small amounts that don't require changing each time. An older baby probably needs fewer diaper changes a day—and is more likely to let you know when a clean diaper is needed.

Turn diaper-changing time into a period of interaction. Sing or hum while you work, or talk about what you are doing. A young baby will enjoy hearing your voice—and may even babble in response.

Keep your diapering supplies near a sturdy, padded surface such as the crib or a changing table. Cloth diapers must be folded to the correct size—the illustration on page 286 shows a good method. Disposable diapers come in several sizes, with thicker

Fold a square diaper in thirds lengthwise so that it is a little wider than the baby's hips. Then turn up one end of the diaper part way.

diapers available for nighttime wear. In addition to the diaper, you will need a wet washcloth, soft tissues or toilet paper, cotton, and baby oil. Disposable baby washcloths are also available.

How to Diaper

It is never safe to leave a baby alone on a raised surface. Always keep at least one hand firmly on the baby. If you need to leave the work surface, for however short a time, take the baby with you. Babies can wriggle, squirm, or roll themselves right off the surface onto the floor, causing serious injury—and even death.

Follow these steps to change a diaper:

1. **Remove the diaper, and clean the baby.** If the diaper was merely wet, clean the baby with cotton and baby oil. If the baby had a bowel movement, use soft tissue or toilet paper to remove the soil from the baby. Then wash with a washcloth and apply baby oil.

2. **Put on a fresh diaper.** Hold the baby's ankles, and lift the body enough to slide the diaper under. If you are using cloth diapers, place the extra thickness in the back for girls, in the front for boys. With disposable diapers, be sure the adhesive tabs are under the baby. Bring the diaper up between the baby's legs. Use the adhesive tabs to fasten a disposable diaper. Use large safety pins or diaper pins to fasten a cloth diaper. If you use pins, be sure to keep your finger between the pin and the baby's skin. You can also use diaper tape, which comes off a dispenser, or diaper wraps, which are put around a diaper and closed with hooks and loops. Waterproof pants may be put on over the cloth diaper.

3. **Dispose of used supplies.** Cleanliness is important. Dispose of used tissues, cotton, and other supplies. Roll a disposable diaper up and place it in a covered trash container. (Never flush one down a toilet. It will clog the plumbing.) Place a wet cloth diaper in a covered container filled with a mixture of water and borax or vinegar. If the diaper is soiled, rinse it before placing it in the container. A good method for rinsing is to hold the diaper firmly in a clean, flushing toilet. Be sure to wash your own hands with soap and hot water after changing a diaper.

Washing Cloth Diapers

Washing cloth diapers requires special care. Washing machines don't always wash out all the bacteria, and bacteria can cause skin problems. Wash diapers separately in the hottest water with a mild soap. Regular detergent leaves the fabric rough. Laundry sanitizers added to the wash help destroy bacteria. Be sure, too, that the diapers are thoroughly rinsed to avoid skin irritation.

Diapers may be dried in a dryer. However, drying them outdoors on a line in the sun destroys even more bacteria.

Diaper Rash

Controlling bacteria in diapers helps prevent **diaper rash**, patches of rough, irritated skin in the diaper area. Sometimes diaper rash includes painful raw spots. Sensitivity to disposable diapers can cause similar symptoms.

Treat a mild case of diaper rash by changing diapers more frequently and cleaning the baby thoroughly after a bowel movement. Spread the area with a product that contains zinc oxide and cod liver oil, which protects against diaper rash and helps it heal more quickly. Also, expose the diaper area to the air as much as possible, and avoid putting waterproof pants on the baby. If the rash continues or gets worse, ask a pediatrician for help.

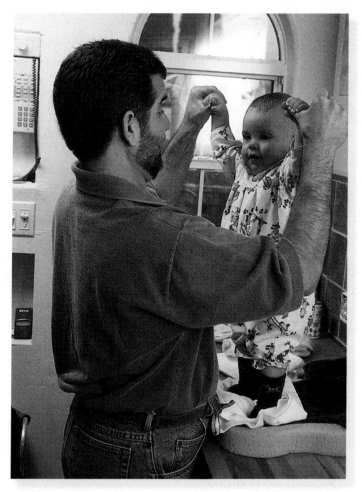

Having a set place and routine for diapering makes the process easier. Use the opportunity as a time to talk, sing, or play.

A few minutes of rocking before bedtime can help a baby settle down more easily.

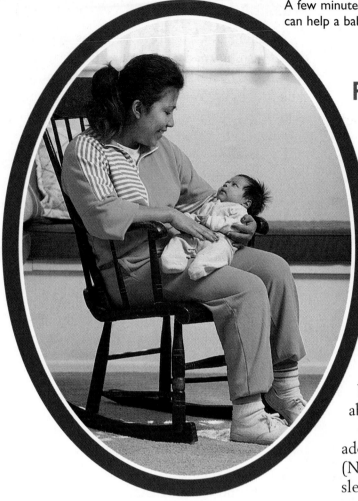

Preparation for Sleep

Putting the baby to bed for the night should be a relaxed and pleasant experience—for both you and the baby. Begin by washing the baby's face and hands and by changing the baby's diaper and clothes. Specific sleeping garments remind the baby that it is time to go to sleep.

Spend a few minutes rocking the baby or singing a soothing lullaby. This will be comforting and reassuring. As you put the baby to bed, keep your manner calm and unhurried, even if you don't feel that way. If not, the baby will pick up your feelings and probably not settle into sleep.

Finally, put the baby down in bed with adequate covering. (Never let a baby sleep in a draft, even in very hot weather.) If the infant is too young to roll over independently, put the baby on his or her back. This practice is recommended to help prevent Sudden Infant Death Syndrome.

INFOLINK

SIDS

To read more about *SIDS*, see Chapter 7, page 238.

Try to follow the same routine every night. The baby learns the routine and is likely to find comfort in the ritual.

Sleep should never be brought about by the use of drugs or sleep medicines of any kind. Talk to the pediatrician if sleep problems continue.

Sleep

All babies need sleep in order to grow and develop. The amount of time an infant spends sleeping decreases considerably during the first year. A newborn may sleep from 12 to 20 hours a day. By one year, however, a baby often has as few as two or three sleep periods, including naps.

The amount of sleep needed also depends on the individual baby. An active baby needs more sleep than an inactive one, just as they need more food. Babies also need more sleep on some days than others.

Crying to Sleep

Many parents wonder what to do about a baby who cries when put down to sleep. Should they comfort the child? If they do, will crying and comforting become a habit that prolongs bedtime every night? If they don't, will the baby be harmed?

Some experts argue that babies should be left alone to "cry it out" so they can learn to settle themselves. Others say that this hurts the child emotionally. They urge a parent to pick up and the baby and offer any kind of comfort that will settle the baby down, even if it means letting the baby sleep with the parent.

A middle ground can be useful. If an infant cries when put to sleep, stay out of the room for two or three minutes to see if the baby settles down. If not, go in and comfort the child with voice and touch, then leave. If the crying starts again, stay away a bit longer than before. This process gives the baby some reassurance without creating an unwanted habit.

Bedtime Problems

Babies—especially active babies—often become restless while they sleep. During the night, they may waken partially and suck their fingers, cry out, or rock the crib. If you respond, your presence may become a necessary part of the baby's pattern for getting back to sleep. Infants need to learn to return to sleep on their own. Of course, provide care for a baby who needs feeding or a diaper change. A baby whose restlessness develops into crying also needs your attention.

SECTION 8-4 REVIEW

✔ Check Your Understanding

1. What should you do if you have to leave the room while you are giving a baby a sponge bath? Why?
2. At what point can a baby have a tub bath?
3. Explain what cradle cap is. What would you do to treat cradle cap?
4. How warmly should you dress an infant?
5. What are the advantages and disadvantages of cloth diapers and disposable diapers?
6. List the three main steps in changing a baby's diaper.
7. What is the benefit of a bedtime routine?

Putting Knowledge Into Practice

1. **Applying.** Using actual garments or magazine pictures, select four items of infant's clothing, ranging in size from newborn to twelve months. Evaluate each item for comfort, practicality, ease in dressing the baby, and required care. Which garment ranks highest on your list?
2. **Applying.** Tran has diaper rash. What should his caregiver do?
3. **Observing and Participating.** Using a doll, practice putting a disposable and a cloth diaper on a baby. How would this be different with a real baby?

Parenting With Care

Spending Quality Time with Baby

As a baby grows older, you will find more opportunities to play games.

For many games, you need no toys at all—just you, the baby, and some creative imagination. Here are a few ideas:

Looking Games

- **Funny face.** Shake your head; stick out your tongue; make funny faces.
- **Shadow figures.** Shine a flashlight on the wall of a partially darkened room. Make shadow designs by placing your fingers in front of the beam.
- **Mirrors.** Sit with the baby in front of a mirror. Point to the infant's eyes, nose, mouth, and other features, and name each feature. Do the same with your own features. Eventually, the baby will point to the features you name.
- **Ping-pong.** In a variation on "Mirrors," let the baby be the leader. Watch the baby closely, and mimic everything he or she does.

Listening Games

- **Musical games.** Play or sing music and nursery rhymes. Encourage the older babies to respond by swaying or humming.
- **What's that?** Point out everyday sounds like running water, the washing machine, and the telephone. Name the sound, and then help the baby see what is making it.
- **Mimic.** Make fun sounds—the noises of cars, animals, motorcycles, and so on. Encourage the baby to imitate you.

Baby Exercises

- **Bicycle.** Lay the baby on his or her back and gently hold both ankles. Revolve the baby's legs as if riding a bicycle.
- **Tug-of-war.** Grasp one side of a large rubber ring, and let the baby grasp the other side. Gently play tug-of-war. Remember—the baby gets to win. If the baby is sitting up, don't let go entirely of the rubber ring, or the baby will tumble backward.

- **Airplane.** Playing airplane can help strengthen the back and neck muscles of a baby who can already hold his or her head steady. Hold the baby just above the waist, and then slowly lift the baby above your face. Avoid a sudden lift, which could cause the baby's head to wobble. The baby's back will arch and arms and legs will stretch out. You may want to make airplane noises, too.

Old Favorites

- **Peekaboo.** Establish eye contact with the baby. Quickly turn your head away, and then turn back again, saying "peekaboo." For older babies, cover your eyes and then uncover them.
- **Hide-and-seek.** Make a toy disappear behind your back. Let the baby crawl to find it. Help the baby find toys that you have hidden. Try hiding from the baby yourself, and then reappear quickly.

Following Up

1. **Communication.** Which of these games also builds a baby's language skills?

2. **Thinking Skills.** Why should you not play airplane with a baby until the baby can hold his or her head steady?

Summary

✔ Children grow and develop most rapidly in the first year. (Section 8-1)

✔ Development proceeds from head to foot, near to far, and simple to complex. (Section 8-1)

✔ Parents can provide a rich environment to help a baby's brain develop. (Section 8-2)

✔ During the first year, babies begin to eat solids. (Section 8-3)

✔ An infant's clothing should be comfortable and easy to put on and take off. (Section 8-4)

✔ Babies sleep best if bedtime is handled with a soothing, familiar routine. (Section 8-4)

8. Describe how to give a baby a tub bath. (Section 8-4)

9. Why is it important to stay calm when preparing a baby to sleep? (Section 8-4)

Thinking Critically

1. **Charting.** Make a chart with three headings: "Head to Foot"; "Near to Far"; "Simple to Complex." Under each heading, list at least three examples of each pattern of development.

Reviewing the Facts

1. What is the difference between growth and development? Give an example of each from the first year of life. (Section 8-1)

2. Describe how one of the five senses changes in a baby's first year. (Section 8-1)

3. What functions do the cerebrum and thalamus control? (Section 8-2)

4. What role does repetition play in brain development? (Section 8-2)

5. Give two guidelines caregivers can follow to help an infant's brain develop. (Section 8-2)

6. What do parents always have to do when handling a newborn? (Section 8-3)

7. How can inadequate nutrition be prevented? (Section 8-3)

2. **Diagramming.** Create a flow chart showing how nerves send information to the brain and receive instructions from it.

3. **Sequencing.** Write out the proper steps for diapering a baby.

Taking Action

1. **Holding a Baby.** Hold a 10-pound (4.5-kg) sack of flour or rice in the crook of one arm while you perform various routine activities—preparing a bottle, opening the mail, putting clothes away, and so on. How much more difficult would these tasks be with a baby? *(Thinking Skills)*

2. **Dressing a Baby.** Using a doll, show the proper technique for dressing a baby. *(Management)*

CONNECTIONS

Cross-Curricular Connections

1. **Health.** Make a chart showing how you would introduce seven foods to an infant, starting with cereals and followed by vegetables. Follow the rule of allowing four days to pass between each new food.

2. **Social Studies.** Find out how many cases of Sudden Infant Death Syndrome occurred each year from 1990 to the most recent year for which statistics are available. In 1992, pediatricians began saying that babies should sleep on their backs. What happened to the rate of SIDS since then?

with all the stores and the prices they charged. Identify the lowest and highest prices and brands. How much can a shopper save?

2. **Evaluating Options.** Ask your parents and others their opinions about different kinds of infant garments: slipover gowns or shirts; one-piece shirts; and one-piece garments with feet. Which did they find most convenient? Why? Share your findings with the class.

Workplace Connections

1. **Resources.** Look through parenting magazines or books to find out how women who work outside the home handle feeding. Do they breast-feed or bottle-feed? If they breast-feed, what do they do when they are at work and the baby is hungry? Report your findings to the class.

2. **Personal Qualities.** What personal qualities does the parent of an infant need?

Family and Community Connections

1. **Pricing Formula.** Check the cost of formula at a local store. Compare your findings to those of classmates. Make a chart

Technology Connections

1. **Technology.** In what ways have technological advances made it easier to keep infants safe? Has technology created any new dangers?

2. **Internet.** Research on the Internet for advice about caring for a baby. What sites offer such advice? What kind of information do they have? How can you judge the reliability of the information?

Kim looked forward to this time every evening. After the long day at work and the many things that needed to be done at night, this was her chance for some quiet time with Nick. The routine was simple. First Nick ate, and then she gave him a bath. After he was all cleaned up, Kim put a clean diaper and sleeper on him. Then they sat down for a book.

Of course, Nick was still too young to read, but Kim knew that he understood something. Each night, she showed him three books that he could choose from. Each night, he picked the same one.

Kim sat down in the chair and put Nick on her lap. She opened the book and said, "Look, Nick. Here's a cute little bear just like your friend Andy." The baby cooed in delight. "Let's read about the little bear. What's he going to do?"

"She opened the book and said, 'Let's read about the little bear.'"

SECTION 9-1

Understanding Emotional and Social Development

Two babies show clear differences in their physical growth—one weighs more or is taller than the other. The same is true of social and emotional development. Watch how two babies respond to the same situation. Where one squeals in delight while crawling on the grass in the park, another may sit still. Each is becoming a unique person.

KEY TERMS

attachment
emotional development
failure to thrive
social development

OBJECTIVES:

- Define emotional and social development.

- Explain the importance of attachment to emotional and social development.

- Explain how a baby's care affects emotional and social development.

- Analyze people according to different temperament traits.

Comparing Emotional and Social Development

Emotional development is the process of learning to recognize and express one's feelings and to establish one's identity as a unique person. A child with healthy emotional development becomes an adult who has self-confidence, can handle stress, and shows empathy toward others.

Social development is the process of learning to interact with others and to express oneself to others. Healthy social development results in an adult who shows tolerance for others. A socially healthy adult can communicate well with others and listens to different points of view before acting.

Emotional and social development are connected to each other. A child's feelings about himself or herself and behavior toward others depend on one another.

Emotional and social development begin at birth and continue throughout life. Many influences shape how a child develops in these areas. The bond formed between parent and child is one. The atmosphere of the home is another. A final influence is the temperament of the child.

The first studies in this area were done with monkeys, not humans. An American experimental psychologist, Harry Harlow, made monkey-shaped forms out of chicken wire and out of soft cloth. He then used these substitute "mothers" to raise baby monkeys. He found that the baby monkeys clung to the "mothers" made of soft cloth—even if the chicken-wire "mothers" held their feeding bottles. Clearly, the monkeys needed to feel physical closeness as well as receive a feeding.

Harlow found that attachment requires more than physical contact. Once the baby monkeys were grown, they didn't know how to relate to other monkeys. They did not develop normal social relationships.

Attachment

Each day, Jo makes a point of going into her baby Franklin's room and giving him a hug to start the day. She does the same thing at day's end. As Jo knows, babies have a basic need for physical contact—holding, cuddling, rocking, or even just being near another person. This contact builds a bond between a parent or caregiver and a child, a bond called **attachment**. Some famous research studies have shown how important that bond is.

Social relationships are important for many animals as well as for humans. A famous example is Koko the gorilla's attachment to a kitten. *What animals do you know of that live in social groups?*

Harlow believed this was caused by the lack of interaction between the babies and real mothers.

Monkeys, of course, aren't humans, but other research suggests that human babies have a similar need for contact. In the 1990s, child care experts were alarmed at the children they found in government homes for orphaned and abandoned babies in Romania. The conditions in the country were desperate, and the children had little personal care from adults. As a result, the physical and emotional development of these children was slower than normal.

The World's Children

Attachment Around the World

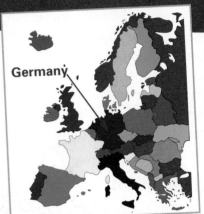
Germany

*P*sychologist Mary Ainsworth developed a way of testing an infant's attachment to his or her mother. In the test, mother and child are placed in a room that has many toys. During the test, a stranger enters and then leaves the room and the mother leaves and returns several times. Observers watch how the infant reacts to these changes. Researchers found four kinds of responses:

- About two-thirds of the babies are somewhat disturbed by the parent's leaving but then returned to the toys. When the mother came back into the room, they went to her. These children are said to be securely attached.

- About a quarter of the babies didn't show much unhappiness when the mother left. When she returned, they ignored her.

- Another group stayed near their mother and were very unhappy when she left. When the mother returned, though, they showed anger toward her.

- A last group showed signs of both going toward and moving away from the mother when she returned.

Studies using this test have been conducted on children all over the world. Researchers have found that babies worldwide show similar responses. However, the percentage of children in each group may differ. The differences can even be within the same country. In one part of Germany, for instance, the percentages for the groups were about the same as in the United States. In another region of Germany, though, more children ignored the mothers.

SHARE YOUR THOUGHTS

1. How do you think the test shows attachment?
2. Why do you think that the percentage of children found in each group would differ from country to country?

More recent research has shown the benefits of giving children a gentle massage. This can sooth a baby and promote bonding. Babies need lots of love. Even young babies can experience loneliness. A baby who is left alone most of the time except for physical care, may fail to respond to people and objects. Researchers at Baylor University studied abused and neglected children. Those who failed to receive love, touch, and opportunities for learning had brains 20 to 30 percent smaller than average.

This problem is most likely to develop when physical needs are met but babies receive no emotional or social care. This may happen in institutions, but it can happen in families as well. When infants get little attention and encouragement from caregivers, their cries weaken, their smiles fade, and they become withdrawn.

Lack of love and attention may result in **failure to thrive**, a condition in which the baby does not grow and develop properly. If these babies are not helped, they become unattached. Even as adults, they will be unable to develop caring, meaningful relationships with others.

Fortunately, these children can be helped. The children in the Romanian institutions improved when they went to live in loving and supportive homes. Caregivers can be given instruction and support so that they can help the baby recover and grow.

Young babies who cry to communicate their needs, gaze into the eyes of caregivers, track the movements of caregivers with their eyes, snuggle, cuddle, and become quiet when comforted show signs of growing attachment. As babies mature, they make sounds to their caregivers, embrace them, and eventually crawl or walk to them.

Building Trust Through Care

The world is a strange new place for newborns. Depending on a baby's early experiences, it may be a comfortable, secure place or a confusing, difficult one. The attitude newborns develop about their world depends on how their needs are met.

By studying a baby's responses, parents can tell if he or she is developing a healthy attachment to others. *What signs should they look for?*

If the newborn is kept warm and dry, fed when hungry, soothed when fussy, and talked to when awake, the infant comes to feel that the world is a comfortable place. That baby develops a sense of security.

On the other hand, if the newborn is made to conform to a rigid schedule of feeding, and crying brings no comforting adult response, the baby learns that the world is not a very friendly place.

The same result occurs when caregivers are inconsistent in their care or responses to the infant. If schedules change often, or if parents are sometimes gentle and loving and other times sharp and impatient, the baby has difficulty building trust.

Emotional Climate of the Home

Like everybody else, you probably have days when you are grumpy. Have you ever noticed how contagious such feelings are? If you snap at someone, chances are that person will snap back at you—or at someone else. Babies react the same way. Long before they know the meanings of words, babies catch the tone of adults' feelings. Worried or angry caregivers are likely to be tense in handling their baby. The baby senses these feelings and, in turn, becomes irritable and fussy.

Every family has ups and downs, and a baby adapts to them. It is essential, however, for a baby to feel that affection and caring are the basis of the family's interactions. Bitterness and mistrust can hinder a baby's healthy development.

Jess and Twana were excited when Andrea was born, but soon their feelings began to change. Jess felt left out because Twana seemed closer to the baby. Twana

loved her baby, but some days felt trapped with a child who only wet herself and cried. One night, these feelings erupted. When Andrea cried, Twana thrust her into Jess's arms, shouting, "Here, you take care of her for a change!" She stalked off into the bedroom and slammed the door.

What Jess and Twana felt isn't unusual. One outburst won't ruin the emotional climate in which Andrea lives. If their negative feelings continue to fester, though, the trouble may become more serious. They need to talk about their frustrations—when they are both calm. They need to find ways they can help each other so they can help their baby.

Conditions in a baby's home will have a big influence on how the baby develops. *How do you think a baby will be affected by having many brothers and sisters?*

Parents need to find time for each other to keep their relationship healthy. *How does this benefit the baby?*

The challenge can be greater for single parents. With no other adult to share the work—or their worries—with, they may feel alone. It's important to find ways of releasing negative feelings away from the child. That way, they can have the patience and calmness to create a caring environment for their baby.

The Baby's Own Temperament

Every baby copes with life in a very personal way. This is because each baby brings his or her own individuality to a situation. For example, all babies react if the surface on which they are lying is suddenly shaken. However, one baby may respond by screaming, whereas another simply squirms a bit and quickly settles down again.

These different responses are based on the baby's temperament—his or her style of reacting to the world and relating to others. Different temperaments are revealed in how children react to a situation. Shanta, for instance, was trying to reach the mobile above her crib. She kept trying many, many times. Finally, when her father picked her up, she grabbed it. Luke, on the other hand, tried only once to reach a toy that was just out of reach. When he couldn't put his hand on it, he returned to the toy he had.

Researchers have found nine different ways of looking at temperament. Each of them has a high and low side, meaning that a child has the trait to a greater or lesser amount. Each baby—each person—needs to be looked at in terms of all of the traits together:

- **Intensity.** How strong or weak are a child's emotional responses to events or to others? A highly intense child is marked by deep and powerful responses. An intense baby may cry heartily. A less intense baby will cry weakly. Intense children are often very loud.
- **Persistence.** A persistent child is one who is determined to complete an action. Such a child may become very upset if unable to finish what was begun. A less persistent child can be easily persuaded to begin a new activity. A less persistent child accepts "no" for an answer. A highly persistent child

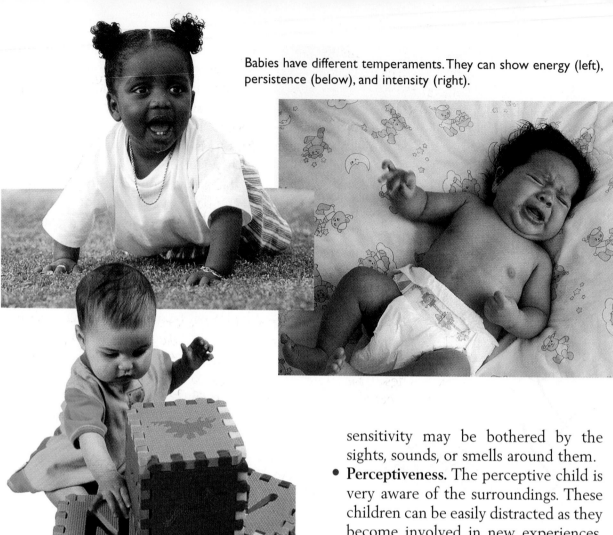

Babies have different temperaments. They can show energy (left), persistence (below), and intensity (right).

won't. These children want to attain a goal and are unwilling to give up on it.

- **Sensitivity.** A child who is high in sensitivity has strong reactions to his or her feelings. Such a child may be a fussy eater or may complain about clothes being uncomfortable. A less sensitive child is more likely to accept what comes. Children who are high in sensitivity may be bothered by the sights, sounds, or smells around them.

- **Perceptiveness.** The perceptive child is very aware of the surroundings. These children can be easily distracted as they become involved in new experiences. They have a hard time following directions that include several different things to do—they often lose track in some new activity after finishing the first task. Children lower in perceptiveness can handle many directions at once. They are less likely to notice things in the world around them.

- **Adaptability.** Some children find it easier than others to adjust to changes. A child who is low in adaptability wants to continue doing whatever activity is going on at the time. He or she resists change. A highly adaptable child will not be bothered by surprises. A child who is low in adaptability will dislike surprises—even pleasant ones.

- **Regularity.** Children who are highly regular follow strong patterns. They get tired and go to sleep at the same time. They go to the bathroom at the same time. They are hungry at the same time. Children who are low in regularity are just the opposite: each day is different for them and their parents.
- **Energy.** High energy children are physically active. Even when they are sitting, they often squirm and move around in the seat. Once they are able to walk, they seem always to run. Low energy children move much less. They can play in one spot for long periods of time.
- **First reaction.** Children differ in how they face new situations. Some dive right in and take part. These children are probably open to new activities and willing to try new foods. Others hold back and watch what others do before joining. They are less comfortable in new situations and may resist new foods.
- **Mood.** Is a child usually cheerful or cranky? Is he or she more often positive or inclined to point out the problems?

Parents and other caregivers have personal temperaments, too. Problems can arise if the adult's temperament conflicts with the child's. Understanding such a differences can help prevent clashes. For instance, a parent who is low in energy has to be prepared to accept the activity level of a high-energy child. If the high energy becomes bothersome, a trip to the park or other opportunity for vigorous play might help.

SECTION 9-1 REVIEW

✔ Check Your Understanding

1. What is emotional development?
2. What is social development?
3. What happens to children if they don't develop attachment?
4. How can a child who suffers from failure to thrive be helped?
5. How should parents and caregivers respond to a baby's needs to help the baby build a sense of trust?
6. Does it matter to a baby how the adults in the family treat each other? Why or why not?
7. How can temperament be used to understand children?

Putting Knowledge Into Practice

1. **Analyzing.** What can parents do to provide consistency in the care and attention their babies receive? What issues should they discuss with each other? What issues should they discuss with others who care for their baby?
2. **Synthesizing.** Explain how one of the following factors might affect the emotional climate in a home: the emotional maturity of parents; education; unemployment; substance use and abuse.
3. **Observing and Participating.** Look at the nine temperament traits described in the chapter. Rate yourself in each area on a scale of 1 (low in that characteristic) to 5 (high in that trait). Summarize your temperament.

Nanny

A CONVERSATION WITH NICHOLE JENKINS

How did you become interested in becoming a nanny? I started babysitting in junior high school. Right then, I decided I wanted a career where I could be with children all the time. They're just such joys. I chose being a nanny instead of working in a child care center because I wanted closer involvement with children.

What are the tasks and responsibilities of a nanny? Everything that a parent would do—we feed, bathe, change, dress, and play with children. We take them to the doctor and dentist and to the park and the zoo. You name it, we do it.

What is the work environment like? That really depends on the home. The people I work for now have an apartment with an extra room for me.

What are the working hours like? Weekdays, I work from six in the morning until six at night, when both parents come home. I watch the baby some evenings when the parents are out and usually a half day or so on the weekend.

What aptitudes are needed to be a nanny? Well, you have to love children, obviously. You need patience and the ability to comfort a child. You need to watch the child at all times to make sure of safety, and you need to be creative to provide a stimulating environment. It helps to have a sense of humor. And you have to be a good communicator to let the parents know how you see the child developing.

NANNY

Education and Training. Nannies have a high school diploma and some additional training in child care. Some receive that training at nanny schools.

Career Outlook. The demand for nannies is expected to grow faster than average in the coming years.

CONNECTING SCHOOL TO CAREER

1. **Information Systems.** What kinds of information do you think nannies would communicate to parents?
2. **Resources.** Why do nannies receive room and board as part of their pay?

Emotional and Social Development of Infants

Jo remembers how sweet the feeling was when she first felt Franklin in her arms. He had just been born. After feeling immense relief that her labor was over, she was swept up in a powerful wave of love. She promised herself—and Franklin—that she would never forget that feeling.

KEY TERMS

colic
pacifier
stranger anxiety

OBJECTIVES:

- Describe how behavior is learned.
- Describe how emotions change during infancy.
- Recognize signs of social development in babies.

How Behavior Is Learned

As studies of attachment show, an infant learns how to behave toward others through his or her relationship with others. The type of behavior a baby learns depends on the messages he or she receives from caregivers.

Babies learn about physical care through their daily routine. Running water may signal bath time; rocking signals time to sleep. They learn social behavior the same way—by seeing the same action bring about the same response repeated times. Babies learn that certain kinds of behavior are rewarded with positive responses, such as smiles, hugs, or praise. Because love is important to them, they repeat those behaviors. Babies also learn to avoid behavior that provokes negative responses like frowns or scolding.

Caregivers have to be sure to provide more positive than negative attention. When babies receive negative attention more often than positive, problems may result. The children are likely to do those things that bring on the negative response. They do so because they crave any kind of attention.

Babies are more sensitive to attitudes than to words. For example, if a mother says "no" as her ten-month-old blows food all over the high chair tray, yet laughs at the same time, the baby thinks she approves. This kind of mixed message can be very confusing.

To help a child understand what behavior is expected, parents and other caregivers must provide consistency. They must repeatedly act the same way. A baby will become confused if the same behavior provokes a positive response one time and a negative response the next. When adults change their mind often about expectations or frequently switch moods, it's difficult for their children to learn appropriate behavior.

Emotions in Infancy

Think about all the different emotions you experience. You may feel happy, angry, anxious, fearful, or excited. Babies only gradually develop such emotions.

At birth, the range of emotions is limited to pleasure or satisfaction—when the baby is quiet—and pain or discomfort—when the baby cries. Between the end of the first and second months, babies show a new emotion that most parents welcome gladly—they feel delight, which they show by smiling. In the second month, babies also show different feelings with different kinds of crying. The chart on pages 308-309 shows when other emotions develop.

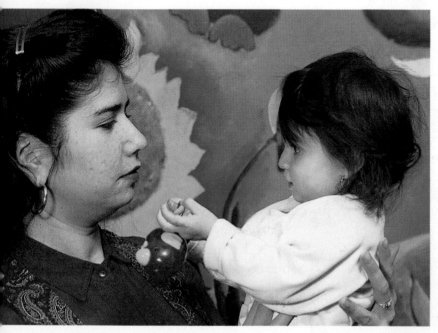

Why is it important to have tone of voice match your words when talking to a baby?

Ask the E?perts

Jean Illsley Clarke
Director of J.I. Consultants in
Minneapolis, Minnesota

BABIES *and Crying*

Q Our one-month-old baby cries and cries some evenings, and nothing seems to help. Should we just leave her alone and let her "cry it out"?

A This is a question many parents have. Most babies between the ages of three and twelve weeks have a fussy period at the end of the day.

My answer to your question really depends on what you mean by letting your baby "cry it out." For some parents, this means completely ignoring their baby. These parents believe—mistakenly—that a baby's crying is pointless and it isn't necessary to respond. This approach to crying is never appropriate.

Other parents let a baby "cry it out" during a fussy period by trying various methods of comforting the baby, one method at a time. Then they leave the baby alone for a short period—perhaps five minutes—between attempts to provide comfort. With this approach, the parents might try feeding, rocking, singing, talking, patting, carrying, adding more covers, removing covers, bundling, and loosening clothing all in turn. When they are out of the room, the baby can perhaps start learning to comfort himself or herself. This approach to crying it out can help both the baby and the baby's parents.

Crying is a baby's method of letting parents and other caregivers know about his or her needs. When the baby cries, they should be willing to listen, to respond by trying to figure out what the baby needs, and to meet the baby's needs as directly as possible. Check with a pediatrician if the problem is severe to rule out other causes.

Thinking It Through

1. What effect can letting a baby "cry it out" without any response have on the baby?
2. In the second method, why leave the baby alone after each attempt to comfort him or her?

When Emotions Develop

Babies develop their emotions gradually over time—just as their physical skills develop. They begin to show more specific responses to their world as they learn to connect their feelings to what they experience and the sensations that those experiences cause.

Delight: Babies show delight by smiling, perhaps in response to an adult who is making funny faces at them.

PLEASANT EMOTIONS

| Month 1 | Month 2 | Month 3 | Month 4 | Month 5 | Mo |

UNPLEASANT EMOTIONS

Distress: Very young babies express any discomfort or unhappiness by crying.

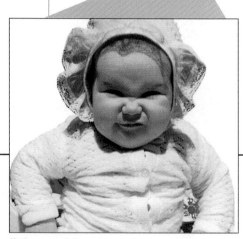

Disgust: Babies begin to show their dislikes very clearly.

Elation: Babies show high spirits with their whole body.

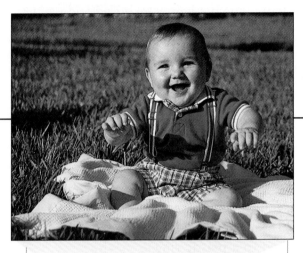

Affection: Babies first show affection for care-givers. Affection for other children comes later.

| Month 7 | Month 8 | Month 9 | Month 10 | Month 11 | Month 12 |

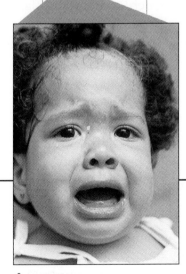

Anger: Babies first show their anger when they don't get their own way. Older babies show anger at objects as well as at people.

Fear: Babies begin to show fear of strangers at about eight months of age.

Crying and Comforting

The most obvious sign of an infant's emotions is crying. Newborns vary greatly in the amount and intensity of their crying. Some babies don't cry very often and are usually easy to comfort. These are what parents call "easy" or "good" babies. Other babies cry often and loudly, and it is usually hard to comfort them. These babies can be considered "difficult," because parents become frustrated when they can't calm the baby.

A young baby who is crying needs attention and care. The first step is to check for a physical problem. Is the baby hungry or in need of a diaper change? Is the infant too cold or too hot? Is there a burp left over from the last feeding? If none of these is the cause of the crying and the baby doesn't seem ill, the baby probably needs something else—your company, your cuddling, or your comforting. Remember that these are real needs, too.

As you and the baby get to know each other, you will probably discover which comforting measures work best. Here are a few to try:

- **Cuddle up with the baby in a rocking chair.** The combination of being held and rocked often soothes a crying baby. You can provide a similar combination by holding the baby close as you walk around.
- **Move the baby to a new position.** Perhaps the baby wants to lie in a different position but can't yet roll over. Maybe the baby wants to sit in an infant seat and feel involved with the rest of the family.
- **Talk softly to the baby or sing to the baby.** Even if you're not a great singer, the tone and rhythm of your voice, and the attention they indicate, may comfort the baby.
- **Offer a toy to interest and distract the baby.** The baby may be bored and want something to do. A favorite toy may end the crying.
- **Stroke the baby's back to give comfort.** Place the baby face down across your legs as you sit. Support the baby's head with one hand while gently rubbing the baby's back with the other.

Babies also develop their own techniques for comforting themselves. The most common comforting technique is sucking—on a thumb, a fist, or a **pacifier**—a nipple attached to a plastic ring.

Pacifiers, if used, must be used safely. *Never* tie the pacifier on a string around the baby's neck. To keep it from falling, use a short pacifier ribbon, which is attached both to the ring of the pacifier and to the baby's clothing. Check the pacifier often for cuts and tears on the surface. Also, clean it regularly.

Many babies also comfort themselves with a soft object such as a certain blanket or stuffed toy. They develop a special attachment to this object and use it for comfort when they are sleepy or anxious.

The Developing Brain

Most babies love to be rocked, and rocking has a variety of benefits—including for the baby's brain. Gentle rocking stimulates the cortex of the brain. This stimulation helps the baby gain weight, develops the baby's sight and hearing, and promotes regular sleep habits.

Other babies comfort themselves by twisting their hair or by rocking themselves back and forth in their crib.

The baby's special self-comforting technique is an indication of his or her individuality and development. Children typically outgrow their need for such techniques and, when they are ready, give up these habits without a problem.

Colic

Catrina was at her wit's end. Little Brandon seemed to cry constantly every night, starting at about nine o'clock and going on until midnight. During the day, he was a cheerful, happy baby, but at night—when Catrina was tired and impatient—he became impossible to comfort.

When Catrina talked to the pediatrician, the doctor explained that Brandon had **colic** (COL-ick). Colic is marked by a baby's being extremely fussy every day. The periods of crying usually come any time between six o'clock in the evening and midnight. Colic is usually the worst when the baby is about six weeks old. The fussy periods then begin to grow shorter until they finally end.

If intense crying happens at all times, the problem may be something else. The baby's parents should check with the pediatrician if they are in doubt. Sometimes the baby's partially digested food comes back up.

This problem called "reflux," can cause colic-like symptoms.

Doctors don't understand why babies get colic. It may have to do with gas gathering in the stomach. One step to try to prevent colic is to eliminate food that may be causing it. Breast-feeding mothers should try avoiding milk products, cabbage, caffeine, and onions, any of which may be irritating the baby. If the baby is bottle-fed, pediatricians recommend using a soy-based, rather than a milk-based, formula.

Signs of Social Development in Infancy

Like physical and emotional development, social development follows a predictable pattern. The following list shows the common signs of social development for babies during the first year. Like all such lists, this one shows typical development for many babies. It is a general guide for what

Some parents feel frustrated until a baby begins to smile at about two months of age. *Why do you think that changes how parents feel?*

children ordinarily go through, not a checklist for helping you understand an individual baby. As you read, think about the brain development that makes each step possible.

- **The first days of life.** From birth onward, babies respond to human voices. A calm, soothing voice will quiet a baby, a harsh or loud voice will upset a baby.
- **One month.** Most babies stop crying when lifted or touched. A baby's face brightens when he or she sees a familiar person such as a parent.
- **Two months.** By two months, babies smile at people. Because their eyes can now follow moving objects, they enjoy watching people move about the room.
- **Three months.** Babies turn their head in response to a voice. Now they want companionship as well as physical care.
- **Four months.** Babies laugh out loud. They look to others for entertainment.
- **Five months.** Babies show an increased interest in family members other than parents. They may cry when they are left alone in a room. At this age, babies babble—to their toys, dolls, stuffed animals, or themselves.
- **Six months.** Babies love company and attention. They delight in playing games such as peekaboo.
- **Seven months.** Babies prefer parents over other family members or strangers.
- **Eight months.** Babies prefer to be in a room with other people. Babies who can crawl by this age may move from room to room looking for company.
- **Nine and ten months.** Now active socially, babies creep after their parents and are often underfoot. Babies love attention. They enjoy being chased and playing games in which they throw toys again and again—with someone else picking them up each time.
- **Eleven and twelve months.** Babies are most often friendly and happy at this age. They are also sensitive to others' emotions—and know how to influence and adjust to the emotions of people around them. Babies like to be the center of attention. By this time, they are usually tolerant of strangers.

Stranger Anxiety

Another important sign of social development may seem difficult to parents and caregivers but is still a significant stage for each baby. Parents see it in the second half of the first year, often around the age of eight months. At this time, babies develop

At eight months, the baby begins to crawl and seek out company. *What dangers does this present?*

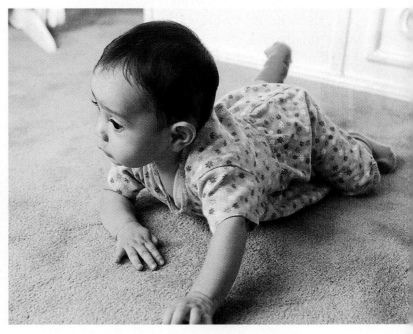

stranger anxiety, a fear, usually expressed by crying, of unfamiliar people. During this period, a baby who used to sit cheerfully on anyone's lap suddenly screams and bursts into tears when an unfamiliar person approaches.

Stranger anxiety shows that the baby's memory is improving. The child can now better remember the faces of parents and caregivers. These are the people who provide comfort and security. Most other faces suddenly seem strange and make the baby feel fearful.

At this stage by remind new people to approach the baby slowly and to give the baby time to adjust. Try to keep the baby's routine as regular as possible. This is not a good time to introduce sudden changes in activities or caregivers.

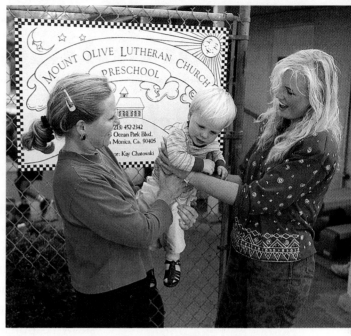

How is stranger anxiety related to intellectual growth?

SECTION 9-2 REVIEW

✔ Check Your Understanding

1. How do parents' smiles and frowns help babies learn good behavior?
2. When do babies begin to smile?
3. Name two measures that might comfort a crying baby.
4. What is colic?
5. What are two signs of social development that many one-month-old babies exhibit?
6. What two signs of social development appear around the fifth month?
7. What is stranger anxiety? When does it develop?

Putting Knowledge Into Practice

1. **Analyzing.** What toys and equipment encourage caregiver-infant interaction? Which would discourage it? How could this be conveyed to parents and other caregivers?
2. **Applying.** Myong Ok's little baby is afraid of her younger brother, Sung. Suggest specific ways Myong Ok can help the baby develop a sense of comfort with her brother.
3. **Observing and Participating.** Watch one or more one-year-olds. What signs of emotions do you see? How are those emotions expressed? Share your findings with the class. Can you see any patterns?

Parenting With Care

Helping a Baby Develop A Sense of Trust

The kind of care babies receive in their first year determines how they view themselves and the world around them.

For every baby, the foundation of a strong and healthy self-concept is trust.

Responsive Care
An infant who is upset or fussy needs to be soothed. However, a content baby needs attention as well. Here are some ways to show responsiveness:

- Hold and cuddle the baby often. Carry the baby close to you as you walk, both indoors and outdoors.
- Give the baby who can crawl the freedom to explore in a safe environment, not just in a playpen.
- Answer the baby's babbles and "funny noises" with your own noises, words, and sentences.
- Let the baby sense your love in your face, voice, and touch.
- Learn to read the baby's signals. Smiling and cooing might mean, "Let's play." Turning or looking away may be the baby's way of saying, "That's enough—time to rest."
- Calm an unhappy baby with close, rhythmic movement, and soothing sounds.

Routines
Babies seem to need a predictable daily routine in order to thrive. Start with the baby's unique pattern of eating, sleeping, and waking. Then work out a routine that makes sense for you and the baby. For example, if you always hold the baby and sing to him or her after a feeding, the baby learns to look forward to it.

New Faces, New Places
Babies also need to learn to accept new situations. A caregiver can soothe fears and help the baby feel secure in unfamiliar surroundings.

Most babies go through a stage of fearing strangers. During this period, don't force a baby to sit on an unfamiliar person's lap. Instead, allow the baby time to get used to the new person. Stay close by and show the baby that you trust this person.

You can help the baby get used to strangers by taking him or her to stores, parks, and other places where young children play. Talk to the baby in a calm, reassuring voice about what to expect and about what is happening.

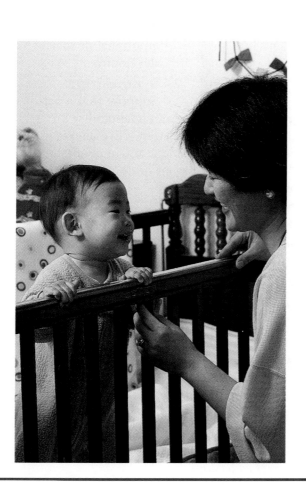

Following Up

1. **Management.** Some parents use cloth carriers that allow them to carry a baby on their chest when the baby is younger, and on their backs when the baby is older. What emotional benefit would this have for the baby?

2. **Thinking Skills.** Strangers often come up to Stephanie and Jamar to comment that their baby Calvin is very cute. Calvin, however, often cries when strangers come too close. How should Calvin's parents handle such situations when they are out shopping?

Summary

✔ Emotional development deals with feelings. Social development deals with relationships with others. (Section 9-1)

✔ Attachment to caregivers is necessary for normal emotional and social development. (Section 9-1)

✔ Children and adults have different temperaments, which affect how they interact with the world. (Section 9-1)

✔ Children learn behavior through their relationships with others. (Section 9-2)

✔ Babies develop emotionally and socially through patterns. (Section 9-2)

8. How should parents and caregivers respond to babies who cry? (Section 9-2)

9. How does a baby's growing mobility help his or her social development? (Section 9-2)

Thinking Critically

1. **Evaluating.** Which do you think is more important, emotional or social development? Why?

2. **Synthesizing.** Suppose that a parent was high in the trait adaptability but a child was low in that trait. Give an example of how they could come in conflict. What could the parent do to prevent problems from arising?

3. **Diagramming.** Use the information in the chapter about the stages of social development to create a chart showing how these stages appear at different ages.

Reviewing the Facts

1. Define emotional and social development, and explain how they are related? (Section 9-1)

2. What did Harry Harlow's experiments with monkeys show? (Section 9-1)

3. How do human babies respond when they are denied emotional support and social interaction? (Section 9-1)

4. What can parents do to create a good climate for raising a baby? (Section 9-1)

5. What is temperament? (Section 9-1)

6. Give an example of how babies learn emotional and social skills from caregivers. (Section 9-2)

7. What emotion is related to stranger anxiety and develops about the same time? (Section 9-2)

Taking Action

1. **Children's Rights.** Work with a partner to write a "Baby's Bill of Rights" that lists everything you think babies have the right to receive from their parents. Make your list into a poster. *(Communication)*

2. **Helping Out.** A mother you know has become frustrated with how much her baby cries. What advice would you give her? *(Leadership)*

CONNECTIONS

Cross-Curricular Connections

1. **Health.** Find out how a child's emotional and social development is affected when a parent abuses drugs or alcohol. Report to the class.

2. **Language Arts.** Research to find suggestions to help parents who have babies who suffer from colic. Create a brochure that communicates these suggestions.

3. **Social Studies.** Choose two of the temperaments described in this chapter. Develop a list of questions that could be used on a test to determine whether a person was high or low in those temperaments.

Workplace Connections

1. **Personal Qualities.** Choose three traits of temperament. Write a paragraph explaining why you think it would be very useful for a child care worker to be high in those qualities.

2. **Basic Skills.** Create a chart showing new parents how they can expect their newborn to develop either emotionally or socially.

Family and Community Connections

1. **Father's Role.** What do you think the father's role can be in building trust? Write a list of suggestions for fathers to help build their child's emotional health.

2. **Forming Attachment.** Make a list of things parents can do to build a strong attachment to a baby.

3. **Talking to Others.** When Elijah gives his son a pacifier, his aunt criticizes the action. She says that a pacifier is bad for the child. What should Elijah say?

Technology Connections

1. **Internet.** Find an Internet site that offers advice to parents of babies. Find out what advice it gives for dealing with children who are high in any one of the nine temperament traits. Report your findings to the class.

CHAPTER 10

Intellectual Development During the First Year

Seven-month-old Daniel sat in a playpen beside a park bench. His mother was nearby, helping Daniel's four-year-old sister play on the swing and slide.

Daniel watched them from time to time, but he gave most of his attention to a red plastic cup. He turned the cup over and over, staring at it intently. Then he started chewing on its bottom, rim, and handle. Occasionally, he stopped chewing on it and banged the cup on the playpen floor.

After a while, Daniel grew tired of the cup and dropped it. He began pulling himself up to a standing position. When he succeeded, he held onto the edge of the playpen and laughed. Suddenly, he sat down again. He looked like he might cry, but instead tried to stand another time. After several tries, he managed to do so. While he stood, his mother said "Look at you, Daniel," and applauded. After two or three minutes, Daniel lost his balance and fell to a sitting position.

"When he succeeded in pulling himself up to a standing position, he laughed."

Understanding Intellectual Development of Infants

Consider the differences between a newborn and a one-year-old. The newborn can't move; the one-year-old can move where desired by crawling or walking. A newborn communicates only by crying; a one-year-old can use gestures and perhaps even words. A newborn can't pick up an object; a one-year-old can play with a stacking toy. In the first year of life, babies make amazing advances in their intellectual abilities.

KEY TERMS

attention span
cause and effect
concrete operations period
formal operations period
object permanence
perception
preoperational period
sensorimotor period
symbolic thinking

OBJECTIVES:

- Give examples of signs of intellectual growth in infants.
- Identify and give examples of Piaget's stages of learning.
- Explain how caregivers can make use of Piaget's ideas.

Learning in the First Year

Right from birth, babies have a number of capabilities. Newborns can hear, see, taste, smell, and feel. They use these abilities as the building blocks of learning.

A baby's brain is fed by what he or she experiences through the senses. These experiences help the brain become organized. Babies' ability to learn from the senses, called **perception** (purr-SEP-shun), improves. As you have learned, newborns can't see objects in three dimensions, but three-month-olds can. In time, babies develop the hand-eye coordination to grasp and handle objects. They develop many skills, as shown in the chart on pages 322-323.

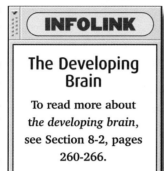

INFOLINK

The Developing Brain

To read more about *the developing brain*, see Section 8-2, pages 260-266.

In just the first year of life, babies also develop four abilities that show growing thinking power:

- **Remembering.** In the first few months, babies develop the ability to remember. The information from the senses can be interpreted in light of past experiences. A two- or three-month-old baby may stop crying when someone enters the room because the baby knows that he or she is now likely to be picked up and comforted.
- **Making associations.** This act—the baby's ceasing to cry—also indicates association. The baby associates a parent or other caregiver with receiving comfort.
- **Understanding cause and effect.** Babies also develop an understanding of **cause and effect**, the idea that one action results in another action or condition. When a baby closes his or her eyes, it gets dark. When the baby opens them again, it gets light. Sucking causes milk to flow. If the baby stops sucking, the milk stops. In short, every time the infant does something, something else happens.

As babies' motor skills develop, cause-and-effect learning changes. By seven or eight months, babies can throw things deliberately. They can pull the string on a toy and make the toy move. At this age, babies have a better understanding of their own power to make certain things happen.

Of course, babies learn by repetition. That's why eight-month-old Jenny continues to drop her bowl from her perch in the high chair onto the floor.

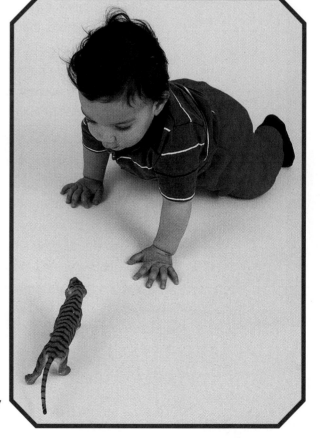

When babies' memories improve, they will seek out a toy that they want.

AGES	DEVELOPMENTAL CHANGES
1-2 months	• Follows moving objects with eyes. • Gains information through senses. • Prefers faces to objects. • Cries to indicate needs. • Can distinguish between familiar and unfamiliar voices.
3-4 months	• Recognizes caregivers' faces. • Can distinguish between familiar and unfamiliar faces. • Grasps objects that touch hand. • Tries to swipe at objects. • Interested in own hands and feet. • Practices making sounds. • Responds when caregiver talks.
5-6 months	• Is alert for longer periods of time, up to two hours. • Reaches for objects and grasps them with entire hand. • Studies objects carefully. • Looks for objects that are dropped. • Plays peekaboo. • Recognizes own name. • Distinguishes between friendly and angry voices. • Makes sounds to indicate pleasure and displeasure.
7-8 months	• Imitates the actions of others. • Begins to understand cause and effect. • Remembers things that have happened. • Smiles at self in mirror. • Sorts objects by size. • Solves simple problems. • Recognizes some words. • Babbling imitates inflections of speech.

Continued

Average Intellectual Development: Birth to Twelve Months (Continued)

AGES	DEVELOPMENTAL CHANGES
9-10 months	• Searches for hidden objects. • Handles medium-sized objects skillfully. • Takes objects out of containers and puts them back in. • Plays pat-a-cake. • Responds to some words. • May say a few words. • Obeys simple commands or directions.
11-12 months	• Manipulates objects skillfully. • Likes to look at picture books. • Fits blocks or boxes inside one another. • Knows parts of body. • Can pick up small objects with forefinger and thumb. • Recognizes many words. • Speaks some words regularly.

She simply wants to be sure that *every time* she drops the bowl, it will fall to the floor. Parents can become frustrated with these repeated actions—after all, for Jenny to repeat her experiment, someone needs to pick the bowl up! If they remember that their little scientists are simply learning about the world, they may find the patience to allow the game to continue.

Repetition has another benefit. Repeated actions strengthen connections between nerve cells in the brain. As a result, they can work together in a coordinated way more smoothly and quickly.

• **Paying attention.** A baby's **attention span**—the length of time a person can concentrate on a task without getting bored—grows longer. If the same object is presented over and over again, the baby's response to the object will eventually become less enthusiastic. The baby's diminishing response is a way of saying, "That's old stuff. I've seen it before." Generally, bright babies have a short attention span—they tend to lose interest sooner than babies of average or below-average intelligence. (Beyond infancy, children with above average intelligence typically have a longer attention span than others their age.)

Piaget's Theories

Jean Piaget, a Swiss psychologist who died in 1980, had a great influence on what we know about how children learn. Piaget was trying to understand how children's intellectual skills developed. He found that intellectual development followed a pattern. Children learn to master one thinking skill before they can master another.

Children can't be forced by parents or teachers to develop understanding any faster than their abilities mature. On the other hand, children who don't get the chance to apply their developing skills may never reach their full potential. For this reason, it is important for children to have the constant opportunities for learning.

According to Piaget, learning stages appear in the same order in all children. What differs is the ages at which the stages develop, although average ages can be given. He identified four major periods.

The Sensorimotor Period

The **sensorimotor period** (SEN-suh-ree-MOE-tur), from birth to about age two, is Piaget's first stage of learning. During this period, babies learn primarily through their senses and their own actions.

During the sensorimotor period, babies come to understand an important concept. Usually at about ten months, they realize that objects continue to exist even when they are out of sight. This concept is called **object permanence.** At four months, Maria drops her rubber ring toy and it rolls behind her. She simply looks for something else to play with. At eleven months, when her ball rolls out of sight, Maria actively looks for it. She has learned the concept of object permanence.

The sensorimotor period can be broken down into six shorter stages. At each stage, a baby has specific intellectual abilities. The

Swiss psychologist Jean Piaget carried out pioneering studies of how children learn. *How can caregivers use what Piaget discovered about children's thinking?*

PERIOD	APPROXIMATE AGES	CHARACTERISTICS
Sensorimotor	Birth to two years	Children learn through their senses and own actions.
Preoperational	Two to seven years	Children think in terms of their own activities and what they perceive at the moment.
Concrete operations	Seven to eleven years	Children can think logically but still learn best through experience.
Formal operations	Eleven years to adulthood	People are capable of abstract thinking.

chart on page 326 explains these six stages. It will better help you understand how learning occurs.

The Preoperational Period

The **preoperational period** (pree-OP-ur-AY-shun-ul), Piaget's second stage, typically lasts from age two to seven. In this period, children think about everything in terms of their own activities and of what they perceive at the moment. Children may believe that the moon follows them around. A child in this stage may think that the same amount of a liquid becomes more to drink when it is poured from a short, wide glass into a tall, thin glass. Because the water is higher in the second glass, the child concludes that there must be more of it.

In the preoperational period, children begin to understand abstract terms like *love* and *beauty*. Concentration, though, is limited to one thing at a time. Children this age

Babies enjoy playing peeka-boo, which helps them learn object permanence. *How does this game also involve interaction?*

STAGE	APPROXIMATE AGES	CHARACTERISTICS
Stage 1	Birth to one month	• Practices inborn reflexes. • Does not understand self as separate person.
Stage 2	One to four months	• Combines two or more reflexes. • Develops hand-mouth coordination.
Stage 3	Four to eight months	• Acts intentionally to produce results. • Improves hand-eye coordination.
Stage 4	Eight to twelve months	• Begins to solve problems. • Finds partially hidden objects. • Imitates others.
Stage 5	Twelve to eighteen months	• Finds hidden objects. • Explores and experiments. • Understands that objects exist independently.
Stage 6	Eighteen to twenty-four months	• Solves problems by thinking through sequences. • Can think using symbols. • Begins imaginative thinking.

tend to solve problems by pretending or imitating, rather than by thinking the problems through. During this period, children may not even be aware of what is real and what is make-believe.

The Concrete Operations Period

The **concrete operations period** is Piaget's third stage of learning, lasting usually from seven to eleven years of age. In this stage, children can think logically but still learn best from direct experience. When problem solving during this stage, children still rely on actually being able to see or experience the problem.

However, logical thinking is possible. Children understand that pouring water from one container to another doesn't change the amount of water. They can also comprehend that operations can be reversed. For example, subtraction will "undo" addition and division is the reverse of multiplication. During this stage, children also learn to make more complex categories, such as classifying kinds of animals or types of food.

The Formal Operations Period

The **formal operations period**, the fourth stage, lasts from about age eleven through adulthood. In this period, children become capable of abstract thinking. In other words, people in this stage are able to think about what might have been the cause of an event without really experiencing that cause. This ability allows problem solving just by thinking. People in this stage can also form ideals and understand deeper, less obvious meanings or subtle messages.

Using Piaget's Ideas

In recent years, other thinkers have raised questions about Piaget's ideas. They point out that his experiments focused on only a certain kind of learning. They charge that the boundaries of his stages are sometimes set too rigidly. They argue that in different kinds of experiments, children have been shown to understand concepts before the stage that Piaget said they should.

Still, his work remains important. Piaget showed that young children learn in their own ways—not as adults do. Older children can learn through **symbolic thinking**, the use of words and numbers to stand for ideas. Younger children, who can't yet think in symbolic ways, rely on concrete experiences. For example, the statement "I have three blocks" means nothing to a young

In the preoperational period, children sometimes have difficulty separating what is real and what is make-believe. *What implications does this have for children when they watch television?*

Why will a young child hold up three fingers while saying "three"?

child. The child has to see the blocks. A three-year-old will hold up three fingers when asked how old he or she is, even though the child may say the words, too.

The preschool child needs lessons presented with objects or activities, not just symbols. Verbal instruction from a teacher or parent has only a minor role in learning during the early years.

SECTION 10-1 REVIEW

✔ Check Your Understanding

1. What is perception? Give an example of how a baby's perception changes during the first year of life.
2. How can pull toys help a baby learn cause and effect?
3. Explain what an attention span is.
4. What are Piaget's four periods of learning and what are their approximate time spans?
5. What do babies use to learn during Piaget's first period of development?
6. Give an example of how a person can use abstract thinking, which begins in Piaget's fourth period.
7. What is the significance of Piaget's findings about symbolic thinking?

Putting Knowledge Into Practice

1. **Analyzing.** What learning ability does the game pat-a-cake build?
2. **Synthesizing.** How does the game of peekaboo contribute to the development of object permanence? How is memory linked to object permanence?
3. **Observing and Participating.** Try conducting one of Piaget's experiments with a younger child. Fill a short, wide glass with liquid and show it to the child. Then pour the liquid into a taller, thinner container and ask whether the taller glass has more liquid, less liquid, or the same amount. How do your findings compare to those of your classmates? What difference does the age of the child make?

CAREER OPPORTUNITIES

Toy Store Worker

A CONVERSATION WITH TONY NUNEZ

How did you become interested in becoming a toy store worker? Well, I've always loved to play with toys myself. In high school, I took a child development course and learned why toys are so important to children's learning. I had always enjoyed working in stores, so I thought I would combine these interests.

What are the tasks and responsibilities of a toy store worker? Much of our work is very simple—we stock the shelves, handle purchases when people know what they want, and take care of returns. What I enjoy most, though, is when customers ask about particular toys. Because I hear all the time about what children play with and like, I can give others good suggestions.

What is the work environment like? A store is a very busy place. We have areas where children can watch videos. There's music playing, so it can get noisy.

What are the working hours like? The store is open from 10:00 a.m. to 10:00 p.m. I usually work 40 hours a week except at the end of the year. Come holiday season, I work lots of overtime.

What aptitudes are needed to be a toy store worker? You have to be good with math. You really need to like children. Good communication skills and an understanding of children help you find out what people are looking for and give them advice.

TOY STORE WORKER

Education and Training. Toy store workers need a high school diploma. They usually get the training they need on the job.

Career Outlook. The demand for toy store workers should be steady in the near future.

---CONNECTING SCHOOL TO CAREER---

1. **Technology.** Why would a toy store worker need to be good at math if scanners and cash registers calculate the amount of a sale?
2. **Interpersonal Skills.** Suppose you were a toy store worker during the holiday shopping period. What would you say to a parent who was angry because the item he or she wanted was out of stock?

Helping Babies Learn

Intellectual development of an infant is closely linked to the responsiveness of others. That is, babies learn more and learn faster when parents and caregivers comfort them, smile at them, talk to them, and play with them. A baby treated this way is likely to be brighter than a similar child who does not receive loving, attentive care. Parents are babies' most important teachers.

KEY TERMS

age appropriate
childproof
recall

OBJECTIVES:

- Discuss ways parents and caregivers can help babies' intellectual growth.
- Identify toys appropriate for a baby's age.
- Explain how babies develop communication skills.

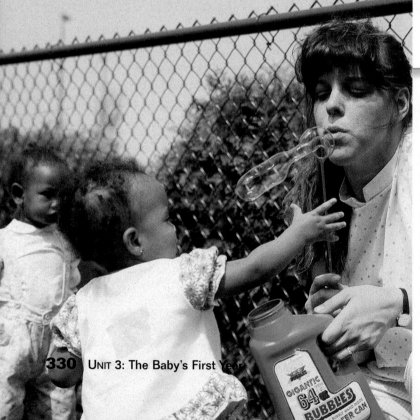

Encouraging Learning

Even the youngest babies learn about the world from the care they receive. When Tyler feels uncomfortable in his stomach, he cries. Then his mother picks him up and nurses him. That makes the discomfort in his stomach go away. The events—discomfort, crying, cuddling, being fed—are connected. There is a pattern.

Age-appropriate toys help children develop both physically and intellectually. *How might this toy promote development?*

If the baby's cries are not answered, the baby sees no relationship between its needs and the caregiver's actions. There is no pattern.

Giving a child basic care, then, helps build that child's mental abilities. Those who care for children can influence the children's intellectual development in other ways. Encouraging learning doesn't require money or special toys. Rather, it depends on the attention, knowledge, and time of parents and other caregivers.

Here are some ways that caregivers can encourage learning:

- **Learn about child development.** Understanding how an average child develops can help you provide learning experiences that are **age appropriate**. That means they are suitable for the age and individual needs of a child.
- **Give your time and attention.** No baby needs attention every waking moment. However, you can help a baby thrive—and learn—just by talking to the baby and playing simple games.
- **Provide positive feedback.** When the baby demonstrates a new skill or tries out a new activity, show your pleasure and respond with praise. Your reaction will encourage the baby to keep trying new things.

- **Express your love.** Use your personal style to show your love for the baby. You'll be helping the baby grow self-confident and encouraging him or her to try more—and to learn more.
- **Talk, talk, talk.** Talking has many benefits. When parents talk to infants, they help them learn about their environment. Current research shows that the more caregivers talk to a baby, the faster the child's brain develops. Talking builds feelings of security, too.

The "Parenting with Care" feature on pages 340-341 presents more ideas for creating a stimulating environment and helping babies learn.

INFOLINK

Reading to Children

For more about *reading to children*, see page 338.

Safe Learning

To encourage learning, allow the baby as much freedom of movement at home as possible. In the first few months, move the baby from room to room to be with the family. A baby who spends times in different rooms and with the family learns more than a baby who is kept alone in a crib. Older babies who can crawl or walk should not be restricted to playpens for long periods of time.

It is better to **childproof** as much of the home as possible and to monitor the child's activities. Childproofing is a matter of taking steps to protect a child from possible dangers. For example, placing gates at the top and bottom of stairways prevents a child from falling. Learning occurs best when children can explore and try new things—safely.

INFOLINK

Childproofing

For more about *child-proofing*, see the "Parenting with Care" feature at the end of Chapter 11.

The Importance of Play

Ten-month-old Beth sits on the kitchen floor, thumping a spoon against the bottom of a saucepan. She has discovered her own "educational toy." With it, she learns that a certain action will produce a particular sound. She delights in the sound and in her own power to produce it.

For children, play is work as well as pleasure. Researchers have clearly established that playtime is essential to intellectual development. Toys are the tools for learning.

Play is also a physical necessity through which development takes place. When a baby shakes a rattle, stacks blocks, throws a ball, or chews on a teething toy, the activity is not just for amusement. These are serious, absorbing tasks through which babies strengthen their muscles, refine their motor skills, and learn about the world.

Different Toys for Different Ages

Because babies mature and change rapidly during the first year, their toys need to change, too. Here are some ideas about appropriate toys for different stages:

Add locks to low cabinets. This will provide a safe environment that gives a baby an opportunity to explore.

- **Birth to three months.** A baby at this age can do little except look and listen. Bright colors and interesting sounds stimulate development of the senses. A mobile hung safely above the crib is interesting for the baby to watch. The baby's random arm and leg movements can set the objects in motion and produce sounds. Brightly colored crib liners, wallpaper, and pictures also provide interest.
- **Four to six months.** The sense of touch is important in this period. Babies need things to touch, handle, bang, shake, suck, and chew. Choose toys that are small enough to handle easily but too large to swallow. All items and pieces should be at least 1½ inches (3.8 cm) across. Teething rings, cups, rattles, and plastic toys are good choices. Stuffed toys are fun to touch, and toys that squeak give results when the baby acts. Providing objects with different textures helps the child learn by touch. Babies this age like simple picture books. Choose washable books with colorful pictures of familiar objects.
- **Seven to nine months.** Babies still need things to handle, throw, pound, bang, and shake. Anything that makes a noise fascinates babies of this age. They enjoy blocks, balls, large plastic beads that pop apart, and roly-poly toys. Safe household items are just as interesting as purchased toys. Pots and pans with lids, and plastic containers to stack make great playthings.
- **Ten to twelve months.** Babies of this age need things to crawl after. Those who are already walking like toys to push or pull. During this period, children especially enjoy toys to manipulate. Baskets, boxes, and other containers are fun. Babies like to put things into them and then dump them out again. Picture books are good for looking at alone or for brief story times during the day or before bed.

Some books not only have pictures but also different textures for a baby to touch. *Why would these be particularly good for babies four to six months old?*

Choosing Toys

When choosing playthings for a young child, look for toys that encourage participation and use. Younger children need simple toys. As a baby's abilities increase, toys can be more complex.

Toys, especially those labeled "educational," can be expensive. Sometimes they have limited usefulness. You can provide a baby with as much fun and learning by making common household items available. Try offering the baby items such as plastic measuring spoons, plastic measuring cups, a clean bucket, plastic bowls, a metal pan or mixing bowl and a large spoon, or a large cardboard box with a "window" cut in it. You'll be surprised at the variety of ways young children play with these items.

When you buy toys, look for ones that will remain interesting and appropriate for a number of years. A set of blocks is a good example. At the age of six months, Reynaldo grasped and inspected his blocks. By his first birthday, he could stack several blocks into a tower. At the age of three, he used the blocks to make roads for his cars. Now, at age six, Reynaldo creates elaborate houses and castles, using every available block.

Developing Communication Skills

One of an infant's major tasks is to learn to communicate with others. This skill depends on development in all areas—physical, emotional, social, and intellectual. There are wide differences in the rate of development from baby to baby. However, a normal baby should show steady improvement in communication skills.

The same type of toy can serve different purposes at different ages. At five months (left), a baby explores shaped objects with his mouth to learn about texture. At eleven months (right), a child can sort the shapes.

Safe Toys

Common household objects often make the best toys for babies—but make sure they are safe. Never allow a baby or young child to play with plastic bags. These may end up over the child's head and can cause suffocation. Small objects that could be swallowed should be off limits as well—they may cause choking. Stay away from objects that could splinter, tear, or break, especially if they can produce sharp corners that could cut the child. Finally, avoid giving a child any sharp or pointed objects. Even something as common as a pen or pencil could cause an injury.

Consumers can check on the safety of store-bought toys or equipment. From time to time, the Consumer Product Safety Commission decides to **recall** a toy—ordering that it be taken off the market or brought back to the manufacturer for needed repairs. If you have access to a computer and the Internet, you can check on product recalls by visiting the web site of the Consumer Product Safety Commission.

FOLLOWING UP
1. Would it be safe to let an infant play with a plastic container that used to hold medicine? Why or why not?
2. If you don't have access to the Internet, how could you find out if a toy was safe?

The Developing Brain

At four months, babies can respond to the different sounds of many different languages. By nine or ten months, they show more interest in the language of their parents and tend not to focus on other sounds.

Communicating Without Words

Babies communicate long before they can talk. By the end of the first year, they can effectively make most of their needs and wants known without words.

Crying is a baby's first means of communication. Babies quickly learn that crying produces a response—someone usually comes and tries to relieve their discomfort. Within a month or so, the crying takes on a pattern. A cry is followed by a pause to listen for reactions. If no response arrives, the baby resumes crying.

The World's Children

Speaking in Signs

Of course, children can learn to communicate in complex ways without words, too. Deaf children learn to speak using sign language. Deaf people in Nicaragua recently developed their own sign language—and may have given us a glimpse into how languages developed.

In the late 1970s, the Nicaraguan government brought deaf people in the country into the same schools for the first time. Each of these people had developed their own way of communicating with their families by using signs. As they met one another, they began to adopt some of those signs and reject others. The result—a common sign language where none had existed before.

SHARE YOUR THOUGHTS

1. How can signs be used by people from two different cultures to talk to one another?
2. If you were developing a sign language, how would you communicate abstract ideas like cooperation and love? Think of two abstract ideas and try to identify a way to communicate them.

The baby soon develops different cries for different problems. A cry indicating hunger may be interrupted by sucking movements. A cry of pain may include groans and whimpers. You can learn to identify the baby's problem by the type of cry.

Babies also send messages with movements and gestures. It's clear that a wiggling baby doesn't want to get dressed. An eleven-month-old who pushes away a bowl of a usually favorite food has had enough to eat. The baby who clings with both arms to a parent's leg is showing a sure sign of fear or shyness. The use of gestures continues into adulthood, but they are used more to reinforce words than as a substitute for words.

Finally, a baby communicates by making special sounds. Some sounds, such as giggles, grunts, and shrieks, carry obvious messages.

Learning to Speak

Before learning to talk, a baby must learn to associate meanings with words. This is a gradual process. It depends on caregivers talking to the baby, even when the baby doesn't appear to respond. For example, when you take a baby for a walk, talk about what you see. Use simple words, but not baby talk. Although the infant won't understand much of what you say, you are beginning to establish an important habit. Listening to other people talk—especially directly to the baby—is essential for an infant's language development. This interaction also helps build the child's brain.

A newborn is physically unable to speak. Over the first year, physical changes take place that allow the baby to make the sounds necessary for speech.

Babies get ready for real speech by babbling—repeating syllables and sounds. You may have heard babies endlessly repeating consonant and vowel sounds such as "mamamamama" or "gogogogo." Babbling is a baby's preparation for saying recognizable words. You can encourage babbling—and thus language development—by responding to and imitating the baby's sounds.

You can help a baby learn language by naming objects and talking about them. *What other occasions, besides mealtime, could this be done?*

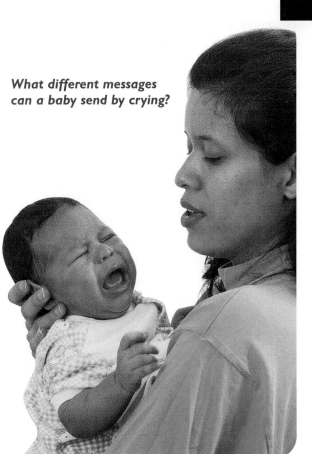

What different messages can a baby send by crying?

A child's first real words are usually understandable between the ages of eight and fifteen months. Because the infant typically has been babbling and coming close to real word sounds for some time, it isn't always easy to know exactly when a specific word is purposely spoken. First words are usually common, simple words that have special meaning for the baby, such as "mama," "dada," or "bye-bye." Most children don't have a large vocabulary or combine words into simple sentences until after their first birthday.

Ask the Eperts

Rachel Perkins
Child Development Technology
Instructor
Hinds Community College
Utica, Mississippi

READING *to Children*

Q When should I begin reading to my child?

A It's never too early to start reading to a child. In fact, I think parents should start reading to their babies even before the babies are born. This kind of reading is an extension of the natural conversing that parents do with their children, both before and after birth.

Reading is much more than a method of communicating information to a young child. Reading is a social event, and reading to a young child can help establish close emotional bonds. When you read to a young child, you have an opportunity for a special kind of personal communication and relationship.

The sense of competency and accomplishment that children gain from reading begins long before they start reading for themselves. They enjoy being part of the close relationship of adult and child.

Parents who especially enjoy reading offer their child another special gift by reading aloud. They have the opportunity to demonstrate and share a valued behavior. Of course, parents who aren't themselves avid readers shouldn't feel at a disadvantage in this situation. Whenever they take the time to read to young children and to enjoy sharing books and pictures together, they are also developing both attitudes and skills that will benefit their chil-

dren. Even parents whose own reading skills are limited can participate in these activities. They can look at books with young children, talk about the pictures and enjoy reading-related games and activities together.

Whatever the age of the child, and whatever the reading skills of the adult, the most important aspect of reading to young children is enjoyment. Don't rush, and don't make reading a daily chore. Instead, enjoy sharing books, and enjoy sharing time together.

Thinking It Through

1. How does reading aloud set a good example?
2. If parents don't know what books their child would like, what can they do?

Recent research has identified certain milestones of language development and roughly at what ages they occur:

- **One to six months.** At first, the child makes sounds such as coos, gurgles, and squeals. By the end of this period, the baby begins to experiment with making different sounds by changing the shape of the mouth.
- **Seven to twelve months.** The baby starts to make more different sounds. Babies may respond to their own names at these ages and add actions to words, waving when saying or hearing "bye-bye." By the end of this period, babies connect words to their meanings.
- **Thirteen to eighteen months.** Children slowly build their language abilities in this period. At around eighteen months, vocabulary begins to grow very quickly and children use words in combinations such as "no nap" and "want juice."
- **Eighteen months to two years.** In this time, children learn as many as twelve words a day. By two years, most know a few thousand words and begin to use words to express their feelings.
- **Two to two-and-a-half years.** Children begin to construct three- and four-word sentences. They begin to use pronouns.
- **Two-and-a-half to three years.** Children speak in longer sentences that follow the rules of grammar for tense (past and present) and using plurals. They also understand that the order of words in a sentence can affect meaning.

SECTION 10-2 REVIEW

✔ Check Your Understanding

1. How does a baby learn from the care he or she receives?
2. Why should caregivers choose toys that are age appropriate?
3. What are five guidelines for parents to help children learn?
4. What is childproofing?
5. Why are bright colors and toys with sounds good for babies from birth to three months?
6. Before they learn to talk, do babies communicate? If so, how? If not, why not?
7. What age period is marked by rapid vocabulary growth and using words to express feeling?

Putting Knowledge Into Practice

1. **Applying.** Look at the list of developmental milestones on pages 322-323. Based on the skills shown, create a list of toys suitable for each age.
2. **Synthesizing.** Explain how communication skills are related to a child's physical, social, emotional, and intellectual skills.
3. **Observing and Participating.** Visit a store and identify four toys for infants. Evaluate each toy, considering appropriateness, appeal, and price. Combine your findings with those of your classmates.

Parenting With Care

Creating a Stimulating Environment

Babies begin learning the moment they are born.

Parents and other caregivers influence both what and how a baby learns. Here are some suggestions for how they can help infants develop their senses and abilities.

Stimulating an Infant's Senses

Holding, cuddling, and gentle stroking all stimulate an infant's senses. Very young babies should have something interesting to look at, but just one or two things at a time. Simple shapes and bright or contrasting colors attract babies' interests.

A mobile hung over the crib provides both color and movement for the baby to watch. You can also hold a bright toy not close to the baby's face and then move the toy slowly, letting the baby's eyes follow it.

Infants like human faces even better than colorful pictures or toys. Let the baby look into your eyes as you hold and play with him or her or when you change a diaper.

Providing Objects the Baby Can Feel

You can also stimulate learning by surrounding the baby with interesting things to touch. Offering a variety of textures is more important than providing a great number of toys. Stuffed toys can have different textures, from a furry teddy bear to a simple beanbag. Different shapes encourage the baby to touch and explore, too. Small plastic squeeze bottles and empty plastic containers with lids are both educational and inexpensive.

Encouraging Listening Experiences

Babies learn from listening, too. The familiar voice of the primary caregiver is the first sound a baby learns to recognize. Rattles and squeak toys introduce different sounds.

Babies delight in music— from a wind-up toy, a CD, or a caregiver's singing. They can also enjoy different rhythms. With exciting music, they can "dance" in the arms of a caring adult. With soothing music, they can cuddle and be rocked.

As babies begin to experiment with their voice, they soon learn that their sounds bring responses from an attentive caregiver.

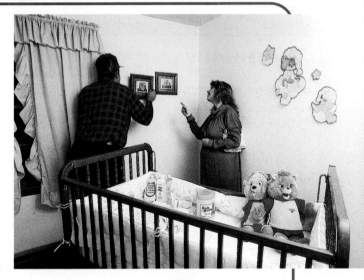

Developing Motor Skills

A stimulating environment can help babies learn about their own abilities to move. As the baby starts to reach and grasp, reinforce these skills by encouraging the baby to reach for a special toy. As the baby's large muscle skills develop, gently pull the baby into a sitting or standing position on your lap. Once the baby is ready to take a few steps, be sure your hand is there for the baby to hold.

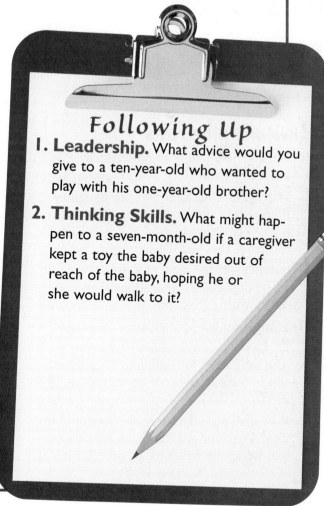

Following Up

1. **Leadership.** What advice would you give to a ten-year-old who wanted to play with his one-year-old brother?

2. **Thinking Skills.** What might happen to a seven-month-old if a caregiver kept a toy the baby desired out of reach of the baby, hoping he or she would walk to it?

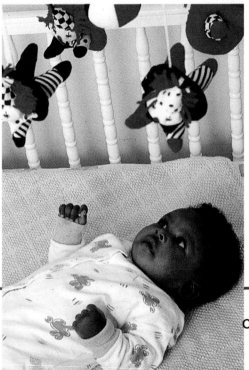

REVIEW &

Summary

✔ Babies learn through the senses, but in their first year they develop some key mental abilities. (Section 10-1)

✔ Based on his experiments, Swiss psychologist Jean Piaget said that all children go through the same four stages of learning. (Section 10-1)

✔ Children learn to think abstractly at about age eleven. (Section 10-1)

✔ Babies need a safe, stimulating environment for learning. (Section 10-2)

✔ Growing communication skills depend on a combination of mental, physical, emotional, and social development. (Section 10-2)

7. Give at least two ways to childproof a home. (Section 10-2)

8. What two ways of communicating other than crying do babies use? (Section 10-2)

9. How can a parent help a child develop language by responding to babbling? (Section 10-2)

Thinking Critically

1. **Making Inferences.** Why do you think care givers should avoid using baby talk when talking to infants?

2. **Sequencing.** Put the following six activities from Piaget's sensorimotor period in the correct order: (a) can think using symbols; (b) uses reflexes; (c) imitates others; (d) develops hand-mouth coordination; (e) develops hand-eye coordination; (f) understands that objects exist independently.

Reviewing the Facts

1. What are four signs of intellectual development in a child's first year? (Section 10-1)

2. Whenever Dierdra brings her daughter Brenna into the kitchen, the little girl says "Foo, Foo." What mental ability is Brenna showing? (Section 10-1)

3. In what shorter stage of Piaget's first period do children act intentionally to produce results? (Section 10-1)

4. What is object permanence? (Section 10-1)

5. In which stage, according to Piaget, are children likely to show abstract thinking? (Section 10-1)

6. Why give an infant only age-appropriate toys? Why not give the baby something that he or she will have to stretch mentally to master? (Section 10-2)

Taking Action

1. **Analyzing Toys.** Think of the earliest toy of yours that you can remember. When did you start playing with it? How did you play with it? *(Thinking Skills)*

2. **Making a Mobile.** Infants enjoy mobiles. Design a mobile to hang above an infant's crib. Make the mobile or draw a picture of it in color. *(Management)*

CONNECTIONS

Cross-Curricular Connections

1. **Health.** Find out more about childproofing. Make a poster instructing parents how to childproof their homes for infants.

2. **Language Arts.** Write a scene that shows how a caregiver can provide an infant with encouragement while the baby is trying to master a new skill in intellectual development. Read your scene to the class.

Workplace Connections

1. **Information Systems.** Design a system that could be used in a child care center to record and store information on what toys children of different ages played with.

2. **Technology.** Suppose you worked in a child care center. What technology do you think would be most helpful with infants- a computer, a tape player, or a television? Explain why.

Family and Community Connections

1. **Stacking.** Infants enjoy playing with stacking toys. What objects around the house could safely be used for stacking games?

2. **First Words.** Ask an adult who has had an infant what the baby's first few words were. Compare your findings with those of your classmates. Do any words appear frequently? If so, why?

Technology Connections

1. **Print Technology.** Some books for infants show pictures of objects and include a material that shows the texture of that object. Why are these appropriate toys?

The Child from One to Three

"EVERYBODY SAYS"
Everybody says
I look just like my mother.
Everybody says
I'm the image of Aunt Bea.
Everybody says
My nose is like my father's.
But I want to look like ME.

Dorothy Aldis

Shamal watched his son Grant with pride. It seemed like just a few months ago when he or Amber had to do everything for Grant. Now, here he was putting on his own shoes and jacket. Of course, the shoes had loop and hook fasteners, and someone still had to zip up the jacket. Still, there was no doubt in Shamal's mind that Grant had made great progress—and more was sure to come. Grant's progress went beyond dressing, too. He could feed himself and wash his hands and face. Next up, Shamal thought, would be toilet training.

Before he could think any more, though, Grant spoke up. "I'm ready!" he said. "Daddy put his shoes on! Let's go outside!"

"I'm ready! Daddy put his shoes on! Let's go outside!"

Physical Growth and Development from One to Three

The transition from babyhood to childhood is dramatic! The one-year-old still moves with some uncertainty, needs help dressing, and eats messily. By age three, the child is running and jumping, dressing and washing himself or herself, and using a fork and spoon.

KEY TERMS

developmentally appropriate
dexterity
large motor skills
preschoolers
small motor skills
toddlers

OBJECTIVES:

- Describe average changes in height, weight, proportion, and posture from ages one through three.

- Identify habits that build healthy teeth.

- Distinguish between large and small motor skills, and give examples of each.

Toddlers to Preschoolers

Physical growth slows considerably after the first year. However, the child's physical skills improve dramatically from the first to the fourth birthday. Most children begin to walk a few unsteady steps around age one. The term **toddlers** refers to children who make this uncertain movement. By age three, however, these children are far from "toddling." They become **preschoolers,** as children ages three to five are called. Three-year-olds not only walk steadily, they also hop, jump, and run. They make similar advances in most other physical skills.

As physical skills develop, these children need lots of space. They need time each day for active play so they can exercise their muscles and use their stored-up energy. Although their attention span is longer than that of infants, they still want to change games and activities often.

Height and Weight

Growth in both height and weight is slower in this period than among babies. Children from one to three gain only about ½ pound (0.2 kg) per month. That is less than half the average monthly weight gain during the first year of life. Growth in height also slows by about half. The chart on page 350 shows average heights and weights for children one through three.

HEALTH TIP

Active Play for Growth and Development

*H*ere are some fun activities for children aged one to three:

- **Roll the Dice.** Say that each number on a die stands for an activity. Roll it once to see what the child is supposed to do—run, jump, skip, or hop. Roll a second time to see how many times he or she has to do it.

- **Batting the Balloon.** Fill a balloon and hit it into the air. Then tell the child to keep it aloft.

- **Dancing.** Pop a cassette into the tape player or just turn the radio on. Then have the child dance, dance, dance.

- **Racing Against Time.** Set a task for the child, such as running around the house or to a neighbor's and back. Time the trial run. Then have the child repeat the task to see if he or she can better the time.

- **Playing "I Spy."** You can liven up a simple walk by calling out objects the child should try to see. Each time he or she sees the desired object, the child calls out "I spy a . . ."

FOLLOWING UP

1. Which activity helps build verbal, as well as physical, skills?
2. Invent your own activity that would be fun and get a child moving. Describe it to the class.

Infants tend to be more similar in height and weight. When children are toddlers and preschoolers, however, height and weight differences begin to show. *What factors influence these differences?*

Hereditary and environmental influences on height and weight are more noticeable among children one to three than among infants. After the first birthday, children begin to show greater variation in size. Some are much larger than average; others are much smaller. Height differences are particularly significant.

These differences will probably continue throughout life. A tall two-year-old usually grows to be a tall adult. An unusually short toddler will probably be shorter than average as an adult.

Proportion and Posture

Because of changes in proportion, posture improves during the period from one to three. Until age two, a child's head, chest, and abdomen all measure about the same. All three also grow at the same rate. Between ages two and three, however, the chest becomes larger than the head and abdomen. Also during this period, the arms, legs, and trunk grow rapidly. These changes in proportion help improve the child's balance and motor skills.

By two years of age, the child stands straighter, but the posture is not completely erect. The abdomen still protrudes, and the head is somewhat forward. The toddler's knees and elbows are slightly bent. By the

Average Heights and Weights: Ages One to Three

AGE	HEIGHT		WEIGHT	
	Inches	**Centimeters**	**Pounds**	**Kilograms**
One year	29.8	75.7	22.5	10.2
Two years	34.0	86.4	27.7	12.6
Three years	37.7	95.8	32.4	14.7

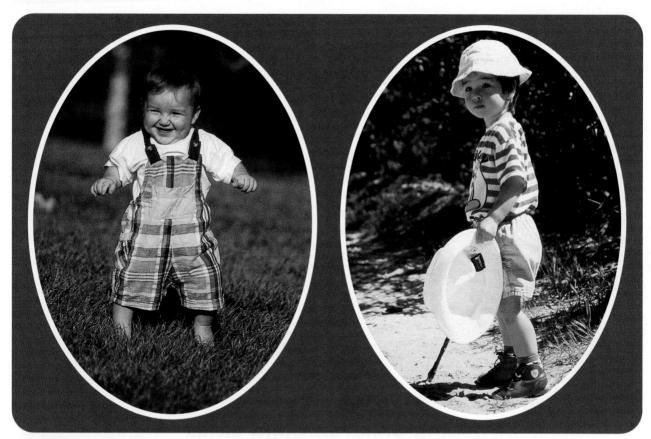

Children's bodies change a great deal from age one (left) to age three (right). The older child stands much straighter and has different body proportions. *What other differences do you notice?*

third birthday, the child's posture is more upright. The spine has strengthened, so the back is straighter. The child has lost some—but not all—baby fat.

Teeth

One-year-olds have an average of eight teeth, but there is a great deal of variation. During the second year, eight more teeth usually come in. For most children, the last four back teeth emerge early in the third year, giving them a complete set of 20 primary teeth.

The quality of a child's teeth is greatly influenced by diet. The diet of the mother during pregnancy and the diet of the child during the first two years lay the foundation for a lifetime of good—or poor—teeth. (A child's adult teeth are forming under the primary teeth.) Dairy products, which are rich in calcium and phosphorus, are especially important. The vitamin D in milk also helps the development of strong and healthy teeth and bones.

Diet can also cause tooth decay. Avoid giving children sweets, especially candy. Sugar-coated cereals often stick between the teeth and can cause decay. Avoid putting a child to bed with a bottle, unless it contains water. Other liquids can pool in the mouth and cause cavities.

Heredity appears to play a role in tooth quality. Dentists have identified a protective mechanism that discourages decay. Some children inherit this trait from their parents; others lack it.

Motor Skills

As you recall, physical development follows three patterns: from head to foot, from near to far, and from simple to complex. When you compare the skills of children at age one and at the end of the third year, these patterns are easy to see. Hand skills, for instance, show the pattern of simple to complex. At thirteen months, a child can bang blocks together or may stack two of them. By the fourth birthday, the same child uses blocks to make high towers, houses, and roads.

Motor skills are often divided into two types. **Large motor skills** involve use and control of the large muscles of the back, legs, shoulders, and arms. Walking, running, and throwing balls are all large motor skills. **Small motor skills** depend on the use and

Practicing Parenting

Helping Children Build Skills

*T*o develop their large and small motor skills, children need two things from caregivers—opportunities and encouragement. No one can learn to run without the chance to practice running. Learning to color requires crayons and paper. Caregivers are responsible for giving children plenty of opportunities to practice their skills.

How can you encourage children to improve their skills? First, avoid making a fuss over less-than-perfect performance. When Toby took a tumble while running, his dad made sure he wasn't hurt and then simply said, "You look fine—ready to go again?" Toby was off and running again. You can also encourage children by offering praise. Children love to know that adults recognize their efforts and accomplishments.

Practice and encouragement help children develop self-confidence. Children believe that if they keep trying, they can do it! That attitude promotes additional learning.

APPLY YOUR KNOWLEDGE
1. What are two ways of providing encouragement?
2. Suppose Valerie is having trouble with a jigsaw puzzle. How could you encourage her?

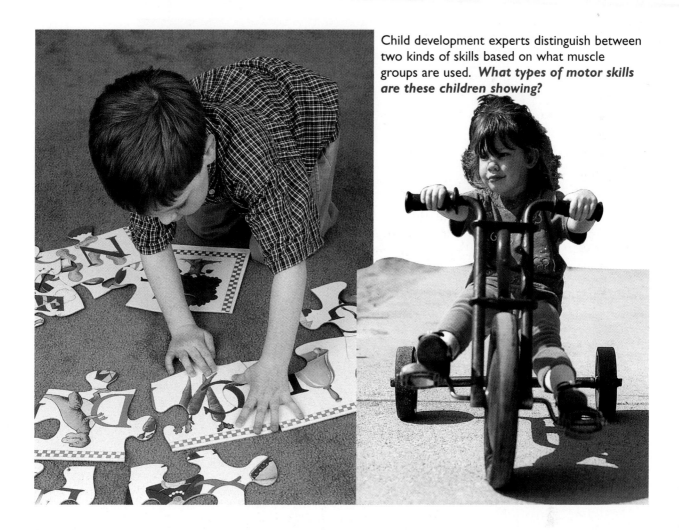

Child development experts distinguish between two kinds of skills based on what muscle groups are used. *What types of motor skills are these children showing?*

control of the finer muscles of the wrists, fingers, and ankles. Many of these skills—from using crayons and paintbrushes to turning pages of books and eating—require hand-eye coordination. This is the ability to move the hands precisely in relation to what is seen.

Children don't acquire physical skills as predictably during the period from one to three as during the first year of life. Most children learn some skills earlier than average and others later than average. These variations can be caused by differences in physical size, health and diet, interests, temperament, opportunities for physical play, and many other factors.

Experts speak of tasks or skills being **developmentally appropriate** for children. By this they mean the tasks are suitable for the child given his or her age and interests. For groups of children, caregivers need to consider the ages and interest level of all the children.

Large Motor Skills

Physical exercise and repeated practice promote the development of large motor skills. A child's improvement in any one skill is typically slow but steady. The chart on page 354 shows average large motor development of one-, two-, and three-year-olds.

Average Large Motor Skills Development:

Ages One to Three

Ages 3 to 4
- Jumps up and down in place.
- Walks on tiptoe.
- Rides a tricycle.
- Catches a ball with arms straight.

Ages 2½ to 3
- Runs, but may not be able to stop smoothly.
- Alternates feet going up stairs, but not going down.
- Throws a ball overhand, but inaccurately.
- Kicks balls.

Ages 2 to 2½
- Walks with more coordination and confidence.
- Climbs, even in unsafe places.
- Jumps off the bottom step.
- Pushes self on wheeled toys.

Ages 1½ to 2
- Runs fairly well.
- Stands on one foot.
- Learns to walk up and down stairs, while holding on, with both feet on each step.
- Throws objects overhand.

Ages 1 to 1½
- Improves from walking a few unsteady steps to walking well.
- Slides down stairs backward, one step at a time.
- Stoops to pick up toys.

As you know, most children begin to walk near their first birthday. This is an important accomplishment. It gives the child a feeling of pride—and much more mobility for exploration. At first, the toddler walks by holding on to furniture. The child's first steps are wobbly, with toes pointed outward and arms held out for balance. After a few shaky steps, the child collapses into a sitting position. Constant practice helps children improve in steadiness, balance, and body control.

Climbing skills follow a similar sequence. Even children who have learned to walk continue to climb stairs on their hands and knees for a while and slide backward when going down the stairs. Next, they begin walking up stairs with help, placing both feet on each step. Then they try walking up and down stairs on their own, holding on to a railing. They continue putting both feet on the same stair before moving down to the next stair until about age three. At that point, they can alternate feet.

Climbing isn't limited to stairs. Nothing is safe from the climbing toddler—furniture, counters, ledges, and sometimes even people are conquered like mountains! This activity, of course, makes safety an important concern for parents and other caregivers. The "Parenting with Care" feature on pages 372-373 suggests ways to make areas safe for children's explorations.

Small Motor Skills

During this stage, children's small motor skills also improve. The chart on page 356 shows average small motor development in these years.

Between their first and second birthdays, children learn to feed themselves and to drink from a cup fairly well. At first, poor

Which individual skills does this toddler need to kick the ball?

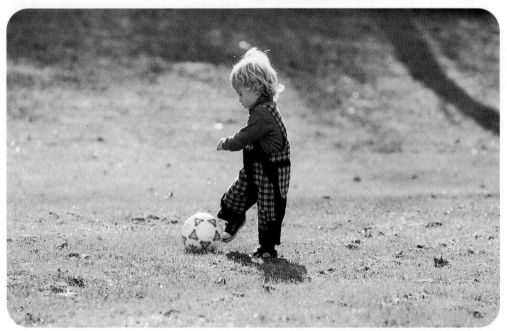

Average Small Motor Skills Development:

Ages One to Three

Ages 3 to 4

- Builds towers of about nine or ten blocks.
- Makes a bridge from three blocks.
- Cuts with scissors.
- Draws recognizable pictures.
- Uses fork and spoon with little spilling.

Ages 2 to 2½

- Turns one page of a book at a time.
- Strings large beads.
- Builds towers of about six blocks.

Ages 2½ to 3

- Builds towers of about eight blocks.
- Draws horizontal and vertical lines and circles.
- Screws lids on and off containers.

Ages 1 to 1½

- Turns several pages of a book at a time.
- Picks up small objects with thumb and forefinger.
- Scribbles.

Ages 1½ to 2

- Buttons large buttons.
- Pulls down zippers.
- Turns doorknobs.
- Stacks several blocks to form a tower.

hand-eye coordination causes many spills. With practice, however, their success and neatness improve. One-year-olds usually enjoy playing with blocks, large pop beads, and pyramids of different-sized rings. They also like jack-in-the-box toys, musical rolling toys, and toy pianos. Playing with these toys helps develop small motor skills.

Two-year-olds show improved **dexterity**, or skillful use of the hands and fingers. They can turn the pages of a book one at a time, peel a banana, and turn on a faucet. They enjoy using crayons—typically with a happy abandon that results in marks running haphazardly off the paper and onto the table or floor. They build towers of blocks, which usually topple once they reach five or six blocks high.

Three-year-olds show considerably more skill. They typically delight in taking things apart and putting them back together again. Children this age can draw circles as well as horizontal and vertical lines. They can also draw a cross.

SECTION 11-1 REVIEW

✔ Check Your Understanding

1. Why are children called toddlers?
2. What height and weight changes take place in these ages?
3. How do a child's posture and proportion change from age one to age three?
4. At about what age do most children have a complete set of primary teeth?
5. How do milk and milk products contribute to healthy teeth?
6. Choose a large motor skill and explain how children develop this skill from ages one to three.
7. How does improved dexterity show development of small motor skills?

Putting Knowledge Into Practice

1. **Synthesizing.** Name three toys for children ages one to three. For each, list the motor skills involved in playing with that toy.
2. **Comparing.** How do safety concerns in the home change as a child becomes one, two, and three years old? Why does this happen?
3. **Observing and Participating.** Watch a group of young children on a playground or other public place. Identify at least two children from these ages and write descriptions of their actions, explaining why you think they are one to three.

CAREER OPPORTUNITIES

Pediatrician

A CONVERSATION WITH EMILY RUTHERFORD

How did you become interested in becoming a pediatrician? When I was in medical school, I had to spend some time in pediatric care. I thought it was the most rewarding part of medicine because it gives you a chance to get people off to a healthy start in life.

What are the tasks and responsibilities of a pediatrician? We try to protect children's health by monitoring how children grow and by giving vaccinations to prevent them from catching diseases. When they are sick or injured, we help them recover. Finally, we give advice about children's diet, exercise, and behavior to parents.

What is the work environment like? I work in a practice with three other doctors. I also visit patients who are in the hospital.

What are the working hours like? Long! I see children at the hospital from 7:00 to about 9:00 each morning. Then we have office hours to either 5:00 or 8:00 P.M. We have one weekday and one weekend day free.

What aptitudes are needed to be a pediatrician? You need to know science—and psychology. It helps to be very patient and gentle. Some children are afraid of the doctor, and they need to be reassured. You need good communication skills to get information from parents— and to give it to them.

PEDIATRICIAN

Education and Training. Pediatricians first must complete a bachelor's degree. Then they need four years of medical school and three more years of additional training. They must also pass a state examination to receive a license to practice medicine.

Career Outlook. The demand for pediatricians should continue to grow.

CONNECTING SCHOOL TO CAREER

1. **Information Systems.** What kind of information do you think pediatricians should keep about their patients? How would you organize it systematically?
2. **Interpersonal Skills.** How would you explain to a three-year-old that he or she needed a vaccination?

SECTION 11-2

Caring for Children from One to Three

By their first birthday, children are already beginning to do things for themselves. If they are encouraged to practice, three-year-olds can be responsible for many self-care tasks. The typical three-year-old can dress, eat, brush teeth, and go to the bathroom independently.

KEY TERMS

hygiene
sphincter muscles
synthetic fibers
training pants

OBJECTIVES:

- Plan meals for young children.
- Explain how to help children learn and practice good hygiene.
- Choose appropriate clothes for children ages one to three.
- Describe common bedtime problems, and discuss how to minimize them.
- Discuss how to toilet train a child.

Feeding

The habits and attitudes toward food that children learn at this stage will influence their food habits throughout life. Self-feeding both depends on and helps improve their small motor skills.

Because they are growing less rapidly than in their first year of life, children these ages don't eat as much. However, most do need food every three or four hours because their stomachs are still small. Snacks can bridge the gap between meals, as long as they are nutritious. The amount that any child eats can vary greatly from day to day, depending on appetite and level of activity.

Meals can become a battle of wills between caregivers and young children, as many strong food likes and dislikes are developed. Children accept new foods more easily if they aren't pressured to or rewarded for eating them.

Self-feeding skills improve greatly during these years.

- **One-year-olds.** The one-year-old still eats a variety of baby foods. In addition, simple foods from the family's meals can be added. Choose foods that are low in sugar and salt. Until more teeth come in, cut foods into small pieces to aid swallowing.

Finger foods—those easily picked up and eaten—are popular with most children this age. Most children are eighteen months or older before they can use the spoon to feed themselves with little spilling. By their

INFOLINK

Finger Foods

For more about *finger foods*, see Chapter 8, page 275.

The bowl is attached to the high chair's table by suction. *What purpose does this serve? How might the high sides help this toddler learn self-feeding?*

The Food Guide Pyramid

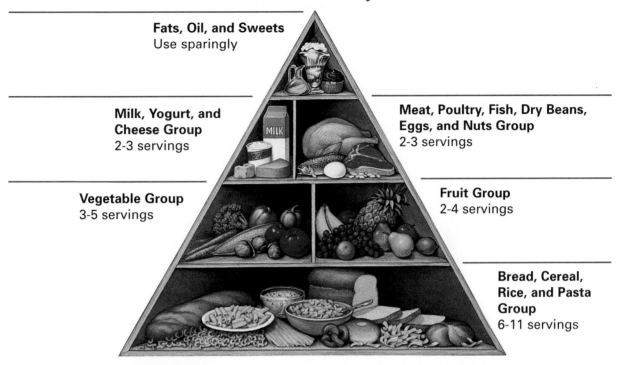

Fats, Oil, and Sweets
Use sparingly

Milk, Yogurt, and Cheese Group
2-3 servings

Meat, Poultry, Fish, Dry Beans, Eggs, and Nuts Group
2-3 servings

Vegetable Group
3-5 servings

Fruit Group
2-4 servings

Bread, Cereal, Rice, and Pasta Group
6-11 servings

second birthday, most children drink from a cup fairly well.

- **Two-year-olds.** Two-year-olds can usually feed themselves and learn to use a fork. Be patient. Remember that children often take a long time to eat. Eating not only provides nutrition, but also allows children to improve their motor skills.

  Try to schedule meals so the young child eats with the rest of the family. Conversation is an important way to help establish the social nature of meals and to reinforce family bonds.

- **Three-year-olds.** Three-year-olds have a full set of primary teeth, so chewing foods is not a problem. However, meats and other tough foods should still be served in small pieces. By this age, most children are quite handy with eating utensils.

Choosing Foods for Children

Like adults, children need a variety of nutritious foods daily. The best way to make sure a child gets this variety is to plan meals using the Food Guide Pyramid. The chart on page 362 gives some examples of a child-size serving in each food group.

Pediatricians recommend that milk or milk products not be given to a child until his or her first birthday. From one to two years, the child should drink whole milk, if not breast-fed. After the child is two, reduced-fat or lowfat milk can be given.

Be cautious in serving convenience foods to children. Many contain a great deal of salt and preservatives, colorings, and artificial flavors. Choose fresh foods when possible. Use the nutrition labels and ingredients lists on frozen, canned, and dried foods to help you make nutritious choices.

Serving Sizes for Children Two and Three

MILK, YOGURT, AND CHEESE GROUP
2-3 servings

Milk, yogurt—½ cup
Frozen yogurt, pudding—¼ to ½ cup
Cheese, processed, American—½ to 1 oz.

VEGETABLE GROUP
3-5 servings

Carrots—¼ to ½
Corn, green beans, peas, mashed potatoes—¼ cup

BREAD, CEREAL, RICE, AND PASTA GROUP
6-11 servings

Bagel, hamburger bun—¼ to ½
Crackers—2 to 3
Whole-grain bread—¼ to ½ slice
Spaghetti, rice, macaroni—¼ to ⅓ cup
Ready-to-eat cereal—¼ to ⅓ cup

MEAT, POULTRY, FISH, DRY BEANS, EGGS, AND NUTS GROUP
2 servings

Egg—1
Chicken, hamburger, fish—1-2 oz.
Baked beans—¼ cup
Peanut butter—1-2 Tbsp.

FRUIT GROUP
2-4 servings

Apple, banana— ¼ to ½
Fruit juice—⅓ cup
Grapes, peaches, strawberries—¼ cup

A healthy diet includes at least the minimum number of servings from each food group *each day*. This chart will help you see how much of several different foods equals a servings. Older children need more food.

To promote interest in nutritious foods, give children appealing meals. Color, texture, shape, temperature, and ease of eating are the keys.

- **Color.** A variety of bright food colors adds interest. A meal of cream of chicken soup, applesauce, milk, and vanilla pudding looks boring. Changing the soup to split pea and serving cut-up apple slices instead of applesauce would make the meal more visually appealing.
- **Texture.** Include foods with different textures at the same meal. Crunchy crackers, chewy cheese, and juicy grapes, for example, all give different sensations.
- **Shape.** Foods with a variety of shapes add appeal. Cut sandwiches into rectangles or squares—or even triangles. Carrot coins, zucchini sticks, and orange wedges might round out the meal. Help the child identify each shape. Another day, use a cookie cutter to cut bread into special shapes or shape pancakes like animals.
- **Temperature.** Try serving both hot and cold foods at a meal. Safety is also a concern, so check the temperature of all hot foods before serving them. If a food has been cooked or warmed in the microwave, stir it thoroughly to even out the temperature. "Hot spots" can burn the mouth.
- **Ease of eating.** Certain foods are easier than others for young children to eat. Ground beef is easier to chew and swallow than a pork chop. Many children like spaghetti, but they can handle it more easily if it is cut into short pieces.

Mealtime Tips

Are you prepared for the challenge of planning and preparing nutritious, appealing meals for young children? Meals are important events in the child's day. They provide a chance to practice skills, learn independence, explore the texture of foods, and talk to others. The following guidelines can help you make mealtimes with a young child more enjoyable:

Meals need to be nutritious, appealing, and easy for young children to eat. *How does this meal satisfy those requirements?*

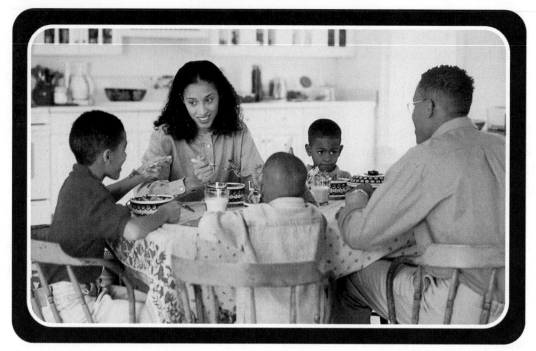

Some parents tell their children to eat all the food that they are served. *How can this lead to the child being overweight? What guidelines should parents follow in terms of how much children should eat?*

- Include children in meal preparation whenever possible. For example, young children can mix raisins in applesauce, wash potatoes with a scrub brush, and wash vegetables.
- Follow a regular schedule for meals and snacks. Children find it difficult to wait—especially when they're hungry.
- Keep meals pleasant. Remember that the child's table manners will improve with age. Be sure to model the behavior that you want the child to follow.
- Use a sturdy, unbreakable dish or plate with sides for serving the child's food. Food can be scooped up against the sides for easier eating.
- Choose a cup that the child can hold easily and that doesn't readily tip.
- Provide child-sized eating utensils. Young children have trouble handling full-sized forks and spoons.
- Let a toddler sit in a high chair for meals. As the child grows, use a high stool with a back or a booster seat on a regular chair.
- Remember that children imitate others. Set a good example in food choices and in table manners.

Avoid using food as a punishment or a bribe. If you say, "You can't have a cookie until you finish your vegetables," you give the impression that vegetables are bad and cookies are good.

Bathing

Parents and other caregivers need to help young children develop both good attitudes about hygiene—personal cleanliness—and good hygiene skills. For instance, when they begin toilet training, children should be taught to wash their hands each time they use the bathroom.

A daily bath also helps develop good habits. Evening baths are usually most practical and can become an enjoyable part of getting ready for bed. Children these ages typically have fun in the water.

One-year-olds begin to want to wash themselves. At first, this means merely rubbing the washcloth over the face and stomach. By age two, however, most children can wash, rinse, and dry themselves fairly well, except for the neck and back. By age three, children can bathe themselves with little supervision.

Bathtubs are still dangerous for children, though. A child can drown in as little as one inch of water. You should never leave a young child alone in the bath—not even for one minute. Another way of making the tub safe is to cover the bottom of the tub to prevent slipping. Attach rough plastic stickers or place a rubber mat on the bottom of the tub.

There is no set age at which all children can safely shower. It depends on the child's ability to control the water temperature, stand in the shower safely, and get himself or herself clean. If a child does shower, some kind of covering for the shower floor is a good idea. This will prevent the child from slipping and falling.

Caring for the Teeth

At age one, most children have several teeth. Teach them to brush their teeth right after eating. The longer food remains in the mouth, the more it can damage the teeth.

To encourage children to begin brushing, give them a small, soft toothbrush and a bit of toothpaste. Their first attempts will

Bath time provides an opportunity for positive parent-child interaction, as well as learning about hygiene.

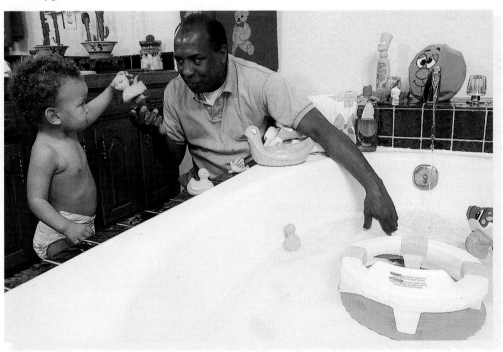

One way that parents teach children good hygiene is by setting a good example. If they brush after every meal, children will learn this habit. *How else can parents help children have clean teeth?*

not be very successful, but the opportunity to try is important. Even up to age three, children still need adult help.

Many dentists recommend that parents also begin flossing the child's teeth and showing the child how to hold and use dental floss. Start with the top teeth one night and do the bottom teeth the next. Creating the habit of flossing is the most important thing. Dentists also suggest that eighteen months is a good age for children to have their first dental checkup.

Dressing

Children are eager to learn dressing skills; adults and other caregivers should encourage self-dressing whenever a child begins to show interest. Dressing involves a number of large and small motor skills that must be learned one step at a time. Patience is important! A child learns these skills only through practice. If others insist on dressing the child because they can do it faster, they will probably have to continue dressing the child when older.

A child usually starts trying to help with dressing around the age of thirteen or fourteen months, perhaps by holding out an arm

As children become older, they wish to have greater power over issues that touch their lives. Giving them choices of what outfit to wear helps them gain that feeling of power.

for the sleeve of a shirt. Next, the toddler may learn to actually push his or her own arm through a sleeve. By two years, the child can pull up pants, but putting on shirts continues to be difficult. At this age, children often end up with their garments inside out or backwards. By age three, the child can dress independently, except for some help with difficult fasteners like buttons and with shoelaces.

With self-dressing, a child learns independence, responsibility, and self-esteem. You can encourage it by providing clothes that are easy to put on and take off.

Choosing Clothing

Comfort, durability, and economy are the most important characteristics to look for in clothing for young children.

- **Comfort.** Look for clothes that allow freedom of movement. Knits that stretch as the child moves are good choices. Avoid stiff or scratchy fabrics.

Size is an important factor in comfort. Clothes that are too small restrict movement. Clothes that are a little large allow the child to move comfortably. Of course, even clothes labeled the same size may not fit the same way. If the child will cooperate, let him or her try on clothing before you buy. Otherwise, have the child try the clothes on at home. Remember to allow for some shrinkage.

- **Durability.** Children's clothes must withstand hard wear and repeated washing. Durability is influenced by the quality of the fabric and the construction of the clothing. Denim, used for jeans and overalls, is an example of a durable fabric. In checking construction, look for close, even stitching with strong thread. The stitching should be

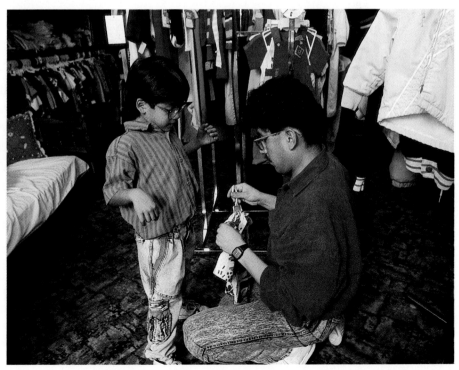

What factors should you consider in buying clothing for children these ages? How can labels help you as you shop for clothing?

reinforced at points of strain. All fasteners and trims should be firmly attached.

Cotton is a good choice, especially for T-shirts and underwear. Cotton wears well, doesn't irritate the skin, and washes well—though it may shrink. Since it absorbs moisture, cotton is also comfortable.

Synthetic fibers are made from chemicals rather than natural sources. Fabrics made from synthetic fibers—like polyester and acrylic—are durable, wrinkle resistant, and quick drying. Unlike cotton, though, most synthetic fibers don't absorb moisture well. They hold heat and perspiration against the body.

A blend of cotton and synthetic offers the benefits of both kinds of fibers. By law, all clothing must have a label that identifies the fibers used.

Clothing labels also state how to care for each garment.

- **Economy.** Since young children grow rapidly, they outgrow their clothes often. Many parents exchange outgrown clothes to cut costs. Others find good used clothes at yard sales, secondhand stores, and thrift shops.

Choose clothes that allow for growth. Look for deep hems or cuffs that can be let down after the child has grown. Check that the straps on overalls or jumpers are long enough to allow the buttons to be moved. Pants often can be bought a size larger and the pant legs rolled up.

When possible, let children help choose their own clothes. They usually love bright colors. In fact, young children choose their clothes more by color than by anything else. Other favorites include clothes printed with pictures of animals, toys, or story characters.

Sleeping

Near their second birthday, the sleeping habits of most children change. They usually require less sleep than before, and they may not go to sleep as easily or as willingly. By age two, most children no longer take a morning nap. Most three-year-olds give up the afternoon nap as well.

Children often need comfort at night. Younger toddlers may fuss before settling down. They may also suffer from nighttime fears. *How might these nighttime demands make a parent feel?*

The Developing Brain

Sleep benefits a child's developing brain. Children who get enough sleep have better memories than those who don't sleep enough.

Bedtime and sleep patterns can change in another way. A two-year-old may seem to be more emotionally dependent on adults than during the previous year. Many two-year-olds call a parent back repeatedly at bedtime. They may ask for a drink of water, another story, and one more trip to the bathroom. What they really want is someone near. Children of this age often use self-comforting techniques at bedtime, such as thumb sucking, rocking the crib, or cuddling a favorite blanket or soft toy.

It isn't unusual for three-year-olds to wake in the middle of the night and even get out of bed. Emotional experiences of the day, excitement at bedtime, or nighttime fears may cause them to feel insecure at night.

Fear of the dark is common among two- and three-year-olds. There are many possible causes. For example, the child may have overheard talk or news reports about prowlers, fires, accidents, or other dangers. The child's fears are very real and usually very troubling. Unfortunately, there is rarely a quick solution. A calm discussion may help some children. Others may feel more comforted by a night-light. All children who feel afraid of the dark need patience and understanding. Ridicule or shaming the child only makes the problem worse. If you were afraid of the dark as a child, try to remember what it felt like.

Toilet Training

Most children begin toilet training sometime after eighteen months of age. There is no set age at which the process should begin. Rather, each child should start toilet training when he or she is physically mature and emotionally ready.

Readiness

To be physically mature enough for toilet training, a child must be able to control his or her **sphincter muscles** (SFINGK-tur), the muscles that control elimination. The child must also be able to recognize the body sensations that precede elimination. Only then is the child ready to start learning to control and release these muscles.

A child who is emotionally ready is happily settled into a familiar daily routine. During a family move or any similar event that requires adjustments is not a good time to start toilet training.

Giving Help

The attitudes of parents and other caregivers toward toilet training are very important. Calm encouragement is more effective than rules and punishment. It also helps build self-esteem. Remember that the child who is physically and emotionally ready for toilet training genuinely wants to succeed. If the child resists, wait for readiness. Even after a child is toilet trained, some accidents should be expected.

When children begin to use the toilet, they may prefer to use a special child seat on the toilet or a separate potty chair. Using a child seat eliminates the need for another adjustment later, when the child is ready to

Ask the Experts

Dr. Van Stone
Pediatrician
Tupelo, Mississippi

SIGNS OF *Readiness for Toilet Training*

 Q What are the signs that a child is ready for toilet training?

A The most important thing to remember about toilet training is not to begin it until the child is ready. Beginning this training before the child is ready can make it longer and more difficult.

A child who is aware of the process of going to the bathroom is probably ready to use the toilet. If your child stops playing and grunts while having a bowel movement, he or she can probably begin toilet training. A child who is curious about the body and about elimination is probably ready as well.

The child with a less frequent need to urinate—sometimes going from one meal to the next—is ready for bladder training. So is a child who tells you that his or her diaper needs changing.

A child will do better at potty training if he or she has mastered self-dressing. Some children have accidents because they head to the bathroom without enough time to manage their clothes.

Having the language skills to talk about elimination can help with training as well. Some children make it fairly easy for parents. They simply announce that they're ready to get out of diapers!

When you do begin toilet training, be sure to keep the whole process as free of stress as possible. Avoid pushing the child, and be sure not to punish him or her for the accidents that will inevitably occur. Instead, praise the child when he or she does use the toilet correctly.

Thinking It Through

1. Why does a child's saying that a diaper needs changing suggest the child is ready for toilet training?
2. What role does self-dressing play in readiness for toilet training?

move from a potty chair to the toilet. On the other hand, using a potty chair allows the young child more independence than the special seat.

Some children are frightened by the flushing of a toilet. Unless the child is particularly interested in flushing, it may be better to flush the toilet after the child has left the bathroom.

Bowel training usually comes before bladder training. Most children are ready when they show an awareness that a bowel movement is imminent. When you see this awareness in the child's facial expressions or gestures, suggest that he or she might try sitting on the toilet seat or potty chair. Be available and encouraging. However, being too forceful or demanding will make toilet training more difficult both for the child and for you.

Bladder training typically follows bowel training by several months, although some children learn both at the same time. Many young children are encouraged in toilet training when they are given **training pants**, heavy, absorbent underpants, in place of diapers. Wearing training pants makes it possible for a young child to use a potty independently. Most children also recognize that wearing underpants instead of diapers is a sign of maturity.

SECTION 11-2 REVIEW

✔ Check Your Understanding

1. What is the most important consideration in preparing meals and snacks for young children?
2. What choices in plates, cups, and utensils can make it easier for toddlers to learn self-feeding?
3. How can parents build the bathing skills of children from one to three?
4. What should caregivers do to teach children to care for their teeth?
5. Why are comfort, durability, and economy important in children's clothing?
6. How should caregivers respond to a young child's fear of the dark?
7. How are sphincter muscles involved in toilet training?

Putting Knowledge Into Practice

1. **Comparing.** How do an infant's sleep patterns compare to those of a two-year-old? How do they compare to those of a three-year-old?
2. **Applying.** When Michael was one year old, his older sister Maria dressed him every day. Now that Michael is one-and-a-half, what should she do?
3. **Observing and Participating.** Plan a lunch or dinner for a toddler that takes into account nutrition and the color, texture, shape, and ease of eating the foods.

Keeping Children Safe and Healthy

Children from one to three are capable of—and interested in—exploring their environment.

They open drawers and cabinets. They turn knobs and stick their fingers into tiny holes. As they try to learn about their world, they often put themselves in danger. It's not fair to the child to put a stop to this exploration. The best solution is to childproof the home, making it as safe as possible for the child.

Parents can follow these tips to make a safe environment for a child:

To Prevent Falls
- Keep the floor and stairs free of anything that the child might trip over.
- Wipe up spills immediately—before someone slips and falls.
- Use safety gates on stairways until the child can navigate them independently.
- Always use the seat belt when the child is in a high chair.
- Be sure that all open windows have secure screens. Windows in high-rise buildings should have safety latches the child cannot open.
- Remove loose rugs and any furniture that might tip easily.

To Prevent Burns
- Teach the child that the range is hot and must not be touched.
- Always turn the handles of pots and pans toward the center of the range.
- Check the temperature of the hot water. It shouldn't be higher than 120° to 130°F (49° to 54°C) to prevent burns. If the water is hotter than that, lower the thermostat of the hot water heater.
- Put safety caps on all unused electrical outlets.
- Keep small appliances, such as toasters and irons, unplugged and out of reach when they are not in use.

To Remove Other Hazards
- Keep all dangerous materials, such as cleaning supplies, medicines, paints,

and insecticides, out of the child's reach. Keeping these materials on a high shelf is not enough—children like to climb. They should be stored in locked cabinets or containers.

- Keep sharp knives, razor blades, scissors, and matches locked out of children's reach as well. Never let a child have such an object.
- Check toys and equipment for broken parts or sharp edges.
- Keep the toilet seat down whenever the toilet isn't in use.
- Lock unused refrigerators and freezers or remove their doors.

Following Up

1. **Leadership.** One way to identify dangers in the home is to crawl around on the floor and look in all directions. Why is this a good idea?

2. **Thinking Skills.** How could a two-year-old be in danger if an older brother or sister often ran up and down stairs?

Summary

- ✔ Children one to three years old grow more slowly than infants. (Section 11-1)
- ✔ Large and small motor skills improve greatly during this period. (Section 11-1)
- ✔ Children from one to three develop eating and cleanliness habits that will last throughout their lives. (Section 11-2)
- ✔ Clothing for children these ages should be comfortable, durable, and economical. (Section 11-2)
- ✔ Bedtime problems are common in this stage. (Section 11-2)
- ✔ Toilet training should begin when a child is physically and emotionally ready. (Section 11-2)

Reviewing the Facts

1. How do body proportions and posture change from ages one to three? (Section 11-1)
2. Explain how heredity and diet affect the health of teeth. (Section 11-1)
3. What is the difference between large and small motor skills? (Section 11-1)
4. List two large and two small motor skills of two-year-olds. (Section 11-1)
5. Why are the attitudes of children ages one to three toward food so important? (Section 11-2)
6. What can caregivers vary to make meals appealing? (Section 11-2)
7. Why shouldn't children wear clothes that are too small for them? (Section 11-2)
8. What bedtime problems may arise with children these ages? (Section 11-2)
9. What are training pants? How can they help with toilet training? (Section 11-2)

Thinking Critically

1. **Making Inferences.** What should a parent do if a child doesn't master large motor skills at the average ages described in the chapter?
2. **Supporting.** The text says "Self-feeding both depends on and helps improve small motor skills." Explain how that is true.
3. **Analyzing.** Make a display for the bulletin board that includes a picture of a child's garment and captions explaining what features the garment should have to be useful to a child one to three.

Taking Action

1. **Handling Food Preferences.** Write a scene showing how a parent should respond when a two-year-old refuses to eat a particular food. *(Leadership)*
2. **Scheduling.** Make a chart of a day's activities for a three-year-old. The schedule should include time for physical activity, meals, practice in small motor skills, and good hygiene. Explain why such a schedule would—or would not—work. *(Management)*

CONNECTIONS

Cross-Curricular Connections

1. **Language Arts.** Write a brochure giving parents advice on how to choose clothes for toddlers.

2. **Math.** A cup of whole milk has 8 grams of fat, a cup of reduced-fat milk has 5 grams of fat, and a cup of lowfat milk has 3 grams of fat. If a three-year-old drinks 3 cups of milk a day, how much less fat does he or she drink by switching from whole milk to reduced-fat milk? From whole milk to lowfat milk?

Workplace Connections

1. **Interpersonal Skills.** Suppose you work in a toy store. What would you suggest to a customer who asked for your help in buying a toy for a niece aged three?

2. **Basic Skills.** Calculate the average weight of ten three-year-olds with the following weight in pounds: 25, 30, 32, 24, 28, 29, 23, 27, 26, 27. Then multiply the answer by 0.45 to find their average weight in kilograms.

Family and Community Connections

1. **Analyzing Meals.** Write down the food eaten by your family at dinner for two nights. Analyze the foods according to the Food Guide Pyramid. Would these meals be appropriate for a three-year-old? If not, what changes would need to be made?

2. **Evaluating Options.** Compare prices for children's clothes at two different stores in your community. Check a pair of pants, a shirt, and a sweatshirt in each store. Bring your findings to the class and compare them with those of classmates. What store or stores offer the best prices?

Technology Connections

1. **Internet.** Search the Internet for reliable advice on toddlers' sleeping problems. You could visit the sites of the American Academy of Pediatrics or some other authoritative source. Based on your research, devise a list of ten tips for parents. Include a list of the sites you visited.

Emotional and Social Development from One to Three

Mark and Michael watched their children on the seesaw. Matt and Jordan were having so much fun together. The two fathers enjoyed seeing it. "Remember how they used to play?" asked Mark. "They would sit back to back in the sandbox as though the other one wasn't even there."

Michael nodded. "There has been a real change," he said. "Now Jordan really looks forward to getting together with Matt. It's great, actually. Most mornings it takes a long time for him to get dressed—he gets distracted by everything in the room. But on days that we're meeting Matt, well, it's all different. He cleans up after breakfast and has his clothes on in a hurry. Then he's ready to play!"

"Remember how they used to play? They would sit back in the sandbox as though the other one wasn't even there. Now Jordan really looks forward to getting together with Matt."

SECTION 12-1

Emotional Development from One to Three

Between one and four, children undergo many emotional changes. They develop new emotions, such as jealousy, they had not felt before. They display their emotions very clearly. By the end of their third year, children begin to control their emotions and to express them in more socially acceptable ways. Emotional development depends upon brain development and personal experiences.

KEY TERMS

empathy
negativism
self-centered
self-concept
separation anxiety
sibling rivalry
temper tantrums

OBJECTIVES:

- Describe patterns of emotional development from ages one to three.

- Identify the common emotions of young children and the changing ways they express those emotions.

- Analyze how individual differences affect emotional development.

- Explain how self-concept develops.

General Emotional Patterns

Throughout childhood, emotional development tends to go in cycles. That is certainly the case with children at this stage. They go through periods of negativism and rebellion, but also periods of happiness, calmness and stability. These periods tend to alternate, and they are generally related to the age of the child.

Of course, each child is an individual. Jasmine may not go through the negativism of eighteen months until she is two. Manuel may not seem to go through it at all. Generally, however, you will find the following characteristics in children at about the ages given.

Eighteen Months

Eighteen-month-old children are primarily **self-centered**, that is, they think about their own needs and wants, not those of others. This isn't surprising. During infancy, caregivers promptly meet a child's needs and desires. At eighteen months, however, they begin to teach the child that some desires won't be met immediately—and others never will be met. This is a difficult lesson, and the eighteen-month-old is only beginning to learn it.

Spoken instructions aren't always successful with children this age. The young toddler is likely to do the opposite of what is requested. At this age, the child's favorite response to everything is "No."

Negativism, or doing the opposite of what others want, is normal for a young toddler. It has a number of causes:

- **The desire for independence.** Saying "no" is a way of saying, "Let me decide for myself." The child may even say "no" to things he or she would really like to do—just for the chance to make the decision!
- **Frustration.** The bodies of toddlers aren't developed enough to obey their wishes, and they don't have the language skills to express their feelings.

The frustration that results is often expressed in a simple and emphatic "No!"

- **The child's realization of being a separate person.** This idea is both exciting and frightening. The child likes the power of being a separate person but misses the close bond with a primary caregiver.

This negativism might produce a battle of wills between child and caregiver. Some strategies can help prevent clashes. One is to eliminate as many restrictions as possible. For example, rather than asking an eighteen-month-old not to touch certain objects, put them away. As the child gets older, they can be put back in place.

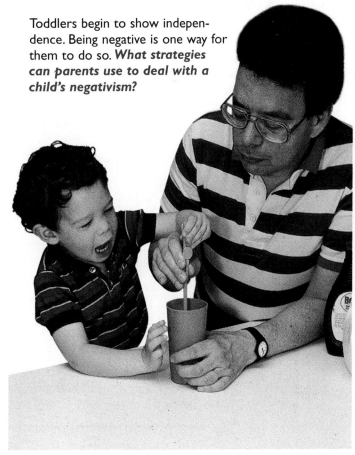

Toddlers begin to show independence. Being negative is one way for them to do so. *What strategies can parents use to deal with a child's negativism?*

Positive guidance can help caregivers handle a child who is negative:

- **Give choices.** Cleaning up can become a game when the caregiver asks, "Which will you pick up first—the books or the toys?" Having choices allows the child to exercise control. Limit choices to two alternatives, however. Toddlers can't think about three or four things at a time.

- **Redirect the child.** If possible, take the child's attention off the issue that is causing the negative response. You may be able to return to it later when the child is calmer.

- **Encourage talking.** Help children learn to use words to communicate how they feel. This will help both you and the child understand and deal with those feelings.

An Emotional Roller Coaster

Parents may be bewildered when a cheerful three-year-old suddenly becomes insecure and uncertain at three-and-a-half. Shifts in behavior become easier to bear when parents realize that they are normal—and that the times when children are more difficult to handle will pass.

Eighteen Months
The eighteen-month-old shows defiance as he tries to establish some control over his life.

Two Years
The two-year-old is affectionate—and may often be in the caregiver's way.

Around eighteen months, many children start to have **temper tantrums**. In a tantrum, the child releases anger or frustration by screaming, crying, kicking, pounding, and sometimes holding his or her breath. These tantrums may occur until age three or four. Sometimes, even seemingly minor frustrations can cause temper tantrums. Try to help the child find less explosive ways of expressing these feelings.

Two Years

Emotionally, the two-year-old is less at odds with the world than he or she was at eighteen months. Speech and motor skills have improved, relieving much frustration. The child also understands more and is able to wait longer for needs to be met.

The two-year-old expresses love and affection freely and seeks approval and

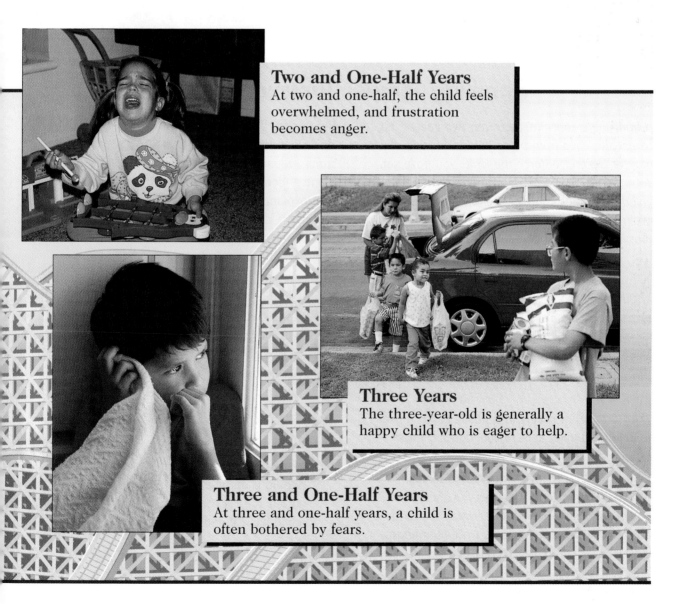

Two and One-Half Years
At two and one-half, the child feels overwhelmed, and frustration becomes anger.

Three Years
The three-year-old is generally a happy child who is eager to help.

Three and One-Half Years
At three and one-half years, a child is often bothered by fears.

praise. Though the child still has some emotional outbursts, they are fewer and less intense. Two-year-olds are easier to reason with. They usually get along better with parents and other children because they tend to be more outgoing and friendly and less self-centered.

Two and One-Half Years

Just as parents and caregivers begin to adjust to a smoother, less intense toddler, the child enters another difficult stage. In fact, this period may seem even more difficult for caregivers than the eighteen-month-old stage. At two and one-half, tod-

Practicing Parenting

Handling Temper Tantrums

In handling a tantrum, there are two goals. First, prevent the child from being hurt or hurting anyone else. Second, enforce the limits you have set. Tantrums usually occur when the child has been denied something that he or she wants. If you give in to the child's demands, tantrums are more likely to be repeated.

If you see a tantrum coming, try to distract the child to head it off. Sometimes holding the child in a firm hug will work. Some children, though, react strongly against that technique.

If a tantrum occurs at home, the caregiver may be able to ignore it. The child who finds that tantrums produce no attention is likely to stop having them.

When a tantrum occurs in a public place, move the child to a quiet spot to cool down. If possible, take the child home.

The most important thing is always to remain calm. Resist giving in to your own frustration by raising your voice—it will only heighten the tension. Acknowledge the child's feelings while reemphasizing why his or her demands can't be met.

Remember that the child isn't old enough to understand rational arguments—don't bother with long explanations. A firm and direct statement of the rule or your decision with a brief reason is enough.

APPLY YOUR KNOWLEDGE

1. Renee was shopping in the supermarket with her father. When her father said he would not buy some candy she wanted, Renee began to have a tantrum. Her father then put the candy in the shopping cart. What problems might this action cause?
2. Many tantrums arise when a child is denied something he or she wants. Why would it be helpful to talk to a child about the reason for the denial after the child has calmed down?

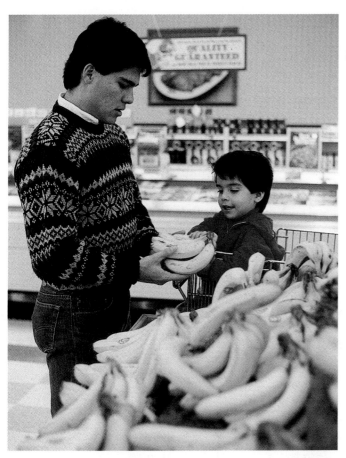

Have you ever seen a child have a temper tantrum in a supermarket? It can be very tempting for a parent to give in so that the noise and emotional turmoil end. *What is the negative result?*

but can't always make themselves be understood. These situations produce frustration that may boil over.

At two and one-half, the drive for independence is strong. This causes children to resist pressures to conform. They are sensitive about being bossed, shown, helped, or directed. Independence and immaturity clash head-on during this stage. Children this age can be stubborn, demanding, and domineering. However, their moods change rapidly, and within a short time they can become lovable and completely charming.

dlers are not so easily distracted as they were at eighteen months.

Children this age are learning so much that they often feel overwhelmed. Their comprehension and desires exceed their physical abilities. For example, they may want their blocks placed in a certain way but succeed only partially before accidentally knocking them over. Two-and-one-half-year-olds know what they want to say

Since two-and-a-half-year-olds like things to be in the same place and like to do things themselves, they can begin to learn to pick up their toys. *What emotional tendency of children this age might make it more difficult to convince them to pick up toys?*

Children this age have a need for consistency. They want the same routines, carried out the same way, every day. This is their way of coping with a confusing world. Following a routine helps build confidence and a feeling of security.

At two and one-half, children are both independent and dependent. Sometimes they seek help; at other times, they want to do things themselves. Love and patience are essential—especially when the child is neither lovable nor patient. Two-and-one-half-year-olds need flexible limitations rather than hard-and-fast rules.

Three Years

Three-year-olds are generally sunny and cooperative and are learning to be considerate. As preschoolers, they are more physically capable. They don't have to deal with as many frustrating situations as two-year-olds.

Three-year-olds are more willing to take directions from others. They will modify their behavior in order to win praise and affection—which they crave. Three-year-olds generally have fewer temper tantrums than younger children.

At three, children like to talk and are much better at it. They talk to their toys, their playmates, their imaginary companions, and themselves. They also respond to others' talking; they can be reasoned with and controlled with words.

Three and One-Half Years

The self-confident three-year-old is suddenly very insecure at three and one-half. Parents may feel that the child is going backward rather than forward emotionally.

Fears are common at this age. The child may be afraid of the dark, lions and tigers, monsters, strangers, or loud noises—even

While three-year-olds play, they may talk for the imaginary people in their games. When they take the parents' role in these games, they often imitate the way their caregivers speak to them. *How can this help caregivers?*

though none of these was frightening before. Emotional tension and insecurity often show up in physical ways, too. Some children may start habits—such as thumb sucking, nail biting, or nose picking—to release tension. Others stumble or stutter.

At three and one-half, children try to ensure their own security by controlling their environment. They may issue insistent demands, such as "I want to sit on the floor to eat lunch!" or "Talk to me!"

Specific Emotions

Children express their emotions openly until the age of two or three. The three-year-old begins to learn socially acceptable ways of displaying feelings. For example,

eighteen-month-old Marta shows anger by kicking and screaming. Three-year-old Jonathan uses words.

Anger

Anger, as we have seen, is often the child's way of reacting to frustration. How children in this stage show that anger changes over the years. Three-year-olds are less violent and explosive—they are less likely to use hitting or kicking. Physical attacks give way to name-calling, pouting, or scolding.

The target of anger changes in these years as well. An eighteen-month-old who has a tantrum usually doesn't direct the anger toward a particular person or thing.

SAFETY TIP

Biting and Hitting

Children ages one to three sometimes express their anger by biting or hitting another person. This can be a serious situation. Children do need to be told that biting and hitting are inappropriate ways to express their anger. They should be told that physical attacks can hurt others. Of course, caregivers need to take the situation into account, too. If the child lashes out during a temper tantrum, that is not the time for a discussion of how it is wrong to hit.

At the same time, children may need physical release for their anger. One way is to provide a safe substitute. A child who is prone to biting may be given a soft cloth or a teething ring—something the child can bite into without hurting others. A child who hits could be given an air-filled punching bag or a pillow to strike.

FOLLOWING UP
1. Why isn't it a good idea to talk to a child about not hitting while the child is having a tantrum?
2. Give some examples of objects that it would be safe for a child to hit.

At age three and a half, children often feel fears at night. *How can parents best respond?*

From age two to three, children are more likely to aim their anger at the object or person they see as responsible for their frustration.

A number of factors can cause a child to be angry more often than normal. Anger is more frequent in anxious, insecure children. The child who hasn't learned self-control also tends to have frequent outbursts. Children whose parents are overly critical or inconsistent become frustrated easily and show anger. Make sure that the demands on children are both limited and reasonable as they are learning self-control.

Some common causes of anger are temporary—and felt from time to time by almost all children. If a child is sick, tired, uncomfortable, or hungry, frustration is more likely to turn into anger.

Caregivers must remember to respond to a child's anger in a controlled way. Reacting angrily themselves will only make the situation worse.

Fear

At each age, children have particular fears. A one-year-old may be frightened of high places, strangers, and loud noises. A three-year-old might be afraid of the dark, animals, and storms. Some fears are actually useful, since they keep the child from dangerous situations. Others must be overcome for the child to develop healthily.

Adults sometimes communicate their own fears to children. Even if the fear is never discussed, the alarmed call of a parent whenever a dog comes near may cause a child to become afraid of dogs.

One fear commonly arises some time or another between the first and fourth birthdays. Many children suffer from **separation anxiety**, a fear of being away from parents, familiar caregivers, or their normal environment. Nicole cried when her parents left her with a new babysitter. Jake cried when his father left on the first day of preschool.

Separation anxiety can upset parents. If they have placed the child in a child care situation, the child's fears may make them feel guilty. The parents need to remind themselves that they chose a safe, secure caregiver for the child. This is simply a stage that the child will go through—and grow out of. Parents can try to speed that process by spending special time with the child at home. They can also be specific about when they will return. "I'll be back after you've had your nap," gives the child a better sense of what to expect.

Many children who feel separation anxiety have trouble going to sleep at night. Some have nightmares. A bedtime routine and a reminder that a parent is nearby can help lessen these fears. Asking the child to describe a nightmare can help as well. It can be a relief to talk about the bad dream, instead of holding it inside. Also, by hearing what the child dreamt, the parent may understand the underlying cause of the nightmare.

The following suggestions will help you deal with the fears of toddlers:

- Offer support and understanding. Avoid shaming a child for his or her fears.
- Encourage the child to talk about the fears and listen seriously. Admitting to fears might diminish their impact.
- In some cases, it is best to accept the fear and avoid trying to force the child to confront it. Often, it will simply go away on its own.

- Read books together about a child who experiences fear. Talking about the book can help relieve the toddler's fears.
- Make unfamiliar situations more secure. Discuss new experiences and events in advance to help the child know what to expect. If possible, accompany the child. A first visit to the dentist, for example, goes more smoothly in the company of a caring adult.
- Teach the child how to control frightening situations. Fear of the dark can be lessened by knowing how to turn on the light.

Jealousy

Jealousy becomes a recognizable emotion some time in the second year. The one-year-old shows no jealous reactions, but by eighteen months, jealousy is very pronounced. It reaches its peak at age three and then lessens as outside relationships begin to replace the close ties to home and parents.

A new baby sometimes causes jealousy. Giving the older child a caring role can help minimize these feelings. *Why might a preschooler handle this situation better than a toddler?*

One focus of jealousy may be the parents. The toddler may resent any show of affection between parents. Children may not understand that parents have enough love for everyone.

Sibling rivalry, or competition between brothers or sisters for parents' affection and attention, is another common cause of jealousy. This often arises when a new baby is born. Suddenly, a child finds that the attention he or she once received is now focused on the baby. For this reason, many experts say it is never safe to leave a baby alone with a toddler.

Some children react to a new baby by trying to get attention. They may show off, act in inappropriate ways, or revert to baby-like behaviors, such as wetting the bed or using baby talk.

If parents act shocked or threaten not to love the child anymore, they only make the problem worse. Fear of losing the parent's love caused the negative behavior in the first place. What the child needs is more affection and reassurance.

Sibling rivalry doesn't occur only when there is a newborn, however. Ask Todd, who came home from work to find himself overwhelmed by hugs from both four-year-old Becky and three-year-old Curt. Soon each child was trying to gain a position that would block the other from their father.

There are steps a parent can take to cut down on sibling rivalry:

- Make sure that all children know that they are loved and appreciated.

> **INFOLINK**
>
> **Accepting a New Baby**
>
> For more about *preparing an older child to accept a new baby*, see Chapter 6, pages 194-195.

- Try to set aside time to be with each child so that there is less need to compete for attention.
- Avoid making comments that compare one child to the other.
- Let the children take turns in choosing activities—the game the family plays together or the video that's rented.
- Make clear that you will not accept one child tattling to get the other in trouble.

Love and Affection

The relationships that children have with others in these years form the basis of their capacity for love and affection in later life. Young children must learn to love.

┌─ **The Developing Brain** ─────────┐
In studying brain scans of children who have suffered severe neglect, researchers found that the area of the brain used for attachment to others is smaller than usual.
└────────────────────────────────┘

First comes "love" of those who satisfy the baby's physical needs. Gradually, the baby's affection expands to include siblings, pets, and people outside the home.

Relationships between parents and children should be strong, but not smothering. A child who depends too much on caregivers has difficulty forming other relationships.

Empathy

For years, people believed that infants and toddlers were so self-centered that they wouldn't feel anything toward another person who was unhappy. Research has overturned that view. Between their first birthday and eighteen months, children begin to understand that their actions can hurt others. This is the first step toward **empathy**, or the ability to put oneself in another's place. Children as early as a year old may pat and talk to an unhappy child. By two, a child can show empathy. When Jesse saw that Nathan was upset, he offered Nathan his favorite stuffed animal to try to cheer him up.

Caregivers can teach children to show empathy. If a child does something to hurt another's feelings—taking a toy, for instance—tell the child to apologize. Then the child should also take an active step to making the wronged child feel better.

Individual Differences

Each child, of course, is unique and will develop emotionally in a special way. Individual differences can be very striking during this stage. These differences grow in part out of the different set of experiences that each child has. Roberto, an only child, will have different opportunities than Andrea, one of five children. Larissa's and Nadia's development will be affected by the fact that they are twins. Muhammad's experience will differ because his only brother, Rasheed, is ten years older.

Another factor is the child's temperament. As you recall, temperament is how a child naturally responds to other people and to events. An intense child may react more strongly to frustration than an adaptable child. A more perceptive child may show more empathy than one who is less perceptive.

Keep these differences in temperament in mind as you teach children how to control their emotions. Cody is very perceptive—he is very aware of his environment. At the same time, he can be easily distracted. When his mother sees a temper tantrum coming, she can try to turn his attention to something new. Such a technique may not work with a child with a different temperament. Nicole

INFOLINK

Temperament

For more about *Temperament*, **see Chapter 9, pages 301-303.**

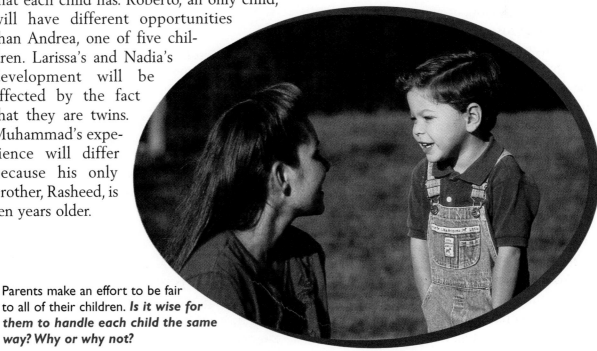

Parents make an effort to be fair to all of their children. *Is it wise for them to handle each child the same way? Why or why not?*

adapts to change slowly. Her parents have to be sure to give her plenty of warning and time before any upcoming changes. She also dislikes surprises—even pleasant ones.

Parents have a range of tools that they can use to try to lead a child to a desirable behavior. This is true whether the issue is negativism, tantrums, sibling rivalry, or changing activities. For each child, with his or her unique combination of experiences and own temperament, some of those tools are more effective than others.

Developing a Positive Self-Concept

As children grow, they become more aware of their individual differences. Those traits that make them special become part of their **self-concept**—how they see themselves. Self-concept can be positive—if you see yourself as a good person, or a capable person, or one who can control emotions. It can also be negative—you could see yourself as a bad person, or an incapable person, or one who loses emotional control.

Self-concept is different from self-esteem. Self-concept is what you think you are like as a person. Self-esteem is how highly you value yourself.

A child forms his or her self-concept in response to the actions, attitudes, and comments of others. Parents usually spend the most time with the young child, so they have the strongest influence on the child's self-concept. The years from one to three are crucial in the child's development of self-concept.

Young children believe what others say about them—and that belief influences how they behave. If children hear they are good, they try to act the part. However, if

they constantly hear that they are "bad" or "stupid," they will live up to that image. Even young toddlers are tuned in to adults' body language and tone of voice. The strong influence of adults' words and actions doesn't diminish until children are older and can judge their own actions. By that time, however, their self-concept is firmly established.

Another factor in building a positive self-concept is mastery of skills. For this reason, it is important to give infants and toddlers the chance to explore their world. Then they have the opportunity to master skills. Success gives a sense of competence, which leads to a positive self-concept.

Some parents unintentionally act in ways that hurt a child's self-concept. For example, when three-year-old Jackie set the table her mother smiled and said, "You did a very nice job, Jackie!" Then, however, the mother moved the forks to their correct positions. This showed Jackie that her efforts weren't worth much. A better approach would have been for Jackie's mother to avoid making any changes. Then at dinner she might have said,

The child's first important relationship is with parents. *How can that relationship be used to gauge emotional development?*

"Jackie set the table tonight. Didn't she do a nice job? She already knows where the knives and spoons go."

Evaluating Emotional Adjustment

How can parents tell whether their child is developing well emotionally? Between the first and fourth birthdays, the most important clue is the child's relationship with his or her parents. The early pattern established between parents and child will shape the child's relationships later in life as a friend, a co-worker, and a spouse.

These are signs of a healthy relationship between parents and child:

- The child seeks approval and praise from parents.
- The child turns to parents for comfort and help.
- The child tells parents about significant events so that they may share in the joy and sorrow.
- The child accepts limits and discipline without unusual resistance.

Another indicator of emotional adjustment is a child's relationship with siblings. Some quarreling with brothers and sisters is bound to occur. However, the child who is continuously and bitterly at odds with brothers and sisters, in spite of parents' efforts to ease the friction, may need counseling. If emotional problems are dealt with early, it can make a difference for a lifetime.

SECTION 12-1 REVIEW

✔ Check Your Understanding

1. Explain what it means to be self-centered.
2. What is negativism? What does negativism in a toddler indicate?
3. What changes occur in emotions between three and three and one-half years?
4. What children are more likely than others to feel anger?
5. What is separation anxiety?
6. What emotional problems do nightmares often reveal?
7. What individual factors affect a child's emotional development?
8. Distinguish between self-concept and self-esteem.

Putting Knowledge Into Practice

1. **Comparing.** Compare two- and two-and-one-half-year-olds in terms of how they handle being told what to do.
2. **Applying.** Suppose a toddler who was toilet trained begins to have accidents after a new baby enters the family. What would you do?
3. **Observing and Participating.** Write down your self-concept—what you think you are like. With each idea you write down, try to determine when in your life it arose.

CAREER OPPORTUNITIES

Clown

A CONVERSATION WITH DAVE JACKSON

How did you become interested in being a clown? I saw the circus when I was a child. I just loved the clowns—they were so funny. I guess the experience stayed with me.

What are the tasks and responsibilities of a clown? Well, to entertain! I try to help children see the magic and fun of life. What I do depends on where I'm working. At a birthday party, we're in a small space, and I'll do simple things like make balloon animals or paint the children's faces—if they want. At a child care center, I'll try to get the children involved in dancing games. In a larger setting, like a fair, I'll do funny routines with my dog.

What is the work environment like? As you can see, I work in many different places—in people's homes, in centers, or at county fairs. I also visit children in hospitals.

What are the working hours like? I work part-time as a clown and part-time at another job. My clown work is usually a few days a week, but it varies from week to week.

What aptitudes are needed to be a clown? You need creativity, a sense of humor, and a real interest in children. For clowning, you need good physical skills because sometimes we do pantomime. The actions need to be clear so children can understand them.

Career Facts

CLOWN

Education and Training. Many clowns take courses in clown or acting schools.

Career Outlook. The demand for clowns is expected to remain steady, though the number of people trying to become clowns is expected to grow.

CONNECTING SCHOOL TO CAREER

1. **Personal Qualities.** Should a clown performing at a three-year-old's birthday party use a loud or soft voice? Why?
2. **Thinking Skills.** Is clowning a very competitive career? Why or why not?

Social Development from One to Three

The period between ages one and four is also an important time for social development. In these years, children develop attitudes and skills that remain with them throughout their lives. Their experiences in the family help them learn how to live with others.

KEY TERMS

cooperative play
parallel play
socialization

OBJECTIVES:

- Describe patterns of social development from ages one to three.
- Explain how children make friends.
- Give principles for guiding toddlers.

General Social Patterns

Young children gradually learn to get along with other people, first in their own families and then in groups. This process is called **socialization**. Through this process, children can be expected to learn certain social skills at different ages. Of course, as with other areas of development, individual differences may influence these patterns.

Eighteen Months

At eighteen months, children begin developing independence from the family. For most children, the closest relationships are—and remain—those with family members. However, toddlers need to learn about the outside world. This may mean trips to the playground or other opportunities to be with children and adults who are not part of the family. Some children attend child care all day.

At about eighteen months, there is little real interaction between children, even when they are playing in the same area. Instead, children engage in **parallel play**, meaning that they play independently near, but not actually with, another child. More than one child may want—and grab for—the same toy, but the children aren't really playing with one another.

Eighteen-month-olds often seem to treat other people more as objects than as human begins. At this stage, the toddler is intent on satisfying strong desires without regard for anyone who interferes. There may be conflicts over toys that result in screaming, hitting, biting, or hair pulling.

The child this age can understand that his or her actions have consequences for others, though. This understanding is limited to actions that have direct, immediate, and physical results, however. When an eighteen-month-old hits another child, and that child cries, the first child can see that he or she caused the upset.

Parents look forward to when their children begin to play with other children, since this is a step in the child's social development. Many parents are surprised, then, when eighteen-month-olds play not *with* but *alongside* children their own age. ***What is this kind of play called?***

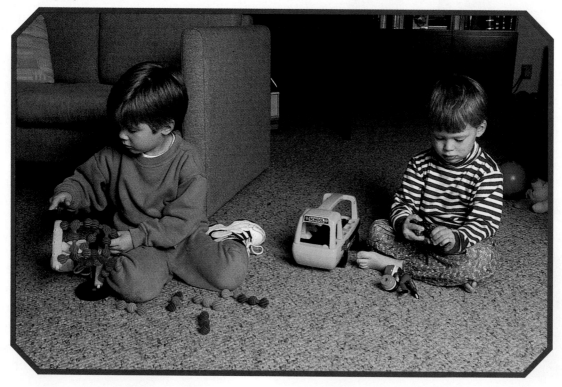

Two Years

By age two, children already have an impressive list of social skills. A two-year-old is especially good at understanding and interacting with his or her main caregiver. The child can read that person's moods and gauge what kind of behavior he or she will accept. As speech develops, the young child is increasingly able to communicate with others.

Two-year-olds find it is fun to have someone to play with, although they usually still engage in parallel play. At two, they begin to be able to understand the ideas of sharing or taking turns. Children this age like to please other people. Occasionally, they are willing to put the wishes of someone else (usually an adult) above their own wishes.

Two and One-Half Years

The negativism that is characteristic of the child at two-and-one-half carries into the child's social relationships. During this stage, a child who refuses to do anything for one person may do things happily for another. The reasons for these different responses are impossible to understand.

At this age, children are beginning to learn about the rights of others. They can respond to the idea of fairness—though at first, they are more concerned with what is fair to them. Social play is still parallel and works best with only two children. Squabbles are frequent, but brief. Children forget them quickly and resume their play.

Three Years

Most three-year-olds are sunny and agreeable. This shows in their relationships

What type of play is shown by these children? At about what age do children begin this kind of play?

with others. People are important to children of this age. A three-year-old will share, help, or do things another person's way—just to please someone.

Three-year-olds begin **cooperative play**, actually playing with one another. They build sand castles together, push toy tractors down the same roads, and park their toy cars side by side in the same area—with little friction. They can also work together in small groups to build with blocks, act out events for doll families, and fit puzzles together.

Parents, though still very important to three-year-olds, are no longer all-powerful in children's social lives. Most children this age seek friends on their own. They may prefer some companions over others.

Three and One-Half Years

By three and one-half, children's play becomes more complex and includes more conversation. Disagreements with play-

Patterns of Talking

From eighteen months to four years, the patterns of children's conversations change. The thick arrow shows the person they speak with the most. The thinner arrow shows other targets of talk. If there is no arrow, the toddler directs little or no talk to that person.

Eighteen Months

Other Toddlers   **Toddler**   **Adults**

Two Years

Two and One-Half Years

Three Years

Three and One-Half Years

Four Years

mates occur less often. Because children this age enjoy the company of others, they realize they must share toys and put up with some things they don't like in order to have it.

Children this age can use several different strategies to solve these conflicts. Jorge tried to take a block that was nearer to Ramon, who was also playing with blocks. When Ramon said, "That's my block," Jorge replied, "Oh, OK" and put it down. Julia and Latishia were playing with trucks. When Julia reached for one of Latishia's trucks, Latishia objected and then said "You can have it if you give me that one of yours."

There is an increasing ability to evaluate friendships. For example, a three-and-one-half-year-old may say, "I don't like to have Kevin come here. He doesn't play nice."

Close friends begin to exclude others, although most friendships don't last.

Children this age also take more notice of what other children are like. They become more likely to compare themselves to other children—not always to their own advantage. One day, Allison asked her mother, "Why does Libby always win when we race?" Her mother agreed that Libby was faster, but pointed out things that Allison did well. In this way, she acknowledged that Allison wasn't as skilled as the other child in one area but had other skills of her own.

Making Friends

The ability to make friends is important to normal social development. A child who is comfortable and friendly with others and who has at least one friend at a time is usually developing normally. However, if a child is unable or unwilling to make friends, try to discover the cause and take steps to help.

Even very young children need contact with other people. This is how they learn the give-and-take of socializing. Sometimes a caregiver needs to help a child learn what to say or how to act to join others in play. Those who begin to play with others early aren't as likely to be afraid of other children. They learn to cope with the occasional blows and snatching of other one- and two-year-olds.

Three-year-olds begin to develop friendships. They also begin to compare themselves to others. *What impact might that have on their self-esteem?*

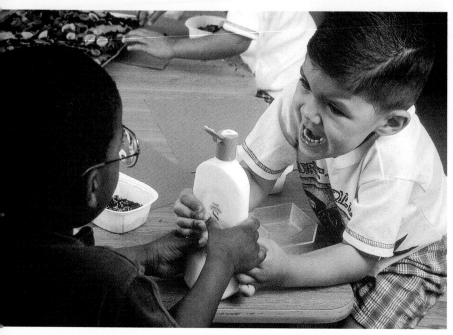

Give an example of a situation when caregivers should take action when children these ages disagree. What action would you take?

Imaginary Friends

In this period, many children begin to have imaginary friends. Some have the same friend for a long period of time—from several months to a year. Others have different friends. Some have imaginary animals rather than friends.

Imaginary friends may start as early as age two. They are more common from ages three to four. In that year, children have rich imaginations and are interested in fantasy and reality.

Some parents are concerned that children invent imaginary friends because they are unable to make real friends. They worry that an imaginary friend is a sign of unhappiness or problems coping with life.

In fact, an imaginary friend can be a very helpful way for a child to experiment with different feelings. Some children use an imaginary friend as a way of working through their negative feelings. For others, the friend mirrors everything the child does or experiences. Then the child talks to the family about how the imaginary friend felt about these experiences. In this way, the child finds a way to examine his or her own thoughts and feelings.

Usually imaginary friends fade away. Crystal simply stopped talking about her

Children who have only adult companions may have difficulty interacting with others their own age. Adults are more polite and considerate than children. Each child needs to learn to enjoy the rough-and-tumble companionship of other children. If this learning is delayed until school age, the child may face a difficult adjustment. At five or six, feelings are more easily hurt.

All children sometimes have disagreements and arguments. Whether or not a caregiver should step in depends on the situation. If two children are relatively evenly matched and there is no physical or emotional harm being done, the caregiver can simply observe the situation. Children need to learn how to solve their problems.

If the situation is more hurtful to one child, the caregiver will probably need to step in and help the children solve the problem. It is best for the children if the caregiver doesn't impose a solution but instead guides the children to find one for themselves.

friend when she started school. Paul had an imaginary friend when he was three, but he was gone by age four. There is no cause for concern unless the imaginary friend continues into adolescence.

Guiding Toddlers

The purpose of guidance is to help children learn self-discipline—the ability to control their own actions. There is no single best approach to guidance. Parents should consider the individual personality of each child, as well as their own personal beliefs. They should also consider each child's age and stage of development and understanding. Different approaches may be especially effective at various ages.

- **Eight to twelve months.** At this age, inappropriate behavior can usually be controlled by distraction. If the baby is chewing on a newspaper, for example, you might jingle a bright rattle in front of the child. As the rattle catches the baby's attention, simply move the newspaper out of the way.
- **Twelve to fifteen months.** Distraction and physically removing the child from forbidden activities or places work best. For example, Jared was fascinated by the lawn mower and tried to follow it around the yard. His older sister picked Jared up and took him into the house, saying, "Let's see if we can find the book about the teddy bear."

- **Fifteen to twenty-four months.** Children this age require distraction, removal, and spoken restrictions. Hassan started playing with toy cars on the driveway, where a repair truck was parked. His father said, "Let's take your cars into the backyard. You'll have more room there. The driveway isn't a safe place to play."
- **Two to three years.** By the age of two, children are better at responding to spoken commands and explanations. Two-year-olds can more easily understand adults' reasoning. Caregivers who explain their reasons get better results than those who only issue sharp commands. When she saw that her two-and-one-half-year-old was still not dressed, Kerri's mother said, "Kerri, you need to get dressed now because Grandma will be here soon to go shopping with us. We can't go unless we are ready."
- **Three to four years.** Three-year-olds take reasonable, loving guidance more readily than children of other ages.

Children learn how to behave as a result of parents' guidance. *Why is it a good idea for parents to discuss guidance issues together? How should parents interact with other caregivers?*

Ask the Eperts

Jacqueline Mault
Director of Special Services for the
Toppenish School District in
Toppenish, Washington

GUIDING *Toddlers' Behavior*

Q How can I guide my toddler's behavior?

A One of the best ways of guiding a toddler's—or any child's—behavior is by setting a good example. Children learn by imitating.

As toddlers grow older, they become increasingly able to take verbal direction. Caregivers get the best results by speaking in certain ways:

- **Be clear and specific.** *Speak to the child using very specific language. To say "I want you to behave at dinner" does not tell a child how to act. It's more effective to say, "I want you to sit still at the table" or "Remember to use your knife and fork."*

- **Limit the instructions.** *Focus on just one behavior at a time. You can't expect a young child to sit still at the table <u>and</u> eat with a knife and fork <u>and</u> stop talking with a mouth full of food <u>and</u> use the napkin. Work on one behavior. When the child learns that, it is time to move to the next one.*

- **Use positive words.** *Avoid saying "don't." Tell the child what he or she <u>can</u> do, not what is not allowed.*

- **Keep it simple.** *Use as few words as possible while still being clear. Toddlers can't remember too many directions at once. Some caregivers give lengthy reasons, explaining why they gave a child a certain direction. Give the next direction after the child has completed the first.*

- **Be firm.** *State the direction firmly and without apologizing so the child knows you mean it.*

Thinking It Through

1. Reword the following direction to make it more effective: "Don't track mud into the house."
2. Does this advice mean a caregiver shouldn't give any explanations for a direction? Why or why not?

They like to please, and they may be quick to remind a parent that they are obedient. Marcus came inside on a rainy day and said, "I remembered to wear my boots today. See my clean shoes? I'm a good boy, right?"

Promoting Sharing

One of the first social skills that children learn is to share, and that learning begins at this stage. Caregivers can help children develop this skill in various ways:

- Lead children to activities in which they need to share—or at least take turns—such as the seesaw or going down a slide.
- Limit the materials on hand for an activity so that sharing or taking turns is required. If there is only one pair of scissors, for instance, children will have to take turns.
- When you're handing out snacks, use the children to pass them to one another. That gives children an opportunity to practice sharing.
- Make clear what behavior you're trying to encourage. Call it "sharing" or "taking turns."

Some toys are very special to a child. They may have a strong emotional attachment to a stuffed animal or be very pleased about a new birthday present. It can be very difficult for the child to share these objects. Sometimes, too, there is legitimate concern that another child may accidentally break it. If the toy is visible, however, odds are that another child will see it and become interested in it. In these cases, it might be a good idea to put that toy away when other children visit.

SECTION 12-2 REVIEW

✔ Check Your Understanding

1. What is socialization?
2. Compare parallel and cooperative play. At about what age does cooperative play begin?
3. How do two-and-one-half-year-olds often show negativism in their social relationships?
4. How do children change in the way they handle disagreements from eighteen months to three and one-half years?
5. Why is it important to give young children opportunities to play with friends?
6. Distraction is effective for children of which ages?
7. What can parents do to promote sharing?

Putting Knowledge Into Practice

1. **Synthesizing.** Jeremy has an imaginary friend. If you were his parent, what would you do?
2. **Applying.** Eric and Chris, both two years old, were playing when they suddenly began to argue. What would you do?
3. **Observing and Participating.** Visit a park or a child care center and observe one or more groups of one- to three-year-olds. Report to the class on how they played.

Parenting With Care

Encouraging Independence

Between one and four, children long to be more independent.

Caregivers can help them achieve that. Of course, caregivers still have the main responsibility of meeting a child's basic needs. They can, however, help toddlers and preschoolers help themselves grow toward independence.

Self-Feeding
- Expect—and accept—some messiness as a child learns self-feeding. Minimize that mess with unbreakable dishes and a child-sized spoon and fork. Serve food in small servings. Use a cup with a spill-proof lid in this learning stage.
- Choose foods that are easy to handle and eat. Cut food into bite-sized pieces before serving.
- Be sure the child is comfortable. For eating at a table, use a high chair with the tray removed or a booster seat to raise the child to the right height.

Self-Dressing
- Choose clothes that are easy to put on and take off. Look for roomy shirts that slip on easily. Elastic waistbands make pants, skirts, and shorts easier to handle. Clothes with buttons or zippers in the front are more convenient than those with back openings.
- Fasteners often cause problems. Hook-and-loop fasteners, large buttons, and zippers are easiest for toddlers to manage.
- If a dressing task is too difficult for the child to do completely, let him or her do at least one part of it. Pulling up a zipper or slipping a foot into a shoe can be the first step toward learning a more complex task.

Grooming Skills
- Provide the child with his or her own towel, washcloth, brush or comb, and toothbrush. Be sure that all are within easy reach.
- A small stool can help small children cope with adult-sized bathrooms.
- Establish grooming routines, and help the child follow them every day.

- Set a good example yourself. The child is more likely to wash hands before eating if you do it, too.

Helping Others
- Putting away toys can start as a game. Be sure there is adequate storage space within the child's reach.
- Let young children help with simple chores around the house, such as sweeping, carrying laundry, and setting the table.

Above all, remember to be patient. A child's efforts will always be slower and less efficient than your own, but learning can't take place without practice.

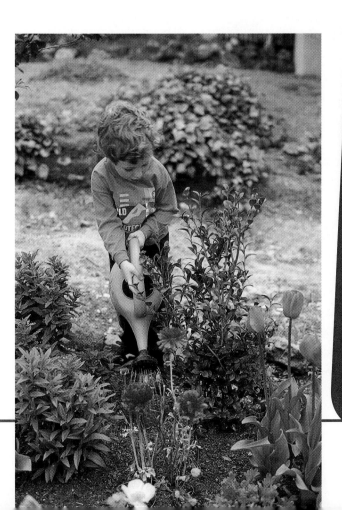

Following Up
1. **Thinking Skills.** Why do toddlers have difficulty opening and closing clothes with small buttons?

2. **Management.** Young children sometimes feel uneasy about independence. How can caregivers handle those situations?

REVIEW &

Summary

✔ Young children pass through emotional ups and downs but become increasingly able to control emotions. (Section 12-1)

✔ Toddlers show negativism as they try to exert control over their lives. (Section 12-1)

✔ Individual differences affect emotional development. (Section 12-1)

✔ As they grow, young children become more interested in other children. (Section 12-2)

✔ Learning to be friends helps toddlers and preschoolers develop skills they use later. (Section 12-2)

✔ Caregivers can help toddlers learn to share. (Section 12-2)

9. What techniques can caregivers use to teach children to share? (Section 12-2)

Thinking Critically

1. **Synthesizing.** Rosalie often tells her son Eric, "You're always messy" and "You never do anything right." How can such statements, when said frequently, affect his self-concept?

2. **Drawing Conclusions.** Are all children in a family likely to have the same temperament? Why or why not? What impact will that have on how parents interact with each of the children and the children as a group?

3. **Diagramming.** Make a time line that charts the typical social development of a child from one to three.

Reviewing the Facts

1. Describe the emotional ups and downs during ages one to three. (Section 12-1)

2. Contrast how younger and older toddlers and three-year-olds express anger. (Section 12-1)

3. What concern often underlies children's fears? (Section 12-1)

4. What is sibling rivalry? (Section 12-1)

5. About when do children begin to show empathy? (Section 12-1)

6. Explain the difference between parallel and cooperative play. About what age does cooperative play begin? (Section 12-2)

7. Why is it important for children to spend time with other children and not just adults? (Section 12-2)

8. How can a child benefit from having an imaginary friend? (Section 12-2)

Taking Action

1. **Living with Differences.** Claire and Carrie are twins. Claire finds it very easy to switch from one activity to another, but Carrie needs more time. If pressured to move faster, she has a tantrum. What can their parents do? *(Leadership)*

2. **Learning to Get Along.** Draw up a set of a few simple rules about getting along with other people that you think two- and

CONNECTIONS

three-year-olds can—and should—follow. Word the rules so that the children could understand and follow them. *(Communication)*

Cross-Curricular Connections

1. **Language Arts.** Write an objective description of a scene in which two toddlers at a child care center become involved in a conflict over toys. Write from the point of view of a center worker who describes what happened and what he or she did about it.

2. **Social Studies.** Explain how a child's culture and how his or her caregivers handle their own emotions could influence the ways the child expresses emotions.

Workplace Connections

1. **Interpersonal Skills.** You and a partner should each write down six negative statements that a caregiver could make about a toddler or preschooler. Then exchange papers and turn each negative statement into a more positive one. In what ways would this skill help in working with adults?

2. **Information Systems.** Create a poster that would remind child care center workers about how to guide children's behavior.

Family and Community Connections

1. **Guiding an Only Child.** Children with siblings have many opportunities to learn to share in the home. How can parents of an only child encourage the child to learn sharing?

2. **Handing Tantrums.** Ask a parent to describe how he or she once handled a child's tantrum. Report your findings to the class and evaluate them to determine which are the best techniques.

Technology Connections

1. **Internet.** Search on the Internet for advice to parents in handling any of the following topics: temper tantrums, separation anxiety, sibling rivalry, nighttime fears. Keep track of your sources. Compare the advice you found with others in your class. What might be the reasons for the differences?

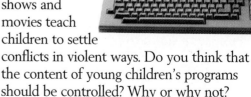

2. **Television.** Some people argue that violent television shows and movies teach children to settle conflicts in violent ways. Do you think that the content of young children's programs should be controlled? Why or why not?

First, Drew, age three and one-half, molded the clay into a flat, round shape. Then he rolled up a smaller ball and attached it to the top of the first shape. He put two small cylinders of clay on the front and then picked up his creation. "Emperor," he said, "the new Star Avenger has been completed." As he spoke, he moved his clay spaceship through the air, making zooming sounds.

Drew put down his spacecraft and began to make something else. This time he made a long cylinder of clay and attached another piece of clay to it. He picked that creation up. "The rebel attack force nears the imperial base," he said. Then he picked up his first ship again and began to maneuver the two clay models through the air.

"He moved his clay spaceship through the air, making zooming sounds."

SECTION 13-1

Understanding Learning and the Mind

Tiffany put the toy stethoscope on. She bent over the doll to listen to its heart. Then she looked into its ears. As she put her tools away, she smiled at the doll and said, "You healthy girl!"

KEY TERMS

concepts
creativity
directed learning
imitation
incidental learning
intelligence
trial-and-error learning

OBJECTIVES:

- Identify ways children learn.
- Explain how children develop concepts.
- Explain how one- to three-year-olds develop in several areas of intellectual activity.

The Role of Intelligence

Tiffany, age two, recently had a checkup. A few days later, she checked on the health of her doll. In the process, she revealed the growing power of her own mind.

A one-year-old is still much like a baby, just learning to make sense of the world. In contrast, a child of three and one-half talks freely, solves simple problems, and constantly seeks out new things to learn.

Intelligence is the ability to interpret or understand everyday situations and to use that experience when faced with new situations or problems. Intelligence is shaped by heredity and by environment. Everyone is born with certain limits of intellectual development. However, the extent to which an individual's potential is actually developed is greatly influenced by that person's environment.

It is crucial for young children to have an environment that promotes learning. Such an environment includes interactions with family members, the availability of playthings, and encouragement. Toddlers and preschoolers form attitudes toward learning that last a lifetime. If curiosity—a natural quality—is encouraged and enhanced, the child develops a positive attitude toward learning.

Methods of Learning

Children learn on their own through everyday experiences and through play. In the course of this learning, they use four different methods.

Incidental learning is unplanned learning. Five-month-old Josh happens to push both feet against the bottom of the crib and discovers that this motion moves his body forward. After this happens accidentally a few times, Josh sees a cause-and-effect situation. He then pushes against the crib on purpose.

Trial-and-error learning takes place when a child tries several solutions before finding one that works. At twelve to eighteen months, this means experimenting: "What happens when I touch the cat? Try to pick up the cat? Pull the cat's tail?" Krista, age three, uses trial-and-error learning differently when she wants her younger brother's truck. First, Krista grabs the truck from her brother, but he screams and her mother makes her give it back. Next, she tells her brother to go outside and play, but he doesn't want to. Finally, Krista offers to let her brother use her clay if she can play with his truck. He agrees, and Krista gets what she wants.

Imitation is learning by watching and copying others. Perhaps you have been annoyed by a younger brother who copied everything you did. Did you realize that he was trying to learn from you? Both skills and attitudes are learned by imitation.

Directed learning is learning that results from being taught. Umberto's first grade teacher helps him learn to read. Kara's mother teaches her the names of parts of her body by saying them while pointing to them. That's directed learning, too—it's just less formal. Directed learning begins in the early years and continues throughout life.

What type or types of learning help a child develop food preferences?

409

What kind of learning is each child demonstrating?

Concept Development

As they learn to think, young children begin to organize the information they receive from their senses. They start to form **concepts**, general categories of objects and information. Concepts range from categories for objects such as "fruit" to qualities such as color or shape and to abstract ideas such as time.

Children learn words and concepts by using three principles. Suppose Desmond's father points to an animal and calls it a dog. How does Desmond know that the label "dog" applies to that animal and not to its legs or its nose? Children start by thinking that labels are for whole objects, not parts. Also, children believe that labels apply to the group to which the individual objects belong, not the particular object. Dog means creatures like that one, not that particular dog. Finally, young children believe that any object can only have one label. That may be why it takes time for children to learn to use pronouns. It is hard for them to understand that "mommy" and "she" can mean the same person.

As a child matures, concepts become more accurate. Babies begin with two broad concepts—"the baby" and "not the baby." Young toddlers make very broad distinctions between people and things. For example, at first all women are "mama." A three-year-old understands the concepts of "woman," "man," "girl," and "boy."

Young children also learn to categorize objects by shape, color, and size. Balls are round, and so are biscuits and plates. Grass and trees are both green. Size distinctions come in two steps. The relationship between two items—"big" and "little"—may be recognized as early as eighteen months. Not until age three, however, can children pick out the middle-sized ball from three possibilities.

Concepts of life are not learned until later. A young child believes that anything that moves or works is alive—clouds, toys, and the washing machine!

Concepts of time improve during the second and third years. Two-year-olds may show more patience because they know what "soon" means and can wait a short time. They know the difference between "before" and "after." However, a child may not understand "today," "tomorrow," and "yesterday" until kindergarten.

The Mind at Work

Intellectual activity can be broken down into seven areas: attention, memory, perception, reasoning, imagination, creativity, and curiosity. All these areas develop throughout life. However, their development from one to three is especially remarkable.

INFOLINK

Piaget

For more on Piaget's preoperational period, see Chapter 10, pages 324-328.

Attention

Every moment, the five senses are bombarded with information. Right now, for instance, you see the words on the page. At the same time, you are also aware of such things as the size, shape, and color of the book and the amount of light in the room. You can probably hear pages being turned. You may be able to smell lunch being prepared in the cafeteria. Your skin can tell you that the paper of the book is smooth and cool.

You have the ability to block out most of this sensory information and focus only on the book. You can concentrate. A baby isn't able to concentrate. The infant's attention flits from one bit of sensory information to another.

As children mature, they gradually develop the ability to ignore most of the information their senses provide and to concentrate on one item of interest. Their learning is more focused on a particular topic. One- to three-year-olds have short attention spans. However, a three-year-old can focus on one activity for much longer than a one-year-old.

Toddlers can describe their experiences during the day to adults who did not share them. *What intellectual development makes this possible?*

Memory

Without memory, there would be no learning. Experiences that leave no impression cannot affect later actions or thoughts.

The Developing Brain

Memories linked to strong emotional reactions are most firmly imprinted in the brain.

As children develop, they become able to react to a situation by remembering similar experiences in the past. A one-year-old who was frightened by a dog may be afraid of all animals for a time. A three-year-old can remember the particular dog and compare it with others.

By age two, a toddler has a fairly good memory. Tyler knew his daddy who had been away for ten days. He can deliver simple messages. He also can repeat bits of favorite stories and talk about going to the park. Three-year-old Keisha remembers simple requests or directions, uses numbers as if counting, and is able to identify most colors.

Perception

A newborn learns about the world through perceptions—the information received through the senses. This sensory information reinforces established connections in the brain and sparks new ones. Gradually, the brain organizes itself for increasingly complex learning. The newborn, however, is just beginning to interpret this information.

Caregivers play a key role in toddlers' and preschoolers' development of perception. By talking about what they and the children are doing, they help the children become more perceptive. Use descriptive observations that the child can understand and expand on. For example, when passing a store window, you might say, "Look at the blue coat. Your shirt is blue, too. Let's see what other blue things we can find as we walk."

Two- and three-year-olds seem to ask questions constantly. Answering questions of "Why?" "What is that?" and "How does it work?" helps improve a child's perception. When questions are ignored or brushed aside, though, a child loses opportunities for learning. If the response is usually an absent-minded "Uh-huh" or "Don't bother me right now—I'm busy," the child eventually stops asking questions.

Reasoning

Reasoning is basic to the ability to solve problems and make decisions. It's also important in recognizing relationships and forming concepts.

Babies show the beginning of simple problem-solving ability at about four to six months of age. One-, two-, and three-year-olds gradually learn more sophisticated reasoning skills. At fourteen months, Omar solves problems by actually trying out all possible solutions. For example, when playing with a shape sorter box, he picks up a triangle and tries to fit it into each shape of hole until one works. By his third birthday, Omar's problem solving is less physical and more mental. He can think through possible solutions and eliminate those that won't work without actually trying out each one. He can usually find the triangle hole on the first try!

Practicing Parenting

Learning from Nature

*S*tep outdoors for a new world to explore! Children learn through their senses, and nature has many different sounds, smells, textures, and tastes.

Outdoors, children discover that sticks make wonderful pencils for scratching designs or letters in the earth or sand. They find that rocks come in a variety of shapes and sizes. Flowers have different scents. Some birds feed in the water and others on land. The bark of trees can feel rough or smooth. Help children make these discoveries by talking about nature and providing opportunities for children to ask questions.

APPLY YOUR KNOWLEDGE

1. How can children learn from nature even in cold or rainy weather?
2. Is it safe to let children experiment with the different tastes of nature? Why or why not?

As children solve problems, they basically are answering these questions:

1. What is the problem?
2. What do I already know about it?
3. What are the possible solutions?
4. Which is the best solution?
5. Did I make the right choice?

Decision making involves choosing between alternatives. Children learn to make good decisions through practice. It's important to give one- to three-year-olds opportunities to make real decisions. At first, these decisions should be based on limited choices in which either choice couldn't cause any harm. An eighteen-month-old can choose between two toys. At two, "Would you rather wear your yellow shirt or your green striped shirt?" What kinds of decisions might be appropriate at age three?

Imagination

Imagination becomes apparent at about two years of age. (No one knows whether babies may have an imagination.) An active imagination enhances learning because it allows the child to try new things and to be different people—at least in the mind. Chairs become trains, boxes are buildings, and closets are caves. The child becomes a ferocious lion or a busy mail carrier.

Children use their imagination to connect what they see and hear with themselves. A child may see an airplane and wonder, "Will I fly in a plane someday?" A child may hear about death and ask, "Will I die, too?"

Respect a child's imagination and respond carefully. When three-year-old Emma makes up a story, she isn't lying—she's using her imagination. In fact, until about the age of five, children are simply not sure where reality ends and imagination begins. However, if Emma's mother says, "Don't be silly. You know that didn't really happen," Emma will be discouraged from using her imagination.

Creativity

A related mental ability is **creativity**, in which the imagination is used to produce something. The product is usually an object that others can see, such as a finger painting.

Children can be and do almost anything through imagination. They can play with ordinary objects like an empty box, turning it into a house, a spaceship, a fort, or many other things.

Ask the Experts

Rachel Perkins
Child Development Technology
Instructor
Hinds Community College
Utica, Mississippi

ENCOURAGING *Creativity*

Q How can I encourage creativity in my toddler?

A Encouraging creativity is very important for children. Fortunately, it is not that difficult.

- *Encourage play activities that depend on exploration and imagination. Drawing, playing with clay, building things, dressing up in grown-up clothes, and telling stories are all examples. You can make up part of a story and ask the child to finish it.*

- *Provide toys that can be used in more than one way. Small wooden blocks can become microphones, cars, sandwiches, or the walls of a castle. Empty cardboard boxes can be caves, fire trucks, or doll beds.*

- *Provide unstructured time. Children need time to themselves to have a chance to let their imagination roam. The less television they watch, the better for their imagination, too.*

- *Remember that the process of creating is more important than the product. You might respond to a child's drawing this way: "Amanda, I've never seen a cat with three eyes before! I wonder what it would be like to have three eyes."*

- *Praise the child's efforts with deeds as well as words. Display the picture of the three-eyed cat on the refrigerator and let the child hear you tell others about it.*

Of course, the main idea behind all these methods is a simple one. To encourage a child's creativity, you need to provide opportunities—and then sit back and watch. Allow the child to control and direct the creative play. Try not to set limits—as long as the child is safe. You'll be amazed at what your child can come up with!

Thinking It Through

1. Why are toys that can be used in more than one way good for developing creativity?

2. Why do you think television does or doesn't promote creative play?

Sometimes, though, the creative product is not an object. Examples are daydreams and dramatic play. Creativity, an asset throughout life, is most readily developed in early childhood.

Curiosity

Children are curious about the world around them, and that curiosity fuels brain development and learning. It's curiosity that causes children to wonder why or to try new activities. However, parents sometimes sti-

fle that curiosity by overprotecting the child—or by overprotecting the home. Children need a safe environment and the freedom to explore it.

Young children seem to be into everything. They poke into every corner and closet. They touch and examine everything within reach. It's impossible to anticipate what a one-, two-, or three-year-old may do next. A doll or truck may turn up in the washer because "it was dirty." Patience and a healthy dose of humor are essential!

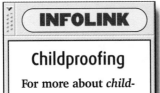

INFOLINK

Childproofing

For more about *child-proofing*, see Chapter 11, pages 372-373.

SECTION 13-1 REVIEW

✔ Check Your Understanding

1. What is intelligence?
2. Which method of learning is based on watching and copying others? Which type is based on trying different approaches to solving a problem?
3. What concept is developed by a shape sorter toy? By stacking boxes?
4. How does memory support learning?
5. How can caregivers help children sharpen their perception?
6. Why is curiosity important?

Putting Knowledge Into Practice

1. **Comparing.** Which of the four methods of learning do you use most? Why? Which do you think you found most useful and enjoyable as a three-year-old? Why?
2. **Applying.** Choose a toy for children ages one to three (other than one mentioned in this chapter). Identify the concepts that the toy helps a young child learn.
3. **Observing and Participating.** In writing, describe a learning situation that occurred in one of your classes this week. Identify the learning method used. Develop another version of the same situation in which a different learning method could have been used.

CAREER OPPORTUNITIES

Preschool Teacher

A CONVERSATION WITH RACHEL QITSAULIK

How did you become interested in becoming a preschool teacher? I always wanted to be a preschool teacher. The early years are crucial for children. I help them get off to a good start.

What are the tasks and responsibilities of a preschool teacher? Our main goal is to help children develop and learn. We provide opportunities to experience new things and explore new situations. We help them learn to get along with others. Of course, we stay in close contact with parents.

What is the work environment like? The classroom is a friendly place with lots of light and bright colors. You have to get used to being busy all the time. Still, the children bring energy, curiosity, and joy so that it's easy to stay energized.

What are the working hours like? We have morning and afternoon sessions. We also prepare materials for classes. I have summers off, but some programs run year round.

What aptitudes are needed to be a preschool teacher? It's a long list—energy, creativity, patience, self-control, initiative, flexibility, knowledge of child development. We need skills in problem solving, time management, and communication. We also need to be able to work with others.

Career Facts

PRESCHOOL TEACHER

Education and Training. Preschool teachers usually have a college degree in early childhood education. In some states, a degree from a two-year college is accepted. In most states, teachers have to be certified. This means getting an official document that declares they meet minimum qualifications.

Career Outlook. The demand for preschool teachers should rise.

---CONNECTING SCHOOL TO CAREER---

1. **Thinking Skills.** Why would states require preschool teachers to be certified?
2. **Basic Skills.** Why would preschool teachers need good communication skills?

SECTION 13-2

Encouraging Learning from One to Three

Caregivers have a major effect—either positive or negative—on a child's learning. Those who provide a relaxed, accepting atmosphere and a variety of experiences encourage young children to learn. But adults who are overly harsh, too busy with their own lives, or who show children that they don't really care about learning discourage it.

KEY TERMS

articulation
flammable
speech-language pathologist

OBJECTIVES:

- Suggest ways to encourage young children to learn.
- Choose safe, appropriate toys that promote mental, physical, and social skills.
- Describe how speech develops.
- Name common speech problems and approaches to solving them.

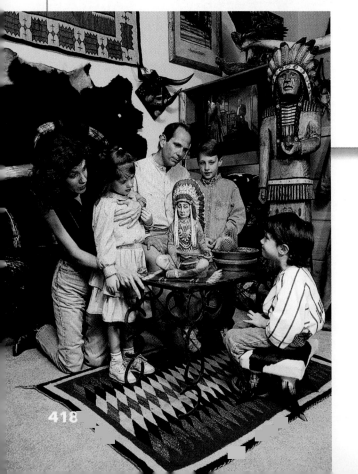

Readiness for Learning

Children can learn a new skill only when they are physically and intellectually ready. It's a waste of time trying to teach a six-month-old to pull a zipper closed—the baby has neither the physical nor intellectual maturity that skill requires. In the same way, most two-year-olds lack the physical and intellectual development needed to

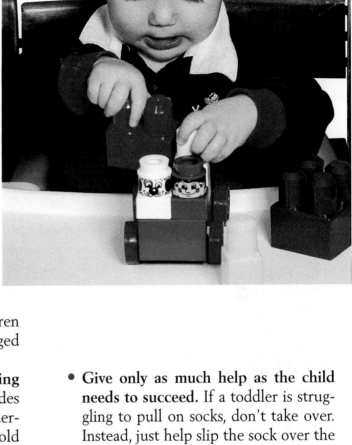

Toddlers can enjoy many different organized activities, but they also need unstructured time in which they can simply do what they are interested in. Caregivers help children by allowing some of this free time every day.

learn to print letters. When adults push children to learn things they aren't ready for, the children can't succeed. A sense of failure may slow the child's learning, rather than increase it as the adult had intended.

Avoid delaying skills that children are ready to learn. Because he struggled with the task, Ben's mother put his shoes on for him. She later discovered that this "helping" caused problems. When Ben was well past the age when he should be able to put on his own shoes, he continued to ask for help.

Guiding Learning

These suggestions will help you guide the learning of young children:

- **Give your time and attention.** Children learn best when they are encouraged by someone who cares about them.
- **Take advantage of simple learning opportunities.** Everyday life provides many chances to help a child's understanding grow. Erin took two-year-old Colin to the supermarket. As she chose oranges, she said, "I'll buy five oranges" and then counted out five. This helped Colin learn the concept of five, counting skills, and the name of the fruit.
- **Allow time for thinking.** Problem solving and decision making are new experiences for young children. They need time to consider choices and make decisions.
- **Give only as much help as the child needs to succeed.** If a toddler is struggling to pull on socks, don't take over. Instead, just help slip the sock over the child's heel before it gets caught. The child learns how to put on socks and enjoys the sense of accomplishment. If at all possible, let children do the final step in any task they are struggling with.
- **Encourage children to draw their own conclusions.** "Let's find out" is better than an explanation. Seeing and doing helps reinforce learning.

- **Show how to solve problems.** When a toddler's tower of blocks keeps toppling, demonstrate that stacking one block directly on top of another provides balance. Then leave building the tower to the toddler.

  You can also model problem solving. Talk out loud as you solve problems or make decisions. That way, the child can hear the way you think your way to a solution.
- **Maintain a positive attitude.** Express confidence in the child's abilities. One way is to praise the child's efforts: "You worked very hard putting your toys away."
- **Keep explanations simple and on the child's level.** Too much information can cause a young child to stop listening. When a child asks about the fish in the aquarium, explain, "The fish live in water. People live outside the water. We need air to breathe."
- **Allow children to explore and discover.** Let them roll in the grass, climb trees, and squeeze mud through their fingers and toes. Constantly saying "Don't do this" and "Don't touch that" limits the sensory and motor experiences needed for learning.
- **Help the children understand the world and how it works.** Take young children along, even on routine errands. The library, the supermarket, and the gas station can all be learning experiences. Talk about what is happening and why it's happening. Helping at home also boosts learning.

The outdoors is a great place for learning. An adult's participation can increase the fun.

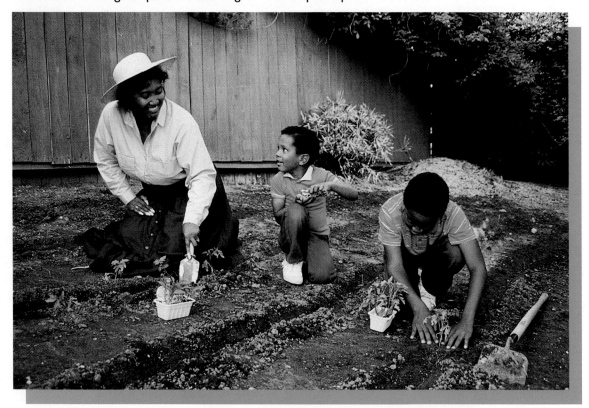

The World's Children

Dolls Around the World

AFRICA

Southern Africa

*D*olls hold a special fascination for children—all over the world. Among the Zulu people of Southern Africa, women spend the winter months making dolls. They use fabric, discarded clothes, and decorative items that have been collected all year.

Sometimes, dolls are more than simple playthings. Among another African people, the Ndebele, mothers make a ceremonial initiation doll for their daughters when the young girls come of age. The doll symbolizes a new beginning.

SHARE YOUR THOUGHTS

1. What can North American children learn by playing with dolls?
2. Why do you think dolls are found in many different cultures?

As toddlers help rake leaves, for example, call attention to the different colors and the crackling sounds. Discuss the changing seasons.

- **Take frequent breaks.** A child needs stimulation—but a child also needs a chance just to have fun. Watch for clear signals that a child has had enough of an activity. Fussing, wiggling in a chair, or a distracted look all suggest that it's time to stop.

Play Activities and Toys

Toys are an important part of play. They allow children to experience imaginary situations and act out different roles. They encourage the development of large and small motor skills. They also help children learn to share and cooperate with others.

Evaluating Toys

With thousands of toys to choose from, knowing what to buy is important. Ask yourself these questions:

- **Is the toy safe?** This is the single most important consideration. Make sure there are no small parts that could be swallowed or sharp edges that could cut a child. Make sure that the toy is not **flammable,** or easily burned. Finally, make sure that the toy has no lead-based paints, which are poisonous. The government's Consumer Products Safety Commission alerts the public about toy safety problems.
- **Is it well made and durable?** There is nothing more discouraging for a child—or an adult—than having a toy break the first time it's used. Is the toy

CHAPTER 13: Intellectual Development from One to Three **421**

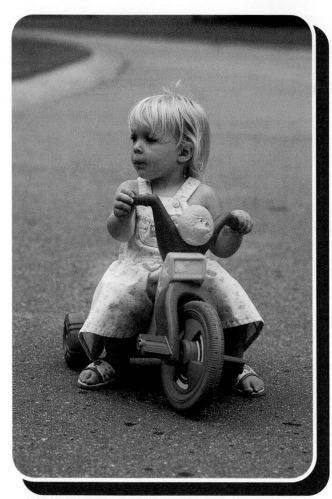

Different toys provide different learning opportunities. Playing with dolls or small figures encourages language development and dramatic play. Blocks and construction toys build spatial and small motor skills. *What skills are developed by a riding toy?*

made to withstand the use it will receive?

- **Will it be easy to care for?** A stuffed bear that takes a ride through a mud puddle may be ruined unless it can be washed. Similarly, books with wipe-clean covers are the most practical choice for young children.
- **Will it encourage the use of imagination?** Many toys do everything for the child. With no need to pretend, the child's imagination develops more slowly. Look for simple toys that can used in a variety of ways. A talking doll may say ten phrases, but a child can make a nontalking doll say anything!
- **Is it colorful?** Young children respond more readily to colorful objects. They also encourage children to learn the names of colors.
- **Will it be easy for the child to handle?** Think about the size of the child in relation to the toy. The excitement of a new tricycle is quickly lost if the child's legs are too short to reach the pedals.

Age-Appropriate Toys

Toys should also be appropriate for a child's age. Infant toys are usually not challenging enough for three-year-olds. Neither will an older child's toys hold the attention of most fourteen-month-olds for long.

Children at different ages enjoy different kinds of toys:

- **One to two years.** At this age, a child practices body control and learns through exploration. Many of the best "toys" are items found in the home, such as metal pans, wooden spoons, and plastic storage containers. Anything that allows the child to use large muscles is popular. This may include swings, riding toys with wheels, balls, small wagons, boxes, and low furniture. Children of this age also enjoy small dolls and stuffed animals, sturdy books, simple puzzles, and toy cars. Be careful to avoid small toys or toys with small parts that could be swallowed.
- **Two to three years.** Coordination and understanding improve greatly during this year. In addition, the child wants to do what adults are doing. The desire to

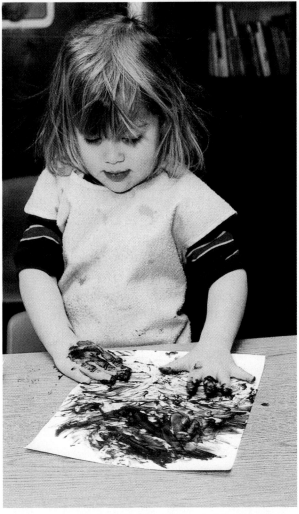

How does finger painting help children express their creativity?

imitate suggests a variety of toys: a child-sized broom, a small shovel, plastic or wooden tools, play dishes, and empty food containers. Crayons, clay, large beads to string, books, large blocks, and blunt scissors are popular. A sandbox can provide hours of enjoyment.

- **Three to four years.** Preschoolers' improved motor skills and increased imagination bring interest in toys requiring small motor skills. Dolls to dress, cars and trucks, and similar toys are popular. Children of this age love to mold clay, color, and paint—especially with finger paint. Three-year-olds spend longer periods with books and enjoy listening to records or cassettes. They enjoy puzzles and using ladders, swings, and slides. Most three-year-olds love the mobility of a tricycle.

Speech Development

In the toddler and preschool years, language abilities grow at a very rapid pace. As with other areas of development, though, children vary greatly in the timing of their speaking skills.

One of the early signs of developing language is that a child can point to or pick up an object that has been named. *What does this show?*

From age one to age two, children learn to understand words more quickly by recognizing a word just from its initial sounds. At 15 months, a child needs more than a second to recognize "baby." By two years, the child understands the whole word from the opening sound "bay"—in just 600 milliseconds.

Brain development research has brought new insights into how children learn to use language. They appear to have an inborn instinct to decode sounds, words, sentences, and grammar from the language they hear. The first three years of life are a window of opportunity for learning words.

Between their first and second birthdays, children work at learning new words. They like to learn the names of everything, and they enjoy listening to the sounds the words make. At twelve months a child may speak two to eight words. By age two, that jumps to about 200 words. During this period, most children use one or two words rather than a whole sentence to express a thought. For example, a child might hold out a cup and say "water" to mean "I want a drink of water."

A child's language development is strongly influenced by how caregivers and older children speak to him or her. For example, Jason's mother usually used baby talk with him. Not surprisingly, at three and one-half, Jason still has trouble speaking plainly enough for others to understand him.

Listening to a young child and giving a personal response help encourage language development.

Signs of Language Development

Children's language abilities develop at different rates. Still, most three-year-olds can do the following:

- Say their name and age.

- Make all the vowel sounds and speak the consonants P, B, M, W, H, D, T, and N.

- Speak without repeating a word or syllable.

- Use sentences of at least four words.

- Usually be understood by others, even strangers.

- Answer questions of "what" and "where."

- Understand what is meant by "on," "in," and "under."

- Follow a command with two or three parts.

FOLLOWING UP

1. Why would it be significant that a child can be understood by strangers rather than by usual caregivers?

2. How does following a multiple-part command indicate improved memory as well as language skills?

Encourage language development and learning in toddlers by talking to them about their lives. Speak in a clear and engaging way. For example, you can take the time to describe—and guide children in talking about—whatever they are seeing or doing. "Look at the big bite you've taken out of that shiny red apple. Can you hear the crunch it makes when you put your teeth into it?"

At about age two, the child usually starts combining a few words to make short sentences: "Doggie bark." "Jimmy fall down." From age one to two, a child typically calls himself or herself by name. At about two years, children begin to use pronouns.

At about two and one-half, children begin to learn some of the rules of grammar.

They learn by listening to other people talk rather than by any formal teaching. For example, a child begins to add an *s* to words to make them plural. The child then—quite logically—applies this rule to all words. At two and one-half, *foots* and *tooths* make as much sense as *hands* and *eyes*. At three, Katie responded to "I'm going to Eureka" with "You're going to *my* reeka?"

Speech Difficulties

Many parents are concerned about "late talkers." Some make the mistake of pressuring the child who talks late or whose speech is unclear. Most often, this pressure just makes the child aware of the problem and may make it worse.

What speech difficulties may require the help of a speech-language pathologist?

A child who doesn't seem to understand what is said and doesn't speak at all or who speaks very little should have a thorough examination. Free screenings may be available from a **speech-language pathologist** through the local public school. These specialists are trained to detect and correct speech problems. It is important to identify, as soon as possible, any physical problem that may be hindering the child's language development. Poor hearing, mental retardation, learning disabilities, and emotional problems may all slow a child's speech.

Problems with **articulation**, the ability to use clear, distinct speech, are common until at least age three or four. Some children skip syllables or leave off the endings of words. These problems usually correct themselves in time. A speech-language pathologist can determine whether a problem is likely to go away over time or if therapy is needed.

Avoid constantly correcting a child's pronunciation. Instead, be careful to set a good example with your own speech. If the toddler says "ba" and reaches for a bottle, hand the bottle over, saying, "Bottle. Selena wants her bottle."

Stuttering is a more serious speech difficulty for young children. However, many adults mistake normal speech hesitations for stuttering. A child may repeat whole words or phrases: "Johnny... Johnny... Johnny. He... he... he hit Zoe!" This is not true stuttering. In this case, the child's speaking and thinking abilities are still immature. He or she simply can't get the words out as rapidly or smoothly as desired.

A true stutter can be identified by the rhythm, pitch, and speed of speech. It is rapid, forced, and short and sharp in sound. Usually, the child repeats only the beginning sound of a word: "I c—c—c—can't g—g—g—go outside." The child often also shows tenseness in some way—with gasping, sputtering, or rapid blinking, for instance.

The cause or causes of stuttering are still not clearly understood. Some children need the help of a speech-language pathologist to overcome the problem. Most children who stutter, however, outgrow it. Experts advise against finishing words for a child. Children who stutter need time to say the word on their own.

Children with speaking difficulties need to know they are loved. Such an attitude will help the child cope with—and perhaps even overcome—the problem. Ridicule or constant corrections only make the problem worse.

SECTION 13-2 REVIEW

✔ Check Your Understanding

1. What kind of readiness is needed before a child can learn a skill?
2. Choose one of the principles of how to guide a child's learning and give an example of a caregiver putting it into practice.
3. Which kinds of development—physical, emotional, social, or intellectual—does play promote?
4. What should be the most important consideration when choosing toys for children? Why?
5. List at least four toys that are appropriate and fun for toddlers between the ages of one and two.
6. What age group most enjoys songs, playground equipment, and tricycles?
7. What is the disadvantage of speaking to a child using "baby talk"?
8. What kinds of problems might indicate that speech therapy is needed?

Putting Knowledge Into Practice

1. **Making Inferences.** Identify three local activities or events appropriate for young children. Explain what you think children would learn from each.
2. **Applying.** While at a friend's birthday party, the friend's mother asks Jake which balloon he wants. He answers, "I . . . ah . . . ah . . . want the . . . ah . . . green one." Does Jake's answer suggest that he needs speech therapy? Why or why not?
3. **Observing and Participating.** Write a description of a routine chore such as shopping for food, washing dishes, or cleaning. Then describe how you could talk about this activity to a toddler who was watching you do it. How could the child help?

Parenting With Care

Reading to Children

Sharing a book with a child can be a special experience, both for you and for the child.

Books are wonderful learning tools. In addition, reading to a child nourishes close relationships, builds vocabulary, encourages language and listening skills, and helps the child separate reality from fantasy.

Children who learn early in childhood that books are fun are more likely to remain readers throughout life. They also learn to read more easily. Chapter 16 gives more information on reading to children.

Choose Appropriate Books

Children of different ages respond to different types of books:

- One-year-olds need short, simple books with large, uncomplicated pictures. They like picture books with objects they can name and books with rhymes.
- Two-year-olds prefer simple stories they can relate to. Like one-year-olds, they never tire of hearing their favorite stories again and again.
- By age three, children enjoy longer stories with more of a plot. They like realistic stories and stories that help them use their imagination. They enjoy books about how things work and why things happen.

Become a Master Storyteller

Reading a story is like putting on a play. Create excitement and interest by varying the tone of your voice, giving each character a different voice, and using gestures and facial expressions.

If you are reading to one or two children, snuggle up close and hold the book so they can see. If you are reading to a group, arrange the children in a semicircle facing you. Read loudly enough for everyone to hear. Take time to learn the book beforehand so you can keep the pictures facing the children.

Encourage Participation

Even before they can read, children can participate in stories to increase learning and fun.

- Very young children can turn the pages, which builds hand-eye coordination.
- Relate the action and pictures in the book to the child's own life. "You have a red ball, too, don't you?"
- Ask questions as you read. "What do you think Melissa will find when she opens the box?"
- With familiar books, let the child play the part of one character.
- With older children, point out the words for familiar objects. Practice recognizing letters and their sounds.
- Encourage children to dramatize a story by themselves or with puppets. Have them draw pictures to go with a story.
- Remember to keep your focus on the child—not on the story. Reading together should be fun. If the child has stopped enjoying the story, put the book away.

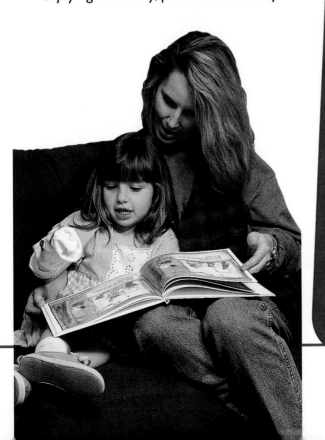

Following Up

1. **Leadership.** Some books have complex drawings that children have to search to find specific people or objects. Would those books be suitable for one-year-olds? Why or why not?

2. **Thinking Skills.** What changes in the toddler's mind make fantasy stories suitable beginning at age three?

REVIEW &

Summary

✔ Intelligence is determined by heredity and environment. (Section 13-1)

✔ Children use four different methods to learn. (Section 13-1)

✔ Imagination and creativity are areas of intellectual activity. (Section 13-1)

✔ Toys should be safe, appealing, and appropriate for a child's age. (Section 13-2)

✔ The way in which caregivers speak to children shapes language development. (Section 13-2)

8. In what way should caregivers talk to children to help them learn speech? (Section 13-2)

9. How should parents respond to children who have problems with articulation? (Section 13-2)

Thinking Critically

1. **Drawing Conclusions.** What can parents do to persuade children to value learning? Why would their actions matter?

2. **Charting.** Make a chart that shows the kinds of skills—large motor, small motor, or language—that children can learn from three of the toys listed on pages 422 to 423 for each age group.

3. **Synthesizing.** What method of learning do children use as they build language skills? Explain how they use that method.

Taking Action

1. **Promoting Creativity.** Write the beginning of a story that would inspire children to use their creativity by finishing the story or by drawing a picture of it. *(Leadership)*

2. **Testing Memory.** Create a simple memory game that could be played by toddlers to improve their memory. *(Thinking Skills)*

Reviewing the Facts

1. Give an example of the effect of environment on intelligence. (Section 13-1)

2. Noemi used the hose to wash her toy trucks, just as her father washed the car. What kind of learning is this an example of? (Section 13-1)

3. When do children learn concepts of time? (Section 13-1)

4. What is the difference between an infant and a three-year-old in terms of attention? (Section 13-1)

5. How can caregivers teach children to solve problems? (Section 13-1)

6. What may happen to children who are pushed to learn something before they are ready? (Section 13-2)

7. Name a principle for guiding learning and give an example of that principle at work. (Section 13-2)

CONNECTIONS

 Cross-Curricular Connections

1. **Art.** Draw a series of pictures that you could show to toddlers to help them learn the concepts of color, shape, or size.

2. **Science.** Find out what scientists have learned about how the brain stores memories. What sights, sounds, words, or colors are remembered? What makes them memorable? Prepare a summary of your findings.

 Workplace Connections

1. **Resources.** Suppose that you are about to start a child care center for children from one to three years old. Choose one kind of activity—such as art or music or reading—and make a list of the toys and play activities that you would have to promote that activity.

2. **Basic Skills.** Write a brochure that explains to parents the philosophy and goals of a fictional child care center in terms of children aged one to three.

 Family and Community Connections

1. **Learning in the Garden.** Suppose you had a two-year-old and your house had a garden. List the concepts and skills the child could learn in that garden.

2. **Learning in the Home.** Identify an object or activity that is commonly found in the house. List ways that this object or activity could be used for learning. Find at least one example for each of the four methods of learning.

 Technology Connections

1. **Internet.** Search on the Internet to find information about stuttering. About how many children stutter? At what ages does stuttering commonly develop?

2. **Television.** Watch a half hour of an educational children's television show such as *Sesame Street, Mister Rogers' Neighborhood,* or *Reading Rainbow.* Describe the show to your class, pointing out what skills or concepts a toddler or preschooler could learn from the show.

UNIT 5

The Child from Four to Six

THE END

When I was One,
I had just begun.

When I was Two,
I was nearly new.

When I was Three,
I was hardly me.

When I was Four,
I was not much more.

When I was Five,
I was just alive.

But now I am Six, I'm as clever as clever.
So I think I'll be six now for ever and
ever.

—A.A. Milne

433

CHAPTER 14

Physical Development from Four to Six

Shawna Simons teaches kindergarten at Great Oaks Elementary School. Today she is the guest speaker on motor skill development at Jefferson High.

"You only have to look at my class of four- and five-year-olds," Mrs. Simons said, "to realize that motor development varies greatly from child to child. You can't necessarily tell a child's age just by how well the child runs or colors. I have one child who's among the youngest but skips better than anyone else in class.

"Think back to the activities during your own days in kindergarten. Many are chosen to help children improve their large and small motor skills. Painting is not only a great creative activity, but it also helps hand-eye coordination. Cutting and coloring do, too. We play games that involve running, jumping, and throwing—all large motor skill activities.

"Children need well-developed motor skills to learn to read and write successfully. Forming letters takes the same kind of small muscle control and hand-eye coordination as coloring, doesn't it?

"Your teacher will be bringing you to observe my kindergarten class next week. I think you'll find the kids interesting and very individual. If you look closely, you will also see lots of learning going on—whether they are flying a kite or listening to a story. I'll be back to answer questions after you have observed my class."

"We know that children need well-developed motor skills to learn to read and write successfully."

Physical Growth and Development from Four to Six

If you've ever been around a four-, five-, or six-year-old, you know how active children are during this period. They run rather than walk, and they wiggle when they sit, yet there is a purpose behind all this activity. Children are constantly practicing and refining their physical skills.

KEY TERMS

permanent teeth
ambidextrous

OBJECTIVES:

- Describe how an average child's height, weight, proportion, and posture change from ages four to six.

- Explain the changes to a child's teeth that generally begin around age six.

- Compare average motor development of four-, five, and six-year-olds.

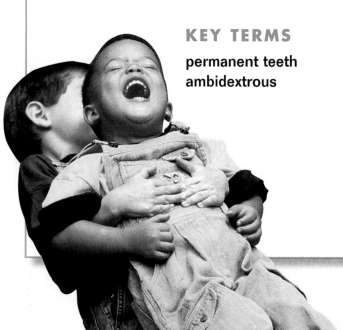

Height and Weight

The rate of physical growth from ages four to six is only slightly slower than from ages one to three. The average yearly increase in height during these years is 2½ to 3 inches (6.4 to 7.6 cm). Most children gain about 4 to 5 pounds (1.8 to 2.3 kg) per year during this period. However, larger or smaller gains are quite common. Boys are often slightly taller and heavier than girls.

The chart below shows average heights and weights for four- to six-year olds. Of course, height and weight charts give average measurements. Most children who are smaller or larger than the averages are still developing normally.

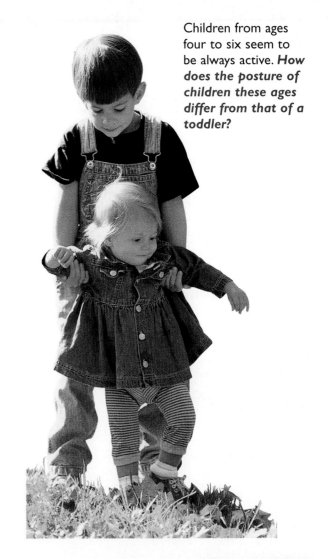

Children from ages four to six seem to be always active. *How does the posture of children these ages differ from that of a toddler?*

The Developing Brain

One of the fastest-growing parts of the child ages four to six is the brain. At age three, the brain is about 75 percent of its adult weight. Over the next three years, it grows to around 90 percent of its adult weight.

Proportion and Posture

Between a child's fourth and seventh birthdays, the body becomes straighter and slimmer. The protruding abdomen of babyhood flattens. The shoulders widen and are held more erect. The chest, round from birth to age three, broadens and flattens. The neck also becomes longer. The legs lengthen rapidly, growing straighter and firmer.

Average Heights and Weights for Four- to Six-Year-Olds

YEARS	HEIGHT	WEIGHT
Four Years Old	40.7 inches *(103 cm)*	36.0 pounds *(16.3 kg)*
Five Years Old	43.5 inches *(110 cm)*	40.5 pounds *(18.4 kg)*
Six Years Old	46.0 inches *(117 cm)*	45.0 pounds *(20.4 cm)*

Differences in height and weight increase as children grow older. *What differences do you see in your own class?*

The child's balance and coordination improve in these years as well. Four- to six-year-olds hold their arms nearer their body when they walk or run.

Teeth

A smile showing missing teeth is typical of a six-year-old. At about that age, children begin to lose their primary teeth. Over time, the primary teeth are replaced by **permanent teeth**, the set of 32 teeth that will not be naturally replaced.

The six-year old molars, or "first molars," are the first permanent teeth to appear.

There are four of them—two upper and two lower—positioned in back of the 20 primary teeth. Because they appear first, these molars act as a lock to keep all the teeth in position. Later, when the child's front teeth are replaced by their larger permanent front teeth, the molars prevent the new front teeth from pushing other teeth farther back in the jaw.

In general, the primary teeth are lost in the same order as they came in. The two lower front teeth are the first to be replaced, followed by the two upper front teeth.

Thumb Sucking

Some four-, five-, and six-year-olds continue to suck their thumb, usually to comfort themselves or to handle tension. Adults may worry about this habit, but in most cases, it is best ignored. Trying to force a child to quit can cause more problems than the habit itself. Generally children stop on their own.

If thumb sucking seems excessive or continuous, check with a dentist. A problem exists if the position of the permanent teeth and the shape of the jaw are being altered.

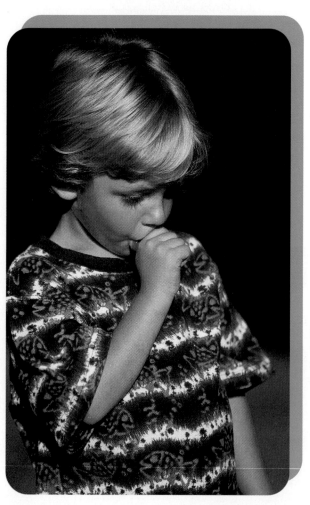

Some children from ages four to six continue to suck their thumbs. *What are some reasons that children suck their thumb, and what should parents do about the habit?*

CAREER OPPORTUNITIES

Dental Hygienist

A CONVERSATION WITH RAMON REYES

How did you become interested in becoming a dental hygienist? At eleven, I needed braces. I spent lots of time in the dentist's office and got to know the people well. I love science, and helping other people always gives me a boost.

What are the tasks and responsibilities of a dental hygienist? My main job is to clean and polish people's teeth. I also take x rays. I keep records and let the dentist know about any problems. I also teach patients how to care for their teeth.

What is the work environment like? Dental hygienists work indoors in offices. Working in health care, we have to be clean and well organized, and our work space must be that way too. Safety guidelines require us to wear masks, gloves, and glasses while we work to prevent the spread of infection.

What are the working hours like? The office where I work is open six days and three evenings a week. That makes it easier for patients to schedule visits. Some hygienists work two or three days a week for two different dentists.

What aptitudes are needed to be a dental hygienist? You need good hand-eye coordination and a sensitive touch so you don't hurt or bother the patients. You need to able to work carefully and thoroughly. Hygienists must be clean and neat, giving a professional appearance. If you are pleasant and reassuring, you can help patients feel more comfortable. Finally, hygienists have to be able to communicate well with people.

Career Facts

DENTAL HYGIENIST

Education and Training. Hygienists can either earn a certificate in a two-year program or receive their training at a four-year college. To practice, they need to pass a state licensing test.

Career Outlook. Jobs for dental hygienists are expected to grow faster than the average in coming years.

CONNECTING SCHOOL TO CAREER

1. **Interpersonal Skills.** If you were a hygienist, how would you introduce yourself to a six-year-old having her teeth cleaned for the first time?
2. **Personal Qualities.** Self-management involves setting personal goals, having self-control, and evaluating one's own work. Why would these characteristics be essential in this career?
3. **Technology.** What are some ways dental hygienists could stay up-to-date on new technological advances in their field?

Motor Skills

During this period, most basic large and small motor skills improve significantly. *How Motor Skills Develop* on the next page gives examples of average physical skills by age. The timing of the development of these skills varies, of course. Ahmad can put together puzzles with 75 to 100 pieces but has not yet mastered skipping. Reilly is more comfortable with puzzles of 35 pieces and loves jumping rope.

Four-, five-, and six-year-olds are very energetic. Their favorite activities are usually physical—running, jumping, climbing, and turning somersaults. At four, children are learning to throw and catch both large and small balls. Five-year-olds show improved speed and coordination in all their activities. The movements of six-year-olds are smoothly coordinated. They enjoy balancing activities, such as walking a curb or riding a bicycle. Rhythm intrigues them—they like keeping time to music and jumping rope to chanted jingles.

Four- and five-years-olds show improved dexterity, the skilled use of the hands and fingers. Most four-years-olds learn to lace their shoes, but generally cannot tie them until about age five. Five-year-olds can pour liquids from a pitcher into a glass, showing improved hand-eye coordination. They like to cut and paste and can print some letters, but often not words. Six-year-olds show even greater ease and skill.

Children need plenty of opportunities for skill development. Giving them time and space to run, jump, and climb helps them develop their large motor skills. Providing activities such as coloring, painting, drawing, tracing, cutting, and writing helps them build small motor skills. Children with well-developed small motor skills will find learning to read and write easier.

Hand Preference

By about age five, most children consistently use either their right or left hand for most activities. The hand used most often becomes the most skillful. Only a few people are **ambidextrous**, or able to use both hands with equal skill.

With better fine-motor skills, children of these ages can paint with brushes instead of using finger paint. Hand preference is becoming established. *What other fine-motor activities are good practice for children ages four to six?*

► HOW MOTOR SKILLS DEVELOP

Small Motor Skills	Large Motor Skills

4 Years

- Laces shoes
- Dresses and undresses self
- Cuts on line with scissors

- Gallops and hops
- Jumps forward as well as in place
- Throws overhand with body control

5 Years

- Ties shoelaces
- Draws recognizable person
- Skillfully picks up very small items
- Buttons, snaps, and zips clothing

- Stands and balances on tiptoe for short period and skips, alternating feet

6 Years

- Builds block towers to shoulder height
- Cuts, pastes, molds, and colors skillfully
- Writes entire words

- Throws and catches ball with more ease and accuracy
- Rides a bicycle

Although handedness becomes apparent about age five, preference for one hand actually begins early in life. Researchers still don't know how hand preference develops. Some point to heredity as the probable source. Others think it depends on which hand parents usually put objects into during the first years of a child's life. Whatever the cause of hand preference, professionals agree that there is no reason to try to influence a child to prefer one hand rather than another.

Practicing Parenting

Making Compliments Count

For children ages four to six, the praise and compliments that they receive play a hidden, but important, role in development. Giving praise does more than just build self-esteem. That self-esteem encourages the child to try and master even more difficult tasks. When Janette learned how to do a forward roll, her dad commented, "Look how well you tucked your head under!" At her next tumbling class, Janette was ready to try doing somersaults. All areas of development can be enhanced through positive reinforcement. How can you use praise effectively?

❤ **Make it special.** Don't just give automatic compliments. Constant praise loses its power. Children know whether you really mean what you say.

❤ **Make it specific.** "You did a fine job putting your books away. They're so neat and organized," tells the child more than "You did a great job!"

❤ **Target problem areas.** If a child needs to work on learning to button clothes or share toys, look for opportunities to encourage improvement of those skills.

❤ **Notice positive behavior.** Children crave attention. By complimenting what the child does well, less desirable behavior will diminish.

APPLY YOUR KNOWLEDGE

1. How might you compliment a child who just learned to jump rope?
2. Why might some people feel children should not be praised very often?

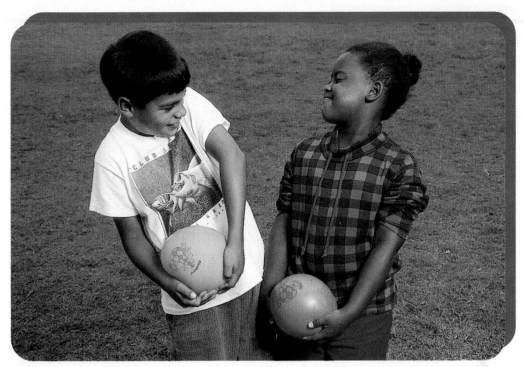

Outdoor play with friends promotes development in all areas, not just physical.

SECTION 14-1 REVIEW

✔ Check Your Understanding

1. What changes in height, weight, and proportion generally take place in four- to six-year-olds?
2. Describe the posture of children ages four to six.
3. Which are the first permanent teeth to appear? What function do these teeth perform?
4. What would you say to a parent who asked you for advice on how to handle a five-year-old who sucks his thumb?
5. List at least four large motor skills you could place on a developmental checklist for four-year-olds.

Putting Knowledge Into Practice

1. **Analyzing.** Six-year-olds—especially boys—are very active and have difficulty sitting still. What effects might that have on their behavior in school?
2. **Synthesizing.** Put together a list of typical activities for a half day of kindergarten. For each appropriate activity, indicate which specific small and/or large motor skills would be practiced.
3. **Observing and Participating.** Go to a park or playground where young children are playing. Watch them play and record what they do and how they behave. Try to determine which of the children are aged four to six based on their behavior. Share your notes and your conclusions with the class.

Providing Care for Children from Four to Six

Four-, five-, and six-year-olds need less actual physical care than younger children. However, they still need guidance in developing self-care skills. This increasing independence is needed as children start school. Many four-year-olds go to preschool programs, and most five-year-olds go to kindergarten for a full or half day. By age six, children are typically in school for a full day.

KEY TERMS

fluoride
group identification
sealant

OBJECTIVES:

- Explain why good nutrition is essential for children ages four to six.

- Give examples of ways to encourage good nutrition in children of these ages.

- Explain how to help children ages four to six develop good self-care habits.

Feeding

The energy children need for growth, learning, and activity depends on a steady supply of nutritious foods. Following the Food Guide Pyramid, shown on page 361, is an easy way to ensure good nutrition. Serving sizes are smaller for children. Young children often eat the minimum number of servings from each food group.

Children four to six need a good diet to have the food energy to stay active. *Of what kinds of food do they need the most servings?*

Of course, the actual amount of food an individual child needs varies. It depends on such factors as height and weight, temperament, and level of physical activity. A girl who runs and bikes a great deal needs more food energy than one who spends more time playing quietly indoors.

Research has shown that many children do better with five or six small meals and snacks a day than three large ones. Why? A child's stomach is still small. Eating more frequently provides a more constant level of energy.

Poor Nutrition

Poor nutrition—not getting the key nutrients needed through food—has many causes. Lack of money to buy healthful foods is *not* the most common one. Some caregivers don't understand the need for or principles of good nutrition. Others have poor eating habits themselves and set a poor example. Sometimes children are simply allowed to choose their own food. It is the responsibility of parents and other caregivers to provide children with healthful food choices and make sure they are well-nourished.

Poor nutrition has negative effects. Children with inadequate diets have less resistance to colds and other illnesses. Their growth may be limited. Learning, too, may be more difficult because they are tired and easily distracted.

Weight Problems

During this age span, children may look chunky or slim and still be healthy. Check with a doctor before deciding that a child is overweight or underweight. If a problem is detected, the doctor or a dietitian can help determine what eating and activity changes are needed. What works for adults may not be appropriate for children. For an overweight child, for example, a low-calorie diet may not supply the nutrients and energy needed for growth, development, and learning.

When a child consistently consumes more calories than the body uses, the extra calories are stored as fat to meet future energy needs. A child who is underweight is not eating enough food to supply his or her energy needs. Neither of these conditions occurs suddenly, although a child may lose weight quickly when ill. Both result from long-term eating habits that do not match the child's needs. Often it's not just the quantity of food eaten, but the quality that's the problem.

Poor food choices can also be a cause of weight problems. With help, children can learn to balance the types and amount of food they eat with the specific needs of their body.

Ask the Eperts

Pat Brodeen
Teacher and Teen Parent Coordinator
at Theodore Roosevelt High School
San Antonio, Texas

PROMOTING *Good Eating Habits*

Q How can I encourage my child to eat a balanced diet now, and how can I help her build healthy eating habits that will last a lifetime?

A Many parents worry about their children's eating habits. It's a natural concern, but worrying isn't part of the solution. Because children begin to eat less and become more choosy as they get older, the best approach to helping a child develop good eating habits has three steps:

1. *Understand children's nutritional needs.*
2. *Make nutritious foods available and attractive.*
3. *Set a good example, but don't make eating an issue.*

The first step is easy. Become familiar with the Food Guide Pyramid. The pyramid makes it clear that children—like the rest of us—should be eating more foods made from grain, fruits, and vegetables than from meat.

The second step can be fun for both parents and children. Involve the children in selecting, preparing and serving nutritious foods. Find ways to enjoy familiar foods and to experiment with new ones. Try making frozen pops from juice or dipping broccoli "trees" in cheese. Let children create—and then eat—their own necklaces of oat cereal rings.

For many parents, the third step is the most challenging. Offer your child nutritious, appealing foods; then let go. Treat your child's food preferences—and your child—with respect. Forcing a child to eat can cause problems beyond food choices. Given opportunities, good examples, and respect, children will likely develop healthy, long-lasting eating habits.

Thinking It Through

1. Children these ages enjoy silly names and rhymes. Suggest specific ways you could build on these interests to encourage good nutrition.
2. In many families, parents work outside the home so preparing a nutritious dinner quickly is a challenge. What techniques could parents use to avoid frequent take-out meals which often are high in fat?

Teaching Children About Nutrition

One of the best gifts parents and other caregivers can give young children is good eating habits. Nutrition lessons learned at this stage can lead to a lifetime of better health.

As children begin school, they start making more decisions on their own about what they will and will not eat. By learning about nutrition, children can make wise food choices. They are more than happy to tell others what they have learned, too. Just before four-year-old Chris popped a carrot stick in his mouth, he announced, "This gives me good eyes." Both home and school play a part in teaching good food attitudes and habits.

At Home

Parents can take advantage of children's natural curiosity at this stage. Food is a rich resource for learning. For example, involving children in caring for a garden has been shown to increase the variety and quantity of vegetables they eat.

Children also can help in the kitchen in many different ways. They can tear lettuce for salads, scramble eggs, or mix batter. They enjoy cutting shapes out of bread. They can make mini pizzas by flattening biscuit dough, pouring on tomato sauce, and sprinkling on cheese or other toppings.

Teaching children about nutrition in this way offers other advantages as well. Children

Children aged four to six are eager to help around the kitchen. *What tasks can parents ask them to perform?*

feel proud of the contributions they have made to a meal. The parent and child spend positive time working together. Such activities also help children improve their small motor skills.

At School

Schools, too, use food as learning tools. For a preschooler, spreading peanut butter inside a celery stick and sprinkling raisins on the top provides lots of lessons. Celery, peanut butter, and raisins are all good for you and help you grow. The textures of these ingredients are quite different. What words describe their texture? How many raisins are on the peanut butter? How does

- **Let them choose their own lunch box or bag.**
- **Don't get in a rut**—send different foods each day.
- **Make foods easy to eat.** Try pita bread or a tortilla wrap to keep the filling inside.
- **Think finger foods**—chunks, strips, cubes, and shapes.
- **It doesn't have to be a sandwich.** Lowfat yogurt with sprinkles, a hearty soup, crisp salad, or casserole favorites can travel in insulated containers.
- **What about sweets?** Ripe fruit, raisins, fig bars, and graham crackers are all good choices.
- **Add a surprise!** This could be a special treat, a fancy napkin, a riddle, or a note that says you care.

the celery sound when you bite it? What does the finished snack look like? Maybe ants on a log!

Children who are in school all day usually bring their lunch from home or eat one provided by the school. However, what children are given to eat and what they actually eat may be quite different. Food is often traded or thrown away. To entice children to eat all of their packed lunch, try the tips shown above.

Teaching Self-Care Skills

As four- to six-year-olds' physical abilities improve, they are increasingly able to care for themselves. They can keep themselves clean, dress themselves, and begin to care for their clothes.

Washing and Bathing

Many children this age are less interested in washing and bathing. Performing these tasks has lost its novelty. Praise for a job well done works better than nagging and scolding.

Setting up and maintaining hygiene routines helps children accept these tasks as expected behavior. Malcolm and his sister take turns using the bathroom to wash up before bed. While one is washing, the other gets his or her backpack ready for the next day.

Brushing Teeth

Regular tooth brushing is another essential routine. Make sure children know how to brush effectively and learn how to floss their teeth.

Tooth decay is a real concern at this age since permanent teeth are beginning to emerge. The dentist may recommend using **sealants**, thin plastic coatings that prevent plaque from developing. Toothpaste with **fluoride**, a chemical that strengthens the outer coating of teeth, helps also. These two steps can prevent about 90 percent of cavities from developing.

Dressing and Choosing Clothes

Four-, five-, and six-year-olds are usually able to dress themselves independently.

Molars, in back, are the first permanent teeth to appear. *What order do the remaining teeth follow?*

of belonging—begins to be important. That may bring a desire to wear clothes that are popular with others. Take the child along on shopping trips, if possible.

Caring for Clothes

Once children begin to care about what they wear, they can learn basic clothing care. To start, they can fold and hang up clothes and put dirty items in the appropriate place. Putting clothes away is simpler if the child has storage within reach. Hooks at eye level, low rods, and handy shelves encourage children to take care of their clothes.

Developing these habits will probably take a long time and require consistent reminders. To some parents, it just seems easier to continue doing such tasks for their

Children will be interested in taking care of clothes that they were able to choose themselves. *What kind of clothing is best for active children?*

Some may need help with complicated fasteners, such as shoelaces or buttons down the back of a garment.

Many children have difficulty figuring out which clothes match. Mismatched outfits can usually just be ignored. Another approach is to help children select coordinating outfits ahead of time and store them together.

Comfort, durability, and economy remain the guidelines for choosing clothes. Two other factors are important in selecting clothes. First, children this age have definite likes and dislikes. Some become attached to a favorite garment, as they do to a particular toy. Second, **group identification**—a feeling

Handling Bedwetting

*I*t is not unusual for children who have completed toilet training to occasionally wet the bed at night. Bedwetting tends to happen more frequently soon after a child learns bladder control. Over time, it usually happens less often, and by five it typically disappears.

Still, about 10 percent of children older than five occasionally wet their bed at night. About two-thirds of these children are boys. There are several possible causes. Either the child's bladder is not large enough to hold urine during the night, or he or she is not awakened by the feeling of a full bladder. Sometimes the cause is an infection in the urinary tract.

Treat toileting accidents casually. Shaming or scolding the child doesn't help. Concerned parents should talk to the child's pediatrician.

FOLLOWING UP

1. How are children older than five likely to feel when they wet the bed at night?
2. If you were a parent of a six-year-old who occasionally wets the bed, how, specifically, would you handle the situation?

---

children. However, this is the stage of development when children need to increase their independence and sense of responsibility. Parents who pick up and put away clothes for a five-year-old shouldn't be surprised when the child expects the same service as a teen.

Sleeping

By four, many children no longer take an afternoon nap. Some continue a daily nap until they begin a full day of school. It depends on the needs of the individual child.

Children this age are generally more cooperative about going to bed. A few use delaying tactics, but many actually ask to go to bed. After saying goodnight and perhaps looking at a book or listening to soft music for a while, most go to sleep easily. Some children may need conversation, compan-

ionship, or a stuffed toy to sleep. Bedtime stories offer a time for closeness and develop an interest in books and reading.

Toileting

By their fourth birthday, most children have few toileting accidents. When accidents do occur, it is often because the child is concentrating so fully on an activity that he or she forgets to go to the bathroom. Sometimes a child is in a new place and feels uncomfortable asking where the bathroom is. Sickness—even a cold—may also lead to accidents. A persistent problem should be checked by a doctor.

These steps can minimize accidents:

- Before leaving home for an activity, make sure the child goes to the bathroom.

A bedtime story can help settle a child after an active day. *What other benefits does reading together provide?*

- When arriving at a new place, help the child find where the bathroom is.
- Keep an extra outfit available so that if an accident does happen, the child has clean clothes to wear.

When they begin school, some children may suffer from constipation or sometimes wet their pants. These problems can be caused by the tension children feel in their new school surroundings. The length of time for adjustment depends on the individual child. Most children adjust within a few weeks. For some children, the problem may recur at the beginning of school for several years.

SECTION 14-2 REVIEW

✔ Check Your Understanding

1. What factors influence the amount of food a child needs?
2. How can parents and other caregivers help children learn good nutrition in the home?
3. What would you do if you found out that a child you care for usually trades away her school lunch for others' cookies and candy?
4. How can caregivers teach children to make cleanliness routines a habit?
5. What practices should children follow to care for their teeth?
6. Why is it helpful to take children along when shopping for their clothes?
7. What steps can be taken to make it easier for children to care for their clothes?
8. How should parents and other caregivers handle toileting accidents by four- to six-year-olds?

Putting Knowledge Into Practice

1. **Comparing and Creating.** Compare the three-year-old's interest in bathing and washing to that of a four- to six-year-old. Working with a partner, brainstorm a list of suggestions for increasing interest.
2. **Applying.** Imagine that you are the parent of a six-year-old who wets the bed about once a month. What might be your reactions? What would you actually do?
3. **Observing and Participating.** Watch a group of four- to six-year-olds eat a meal. Choose one child and analyze his or her food choices. Were they nutritious? If not, what would you do to make them more nutritious? Share your notes and conclusions with the class.

Parenting With Care

Monitoring Television Viewing

If you ask whether young children should watch television, you'll likely get strong opinions.

Actually parents and other caregivers should think about different questions: Which TV programs are right for young children? How much TV should they watch? With whom should they watch TV?

There are certainly many valuable TV shows. Shows like *Sesame Street*, for example, teach the alphabet and numbers, help children learn about different cultures, and help them understand their feelings. Nature shows teach and entertain at the same time.

Programs about current events can help children develop an interest in the world around them. Letting the TV serve as an "electronic babysitter," however, isn't healthy. The more children watch TV, the less time they have for other activities. Drawing and cutting and pasting, running and jumping, and playing with other children are all important to the child's physical, social, emotional and intellectual development.

Many TV programs simply aren't suitable for children. Some programs frighten or confuse them. Others present topics that are too mature for them to understand. The amount of violence shown on TV—even in children's programs, such as cartoons—is a particular problem. Research is still being conducted on the effect of TV violence on children, but the extent of violence is clear. One study found that more than 60 percent of all TV shows surveyed had violence—and in almost three quarters of them, the person who committed the violence suffered no punishment. The American Academy of Pediatrics has taken a firm stand on the issue:

"We believe that televised violence has a clear effect upon the behavior of children and contributes to the frequency with which violence is used to resolve conflict."

TV watching can be helpful or harmful to a child's development. These steps can help make it a positive experience.

- Limit the amount of time children spend watching TV.
- Choose programs that are appropriate for the child's age and promote development.
- Check out shows the child wants to watch to see if they are acceptable.
- Whenever possible, watch along with the child. You can help the child separate reality and fantasy by explaining things that may be confusing. If violence is shown, explain other ways that the problem could have been solved.

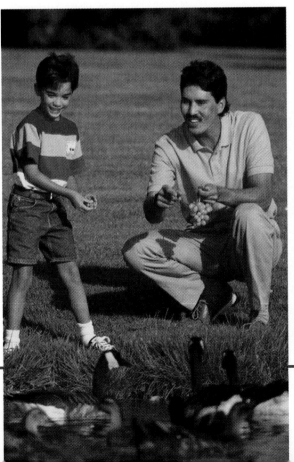

Following Up

1. Choose one development task described in the chapter and explain how watching TV could interfere with or promote it.

2. **Communicating**. How would you tell a six-year-old that TV viewing will be limited to one hour a day on school days?

Summary

✔ Children ages four to six grow rapidly, and their body shape changes. (Section 14-1)

✔ Permanent teeth begin to appear around age six, replacing primary teeth. (Section 14-1)

✔ Children ages four to six refine their large and small motor skills. (Section 14-1)

✔ Good eating habits can influence nutrition habits as an adult. (Section 14-2)

✔ Four- to six-year-olds can wash and dress themselves and can help care for their own clothes. (Section 14-2)

✔ Children ages four to six may still have toileting accidents. (Section 14-2)

8. Name two possible causes for toileting accidents by children ages four to six. (Section 14-2)

Thinking Critically

1. **Analyzing.** By the end of kindergarten some children haven't yet mastered such small motor skills as writing letters. Do you think these children should repeat kindergarten or be allowed to advance to first grade? Explain your answer.

2. **Synthesizing.** Suppose you worked at a child care center. Describe three steps you could take to help the children prevent bladder-control accidents.

Reviewing the Facts

1. Describe how children ages four to six change in height, weight, and posture. (Section 14-1)

2. In what order do permanent teeth appear? (Section 14-1)

3. Why do some children continue to suck their thumb? (Section 14-1)

4. How do children's large motor skills improve during this age span? (Section 14-1)

5. Give at least four examples of activities which can help four- to six-year-olds improve their dexterity. (Section 14-1)

6. What are three ways parents can help young children learn good nutrition? (Section 14-2)

7. How can parents make it easier for children to choose clothing that matches? (Section 14-2)

Taking Action

1. **Which Hand Is It?** Draw two pictures of a house with trees and flowers—one with your right hand and one with your left. (Mark them with an "R" and "L".) As a class, compare all the right-handed drawings and all the left-handed ones. Can you identify which were drawn with the preferred hand? How might drawing with your "wrong" hand be similar to a young child's experience drawing pictures? (*Thinking Skills*)

CONNECTIONS

2. Tie It Up. How would you teach a five-year-old to tie shoelaces? Make a simple chart or give a visual demonstration of the steps you would use. Be sure your verbal explanation will be understood by the child. *(Leadership)*

 Cross-Curricular Connections

1. **Math.** Using the heights and weights of the children in a preschool or kindergarten class, calculate the children's average height and weight. Next find the range of differences in weight and height. Make a visual of your findings.

2. **Language Arts.** Ask a librarian to recommend a book that would be suitable as a bedtime story for a four- to six-year-old. Read the book and tell the class why you agree or disagree with the recommendation.

 Workplace Connections

1. **Interpersonal Skills.** You see Tonya, a five-year-old, bouncing a ball near a group of three-year-olds. Being older, Tonya is faster and more sure on her feet, but she still isn't very aware of others. As she bounces the ball harder and harder, you are concerned that it may hit and knock down one of the younger children. What would you do?

2. **Basic Skills.** You work in a child care center and have been asked to devise a set of cleanliness rules for the children. The rules should include what children should do before and after meals or snacks and after they have used the bathroom.

 Family and Community Connections

1. **Eating Right.** Design a poster about good nutrition or healthful snacks for kindergarten students. Display the posters in a classroom or other appropriate community site.

2. **Clothing Care.** If you have a younger child living with you, look at how his or her clothes are stored. Would you recommend any changes to make it easier for the child to care for his or her clothes?

Technology Connections

1. **Computer.** Using a nutrition analysis program, find the nutritional value of the foods that you ate today for breakfast and lunch. Include serving size, number of calories, and grams of fat, protein, and carbohydrates. Based on your findings, what would you do to improve your diet to be a good example for a child? Explain whether or not you would use this software to analyze a child's diet.

Emotional and Social Development from Four to Six

The children crowded around the aquarium's children's exhibit to touch the baby shark. Angela pushed her way through the rest to get right to the front where she could feel it. Dustin hung back from the others although he moved to a position where he had a good view. Rachel and Briana talked the whole time—although their conversation did not seem to be about the shark. Kaleel told Bobby what kind of shark it was, and what it ate. Molly named it, and Shoma tried to tell a story about sharks.

Jed Washburn, who taught this preschool class, simply watched the children be themselves. He smiled to himself and realized how much the children had changed since the class started in the fall. "They're really growing up," he thought, and then said aloud, "OK, Briana, tell me what you know about sharks."

"He realized how much the children had changed over the year."

SECTION 15-1

Emotional Development from Four to Six

Heather walked to school with Justin on his first day. As they reached the block where the school stood, Justin turned to his mother. "OK, Mommy," he said. "You can go home now." Heather gave him a hug and a kiss, and Justin walked the rest of the way, swinging his lunch bag. Heather's eyes clouded as she thought of how her baby had grown up in just five years.

KEY TERMS

initiative

OBJECTIVES:

- Describe emotional development in children ages four, five, and six.
- Identify ways children show anger, fear, and jealousy.
- Develop ways to respond to anger, fear, and jealousy in children ages four to six.
- Analyze the effects of competition on children.

General Emotional Patterns

Four-, five-, and six-year-olds face many changes. Many, like Justin, begin regular school attendance during this period. School takes children away from their home and into a new environment that they share with unfamiliar adults and large groups of other children. In addition, children of this age begin to assume more responsibility and become aware that they have left babyhood forever. Feelings of independence and self-worth help children develop initiative—motivation to accomplish. Each child differs in response to these challenges.

Four Years

Most four-year-olds seem intent on asserting their independence. They are more self-centered, impatient, defiant, and boastful than they were at age three. They often argue and compete, and they are bossier than in the past.

Children four years old spend more time playing with others than do younger children, but relations are not always smooth. This four-year-old is telling her playmates where to play. *What quality typical of four-year-olds is she showing?*

Four-year-olds can also be unusually loving and affectionate. They need and seek parental approval. One minute, a four-year-old may stamp her foot and scream, "I hate you, Mommy!" Three minutes later, she may smilingly offer her mother a flower.

Because they feel more independent and have more skills, four-year-olds can wash and dress themselves. They are typically proud of their accomplishments, abilities, possessions, and creations. They can still fall back into younger behavior, though, when you least expect it.

Four-year-olds use language with enthusiasm. They enjoy the sounds of language. "Antsy-Wantsy-Nancy"—or some similar nonsense—can send them into hysterical laughter. They enjoy trying out bathroom-related words and seeing how others react. They also want to talk the way adults do, although they don't yet have the language skills for mature conversations.

Four-year-olds enjoy having other people laugh at their jokes, but they dislike it when people laugh at their mistakes. It is important to them that they are no longer seen as babies.

Most four-year-olds are in a rather difficult phase of normal emotional development. You can help children of this age by respecting their need to explore and test themselves. Avoid treating four-year-olds like toddlers. Try to use flexible rules when guiding their behavior.

Four-year-olds can be difficult, but they are also very loving. *What needs mark their relationship with parents?*

Having learned that others won't accept tall tales and lies, five-year-olds are increasingly realistic. Like four-year-olds, they continue to enjoy slapstick humor. At the same time, they are more able to carry on real discussions and ask meaningful questions than four-year-olds.

At this age, children conform to rules more easily. They willingly mind their parents and teachers—at least most of the time. However, adult criticism is very hard for them to take.

Children at age five are more patient, generous, persistent, and conscientious than earlier. They sometimes feel anxious, often out of a desire to achieve acceptable results rather than as a result of general insecurity.

Five Years

Five-year-olds enter a quieter period of emotional development, similar to that of age three. Children of five are generally rather practical, sympathetic, and serious. Their improved attention span allows them to finish what they have started, rather than moving from one thing to another. Having a better memory allows them to go back and finish uncompleted tasks.

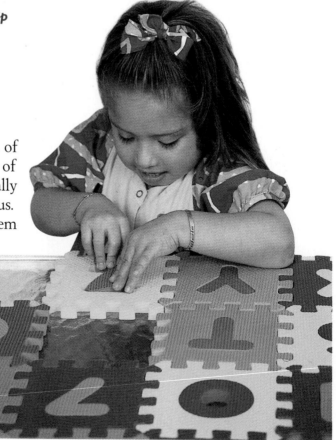

Because they have improved attention spans, five-year-olds can take on more complex tasks than they could before. *How will this help them in the future?*

Six Years

Like children of four, six-year-olds are often stubborn and quarrelsome. They resent directions, and they think they know everything. They are the center of their own universe—and determined to stay there. Six-year-olds are often at their worst with their own parents.

At six, children have rapidly changing moods. They love and hate, accept and reject, smile and storm—sometimes for no apparent reason. Even a favorite playmate is likely to get a swift whack before being told, "You bumped into my truck." Of course, a six-year-old playmate will probably immediately hit back.

Six-year-olds are learning to appreciate humorous situations and jokes. They throw themselves into their fun with the abandon that characterizes all they do.

It is easy to understand why six is a difficult age for children. Many are in school all day for the first time. They are faced with the task of finding their status outside the home. It's also a time when children long to feel grown-up—but often feel small and dependent. Six-year-olds crave praise and approval. They are easily hurt and discouraged.

Specific Emotions

During the years from four to six, children need help in recognizing and expressing their emotions. Caregivers should accept and help children identify all the emotions they experience.

Six-year-olds have rapidly changing moods. *What new change in their lives contributes to their emotional upheaval?*

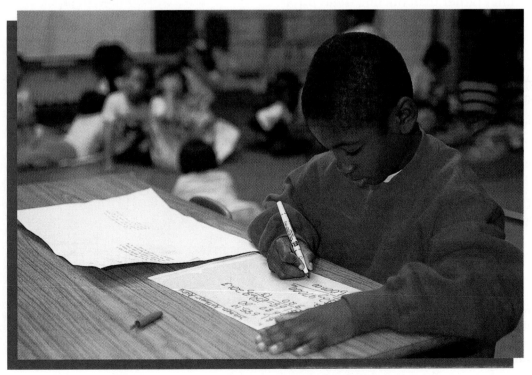

Self-Confidence

As children find success at accomplishing new skills and facing unfamiliar situations, their confidence improves. These feelings of independence and self-worth help them develop **initiative**—motivation to accomplish more.

Anger

How children express anger changes more during childhood than any other emotion. Young children show anger freely, with no effort to restrain themselves. As children grow, they use more subtle means of expressing their anger:

- **Four years.** Four-year-olds may still show anger by physically fighting. Their anger lasts longer than before. They often threaten and attempt to "get even."
- **Five years.** Five-year-olds are more likely to try to hurt other children's feelings rather than hurting them physically.
- **Six years.** Six-year-olds are even more stinging with words. They tease, insult, nag, and make fun of others.

The frequency of anger decreases from age four to age six, but the effects of anger last longer. There are a number of reasons for these changes. A child's tolerance for frustration generally increases with age. Also, some sources of earlier frustration are eliminated as the child's skills improve. Finally, by age six, children have better social skills, which can reduce situations that lead to anger. They usually recognize some things belong to other people, can work well in groups, and begin to learn about and accept the differing personalities of others.

Disagreements with other children are the most common cause of anger. Although quarrels are still loud and verbal, five- and six-year-old children begin to conceal and disguise their feelings. Sometimes their methods of revenge are indirect. They may pretend indifference, sneer, or make sly remarks. Often they make exaggerated threats. Occasionally, they take their anger out on a scapegoat, such as a younger sibling, a pet, a toy, or the furniture.

Parents can also be the object of the child's anger. Children who are chided for

Because parents are the ones who make rules, children may turn their anger toward their parents. *Who are children more commonly angry with?*

The fears felt by children in this age group may lead to nightmares. *What kinds of fears are common in these ages?*

Fear

Children from four to six have a well-developed imagination, and many of their fears center on imaginary dangers. They may be afraid of ghosts, robbers, kidnappers, or vampires. Sensitive and insecure children are especially prone to fears. Many children of this age are afraid of the dark. Some may worry about the possibility of being left alone or abandoned.

Many children fear school. Some are afraid to be leaving the security of home. Others may fear a bully or a teacher. Social acceptance is very important at this age, and the threat of losing it worries children.

You can help children overcome these fears in three ways:

- **Accept the fear.** Having someone older who listens and understands can greatly help a fearful child. Don't just say that what the child fears doesn't exist. It's very real to the child.
- **Let the child express the fear without ridicule.** If they worry that they will be made fun of, children may not show their other fears openly.
- **Help the child feel able to face the fear.** Use talking and acting out to help the child learn to face the fearful situation. By practicing how to face a large dog, Kyle found the strength to overcome his fear of large dogs.

Sometimes, of course, a child's concern over a situation is justified. A bully at school or danger on the streets are reasonable con-

doing something wrong will "punish" a parent by breaking yet another rule. When six-year-old Hanna was told to go to her room for kicking her brother, she retorted, "Okay, I'm not going to hang my clothes up for a week—or maybe a year!"

Children vary greatly in how much anger they show and how they show it. Some of these variations depend on a child's personality, but the way parents express their own anger—and respond to the child—are also important. Caregivers need to set an example by sharing and talking—but not acting out—their own anger. It's important to teach the child self-control early in life before inappropriate expressions of anger become a habit. Encourage children to use words—not their bodies—in expressing anger.

A child who is very physical may need action to release the anger. Teaching the child to hit something soft, like a pillow, may help.

cerns. In these cases, parents need to take action to help remove the source of those fears.

Jealousy

Sibling rivalry—jealousy of brothers and sisters—is common during this period. Some parents worsen the problem, often without meaning to, by showing favoritism to one child. Sometimes they try to improve behavior by comparing one child with another. For example, one father asked his daughter, "Why can't you be neat and clean like Jennifer? I never have to tell her to put her toys away." Such comparisons are rarely effective. Instead, they damage a child's self-esteem and undermine good family relationships.

At this age, jealousy often takes the form of tattling, criticizing, or even lying. Some children react to their own feelings of jealousy by boasting. Jealousy may also result in tensional outlets such as nail biting, bed-wetting, and tantrums. By encouraging empathy you can help lessen jealousy. Sometimes a bit of additional attention helps. Sibling rivalry tends to fade as the child matures and finds interests outside the family.

Children and Stress

Children, like teens and adults, lead stressful lives. Children may worry about everything from fires to their own popularity, the illness or death of a family member, or news about missing children. One expert says that more than one in three children suffers from stress.

As with adults, this stress can result in problems. Stress can cause stomachaches, headaches, moodiness, irritability, and trouble eating or sleeping. Other signs of stress include problems at school, pulling away from groups, clinging to adults, or stuttering. A child who often blinks rapidly, taps pencils or pens, or shuffles his or her feet may be under stress as well.

What should parents and other caregivers do? Hugs help. The "Health Tip" on the next page has other suggestions.

Is Competition Good or Bad?

People have differing views about the role competition should play in children's

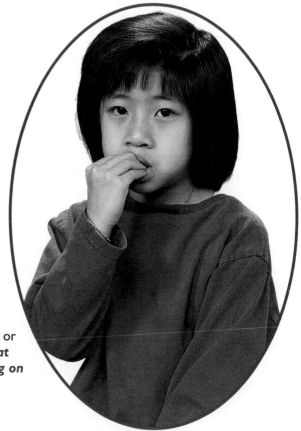

Habits like twirling hair, rapid blinking, or biting nails can be signs of stress. *What kinds of events or feelings can bring on this stress?*

HEALTH TIP

Handling Stress

*Y*ou can take these steps to help children reduce stress:

- **Find the cause.** Children's drawings can reveal the causes of stress. A child whose parents had just divorced drew a picture of herself split in two. Another approach is to say that a favorite puppet or stuffed animal is not feeling well and then ask the child what the problem is. The child may describe his or her own problems. Once the cause of the stress is known, work on that problem.

- **Give them chances to get rid of tension.** By giving children a physical way of releasing tension, you can relieve their stress. Have them run around the home, jump off a cushion, or color very rapidly.

- **Read a book about the issue causing the stress.** There are books that deal with issues that can cause stress in children, from moving to a new home to facing someone's death. Reading a book can help the child learn ways to handle the situation.

- **Maintain normal limits on behavior.** Some parents ease up on rules because they want to make life easier for a child feeling stress. Such an approach can actually backfire by confusing the child—and causing additional stress.

FOLLOWING UP

1. Chad, a five-year-old, has three brothers and sisters, including a newborn. He drew a picture of himself and his whole family, but he was toward the edge of the page and smaller than the other figures. What might this drawing reveal as a likely cause of the stress he is experiencing?

2. What techniques for handling stress have you found to work? Would they work with young children? Why or why not?

lives. Some say that children benefit from it because competition:

- Stimulates individual effort.
- Promotes higher standards.
- Creates an interest in completing tasks.
- Helps a child gain a realistic view of his or her own ability in relation to others.
- Encourages speed in accomplishment.
- Helps children excel and prepares them for the adult world.

Others feel that competition harms children because it:

- Instills the idea that success depends on the ability to outdo others.
- Leads to hostile relationships with others.
- Results in lack of effort among those who never or rarely win.
- Points out children's inadequacies.
- Lowers the status and self-esteem of those who lose.

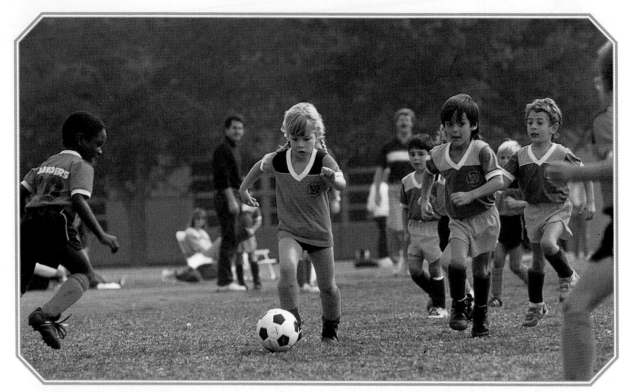

Many children these ages begin to play competitive sports on teams. *How can parents take part in these activities?*

Competition can be very difficult for six-year-olds. Children this age don't take criticism well, and they hate to lose. Cal, playing a board game with his father, tried a six-year-old's typical solution to losing. When his father wasn't looking, he cheated. Such behavior fades after a year or so. If a child shows that he or she has difficulty handling losing, it may be best to set aside competitive games for a while. As the child matures, they can be played again. Of course, caregivers who show what it's like to be good sports help children learn to lose graciously.

When competitive games are played, be aware of the possible impact on children's feelings. If children are being grouped into teams, use some system other than letting the children choose teammates.

Another issue with competitive games is playing time. Most children, regardless of their skill level, want to join in when games such as soccer or kickball are being played. If only a few children are given a chance to play, others feel left out. Not only do these children feel rejected, they also lose the chance of working to improve their skills. At this age, choose games that give everyone a chance to play.

Teamwork and Cooperation

Most four-, five-, and six-year-olds prefer cooperative play to competitive games. You can encourage children to play cooperatively in competitive games by working together with their teammates. Any children who are not playing at a particular time can cheer for their teammates. When they are playing, children can share by, say, passing the ball to one another.

Whatever the game, teach children not to compare themselves to others. Instead, they can compare their skills today to their skills in the past. Is Jennie dribbling the ball better? Is Carlos running faster than last month? Most children can see improvement—and feel some satisfaction.

SECTION 15-1 REVIEW

✔ Check Your Understanding

1. What major change takes place for most children between the ages of four and six?
2. Compare four- and five-year-olds in terms of their willingness to cooperate.
3. Which group—four-, five-, or six-year-olds—is most likely to have major swings in mood?
4. How do children aged four to six show anger? How should a caregiver respond?
5. Mandy's mother said, "Silly, don't be afraid of the dark. There's nothing that can hurt you." Was that an effective way of dealing with Mandy's fear? If not, what would have been better?
6. What behaviors may be signs of stress in a child?
7. List three advantages and three disadvantages of competition among children.

Putting Knowledge Into Practice

1. **Applying.** Children in all three ages from four to six have difficulty handling criticism. Develop a list of four rules for caregivers to use when they try to correct the behavior of a child during this period.
2. **Interpreting.** Derrick was angry when he was kicked by another child. Instead of hitting, he said, "That felt just like a minnow swimming by me." What age is Derrick likely to be? Why?
3. **Observing and Participating.** Working in a small group, develop a game that children four to six could play that would encourage cooperation. Explain the rules of the game to your class.

CAREER OPPORTUNITIES

Children's Book Writer

A CONVERSATION WITH PAUL ZARSKY

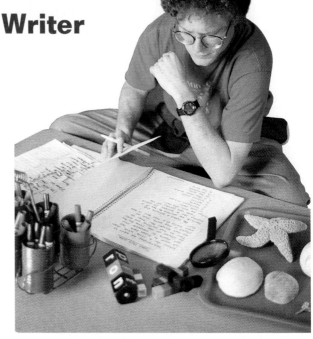

How did you become interested in becoming a children's book writer? I've loved to read ever since I was a child. It's just something I naturally moved into.

What are the tasks and responsibilities of a children's book writer? As a writer, you have to craft a story that will capture a child's interest and imagination. It helps if your story can reflect the real concerns that children have, like getting along with others, feeling different or alone, or adjusting to changes in life. You have to create characters who behave in realistic, understandable ways—even if you're putting them in unusual, unreal situations, like a magical trip to another world.

What is the work environment like? Most writers work in offices in their own homes. What that is like is really what you make it like.

What are the working hours like? Because you're working at home, you can create the hours that you want. Of course, when a deadline looms, you have to put in extra hours if you're behind.

What aptitudes are needed to be a children's book writer? You need a good imagination and excellent language skills. You need to know the meanings of words and their sounds so you can put them together in pleasing ways. You need to be able to do research—for instance, if you're writing about a medical problem, you need to learn about it to make your story convincing. You must have self-discipline when you work at home.

CHILDREN'S BOOK WRITER

Education and Training. Writers usually have college degrees in English. Some begin writing in their teens or college years.

Career Outlook. The demand for writers is expected to continue to grow in the future, but competition for writing jobs is high.

CONNECTING SCHOOL TO CAREER

1. **Thinking Skills.** Why is it important for characters to behave realistically even if they are in fantasy worlds?
2. **Technology.** How could children's book writers use the Internet in their work?

SECTION 15-2

Social and Moral Development from Four to Six

School brings four-, five-, and six-year-olds into contact with many new people. Children must learn how to meet strangers, make friends, work and play in groups, and accept authority from new people. As they enter school, children broaden their world.

KEY TERMS

moral development
peers

OBJECTIVES:

- Describe social development in children ages four, five, and six.
- Describe a child's relationship to family at ages four, five, and six.
- Create strategies for helping children develop a sense of right and wrong.
- Debate ways of handling outside influences on children's behavior.

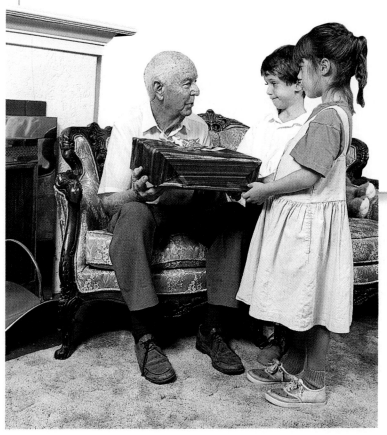

General Social Patterns

During the preschool and early school years, development of social skills is a major task. As children spend more time outside the home, they refine skills in getting along with **peers**, others their age.

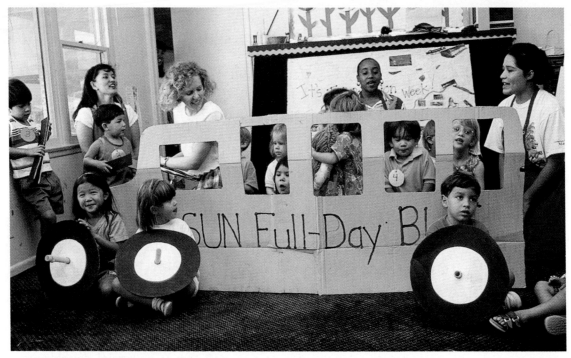

Preschool gives children opportunities for social relationships outside the home. *Do you think children who attend preschool are more likely to make the transition to grade school more easily? Why or why not?*

The World's Children

Child's Play in China

Children in the People's Republic of China approach play differently than North American children. If North American children are running a race and one falls, the other children are likely to continue running, hoping to win. In China, another child is likely to stop to help the one who has fallen—even though stopping means losing the race. Teachers in China encourage this behavior by praising the child who helps the other.

SHARE YOUR THOUGHTS

1. What values are being promoted in each culture? How do they fit in with what you know about these cultures?
2. What are other examples of values that young children are taught through play?

Adult authority figures other than parents also gain more importance. Although the rate at which individual children learn social skills varies, there are general patterns common at each age.

Four Years

Four-year-olds form friendships with their playmates. At this age, children spend more time in cooperative play than they do playing alone. They seem to play best in groups of three or four. Children this age share toys and take turns. Since four-year-olds are still often bossy and inconsiderate, fighting can be common.

Although friends are important to four-year-olds, the family is still more important. Children this age often ask for approval by making such remarks as "I'm a good builder, right?" or "Look how high I can climb!" If things go wrong, they look to adults, including teachers, for comfort.

At age four, children enjoy helping around the house. *What kinds of tasks could they be given?*

Five Years

Most five-year-olds are more outgoing and talkative than they were at age four. They play best in groups of five or six, and their play is more complicated. Quarreling is less frequent. When they do quarrel, five-year-olds typically resort to name-calling and to wild threats.

At age five, children have more respect for others' belongings. This doesn't mean that a five-year-old will never snatch someone else's toy. Such behavior, though, is less common than in earlier years.

As children begin school, social acceptance by peers becomes more important. Children are concerned about what their friends say and do. They don't like to be different, and they fear ridicule. This is why teasing can be very hurtful for children this age.

At about this age, children often begin to gossip about other children. Typically, this talk involves which children are friends or who has what toys. Sometimes, though, the talk can be personal—and very critical. Gossip indicates what behaviors children as a group value. Undesirable actions are criticized. If such talk turns nasty, though, discuss the matter with the children, pointing out that gossip can be hurtful.

Six Years

At age six, social relations are often characterized by friction, aggression, threats, and stubbornness. Children this age want everything, and they want to do things their own way. When playing with other children, they may not want to share their own toys, and they are likely to be jealous of others' toys.

Children in this stage follow rules to avoid being punished. They do not yet have the ability to understand the reasons for these rules. *What development shows that they are beginning to internalize rules of behavior?*

Best friends are usually of the same sex, although six-year-olds play readily in mixed groups. Friendships are closer and longer lasting now than at age five.

At this age, children like the group play and organized teams of school games. As soon as they tire of playing, though, they will drop out of a game with no regard for the team effort.

Family Relationships

Four-year-olds have a strong sense of family and home. They want to feel important in the family. They are proud to perform household chores. However, they are also apt to quarrel and bicker with their brothers and sisters.

The family relationships of five-year-olds are similar to those of four-year-olds. They are proud of their parents and delight in helping. At five, though, children play much better with their younger brothers and sisters. They are usually protective, kind, and dependable with younger siblings.

Six-year-olds are less in harmony with their family members, in part because children this age are more self-centered. Their own opinions and needs come first. Arguing with adults is common. At six, children are often rough and impatient with younger brothers and sisters, and they may fight with older siblings.

Moral Development

Moral development—the process of gradually learning to base one's behavior on personal beliefs of right and wrong—begins early in life. Parents have a responsibility to help their children develop a moral sense that will guide their behavior.

As toddlers, children begin to learn the rules their parents and other caregivers set. At this age, though, they can't understand the reasons behind the rules or the difference between right and wrong. They just know that some actions—such as hitting another person—make their caregivers unhappy with them. They learn to avoid such behavior because they don't want to lose love and approval.

Between the ages of five and seven, children gradually develop the beginning of a conscience, that inner sense of right and wrong that leads people to good behavior and causes them to feel guilt following bad behavior. The rules learned in early childhood form the basis of the conscience in the early school years.

Lying

As children begin to learn the difference between truth and lies, that understanding isn't always accurate. For example, they may exaggerate the details of stories they tell.

During this process, help children separate fact from fiction. At the same time, punishing children when they are simply being imaginative isn't appropriate. Children need to know that telling the truth is important because people rely on what others say as they decide how to act. Point out that someone who consistently tells the truth is trusted by others. Telling the story of "The Boy Who Cried Wolf"—who suffered because he couldn't be trusted—can help the child see this point.

Sometimes children lie because they fear the consequences of something they did wrong. Punishment for undesirable behavior shouldn't be so severe that a child would rather lie than accept responsibility for an action.

As children learn right from wrong, try to avoid direct confrontations. When Brad saw the flower pot overturned, he didn't challenge his son Lee directly. He simply said, "Look at this! I wonder how this happened?" Then Lee explained that he had accidentally knocked it over. If Lee hadn't offered the information, Brad could have asked him, "Do you know anything about it?" to try to prompt a response. When asked in a nonthreatening way, children can be more willing to tell the truth. This helps establish the pattern of truthfulness.

Guidelines for Moral Development

Here are some guidelines for teaching moral behavior:

- **Consider the child's age and abilities.** For example, at preschool, Chrystal was playing at the shallow table filled with rice and containers. She started tossing the rice into the air and watching it land on the floor. The teacher

There are many ways that parents can use to guide children in their moral development. *Why is setting a good example such an important one?*

Ask the Experts

Jean Illsley Clarke
Director of J.I. Consultants in
Minneapolis, Minnesota

CHILDREN *and Lies*

Q Do young children lie?

A Of course children lie. Children learn about their world by exploring it, by trying it out. So we can expect children to learn about lies by lying. However, their lies are often not deliberate attempts to deceive.

Many children, especially four- and five-year-olds, tell tall tales. Telling such tales helps children develop their imagination and creativity. It may also help them deal with their own fears and frustrations.

It's not unusual for young children to mix exaggerated stories with reality. When you need information from a child, you can show the child that you know the difference. You might explain, "I will listen to your story, and then I need to know what really happened."

Sometimes a statement that sounds like a lie really reflects the child's misunderstanding. For example, a child might feel that he or she has completed a task, but a caregiver is not satisfied that it has been done fully. When the child says, "I did what you told me," he or she is not lying.

Children sometimes tell lies simply to get a response from adults. In these cases, it's usually best to give the child more attention at other times, but to avoid special attention in response to the lying. Remember that all children want—and need—to be noticed.

Children may also lie to protect themselves or to please others. They may not want to risk an adult's anger or disappointment, so they lie about their behavior. Parents and other caregivers can help by encouraging children to accept and deal with their own mistakes or with their own deliberate misbehavior.

As we help children learn when and where and how to tell the truth, we should remember that the development of a conscience as an internal behavior guide takes many years. We should remember, as well, that children learn from our examples.

Thinking It Through

1. Can you remember a time when you were younger that you lied? Why did you lie? What happened?
2. What would you do if a five- or six-year-old lied to you about having taken a cookie?

reminded Chrystal to keep the rice in the table. Then she handed her a broom and a dustpan to sweep up the mess. Chrystal's teacher knows that children this age can't always remember the rules but will learn from the consequences of their actions.

- **Set a good example.** Children learn best by following an example. They receive a mixed message if, for example, they are told that lying is wrong, but hear their parents telling lies. You must behave around children the way you want them to behave.

- **Remember that learning self-discipline is a lifelong task.** It is unfair to expect perfection from children. Instead, help children learn from their mistakes—and recognize their steps in the right direction.

- **Talk about mistakes in private.** Children don't like to be put in a position where others can ridicule or make fun of them. Correcting their behavior in front of others may make them feel humiliated. The teacher took Jason to the side to talk to him about his loud talking.

- **Continue to show love despite misbehavior.** Children need to know that, although you don't like what they did, you continue to love them. Separate the deed from the doer.

Handling Outside Influences

The influence of peers increases as children spend more time away from home. They pick up the words and speech patterns of their friends. They come to want toys or clothes like other children have. Of course, every request can't be met. Children need to learn that each family has its own set of rules.

As they gain independence, many children watch more television. Some of the shows they see may reflect values that run counter to those of the family. Some preschoolers spend time on the computer,

Talking about a behavior problem can help a child improve. Remember that such changes take time.

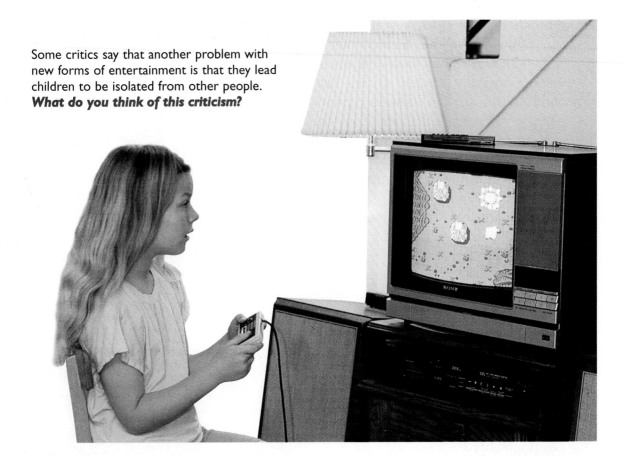

Some critics say that another problem with new forms of entertainment is that they lead children to be isolated from other people. *What do you think of this criticism?*

where games may include images that parents object to. What can parents do about these issues?

The television industry has adopted a series of ratings meant to advise parents of the content of each show. One study argued that the rating system doesn't work. The study identified shows that had "fantasy violence"—the kind found in cartoons, in which characters act violently but don't suffer any harm. Researchers said that only one-quarter of the shows they identified as being violent in this way were given the appropriate rating. The study also found that of all the shows that networks said were educational, under one-third were highly educational.

Parents and caregivers are responsible for what children watch and how much they watch. One way to prevent television from having a negative effect is to lead young children away from television as a way of passing time. If children develop other ways of learning and playing, watching television is less likely to become a habit.

Video and computer games can be violent as well. Software boxes have labels indicating the level of violence. Parents can check with store personnel for more details if they are unsure of what the labels mean.

> ### INFOLINK
>
> ### Children and Television
>
> **For more about** *children and television,* **see** "Parenting With Care," **pages 452-453.**

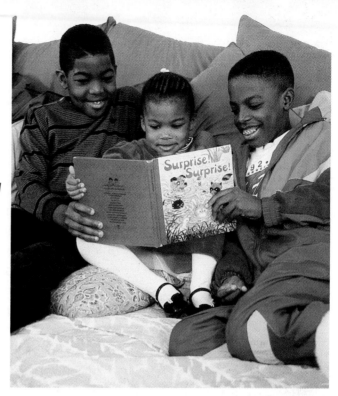

What social and moral values would this type of activity encourage?

SECTION 15-2 REVIEW

✔ Check Your Understanding

1. Who are a person's peers?
2. What kind of play is typical for four-year-olds?
3. How do five-year-olds' feelings about teasing show the influence of peers?
4. Compare how four- and five-year-olds typically play with younger siblings.
5. What is moral development?
6. Give three suggestions for helping children learn right from wrong.
7. How can parents minimize the effects of television violence on children?

Putting Knowledge Into Practice

1. **Comparing.** What is the difference between a four-year-old's imaginative story and a teen's lie? How would you, as a parent, handle each situation?
2. **Applying.** Five-year-old Savanna often takes playthings away from neighbor children in the child care center. You work at the center. What would you do?
3. **Observing and Participating.** Based on how you and your friends interact, how would you define "friend"? How differently do you think a child four to six would define "friend"?

Parenting With Care

Teaching Manners

As children become older, they are ready to learn how to behave politely.

As with all behavior, children learn manners from the example set around them. When parents say "Pass me the bread, please" at the dinner table, children learn that this is the way requests are made.

What kinds of manners are young children capable of learning? Although they can't be expected to act with all the polished manners of an adult, they can manage some simple steps:

- To say "please" and "thank you"—although, being children, they may not remember to do it all the time.
- To say "excuse me" when they wish to interrupt a conversation or when they cross in front of someone.
- To say "hello" and "good-bye" to people when they enter and leave the home.
- To speak clearly instead of mumbling and to look people in the eye.
- To follow basic table manners such as using a knife and fork, wiping the mouth with a napkin, and chewing with the mouth closed.

Parents can use the following technique to teach these manners to their children:

- **Focus on one area of behavior at a time.** It's easier for children to learn one skill at a time, rather than trying to master many instructions at once. Parents may choose to focus first on learning to say "please" and "thank you" before moving to table manners in general. Once the child is mastering these two areas, it is possible to move on to, say, greetings or phone manners.
- **Be prepared to accept mistakes.** Children will slip. They should not be berated or severely criticized for these lapses. Give them a chance to show that they know what to do by asking them how they should behave.

- **Notice—and comment on—what children do right.** Caregivers sometimes fall into the trap of only talking about what children do wrong. Children need to hear praise when they have acted correctly so they know that those actions matter.

- **Review the basics.** Before a social occasion, talk to the child about what situations might arise and what the child should do. By being prepared, the child will be more likely to behave as desired.

Following Up

1. **Communication.** How would you tell a child four years old that he or she should say "please" and "thank you"?

2. **Thinking Skills.** When reviewing basic manners before a special occasion, how would it help to have the child act out the desired behavior?

Summary

✔ Children four to six move from defiance to cooperation to defiance. (Section 15-1)

✔ Children four to six become less physical when they show anger. (Section 15-1)

✔ Competition can have both positive and negative effects on children. (Section 15-1)

✔ Peer acceptance grows in importance with children these ages. (Section 15-2)

✔ In this period, children begin to tell right from wrong. (Section 15-2)

✔ Parents can minimize the negative effects of outside influences. (Section 15-2)

Reviewing the Facts

1. At which age do children find it easier to finish what they have started? (Section 15-1)

2. Why is six a difficult age emotionally? (Section 15-1)

3. How should caregivers respond to a child's fears? (Section 15-1)

4. How can cooperation be fostered when children play competitive games? (Section 15-1)

5. Compare children at ages four, five, and six in terms of how they get along with each other. (Section 15-2)

6. Jeremy always seems to be fighting with his parents. Is he most likely to be four, five, or six? (Section 15-2)

7. How can caregivers prevent punishments from leading children to lie? (Section 15-2)

8. Why is it better to correct a child's behavior in private? (Section 15-2)

9. How can early training affect a child's television viewing? (Section 15-2)

Thinking Critically

1. **Analyzing.** Do you think it is possible to treat all children in the family in the same way? If not, how can parents prevent feelings of sibling rivalry?

2. **Drawing Conclusions.** Based on your own experience, do you think that competitive games are helpful or harmful for children? Be prepared to defend your position in a class debate.

3. **Applying.** What would you do if you overheard your five-year-old son and a friend exchanging gossip about another boy in their class?

Taking Action

1. **Teaching Values.** Suppose you are part of a group of adults setting up a league for six-year-olds to play a sport such as T-ball or soccer. Make a list of ten rules of behavior you want all players to follow. Make sure that the rules address the children's behavior, not athletic concerns. *(Leadership)*

2. **Avoiding Sibling Rivalry.** With a partner, develop a list of ten things parents say that might cause five- or six-year-olds to feel jealous of a sibling. Working with the same partner, find more positive ways to express those thoughts. *(Communication)*

Cross-Curricular Connections

1. **Language Arts.** Write a story that begins with this paragraph: "Sandy came home in tears from her first day in kindergarten. She dropped her backpack and slumped on the floor at her mother's feet. 'I'm never going back there!' she said."

2. **Language Arts.** Read the story "The Boy Who Cried Wolf." Write a new version of the story for a five- or six-year-old. Update it to situations a child might encounter in your neighborhood. Include illustrations if you wish.

Workplace Connections

1. **Interpersonal Skills.** You work in a child care center and notice that in the past week four-year-old Callie has been blinking and spending more time alone. You also notice that Callie's father no longer comes to pick her up at the end of the day. What might be Callie's problem? Describe how you would handle the situation.

2. **Interpersonal Skills.** Suppose you were the head of a preschool. Write a list of rules you would expect children to follow in terms of their behavior with one another. Make sure the rules are appropriate for four- and five-year-olds.

Family and Community Connections

1. **Handling Outside Influences.** Ever since Jem started kindergarten, he's been talking about a video game that other children have. He wants it badly, but his parents have heard that it is extremely violent, and they don't want him to have it. Join with a partner to write and act out a scene between Jem and one of his parents when Jem asks for this game—and nothing else—for his birthday.

Technology Connections

1. **Ratings for Violence.** Television programs, movies, and video and computer games all have ratings that indicate the presence of violence or other possibly objectionable content. Research one of these rating systems and report on it to the class. If you don't think the system is effective, make suggestions to improve it.

RATINGS

G   PG

PG 13   R

Marcus patiently connected the blocks. He started with a long base and stacked medium-sized pieces atop it. After putting down a few pieces, he would stop and examine the results. Sometimes he pulled off a piece or two after these reviews, then quickly put others in a different position. On one side, the blocks rose like a wall with a gap in it. "What's that?" his father asked. "That's a window," said Marcus, not looking up from his work. He had trouble figuring out how to build above the window to reconnect the two sides of the wall, however. He couldn't find pieces that were long enough to bridge the gap. Marcus's father wanted to help, but he decided that it was best to let his son solve the problem on his own.

The solution would not come to Marcus right then, however. As he was still struggling with his problem, his father looked at his watch and said, "OK, Marcus, it's time for your bath."

"Sometimes Marcus would pull off a piece or two, then quickly put others in their place."

Intelligence and Learning from Four to Six

Do you enjoy reading, art, or music? Think back to your first experiences in school. It's quite possible that your liking for these subjects started during this period of your life. When they enter school, children aged four to six become exposed to new people, activities, and ideas. These experiences have an impact on their growing minds.

KEY TERMS

bilingual
dramatic play
finger plays
intelligence quotient (IQ)
multiple intelligences
phoneme

OBJECTIVES:

- Identify signs of preoperational thinking in children aged four to six.

- Discuss different kinds of intelligence.

- Find ways to help children learn from everyday experiences.

- Use techniques to encourage children's interest in reading, art, and music.

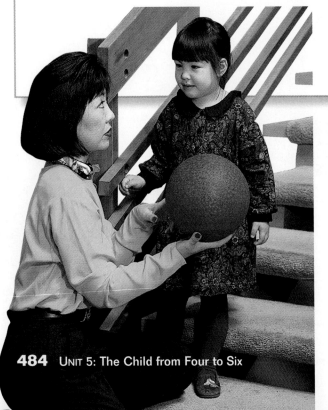

Preoperational Thinking

As you recall, Jean Piaget identified the time between ages two and seven as the preoperational period. In this period, children think in terms of their own activities and what they perceive at the moment. Four-, five-, and six-year-olds show by their thinking and actions that they are still in this period:

- **Use of symbols.** Children learn that objects and words can be symbols—that is, they can represent something else. A child this age can recognize that a stop sign means stop.
- **Make-believe play.** Children continue to learn through fantasy play and **dramatic play**, in which they imitate real-life situations, such as playing house or school.
- **Egocentric viewpoint.** In this period, children view the world in terms of their own thoughts and feelings. When the mother of a five-year-old wasn't feeling well, the child gave her mother her favorite stuffed animal for comfort.
- **Limited focus.** Children find it difficult to focus on more than one feature at a time. Suppose you show a child three white tennis balls and seven yellow ones. If you ask whether there are more yellow balls or more tennis balls, a four-year-old will probably say more yellow balls. The child can't focus on both the color and the type of ball at once. An older child would see that all the balls are tennis balls, of which only some are yellow.

INFOLINK

Preoperational Period

For more on *preoperational period*, see Chapter 10, pages 325-326.

What Is Intelligence?

Although children these ages are still in the preoperational period, their mental abilities are clearly growing. Children learn to read and count in this period—the basis of later work in school. As children begin school, many parents wonder how intelligent their children are. Will they thrive in school? How will their school experiences shape their lives?

Traditional Views of Intelligence

Educators use formal intelligence tests to try to determine the thinking skills of children. The test results can help teachers, principals, and learning specialists understand and meet students' educational needs.

The first intelligence test was developed by a French psychologist, Alfred Binet, in 1905. In 1916, Lewis M. Terman of Stanford University made a major revision of the Binet test.

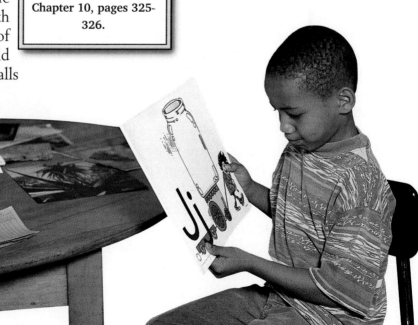

In ages four to six, children learn that numbers represent quantity and letters stand for sounds. *What mental ability does this indicate?*

Today the test is commonly called the Stanford-Binet, and it is one of many tests used to measure intelligence in children.

By having many children take the test, Terman created a mathematical formula that could be used to give a child's intelligence a number value. This **intelligence quotient**, or **IQ**, is a number obtained by comparing a person's test results to that of other children the same age. The average child of any age has an IQ between 90 and 110. Those who score higher or lower than this average are said to be of higher or lower intelligence.

Intelligence tests are composed of tasks and questions. These correspond to the expected abilities of children at different age levels. Two-year-olds, for example, cannot read. An intelligence test for them might include building a tower of blocks, identifying parts of the body, and fitting simple geometric shapes into corresponding holes.

There are several problems with using intelligence tests, however:

- No one test gives an accurate measure of a child's mental ability. Also, these tests only measure one kind of mental ability, ignoring other kinds.
- Many factors that have nothing to do with intelligence can influence test results. A child's physical or emotional state when taking the test can affect his or her score. Thus, test results are not consistent. The same test given to the same child at two separate times may show a wide difference in scores.
- The tests don't tell much about specific abilities. Two people with the same IQ may have very different strengths and weaknesses.

Because of these problems, educators must use intelligence tests cautiously. The National Association for the Education of Young Children (NAEYC) warns that no decision about a child's placement in school should be made on the basis of one test alone. Today, preschools and kindergartens are more likely to use different techniques to gain an overview of a child's level of development in all areas, not just thinking skills. If the child falls outside the norms of development for his or her age, then an in-depth assessment of skills can be done. In this way, educators can identify problem areas and plan activities that will help the child.

Multiple Intelligences

In recent years, psychologist Howard Gardner has advanced a new way of looking

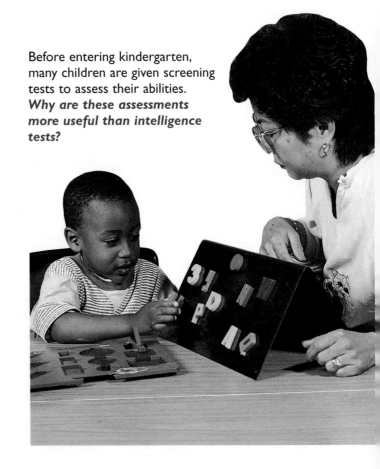

Before entering kindergarten, many children are given screening tests to assess their abilities. *Why are these assessments more useful than intelligence tests?*

Researchers have identified many different kinds of intelligence. *Which types are shown here?*

at intelligence. He argues that humans have **multiple intelligences**—many different ways of using the mind and body to experience the world. He outlines eight such intelligences:

- **Verbal-linguistic.** This is linked to language. A person strongest in this intelligence learns best through words.
- **Logical-mathematical.** This is shown by skill in arithmetic and many areas of science. People try to find patterns to connect facts and observations.
- **Visual-spatial.** This is shown by ability in drawing and construction. Learning is easiest through pictures and colors.
- **Musical.** This intelligence has to do with rhythm and sounds. Hearing rhythms and melodies helps promote learning.
- **Bodily-kinesthetic.** This intelligence is skill in moving the body through space. Athletes, dancers, and those who are skilled in crafts are high in this intelligence.
- **Interpersonal.** This intelligence has to do with social skills. A person with these abilities is good at communicating with and empathizing with others.
- **Intrapersonal.** This intelligence is revealed by a person who is more private and less social. A person who keeps a diary, has a strong will and much independence, and prefers to play alone has this intelligence.

- **Naturalistic.** This intelligence is revealed by an understanding of the natural world—plants, animals, and the processes of nature. A person who has naturalistic intelligence is likely to be interested in being outdoors and may enjoy books about animals.

Of course, people—including children—have abilities in various intelligences. Those who study multiple intelligences point out that caregivers shouldn't label a child as being one particular way and then try to enhance that intelligence at the expense of all others. Children need to grow in many areas.

Still, it can help caregivers to recognize a child's particular strengths in one or more areas. They can provide that child with opportunities in that area to challenge and interest the child in learning.

Practicing Parenting

Activities for Multiple Intelligences

Each type of intelligence can be fostered with particular activities:

- **Verbal-linguistic.** Word games and puzzles, reading, writing, jokes and tongue twisters, games involving memorizing.
- **Logical-mathematical.** Number games; chess and checkers; maps and diagrams; tests of logic; experiments.
- **Visual-spatial.** Play with pictures, drawing, modeling clay, construction toys, jigsaw puzzles.
- **Musical.** Toy instruments, household objects that can be banged, music tapes, music lessons.
- **Bodily-kinesthetic.** Physical activities such as gymnastics or soccer, using playground equipment, dancing.
- **Interpersonal.** Activities that involve other children such as joining clubs or other groups.
- **Intrapersonal.** Time to be alone and think, writing in a diary.
- **Naturalistic.** Opportunities to experience nature, such as gardening, walking in the woods, or watching birds.

APPLY YOUR KNOWLEDGE

1. What kind of intelligence is a child who enjoys cooperative play likely to have? What child would be least likely to join in such play?
2. What kinds of intelligences, other than logical-mathematical, do you think would be connected to playing chess or checkers?

A child's world is full of opportunities for learning. *What can this child learn from helping in the kitchen?*

Helping Children Learn

In this period, children can be excited about learning. Parents and caregivers can help build that excitement in many ways.

Learning from Everyday Life

A four-, five-, or six-year-old learns from a wide variety of experiences, especially when a parent or other important caregiver shares them.

Talk with children about what they are doing. A few positive comments, such as "Wow, the building you are making is so tall—and it has so many windows!" can encourage interest. Questions help children think in new ways about what is happening and encourage them to organize their thoughts into answers.

Explanations and suggestions can also be helpful. You might explain in simple terms why water turns to ice. If a child is trying to lift a heavy box full of toys, you could suggest that pushing the box might be easier.

Asking a child's advice is another effective technique for promoting learning. For example, ask how to arrange the carrot sticks and radishes on the serving plate and then do so.

Trips and activities are important to learning. A ride on a bus, train, or plane can be an adventure that leads the child to discuss what is seen and to ask questions.

Nature walks are fun—and free. Everyone in the family can learn by looking closely at leaves, flowers, and birds.

Helping around the house provides great learning opportunities. Sharing such tasks also strengthens the family bonds and helps children develop responsibility, maturity, and independence.

Children of this age are curious to learn more about their own bodies and about where babies come from. Answer their questions in simple terms they can understand, and help them learn the correct names for body parts. Encourage children to have positive attitudes by answering their questions in an unembarrassed, natural way.

Visits to the library can help build a love of reading. Many libraries have story hours, in which librarians read to children. *How do children benefit from story hours?*

Appreciating Reading

Developing an interest in reading is important. Books provide an opportunity to learn about and understand the world and the people in it. Children who enjoy reading will find learning easier—and more fun.

An important factor in learning to read is the ability to hear **phonemes** (FOH-neems), or the individual sounds in words. Rhyming words help develop this awareness, so reading rhyming books to children is a good learning activity. When a book becomes familiar, stop from time to time and let the child fill in the missing sounds.

Another way to develop this awareness is through alliteration—words that begin with the same sound. Many alphabet books provide an opportunity to hear alliteration because they collect many words that begin with each letter. After children have learned the sound, they will begin to connect the letter to it.

Research suggests that being **bilingual**, or able to speak two languages, may make reading easier. Children who are bilingual understand that printed words convey a particular meaning sooner than do children who speak one language. This may give them an edge in reading.

Choosing Books

Fortunately, young children love books and stories. If this interest is encouraged, children are likely to enjoy reading as they grow older.

Most communities have free public libraries that lend children's books. Many libraries also offer story hours for young children. Some schools and preschools allow children and families to borrow books for a short time.

When choosing books for children, use these questions to guide you:

- Are the pictures colorful, interesting, and easy to understand?

- Will the story appeal to the child's interests?
- Does the story include action that will hold the child's interest?
- Will the child understand most of the words?
- Does the book use descriptive language that brings the story alive?
- Is the story short enough to read in one sitting?
- If you are considering buying the book, is it made well to stand up under hard use?

What kind of books do four- to six-year-olds like? Many like stories about experiences that are different from their own. Through books, city children can learn about farm life and children who live in rural areas can experience buses, apartments, and other parts of city life.

Children this age also enjoy humor, including funny rhymes, and unusual situa-

tions. When they giggle over the picture of a horse in the bathtub, they show that they are beginning to separate reality from fantasy.

Introducing Art and Music

Art helps children express their feelings, learn to control their body, and show creativity. Four- to six-year-olds benefit from using many different art materials, such as play dough, crayons, paper, paste, paint, and scissors. Even dried macaroni can be strung into a necklace or pasted onto a sheet of construction paper to make a design.

Children should be encouraged to experiment with art materials. Don't correct or criticize their work. Experiencing creativity rather than the product itself is what is important. Parents and other caregivers need to follow this guideline.

Children enjoy talking about their art—and this talking helps them build their ver-

Children enjoy experimenting with many different art materials. *If they are doing painting in the home, what precautions might a caregiver wish to take? Why?*

bal skills. Ask "How did you make that?" to prompt the child to explain the process used. Instead of guessing what a picture represents, ask the child to tell you. Then find specific aspects of the work that you can praise. For example, you might say, "I really like the bright colors you used for the flowers."

The Developing Brain

Math and music are interconnected. Researchers have found that children's reasoning about space and time improved when they had weekly piano lessons. That's the reasoning that underlies math.

All children respond naturally to rhythmic sound, which is a part of music. A boy rubs a stick against a fence as he walks, hearing the rhythm. A girl listens to her footsteps as she runs.

Three- to six-year-olds enjoy rhythm games and singing simple, repetitive songs. Many children are introduced to singing by **finger plays**, songs or chants with accompanying hand motions. "The Itsy-Bitsy Spider" is a finger play.

The opportunity to play simple instruments helps develop children's interest in music. Children enjoy using bells, drums, tambourines, or almost anything that makes a noise. There is no need to buy instruments; old kitchen pans and mixing spoons work well.

SECTION 16-1 REVIEW

✔ Check Your Understanding

1. List three signs of preoperational thinking.
2. What does an IQ score of 100 tell you about a child? What does it *not* tell you about the child?
3. What kind of intelligence is shown by a child who draws well? By a child who spends time riding bikes, practicing gymnastics, and swimming?
4. In terms of Gardner's idea, why would a teacher have to teach a lesson several different ways?
5. Name an everyday activity that could be used as a learning experience and explain how. Use an example other than those in the textbook.
6. What types of books can help children learn phonemes?
7. What are finger plays?

Putting Knowledge Into Practice

1. **Supporting a Position.** Some early childhood educators urge a stop to all standardized testing of young children. Do you agree with this idea? Why or why not?
2. **Analyzing.** When Dawn showed her father a drawing, he said "That's nice." What would have been a better response? Why?
3. **Observing and Participating.** Analyze your own abilities in terms of the eight intelligences. Using a five-point scale, in which 1 is low and 5 is high, rate how skilled you are in each area. Base your ratings on the activities you enjoy and how you learn.

SECTION 16-2

The Child in School

Sarah came home from kindergarten bursting with excitement. "We learned a new song today," she said. "And Mrs. Puhl told us about the leaves changing colors. Then we walked outside and picked up leaves. Then I helped serve the snack, but Janey wouldn't do it. After we ate, we made a drawing. Look!" Sarah thrust a paper into her mother's hand—and finally stopped for a breath.

KEY TERMS

attention deficit hyperactivity
    disorder (ADHD)
dyslexia
gifted children
learning disability

OBJECTIVES:

- Create ways to help a child adjust to starting kindergarten.

- Describe the speech development of children aged four to six, and identify possible speech problems.

- Identify ways to meet the needs of children with learning disabilities and gifted children.

The School Experience

Since children attend school for many years, it is vital that they develop a positive attitude from the start. Children who have a bad experience with classmates or a teacher can develop negative feelings about school.

These feelings can keep them from learning as well as they might. To build that positive attitude, a smooth transition to school life is important.

Preparing for School

Many parents place their children in a preschool so that they can become used to being in a school setting. In preschool, children learn to pay attention, take turns, sit still for various periods of time, and interact with other children.

At age five or six, most children enter kindergarten. The standard for entering the public school system is usually when the child turns five years old. Most systems have a cutoff date, such as September 1 or

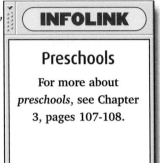

INFOLINK

Preschools

For more about *preschools*, see Chapter 3, pages 107-108.

December 31, after which the child must wait until the following year to enroll.

Many states require that a child have a physical exam by a physician before starting school. Parents also have to show that children have had all needed immunizations (see Chapter 18).

In the past, kindergarten was usually only a half day. Now, though, many school systems offer full-day kindergarten programs. Research has shown that children in full-day kindergarten programs perform better in elementary school.

Making the Transition

Starting kindergarten can be a major adjustment for a child—even one who has gone to preschool. The school is generally bigger than any preschool, and it includes children several years older. A child switching from a half-day preschool to a full-day kindergarten has other adjustments to make. For example many children begin riding on a school bus.

Parents can help their children adjust to this new experience in several ways:

- Be sure the child knows his or her full name, address, and telephone number.

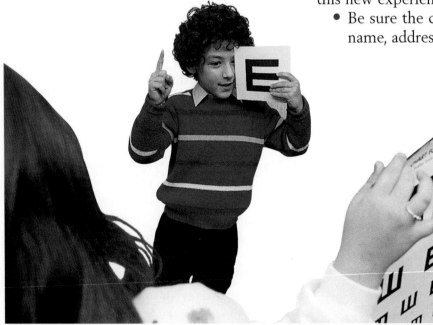

Some children need glasses so they can see the board. Having a hearing test is also a good idea. *Why would that be important?*

Ask the E❓perts

Rachel Perkins
Child Development Technology
Instructor
Hinds Community College
Utica, Mississippi

READINESS *for School*

When should I start my child in school?

The question of school readiness is a difficult one. Children born before the school system's cutoff date may enter school that year, but they do not have to enter. What should parents whose child doesn't seem ready do—put the child in school or wait another year?

For many years, experts said that holding a child out of school for another year would do no harm—and could help by giving a child time to develop more emotional maturity. One study showed that even children with high intelligence had emotional problems if they began school too early.

Another study, however, suggests that the opposite is true. In this research, children who started late had problems with behavior later in their school careers.

What, then, should a parent do? Many school systems offer screening tests for the children to take the summer before the school year begins. Parents who have their children in a preschool can talk to the teachers at that preschool. Those professionals can speak about the child's readiness based on what they have observed.

Parents can also look for certain signs. A child is ready for school if he or she can:

- *Communicate with adults other than his or her parents and be understood.*
- *Put on and take off coats and shoes and go to the bathroom on his or her own.*
- *Complete a task.*
- *Listen to a story and answer questions about it.*
- *Follow directions and take turns.*
- *Be willing to wait for a request to be met or a question answered.*

Thinking It Through

1. How can parents handle the conflicting results of different studies on the issue of school readiness?
2. Why do children need certain self-help skills to be ready for school?

- Explain what to expect at school. If possible, visit the school together before the child's first day. Some schools offer open house days for new students.
- Be sure that the child has plenty of rest by starting an earlier bedtime a few weeks before school begins.
- Let the child choose a lunch box or backpack and pick out the clothes to wear on the first day of school. With these choices, the child will link the new school to pleasant experiences.
- Above all, have a positive attitude. A parent's positive feelings will rub off on the child.

Speech Development

By the time they start school, children have gained an extensive knowledge of language just by listening. They probably don't know what an adjective is, but they can use adjectives confidently and correctly. As children grow older, their vocabulary increases. The sentences they use will become more complex. However, all the basic language forms have already been learned in the preschool years. For instance, children know how to use nouns and verbs to build a sentence, even if they can't label words as nouns and verbs.

A child's vocabulary should increase rapidly during this period. A normally developing six-year-old can understand and use approximately 2,500 words.

Articulation (clear, distinct speech) improves dramatically in this period as well. Three-year-olds typically say only about 30 percent of their words correctly. By age six, that has increased to 90 percent.

Much of this improvement depends on physical development. Some sounds are more difficult to make than others. The sounds represented by *b*, *m*, and *p* are produced simply by moving the lips. By three, most children can make these sounds. The *f* and *v* sounds, among others, involve both the lips and the teeth. Children may not master these sounds until age five. The most difficult sounds are those represented by *j*, *ch*, *st*, *pl*, and *sl*. They require the smooth coordination of the lips, tongue, and throat muscles. Some children may be six or seven before "pwease" becomes "please."

Speech Difficulties

Most children can develop good language skills at home. Some children, though, have problems with language. They may have plenty of opportunity to listen and speak at home, but hear and use only a limited number of simple words. Children need to hear—and be encouraged to use—language that is specific and rich in detail. For example, rather than using the very general verb *go*, encourage children to use a variety of specific verbs: The boys *race* across the field. The women *jog* every morning. The bugs *creep* down the tree.

Children who speak only a language other than English at home often have problems when they begin school. They must learn English language skills and, at the same time, keep up with their class. Children who move from one part of the country to another may also have difficulty because of differences in pronunciation.

Some children have physical problems that prevent normal speech. Others may be emotionally immature.

Some children with hearing loss are taught to communicate using sign language. *How would they benefit if other children learned to sign as well?*

All these situations may cause children to have difficulties at school. They may not be able to understand the teacher or to make themselves understood. As a result, learning becomes more difficult. This situation may cause emotional problems as well. Classmates are often unkind to a child whose speech is different. Teasing and jokes may add to a child's sense of isolation. Whatever the cause, children with speech problems need special help—preferably before they begin school.

Children with Special Needs

Some children have special educational needs. Two common causes of special needs—learning disabilities and unusually high intelligence—are discussed here.

Learning Disabilities

Not all children learn easily. For some, learning is made more difficult by a **learning disability**, a problem in a person's mental processes that prevents him or her from learning in a normal way. The Child Development Institute says that all the definitions of learning disability—and there are many—agree on four points:

1. People with learning disabilities have difficulty mastering academic work.
2. Development for people with learning disabilities is uneven, unlike that for other people.

INFOLINK

Children with Disabilities

For more about *children with disabilities*, see Chapter 19, pages 579-588.

3. The learning problems these people have are not due to living in a disadvantaged environment.
4. The learning problems these people have are not due to mental or emotional problems.

A severe physical handicap, such as blindness, is not a learning disability. Being blind does make learning more difficult, but blindness is not a problem in how the brain processes information. Some children cannot understand what words mean or form their own thoughts into speech. If these problems result from problems in how the brain works, they are learning disabilities. From 6 to 10 percent of all children may have learning disabilities. Two are especially important.

- **Attention deficit hyperactivity disorder**. A child who is not able to control his or her activity or concentrate for a normal length of time may have **attention deficit hyperactivity disorder (ADHD).** Children who have ADHD often fail to finish what they start, don't seem to listen, and are easily distracted. They also may have difficulty staying in their seats or may always be active. Some of these children show signs of a lack of emotional control.

  Young children who first begin school and have difficulty sitting still do not necessarily have ADHD. Children from ages four to six simply need time to learn to settle down.

Researchers think that ADHD is caused by an imbalance of chemicals in the brain. The problem has been linked to heredity—it runs in families—and to environment—taking drugs during pregnancy. Researchers have found they can use a special kind of brain scan to clearly tell whether a child has ADHD. This will help prevent cases of incorrectly diagnosing a child. The test is very expensive, however.

Some children with ADHD are given medication, but the practice is controversial. Studies are still being done. Children with ADHD can benefit by learning techniques that help them change their behavior and relax.

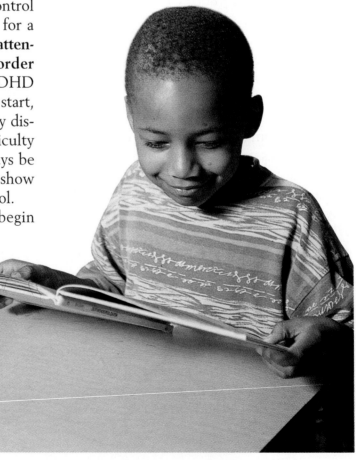

Children with ADHD can learn techniques to control their behavior so they can improve concentration and the ability to sit still. *What causes ADHD?*

CAREER OPPORTUNITIES

Special Education Teacher

A CONVERSATION WITH CARLA RANDISI

How did you become interested in becoming a special education teacher? I was studying for my degree in education. Through working with a scout troop, I became interested in helping children who have mental or physical disabilities.

What are the tasks and responsibilities of a special education teacher? We plan lessons that will help the children learn. Generally we teach each child individually—we have to develop methods of teaching that are suited to that child. We also keep parents informed of their child's progress.

What is the work environment like? We work in the school, either in our own classroom or in regular classrooms. Some teaching is done one-on-one, other times in groups.

What are the working hours like? We work a normal school schedule. After that we spend more time planning lessons and grading students' projects. We also meet with the regular teachers and with parents.

What aptitudes are needed to be a special education teacher? Like all teachers, we need to be well organized and good at planning and communicating. We also need to be flexible, and have patience, because students may take a long time to show progress. Self-control helps us handle students who have emotional problems.

Career Facts

SPECIAL EDUCATION TEACHER

Education and Training. Special education teachers have a bachelor's degree in education and often an extra year of training. All states require these teachers to receive a license before they can teach.

Career Outlook. The demand for special education is expected to continue to grow.

CONNECTING SCHOOL TO CAREER

1. **Thinking Skills.** Why do these teachers generally work with special needs children individually?

2. **Interpersonal Skills.** What do you think would be the most important interpersonal skill for a special education teacher? Why?

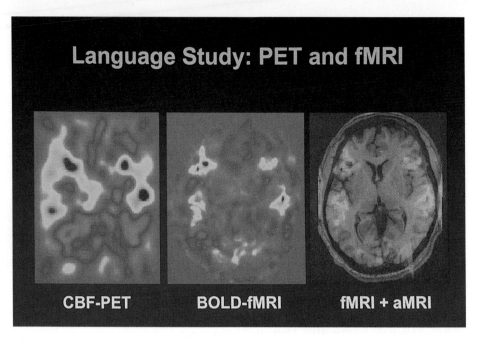

Language Study: PET and fMRI

Sophisticated medical tests such as the PET scan and functional MRI can be used to study and diagnose problems in brain function. This person was completing a language task during testing. The brightest colors show the areas of greatest activity.

CBF-PET   BOLD-fMRI   fMRI + aMRI

- **Dyslexia.** Another important disability is **dyslexia.** This problem prevents a person from understanding printed symbols in a normal way. Children with dyslexia are often intelligent, but their brains do not process some visual information normally. As a result, they have problems with reading, writing, spelling, and math. Children with dyslexia have difficulty understanding directions and repeating what is said to them. They may have problems distinguishing left and right as well.

  Children with dyslexia need special help, particularly during the early school years. The best treatment for children with dyslexia, according to the Child Development Institute, is to use the phonics approach to teaching reading. This technique is based on learning to see that certain letter combinations stand for particular sounds.

The Developing Brain

Normally, when a child reads, the brain shows activity in both the areas of the brain that handle visual information and those that handle language. In the brains of children with dyslexia, however, there is less activity in the language center.

Sometimes the label "learning disabled" can be as harmful as the problem itself. Children who have been found to have learning disabilities are sometimes treated as if they cannot learn. In fact, they can learn—but somewhat differently from most other children. They need special approaches tailored to their special needs.

Parents can find it difficult to accept that a child has a learning disability. One reason is that these problems often appear fairly late—when a child starts school. Until then, the parent was sure that the child was developing normally.

Parents can help these children overcome the disability by treating them with the same love and care shown to other children. Children should also have age-appropriate responsibilities around the house. Parents can help children with disabilities by removing any distractions that might interfere with learning. Finally, praise and reward for what is accomplished is important to these children. It took hard work!

Gifted and Talented Children

From 3 to 10 percent of the nation's students are **gifted children**, children who have unusual intelligence or special talent in an artistic area. Ramon, for example, has exceptional musical ability. Jennifer, though only four, shows remarkable artistic talent.

Educators once believed that gifted and talented children would thrive in any environment. It is now known that these children have special needs that must be met. They need recognition and acceptance— and they need challenging activities in which they can be successful. They benefit from playing with a variety of children, but

Children learn in different ways, based on their particular kind of intelligence. *What must teachers do as a result?*

The World's Children

School Around the World

*R*esearch indicates that the learning abilities of American, Chinese, and Japanese children are similar. At the same time, large differences exist in the three countries in terms of attitudes and beliefs about education. Chinese and Japanese children spend more time at school in academic activities. They also spend more time on homework than do most American children. In fact, homework is assigned in each grade.

The high demands placed on Chinese and Japanese children don't make them dislike school, however. On the contrary, children in these countries appear happy, enthusiastic, and responsive in school. Possibly, the reason is that education is highly prized in China and Japan. Parents spend considerable time helping their children with their work.

SHARE YOUR THOUGHTS

1. How do children's attitudes toward school in these countries compare to those of American children?

2. Do American children's attitudes to school need to change? If so, what would you do to change them? If not, why not?

---

they also need time with other gifted or talented learners.

Avoid overwhelming gifted and talented children with unrealistic expectations or goals. Instead, give these children encouragement and opportunities to explore their gifts.

Gifted children can easily become bored and frustrated in school. They may be labeled "problem children" because they don't follow classroom procedures, they give unexpected answers to questions, and they like to argue. Some gifted children

who are not challenged at school become poor students. Most schools have special programs for gifted students. These may include enrichment programs within regular classes or special classes or even special schools for gifted children.

Most gifted children show recognizable signs by age two. They may talk early, using complete sentences, and show that they have an unusually large vocabulary. Many read before school age—some even by two and one-half. They are highly curious and ask challenging questions.

Giving children opportunities in the areas that interest them can help build their talents.

✔ Check Your Understanding

1. List two steps parents can take to prepare a child for kindergarten.
2. What are two signs of growing language skills among children of this period?
3. Why might children who only hear a language other than English in the home have problems in school?
4. Would deafness be a learning disability? Why or why not?
5. What behaviors are shown by a child with ADHD? By a child with dyslexia?
6. What do schools do to help gifted children?

Putting Knowledge Into Practice

1. **Analyzing.** Why do you think children who attend full-day kindergarten show better performance in school?
2. **Synthesizing.** How does a child benefit when he or she is diagnosed with a learning disability? What problems can such a diagnosis create for the child?
3. **Observing and Participating.** Describe your emotions when you first started high school. How did your earlier school experiences prepare you for high school? How would that compare to a six-year-old starting school for the first time? What could make that child's transition to school easier?

Parenting With Care

Encouraging Make-Believe Play

Between the ages of two and nine, children often engage in make-believe play.

This kind of play aids development in many ways.

What Is Make-Believe Play?

In make-believe play, children act out situations using their imagination.

They may engage in dramatic play, acting out what they see in the adult world. After watching an adult bake a cake, a child may pretend to bake a cake for a favorite stuffed animal. After spending a day at a parent's place of work, a child may play "office." Children might also use fantasy play, acting out a voyage to another planet or being a pirate.

The Benefits of Make-Believe Play

In make-believe play, children themselves choose what to play, and they create a situation over which they have full control. In this pretend world, they can be successful, feel important, and gain confidence. They can make up their own rules and try out new activities without fear of failure or ridicule. Pretend play provides endless opportunities for trying out different roles. This play helps children understand and express their feelings. Stuffed animals, dolls, and puppets can all act as good friends—or perhaps enemies to talk to and act out feelings with.

Guiding Make-Believe Play

The best way to encourage make-believe play is to let it happen. Most children show an interest in this play at some time or another. Adults who allow it to take place naturally do the children a great favor.

Adults can also encourage this play by providing props. Kitchen equipment can help children playing house. A chalkboard and some books can turn a room into a school. Old clothes, jewelry, and shoes can be used for dressing up.

Caregivers should avoid limiting make-believe play. They can, however, let children know how they feel about certain situations. For example, suppose that a caregiver doesn't like shooting games. If children do begin to play such games, the caregiver might explain that he or she doesn't like to shoot people or be shot at. In this way, the caregiver reinforces a set of values without preventing the children from learning about aggressive behavior.

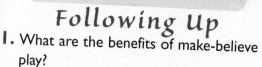

Following Up

1. What are the benefits of make-believe play?

2. **Management.** What materials from around the home could be used by children who wanted to pretend they were detectives?

3. **Leadership.** How might allowing a child to watch many hours of television affect make-believe play?

Summary

✔ Children four to six are in the preoperational stage of thinking. (Section 16-1)

✔ One theorist emphasizes that there is more than one kind of intelligence. (Section 16-1)

✔ Parents and caregivers can lead children to appreciate reading, art, and music. (Section 16-1)

✔ Children starting school have to adjust to new situations. (Section 16-2)

✔ Between four and six, children have rapid language development, but some children need help. (Section 16-2)

Reviewing the Facts

1. What are the signs of preoperational thinking in children these ages? (Section 16-1)

2. List the disadvantages of intelligence tests. (Section 16-1)

3. Choose one of Gardner's multiple intelligences and explain what it means. (Section 16-1)

4. What positive effect does reading have on learning in general? (Section 16-1)

5. Why is it good to ask children about the processes they used to create art? (Section 16-1)

6. What do some states require before students start kindergarten? (Section 16-2)

7. What factors in the home might lead to language problems? (Section 16-2)

8. What is the difference between a learning disability and a physical disability? (Section 16-2)

9. What is meant by a "gifted" child? (Section 16-2)

Thinking Critically

1. **Making Inferences.** Lara is playing with her dolls by sitting them around a table with her. What kind of play typical of preoperational thinking is she playing?

2. **Analyzing.** How can an educator make a distinction between a child who is simply very squirmy because he or she is young and one who may have ADHD?

3. **Synthesizing.** What emotional problems might a gifted or talented child suffer? How might other children contribute to those problems?

Taking Action

1. **Making a Book.** Create a story suitable for a five-year-old about a child just starting kindergarten. Include some of the challenges that the child may face. Show how the child successfully met them. *(Communication)*

2. **Creating Finger Plays.** Think of a song that children enjoy and make up a finger play to go along with it. Show your creation to the class. *(Leadership)*

CONNECTIONS

 ## Cross-Curricular Connections

1. **Art.** Make a poster that explains the eight multiple intelligences.
2. **Music.** Listen to the recording of a singer or group that performs for young children. Perform the song, or read the words, to the class. Discuss why young children would find that song appealing.

 ## Workplace Connections

1. **Resources.** Make a list of resources that you think should be on hand for art activities for kindergarten students.
2. **Interpersonal Skills.** With a partner, write and act out a scene in which a teacher informs a parent that his or her child has a learning disability or a speech problem and needs special help. Assume that the child has been tested to confirm the need and that the parent gave approval for the test.

 ## Family and Community Connections

1. **Learning in the Home.** Make a chart. At the top of each column, list such everyday experiences as cooking, cleaning, doing the laundry, or going shopping. Underneath, list ways that those activities can become learning experiences for children four to six years old.
2. **Finding Intelligences.** Choose three people that each show a different kind of intelligence. Without naming them or their particular intelligence, write a description of their abilities. Read your description to the class and see if they can identify the kind of intelligence.

 ## Technology Connections

1. **Internet.** Research gifted children, talented children, speech problems, ADHD, or dyslexia on the Internet, looking at government sites. What programs are suggested for children in these situations? Report your findings to the class.

UNIT 6

Special Areas of Study

"THE BIGGEST PROBLEM (IS IN OTHER PEOPLE'S MINDS)"

My brother Bobby never listens when I talk;

Pays close attention though, and watches like a hawk.

Took some time for my hands to learn the signs,

But now the two of us, we get along just fine.

Bobby's biggest problem is in other people's minds;

We do things we like to do and have a great time.

Some kids stay away, but if they knew him they would find

Bobby's biggest problem really is in other people's minds.

—*Don Haynie*

CHAPTER 17

The Child from Seven to Twelve

Just before the curtain rose, the students on stage fought down their nerves. This was the big moment they had worked toward. Next year the sixth graders would be moving on to a new school. This would be their last performance at the old school, and they wanted it to be special.

Trisha thought about how much she had grown since she started in kindergarten. She remembered how big the school had looked then. In her first year at the school, the sixth graders seemed so grown up to her—big and knowing everything. Now she was one of them! She smiled when she remembered Mrs. Sanchez, who taught her how to read, and Mr. Nolan, who made social studies so interesting.

Trisha's thoughts were interrupted by Mrs. Robbins, who whispered from offstage. "OK, kids, we're going to raise the curtain now. Do a great job, I know you can!"

> **"This would be their last performance at the old school, and they wanted it to be special"**

SECTION 17-1

Physical Growth and Development from Seven to Twelve

From seven to twelve, children go through two stages. The period from seven to ten is called middle childhood. In this time, children build on the growth and skills that began in early childhood. From ten to twelve, they are in early adolescence. These young teens or "pre-teens" stand poised to enter the path that leads to being an adult.

KEY TERMS

acne
eating disorder
fiber
orthodontist
puberty
saturated fat

OBJECTIVES:

- Describe average changes in height and weight during these years.
- Identify the physical changes that take place in puberty.
- Select foods that meet the guidelines for good nutrition.
- Explain how to fight acne.

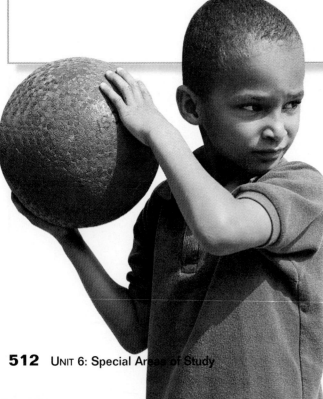

Physical Changes

From seven to twelve, children go through a period of major physical change. A sudden spurt of growth adds to their height. Their bodies also change in profound ways as they begin to take on the physical signs of adulthood.

From eleven to thirteen, girls have a growth spurt and begin to be taller than boys. *What brings about these changes? What happens afterward?*

Height

In middle childhood, children grow an average of 2 inches (5.1 cm) each year. This gain is usually at a regular pace, but many children have spurts in which they grow very rapidly in a short time.

Growth speeds up in early adolescence. Young teens reach **puberty** (PYOO-burr-tee), the set of changes that gives a person a physically mature body able to reproduce. Young teens grow very rapidly, adding from 3 to 5 inches (7.6 to 12.7 cm) a year. During puberty, they add about a quarter of their adult height.

The chart on page 514 shows the average height of children from seven to twelve. Of course, these figures are averages. Children these ages differ greatly in height.

This growth takes place in different parts of the body at different times. Typically, hands and feet grow first, followed by arms and legs and then the torso. Sometimes one part of the body—perhaps the nose—grows faster than other parts. The child may feel awkward and uncomfortable. Fortunately, growth rates even out, and the differences disappear.

Because they grow so rapidly, some children have stretch marks on their skin. These whitish or purplish lines are caused by their skin being stretched. They fade over time.

Weight

On average, children gain about 6.5 pounds (3.0 kg) each year from age seven to twelve. At around age ten or eleven, a boy

Average Height of Boys and Girls Seven to Twelve

AGE	BOYS		GIRLS	
	Inches	Centimeters	Inches	Centimeters
Seven	48.0	121.8	47.4	120.5
Eight	50.0	127.0	49.8	126.5
Nine	52.0	132.0	52.0	132.0
Ten	54.0	137.2	54.0	137.2
Eleven	56.3	143.0	57.0	144.8
Twelve	58.7	149.2	59.6	151.5

or girl may seem to be gaining more weight than that. This is typical just before puberty begins.

Heredity influences a child's weight, but environment plays a very important part, too. A child who eats food low in fat and high in nutrients is less likely to have weight problems than one who eats food high in fat and low in nutrients. Physically active children are less likely to have weight problems.

Some children—especially girls—become overly concerned about their weight. They see themselves as being fat when they really aren't. They may develop an **eating disorder**, a condition in which they starve themselves or eat large amounts of food at a time and then make themselves vomit.

Eating disorders can have a devastating effect on the body. They can even lead to death. These are emotional problems. A person with an eating disorder needs counseling from a trained professional.

The Developing Brain

Exercise helps the brain think, too. The tissue that connects the two sides of the brain benefits from both small and large motor activity. This tissue also plays a role in creative imagination and analytical thinking.

Changes of Puberty

Puberty usually starts about age ten for girls and about a year later for boys. The changes, which take place over many years, are usually completed by about sixteen or seventeen. Of course, some children begin puberty earlier and others do so later. There is no cause for concern if puberty is delayed for up to three years. If no signs of puberty show by the time a girl reaches thirteen or a boy fourteen, a doctor should be consulted.

Puberty causes profound changes to the young teen's body. For both boys and girls, hair appears under the arms and in the pubic area.

In addition, boys experience several other changes. Facial hair begins to appear, and their voice deepens. Sometimes the deepening doesn't take place smoothly, and the boy's voice may "crack," or change tones, from time to time. A boy's shoulders broaden, and muscles grow larger. Also, the boy's sexual organs develop and become capable of producing sperm.

Girls undergo several changes as well. Their breasts enlarge, their waist narrows, and their hips widen. The sexual organs develop and become capable of releasing mature eggs. Related to that change is the beginning of menstruation.

This is the monthly cycle in which the female's body releases an egg and the uterus prepares for a possible pregnancy. Most girls begin to have menstrual periods about two years after puberty begins. The average age for girls is about twelve or thirteen. Girls' menstrual periods may be quite uneven at first. They may not occur every month, and the amount of flow may vary greatly from month to month.

HEALTH TIP

Being Active

American children are less active than they used to be. As a result, about a third of them are overweight. Their physical skills have declined as well. In a recent study, only 64 percent of boys aged six to twelve and 50 percent of girls that age could run a mile in ten minutes. Only 2 percent of the children tested could pass the fitness tests that are part of the President's Challenge award. Parents and educators are worried.

The National Association for Sport and Physical Education recommends that elementary school children need to be involved in active play at least one hour a day. More, says the association, is even better.

Children can take turns between vigorous activity that lasts ten or fifteen minutes and periods of rest. The association points out that the best activities are those that can be continued later in life. Walking, biking, swimming, and tennis are all examples. So are dancing, skating, and basketball.

FOLLOWING UP

1. Why do you think that children are less active now?
2. Why do you think lifetime sports like walking and biking are desirable?

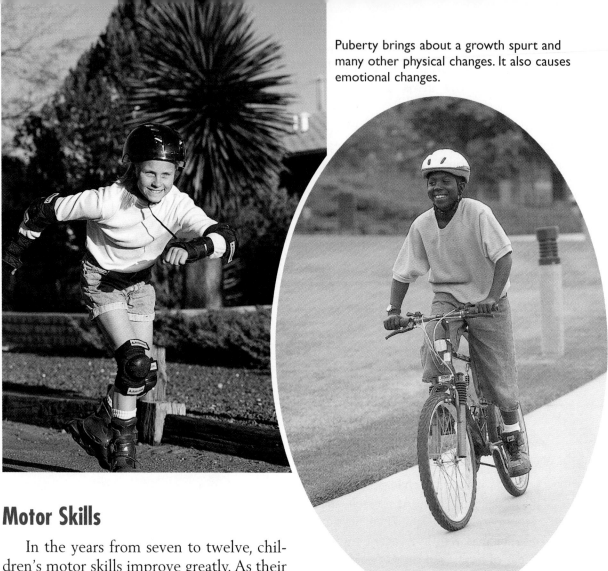

Puberty brings about a growth spurt and many other physical changes. It also causes emotional changes.

Motor Skills

In the years from seven to twelve, children's motor skills improve greatly. As their bodies mature, they build more muscles and become stronger. Children these ages enjoy active play. They have fun running, using playground equipment, playing tag, in-line skating, and bike riding. Many enjoy playing on teams in organized sports.

They also have growing control over those muscles. Improved coordination shows in the greater ease and smoothness of their actions. It also shows in the complexity of the tasks they can perform. Seven-year-olds have trouble catching a baseball, but ten-year-olds can manage it.

Greater control extends to small motor skills as well. Around age seven, children's drawings become neater and more controlled. Younger children learn to write by printing, but around age eight they can learn cursive writing.

Caring for Children from Seven to Twelve

Children ages seven to twelve dress themselves and take care of their own personal hygiene. Parents need to ensure that they care for themselves in healthy ways, however. This is particularly important with nutrition.

Nutrition

As at other ages, the key to good nutrition in these years is to plan meals using the Food Guide Pyramid. Children—and adults—should also follow the Dietary Guidelines to have a healthy diet:

- **Reduce the amount of fat in the diet.** It is especially important to limit the amount of **saturated fat** eaten. Saturated fat is animal fat that is solid when at room temperature.
- **Eat plenty of fiber.** Plant foods and products made from whole grain contain **fiber,** a part of plants that humans cannot digest. Eating fiber helps the digestive system work properly.
- **Limit sugar.** Sugary drinks or desserts have few nutrients.
- **Reduce the amount of salt.** Salt can contribute to high blood pressure and heart disease.

INFOLINK

Food Guide Pyramid

For more about the *Food Guide Pyramid*, see Chapter 11, page 361.

Parents need to make sure that young children eat breakfast. Many skip the meal, but this is a mistake. Breakfast provides vital fuel for children to begin their day. Children who eat breakfast learn better, pay more attention, and are more likely to take part in activities than those who do not. A healthy breakfast includes two servings from the bread, cereal, rice, and pasta food group; one from the fruit group; and one from the milk, cheese, and yogurt group.

Caring for the Teeth

In this period, children lose all of their primary teeth, and most of the permanent teeth appear. The first permanent teeth are a set of molars that appears around age six. Around age twelve, a second set of molars emerges behind the first set. The last set of molars—called the "wisdom teeth"—do not appear until age eighteen to twenty.

As they reach adolescence, children have even greater need for good nutrition, but many teens skip breakfast and eat many snack foods that are high in fat, salt, or sugar. *Why is having a healthy breakfast and choosing nutritious snacks so important?*

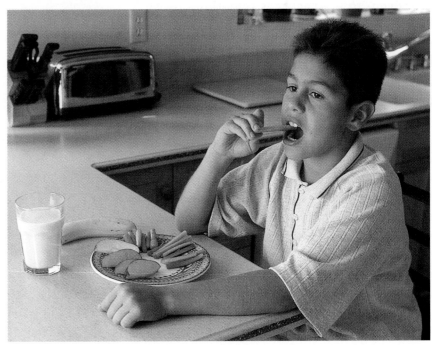

The permanent teeth look different than the primary teeth. They are larger and somewhat more yellow. They are also more jagged looking, although the points wear down over time.

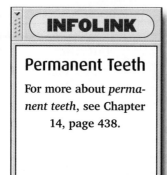

INFOLINK

Permanent Teeth

For more about *permanent teeth*, see Chapter 14, page 438.

Teeth should be brushed at least twice a day and flossed at least once a day. A dental check-up and cleaning, at least once a year, help prevent decay.

Sometimes teeth don't come in straight. A dentist can suggest whether this is a potential problem. If so, the dentist may advise that the child see an **orthodontist**. This dental specialist can decide whether the child would benefit by having braces to straighten the teeth.

Personal Hygiene

Seven- to ten-year-olds sometimes resist keeping clean. It's not that they want to be dirty, they simply can't be bothered to take time out of their active lives. Parents can take various steps to prevent fights over hygiene:

- **Focus on essentials.** Make sure that the child washes before eating and after using the bathroom, but don't insist on the child bathing every day.
- **Give choices when possible.** Katrina lets Ashley choose when to shower, giving her some control over her life.
- **Send positive messages.** After he showered, Eduardo said how refreshed he felt. That signals his children that bathing brings benefits besides simply getting clean.

The lack of interest in hygiene changes around age ten. The timing is convenient, because the physical changes of puberty put new demands for cleanliness. With puberty, the body produces more sweat, so young teens may develop body odor. Washing, especially the feet and under the arms, can remove this odor. Also, the hair becomes more oily. This usually goes away over time, as the body's production of skin oil goes down. Until then, many teens need to wash their hair more often.

Acne

The oil glands bring about another condition as well. About 80 percent of all teens develop **acne**, a skin problem caused by these excess oils in the skin. The oil may plug a pore, or opening in the skin, and form a blackhead. Sometimes it collects below the skin and forms a whitehead. Some

As children's full set of permanent teeth develop, a dentist may recommend that they need braces. *Why do you think braces are used at this time?*

Acne is a normal result of the physical changes of adolescence, but it can make young teens feel very self-conscious. They worry that pimples make them look funny or ugly. *What should a teen do if a case of acne is very severe?*

young teens have more severe forms, with infections forming below the skin. Acne tends to appear on the face, neck, and upper body.

Acne seems to be influenced by heredity. Parents who had serious acne are more likely to have children with the same problem. Diet doesn't affect acne in most cases, although some people find that certain foods worsen the problem. These can simply be avoided. Some make-up can also make acne worse.

Washing with warm water and mild soap can generally help. With more severe forms, it may be necessary to see a doctor. The doctor may prescribe a special cream to be used on the face.

SECTION 17-1 REVIEW

✔ Check Your Understanding

1. What are the ages of middle childhood? What are the ages of early adolescence?
2. What changes in height and weight are typical in these years?
3. What is an eating disorder?
4. How do boys change in puberty? How do girls change?
5. What is better to drink, fruit juice made from concentrate or a fruit flavored soda? Why?
6. Why do some children need braces?
7. How do the changes of puberty increase the need for hygiene?
8. What causes acne? How can it be treated?

Putting Knowledge Into Practice

1. **Analyzing.** Why do you think girls are more likely to suffer from an eating disorder?
2. **Comparing.** Contrast the average ages of puberty for boys and girls. What social impact do you think these physical changes might have?
3. **Observing and Participating.** Compare the handwriting of children seven, ten, and twelve years old. What differences do you see? How do you explain those differences?

SECTION 17-2

Emotional Development from Seven to Twelve

At seven, Chloe often stayed in her room. At ten, she became more outgoing, and her parents adjusted to her new breezy manner and to her frequent shows of affection. A year later, she changed again. She became moody and had no interest in her parents at all. Chloe's emotional shifts are typical of the changes children go through between seven and twelve.

KEY TERMS

gender identity
role model

OBJECTIVES:

- Recognize signs of the child's growing sense of self.
- Identify a child's age based on his or her emotional behavior.
- Recommend strategies for living with children from seven to twelve.

A Sense of Self

One of the most important changes in this period is the developing sense of self. As children grow, they become able to think more abstractly. This shapes how they see themselves.

A researcher asked a girl who was five and one-half whether she could become the

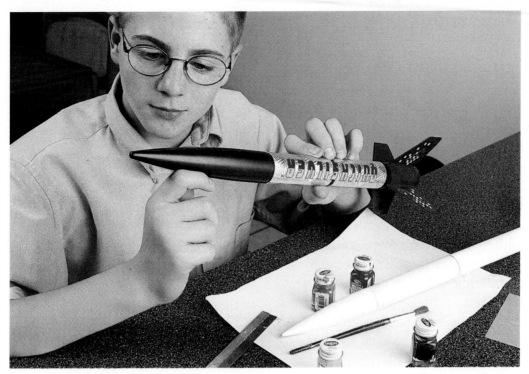

Children can build self-esteem by having pride in their accomplishments. *How can parents contribute to high self-esteem?*

family dog. The girl said no, but based her reasoning on physical traits. The dog, she said, "has brown eyes . . . and walks like a dog." When a nine-year-old was asked whether she could become her brother, she answered no for a different reason: "I'm me and he's him. I can't change in any way 'cause I've got to stay like . . . myself."

In this period, children see that they have a personality that is uniquely theirs. They see themselves as a mixture of many qualities. Some are based on their physical appearance, and others are based on talents or abilities. By ten, children can see themselves as highly skilled in one area and less able in another. By eleven and twelve, children also use personal qualities to define themselves —"I'm honest," or "I'm a good friend," or "I can be counted on."

They also see that they behave differently in different situations. Jeff thought of himself as friendly. Then he went to a party at his cousin's house. He didn't know anyone besides his cousin, and he found it hard to begin talking to anyone. As he thought about it, Jeff realized that he is shy with strangers. How could he be both friendly and shy? Jeff can reconcile these two opposite views by seeing that his approach to people changes as the situation he's in changes.

Young teens like Jeff also realize that different people may perceive them in different ways. This, too, is an example of their growing thinking skills. It shows that they can view themselves from other people's point of view.

Being Male or Female

An important part of that growing sense of self is the child's **gender identity**. This is the awareness of being a boy or girl. Gender identity begins in early childhood and is usually firmly fixed by age four. In middle childhood and early adolescence that identity becomes stronger.

- Children spend more time with those of the same sex. The close friendships they develop are almost always with children of the same sex.
- They show an increased desire to act and talk like children of the same sex.
- They tend to choose adults of the same sex as their **role models,** the people they admire and who they wish to pattern their behavior after.
- In early adolescence, they begin to explore relationships with the opposite sex.

As they form their gender identity, children choose someone of the same sex as a role model. This may be a parent. *Who else might be a role model?*

Emotional Changes

Changes in intellectual development have an impact on how children see themselves. The physical changes of puberty also have a major impact on emotional life. While emotional development has characteristics at each age, a child's own temperament also makes a difference.

Middle Childhood

In middle childhood, how children handle their emotions varies from year to year. In some years, they are fairly negative. In others, they are often happy.

- **Age seven.** Seven-year-olds tend to be somewhat withdrawn and quiet. Many children this age worry a great deal—about all kinds of issues. Like many children aged seven, Jaquala is very sensitive to what others say about her.
- **Age eight.** Eight-year-olds direct their attention outward. Seven-year-olds tend to stay near home. Eight-year-olds are willing to explore and are curious about new things. They are lively and active—and very dramatic. Antuwan often exaggerates when telling stories or describing his feelings. Eight-year-olds take a positive attitude to life.
- **Age nine.** Nine-year-olds can be very harsh about their own failings—even embarrassed by them. They may also show signs of tension such as tightening the lips. They tend to be absorbed in their own thoughts. When Lamar's mother called, he didn't answer. She thought he was being rude, but he was concentrating so much on his own concerns that he simply didn't hear her.

At age seven, children can be very gloomy. They often look at the negative side of things and say, for instance, that other people hate them. *What could parents do to help a child handle these feelings?*

Like nine-year-olds, young teens can be very absorbed in their own thoughts and concerns. They may pay little attention to others—except their peers. Peers are extremely important to young teens. They crave acceptance and become anxious if they stand out in any way from their peers.

Young teens can also hide their true feelings with a mask of not caring. This is a sign of growing emotional control. Younger children show the emotions they feel. Young teens are able to show the emotions they wish—to some degree.

Young teens are better able to verbalize their feelings. Many begin to write their thoughts in a diary. *What is another emotional characteristic of young teens?*

- **Age ten.** Ten-year-olds are more positive and happy. Many would agree with Whitney, who called ten the best age "because you're not too young and not too old."

Early Adolescence

The release of hormones into the body causes the physical changes of puberty. These hormones also bring about emotional changes. Young teens can move from happiness to anger, frustration, or sadness in minutes. These mood swings can just as easily swing in the opposite direction.

Specific Emotions

In early childhood, emotional life centers on the family. In middle childhood and the early teen years, the focus shifts to the wider world. People and events outside the family have more impact on the person's emotions than before.

Anger

As they leave early childhood, children gain greater ability to control their emotions. Still, from time to time, children feel angry—and let others know it. Even ten-year-olds, who are typically quite happy, show anger. When they do, though, it usually passes quickly.

The moodiness of young teens means that anger can erupt at any time. Often, though, occasions of anger are just that—eruptions that boil over and go away. The young teen may slam a door or noisily leave a room. Soon, though, the situation will be back to normal.

Many times, these outbursts have little to do with the small event or comment that triggered them. Courtney became very angry when her mother asked her to hang up her coat after school. Within minutes, though, she was cheerful. Courtney wasn't actually upset at anything her mother said. She was really angry because her friends went shopping without her.

By middle childhood, children generally know to use words to show anger. Sometimes, though, a child lashes out with aggressive actions. It is important to avoid responding in the same way. Setting a good example is the best method of teaching a child. In addition, caregivers can try these approaches:

- **Teach the child how to gain self-control.** Time-outs, counting to ten, or breathing deeply are all ways of helping children learn to calm down.

Eight-year-olds have very strong attachments to their mothers and may be jealous of other children in the family.

The mood swings of young teens can make them difficult to live with from time to time. Fortunately, negative feelings often quickly pass. **When children this age are angry, who is it usually with?**

- **Help the child learn how to resolve conflicts without fighting.** Working through problems at home—say with other siblings—can give a child the tools to settle conflicts at school.
- **Use rewards for controlling anger.** The reward reinforces the value of self-control.

Fear and Worry

Children's fears change during this period. Seven-year-olds may still fear some of the things they feared in early childhood, such as the dark. This can lead, with some, to problems going to sleep. Leaving a light on at night can help relieve this fear.

By age ten, these childhood fears have often disappeared. Many children may be like Summer, who simply announced one day that she was no longer afraid of dogs.

As childhood fears disappear, new worries may emerge. News reports of violent crimes or fatal car accidents or natural disasters lead some young teens to worry about these problems striking them or their families. More aware of the world around them, they realize that there are dangers in that world. They need to be reassured that caregivers will take all the steps necessary to protect them.

Other worries also appear. Most have to do with how others see them. Up to age ten, children may be concerned about how adults, as well as children, see them. By the young teen years, their focus is on the attitudes of their peers.

Living with Children Seven to Twelve

Living or working with children from seven to twelve can be difficult at times. The quiet, withdrawn seven-year-old may not be willing to talk about his feelings. The eight-year-old, though cheerful, often clings to her mother. Here are tips for preventing small emotional problems from becoming large ones:

- **Be patient.** Remember that the child still doesn't have full self-control. The anger young teens show often results mainly from the difficulty they are having adjusting to the changes in their bodies.

- **Avoid taking it personally.** A child who is angry or upset may say some pretty nasty things. Remember that the child doesn't usually mean what is said.
- **Keep the child under control.** Of course, the child also has to stay within acceptable limits of behavior. Actions that break the rules can and

should be dealt with. If the problem wasn't too serious, talking through things may be enough. Remember that as they grow older, children have greater ability to understand abstract ideas and more complex explanations.

- **Listen.** Give the child a chance to explain what happened and why. The child may have a valid grievance. Admitting that does not lessen the force of saying you don't approve of how the anger was expressed.

SECTION 17-2 REVIEW

✔ Check Your Understanding

1. By eleven and twelve, how do young teens define their personalities?
2. How do early adolescents strengthen gender identity?
3. At what age is a child likely to be withdrawn and worry a great deal?
4. At what ages in middle childhood do children tend to be happy and positive?
5. What effect do the hormones of puberty have on the emotions of early adolescents?
6. What new fears may appear in middle childhood?

Putting Knowledge Into Practice

1. **Analyzing.** Charlie was reading when his brother asked for help with his homework. Charlie said, "I always help. Get Kim to help" and returned to his book. When his brother asked again, Charlie grew angry. "No one else does *anything* around here." Then he stormed off to his room and slammed the door. What age do you think Charlie is? Why?
2. **Applying.** What advice would you give a friend who has a seven-year-old sibling who frequently starts fights and tells your friend, "I hate you!"?
3. **Observing and Participating.** Write a paragraph describing what you were like at seven and another one describing what you were like at twelve. Evaluate how you changed and how you stayed the same.

CAREER OPPORTUNITIES

Recreation Worker

A CONVERSATION WITH CHRIS O'BRIEN

How did you become interested in becoming a recreation worker? I've always liked sports and fitness, I enjoy working outdoors, and I love kids. This career seemed like a natural for me.

What are the tasks and responsibilities of a recreation worker? I teach the value of being fit, the basic skills of different sports, and how to be a good sport. All three are equally important.

What is the work environment like? I work at a local center that has a gym, a pool, and other facilities. During the school year, I teach younger children and adults during the day. We have classes in aerobics, swimming, and gymnastics. In the late afternoon, I head leagues for elementary school children. During the summer, I split my time between the gym and soccer and softball leagues.

What are the working hours like? The days are long and full. I work six days because our center is open on Saturday.

What aptitudes are needed to be a recreation worker? You need to be able to explain things to people. You need to have judgment so you can gauge what each person is capable of doing. The goal is not to make everyone a great athlete, but to help each person meet his or her full potential. You have to be well organized so that practices run smoothly. Kids hate standing around with nothing to do. Finally, you need a lot of energy and enthusiasm.

RECREATION WORKER

Education and Training. Most full-time recreation workers have a bachelor's degree, usually specializing in recreation.

Career Outlook. Many people compete for the jobs available in recreation work.

CONNECTING SCHOOL TO CAREER

1. **Thinking Skills.** Look at the three things O'Brien teaches. Do you agree that they are all equally valuable? Why or why not?
2. **Resources.** Why would having experience from summer jobs help someone who was applying for a job as a recreation worker? Where could you get that experience?

Social and Moral Development from Seven to Twelve

Jeannie and Carlton were neighbors. From the time they were two, they played together. First they played in the sandbox behind Jeannie's house. Later, they played on the same soccer team. When they were eight, though, Jeannie and Carlton began to move in different directions. Jeannie spent more time with the girls from school, and Carlton with the boys.

KEY TERMS

conformity
peer pressure

OBJECTIVES:

- Describe changes in friendship in these years.
- Analyze peer pressure.
- Explain changes in how children these ages get along with parents.
- Identify ways to help children learn to act morally.

Friendships

Children begin to play together early in life. By five, they speak of having friends, but these friends are simply playmates. In middle childhood and early adolescence, friendships change in character. They become much more personal, based on the children's thoughts and feelings, and they become deeper.

Friendships are very important to young teens, but relations between friends aren't always smooth. Children may be upset if a friend seems to enjoy the company of another person. *How can children work these problems out?*

- Of course, they still look on friends as people they have fun with.

Not surprisingly, a common pastime of children these ages is talking. Children these ages still enjoy active, physical play, but they spend a great deal more time simply talking.

It is their development in other areas that brings about these changes. The physical and emotional changes of puberty raise new questions about dating and sexuality. Children talk to their friends as they try to think through these issues.

Their intellectual growth makes deeper friendships possible. Able to think abstractly, young teens can better understand how others see them. At the same time, they can more easily see other people's point of view and feel empathy for them. These new skills make it easier to relate to friends in a deeper way.

Friends of the Opposite Sex

As the story of Jeannie and Carlton shows, sex differences become important in these years. Even in early childhood, children are more likely to play with others of the same sex. Still, situations like Jeannie and Carlton's are not unusual.

As children grow older, though, they are more likely to play only with children of the same sex. This is true even though, as puberty begins, they become more interested in and preoccupied with children of the opposite sex.

Beginning around age seven or eight, children see new reasons for friendship.

- Children value friends who are loyal. They appreciate those who stand by them when they are in a difficult situation or feeling low.
- They also look for friends that they can feel comfortable revealing inner feelings to. These older children share their thoughts and ideas with others. Close friends become those they feel they can trust—friends who won't pass these highly personal revelations on to others.

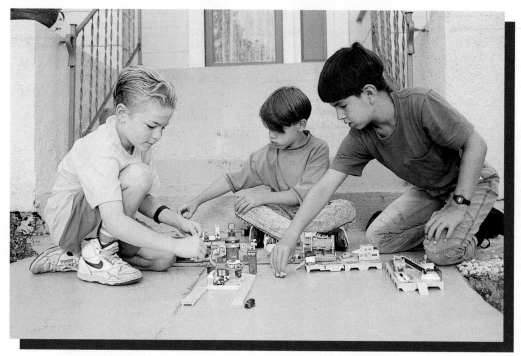

How can belonging to a club or group help develop social skills?

One reason is that opposite sex friendships raise questions of being romantically involved. Many—perhaps most—eleven- and twelve-year-olds aren't yet ready for that step. They wish to avoid the teasing they may hear if they have a friend of the opposite sex.

How Many Friends?

Some children have many friends, some have a few, and some have only one or two. The number of friendships depends on the child's temperament—some children are private and quiet and simply don't need many friends. Another influence is environment. Children in after-school programs, clubs, or teams meet others more easily.

There is no set number of friends that a child should have. Still, young teens may use the number of friends as a way to measure their popularity. Those with fewer friends may feel that they fall short. They might feel unliked and unwanted.

The key to a healthy social life, though, is not how many friends a child has. It is whether a child has the social skills to form the friendships he or she wants to have.

Peer Pressure

Starting in early adolescence, peer groups become the most important set of relationships for children. Children this age loosen ties to parents and identify more with a group of peers.

Because of this, **peer pressure** becomes very strong. The desire for acceptance by children their own age leads young teens to adopt the words, behaviors, habits, and ideas of their group.

Peer pressure can be a powerful influence on a young person's life. It is important for young teens to join a peer group that

Ask the Eperts

Rachel Perkins
Child Development Technology
Instructor
Hinds Community College
Utica, Mississippi

TEACHING *Tolerance*

How can I teach my child to be tolerant of others?

Children start out ready to be tolerant of anyone. Parents need to make sure that they continue to grow that way. One way is to avoid teaching them prejudice.

As with any moral teaching, parents do this best by example—by showing that they are not prejudiced. They can avoid making negative comments about people or groups who are different. If they do make such a remark, they can take it back in front of the child—and explain why it was wrong.

Parents can act in accepting ways towards other people. At work, at home, at school, or at play, they can show that they are willing to get along with anyone who behaves acceptably.

Messages in the media can counter the lessons that parents try to teach their children. Parents can fight those messages by pointing them out and explaining what is wrong with them.

Parents can help children to know and understand traditions of their own heritage as well as to know and respect the traditions of other cultures.

Teaching tolerance is not something that can be done once and then forgotten. Parents can raise the subject any time the opportunity presents itself. Reinforcing the message makes it more likely to be learned.

Thinking It Through

1. What should you do if a friend tells a joke that makes fun of a group of people?
2. Some people charge that taking tolerance too far can lead to acceptance of *any* behavior, even those that are wrong. Is that what tolerance means? If so, why? If not, why not?

shows positive values. These values include staying free of drugs, tobacco, and alcohol and avoiding risky behaviors. It also includes tolerance for others who are different.

A child who is different from others can have a difficult time in this period. Young teens feel a strong drive for **conformity**—being like one another. The person who has different interests—music rather than athletics, gardening rather than video games—or who dresses differently may be ridiculed and teased by others.

How can they handle this teasing?

- Find others with similar interests and spend time with them. Clubs and other social groups can provide opportunities for sharing special interests.
- Recognize that the problem is with the others, not themselves.
- Avoid becoming upset when teased. People who tease are looking for a reaction. If there isn't one, they may stop the teasing. Try to release the frustration at home with a parent, rather than in front of the others.
- Try to break the situation up with humor. Making a joke can weaken the impact of harsh words—and show that he or she can't be picked on.

Parents can help such a child, too. By giving their love and support, they let the child know that he or she is not alone.

Family Relationships

With all the differences between seven- and twelve-year-olds, it's easy to see why family relationships change during this period. Development in all areas moves children from dependence toward more independence. The complex relationships within the family must reflect that change.

Family situations vary greatly. Some families have two parents in the home; others only one. Parents' work schedules make a difference in how much "family time" is available. The number and ages of siblings also affects family relationships.

With children, age does impact how they view their parents. Seven-year-olds depend on their parents but often challenge

When children have problems with their friendships, they may turn to their parents. *Name one good listening technique that parents can use.*

Community service projects can teach children that people can make a difference. *What other lessons can they learn from these activities?*

parental authority. At eight, children tend to cling to their parents. But by nine, children sometimes ignore adults because they are wrapped up in their own thoughts. Ten is a smooth year, while eleven- and twelve-year-olds are critical of their parents. At twelve, children are again more cooperative.

Starting at age seven, children get along well with siblings who are very young or much older than themselves. They are helpful and protective of children under two. They tend to respect and admire siblings in their late teens.

Children often have difficult relationships with siblings closer in age. Fights are more often verbal than physical. They judge each other harshly. Parents need to help them develop empathy and a sense of cooperation.

Moral Development

As children spend more time outside the home, they more often face decisions about right and wrong that they must answer alone, without a parent being around. This is especially true starting in early adolescence, when children feel a growing need to be independent.

What will a child do when classmates tease someone else for not being a good ath-

lete? What will he say if another child challenges him to smoke? What will she do if the group urges her to shoplift? With peer pressure being such a strong force in children's lives, the urge to go along with such wrong actions can be strong.

Parents can help prepare their children to make the right choice in a few ways:

- **Set a good example.** Showing tolerance to others and behaving in a moral way are the best way to teach a child to act in a moral way. If a cashier gives too much money in change, return the extra. That sends a powerful message to a child.

- **Support the child's growing conscience.** Sometimes the wrong thing can seem attractive. Joining the group, even if it's doing something wrong, can win acceptance. Remind the child, though, that doing the wrong thing can leave an uncomfortable feeling afterward.
- **Talk about situations that may occur.** Discussing "what if's" ahead of time can give a child coping strategies when confronted with difficult situations.

- **Reinforce empathy.** Joining in teasing another child can win acceptance by the group doing the teasing. Ask your child how he or she would feel as the object of that teasing. The child will probably remember that lesson in the future.
- **Use the child's sense of fairness.** Children these ages value fairness. That value can be used to lead them to the right decision.

SECTION 17-3 REVIEW

✔ Check Your Understanding

1. What characteristics do children look for in friends starting about age seven or eight?
2. How are deeper friendships in this period linked to changes in other areas of development?
3. What is peer pressure?
4. Why is conformity important to young teens?
5. Why do family relationships change during this period?
6. How do children from seven to twelve tend to get along with siblings?
7. Give an example in which a child's interest in fairness is used to lead him or her to make a moral choice.

Putting Knowledge Into Practice

1. **Synthesizing.** What social skills do you think a person needs to have in order to make friends?
2. **Analyzing.** What strategies would you recommend for coping with being teased over being different?
3. **Observing and Participating.** Think of an occasion in which you saw peer pressure at work. Describe what took place. Was the result good or bad? If it was bad, what could have been done differently to change the outcome?

Intellectual Development from Seven to Twelve

In middle childhood and early adolescence, children make many advances in their intellectual abilities. They find new ways of thinking and develop an awareness of how they learn. The emotional and intellectual needs of young teens are so special, educators have devised a special setting for them—the middle school.

KEY TERMS

conservation
hypothetical
transitivity

OBJECTIVES:

- Compare the thinking skills of children in middle childhood and early adolescence.

- Identify signs of intellectual development in children seven to twelve.

- Explain why middle school benefits young teens.

Thinking Skills

As you recall, Jean Piaget developed a powerful theory to explain how children think. That view divided thinking into four different stages. Children from seven to twelve fall in two of Piaget's stages.

How are small motor skills used in school?

During this period, children develop several important thinking skills. These abilities give them the basis for mastering school work:

- **Classifying objects.** Children as young as three can classify objects, or group them according to one similar characteristic. They can't sort out all the blocks that are both red and a certain shape. By age seven, they can handle two different characteristics at the same time.

- **Putting objects in a series.** In this stage, children can learn to put objects in a series from, say, largest to smallest. This is an important skill. As Piaget pointed out, all objects in the middle of the series have two properties at the same time. They are both smaller than some and larger than others.

- **Extending relationships.** Piaget said that children this age learn **transitivity.** This is the idea that a relative relationship between two objects can extend to another. If 3 is greater than 2, and 2 is greater than 1, then 3 must also be greater than 1.

- **Retaining basic qualities of an object.** Piaget said that in this period, children learn **conservation.** This is the idea that an object or quantity has the same characteristics even if there is a change in how it is presented. Piaget showed children two balls of clay of equal size. Then he rolled one into a long cylinder of clay and asked if one was larger now. Younger children think so—the longer piece of clay looks bigger, so they think it has more substance. By age seven, children see that the amount of clay hasn't changed.

Concrete Thinking

Children from seven to ten are firmly placed in the stage that Piaget called "concrete operations." Their thinking works effectively on concrete objects. They can't yet understand abstract ideas, although they can generalize from their own experiences. A five-year-old probably can't draw a map of the route from home to a familiar landmark, even though the child is perfectly capable of walking the route. An eight-year-old can draw such a map.

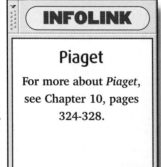

INFOLINK

Piaget

For more about *Piaget,* see Chapter 10, pages 324-328.

Talking About Numbers

*F*or many years, educators and critics have pointed out that the math skills of American students seem to be declining. A recent study compared thirteen-year-olds in math and science around the world. Test results put the American students at the bottom.

Asian students, in particular, are beating American students in math. Two researchers think one reason may be the way numbers are talked about in English and in Asian languages.

Many American children, they say, stumble on the idea of "place value"—whether a number is in the ones, tens, or hundreds place. They point out that in English, place value can be hidden by the words used for numbers above ten, such as "eleven," "twelve," "sixty," and "seventy." Japanese and other Asian languages, though, are different. In these languages, a number's place value is built into the word for the number. "Seventeen" in English is expressed as "ten-seven" in Japanese. "Seventy" is said as "seven-tens."

_____SHARE YOUR THOUGHTS_____

1. Do you know a language other than English? How are the concepts of place value expressed in that language?

2. What other reasons do you think could account for differences in performance on math and science tests?

Formal Thinking

At about age twelve, children move into the formal operations stage. They now have the ability to think abstractly. They can visualize objects that are not in front of them. They can imagine **hypothetical** (HIGH-puh-THET-uh-kal) situations. That is, they can think about things that are not, but could be. This improves their ability to solve problems. It makes it possible for them to think about different situations and prepare for them before they occur. A young teen who begins to show this type of thinking is likely to use it only selectively at first—not in all areas and not at all times.

Other Signs of Intellectual Growth

Other researchers have looked at other aspects of intellectual growth of children from seven to twelve. They have found that children advance in many areas.

In this period, children's memory improves. This enables them to remember basic mathematical operations so they don't

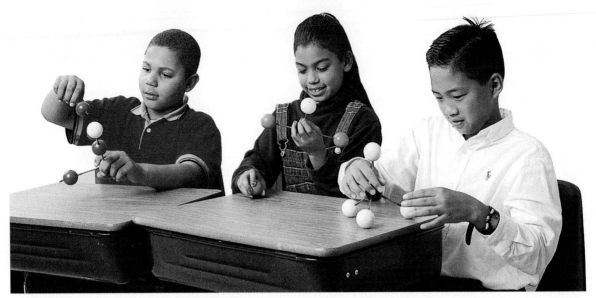

Some children learn best by physically manipulating objects. This is especially true of children from ages seven to ten, when they are in the concrete operations stage. *What is the following stage called?*

Computers provide new learning opportunities for children. *Why are learning games useful?*

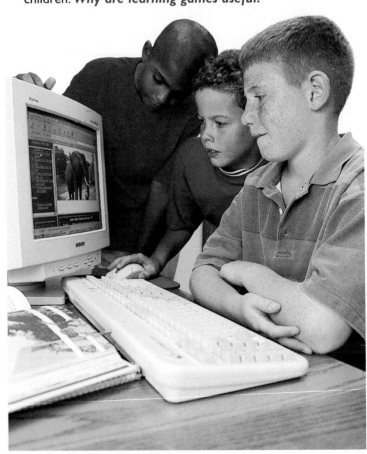

have to count on their fingers. It helps them remember the spellings of unusual words or the names and capitals of the states.

Children also develop a better awareness of how they learn. They can find strategies that work for them. They can plan tasks and organize their work to complete longer term projects.

Other research shows that starting about age twelve, children's capacity for learning generally goes down for about two years. Researchers do not understand why, however. The rapid rate of learning picks up again in the mid teens.

A young teen's attention span also lessens. Children find it difficult to concentrate for long periods of time. They benefit if learning is broken up into small amounts.

As they learn to think abstractly, young teens often see things in sharp terms. They see complex problems, such as social issues, in terms of black and white and believe that the problems can be solved simply. They

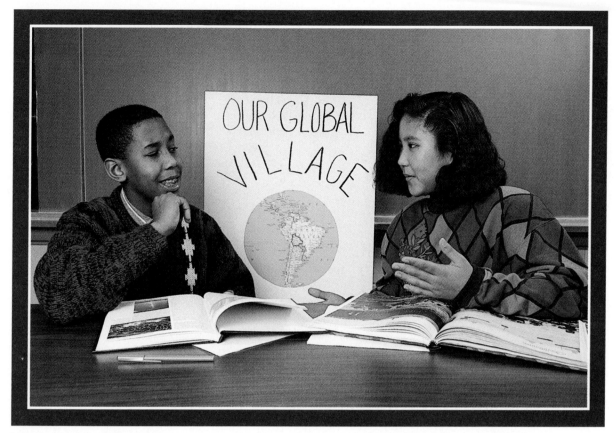

Many school activities call for group work. *How can children benefit from these projects?*

can't understand why people don't put these solutions into practice.

Along with this tendency, they also become very idealistic. They want perfection. They can't yet analyze their ideas to see if they are realistic.

Finally, young teens are interested in exploring. They like to become actively involved in learning, and they enjoy experimenting.

The School Experience

In middle childhood, children continue learning the basic skills that they need in order to succeed in school. In their young teens, they build on those basics and their new thinking skills.

The past few decades have seen a growing movement toward putting early adolescents in middle schools. Educators recognize that these children are too old for the approach of elementary school, in which the teacher is almost like a parent and students have the same teacher for most of their class work. Students this age are more independent and more able to take responsibility for their work.

At the same time, these students are too young for high school. In a high school, students have different teachers for all their classes. They may have an impersonal relationship with teachers. Young teens need more personal contact than that.

The middle school balances these two needs. Students typically have a homeroom

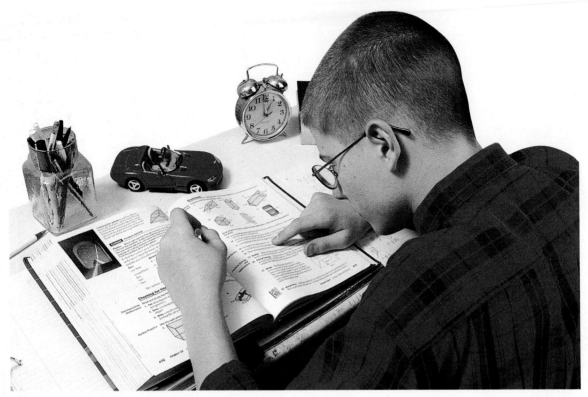

Homework gives students opportunities to practice their skills and to explore new areas of learning. Doing homework also teaches study skills and time management.

with one teacher who meets with them for a brief period every day. This teacher gets to know the students well and gives the students someone they can go to if a problem arises.

Most of the day is spent in a variety of classes. Some of those classes continue traditional subjects, such as English, math, and science. Others bring in new subjects, such as computers. In this way, young teens are prepared for high school.

Homework

As they begin school, children may be excited about the idea of homework. Bringing assignments home gives some children the feeling that they are growing up.

Along with that enthusiasm, though, they may also feel tired after a long day of schooling. They may need a mental break right after school ends for the day. After hours of sitting still at school, physical activity can help work out their stored-up energy. This activity can also revive them, making the homework easier to get done.

Children work most effectively if they have a place where they can spread out their papers and concentrate on their work. Many children work best if the area is quiet and free of distractions.

Homework also becomes more complex over time. In the middle school years, teachers often assign projects that require students to plan over several days or even weeks.

Many parents wrestle with the question of how much help to give. Experts advise that parents remember that homework is the child's responsibility. Although younger children may need to be reminded to finish their work, by middle school children should be ready to take responsibility for their work themselves.

SECTION 17-4 REVIEW

✔ Check Your Understanding

1. How have children age seven advanced in their ability to classify?
2. How is the ability to put objects in a series linked to transitivity?
3. How does the thinking of early adolescents differ from that of children aged seven to ten?
4. How does having more awareness of how they learn help children learn?
5. In what ways is middle school different from elementary school and high school?
6. Give two reasons why children in this age group may need a break after school is over before they begin their homework.

Putting Knowledge Into Practice

1. **Making Inferences.** If hypothetical thinking is so advantageous for children, why don't they use it more often when they first acquire the skill?
2. **Creating.** Devise an experiment to test one of the four mental abilities that Piaget says children acquire in the concrete operations period. Write a description of how you would test this ability.
3. **Observing and Participating.** Watch a teacher in one of your classes. Identify ways that he or she tries to draw out students' ability to think in abstract terms.

Parenting With Care

Becoming Involved in a Child's Education

When parents get involved in their child's education, they send a very important message: school counts.

The children of involved parents are more likely to be engaged by school and to perform well in school. There are many different ways that they can send this message.

- **Meet the staff.** Many schools have a "back to school" or parents' night, when parents can visit their children's classes and meet their teachers. At these group meetings, teachers describe the curriculum for the year, their policy on homework, the behavior they expect, and the level of performance they require.

- **Talk to the teachers personally.** Many schools also schedule parent-teacher conferences. These are one-on-one sessions in which teachers describe the particular child's performance in class. Even if the school has no formal conferences, parents can call the school and arrange to talk to teachers.

- **Read any messages sent by the schools.** Teachers and principals often send home or mail important information about the school.

- **Review the child's homework.** Parents can judge a child's performance by reviewing homework. It is especially useful if they look at assignments that have been graded.

- **Help out with school activities.** When a class takes a field trip, schools usually ask for parent volunteers to come along. Taking part can give a parent a feel for what is going on in the school and how the child gets along with teachers and fellow students.

- **Join the parents' group.** In many communities, parents form an association that has monthly meetings. Often people from the school's faculty or administration speak at these meetings. Parents can learn a great deal about the school by attending these meetings.

- **Talk to the child.** Most important is to talk to the child about school. Dinner every night is a great opportunity to review the day. Students can describe the work they did and any important events that took place.

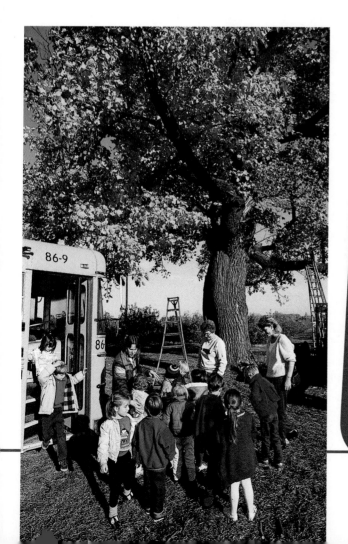

Following Up

1. **Communication.** Many children, when asked what they did in school, answer "Nothing" or something vague like "Stuff." If you were a parent, how would you ask about your child's day in school to be sure to get an answer that had real information?

2. **Leadership.** If you were a teacher, what would you do to help parents become involved in their child's education?

Summary

✔ Once puberty begins, children undergo major physical changes. (Section 17-1)

✔ Children seven to twelve develop more of a sense of self and tend to be more emotional. (Section 17-2)

✔ In these years, children form deeper friendships than earlier. (Section 17-3)

✔ Young teens become capable of abstract thinking and have special needs for schooling. (Section 17-4)

9. How does middle school prepare young teens for high school? (Section 17-4)

Thinking Critically

1. **Analyzing.** In what ways do you and your friends show conformity?

2. **Drawing Conclusions.** Why do you think children in these ages have more problems with siblings near them in age?

Reviewing the Facts

1. How do height and weight increase before and after puberty? (Section 17-1)

2. Make a chart showing the changes of puberty for boys and girls. (Section 17-1)

3. What can a young teen do if he or she has acne? (Section 17-1)

4. What are the signs that a child has a growing sense of self? (Section 17-2)

5. How can parents teach children to control anger? (Section 17-2)

6. Compare friendship at age five and from seven to twelve. (Section 17-3)

7. How many close friends should a child have? Why? (Section (17-3)

8. Explain why Piaget said that putting objects in a series and understanding conservation were advances in mental abilities. (Section 17-4)

Taking Action

1. **Analyzing.** Identify the age that tends to be represented by the following behaviors: (a) telling exaggerated stories; (b) ignoring adults; (c) hiding feelings; (d) being sensitive to others' comments. *(Thinking Skills)*

2. **Memorizing.** Write two lists of random numbers from one to one hundred. Have six numbers in the first list and ten in the second. Ask a child seven to twelve to memorize both lists and repeat them back to you. Ask the child what strategies he or she used. Compare your findings to those of classmates and draw conclusions about how children use memory. *(Thinking Skills)*

CONNECTIONS

Cross-Curricular Connections

1. **Language Arts.** Take the role of someone who writes an advice column. Answer a letter from a parent who wants help handling a young teen who is frequently angry.

2. **Social Studies.** Research the work of Piaget. He used many different experiments to test different aspects of the concrete operations period. Choose one of the experiments. Explain it to the class, then discuss whether you think the test is useful.

Family and Community Connections

1. **Planning Nutritious Snacks.** What snacks could you have in your home that would meet the guidelines on page 517 for a healthy diet?

2. **Sending Positive Messages.** Write a list of ten words or sentences that a parent could use to send reassuring messages to a child who is being teased by peers because he or she is different.

Workplace Connections

1. **Interpersonal Skills.** Suppose you coach a team of ten-year-olds. One child isn't a very good player, but he works hard at practice and cheers for his teammates during every game. The other children on the team make fun of this child every time he makes a mistake. What would you do to help his teammates learn to stop teasing him?

Technology Connections

1. **Television.** Think of a television show that focuses on the lives and concerns of a group of teens. Write the outline of an episode that shows peer pressure at work.

2. **Internet.** Search on-line for information about eating disorders. Create a chart that shows the causes and effects of this condition.

CHAPTER 18

Safety and Health

Max entered the water from the side without making too much of a splash. It was Noah's first trip to the pool, and he wanted to make it a positive one. Then he turned and held his arms up for his wife to hand Noah to him.

Max held Noah right at the surface of the water. He made sure that Noah could touch the water with his arms and legs without getting his face in it. Noah splashed happily as his father kept a secure hold. Max walked along the bottom of the pool so Noah could feel what it was like to move through the water. Noah spread his arms out and splashed some more.

"Isn't this fun?" Max asked. Noah grinned and agreed. "When you're a little older, we'll make sure that you learn how to swim. Would you like that?" Noah laughed, kicked vigorously with his feet, and responded with a loud "Yes." The surge of water hit his father's face, and Max called out in surprise and then he laughed, too.

"It was Noah's first trip to the pool, and Max wanted to make it a positive one."

SECTION 18-1

Preventing Accidents and Handling Emergencies

"**A**n ounce of prevention is worth a pound of cure." That old saying is especially true when it comes to the safety of children. It's easier to prevent accidents than to cope with their effects. Anyone who cares for children, though, has to be prepared for possible emergencies.

KEY TERMS

artificial respiration
convulsion
CPR (cardiopulmonary resuscitation)
fracture
Heimlich maneuver
nontoxic
poison control center
sprain

OBJECTIVES:

- Identify safety hazards for children of different ages.
- Recognize emergency situations and plan appropriate responses.
- Demonstrate appropriate first aid for common ailments.
- Identify basic rescue techniques.

Safety

The safety of the child is the most important responsibility of every caregiver. Each age has its particular hazards because children of different ages have different abilities and interests.

Infants

Falls cause the most injuries among babies, and they account for many deaths. Even before an infant can crawl, wiggling can cause the baby to fall from a bed, a changing table, or an infant seat placed on a table. Babies tend to fall headfirst, which can result in brain damage. Because of these dangers, no baby should ever be left unattended on any kind of furniture where there's a danger that the child could fall.

Babies like to suck and chew on almost anything that comes within reach. This tendency produces three hazards:

- **Choking on small objects.** Anything that an infant might swallow—including small parts that might come off a toy—must be kept away from the baby.
- **Choking or suffocating on plastic bags.** Infants and small children should never be allowed to play with plastic bags. Don't use plastic bags as a protective covering for the mattress in a crib or playpen.
- **Poisoning.** Anything babies could place in the mouth—even the edges of furniture—must be **nontoxic**, or not poisonous. Some paints that contain lead are particularly dangerous for children. Many common household products are poisonous. The chart on pages 550-551 lists many of them. Any substances that are poisonous must be placed well out of a baby's reach.

A small child should never be left alone near water, such as a tub or a wading pool. Water can be very dangerous. Drownings happen quickly, even in the time it takes to answer the phone or go to the door.

Car accidents cause more deaths among children than any other factor. Many deaths and injuries can be prevented if a baby is put in a child safety seat and an older child wears a seat belt. Regular adult seat belts cannot keep babies or young children safe.

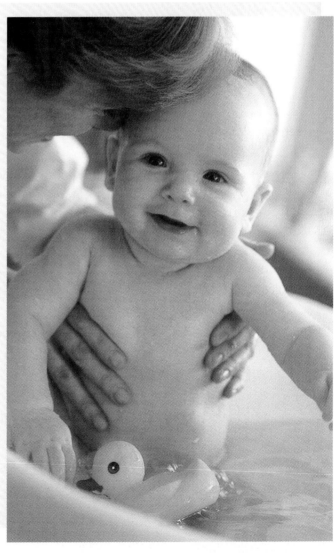

What rule should caregivers always follow when infants are in water?

Common Household Poisons

KINDS OF POISONS	EXAMPLES	TYPE OF CONTACT
Medicines	• Sleeping pills • Aspirin • Tranquilizers • Vitamins • Cold preparations	• Swallowing
Cleaning Products	• Ammonia • Automatic dishwasher detergent • Laundry detergents • Bleach • Drain and toilet bowl cleaners • Disinfectants • Furniture polish	• Swallowing • Skin • Eyes • Inhaling
Personal Care Products	• Shampoo • Soap • Nail polish remover • Perfumes and after-shave lotions • Mouthwash • Rubbing alcohol	• Swallowing • Skin • Eyes • Inhaling
Gardening and Garage Products	• Insecticides • Fertilizers • Rat and mouse poisons • Acids of all kinds • Gasoline • Paint thinner • Charcoal lighter fluid • Antifreeze	• Swallowing • Skin • Eyes • Inhaling

Continued on next page

KINDS OF POISONS	EXAMPLES	TYPE OF CONTACT
Plants	• Some wild mushrooms • English ivy • Daffodil bulbs • Rhubarb leaves • Holly berries • Poinsettias • Poison ivy and poison oak	• Swallowing • Skin

Parents must buy an infant car seat that meets current safety standards. Then they need to use it *every time* they put a baby or young child into the car, no matter how short the trip. This is the law in most states. Putting young children in the center of the back seat gives them the most protection. They should never ride in the front seat. Infants should face the back of the car.

Ages One to Three

One- to three-year-olds need very careful supervision. They are so mobile that they can quickly get into danger. Any area where they spend time should be carefully

INFOLINK

Infant Car Seats

For more about *infant car seats*, see "Parenting with Care," Chapter 6, page 210.

checked for safety. No toddler should be left unattended for more than a few minutes—and even then they should be within hearing distance.

Children can be taught to follow these safety guidelines to prevent choking:
- Stay seated while eating.
- Always take small bites.
- Chew all food thoroughly.
- Swallow before taking another bite.
- Don't talk or laugh with food in the mouth.
- Keep small toys and other small objects out of the mouth.

Some parents stop using child car seats after the child's first birthday. However, they are still essential. A different kind of seat is needed for older, heavier children. Once a child is a year old and weighs more than 20 pounds (9.1 kg), the child seat can face forward.

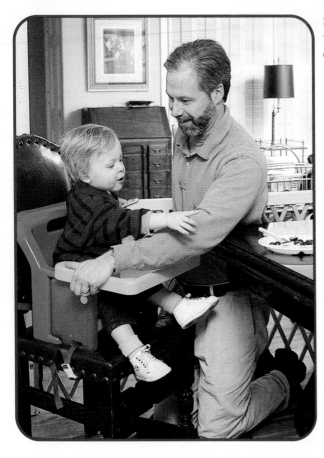

Safety seats and safety belts can also help prevent accidents while eating. *Why are infants and toddlers particularly at risk?*

Ages Four and Older

Children from four to six spend a great deal of time in unsupervised play. They need to learn good safety practices. They won't always remember and follow all safety rules, however. They need frequent reminders and watchful caregivers nearby.

Outdoor play equipment, such as a swing set, should be firmly anchored to keep the set from tipping over. The ground should be covered with a soft material, such as shredded tires, to cushion falls. Caregivers should set and enforce safety rules. For example, there should be only one child on a swing at a time, and no pushing is allowed on a slide. A child riding a tricycle should wear a helmet.

Many young children are fascinated by fire. Even those who have been taught that matches are unsafe may experiment with them. As the match burns closer to the finger, the child often becomes frightened and may drop the match or throw it into a wastebasket. Many fires start this way. All matches should be locked away.

Guidelines for Fast Action

If a child in your care does get hurt:
1. **Above all, try to remain calm.** This will help reassure the child and help you think more clearly.
2. **Evaluate the situation.** What seems to be wrong? You must know what's wrong so you can act properly.
3. **Make the victim comfortable.** If the injury is serious, keep the child warm.
4. **Call for help if necessary.** If you are not certain what the problem is or what to do, call for help. Keep emergency numbers at hand. Does your community have 911 emergency service?

   Know how to call the nearest **poison control center**—a special unit to advise and treat poisoning victims. Hospitals can also give advice.

   On the phone, clearly and concisely state the age of the child and the problem. Tell who you are and your relationship to the child. Follow instructions.
5. **Give the minimum necessary first aid treatment.** Give the most necessary first aid, then seek more qualified help.

Using Standard Precautions

Today, more is understood about the spread of diseases. Medical professionals have developed standard precautions to be used in caring for patients. Child care workers also need to know and follow many of these standard precautions to protect themselves and the children they care for. These include:

- Use of disposable gloves when changing diapers, dealing with bodily fluids (except sweat), or touching contaminated objects or surfaces.
- Thorough, frequent handwashing.
- Proper cleaning of surfaces and disposal of items which may be contaminated (such as disposable diapers and used gloves).
- Use of special devices for mouth-to-mouth resusitation.

First Aid

It is essential for anyone who takes care of children to be familiar with first aid procedures. The following guidelines are very general. For more information, contact the nearest office of the American Red Cross about first aid training classes.

Animal Bites

Wash the area around the bite with soap and running water. Tell the parents, who will probably talk to a doctor.

If the animal was a bat, fox, raccoon, skunk, dog, or cat that bit the child without being provoked, call the local health department. It will send someone to try to catch the animal so that it can be tested for rabies.

Playgrounds can be fun for children—but they can be dangerous too. *Name one safety guideline for playgrounds.*

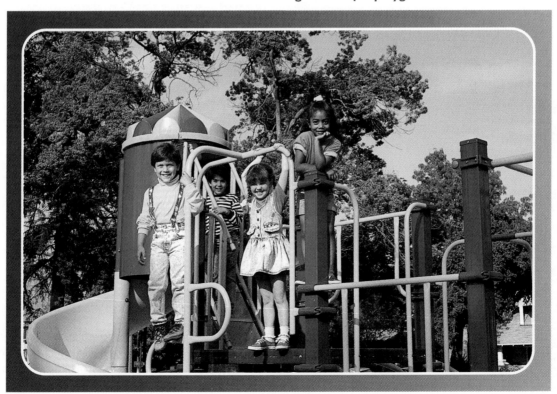

This disease can be very dangerous. The child may need shots for protection from the disease.

Bleeding

The Centers for Disease Control recommends that child care workers always wear disposable plastic gloves when giving first aid to any person who is bleeding.

- **Minor cuts or scrapes.** Stop the bleeding by placing a clean cloth or gauze pad on the wound and pressing hard for ten to fifteen minutes without releasing. Once the bleeding has stopped, clean the area with soap and warm water. Apply a mild antiseptic, and cover it with a bandage.
- **Deep cuts or wounds.** These may need medical help. If the child's breathing is shallow and rapid, send for medical help. In a light-skinned child, the skin may turn pale and bluish. Continue to try to stop the bleeding until help arrives. Elevating the affected area may stop the bleeding. Do not apply a tourniquet. (A tourniquet is a bandage that cuts off the blood supply to a portion of the body.) An improperly applied tourniquet can harm the victim.
- **Nosebleeds.** Have the child sit down and lean slightly forward over a basin or sink. Using the thumb and forefinger, squeeze the child's nose firmly just below the bones in the nose. After squeezing for several minutes, check to see whether the bleeding has stopped. If not, reapply pressure for five to ten minutes. Sometimes putting cold packs on the nose and forehead also helps. If you can't stop the bleeding, or if the child becomes dizzy or pale, seek medical help.

Bumps and Bruises

Treat bruises with a cold cloth or ice pack to minimize swelling. An injured arm or leg can be elevated. If the child complains of pain for more than a day, call a physician. A fall or bump on the head can be serious. Call a doctor if the child loses consciousness, is drowsy or irritable, complains of a headache, or vomits.

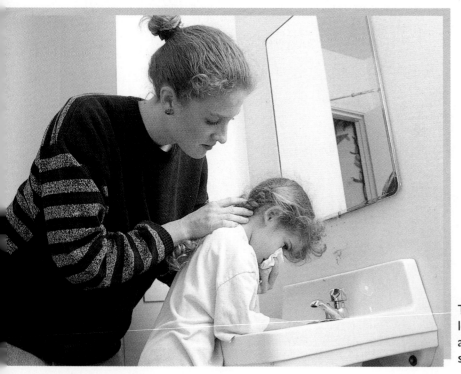

To stop a nosebleed, have the child lean forward slightly. Firmly press above the nostrils and hold for several minutes.

Burns

How you treat a burn depends on what caused the burn and how bad it is. All but small surface burns are serious because they may cause scarring, infections, or shock. Burns are classified by degree.

- **First-degree burns look red and slightly swollen.** They may be caused by too much sun, hot objects, hot water, or steam. Cover the area with cold water or a cold, wet cloth until the pain stops. These burns heal rapidly.
- **Second-degree burns are deeper, redder, and blistered.** The burned area remains swollen and somewhat moist for several days. These burns may be caused by very deep sunburn, hot liquids, and flammable products like gasoline. Second-degree burns should be treated by a physician.
- **Third-degree burns destroy the skin.** These burns may look white or charred. There may be little pain at first because nerve endings have been destroyed. Third-degree burns can be caused by flames, burning clothing, hot water, extremely hot objects, or electricity.

  These burns are extremely serious and require immediate medical care. Cover the burn with a clean, dry cloth and keep the patient warm. To help ease the pain, elevate the burned area slightly. Get the victim to a hospital as soon as possible.
- **Chemical burns.** Household products such as toilet bowl cleaners, drain cleaners, and disinfectants can cause chemical burns. Using protective

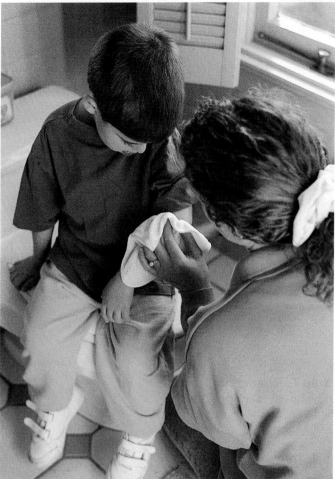

Minor burns can be treated with a cold, wet cloth and then covered with a clean, dry cloth. *What should be done with more serious burns?*

gloves or a towel, wash off the affected area immediately and completely with cold water. Remove any clothing with the chemical on it, unless the clothing is stuck to the skin. Apply a clean bandage, and call a doctor.
- **Electrical burns.** These burns may be deep, but they often appear minor, leaving only a small black dot on the skin. Cool the burned area with cold water, and cover it with a clean, smooth cloth such as a handkerchief.

Then have the patient lie down with legs elevated and head turned to one side. This prevents shock. (See page 560 for more about shock.) Take the child to a hospital emergency room, or call an ambulance.

Choking

Choking occurs when something is caught in a person's throat. The danger is that choking can cut off the supply of air. When oxygen is restricted, brain damage can occur within a few minutes.

First, recognize the signs of choking. They are an inability to speak, breathe, or cry; bluish lips, nails, and skin; high-pitched noises or ineffective coughing. If a person is choking, you must act quickly to dislodge the object that is blocking the breathing passage.

If an infant less than one year old is choking, follow the steps shown in the drawings below. With children older than one year and with adults, use the **Heimlich maneuver** (HIME-lick muh-new-vur). This technique uses pressure on the air in the body to expel an object that is blocking

Rescue Maneuver for Choking Infants

Step 1: Turn the infant face down over your arm.

Step 2: Using the heel of your other hand, give four quick blows between the infant's shoulder blades.

Step 3: Turn the infant over, supporting the head, neck, and back. Position your two middle fingers below the rib cage and above the navel. With your fingers in that position, give four quick thrusts toward the chest. Repeat these three steps until the object is expelled.

breathing. The drawings below show its steps.

The amount of pressure to use in the Heimlich maneuver depends on the age and size of the victim. Too much pressure can harm a young child. It is best to get training in using the Heimlich maneuver—before you need to use it.

If the child who is choking has lost consciousness or stops breathing, you must take different steps. First, call for emergency medical help. You can try to remove the object from the child's throat, but do so only if you can see the object and remove it safely. Use your thumb and forefinger to try to locate the object and pull it out. Then begin artificial respiration immediately. (See page 561 for more information on artificial respiration.) If you can't remove the object, try to help the person breathe until help arrives.

Heimlich Maneuver for Children One Year and Older and Adults

If the victim is standing or sitting:

Step 1: Stand behind the victim. Clasp your hands with your fists just below the victim's rib cage.

Step 2: Press your clasped hands into the victim's abdomen with a quick upward thrust. Repeat step 2 if necessary until the object is expelled.

If the victim has collapsed:

Step 1: Kneel above the victim's hips. Place both your hands, one over the other, on the victim's abdomen. The heel of your bottom hand should be slightly above the victim's navel and below his or her rib cage.

Step 2: Use the force of both hands to press with a quick upward thrust. Repeat Step 2 if necessary until the object is expelled.

Convulsions

A **convulsion** or a seizure is a period of unconsciousness with uncontrolled jerking or twitching of the muscles. There are many causes of convulsions. They occur most often in infants, usually as a result of high fever.

If a child has a convulsion, place the child on his or her side on the floor. Move any hard objects out of the way. Don't attempt to hold the child down, and don't force anything between the teeth. After the convulsion stops, be sure the child's head is turned to one side to reduce the risk of choking. Check with a doctor for further instructions. If the convulsion lasts more than fifteen minutes, take the child to a hospital emergency room or call an ambulance.

Fainting

A child who faints loses consciousness. The child may collapse without warning, or he or she may first experience sweating, cold skin, nausea, or dizziness. A light-skinned child who is about to faint may look pale. Anyone who feels faint should lie down or sit with the head between the legs.

If a child has fainted, loosen any tight clothing. Position the child's head to one side. Check to be sure the child is breathing. If breathing has stopped, have someone call for medical assistance, and begin artificial respiration. (See page 561 for information on artificial respiration.) If the child is breathing, expect him or her to revive within a minute or two. If the child does not gain consciousness within two minutes, call for help.

Fractures and Sprains

A **fracture** is a break or a crack in a bone. A **sprain** is an injury caused by sudden, violent stretching of a joint or muscle. Both may cause pain, swelling, and bruising. It is often difficult to tell a sprain from a fracture without an X ray.

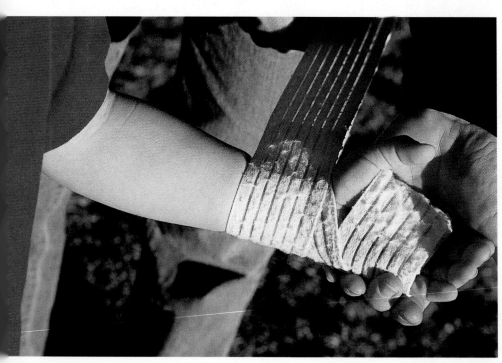

Sprained wrists are sometimes treated by wrapping the joint in an elastic wrap.

This symbol—called "Mr. Yuk"—is used to show small children that they should not eat or drink a substance. It can help protect them from taking in any poison.

If you suspect that a child has a fracture or a sprain, don't move the child until you know how serious the injury is. This is especially important for injuries to the back, ribs, neck, or collarbone. You can cause further damage by moving the child. Call for qualified medical help, and use artificial respiration if necessary.

You can treat a mild sprain by elevating the injured area and putting cold packs on it to help reduce the swelling. If the pain persists, check with a doctor.

Insect Stings and Bites

If a child has been stung by a bee, wasp, hornet, or yellow jacket, scrape off the stinger. Apply a cold cloth, an ice pack, or ice water to the area. Then cover it with a paste made from baking soda and water.

Some people are very allergic to insect stings. For them, a single sting can cause serious illness or even death. Anyone with a known allergy to stings must be taken to a hospital or doctor immediately after being stung. The same is true of anyone who becomes dizzy, feels faint, has difficulty breathing, vomits, develops hives, or perspires heavily.

Ticks are small insects that cling to the skin or scalp. They carry diseases. If you find a tick on a child, use tweezers to grab the tick as close to the skin as possible. Then pull the tick off in one smooth motion. Wash the area well with soap and water.

Mosquito, ant, and chigger bites are annoying but usually not dangerous. A paste of baking soda and water or rubbing the spot with witch hazel or rubbing alcohol will give relief.

Poisoning

Recognizing that a child has been poisoned is not always easy. Here are some symptoms that may indicate poisoning:

- **From swallowed poisons.** Difficulty in breathing, unconsciousness, fever, burns in the mouth and throat, and vomiting may result from swallowed poisons or chemicals.
- **From skin-contact poisons.** Burns or rash on the skin can indicate the presence of these poisons.
- **From eye-contact poisons.** Look for burning or irritation of the eyes or blindness.
- **From inhaled poisons.** Choking, coughing, nausea, or dizziness all may result from fumes, sprays, and poisonous gases.

If a child is poisoned, take these steps:

1. Find out what has poisoned the child. If the child has swallowed something poisonous, try to learn how much he or she swallowed.
2. Phone the poison control center, hospital, or the child's doctor. Have the container that held the poisonous substance with you as you call. That way you can answer any questions you are asked.
3. Follow the directions you receive. Act quickly and calmly.

Anyone who has been poisoned must be seen by a physician. This is true even if emergency treatment has already been given and even if the victim shows no symptoms. Take the container that held the poisonous substance—or a sample of the substance—with you. This will help the doctor decide on the proper treatment.

Shock

When a person suffers a severe injury, the loss of a great deal of blood, or poisoning, the body goes into shock. Important body functions, including breathing and heart action, are impaired. The symptoms of shock include rapid pulse, clammy skin, shallow breathing, enlarged pupils, a glassy stare, and nausea. Sometimes a person in shock loses consciousness.

Shock can be serious. If you suspect a child is in shock, seek medical help immediately. Until help arrives, be sure the child remains lying down, and keep him or her warm.

Splinters and Thorns

Splinters are tiny pieces of wood, metal, or glass that become stuck in the skin. Thorns may also be treated as splinters.

Although splinters are not dangerous, they do hurt, and they can become infected.

If part of the splinter is above the surface, you can use tweezers for removal. Sterilize the tweezers in boiling water or in a flame. Grab onto the part of the splinter that sticks out and pull evenly. Put antiseptic on the wound and cover it with a sterile bandage.

If a nonglass splinter is just under the skin surface, you can take it out with a sterilized needle. Numb the skin over the splinter with a piece of ice. Use the needle to break the skin and lift the splinter out. Clean and cover the wound as described above.

Large or deep splinters and those caused by glass can be more serious. They should be removed by a physician.

Rescue Techniques

When an emergency situation causes the victim to stop breathing or the heart to stop beating, immediate action is vital. Learn the rescue techniques that will enable you to respond quickly.

Artificial Respiration

Artificial respiration (RES-puh-RAY-shun) is a procedure for forcing air into the lungs of a person whose breathing has stopped. Some emergency situations, such as drowning and electrical shock, call for artificial respiration. The technique to use with infants and small children is shown on page 561. Child care workers should wear gloves and use a special protective face mask when giving artificial respiration.

You can learn more about artificial respiration in a rescue training class. Taking such a class will also give you a chance to practice the correct techniques.

Artificial Respiration for Infants and Small Children

Step 1: Turn the child's head to one side. With your finger, carefully clear the child's mouth of any foreign objects or fluid. (If the victim is under a year old, do *not* put your finger into his or her mouth.) If there is an object caught in the child's throat, or to clear the mouth of the young baby, follow the instructions for aiding a choking victim, page 556. Be sure that you can see the object and remove it safely.

Step 2: Tilt the child's head back slightly. Put two fingers just under the chinbone and lift the jaw into a jutting-out position. Check for breathing.

Step 3: If the child is not breathing, take a deep breath. Seal your lips around the child's mouth and nose. (If you can cover only the mouth, pinch the child's nostrils shut with your fingers.)

Step 4: Blow into the child's mouth and nose. (For an infant, use gentle puffs of air.) When you see the chest lift, remove your mouth and let the air come out. Then blow in again. Repeat 15 to 20 times per minute for a child, or 20 times per minute for an infant. Continue until the child resumes normal breathing or until help arrives.

CPR

CPR is the short name for **cardiopulmonary resuscitation** (CAR-dee-oh-POOL-muh-NER-ee ri-SUSS-uh-TAY-shun). This rescue technique is used to sustain life when both breathing and the heart have stopped. Special training from a certified instructor is needed to perform CPR. Many communities offer training programs. To find out where CPR training is offered in your area, call a local chapter of the Red Cross or the American Heart Association.

SECTION 18-1 REVIEW

✔ Check Your Understanding

1. Why should you put an infant or young child in a car safety seat?
2. What three dangers arise from the fact that infants often put things in their mouths?
3. List the five guidelines for responding to an accident or injury.
4. What is a poison control center?
5. What is the possible danger from an animal bite?
6. Briefly describe the three categories of burns.
7. What is the Heimlich maneuver?
8. What is the difference between a fracture and a sprain?
9. What symptoms call for artificial respiration? What symptoms call for CPR?

Putting Knowledge Into Practice

1. **Analyzing.** Why might it be difficult to remain calm if a child in your care was injured? Why would it be especially important to remain calm? What could you do to help yourself stay calm?
2. **Observing and Participating.** Visit a local park, and observe a group of kindergartners or first graders as they play. Describe the playground equipment used by the children. Are there any apparent safety hazards in the equipment? Are there any hazards in the children's behavior? Write a list of safety rules that you think should be posted at the park.

CAREER OPPORTUNITIES

Emergency Medical Technician

A CONVERSATION WITH RON JACOBSON

How did you become interested in becoming an emergency medical technician? I wanted to be an EMT—that's what we're called—because I wanted to help people. I also like the excitement of meeting emergencies. It's tremendously satisfying to help save someone's life.

What are the tasks and responsibilities of an emergency medical technician? We respond to emergencies like car accidents or fires or a heart attack. We have to provide whatever immediate care the person needs, then get him or her to the hospital for further treatment. With us, it's often a life-or-death situation.

What is the work environment like? When we're not on call, we work on the equipment, study, and do paperwork. When an emergency happens, we could be called anywhere—and must get there quickly. We can be called any time of the day or night and in all kinds of weather.

What are the working hours like? In our station, we work eight hour days, six days a week. We have three shifts. Each of us works at least one weekend day every week. We often work on holidays, too.

What aptitudes are needed to be an emergency medical technician? The most important thing is to stay calm and think clearly under pressure. We need good dexterity to use the equipment. We need great teamwork skills. We have to be strong, too.

Career Facts

EMERGENCY MEDICAL TECHNICIAN

Education and Training. An EMT needs a high school diploma and special training. Workers must pass a certification test and retake the test every two years.

Career Outlook. The number of EMTs is expected to grow in the future.

CONNECTING SCHOOL TO CAREER

1. **Personal Qualities.** What do you think would be the most important personal quality of an EMT? Why?
2. **Technology.** What kinds of technology do you think EMTs use?

Preventing Illness and Caring for a Sick Child

It is never easy caring for a child who is ill. Normal routines are upset. The child may cry often, demand attention, and have a short temper. However, the attitude of the caregiver can be as important as the medical treatment in restoring good health.

KEY TERMS

allergy
antibodies
asthma
communicable diseases
contagious
immunize
vaccine

OBJECTIVES:

- Explain how health checkups and immunizations help prevent illness.

- Discuss what allergies are and how they can be treated.

- Give basic guidelines for caring for children who are ill.

- Discuss how to help a child who is hospitalized.

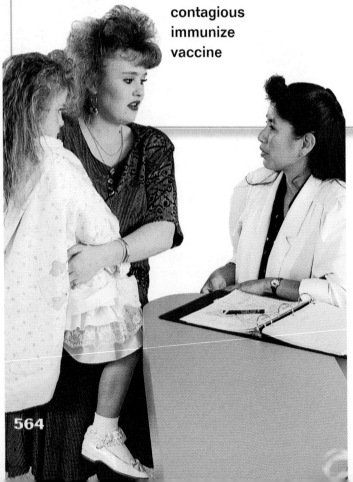

Regular Health Care

Children, like adults, should have regular medical checkups. These can often detect health problems in their early stages. Early treatment may prevent serious illness or serious damage to the child.

Newborns should be examined frequently during the first year. After the first year, healthy children need check-

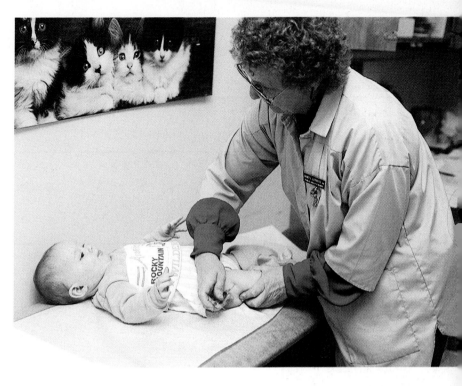

Immunizations have helped many youngsters lead healthier lives. *What diseases can be fought with vaccines?*

ups less frequently, but at least once a year. Because these checkups are so important, most cities have free or inexpensive clinics that provide good medical care.

Call the doctor's office if a child shows symptoms that concern you. In younger children, look for fever, lack of energy, prolonged diarrhea, constipation, vomiting, or difficulty in breathing. In older children, symptoms include fever, persistent cough, vomiting, severe headache, and dizziness.

Immunization

To **immunize** (IM-yuh-NIZE) is to protect a person against a particular disease. People can be protected from many **communicable diseases**—diseases that are easily passed from one person to another—by being immunized.

The most common way to immunize people against diseases is with vaccines. A **vaccine** (vak-SEEN) is a small amount of a disease-carrying germ introduced into the body so that the body can build resistance to the disease. After getting a vaccine, a person's body produces **antibodies** (AN-ta-BAHD-ees) that fight off the germs for that disease. If later exposed to the disease, the person already has antibodies that fight it.

That person will then either not get the disease or have only a very mild case of it.

The chart on page 566 shows what immunizations a child should receive and when. It's up to parents to be sure that children are given these immunizations at these times. They should keep a record of a child's immunizations.

Many states require immunizations for all school children. Many also require that children in a child care center be immunized. In fact, preschool children are most likely to develop complications from the diseases, so parents should not wait until elementary school starts to have their children immunized.

Some parents are afraid that a vaccine could hurt their child. In some extremely rare cases, a child does have a bad reaction to a vaccine. The chances of getting the disease are much, much higher, though.

Schedule of Immunizations

Vaccine	Birth	1 mo.	2 mo.	4 mo.	6 mo.	1 yr.	15 mo.	18 mo.	4-6 yrs.	11-12 yrs.
Hepatitis B 3 dose series	1	2			3					1-3 [a]
Diptheria tetanus, pertussis (DTP) 4 dose series with boosters			1	2	3		4 [b]		Booster	Booster [c]
H. Influenzae, Type B 4 dose series			1	2	3 [d]		4 [b]			
Polio 3 dose series			1	2	3 [b]					
Diarrhea 4 dose series			1	2	3				4	
Measles, mumps, rubella (MMR) 2 dose series						1 [b]			2 [e]	
Varicella (chicken pox) 2 dose series						1 [b]			2	1-2 [f]

Notes

a If the child did not have the Hepatitis vaccine earlier, the three-dose series should be given at ages 11 or 12.

b Can be given any time in this period.

c Booster should be repeated every 10 years after this.

d May not be necessary if a certain brand of vaccine was given in the first two doses.

e May be given at any time after the age of 4 but no later than age 12.

f If the child has not been vaccinated earlier.

Source: *Advisory Committee on Immunization Practices,*
American Academy of Pediatrics, American Academy of Family Physicians.

Allergies

An **allergy** is an oversensitivity to one or more common substances. Individuals may have allergic reactions when they eat, breathe in, or touch specific substances, such as grass, molds, milk products, and pollens. Symptoms of allergic reactions may be mild, such as nonitching rash or a runny nose. Some allergic reactions, however, can threaten a person's life. Sometimes, for instance, the air sacs in the lungs can be constricted, which dangerously cuts the oxygen in the body.

Nearly half of all the children in the United States develop allergies. Specific allergies are not inherited, but the tendency to be allergic seems to be. If both parents have allergies, the child has a 70 percent chance of having at least one allergy.

Although allergies can't be cured, their effects are often preventable. For example, a child who is allergic to a specific food can avoid eating that food. Foods that commonly cause allergies in babies and children include milk, cereal grains, eggs, shellfish, nuts, fresh fruit juices, chocolate, and food additives.

A doctor may prescribe medication to help control an allergy. If the allergy causes severe problems, the child may be given a series of allergy tests to determine which specific substances are causing the problems. Then the child can be gradually desensitized to those substances.

Asthma

A growing health problem is **asthma** (AZ-muh). This condition affects the lungs, where air passages tighten, making it difficult to breathe. About 5 million children suffer from asthma.

Asthma attacks can be brought on by an allergic reaction. They may also be caused by a cold or flu. Cold air can bring on an attack, as can stress. Signs of an asthma attack include a tight feeling in the chest, a wheezing sound when the child breathes, and rapid breathing. The child may cough repeatedly but never be able to clear fluid out of the lungs.

Children with asthma can take medication to open their airways and breathe more easily. The medicine must be prescribed by a doctor. Children can be taught to take it when they need it. The doctor who examines the child can say whether or not the child needs to cut down on physical activities.

Asthma is a growing problem for children. *Can children with asthma still be active in sports?*

DISEASE	SIGNS	TREATMENT
Chicken Pox	A rash of tiny red, raised pimples or blisters appears first. It may cover the entire body. In a day or two, scabs form which fall off in 7 to 10 days. Fever is either absent or no higher than 102°F (39°C). Rash is irritating but child usually does not feel ill otherwise.	Rest in bed during feverish stage. Give acetaminophen to relieve fever, *but do not use aspirin*. Keep the child cool in loose clothing. Use powder or calamine lotion to relieve the itching. Recovery is usually within 7 days. Once scabs form, and no new pox have appeared for 2 days, the disease is no longer infectious.
Common Cold	Runny nose, sneezing or coughing, a mild fever of 101° to 102°F (38.3-38.9° C), lower appetite, and a sore throat.	Give the child plenty of rest and lots of liquids. Give acetaminophen to relieve fever. Don't give a cough or cold medicine to any child under three years of age unless approved by a doctor.
Ear Infection	An infant may pull at the ear and cry; an older child is likely to say that the ear hurts. There is usually a fever, which may go as high as 104°F (40°C).	The child needs to see a doctor, who may prescribe an antibiotic. You can use cool baths and acetaminophen to relieve the fever.
Influenza (Flu)	Sudden onset of fever, chills and shakes, tiredness, and aching muscles. After a few days, a sore throat and stuffy nose may appear. The disease may last as long as a week.	Give the child plenty of rest, lots of liquids, and extra food. Give acetaminophen to relieve fever.
Measles	Usually fever, sometimes as high as 105°F (41°C). The child may also have a cough, a runny nose, and inflamed, watery eyes. About 4 days later a blotchy, dusty-red rash appears, often seen first behind the ears or on the forehead and face. On day 6, the rash quickly fades and by day 7 all symptoms are gone.	The child should be under a doctor's supervision and kept in bed for the duration of the fever. The disease is most contagious during the few days before and after the rash appears. If the child's eyes are sensitive, keep him or her in a darkened room and do not allow reading or other close work.

Continued on next page

DISEASE	SIGNS	TREATMENT
Mumps	Sudden fever, occasional nausea, abdominal pain, and swelling of one or more salivary glands, most commonly those located at the angles of the jaws. Swelling reaches maximum within 24 hours and may last 7 to 10 days. In boys, infection may also cause painful swelling in the testicles.	A hot water bottle and acetaminophen may ease pain. Fluids are easiest to swallow. Mumps is usually a mild disease, leaving no ill effects. However, sometimes deafness occurs.
Scarlet Fever and Streptococcal Sore Throat	Sudden onset, with headache, fever, sore throat. Lymph nodes usually enlarged. In scarlet fever a rash appears, usually within 24 hours, as fine red dots. The rash is seen first on the neck and upper part of the chest, and lasts 24 hours to 10 days. When it fades, the skin peels. The rash is the only sign that differentiates scarlet fever from strep throat.	A physician's care is needed. The child should rest in a warm, well-ventilated room. Patient usually recovers in a week, but watch for such complications as earache or inflamed neck glands.
Whooping Cough (Pertussis)	Begins with a cough that is worse at night. Symptoms may be mild at first. Characteristic "whooping" cough develops in about 2 weeks, and coughing spasms sometimes end with vomiting.	The child should take antibiotics under a doctor's care. Hospitalization is often required for infants. Rest is important, as is a diet that will not irritate the throat. Keep the child isolated from other children until antibiotics have been taken for at least 5 days.

Caring for a Sick Child

Children fall prey to illness from time to time. Caregivers need to recognize the signs of different illnesses. Of course, any caregiver who is unsure exactly what illness is bothering a child should talk to a medical professional. The child's doctor can also explain what treatment to offer the child.

Caring for a sick child often involves no more than keeping the child inside and quiet for a while. Often recovery takes only a few days. It may also be important to keep the child away from other children during the **contagious** period of illness. This is the time when a child can pass the germs on to someone else. A doctor can say how long the contagious period lasts.

Sometimes children need pain relief or a medicine to reduce fever. For children, doctors recommend using a medicine that contains the ingredient acetaminophen. Never give aspirin to a child with a fever. Although it happens only rarely, some children with a fever who take aspirin develop a serious illness called Reye syndrome. Also, be sure to use children's medicines, not products meant for adults.

Comforting a Sick Child

When a child is sick, try to maintain a calm and cheerful attitude. Treat the illness matter-of-factly. Remember, though, that from time to time the child may need some extra sympathy and love.

Children who are very ill don't have much energy for play. They spend most of the time sleeping. If children have only a mild illness or if they are recovering from a serious illness, however, they may be easily bored. Quiet play helps pass the time. Having a caregiver play along increases the child's fun!

Children of different ages have different needs during illness.

- **Infants.** Infants who are ill sleep much more than usual. They tend to be cranky and may want a lot of physical comforting. Gently rocking the baby, talking softly, singing, and holding the baby close (perhaps in a cloth carrier) can provide the needed comfort.
- **Ages one to three.** Young children are likely to need help keeping comfortable and occupied during an illness. Because children one to three are usually very physically active, staying in bed is difficult for them. The doctor will often allow a child who is warmly

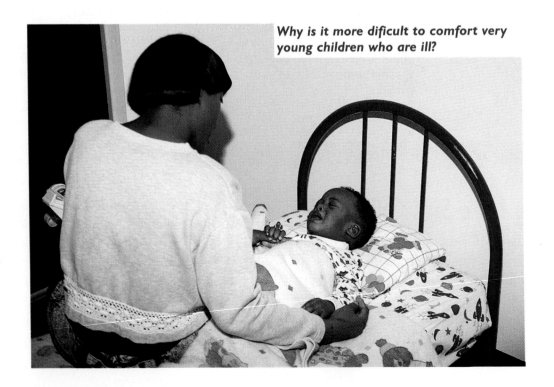

Why is it more dificult to comfort very young children who are ill?

Ask the Experts

Dr. Van D. Stone
Pediatrician
Tupelo, Mississippi

NUTRITION *During Illness*

Q Can you give me any tips about feeding children who aren't feeling well?

A By providing good nutrition during an illness, you can help a child feel more comfortable and often even encourage the child's recovery.

It's usually important to offer a sick child plenty of water and other liquids. The body needs fluids when fighting a fever, and liquids might be the only food that will stay down. A child with a fever should be encouraged to drink as much as possible.

However, if the child's stomach is upset, even water may cause vomiting. Offer very small, but frequent amounts of a commercially available rehydration fluid.

With some illnesses, the child's doctor may recommend a specific diet. In this case, of course, you should follow the doctor's suggestions as closely as possible. In all other cases, it's best simply to offer the sick child small amounts of regular foods. Remember, though, that it is never a good idea to force a child to eat.

In certain cases, a child's doctor may recommend a bland diet or a liquid diet. A bland diet consists of soft, smooth, mild-flavored foods, generally low in fat. If recommended, you might offer the child soups, hot cereals, puddings, gelatin, eggs, and mild cooked vegetables. A liquid diet provides foods in liquid form that can be more easily used by the body. If a pediatrician recommends a liquid diet, rehydration fluid can be used.

Thinking It Through

1. Should a sick child eat more, smaller meals, or fewer, larger meals? Why?
2. If the doctor recommends a bland diet, should a sick child be offered regular foods? Why or why not?

If a child must be hospitalized, the doctor may suggest arranging a visit to the hospital beforehand to minimize fear.

dressed to play quietly around the house. Quiet play may include listening to stories, building with blocks, and playing simple games.

- **Ages four to twelve.** Preschoolers and school-age children can help care for themselves. They also have better verbal skills, meaning that they can more easily communicate how they feel. Children these ages can usually enjoy playing quietly with storybooks, stickers, puzzles, and games.

Going to the Hospital

A hospital stay is a difficult event for almost every child. Hospitalized youngsters may fear that their parents have abandoned them. They may be frightened that they will be hurt, or that they will die. Children have these fears because they don't understand what is happening to them.

A family that knows in advance that a child will be hospitalized can prepare the child for the event. The parents or doctor should explain to the child in simple words just what to expect. If possible, the parents should take the child to visit the hospital. Many hospitals have special tours that include a look in patient rooms and operating and recovery rooms. When the child is admitted, these things are already familiar—and less frightening.

The Hospital Stay

Hospitals realize that children recover better if a parent stays with them. Some move a cot into the child's room so that a parent can sleep nearby. Others have rooms with space for both child and parent. Even when there are no such arrangements, parents can often visit at any time. Of course, if the procedure the child needs is minor, he or she may have it done and go home the same day.

While in the hospital, a child often needs many tests and forms of treatment. When the child asks, "Will this hurt?" the parent should answer truthfully. Parents may be tempted to say, "Oh, no, this won't hurt." It is actually more helpful to the child to hear something more accurate, such as, "Yes, it will hurt for a while, but then you will feel much better. It is all right for you to cry when it hurts, if you feel like it."

If the child needs to go to the hospital for an emergency, it is important for a parent to stay with the child as much as possible. Being nearby can make a difficult situation less frightening to the child.

SECTION 18-2 REVIEW

✔ Check Your Understanding

1. What diseases should a child be immunized against?
2. What is an allergy?
3. How does asthma affect a child? How is it treated?
4. What is the contagious period?
5. Why is physical comforting especially important for an infant who is ill?
6. Why is it particularly difficult to keep toddlers cheerful during illness?
7. What fears are common among young children who are hospitalized?

Putting Knowledge Into Practice

1. **Evaluating a Position.** Some parents fear the risks of giving their children a vaccine and don't have them immunized. What do you think of that practice?
2. **Applying.** Suppose you were caring for a sick two-year-old. Plan quiet activities for the child—enough to occupy an entire afternoon. What else would you expect to do with and for the child?
3. **Observing and Participating.** Write an account of a child's hospital stay from the perspective of the child. What would it feel like? How would the child react to being away from parents?

Parenting With Care

Teaching About Personal Safety

An important responsibility parents have is to teach children basic lessons of personal safety.

Without alarming children, parents should make clear that there are dangers in the world. Following safe practices can reduce the risk of those dangers touching the child.

Basic Safety Information

Each child should know the following information:

- His or her full name, address, and phone number, including the area code.
- The work number of any parents who work outside the home.
- The local number to call in the event of an emergency.
- How to recognize an emergency. To teach this, play the "What If?" game. Ask a child specific questions, such as: What would you do if you woke up at night and smelled smoke? What would you do if you heard scary noises outside your bedroom?
- If separated from a parent in a public place, such as a store or mall, go to a police officer or an employee and explain the problem.

Safety to and from School

To act safely as they go to and from school, children can follow these rules:

- Never go anywhere with a stranger.
- If approached in a threatening way, run in the opposite direction. If they are close to the home of a neighbor they know, go to that home for help.
- If the child walks to school, find the safest route and use it every day. Of course, the child should take care to cross streets only when it is safe. Usually crossing guards are posted to help children walk safely.
- It's safer to travel in numbers—not just to and from school, but anywhere. Parents may wish to ask an older child, either a sibling or a neighbor, to walk with a younger child.
- Avoid isolated or deserted areas.

- If traveling by bus, the child should enter and leave the bus only after it has reached a full stop. Don't do anything that might distract the bus driver during the trip.

When Alone at Home

Some children spend time home alone after school. They should follow these safety guidelines:

- Never enter the home if the door is ajar or a window is open or broken.
- Lock the door right after entering the house. Windows should be kept closed and locked as well.
- Check with the parent or a neighbor right after arriving home.
- Never open the door if a stranger comes.
- Never tell anyone at the door or on the phone that he or she is alone.

Following Up

1. **Management.** Suppose you drove a school bus for elementary school students. How would you want the children to behave?

2. **Thinking Skills.** Many parents label a child's clothes, school bag, and lunch box with his or her name. For safety, though, those labels shouldn't be on the outside. Why?

REVIEW &

Summary

✔ It is much easier to prevent accidents than to handle the effects. (Section 18-1)

✔ The safety of the child is the most important responsibility of a caregiver. (Section 18-1)

✔ Emergencies must be dealt with quickly and calmly. (Section 18-1)

✔ Children should have regular checkups and should be immunized against certain diseases. (Section 18-2)

✔ The attitude of a caregiver toward a sick child can be as important as the care the child receives. (Section 18-2)

8. What are the signs of an asthma attack? (Section 18-2)

9. What is the danger of giving aspirin to a child with a fever? (Section 18-2)

Thinking Critically

1. **Sequencing.** Write the steps for rescuing an infant and a small child who is choking. Put each step on an index card. Use two separate sets of cards for the two different processes. Don't number the steps. Then shuffle the cards and give them to a partner. Have him or her put them in the correct order. When finished, your partner should do the same for you.

2. **Analyzing.** Why do you think people have to take special courses to learn CPR?

Reviewing the Facts

1. What is the leading cause of death among young children? How can it be prevented? (Section 18-1)

2. How would you try to protect a toddler from choking? (Section 18-1)

3. How would you treat a child who has a small cut? (Section 18-1)

4. Angela is having difficulty breathing, is vomiting, has a fever, and complains that her throat hurts. Nearby is an empty bottle of a liquid cleaner. What may have happened? (Section 18-1)

5. What should you do if a child seems to be in shock? (Section 18-1)

6. Why should children have regular medical checkups? (Section 18-2)

7. What is an allergy? How is it treated? (Section 18-2)

Taking Action

1. **Practicing a Rescue.** Using a large doll, practice artificial respiration for an infant. *(Leadership)*

2. **Categorizing.** With the class, brainstorm a list of ideas of activities that could be used with children who are ill. Write the ideas down as they are mentioned. When the list is complete, organize the ideas according to their appropriateness for children of different ages. *(Thinking Skills)*

CONNECTIONS CHAPTER 18

 Cross-Curricular Connections

1. **Art.** Design and make a poster to increase parents' awareness of one aspect of child safety. If possible, display your poster in an area where parents are likely to read it.

2. **Language Arts.** Write a public service announcement that explains to child care workers the five basic guidelines for handling emergencies.

 Workplace Connections

1. **Resources.** Develop a list of first aid supplies you think a child care center should have. Exchange lists with a classmate. Indicate on your classmates' list the situation for which each supply could be used.

2. **Information Systems.** Working with a partner, draw up a list of rules that you think a hospital should establish for children who are hospitalized.

3. **Thinking Skills.** Make a list of ways child care workers can protect themselves from on-the-job hazards. Which emergency situations carry the greatest risks? How can those risks be minimized? Should a parent take the same precautions?

 Family and Community Connections

1. **Finding Emergency Numbers.** Make a list of emergency numbers for your family. Post it near each phone at home.

2. **Protecting Against Fires.** Design an escape plan that your family can use in case of a fire in your home.

 Technology Connections

1. **Genetics.** Researchers are trying to find new ways of developing vaccines by using genes. Find out about this research and report to the class. Does this approach raise any ethical issues?

2. **Internet.** The Red Cross does more than run safety and first aid training. Use the Internet to find out what else the organization does and report to the class about it. How effective does this program seem to be?

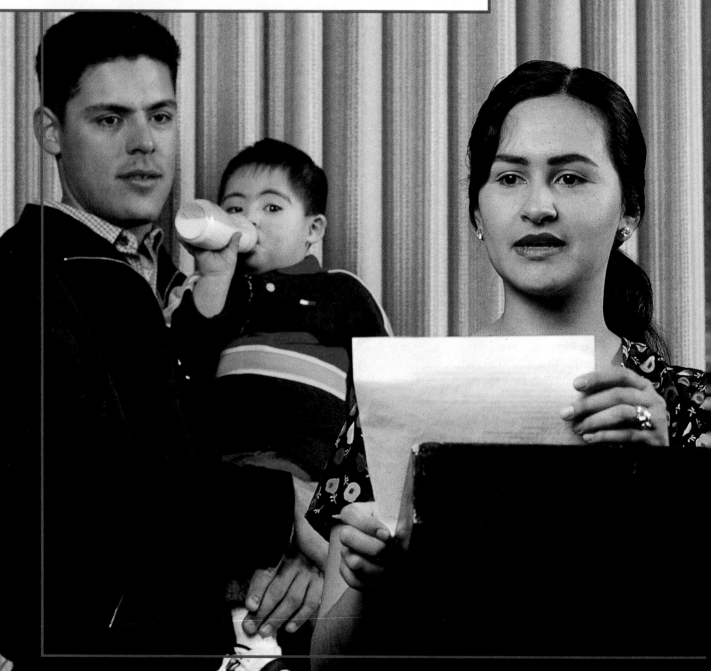

Florinda and Silvio Sanchez hurried to the first meeting of a group of parents of infants with Down syndrome. They were scheduled to talk to the group that evening.

After they had been introduced, Florinda said, "When I look at all of you, I see Silvio and myself sitting there just a few years ago. When you have a baby with Down syndrome, it seems like your world has shattered. I want you to know, though, that your outlook will change—now I laugh much more often than I cry. Our son Luis has made us a happier family."

Silvio continued, "Florinda and I have been actively involved in a local organization for mentally disabled persons. At first, we attended meetings because we needed information and we needed to talk to other parents in the same boat. We've become more involved because we enjoy it—and because we want to help other parents."

"Luis is such a lovable child," Florinda said. "We don't know just how much independence he'll be capable of as an adult. Right now, though, each of his achievements is cause for celebration."

" 'Our son Luis has made us a happier family.' "

SECTION 19-1

Exceptional Children

In the past, babies with disabilities often died at birth or soon after. Today medical science saves the lives of many of these children. With treatment many disabilities can be made less severe. Children can be taught to compensate for their disabilities. With proper care and treatment, disabled children can usually lead happy, productive lives.

KEY TERMS

behavioral therapist
inclusion
support group

OBJECTIVES:

- Describe the needs of children with physical, mental, and emotional disabilities.
- Develop strategies caregivers can use to help disabled children.

Children with Disabilities

The attitude of parents toward a child with a disability shapes that child's future. Parents can help the child become as independent as possible and accept the limitations that cannot be overcome. Parents who pity, resent, or overprotect a child with disabilities hinder his or her emotional and social development. The child may become angry and self-pitying and have difficulty living in society. A child with a positive attitude avoids these problems.

Many states require that public schools provide programs for disabled children and their parents. These programs may start right after the child's birth. Some states give children who have disabilities the chance to go to preschool.

Not all children with disabilities need to be in special programs. Many children do best when placed in regular classrooms. Both the children with disabilities and those without benefit. This approach, called **inclusion**, provides an opportunity for all the children to grow intellectually, develop social skills, and build empathy.

Practicing Parenting

Children's and Parents' Rights

In 1997, Congress passed and the President signed into law a new version of the Individuals with Disabilities Education Act (IDEA). The new law made several changes to the education of children with disabilities:

- ❤ Children have a right to a free public education that meets their needs.
- ❤ Parents must be notified if a school system plans to evaluate a child or change the child's school arrangement.
- ❤ Parents have the right to request that the school evaluate a child.
- ❤ Schools must ask parents to sign a form giving their consent to the initial plan for placing the child.
- ❤ Children must be retested every three years at least and their school situation must be reviewed at least every year.
- ❤ Children can be tested in the language they know best. Parents must be spoken to in the language they know best.
- ❤ Parents can request to see the child's school records.

- ❤ The school must draw up an educational program specifically for the child, and parents can take part in the process of developing that plan.
- ❤ Schools must make every effort to put the child, as much as possible, in a classroom with children who are not disabled.

APPLY YOUR KNOWLEDGE

1. What rights do parents have as a result of IDEA?
2. Why should the child's educational program be reviewed each year?
3. Why test the child in the language he or she knows best?

Special preschool programs give children with disabilities a chance to be with other children. *What law sets the rules for educating these children?*

Physical Disabilities

Physical disabilities take a wide range of forms. A child who must wear leg braces and a child who is missing an arm have obvious physical disabilities. The problems of children who can't hear or who have a heart defect are more hidden.

The Developing Brain

The brains of children who are deaf differ from those of hearing children. Parts of the brain that are usually used for hearing become part of the system for seeing instead.

Some physical disabilities are apparent at birth, but others may not be revealed for months or years. Parents should seek a complete diagnosis as soon as they suspect that their child has a physical disability. If it is true, the child should begin treatment as soon as possible. Early diagnosis and treatment helps children reach their potential.

Each child with a physical disability has the need for individual care. Routines that others take for granted can be difficult or even impossible. For example, a three-year-old with poor coordination may be unable to dress or eat without help.

Special exercises, special equipment, understanding, and patience are the keys to helping children with physical disabilities learn to be independent. Sometimes surgery can help. Independence is essential, not only for the child's future but also for developing a positive self-concept. Self-care skills such as eating, dressing, bathing, and using the toilet are fundamental to this independence.

Learning Self-Care

Bathing is a good example of a self-care skill. A child should be encouraged to handle as much of the task as possible.

Begin by making sure the child feels secure during the bath. This can mean putting a nonskid mat on the bottom of the tub or installing rails on the sides of the tub. Some youngsters need an inner tube or inflated cushion to keep their head above water. For those who cannot sit independently, the water level must be kept very low for safety.

Most children can perform some aspect of washing themselves. Children who have less coordination might participate by splashing water on themselves. Others might use a washcloth made into a mitt, which is easier to handle and less likely to be lost in the water. They can dry off using a towel with a hole cut in the middle. The child can slip the towel over the head to simplify the process of drying.

Parents and others who care for physically disabled children may need to develop similar adaptations for eating and other routine activities. Some children may need special help with only a few tasks. Others may need many adaptations because their physical skills are more limited.

Mental Disabilities

Children with mental disabilities do show some thinking skills. Their rate of development is slower than is typically the case, however, and it stops at a lower level. There are many degrees of mental disabilities. Some children simply have a harder time with normal tasks. Others may never progress past the mental abilities of babies.

Medical professionals can usually diagnose mental retardation early. They can offer some ideas about the child's learning potential, but they can't be exact. This is difficult to predict. Education and treatment must begin early to achieve the best possible results. Often doctors suggest special programs for these children.

Children with mental disabilities learn and respond best when they know what to expect. Directions for these children should be simple and direct. Showing the child what needs to be done and repeating the directions many times is usually the best way to teach.

The goal for children with mental disabilities is to help them become as independent as possible. Many can learn living and job skills that enable them to live alone or in a group home, support themselves, and perhaps marry and raise a family. Some depend totally on others their entire lives.

Some children with physical disabilities have a series of exercises they must do every day. *How do these exercises benefit the child?*

Ask the Experts

Jacqueline Mault
Director of Special Services for the Toppenish School District in Toppenish, Washington

IDENTIFYING *Children with Mental Disabilities*

Q How are children with mental disabilities identified?

A In many cases, parents are the first to suggest that a child has a mental disability. Usually, this is because they have noticed a delay in the child's development in certain areas. Often there are no signs until several months into the child's life. Physical development can proceed normally without there being any signs of problems with mental development. Many times, it is delays in language development that suggest to parents there may be a problem.

Usually, parents ask the child's pediatrician about their concerns. The doctor can comment on whether there does seem to be a delay in the child's acquisition of skills. He or she may not recommend any immediate action, however. If the delay is only slight, the doctor may feel that it is best to give the child a little more time.

Once the doctor feels that it is appropriate, he or she will suggest that the child be taken to a specialist in child development. That professional will give the child a series of tests.

The child's performance on the tests should identify whether he or she is mentally retarded. They should also show the child's strengths and weaknesses.

The tests will suggest how severe the child's problem is. It will also give hints as to what might be expected of the child's development in the future. These are only clues, though. It is impossible to make fully accurate predictions. With time and effort, with the help of professionals, and with the cooperation and dedication of parents, children can learn to master skills.

Thinking It Through

1. Why would language development often be a sign of mental disabilities?
2. Why do you think most parents take their concerns to a pediatrician?

Being accepted by others is important for people with mental retardation. Children with mental disabilities should be taught grooming, manners, and acceptable social behavior. Learning these skills increases acceptance.

Emotional Disabilities

How can parents know when their child is emotionally troubled or needs professional help? The child's behavior is the best indication, but there is no clear-cut line between typical behavior and disturbed behavior. Some troublesome behavior may be a part of a normal stage of development. Sometimes, though, a child's behavior prevents typical development or disturbs the lives of family members. In those cases, parents should try to find out if the child has an emotional problem. Early intervention can help minimize problems.

Behavior that suggests an emotional disability usually becomes more noticeable and more disturbing over time. For example, at age two, Terry began to rock in his crib and bang his head over and over against the headboard. He resisted toilet training and had frequent toileting accidents. He stuttered. Terry's parents hoped that after starting school, Terry would improve.

In school, though, Terry fought with other children and upset classes with loud outbursts. The school suggested that he have a psychological evaluation. It indicated that Terry needed therapy.

Even when a child's behavior shows a pattern that suggests emotional problems exist—as Terry's did—parents may be reluctant to ask for help. They may be ashamed to admit they can't handle the problem themselves. For the sake of the child—and the rest of the family—they need to get help.

What to Do?

When a child does need help, parents need to find a **behavioral therapist**, a professional trained in helping people work through emotional problems. Pediatricians,

Where can parents go for help if they have a child with emotional disabilities?

school counselors, members of the clergy, or a local office of the Mental Health Association can suggest therapists to contact. Parents should take the time to select someone they trust and with whom they feel comfortable.

The therapist will ask for background information on the problem behaviors, get to know the entire family better, and observe the child in various situations. Then he or she will plan treatment for the child. The treatment may involve making a few changes in the ways family members interact. For example, the therapist might suggest that the parents spend individual time with the child each day or that the child be introduced to a special activity, such as gymnastics or music.

The therapist may find that emotional problems have physical causes. If so, the therapist may recommend that the child be examined by a doctor.

Often the therapist works directly with the child—and sometimes with other family members—to improve the child's self-concept and self-esteem. Therapy can change the way children view themselves and, as a result, the way they behave.

The results of therapy depend to a great extent on the child's parents. They must believe in and support the therapist's work. They must be available to listen and talk when the child is ready. They need to accept the changes that result from the therapy. Sharing the children's personal feelings, learning to understand them, and accepting children for who and what they are—not what parents expect them to be—all help children overcome their problems.

Raising a Child with Disabilities

The responsibilities and demands of raising a child with a disability can seem overwhelming. In accepting that their child has a disability, parents may feel guilt, sadness, anger, and frustration.

Children with disabilities are still children. They need to know they have their parents' love. *Since children with disabilities require a great deal of attention, what do parents of more than one child have to be careful about?*

They can get help for themselves in **support groups.** In these groups, parents get together with other parents of disabled children to share comfort, advice, and solutions to everyday problems. In addition, groups can keep members up-to-date on research and treatment options.

Support groups can also help parents find tools to meet the emotional needs of their children. Children who receive emotional support have a strong sense of self—positive self-esteem. This gives them the inner strength, patience, and courage they need to cope with their disabilities.

Children with disabilities can bring as much joy to a family as children without disabilities. Like others, children with disabilities give family members a chance to love and be loved, to give, to receive, and to share.

SECTION 19-1 REVIEW

✔ Check Your Understanding

1. How can parents' attitudes affect children with disabilities?
2. How do children without disabilities benefit when children who have disabilities are placed in regular classes?
3. Why is it especially important to encourage independence for children with physical disabilities?
4. Why should children with mental disabilities be trained in grooming, manners, and acceptable social behavior?
5. What signs suggest that a child may have an emotional disturbance?
6. How do self-concept and self-esteem enter into therapy for emotional disabilities?
7. How can support groups help parents of children with disabilities?

Putting Knowledge Into Practice

1. **Making Inferences.** Many children born with disabilities must remain in the hospital for the first weeks—or even months—of their life. How might this long period of separation affect the baby and the parents? What could the parents do?
2. **Observing and Participating.** Visit a preschool class in which some students are disabled and others are not. Describe how much the disabled children seem to be integrated into the classroom activities. What evidence do you see that all the children are learning empathy?

CAREER OPPORTUNITIES

Physical Therapist

A CONVERSATION WITH ALICIA WAGNER

How did you become interested in becoming a physical therapist? I got hurt playing ball in high school, and a physical therapist helped me recover. We talked a lot while he worked with me. I realized that this could be a great career.

What are the tasks and responsibilities of a physical therapist? We try to help people recover the ability to use their bodies, which they've lost to an extent because of illness, or injury. We also help children with problems caused by some birth defects. To do this, we use massage, and exercise equipment like a stationary bike. We teach some patients how to use canes or walkers or artificial limbs.

What is the work environment like? I work mainly with children. Other therapists work in hospitals, sports medicine centers, or nursing homes.

What are the working hours like? I work forty hours a week.

What aptitudes are needed to be a physical therapist? Therapists have to be able to explain things clearly so that patients know what to do. They need to be very encouraging. With children, I try to make the exercises into games. Sometimes patients become frustrated when they don't make progress as rapidly as they'd like to. Therapists also need good writing skills because they have to write reports. They need to be fairly strong—sometimes it's necessary to lift patients.

PHYSICAL THERAPIST

Education and Training. Therapists need a bachelor's degree in physical therapy. They must also pass a licensing test to practice as a therapist.

Career Outlook. The demand for physical therapists is expected to grow much faster than average in the future.

CONNECTING SCHOOL TO CAREER

1. **Technology.** How might a physical therapist use exercise equipment?
2. **Thinking Skills.** How would the fact that the population is growing older affect the demand for physical therapists? Why?

Child Abuse and Neglect

Child abuse is the physical or emotional mistreatment of a child. The effects of child abuse, of any type, are long-lasting. Abuse can affect the physical, emotional, mental, and social health of its victims throughout their lifetime.

KEY TERMS

child abuse
crisis nurseries

OBJECTIVES:

- Explain what child abuse is and analyze why it happens.
- Discuss what can be done to prevent child abuse.

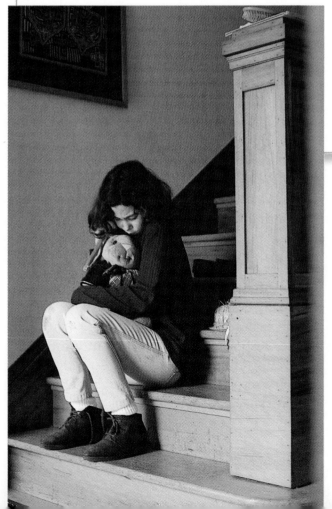

What Does Abuse Involve?

According to the National Committee for the Prevention of Child Abuse, abuse of children has reached epidemic proportions throughout the world. It is believed that abused children number in the millions. According to one report, at least 30 percent of all children are abused by the time they reach age eighteen. Every day an average of five American children are abused so badly that they die.

Child abuse is generally considered in these four categories:

- **Nonaccidental physical injury.** Injury caused by such things as beatings, burns, bites, or scalding water.
- **Neglect.** Failing to provide a child with the basic necessities of life, such as food, clothing, shelter, and health care.
- **Sexual molestation.** Using a child to gain sexual pleasure.
- **Emotional abuse.** Placing unreasonable, unrealistic, or excessive demands on the child. Examples are constant belittling, teasing, or verbal attacks. Some children never receive the love and affection they need for normal emotional development.

A single incident does not generally indicate child abuse. Abuse involves a pattern of behavior. The longer it continues, the more serious the problem becomes for both child and parent.

Experts often speak of the "cycle of child abuse." Once the abuse begins, a pattern of abuse results. A parent who hits a child one day is more likely to do so again—probably more severely. Abuse becomes a pattern of behavior.

Who Are Child Abusers?

Most child abusers are not monsters. They are ordinary people, usually parents or other relatives of the child, who don't intend harm. They are caught, however, in emotional situations that they can't handle. They are often people who feel lonely and

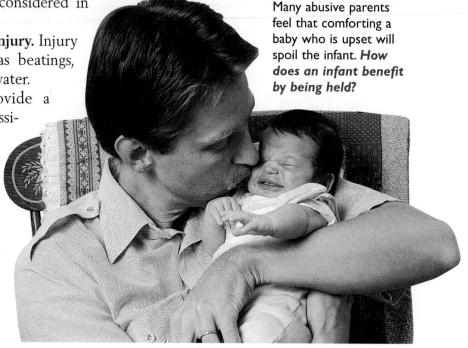

Many abusive parents feel that comforting a baby who is upset will spoil the infant. *How does an infant benefit by being held?*

can't cope with their own personal problems. They typically have low self-esteem. In many cases, they were themselves abused as children. When abuse is the only kind of parenting they have known, they repeat the behavior with their own children.

Child abusers come from all income levels, ethnic groups, and religions. Often, only one parent in a family actively abuses the children. However, the other parent may play a role by refusing to recognize it, by ignoring it, or by refusing to seek help.

Why Does Abuse Happen?

Parents who abuse their children are usually easily provoked and unable to maintain self-control. When they are irritated, they respond quickly and violently, much as a young child does. A three-year-old who is angry responds without thought. The child may kick the cat, smash a toy truck, or throw a doll across the room. An abusive adult displays the same uncontrollable emotions. An argument with a spouse, a car that won't start—almost anything—can trigger an incident of abuse. The child's words or actions are seldom the cause. The child is simply nearby, a defenseless target.

Abusive parents generally have certain beliefs that run against the facts of how children develop:

- They believe that infants will be spoiled if they are picked up and comforted when they cry. They don't recognize that this physical comforting is essential for the development of trust.
- They often have unrealistic expectations of what children can do. For example, they may tell a toddler to "sit up and eat right." They expect the toddler to do just that—promptly—even though the nature and skills of toddlers make this impossible.

- They expect young children to remember commands given only once. Of course, young children learn only after directions have been repeated many times. An abusive parent may see a child's inability to do as he or she is told as stubbornness, meanness, disobedience, or revenge.

Are There Any Answers?

Society doesn't tolerate child abuse. It is against the law to abuse a child. Those who work with children, such as doctors, teachers, social workers, and child care workers, must report suspected cases of child abuse. It is essential for the well-being of children to report these cases to the closest social service agency or child welfare agency.

Once an agency hears of suspected child abuse, it begins to investigate. If the child is in immediate danger, a court may place the

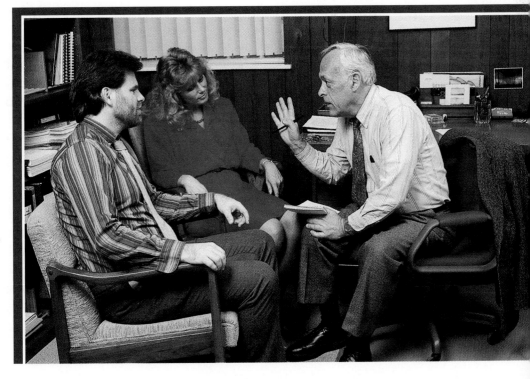

Counselors can help abusive parents understand why they are abusive and learn to change their attitudes and how they respond to situations.

child in a foster home. If there is a history of past abuse or the child's injuries are severe, parents can be charged and tried.

Putting abusive people in jail does give the child temporary protection. It does not solve the problem of the abuse, however. In most cases, treatment and counseling are used in an effort to correct the cause of the abuse—and so bring the abuse to an end.

Most abusive parents must work harder to learn how to care for their children responsibly. There are many types of government, private, and volunteer programs available to help them. Parents Anonymous, one of the best-known groups, is made up of parents who help each other gain self-control.

Some communities have **crisis nurseries,** child care facilities where troubled

parents can leave their children for a short time. Using a crisis nursery gives parents time to cool off and try to cope with their frustrations and anger away from their children. Workers at these crisis nurseries usually work with the abusive parents. They help parents understand their frustrations and resolve their problems. They guide parents in learning how to break the cycle of child abuse.

Many family problems, including child abuse, are directly related to poor parenting skills and to a lack of knowledge about child development. Classes like the one you are taking help give parents—and future parents—realistic ideas about what parenting involves. Are other parenting classes available in your community?

SECTION 19-2 REVIEW

✔ Check Your Understanding

1. What is child abuse?
2. Give an example of one of the categories of child abuse.
3. List three traits common among child abusers.
4. What quality do people who are abusive lack?
5. Where should child abuse be reported?
6. Is putting child abusers in prison the answer to the problem? Why or why not?
7. Who belongs to Parents Anonymous? What do members do?

Putting Knowledge Into Practice

1. **Supporting an Argument.** Child abuse is a personal problem. To what degree is it also a social problem? What can society do to try to solve this problem?
2. **Making Inferences.** How might understanding child development help prevent abuse?
3. **Observing and Participating.** Talk to a counselor or social worker about why people find it difficult to report suspected cases of child abuse. What particular problems would a person have in reporting abuse? Describe what you would say and do to encourage a close friend to report his or her suspicions of child abuse.

Family Stresses

Evan stared out the window. He didn't have the energy to do anything. He couldn't think of anything that would be fun. All he could think of was his friends in his old town—the town he and his family had just moved away from. He liked the new home, but he sure missed his friends.

KEY TERMS

addiction
co-dependency

OBJECTIVES:

- Describe the emotional effects on children of stressful family situations.

- Create strategies for minimizing these effects.

Children and Stress

During times of stress, children need even more support than adults. They are less capable of understanding the events that cause stress and lack essential tools for handling that stress. At these times, children should be encouraged to talk about their feelings.

Divorce

Divorce is more common now than it used to be. Nearly 20 percent of children will have to face a family breakup before they turn eighteen.

If a family is about to break up, the children need to be told about the change in an honest and reassuring way. Experts advise using the following guidelines:

- **Truth.** The children should be told the truth about the upcoming changes. If possible, both parents should discuss the situation. All children, even toddlers, should be included. Young children often understand much more than parents realize. Parents can say something like this to their children: "We're having a hard time right now. We are going to live apart, for a while at least. Still, no matter what happens, we will both always love you and take care of you." The last point—that love will continue—is essential.

- **Elimination of blame.** Parents need to avoid placing blame for the divorce on one another, at least in front of the children. If the parents can't talk about the divorce without placing blame, they can ask a counselor or religious leader to help them. Each parent should remember that the children will continue to need both parents. It is unfair to children to place them in a position where they have to take sides with one or the other.

Children also need to be reassured that they are in no way responsible for the breakup. Parents should stress that they are separating because of their own differences, not because of anything their children have said or done—or failed to say or do. Most children feel guilty when their parents fail

Divorced parents should refrain from criticizing each other when the child is around. *Why?*

In the past, mothers were almost always given custody of the child in a divorce. Today, more fathers are being given custody. *How might boys in particular benefit from this arrangement?*

to get along. Parents should make a special effort to be reassuring on this point.

- **Reassurance.** Parents also need to reassure the children that they will continue to be loved by both parents. After a separation or divorce, children typically live with only one parent. They need to know that the other parent is still there for support and companionship.
- **No false hope.** The children shouldn't be encouraged to hope for a reconciliation if their parents are not considering the possibility. This false hope only delays the children's adjustment to their new situation.

After the divorce, children need stability and continuity. Their lives should be kept the same as much as possible. Siblings should continue living together if possible. Children will feel more comfortable if they don't change homes or schools. The absent parent should spend time with the children often and regularly. Frequent contact with relatives from both sides of the family can help retain a sense of belonging. See the "Parenting with Care" feature on pages 600-601 for more suggestions about living with children after a divorce.

Many children begin to show behavior problems after the family breaks up. Even children who appear to adjust well may be hiding their grief and pain. If these problems continue, it is wise to seek professional help.

Death

The death of someone close causes special problems for a young child. The age of the child, however, influences the youngster's reaction.

- **Under age three.** Children this young cannot understand much more than a brief separation. Often, a toddler will

Many children first experience death when a pet dies. *What are the three steps that children go through when dealing with death?*

react to a parent's death in the same way as to the parent's week-long vacation.

- **Ages three to five.** Children this age think that death is like sleep—you are dead, and then you wake up and are alive again. As a result, they may seem unfeeling when someone dies. They don't understand that death is permanent.
- **Ages five to nine.** As children mature, they accept the idea that a person who has died will not come back. However, they don't view death as something that happens to everyone. They don't recognize that they themselves will die.
- **Age nine or ten.** At this age, children begin to see that they, too, will die. This may make them afraid. At this age, children must come to terms with their fear and put it in proper perspective.

How Children Cope with Death

By age five, most children have had some contact with death and are curious about it. Perhaps a pet has died; or perhaps it was someone in the extended family. Children go through a three-step process in accepting death. Caregivers who understand this process are usually better prepared to help children cope with death and their feelings about death.

1. **Disbelief.** In this early stage, children may express anger, hostility, and defiance.
2. **Despair.** Later, children are often withdrawn and depressed. Some may revert to babyish behavior during this stage.
3. **Reorganization.** Finally, children begin to adjust to life without the person who has died.

If a loved one dies, children should be told about it in an honest way. They may need an explanation of what death is. Children should then be encouraged to talk about their feelings. Parents, in turn, should let children know that they, too, miss the person very much. Sharing memories of the person who has died, looking at photographs, and talking about what made him or her special can help parents and children deal with the death.

Adults must be very careful about the words they use when discussing death with a child. Phrases like "passed away" or "gone to sleep" only add to a child's confusion. Use simple, direct references to death and dying. It's also important to remember that children understand most things in terms of themselves. For example, a child who is told that "Grandpa got very sick and died" may worry about dying the next time he or she gets a cold. The type of explanation an adult offers must fit the age and understanding of the child, but it should always be honest and direct.

When a Parent Dies

The death of a parent is the most tragic thing that can happen to a youngster. A child whose parent dies needs support for an extended period. Many children react with guilt. The child may think, "I wasn't always good when he wanted me to be" or "I wasn't quiet enough when she was sick." Children need the reassurance that nothing they did, said, or even thought caused the death. They also need help coping with their feelings of abandonment.

Even very young children should be allowed to take part in family funerals or memorial services. Doing so will help them heal and make the transition from the presence to the absence of the person who died. Children of any age are capable of mourning. Even infants go through a period of excessive crying and searching for a parent who has died.

Suicide

Some children feel that they can't cope with their problems any longer. They feel overwhelmed and without hope and try to take their own lives.

A person who is thinking about suicide needs help. Comments like "You'd all be better off without me" and actions like giving away prized possessions may be signs that someone is thinking about suicide. If you know of someone who shows these signs, talk to an adult. It may save a life.

Moving

Moving is stressful for children, because their familiar settings and routines are upset. Often, children don't want to leave their present home, where they feel secure and safe.

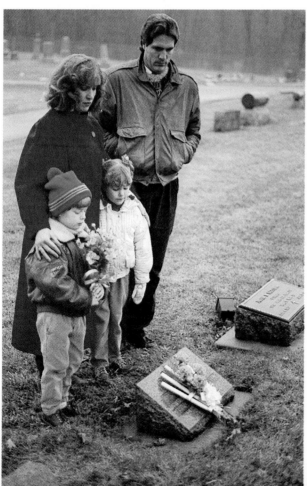

How might a child react to the death of a parent? A grandparent?

Financial Problems

When a family has financial problems, children sense the tensions even though they may not understand them. The parents may be short-tempered or pay less attention to the children than usual. Children typically believe that they themselves have done something wrong.

Children can't understand complex financial situations. Still, parents should talk to them about the family's situation. They may wish to point out a need to limit expenses for a while. Parents must work hard to avoid taking out their own fears and worries on their children.

Illness

When a family member is ill or in the hospital, the routine of family life is upset. Parents can help their children handle this kind of situation by explaining what is happening. If the illness is minor, the child can be reassured that the person will soon be well and everything return to normal. If the illness is serious or terminal, the child should be told the truth, but in a calm, reassuring way.

Children often worry that they will suffer a similar illness or injury. They may grow afraid of doctors or hospitals. Parents should take the time to explain how the relative's illness or injury differs from any the child is likely to have. As with other situations of family stress, parents need to show patience and reassurance.

Substance Abuse

Some people develop an **addiction** to a drug or to alcohol. When this happens, they

Moving can be difficult for children, who have to adapt to a new school and find new friends. *Why should parents let children pack their own things?*

Parents can help soothe children's fears by encouraging them to talk about their feelings. Children should also be encouraged to pack their own belongings as much as possible. This activity helps them feel more in control and more involved in the move. Parents can also stress what the family—and the child—will gain from the move.

After the move, parents need to help the child get settled. They can take walks with the child around the new neighborhood and help the child meet nearby children. They can also take the child to visit his or her new school.

crave the substance even though it has powerful and harmful effects on their minds and bodies. When people abuse substances, they cause many problems for their families.

Some parents who are substance abusers often begin to abuse their spouses or their children, causing further problems. If the drug or drinking problem becomes very serious, a person may lose a job or turn to crime in order to support the habit.

Members of the family often are well aware that a person has a substance abuse problem. They don't always admit it, though. Sometimes they show a kind of behavior called **co-dependency.** This means

they take on responsibilities that the substance abuser should be filling. In that way, they help the person hide the problem.

Substance abusers and their families need to face up to their problems. An abuser will not stop or seek help until ready to. Nagging or threatening won't make it happen. On the other hand, others in the family may need to protect themselves from the abuser's behavior. Groups like Alateen and Families Anonymous give support to the teen children and the families of alcoholics. Other groups are also available to provide help for the families of people who abuse drugs.

SECTION 19-3 REVIEW

✔ Check Your Understanding

1. List some guidelines for telling children about a separation or divorce.
2. What attitude toward death is typical of three- to five-year-olds? At what age do children usually begin to understand that death is inevitable for everyone?
3. Describe the signs of each of the three stages children often go through in accepting a death.
4. Twelve-year-old Danielle has a friend who has been very sad lately. One day, she gave Danielle all her CDs. What should Danielle do?
5. How can parents help children settle in after a move?
6. How might a family member's illness affect a child's own health?
7. What is co-dependency? How can it contribute to a substance abuse problem?

Putting Knowledge Into Practice

1. **Making Inferences.** Make a list of coping skills—techniques that families can use to handle problems such as talking honestly to children about a divorce. On your list, indicate which ideas would be especially effective with young children.
2. **Synthesizing.** When Curtis's grandmother died, his parents said, "Grandma went on a long trip." Was that an effective message to give their five-year-old? Why or why not? If not, what could the parents have said instead?
3. **Observing and Participating.** Think of how you handle stress. Would your techniques be suitable for a child? Why or why not?

Parenting With Care

Living with Children After a Divorce

When parents divorce, one parent is often given custody of the children.

In the past, that parent was almost always the mother. Now, most courts base the decision on a judgment of which parent can provide a loving, stable home.

In more and more families, parents take joint custody—they both agree to take responsibility for children. The children usually split their time between their two parents' homes. Either way, parents can take certain steps to make their children's lives easier:

- If the court orders a parent to send money for child support, that parent must comply.
- The parent whom children don't live with should visit the children as often as possible to maintain healthy relationships.
- Follow the same routines in both homes to help the child feel comfortable.
- Follow the same rules in both homes so that children have consistent standards of behavior. This also prevents the child from being able to play one parent against the other by saying "Daddy lets me watch that show" or "Mommy lets me eat that."
- Use guidance in the same way as before the divorce. Avoid being too harsh or too lenient with the child. The health and welfare of the child should be most important.
- The parent with custody should keep the other parent informed about the child's life. He or she should share news about school events or recent illnesses, for example.
- Both parents should avoid saying negative things about the other. Criticisms of the other parent can let a child feel caught between love for one or the other.
- If parents fight whenever they see each other, use another adult—such as a grandparent—as a go-between.

- Give extra comfort to the child just before he or she is ready to spend time at the other parent's home.
- Don't be surprised if the child begins to revert to the behavior of a younger child. Children do so in an unconscious desire to restore life to an earlier, happier time. Show patience while still making it clear to the child that appropriate behavior is expected.

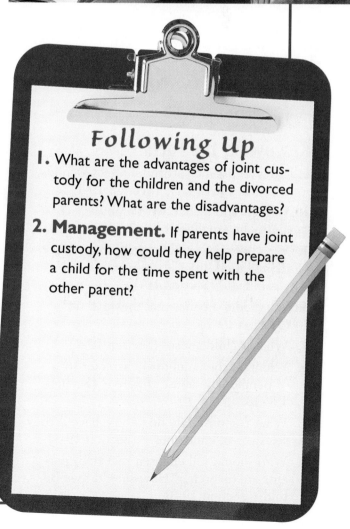

Following Up

1. What are the advantages of joint custody for the children and the divorced parents? What are the disadvantages?

2. **Management.** If parents have joint custody, how could they help prepare a child for the time spent with the other parent?

REVIEW &

Summary

✔ Some children have serious disabilities that make their lives more difficult, but they can usually have productive lives. (Section 19-1)

✔ Treatment and counseling can help abusive parents learn to cope with their problems and stop patterns of abuse. (Section 19-2)

✔ Children need extra support when facing stressful situations. (Section 19-3)

✔ When the family faces problems or stresses, children should be told about the problem honestly and in a way suited to their level. (Section 19-3)

9. Contrast how children of different ages understand death. (Section 19-3)

10. Kevin does all the shopping and cleaning and cares for his younger sister because his mother has a drinking problem. What is Kevin's behavior called? (Section 19-3)

Thinking Critically

1. **Analyzing.** Children with disabilities are more likely to be abused than children without disabilities. Why do you think that is true?

2. **Synthesizing.** Which do you think would be better for a child, living in a home in which the parents often fight or having parents divorce? Why?

Taking Action

1. **Making a Poster.** Make a poster that contains advice for young children whose parents are divorced. *(Communication)*

2. **Helping Out.** Find a local group that offers help to families with any of the problems described in this chapter. Find out what people your age can do to help out. Create a fact sheet that describes the group and the help they are looking for. *(Leadership)*

Reviewing the Facts

1. How do parents' attitudes affect a child who has a disability? (Section 19-1)

2. Why should a child with a physical disability be taught self-care? (Section 19-1)

3. Why is it suggested that children with mental disabilities learn manners and cleanliness? (Section 19-1)

4. What does a behavioral therapist do? (Section 19-1)

5. What is child abuse? (Section 19-2)

6. What are the emotional characteristics of people who abuse children? (Section 19-2)

7. What responsibility do people have if they see signs of child abuse? (Section 19-2)

8. Who should tell children that their parents are divorcing? How should they be told? (Section 19-3)

CONNECTIONS

Cross-Curricular Connections

1. **Social Studies.** Stage a debate in which you argue for or against the idea that parents who abuse children should lose all rights of custody for those children.

2. **Language Arts.** Write a story about a five-year-old child whose family just moved.

Workplace Connections

1. **Basic Skills.** Suppose you wrote a newspaper advice column. A parent writes you to say that her spouse is dying of a serious illness. She wants advice on how to explain his illness and upcoming death to their children, ages six and four. Write a reply to the letter.

Family and Community Connections

1. **Help for the Abused.** Gather information about the work of a group in your area that helps spouses or children who are abused. What kind of help is offered?

2. **In the School.** Learn more about the Individuals with Disabilities Education Act (IDEA). What does the act require of schools? Of parents and children? Write a summary of your findings.

Technology Connections

1. **Internet.** Search online to find a group that provides support to families who have a child with a disability. What kind of help do they give to parents? Write a summary of what you find.

2. **Internet.** Search online to find a group that provides help to those who abuse substances. Examples are Alcoholics Anonymous and Alateen. Choose one of the following issues: alcoholism, crime, mental health, co-dependency, impact on children. Report your findings to the class, and suggest steps society can take to try to solve the problem you addressed.

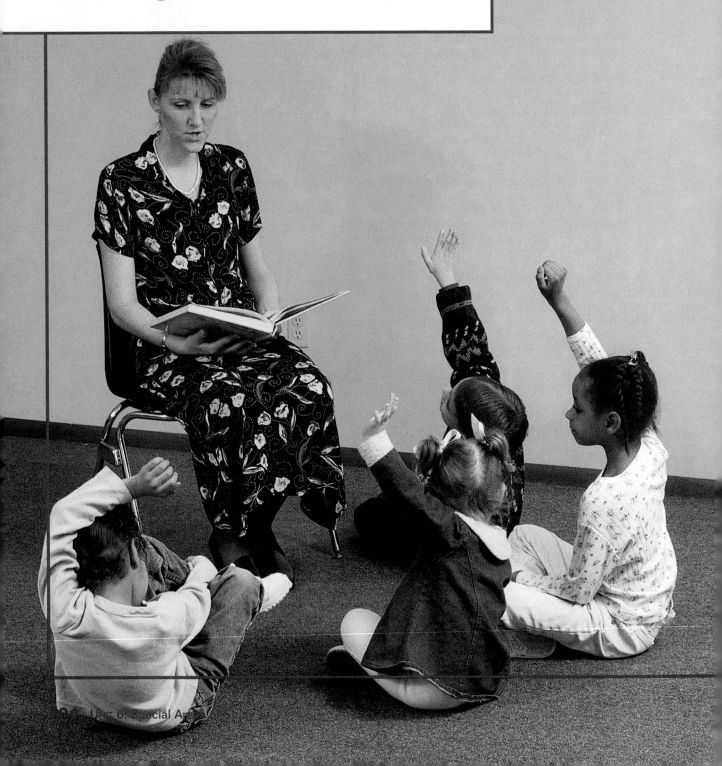

CHAPTER 20

Caring for Children

Margo told the children that it was time to finish their projects and put their materials away. They had been making designs to celebrate Thanksgiving, gluing dried macaroni and colored pieces of construction paper to decorate the outline of a turkey. Margo told the children where to put their projects so they would dry in time to take them home that night. She didn't have to remind them where to put the glue or the construction paper—the children knew from practice where those went.

As the children put things away, there were the usual interruptions. Alex objected to Brock telling him what to do. Lisa needed to go to the rest room. Inez asked if she could go to the reading area already. Eventually, though, the picking up was completed.

Margo brought all the children to the reading area and said, "OK, kids, it's time to hear more of our story." The children settled down on the floor, and Margo sat in the big chair with the book. "Who remembers where we left off yesterday?" she asked. Immediately five hands were raised, and five voices called out, "I do."

"OK, kids, it's time to hear more of our story."

Providing Short-Term Child Care

The most common first child care job is **babysitting,** caring for children for a short time while parents are away from the home. Actually, *babysitting* is not a very accurate term. When you undertake this job, you are really providing care for children. The job allows little time for sitting—unless the children are asleep!

KEY TERMS

authority
babysitting

OBJECTIVES:

- Determine what personal qualities are needed to be a good babysitter or child care provider.

- Describe the responsibilities of a child care provider when caring for children of various ages.

- List safety guidelines that are especially important for child care providers.

Making Arrangements

Whenever you arrange a babysitting job, agree in advance on the rate of pay. Ask how long the parents intend to be gone and discuss how you will get to and from their home. Before you leave for the job, be sure your own family knows the name, address, and phone number of the people you will be working for and the approximate time you will return.

The first time you provide child care for a family, arrive about 20 minutes early. This will give the children a chance to get used to you while their parents are still home. It will also allow you enough time to find out any additional information from the parents. Obvious questions to ask include when bedtimes are, where the parents will be, how the parents can be reached, and emergency procedures.

Caring for Children of Different Ages

When parents are gone, child care providers are completely responsible for the safety and welfare of the children. Good caregivers:

- Are interested in the children, not just in the money they are earning.
- Can behave responsibly.
- Have patience, especially with small children.
- Understand children's physical, emotional, social, and intellectual needs.
- Are flexible and prepared to meet the needs of children of different ages.
- Have a sense of humor.
- Come prepared to meet the children's needs.

Babies

Babies need a great deal of physical care and protection. This means that when you agree to care for an infant, you should have the necessary skills and understand the characteristics of babies.

INFOLINK

Caring for an Infant

For more about *caring for an infant*, see Chapter 8, pages 268-291.

Teens who take a babysitting job should be sure to find out what the parents expect them to do in caring for the children. Will they have to feed and bathe the children? Do the parents want them to play with the children? Knowing this in advance will make the babysitting experience satisfying for everyone concerned.

Remember to follow five three most important rules of caring for infants:

- When handling a young infant, hold the infant firmly, and always support the baby's head and neck.
- Never leave a baby on a bed, sofa, or other raised surface. Even a tiny baby can wiggle enough to fall off.
- Keep harmful objects out of the reach of crawling infants.
- Never shake a baby. Even a few moments of strong shaking can cause permanent damage to the baby's brain.
- Use the time when a child is awake for positive, loving interaction.

When a baby cries, find out what the problem is. Is the baby too cold or warm or perhaps hungry? Is the diaper wet or soiled? Remember, too, that except for very young infants, babies cry when they are lonely. If that is the problem, a few minutes of cuddling will help.

Changing diapers is a frequent duty of child care providers. Be sure to gather all needed supplies so that they are nearby before you start changing the diaper.

Child care providers aren't usually asked to bathe a baby. However, a qualified care provider should be able to undertake this task. Before you agree to do it as part of a child care job, review what is involved and practice bathing a baby while an adult watches.

Toddlers and Preschoolers

Because toddlers and preschoolers sleep less and are more adventuresome, they require more watching. Don't leave them alone—even for a minute—while they are awake. They are also more sensitive than infants to their parents' leaving and may need comforting. They like being read to, played with, or talked to.

Sometimes babysitters have to feed the children they care for. *What can they do to help promote self-feeding?*

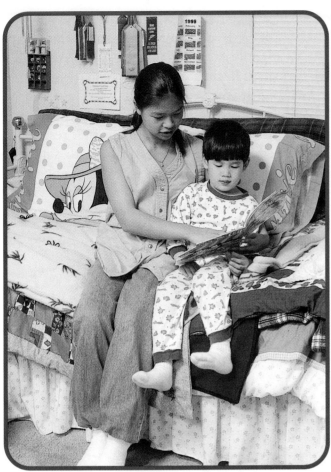

Following the child's normal routine can make bedtime easier when you are babysitting. *What would you do if a child says that parents let him or her stay up later on nights that there is a babysitter?*

Bedtime may be a problem. Toddlers and preschoolers usually don't want to go to bed. Try to follow the child's regular bedtime routine. Ask the parents in advance what bedtime activities the child is used to so you can follow the normal routine.

During the night, a young child may be awakened by a bad dream. Providing a bit of comfort will help the child go back to sleep. Later, tell the parents about the bad dream—and anything else unusual.

School-Age Children

Some older children try to give caregivers a difficult time. Some are jealous of the time and attention given to younger siblings. Others try to get away with behavior their parents wouldn't permit. Still others may feel they are too old for a babysitter.

Get the relationship off to a good start by making friends with older children. If you show interest in their possessions, games, or activities, you'll win over even the most independent youngsters.

It helps if before the parents leave, they make clear to the children that you have **authority**. This means you have the right to make decisions in their absence.

At no time is your maturity as a care provider more important than when a child deliberately misbehaves. You will have better control of the situation if you remain calm. Be fair—but firm and consistent.

No matter how a child behaves, never use physical punishment. Bribery and threats don't work well, either. If you feel you need to punish a child, use reasonable punishment, such as no TV. Be sure to describe the situation to the parents when they return. Tell what the child did, how you responded, and why. Ask if the parents would prefer you to handle such situations differently. In the future, then, you can act accordingly.

INFOLINK

Guidance

For more about *guidance*, see Chapter 3, pages 88-89.

Safety Tips for Child Care Providers

Caring for children requires your full attention. If you are alert and on the scene when something starts to happen, you can usually prevent serious problems. You should never let anything distract you from your primary job—watching the children.

One of the most dangerous situations you might meet is a fire. When you begin a child care job, locate all the outside doors. Note escape routes from various parts of the home. Find out whether the house has

INFOLINK

Accidents and First Aid

For more about *accidents and first aid*, see Chapter 18, pages 548-562.

smoke detectors and a fire extinguisher. Ask whether the parents have a family escape plan to be used in case of fire. If they do, have them review it with you.

If a fire does break out, remember that the children are your first responsibility. Lead or carry them to safety. Then alert anyone else who may be in danger, and call the fire department. After calling the fire department, notify the parents.

How Do You Rate as a Care Provider?

Successful child care requires thoughtful attention to the children. You will rate

When you are babysitting, ask for a phone number where the parents can be reached. *What kind of situation would require a phone call to the parents?*

well with parents if the children are well cared for, safe, and happy. Parents also want a care provider to arrive on time and follow the routines or directions provided. In addition, parents appreciate a care provider who straightens up, making sure that toys, books, and games have been put away and any snacks or meals have been cleared away. Ask ahead of time about any food a child may or should have.

You will rate well with children if you are prepared to spend time with them in activities that appeal to them. Buying toys and bringing them with you is not the only way—or even the best way—to keep children amused and happy. More important are your interests, imagination, and enthusiasm. An attentive care provider with a headful of stories, rhymes, songs, tricks, and games is more welcome than toys. These activities can make a child care job a pleasant and worthwhile experience.

SECTION 20-1 REVIEW

✔ Check Your Understanding

1. What arrangements should be discussed when taking on a babysitting job?
2. List five qualities of a good care provider.
3. What are the five basic rules of caring for an infant?
4. Patricia is babysitting a six-month-old who begins to cry. What should she do?
5. What should a care provider do to help make bedtime easier for a toddler or preschooler?
6. What three steps can a babysitter take to be prepared in case there is a fire?

Putting Knowledge Into Practice

1. **Giving Examples.** How can parents make clear to their children that a babysitter has authority?
2. **Applying.** Imagine that you are providing care for a family with an eight-year-old. The child is clearly interested in finding out how much she can get away with. How would you encourage the child to behave in appropriate ways?
3. **Observing and Participating.** Write down a list of qualities and skills you think a babysitter should have. Then interview at least two parents of small children to ask what qualities and skills they look for. Compare your list to the parents' responses. What differences are there? Why?

CAREER OPPORTUNITIES

Child Care Center Worker

A CONVERSATION WITH
SHANNA RUTHERFORD

How did you become interested in becoming a child care center worker? I started babysitting at fourteen, and just loved it. I mean, young children are so incredibly alive. I wanted to be one of those people to give them a good start in life. I'm a child care aide now, but am working on my college degree.

What are the tasks and responsibilities of a child care center worker? First, care for their physical needs—we need to keep them safe and healthy. Next, give them chances to learn and develop their physical skills, their minds, their language skills, how they get along with others. You name it!

What is the work environment like? Noisy, and fun, and demanding, and exciting. We try to have as much structure as possible so the children know what to expect, but the children make every day a surprise.

What are the working hours like? I work eight hours a day, five days a week. It's a long eight hours, because I have to be alert and upbeat all the time.

What aptitudes are needed to be a child care center worker? I always tell my friends that the main thing is energy. Next is enthusiasm. Being soft spoken and gentle is important. So is having patience. There are so many things, it's hard to narrow the list!

CHILD CARE CENTER WORKER

Education and Training. Child care workers need at least a high school education. They can also take courses in early childhood education at two- or four-year colleges. Degrees are needed for higher-level positions.

Career Outlook. The outlook for child care workers is expected to be good.

CONNECTING SCHOOL TO CAREER

1. **Interpersonal Skills.** How much do you think workers in a child care center need to cooperate with one another—a lot or a little? Why?

2. **Resources.** Do you think that child care workers should have to pass a skills test to earn a license? Why or why not?

SECTION 20-2

Participating in Child Care and Education

As a part of your class in child development, you may have the chance to participate in an early childhood classroom. The following guidelines will help you get started and suggest ways that both you and the children can learn together. These skills can help you move toward a career in child care.

KEY TERMS

circle time
learning centers
transitions

OBJECTIVES:

- Explain the benefits of different learning centers in early childhood classrooms.
- Discuss how to promote health and safety in early childhood classrooms.
- Analyze what makes activity plans effective for young children.
- Discuss how to promote positive behavior.

The Early Childhood Classroom

Classrooms for young children need to be designed to meet their special needs. Think about all you have learned about the physical, social, emotional, and intellectual development of young children.

The first requirement is for the classroom environment to be child-sized. This promotes independence because children are able to use the materials without having to ask adults for help. This independence allows the child to feel successful. Chairs should be low enough to allow children to sit with their feet touching the floor. Shelves should be low so that children can get and return materials on their own.

A classroom for young children must be designed for their activities and needs. Discovery centers should have interesting objects to explore. Play areas must have sturdy equipment. *How do the areas shown here meet these standards?*

Learning Centers

Early childhood classrooms are usually divided into **learning centers.** These are areas of the classroom meant for certain types of play and learning. Learning centers offer children choices. They can select activities, explore different areas of knowledge, and develop skills through hands-on experiences.

The number and type of learning centers varies. The illustration on pages 616-617 shows one arrangement of centers in an early childhood classroom. Guidelines for materials learning centers are described in the "Parenting With Care" feature on pages 626-627.

Early childhood programs use guidelines such as these in setting up learning centers:

- Use different colored floor coverings, wall decorations, low shelves, or storage containers to separate different learning centers.
- Separate noisy centers from quiet centers.
- Place the art center near a source of water. The floor should be easy to clean if it gets wet.
- Leave a large, open area for large-group activities such as dancing to music.

Health and Safety

Ensuring the health and safety of the children is the first responsibility of the staff of an early childhood classroom. Workers must follow health care routines to prevent illness, make sure the environment is safe, and supervise play.

Health Care Routines

Health care routines prevent the spread of illness. They also help make sure the children are well nourished and rested.

As children enter the classroom, staff members usually look for any obvious signs of illness. Children who are sick or become sick aren't allowed to stay with the group.

Children who attend a child care center for a half-day should have a snack in the middle of the morning or afternoon session.

Learning Centers in the Early Childhood Classroom

1 ## Block Center

Include small and large blocks, building logs, trucks and cars, and people and animal figures. Placing the block center on carpeting cuts down on noise.

2 ## Science Center

The science center allows children to explore their world. Include magnifying glasses, scales, magnets, and specimens—rocks, leaves, and other natural objects—for children to use. Have a low table to give children a place to work.

3 ## Math Center

In this area, children can learn such concepts as matching, sorting, classifying, and counting. They can also learn about colors, sizes, and shapes and ideas such as before and after or over and under.

4 ## Music Center

This area can include musical instruments such as tambourines, finger cymbals, triangles, and drums. It can also include records, CDs, audio tapes, and equipment to play them.

8 Art Center

The art center allows children to be creative and exercise their imagination by drawing, painting, and working with clay and fabric. It should include paper, scissors and paste, crayons, paints, chalk, clay, and fabric. There should be smocks for children to wear when they work with these materials.

7 Active Play Area

In this area, children exercise their large muscles. It can include bean bags and streamers for throwing; areas for climbing, tumbling, and sliding; and a work bench for hammering.

6 Language Arts Center

This area includes materials related to speaking, listening, reading, and writing. It should be a quiet area with good lighting and comfortable chairs or throw pillows. The area might include a computer as well.

5 Dramatic Play Center

This area provides children with opportunities for make-believe play. It can include clothes and hats for dressing up, a play kitchen and related equipment, material that can be used to play office or grocery store, play money, and a telephone.

Careful hand washing in one of the best ways to prevent he spread of disease. Children should be taught to wash their own hands thoroughly with warm water and soap, then dry them with a clean paper towel. Hands need washing after using the toilet, after blowing the nose, and before cooking, eating, or playing with materials such as clay.

Make a habit of washing your own hands often, both to protect everyone's health and to set a good example. Be sure to wash them after helping a child in the rest room, after you use the rest room yourself, after using a tissue to wipe a child's nose, and before handling food.

Children should learn several other important health care habits as well:

- To blow and wipe their nose and to dispose of the tissue.
- To cover their mouth when they cough.
- To use only his or her own comb, brush, or head wear—never those of another child.
- To avoid taking bites of each other's food and not to share the same cup or eating utensils.

Safety

To keep young children safe, make sure the environment is childproofed. Check the children's classroom and outdoor play areas for any possible safety hazards.

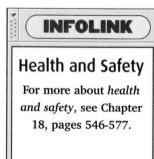

INFOLINK

Health and Safety

For more about *health and safety*, see Chapter 18, pages 546-577.

In addition, you need to supervise the children closely as they work and play. There should always be an ade-quate number of teens or adults present to watch the children in each area. If an emergency arises, some caregivers should stay with the children in the classroom while someone goes for help.

Planning Appropriate Activities

Planning plays an important role in providing appropriate learning experiences for young children. The daily schedule should provide a balance of activities for individuals and for small and large groups of children. Activities also need to provide opportunities in each area of development. Of course, activities must be appropriate to the age and skill levels of the children too.

Learning Through Play

As you plan activities for young children, remember that the more involved the children are and the more realistic their experiences are, the more they learn. A story about a fire truck isn't nearly as effective a learning tool as a trip to the fire station and a chance to climb on a real one.

Children need play experiences that focus on these areas of development:

- Thinking and problem solving.
- Movement of large and small muscles.
- Creativity, including music, dance, dramatic play, and art.
- Relationships with others.

Children need a variety of activities that involve different kinds of experiences. When several children sit at a table each working on a puzzle, they are playing individually but alongside one another. Sometimes children play alone, perhaps looking at books by themselves. Children

Ask the Experts

Pat Brodeen

Teacher and Teen Parent Coordinator at Theodore Roosevelt High School in San Antonio, Texas

What to *Look for in a Child Care Program*

How can I know that I'm choosing the best child care program for my child?

Child care is very important and often a very difficult choice for parents to make. Let me suggest an effective approach to making this decision. Once you have found a program that is convenient and affordable and that offers the hours and services you need, approach that program from the child's point of view.

I want to spend my time with a loving person. Will the caregiver here love and appreciate me? Does he or she know how to communicate with me? Will the caregiver give me gentle but firm guidelines for my behavior? Does the caregiver have a high tolerance for my noisy activity level? If my caregiver's children are also here, will I get the same treatment? Has the caregiver had any educational preparation to work with me? Does he or she treat me the way my parents do, so I will have consistency in my day? Do I really like this person?

The facility where I will stay is also important to me. Are there few enough children so that I can feel secure in getting plenty of attention? Is the food nutritious, attractive, and tasty? Will I get regular meals and snacks, so I won't ever feel too hungry? Will I be safe here? Will I be encouraged to explore and learn, to be creative, to use all of my muscles, to pretend, and to laugh? Is this place clean and attractive? Will I get to go outside often and play on different kinds of equipment? After I have played and am really tired, will there be a special place for me to rest—a spot with soft, clean sheets that only I use?

Of course, these questions are just a start. You know your own child best, and you are the person who can most fully adopt your child's perspectives and interests in selecting a child care program.

Thinking It Through

1. Think of three more questions to add to the list. Explain why they are important.
2. How can a parent try to find out about a child care center to be able to answer these questions?

A field trip gives the children a chance to have new learning experiences. *What places can you think of to take children?*

The Developing Brain

The brains of young children benefit by hearing nursery rhymes. The patterns formed by rhymes and rhythms prime them for later learning of reading and math. Working puzzles has the same benefit.

The Daily Schedule

The daily schedule is the master plan for how the children will use their time. Good schedules for young children in group settings feature a balance of active and quiet activities, small- and large-group activities, and teacher-directed and child-selected activities. Here's a sample schedule for a three-hour session:

8:30-8:45	Arrival and free play
8:45-9:00	Circle time
9:00-9:30	Small-group activities
9:30-9:45	Large-group activities
9:45-10:00	Toileting and hand-washing
10:00-10:15	Snack
10:15-10:45	Outdoor play
10:45-11:15	Learning centers
11:15-11:30	Large-group story time

A good daily schedule allows time for **transitions,** periods during which children move from one activity to the next. During a transition, the children need to conclude one activity, put their materials away, and get ready for the next activity. Always let them know a few minutes ahead of time that they will soon have to make a change. Whenever possible, use a song or a game to help children move from one place to another or from one activity to the next. For

also play in small groups. Sheera, Kyle, and Tessa are pretending they are going to the store. Large group music or movement activities are usually guided by a teacher. The group as a whole may join together in **circle time,** in which a large group sits together for such activities as show-and-tell or story reading.

Planning activities for each day will help make your work with children more successful. *What could happen if you didn't plan?*

example, you might sing a special cleanup song as you and the children put away materials after learning center time.

Writing Learning Activity Plans

A daily schedule outlines the children's day in general. The lead teacher then must plan specific things to do during each activity period. There are two types of forms that can be used to write these plans.

The first form—the planning chart—works from the daily schedule. This form lists the activities that will take place in each learning center during each period of

the day. Suppose you are preparing a one week overview based on the daily schedule on the previous page. If so, you would note which outdoor activities would take place each day and which stories you would tell during story time each day.

The second form allows you to record detailed information about each planned

Putting away is a basic rule that teaches respect for others. *Name another.*

Writing out plans ahead of time helps you think through the appropriateness of each activity. It also provides a list of everything you need so that the materials can be set up before the children arrive. Written plans give workers materials they can discuss with the children's parents. Finally, having a written plan will give you a reference source you and your co-workers can consult when it is time to start the activity.

Promoting Positive Behavior

For a classroom to function smoothly, rules need to be established for the children to follow. Child care providers also need to use positive reinforcement and act as role models. Strategies must be developed for dealing with unacceptable behavior in a safe and nurturing manner.

Establishing Classroom Rules

Young children need classroom rules, but too many rules can overwhelm them. The classroom rules should be stated in positive terms. That is, each rule should tell the children what they should do—not what they shouldn't do. Each classroom rule should also have a clear purpose. Rules should also be appropriate for the age of the children involved. The younger the child, the shorter and fewer the rules should be.

activity. On this form, you would include specific information under these headings:

- Title of the activity.
- Objective, or purpose, of the activity.
- Type of activity (for a learning center, small group, or large group).
- Materials needed.
- Procedures to be followed.
- Evaluation—a recap of the success or problems with the activities.

The form you use isn't as important as the fact that you do have written plans.

The following list shows one possible set of rules:

1. **Use your hands gently.** This discourages hitting or pushing.
2. **Walk, don't run, inside the classroom.** This prevents accidents from falls.
3. **Put materials away when you are finished.** This keeps the room well organized and allows children to find materials when they want them.
4. **Use an inside voice in the classroom.** This prevents the classroom from being too noisy.
5. **Be a friend to other people.** This builds a pleasant atmosphere.
6. **Keep your feet away from others.** This prevents injuries and falls.

Provide activities that help the children understand the rules. For example, for "use your hands gently," you might have a collection of pictures showing friendly touching and hurtful touching. By asking the children questions, you could help them understand what each type of touching feels like. Make it very clear that hurtful touching is not allowed in your classroom.

Using Positive Reinforcement

Children enjoy being recognized and rewarded with attention. They tend to repeat behaviors that are rewarded. To make this technique effective, however, you must be sincere in your response to a child's behavior. If you give only automatic or inattentive comments and praise, the children won't see them as rewards.

Caregivers can reinforce the purpose and importance of basic rules through stories and conversation.

Child care workers need to communicate with parents. *Do you think they should tell parents every time a child does something wrong? Why?*

Being a Good Role Model

In the classroom, your own behavior has a powerful influence on children. Children are more likely to do what you do—not what you say. If you want the children to use inside voices, then you must always use a quiet voice indoors. If you want them to treat each other with kindness, you must treat them and co-workers kindly.

Dealing with Misbehavior

Of course, children will from time to time behave in unacceptable ways. You need to know in advance the program's guidelines for handling such situations. The children should also understand what will happen if they behave in unacceptable ways.

In most cases, a simple statement of what you want the child to do is effective. If a child is using too loud a voice, for example, simply say, "Taylor, please use your inside voice. I can't hear well when you are shouting." In other situations, you may offer the child a choice of more acceptable activities. If a child is not playing well in the block center, you might say, "Qiuhong, you may choose to go to the dramatic play center or the art center. I can't let you stay in the block center because you are still trying to take Emilio's blocks." Notice that each example includes an explanation of why the child's behavior was unacceptable.

For some types of unacceptable behavior, a stronger response is necessary. Behavior that hurts other people or property must not be permitted at any time. Children who break this type of rule should receive an immediate and consistent response. One effective approach is to give the child a time-out. Of course, you need to continue to show that you care for the child—but that the actions aren't acceptable.

INFOLINK

Time-Out

For more about *time-out*, see Chapter 3, page 97.

SECTION 20-2 REVIEW

✔ Check Your Understanding

1. What are learning centers?
2. How can you separate learning centers from one another?
3. When should young children wash their hands? When should child care workers wash theirs?
4. Study the sample schedule in this section. Are the different activity periods long or short? Why?
5. What are transitions? How can teachers help young children feel comfortable during transition times?
6. What elements need to be listed in an activity plan?
7. How lengthy should a child care worker make any explanations about why a child is being disciplined? Why?

Putting Knowledge Into Practice

1. **Analyzing.** What makes an activity plan effective? Why does a caregiver need to look at other plans for the children to do in the same day in order to evaluate an activity plan?
2. **Applying.** Working in a group, brainstorm a list of possible rules for an early childhood classroom. Share these rules with the rest of the class and develop a class list.
3. **Observing and Participating.** Visit a child care center. Describe how attentive the adults seem to be. Do you feel the children are receiving personal, loving care? Why or why not?

Parenting With Care

Choosing Materials for the Classroom

The materials chosen in different learning centers have to be chosen carefully.

These materials can be expensive, and educators can't afford to waste money. They must meet special requirements because they will be used by many children of different ages over a long period of time.

Here are some guidelines for choosing materials for the early childhood classroom:

- Are they safe? Edges should be rounded rather than sharp. Paint must be nontoxic since children often put objects in their mouths.
  Will they withstand heavy or rough use by a group of as many as twenty children? Are the materials durable?
- Will the materials be easy to clean? This is even more important in the classroom than in the home since materials are used by many different children.
- Does the classroom have sufficient storage space for the materials? Are there storage containers available?
- Can children of different ages use the materials?
- Do the materials encourage cooperative play rather than aggressive play?
- Do the materials encourage creative play? Can they be used for more than one purpose?
- Do the materials encourage children's active play rather than passive participation? Will it hold a child's interest?
- Will children learn basic concepts while using the materials? Will the materials support program goals? Will they reinforce curriculum themes and objectives?
- Will the materials allow children to learn from their senses?

- Could both boys and girls use the materials? Are the materials free of racial, cultural, and gender stereotypes?
- Will children have fun with the materials?

Following Up

1. Why is it important for materials to support flexible play—being used for more than one purpose?

2. **Management.** Why is it important for early childhood educators to carefully manage their resources?

3. **Thinking Skills.** List the three guidelines that you think are the most important and explain your choices.

REVIEW &

Summary

✔ Babysitters take responsibility for caring for children for a short time. (Section 20-1)

✔ Caring for children requires being prepared to meet the needs of children of different ages. (Seciton 20-1)

✔ An early childhood classroom includes different learning centers and must be healthful and safe for children. (Section 20-2)

✔ The classroom should stimulate learning by children. (Section 20-2)

✔ Early childhood staff must promote positive behavior. (Section 20-2)

8. Give an example of how being involved in an activity can help children learn. (Section 20-2)

9. What information should be included on an activity plan? (Section 20-2)

10. What are the methods staff can use to teach children appropriate behavior? (Section 20-2)

Thinking Critically

1. **Diagramming.** Make a chart of important skills a child care provider should have to care for children. Put each item under the heading "Infants," "Toddlers and Preschoolers," and "Older Children."

2. **Analyzing.** Evaluate the following sequence of activities. If you think it is not effective, make changes to fix the problems: Arrival and free play; dancing; story time; outdoor play; art activities; snack; toileting and hand-washing; resting.

Reviewing the Facts

1. Why is it important for a babysitter to arrive about 20 minutes early the first time he or she works for a family? (Section 20-1)

2. What problems must a babysitter be prepared for when watching toddlers and preschoolers? (Section 20-1)

3. What can a babysitter do to get along more easily with an older child? (Section 20-1)

4. What should you do if a fire breaks out where you are babysitting? (Section 20-1)

5. What is a learning center? (Section 20-2)

6. What is the first responsibility of the staff of an early education classroom? (Section 20-2)

7. List three practices that contribute to health in the classroom. (Section 20-2)

Taking Action

1. **Making a Book.** Create a cartoon-like book or a series of posters that can teach young children the benefits of basic safety habits. *(Communication)*

2. **Easing Transitions.** Make up a song or game that you could use in an early childhood classroom to ease children in the transition from one activity to another.

CONNECTIONS

Demonstrate the song or game to others in the class and ask for suggestions to improve your idea. *(Leadership)*

Cross-Curricular Connections

1. **Language Arts.** Write a help-wanted ad that a parent might write for a babysitter. The child to be watched could be of any age from birth to eight years old. What qualities would the parent be looking for?

Workplace Connections

1. **Resources.** Make a schedule that could be used for a half-day program for three-year-olds. Be sure to vary activities aimed at different developmental areas and different ways for children to be involved.

2. **Basic Skills.** Take the role of the supervisor of an early childhood classroom. Write a memo to new staff members that explains how children can benefit from each of the learning centers in the classroom. Choose any six centers to write about.

Family and Community Connections

1. **It's in the Bag.** Make a "care provider bag" of materials you find around your home that you could bring with you on babysitting jobs to entertain the children. Bring your bag to class and explain what objects you found and why they would be effective.

2. **Checking It Out.** Suppose you were the parent searching for an early childhood classroom for your four-year-old. Create a checklist of what you would look for.

Technology Connections

1. **Internet.** Search online for information about health in early childhood classrooms. Choose one issue that you find in your research. Develop a list of procedures that could be followed in a classroom to meet the recommendations.

2. **Technology.** Search online or in the library to find out how the computer or other technology is being used in the early childhood classroom. Evaluate the uses described—what impact might these uses have on small motor skills, for instance?

APPENDIX

A basic knowledge of how the female and male reproductive systems work is a key to understanding pregnancy. Information on family planning shows methods for preventing or spacing pregnancies.

The Female Reproductive System

The female reproductive system has three functions. They are to produce and store eggs; to allow fertilization to take place; and to provide a place where the fertilized egg can grow and develop. The illustrations on page 632 show the parts of the female reproductive system and the role that each plays in these processes.

About two years after reaching puberty, a female begins to have a menstrual cycle. She will continue to have cycles for the next thirty or forty years. The average length of a menstrual cycle is 28 days, although individual women vary.

The cycle begins when an egg cell develops in the ovary. Hormones that are released into the body prepare the lining of the uterus in case the egg is fertilized. About the fourteenth day of the cycle, the mature egg is released. If fertilization does not take place, the uterus sheds its lining. It leaves the body as a bloody flow—often called a "period"—that passes through the vagina.

Females can use tampons or sanitary napkins to absorb the blood of the menstrual flow. These should be changed regularly. Using tampons may bring about a serious infection called toxic shock syndrome. Women who use tampons should change them every four or six hours to avoid this problem.

Some women use a product called a "douche" to clean the vagina during menstruation. This is not a good idea. By changing the balance of chemicals in the vagina, these products increase the chances of the women developing an infection.

If a woman notices an unusual discharge coming from the vagina, she should see a doctor. It could be the sign of an infection.

The Male Reproductive System

The male reproductive system has three functions also. It produces, stores, and transports sperm cells. The illustrations on page 633 show the parts of the male reproductive system and describes their role in these processes.

Males should avoid wearing underwear or pants that are too tight. They should also wear protective cups when they play contact sports. Males should also see a doctor if they notice any unusual discharge coming from the penis. They should also check their testicles from time to time. If they find swelling or soreness, they should see a doctor.

The Female Reproductive System

Ovaries: Each woman has two ovaries (OH-vuh-rees), which produce and store eggs. All the eggs a female will have are present at birth. Until they mature—which happens first when the female reaches puberty—they cannot be fertilized. Normally, each month one egg will mature. The ovaries also have two hormones that control the menstrual cycle.

Fallopian Tubes: Near each ovary is a fallopian tube (fuh-LOH-pee-uhn). When an egg is released by the ovary, it enters the fallopian tube. If fertilization takes place, it occurs in the fallopian tube. The fertilized egg then moves down the tube to the uterus.

Vagina: The vagina is a tube that leads from the uterus to outside the female body. When a male's sperm enters the vagina, pregnancy may occur. It is through the vagina—sometimes called the "birth canal"—that the baby must travel in childbirth.

Uterus: The uterus is the organ where the fertilized egg grows and develops.

Cervix The cervix is the opening of the uterus.

Fallopian Tube

Uterus

Ovary

Cervix

Vagina

The Male Reproductive System

Seminal Vesicles, Prostate Gland, and Cowper's Glands: The two seminal vesicles (SEM-uh-nuhl VES-uh-culs), the prostate gland, and the two Cowper's glands all produce semen (SEE-muhn), a liquid that helps nourish and transport sperm cells.

Vas Deferens: Leading from the epididymis is a tube called the vas deferens (vass DE-fuh-runz), which carries the sperm to the urethra.

Testes: Males have two testes (TES-teez), which are the organs that produce sperm. They are also called "testicles." They sit outside the body in the scrotum (SKROH-tuhm), a sac.

Urethra: The urethra (yoo-REE-thruh) is a long tube that carries urine or semen outside the body.

Epididymis: Behind each testicle is a network of tubes called the epididymis (ep-i-DID-uh-mis). These tubes store the sperm, allowing them to mature.

Penis: The penis (PEE-nis) is the external male sexual organ. The urethra is inside it.

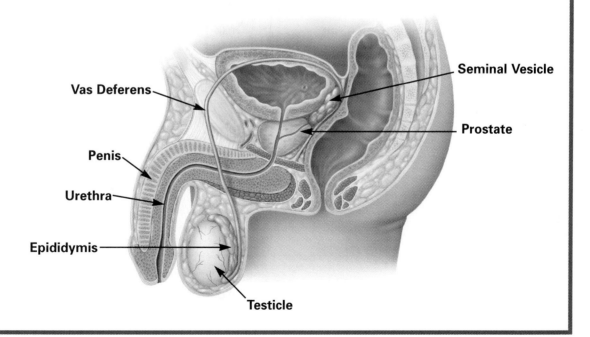

Seminal Vesicle
Prostate
Vas Deferens
Penis
Urethra
Epididymis
Testicle

Family Planning

The only sure way to prevent pregnancy is abstinence—avoiding sexual activity. There are various other methods of contraception, which help prevent pregnancy. Each has been shown to be more or less reliable.

Methods also differ in their ability to prevent sexually transmitted diseases (STDs). Abstinence is the best method for preventing STDs as well.

Most methods of family planning also have side effects. These are problems that develop among some, but not all, people who use the method. The chart below compares the different methods of family planning. It lists some of the possible side effects. Check medical reference books for complete listings of side effects.

Effectiveness is given as a percentage. A method that is 100 percent effective—such as abstinence—works all the time. If a method is 99 percent effective, there is a 1 in 100 chance that a pregnancy could result when that method is used. The higher the percentage, the greater the effectiveness of the method.

Methods of Family Planning

METHOD	EFFECTIVENESS	SIDE EFFECTS INCLUDE
Abstinence	100%	None
Contraceptive implant	99%	May cause changes in menstrual cycle and occasional spotting of blood.
Birth control pill	97-98%	May increase the risk of heart attack and, in females, breast cancer.
Intrauterine device (IUD)	95%	May cause discomfort and heavy bleeding between menstrual periods. Raises risk of complications if pregnancy does occur and of inflammation of the pelvis.
Condom used with spermicide	90%	May break, making it ineffective.
Diaphragm used with spermicide	90%	Raises risk of infections of the vagina and urinary tract. May raise the risk of toxic shock syndrome.
Cervical cap	85-90%	Raises risk of infections of the vagina. May raise the risk of toxic shock syndrome.
Contraceptive sponge	80-90%	May raise risk of toxic shock syndrome. May result in irritation of the vagina.
Spermicide	70-85%	May cause allergic reactions.
Natural family planning	53-80%	None

GLOSSARY

A

abstinence Avoiding sexual activity. (4-1)

accreditation A formal process in which the National Association for the Education of Young Children reviews a child care facility's staff, programs, and environment to see if they meet the association's strict standards. (3-3)

acne (AK-knee) A skin problem caused by excess oils. (17-1)

addiction (uh-DICK-shun) Craving a substance, such as a drug, even though it has powerful and harmful effects on the mind and body. (19-3)

adolescence (AD-uh-LES-unts) The stage of life between childhood and adulthood. (1-2)

adoption A legal process by which children enter a family they were not born into. (2-1)

age appropriate Suitable for the age and individual needs of a child. (10-2)

allergy (AL-ur-jee) An oversensitivity to one or more common substances. (18-2)

alternative birth center A facility separate from any hospital that has homelike rooms for giving birth. (6-3)

ambidextrous Able to use both hands with equal skill. (14-1)

amniocentesis (AM-knee-oh-sen-TEE-sis) A prenatal test performed by withdrawing a sample of the **amniotic fluid** surrounding an unborn baby and testing that fluid for indications of specific birth defects or other health problems. (5-3)

amniotic fluid (AM-knee-AH-tik) Liquid that surrounds and protects the developing baby in the uterus during pregnancy. (5-1)

anecdotal (AN-ek-DOE-tuhl) **record** A method of writing observations in which the observer writes down all the behaviors that have to do with one issue only. *See also* **developmental checklist, frequency count, running record.** (1-3)

anemia (ah-KNEE-mee-ah) A condition caused by lack of iron that results in poor appetite, tiredness, and weakness. (6-1)

antibodies (AN-ta-BOD-ees) Substances produced by the body to fight off germs. (18-2)

Apgar scale A rating system used to evaluate a newborn's physical condition and applied shortly after birth. (7-2)

aptitudes A person's special talents and abilities. (1-4)

articulation The ability to use clear, distinct speech. (13-2)

artificial respiration (AR-tuh-FISH-ul RES-puh-RAY-shun) A procedure for forcing air into the lungs of a person whose breathing has stopped. (18-1)

asthma (AZ-muh) A condition affecting the lungs in which air passages tighten, making it difficult to breathe. (18-2)

attachment The bond between a parent or caregiver and a child. (9-1)

attention deficit hyperactivity disorder (ADHD) A learning disability in which a person is not able to control his or her activity or concentrate for a normal length of time. (16-2)

attention span The length of time a person can concentrate on a task without getting bored. (10-1)

authoritarian style A parenting style based on the idea that children should obey their parents without question. *See also* **democratic style, permissive style.** (3-1)

authority The right to make decisions. (20-1)

axons (AKS-ons) The parts of neurons that transmit instructions from the cell body of a neuron to another neuron. *See also* **dendrites.** (8-2)

B

babysitting Caring for a child for a short time while parents are away from the home. (20-1)

baseline A **frequency count** taken before any steps are taken to change the behavior being counted. (1-3)

behavioral therapist A professional trained in helping people work through emotional problems. (19-1)

behaviors Ways of acting or responding. (1-1)

bilingual Able to speak two languages. (16-1)

birth defects Problems babies are born with which threaten their health or ability to live. (5-3)

blended family A family group that is formed when a single parent marries another person, who may or may not be a parent as well. (2-1)

bonding Forming strong emotional ties between parent and child. (7-2)

budget A spending plan used to help people set financial goals and work toward them. (6-2)

C

cardiopulmonary resuscitation (CPR) (CAR-dee-oh-POOL-muh-NER-ee ri-SUSS-uh-TAY-shun) A rescue technique used to sustain life when both breathing and the heart have stopped. (18-1)

caregivers Parents and others who take care of children. (1-1)

cause and effect The idea that one action results in another action or condition. (10-1)

cervix (SIR-viks) The lower part of the uterus. (7-1)

cesarean birth (si-ZARE-ee-uhn) The delivery of a baby by making a surgical incision in the mother's abdomen. (7-1)

child abuse The physical or emotional mistreatment of a child. (19-2)

child care center A facility in which staff provides care for children whose parents are not available during working hours. (3-3)

child development The study of how children master new skills. (1-1)

Child Development Associate (CDA) credential A document given to someone whose competency in specific areas of child care has been certified. (1-4)

childproof Taking steps to protect a child from possible dangers in the home. (10-2)

chorionic villi sampling (CORE-ee-ON-ik VI-lie) A prenatal test for specific birth defects performed by sampling small amounts of the tissue from the membrane that encases the fetus. (5-3)

chromosomes (CROW-muh-soams) Tiny threadlike particles in the nucleus of every cell. (5-2)

circle time A period in a child care facility during which a large group of children sit together for such activities as show-and-tell or story reading. (20-2)

closed adoption A type of **adoption** in which the birth parents do not know the names of the adoptive parents. *See also* **open adoption.** (4-1)

co-dependency The actions of a member of the family of a substance abuser, in which the person takes on responsibilities that the substance abuser should be fulfilling. (19-3)

colic (COL-ik) A baby's being extremely fussy every day. (9-2)

colostrum The first milk produced by a woman's breast after childbirth, which is easy to digest and rich in antibodies to protect the baby against disease. (7-2)

communicable diseases Illnesses that are easily passed from one person to another. (18-2)

conception The union of an ovum and sperm, resulting in the beginning of a pregnancy. (5-1)

concepts General categories of objects and information. (13-1)

concrete operations period Piaget's third stage of learning, during which children can think logically but still learn best from direct experience. *See also* **formal operations, preoperational period, sensorimotor period.** (10-1)

confidentiality (CON-fuh-den-shee-AL-uht-ee) Privacy. (1-3)

conformity Being like other people. (17-3)

conscience (KON-shuns) An inner sense of what is right. (3-2)

conservation The idea that an object or quantity has the same characteristics even if there is a change in how it is presented. (17-4)

contagious The period during which a **communicable disease** can be spread to another person. (18-2)

contraction The regular tightening and release of the muscle of the uterus during labor. (7-1)

convulsion A seizure or a period of unconsciousness with uncontrolled jerking or twitching of muscles. (18-1)

cooperative play The situation in which children actually play with one another. *See also* **parallel play.** (12-2)

cortex (CORE-teks) Part of the cerebrum, in the brain. (8-2)

cradle cap A skin condition of infants in which the scalp develops patches of yellowish, crusty scales. (8-4)

creativity A mental ability in which the imagination is used to produce something. (13-1)

crisis nursery Child care facilities where troubled parents can leave their children for a short time. (19-2)

D

delivery The birth of a baby. *See also* **labor.** (6-3)

democratic style A parenting style in which parents allow children some input into rules and limits put on their behavior. *See also* **authoritarian style, permissive style.** (3-1)

dendrites The parts of neurons that receive messages from other neurons. *See also* **axons.** (8-2)

deprivation The lack of an enriching environment. (3-1)

depth perception The ability to recognize that an object is three-dimensional, not flat. (8-1)

developmental checklist A method of writing observations in which the observer identifies a series of specific skills or behaviors that a child of a certain age should master and checks off those that are observed in a particular child. *See also* **anecdotal record, frequency count, running record.** (1-3)

developmentally appropriate Tasks that are suitable to a child given his or her age and interests. (11-1)

developmental task Challenge that must be met or skill developed at a particular stage of life. (1-2)

dexterity The skillful use of the hands and fingers. (11-1)

diaper rash Patches of rough, irritated skin in the diaper area. (8-4)

directed learning Learning that results from being taught. (13-1)

dominant The gene that dictates the way a trait is expressed. *See also* **gene; recessive gene**. (5-2)

dramatic play Play in which children imitate real-life situations. (16-1)

dyslexia (dis-LEKS-see-uh) A learning disability in which a person is unable to understand printed symbols in a normal way. (16-2)

E

eating disorder A behavioral problem in which people think they are fat when they really aren't and, as a result, starve themselves or eat large amounts of food at a time and then make themselves vomit. (17-1)

embryo (EM-bree-oh) The developing baby from about the third to the eighth week of pregnancy. *See also* **fetus, zygote**. (5-1)

emotional development The process of learning to recognize and express one's feelings and to establish one's identity as a unique person. (9-1)

emotional maturity Being responsible enough to consistently put someone else's needs before your own. (2-2)

empathy The ability to put oneself in another's place. (12-1)

entry-level job A position for beginners in a field, one which requires limited education and training. (1-4)

environment (in-VY-run-munt) The people, places, and things that surround and influence a person. (1-2)

extended family A family group that includes relatives other than a parent and child who live with them. (2-1)

F

failure to thrive A condition in which the baby does not grow and develop properly. (9-1)

family child care A child care situation in which an adult cares for a small number of children in his or her own home. (3-3)

family life cycle A series of stages that families live through. (2-1)

fetal alcohol effects (FEE-tuhl) A condition less severe than **fetal alcohol syndrome** that still results in damage to the developing baby caused by a pregnant woman drinking alcohol. (5-4)

fetal alcohol syndrome (FAS) (FEE-tuhl) A condition that includes physical and mental problems that result from a mother's drinking alcohol while she is pregnant. (5-4)

fetus (FEE-tuhs) The developing baby from the eighth or ninth week of pregnancy until birth. *See also* **embryo, zygote**. (5-1)

fiber A part of plants that humans cannot digest; eating it helps the digestive system work properly. (17-1)

finger plays Songs or chants with accompanying hand motions. (16-1)

fixed expenses A cost that cannot be changed, such as payments for housing, taxes, insurance, and loans. *See* **flexible expenses**. (6-2)

flammable Easily burned. (13-2)

flexible expenses A cost over which people have some control and which can be cut back if necessary, such as food, household maintenance, clothing, recreation, and similar expenses. *See* **fixed expenses**. (6-2)

fluoride A chemical that strengthens the outer coating of teeth. (14-2)

fontanels (FON-tuh-NELLS) Open spaces in a baby's head where the bones have not yet joined. (7-1)

forceps Specialized tongs made from bands of surgical steel that are molded to fit the shape of a baby's head. (7-1)

formal operations period Piaget's fourth stage of learning, during which children become capable of abstract thinking. *See also* **concrete operations, preoperational period, sensorimotor period.** (10-1)

formula A mixture of milk or milk substitute, water, and nutrients that can be fed to a baby. (6-2)

foster children Children who enter a family temporarily because they need a home until their parents can solve their problems or until the children can find a permanent adoptive home. (2-1)

fracture A break or crack in a bone. (18-1)

frequency count A method of writing observations in which the observer tallies how often a certain behavior occurs. *See also* **anecdotal record, developmental checklist, running record.** (1-3)

G

gender identity The awareness of being a boy or girl. (17-2)

gene The unit that determines inherited characteristics. (5-2)

gifted children Children who have unusual intelligence or special talent in an artistic area. (16-2)

grasp reflex The automatic response of a newborn's hand to close over anything that comes in contact with the palm. (7-3)

group identification A feeling of belonging. (14-2)

guardian Adult who takes all financial and legal responsibility for raising a child when the child's parents die. (2-1)

guidance Using firmness and understanding to help children learn to control their own behavior. (3-2)

H

hand-eye coordination The ability to move hands and fingers precisely in relation to what is seen. (8-1)

Head Start A federal government program that sets up locally run child care facilities designed to help lower-income and disadvantaged children improve their readiness for school. (3-3)

Heimlich maneuver (HIME-lick muh-NEW-vur) A technique for rescuing a person who is choking that puts pressure on the air in the body to expel an object that is blocking breathing. (18-1)

heredity (huh-RED-uht-ee) The passing on of certain characteristics from earlier generations. (1-2)

hormones Chemicals in the body that cause changes. (4-1)

hygiene Personal cleanliness. (11-2)

hypothetical (HIGH-puh-THET-uh-kal) Imagined; used to describe things that are not but could be. (17-4)

I

imitation Learning that occurs by watching and copying the actions of others. (13-1)

immunize (IM-yuh-NIZE) To protect a person from a particular disease, usually by means of giving the person a **vaccine.** (18-2)

incidental learning Learning that is not planned. (13-1)

inclusion Placing children with disabilities in regular classrooms. (19-1)

incubator A special enclosed crib used for premature babies in which the oxygen supply, temperature, and humidity can be closely controlled. (7-2)

infertility The inability to become pregnant. (5-2)

initiative Motivation to accomplish more. (15-1)

intelligence The ability to interpret or understand everyday situations and to use that experience when faced with new situations or problems. (13-1)

intelligence quotient (IQ) A number obtained by comparing a person's score on an intelligence test to the scores of other people the same age. (16-1)

interpret To find meaning in, explain, or make sense of something. (1-3)

L

labor The process by which the baby gradually moves out of the uterus into the vagina to be born. (6-3)

large motor skill An ability that depends on the use and control of the large muscles of the back, legs, shoulders, and arms. *See also* **small motor skill.** (11-1)

lay midwife A person with special training in the care of pregnant women and normal deliveries, but who does not have a nursing degree. (6-3)

learning center Areas of the early childhood classroom meant for certain types of play and learning. (20-2)

learning disability A problem in a person's mental processes that prevents him or her from learning in a normal way. (16-2)

license A document issued by a state which shows that caregivers meet health and safety standards. (3-3)

lifelong learner Person who spends his or her entire life learning new information and skills. (1-4)

M

maternity leave Time off from work that allows a women to give birth, recover, and begin to care for a new baby. (6-2)

miscarriage (MISS-care-uj) The unexpected death of a developing baby before 20 weeks of pregnancy. *See also* **stillbirth.** (5-3)

Montessori (mon-tuh-SORE-ee) **preschool** A facility for the education of children aged three to five that uses special learning materials and follows the ideas of Dr. Maria Montessori. (3-3)

moral development The process of gradually learning to base one's behavior on personal beliefs of right and wrong. (15-2)

motor skills Abilities that depend on the use and control of muscles. (8-1)

multiple intelligences Many different ways of using the mind and body to experience the world. (16-1)

myelin A waxy substance that coats **axons,** making it easier to transmit information from one neuron to another. (8-2)

N

nanny Trained worker hired by a family to provide live-in child care. (3-3)

negative reinforcement A response aimed at discouraging a child from repeating a behavior. *See also* **positive reinforcement.** (3-2)

negativism Doing the opposite of what others want, a normal behavior for a young toddler. (12-1)

neurons (NER-ons) Nerve cells. (1-2)

nontoxic Not poisonous. (18-1)

nuclear family A family group that includes a mother and father and at least one child. (2-1)

nurse-midwife A registered nurse with advanced training in normal pregnancy and birth. (6-3)

nurturing Giving a child opportunities for encouragement and enrichment and showing love, support, and concern for the child. (3-1)

O

objective Using facts, not personal feelings or prejudices, to describe things. *See also* **subjective.** (1-3)

object permanence (PURR-muh-nens) The idea that objects continue to exist even when they are out of sight. (10-1)

obstetrician (AHB-stuh-TRISH-un) A doctor who specializes in pregnancy and childbirth. (6-1)

open adoption A type of **adoption** in which birth parents are told about the adoptive parents and may even get to meet them. *See also* **closed adoption.** (4-1)

orthodontist A dental specialist who sees whether a child needs braces. (17-1)

ovum (OH-vum) Female cell, or egg, needed for reproduction. (5-1)

P

pacifier (pass-uh-FIE-uhr) A nipple attached to a plastic ring. (9-2)

parallel play The situation in which a child plays independently near, but not actually with, another child. *See also* **cooperative play.** (12-2)

paraprofessional (pare-uh-pro-FESH-uhn-uhl) A worker with education beyond high school that trains him or her for a certain field. (1-4)

parent cooperative A child care situation in which part of the care is provided by the parents of children in the program. (3-3)

parenthood The state of being a parent, which begins when one has a child by birth or adoption. (2-2)

parenting Caring for children and helping them develop. (3-1)

paternity Legal identification of a male as the father of a child. (4-1)

pediatrician A doctor who specializes in treating children. (6-2)

peer pressure The influence of people one's own age. (4-1)

peers People one's own age. (15-2)

perception (purr-SEP-shun) The ability to learn from the senses. (10-1)

permanent teeth The set of 32 teeth that replace the **primary teeth** but will not themselves be naturally replaced, which begin to appear at about six years. (14-1)

permissive style A parenting style in which parents give children a wide range of freedom, with children being able to set their own rules. *See also* **authoritarian style, democratic style.** (3-1)

phonemes The individual sounds in words. (16-1)

placenta (pluh-SEN-tuh) A tissue in the **uterus** of a pregnant woman that is rich in blood vessels and plays a role in bringing food and oxygen from the mother's body to a developing baby. (5-1)

play group A child care arrangement in which parents take turns caring for each other's children in their own homes. (3-3)

poison control center A special unit that gives advice for and treats victims of poisoning. (18-1)

positive reinforcement A response that encourages a particular behavior so it will be repeated. *See also* **negative reinforcement.** (3-2)

postnatal The period after birth. (7-2)

postpartum The time after a baby is born. (6-3)

premature Babies born before 37 weeks of development and weighing less than 5 pounds, 8 ounces (2.5 kg). (7-2)

prenatal development Physical changes that take place before a baby is born. (5-1)

preoperational period (pree-OP-ur-AY-shun-ul) Piaget's second stage of learning, during which children think about everything in terms of their own activities and what they perceive at the moment. *See also* **concrete operations, formal operations, sensorimotor period.** (10-1)

prepared childbirth A method of giving birth in which pain is reduced through the elimination of fear and the use of special conditioning exercises. (6-3)

preschool A facility that provides education programs for children aged three to five. (3-3)

primary teeth The first set of teeth that a baby gets, which usually start to appear about six or seven months of age. *See also* **permanent teeth.** (8-1)

professional A worker who has at least a degree from a four-year college or technical school in a particular field. (1-4)

proportion The size relationship between different parts of the body. (8-1)

puberty (PYOO-burr-tee) The set of changes that gives a child a physically mature body able to reproduce. (17-1)

R

recall The order of the Consumer Protection Agency to take a product off the market or bring it back to the manufacturer for needed repairs because it is not safe. (10-2)

recessive The gene that is expressed as a trait only if paired with a matching recessive gene. *See also* **dominant gene; gene.** (5-2)

reflex Instinctive, automatic response, such as sneezing or yawning. (7-3)

Rh factor A characteristic of the blood indicating the presence or absence of a certain protein. (6-1)

role model A person that someone admires and wishes to pattern his or her behavior after. (17-2)

rooming-in An arrangement in which a newborn baby stays in the mother's room in the hospital day and night. (7-2)

rooting reflex A newborn's automatic response, when touched on the lips or cheeks, of turning toward the touch and beginning to suck. (7-3)

running record A method of writing observations in which the observer writes down for a set period of time everything observed about a particular child, group, or teacher. *See also* **anecdotal record, developmental checklist, frequency count.** (1-3)

S

saturated fat Animal fat that is solid at room temperature. (17-1)

sealant Thin plastic coating applied to the teeth that prevents plaque from developing. (14-2)

self-centered People who think about their own needs and wants. (12-1)

self-concept How you see yourself. (12-1)

self-discipline Children's ability to control their own behavior, learned through **guidance.** (3-2)

self-esteem How you value yourself. (1-2)

sensorimotor period (SEN-suh-ree-MOE-tur) Piaget's first stage of learning, during which babies learn primarily through their senses and their own actions. *See also* **concrete operations, formal operations, preoperational period.** (10-1)

separation anxiety A child's fear of being away from parents, familiar caregivers, or the normal environment. (12-1)

sequence A step-by-step pattern. (1-2)

service learning A program that combines some form of community service with schoolwork. (1-4)

sexuality (SEK-shoo-AL-uht-ee) A person's view of himself or herself as a male or female. (4-1)

sexually transmitted disease (STD) An illness spread from one person to another by sexual contact. (4-1)

shaken baby syndrome A condition caused when parents severely shake a baby, which can lead to damage to the baby's brain and perhaps other problems. (8-3)

sibling rivalry Competition between brothers or sisters for parents' affection and attention. (12-1)

single-parent family A family group that includes one parent and at least one child. (2-1)

sleeper A one-piece stretchy garment with feet, meant for an infant. (8-3)

small motor skill An ability that depends on the use and control of the finer muscles of the wrists, fingers, and ankles. *See also* **large motor skill.** (11-1)

social development The process of learning to interact with others and to express oneself to others. (9-1)

socialization The process by which young children gradually learn to get along with other people, first in their own families and then in groups. (12-2)

speech-language pathologist A specialist trained to detect and correct speech problems. (13-2)

sperm Male cell needed for reproduction. (5-1)

sphincter muscles (SFINGK-tur) The muscles that control elimination. (11-2)

sprain An injury caused by sudden, violent stretching of a joint or muscle. (18-1)

startle reflex A newborn's automatic response to a loud noise or a touch on the stomach, in which the legs are thrown up, fingers spread, and arms are first extended and then brought back rapidly while the fingers close in a grasping action. (7-3)

stillbirth The death of a developing baby after 20 weeks of a pregnancy. *See also* **miscarriage.** (5-3)

stranger anxiety A baby's fear of unfamiliar people, usually expressed by crying. (9-2)

subjective Using personal opinions or feelings, rather than facts, to judge or describe things. *See also* **objective.** (1-3)

support group A group that gives people with problems a chance to explore and accept their feelings. (19-1)

surrogate A substitute. (5-2)

symbolic thinking (sim-BOL-ik) The use of words and numbers to stand for ideas. (10-1)

synapses (sin-AP-suhs) Gaps between neurons over which messages are sent between neurons. (8-2)

synthetic fiber Manufactured thread, made from chemicals rather than natural sources. (11-2)

systems Complex networks of people or objects that interact with each other. (1-4)

T

temperament A person's style of reacting to the world and relating to others. (7-3)

temper tantrums Occasions when a child releases anger or frustration by screaming, crying, kicking, pounding, and sometimes holding his or her breath. (12-1)

time-out A short period of time in which a child sits away from other people and the center of activity after he or she has misbehaved. (3-2)

toddlers Children from age one to three, so named for the unsteady steps they use when they first begin walking. (11-1)

training pants Heavy, absorbent underpants that can be worn in place of diapers. (11-2)

transition A period during which children move from one activity to the next. (20-2)

transitivity The idea that a relative relationship between two objects can extend to another object. (17-4)

trial-and-error learning Learning that takes place when a child tries several ways of solving a problem before finding one that works. (13-1)

U

ultrasound A prenatal test performed by using sound waves to make a video image of an unborn baby to check for specific health problems. (5-3)

umbilical cord (um-BILL-uh-cuhl) A long tube that connects the **placenta** to the developing baby during pregnancy; carries food and oxygen to the baby. (5-1)

uterus (UTE-uh-rus) The organ in a woman's body in which a baby develops during pregnancy. (5-1)

V

vaccine (vak-SEEN) A small amount of disease-carrying germs introduced to the body on purpose so that the body can build resistance to that disease. (18-2)

values What is important to people. (2-1)

W

weaning The process of changing from drinking from the bottle or breast to drinking from a cup. (8-3)

work-based learning A program in which students combine in-school and on-the-job learning. (1-4)

work environment The physical and social surroundings at the workplace. (1-4)

Z

zygote (ZY-goat) The fertilized egg. *See also* **embryo, fetus.** (5-1)

GLOSARIO

Los números entre paréntesis después de cada entrada indican el capítulo y sección en que se explica el término.

A

abstinence/abstinencia Evitar la actividad sexual. (4-1)

accreditation/homologación Un proceso formal en que la National Association for the Education of Young Children (Asociación Nacional para la Enseñanza de Niños Pequeños) examina el personal, los programas, y el ambiente de una guardería de niños para asegurar que mantiene el nivel de calidad que la asociación exige. (3-3)

acne/acné Un problema del cutis causado por grasa excesiva. (17-1)

addiction/adicción Ansiar una sustancia, como una droga, a pesar de que tenga malos efectos en la mente y el cuerpo. (19-3)

adolescence/adolescencia La etapa de la vida entre la niñez y la adultez. (1-2)

adoption/adopción Un proceso legal por el cual un niño se hace parte de una familia a la que no nació. (2-1)

age appropriate/apropiado para la edad Adecuado para las necesidades de un niño de cierta edad. (10-2)

allergy/alergia Sensibilidad extrema a una o más sustancias comunes. (18-2)

alternative birth center/centro de nacimiento alternativo Una instalación separada de los hospitales, con habitaciones semejantes a las de una casa para dar a luz. (6-3)

ambidextrous/ambidextro Que puede usar ambas manos con igual facilidad. (14-1)

amniocentesis/amniocentesis Una prueba prenatal en que se extrae una muestra del **líquido amniótico (amniotic fluid)** que rodea al feto para comprobar si hay indicaciones de defectos de nacimiento u otros problemas de salud. (5-3)

amniotic fluid/líquido amniótico Líquido que rodea y protege al feto en el útero durante el embarazo. (5-1)

anecdotal record/expediente anecdótico Un método de anotar observaciones en que el observador escribe todas las conductas que tienen que ver con un solo asunto. *Véase* **developmental checklist/lista de control del desarrollo infantil, frequency count/recuento de frecuencia, running record/expediente continuo.** (1-3)

anemia/anemia Una condición causada por la falta de hierro, que resulta en la falta de apetito, el cansancio y la debilidad. (6-1)

antibodies/anticuerpos Sustancias producidas por el cuerpo para combatir los gérmenes. (18-2)

Apgar scale/escala de Apgar Un sistema de evaluación para determinar la condición física de un recién nacido que se aplica a los pocos momentos de nacer. (7-2)

aptitudes/aptitudes Los talentos y habilidades especiales de una persona. (1-4)

articulation/articulación La habilidad de hablar con claridad. (13-2)

artificial respiration/respiración artificial Un procedimiento para forzar aire en los pulmones de una persona que ha dejado de respirar. (18-1)

asthma/asma Una condición que afecta los pulmones en que las vías respiratorias se contraen, haciendo difícil la respiración. (18-2)

attachment/apego El afecto entre un niño y sus padres u otra persona que lo cuida. (9-1)

attention deficit hyperactivity disorder (ADHD)/alteración hiperactiva por déficit de atención Un trastorno de aprendizaje en que una persona no puede controlar sus propias actividades o concentrarse por un período de tiempo normal. (16-2)

attention span/período de atención La cantidad de tiempo que una persona puede concentrarse en una tarea sin aburrirse. (10-1)

authoritarian style/estilo autoritario Una manera de criar a los hijos basada en la idea que los niños deben obedecer a sus padres sin hacer objeciones. *Véase* **democratic style/estilo democrático, permissive style/estilo permisivo.** (3-1)

authority/autoridad El derecho de tomar decisiones. (20-1)

axons/axones Las partes de las neuronas que transmiten instrucciones del cuerpo celular de una neurona a otra neurona. *Véase* **dendrites/dendritas.** (8-2)

B

babysitting/cuidado de niños Atender a un niño por poco tiempo mientras que los padres están fuera de casa. (20-1)

baseline/punto de referencia Un **recuento de frecuencia** tomado antes de hacer esfuerzos para cambiar la conducta que se está midiendo. (1-3)

behavioral therapist/terapeuta de la conducta Un profesional preparado para ayudar a otros a resolver sus problemas emocionales. (19-1)

behaviors/conductas Maneras de actuar y responder. (1-1)

bilingual/bilingüe Que puede hablar dos idiomas. (16-1)

birth defects/defectos de nacimiento Problemas con que nacen los niños que amenazan su salud o vida. (5-3)

blended family/familia incorporada Grupo familiar formado cuando una persona con hijos se casa con una nueva pareja que puede tener o no tener hijos. (2-1)

bonding/vinculación emocional La formación de lazos emocionales entre padres e hijos. (7-2)

budget/presupuesto Un plan de gastos que ayuda a establecer metas económicas y trabajar para lograrlas. (6-2)

C

cardiopulmonary resuscitation (CPR)/resucitación cardiopulmonar Una técnica de rescate que se usa para mantener a una persona viva cuando han parado la respiración y el corazón. (18-1)

caregivers/cuidadores Padres u otras personas que cuidan niños. (1-1)

cause and effect/causa y efecto La idea que una acción resulta en otra acción o condición. (10-1)

cervix/cerviz El cuello o parte inferior del útero. (7-1)

cesarean birth/cesárea Dar a luz a un niño por medio de una incisión quirúrgica en el vientre de la madre. (7-1)

child abuse/abuso infantil el maltrato físico o emocional de un niño. (19-2)

child care center/guardería infantil Un centro donde los empleados cuidan a niños cuyos padres están trabajando. (3-3)

child development/desarrollo infantil El estudio de cómo los niños perfeccionan nuevas habilidades. (1-1)

Child Development Associate (CDA) credential/credencial de Asociado en Desarrollo Infantil Documento que se da a una persona que ha demostrado capacidad en área particulares del cuidado infantil. (1-4)

childproof/poner a prueba de niños Tomar medidas para proteger a un niño de los peligros que se encuentran en la casa. (10-2)

chorionic villi sampling/biopsia de vellosidades coriónicas Una prueba prenatal para comprobar defectos de nacimiento particulares en que se toman pequeñas muestras del tejido que envuelve el feto. (5-3)

chromosomes/cromosomas Diminutas partículas en forma de hilos en el núcleo de todas las células. (5-2)

circle time/hora del círculo Un período de tiempo en una guardería infantil en que un grupo de niños hace un círculo y se sienta para mostrar cosas que han traído de casa, escuchar cuentos o participar en otras actividades juntos. (20-2)

closed adoption/adopción cerrada Un tipo de **adopción (adoption)** en que los padres de nacimiento no saben los nombres de los padres adoptivos. Véase **open adoption/adopción abierta.** (4-1)

co-dependency/co-dependencia Las acciones de un pariente de alguien que abusa drogas u otras sustancias para cumplir con las responsabilidades de la persona adicta. (19-3)

colic/cólico La profunda molestia que sienten algunos bebés todos los días. (9-2)

colostrum/calostro La primera leche que produce una mujer después del parto; es fácil de digerir y rica en anticuerpos que protegen al recién nacido contra enfermedades. (7-2)

communicable diseases/enfermedades contagiosas Enfermedades que se transmiten de una persona a otra fácilmente. (18-2)

conception/concepción La unión de un óvulo y un espermatozoide que resultan en el comienzo del embarazo. (5-1)

concepts/conceptos Categorías generales de objetos e información. (13-1)

concrete opertions period/período de operaciones concretas La tercera etapa de aprendizaje de Piaget, durante la cual los niños pueden pensar de manera lógica pero aún aprenden mejor de las experiencias directas. *Véase* **formal operations/operaciones formales, preoperational period/período preoperacional, sensorimotor period/período sensoriomotriz.** (10-1)

confidentiality/confidencialidad Privacidad. (1-3)

conformity/conformismo Ser igual que las demás personas. (17-3)

conscience/conciencia Un sentido interno del bien y el mal. (3-2)

conservation/conservación La idea que un objeto o cantidad mantiene las mismas características aunque se cambie su presentación. (17-4)

contagious/contagioso El período durante el cual una **enfermedad contagiosa (communicable disease)** se puede transmitir a otra persona. (18-2)

contraction/contracción El encoger y relajar con regularidad del músculo del útero durante el trabajo de parto. (7-1)

convulsion/convulsión Un espasmo violento o la pérdida de conocimiento con sacudidas incontrolables de los músculos. (18-1)

cooperative play/juego cooperativo La situación en que niños verdaderamente juegan juntos. *Véase* **parallel play/juego paralelo.** (12-2)

cortex/corteza cerebral Parte del cerebro en el encéfalo. (8-2)

cradle cap/dermatitis seborreica Una condición de la piel de niños lactantes en que secciones del cuero cabelludo desarrolla escamas amarillentas y duras. (8-4)

creativity/creatividad Una habilidad mental en que se usa la imaginación para producir algo. (13-1)

crisis nursery/guardería de crisis Centro de cuidado infantil donde los padres con problemas pueden dejar a sus hijos por un período corto de tiempo. (19-2)

D

delivery/parto El nacimiento de un niño. *Véase* **labor/trabajo de parto.** (6-3)

democratic style/estilo democrático Un estilo de criar hijos que les permite a los niños expresar ideas acerca de las reglas y límites que regulan su conducta. *Véase* **authoritarian style/ estilo autoritario, permissive style/estilo permisivo.** (3-1)

dendrites/dendritas Las partes de las neuronas que reciben los mensajes de otras neuronas. *Véase* **axons/axones.** (8-2)

deprivation/privación La falta de un ambiente enriquecedor. (3-1)

depth perception/percepción de la profundidad La habilidad de reconocer que un objeto tiene tres dimensiones y no es plano. (8-1)

developmental checklist/lista de control del desarrollo infantil Un método de anotar observaciones en que el observador identifica una serie de habilidades o conductas que un niño de cierta edad debe dominar y marca las que ha observado en un niño en particular. *Véase* **anecdotal record/expediente anecdótico, frequency count/recuento de frecuencia, running record/expediente continuo.** (1-3)

developmentally appropriate/apropiado para el desarrollo Tareas que están apropiadas para un niño de cierta edad y con ciertos intereses. (11-1)

developmental task/tarea del desarrollo Labor que hay que completar o habilidad que hay que dominar en una etapa particular de la vida. (1-2)

dexterity/destreza El uso hábil de las manos y dedos. (11-1)

diaper rash/salpullido en el área del pañal Erupción o irritación de la piel de la ingle o las nalgas. (8-4)

directed learning/aprendizaje dirigido conocimientos que son el resultado de haber sido enseñado. (13-1)

dominant/dominante El gen que dicta la manera en que se expresa una característica. *Véase* **gene/gen, recessive gene/gen recesivo.** (5-2)

dramatic play/juego dramático Juego en que los niños imitan situaciones de la vida real. (16-1)

dyslexia/dislexia Un trastorno de aprendizaje que no permite a una persona comprender de manera normal los símbolos impresos. (16-2)

E

eating disorder/trastorno alimenticio Un tipo de conducta problemática en que la persona se priva de la comida o come cantidades excesivas y después se hace vomitar porque piensa que está gorda a pesar de no estarlo. (17-1)

embryo/embrión El bebé en desarrollo entre la tercera y la octava semana del embarazo. *Véase* **fetus/feto, zygote/cigoto.** (5-1)

emotional development/desarrollo emocional El proceso de aprender a reconocer y expresar los sentimientos propios y establecer su propia identidad como persona única. (9-1)

emotional maturity/madurez emocional Ser lo responsable suficiente para continuamente poner las necesidades de otra persona antes de las propias. (2-2)

empathy/empatía La habilidad de ponerse a sí mismo en el lugar de otro. (12-1)

entry-level job/trabajo al nivel de principiante Una posición para principiantes en un campo de trabajo que requiere poca instrucción o preparación. (1-4)

environment/medio ambiente Las personas, lugares, y cosas que rodean e influencian a una persona. (1-2)

extended family/familia extensa Un grupo familiar que incluye a otros parientes, además de los padres e hijos que viven juntos. (2-1)

F

failure to thrive/falta de desarrollo Una condición en que el bebé ni crece ni se desarrolla adecuadamente. (9-1)

family child care/cuidado familiar de niños Un tipo de cuidado infantil en que un adulto cuida a un pequeño número de niños en su casa. (3-3)

family life cycle/ciclo de vida familiar Una serie de etapas por las cuales pasan las familias. (2-1)

fetal alcohol effects/efectos del alcoholismo fetal Una condición menos severa que el síndrome de alcoholismo fetal (fetal alcohol syndrome) que aún perjudica al hijo de una mujer que bebe alcohol durante el embarazo. (5-4)

fetal alcohol syndrome/síndrome de alcoholismo fetal Una condición que incluye problemas físicos y mentales que resultan del uso de alcohol por la madre durante el embarazo. (5-4)

fetus/feto El niño no nacido entre la octava o novena semana del embarazo hasta el nacimiento. *Véase* **embryo/embrión, zygote/cigoto.** (5-1)

fiber/fibra La parte de las plantas que los seres humanos no pueden digerir; comer la fibra ayuda al sistema digestivo a funcionar correctamente. (17-1)

finger plays/juegos de dedos Canciones y versos acompañados por movimientos de las manos. (16-1)

fixed expenses/gastos fijos Pagos que no se pueden cambiar, como los del alquiler de la casa, los impuestos, el seguro, y los prestamos. *Véase* **flexible expenses/gastos flexibles.** (6-2)

flammable/inflamable Que se puede quemar con facilidad. (13-2)

flexible expenses/gastos flexibles Costos sobre los cuales una persona tiene algún control, como los de la comida, el mantenimiento de la casa, la ropa, las diversiones y otros gastos semejantes. *Véase* **fixed expenses/gastos fijos.** (6-2)

fluoride/flúor Una sustancia química que fortalece la capa exterior de los dientes. (14-2)

fontanels/fontanelas Espacios en el cráneo de un bebé donde los huesos todavía no se han unido. (7-1)

forceps/fórceps Tenazas especiales hechas de bandas de acero quirúrgico moldeadas en la forma de la cabeza de un niño. (7-1)

formal operations period/período de operaciones formales La cuarta etapa de aprendizaje de Piaget, durante la cual los niños desarrollan la habilidad de pensar de manera abstracta. *Véase* **concrete operations/operaciones concretas, preopera-**

tional period/período preoperacional, sensorimotor period/período sensoriomotriz. (10-1)

formula/fórmula Una mezcla de leche o sustitutos de leche, agua y nutrientes que se le puede dar de alimento a un bebé. (6-2)

foster children/niños acogidos Niños que ingresan en una familia temporalmente porque necesitan un hogar hasta que sus padres resuelvan sus problemas o los niños encuentren una familia adoptiva permanente. (2-1)

fracture/fractura Una rotura o rajadura en un hueso. (18-1)

frequency count/recuento de frecuencia Un método de anotar observaciones en que el observador usa marcas para llevar la cuenta del número de veces que ocurre una conducta en un período de tiempo. *Véase* **anecdotal record/expediente anecdótico, developmental checklist/lista de control del desarrollo infantil, running record/expediente continuo.** (1-3)

G

gender identity/identidad sexual La conciencia de ser varón o hembra. (17-2)

gene/gen La unidad que determina las características heredadas. (5-2)

gifted children/niños dotados Niños que tienen gran inteligencia o un talento artístico especial. (16-2)

grasp reflex/reflejo de prensión La reacción automática de la mano de un recién nacido de cerrarse alrededor de cualquier cosa que la toque. (7-3)

group identification/identificación con el grupo El sentido de pertenecer. (14-2)

guardian/tutor Un adulto que toma la responsabilidad económica y legal de criar a un niño cuando los padres del niño están muertos. (2-1)

guidance/orientación El uso de firmeza y comprensión para ayudar a los niños a controlar su propia conducta. (3-2)

H

hand-eye coordination/coordinación ojo-mano La habilidad de mover las manos y dedos con precisión en relación a lo que se ve. (8-1)

Head Start/Head Start Un programa del gobierno federal que establece guarderías locales para niños de familias en desventaja o de pocos recursos para prepararlos para la escuela. (3-3)

Heimlich maneuver/maniobra de Heimlich Una técnica para salvar a una persona que se está atragantando, poniéndole presión al aire dentro del cuerpo para expulsar el objeto que bloquea la respiración. (18-1)

heredity/herencia La transferencia de ciertas características que vienen de generaciones anteriores. (1-2)

hormones/hormonas Sustancias químicas en el cuerpo que causan cambios. (4-1)

hygiene/higiene Limpieza personal. (11-2)

hypothetical/hipotético Imaginario; se usa para escribir cosas que no son pero pudieran ser. (17-4)

I

imitation/imitación El aprendizaje que ocurre al mirar y copiar las acciones de otras personas. (13-1)

immunize/inmunizar Proteger a una persona de enfermedades particulares, generalmente por medio de una **vacuna (vaccine).** (18-2)

incidental learning/aprendizaje incidental Una lección que no es planeada o intencional. (13-1)

inclusion/inclusión Introducir a niños minusválidos en las clases regulares. (19-1)

incubator/incubadora Una cuna especial cerrada, usada para los prematuros, en que el oxígeno, la temperatura y la humedad se pueden controlar con precisión. (7-2)

infertility/infertilidad La falta de capacidad para concebir hijos. (5-2)

initiative/iniciativa La motivación para llevar a cabo algo. (15-1)

intelligence/inteligencia La habilidad de interpretar o entender las situaciones de cada día y utilizar esas experiencias al enfrentar nuevas situaciones o problemas. (13-1)

intelligence quotient (IQ)/cociente intelectual El número que se obtiene al comparar la calificación de una persona en un examen de inteligencia con las calificaciones de otras personas de su edad. (16-1)

interpret/interpretar Hallar el significado, explicar o darle sentido a algo. (1-3)

L

labor/trabajo de parto El proceso mediante el cual el niño se mueve del útero a la vagina para nacer. (6-3)

large motor skill/capacidad motora de músculos mayores Una destreza que depende del uso y control de los músculos grandes de la espalda, piernas, hombros y manos. *Véase* **small motor skill/capacidad motora de músculos menores.** (11-1)

lay midwife/comadrona Una persona con instrucción especial en el cuidado de mujeres embarazadas y partos no complicados pero sin título de enfermera. (6-3)

learning center/centro de aprendizaje El área de un aula señalado para ciertos tipos de juegos o enseñanza. (20-2)

learning disability/trastorno de aprendizaje Un problema de los procesos mentales de una persona que no le permite aprender de manera normal. (16-2)

license/licencia Un documento que un estado da que demuestra que un lugar donde se cuidan niños llena los requisitos de salud y seguridad. (3-3)

lifelong learner/estudiante por vida Persona que pasa su vida entera aprendiendo nueva información y adquiriendo nuevas habilidades. (1-4)

M

maternity leave/licencia por maternidad Un período en que una mujer deja de asistir al trabajo para dar a luz, recuperarse y comenzar a cuidar a su nuevo hijo. (6-2)

miscarriage/aborto espontáneo La muerte de un feto antes de las 20 semanas de embarazo. *Véase* **stillbirth/aborto espontáneo.** (5-3)

Montessori preschool/escuela preprimaria Montessori Un colegio para la enseñanza de niños de tres a cinco años donde se usan materiales especiales y se siguen las ideas de la Dra. María Montessori. (3-3)

moral development/desarrollo moral El proceso de aprender gradualmente a basar la conducta propia en las creencias personales del bien y el mal. (15-2)

motor skills/capacidades motoras Habilidades que dependen del uso y control de los músculos. (8-1)

multiple intelligences/múltiples inteligencias Distintos modos de usar la mente y el cuerpo para conocer el mundo. (16-1)

myelin/mielina Una sustancia cerosa que cubre los **axones (axons)**, facilitando la transmisión de información de una neurona a otra. (8-2)

N

nanny/niñera Una persona instruida en el cuidado de niños empleada por una familia para vivir en su casa y atender a su hijo. (3-3)

negative reinforcement/refuerzo negativo
Una reacción que tiene como objetivo
desanimar a un niño de repetir una conducta. *Véase* **positive reinforcement/
refuerzo positivo.** (3-2)

negativism/negativismo Hacer lo contrario
de lo que quieren los demás; es conducta
normal para un niño pequeño. (12-1)

neurons/neuronas Las células del sistema
nervioso. (1-2)

nontoxic/no tóxico Que no es venenoso.
(18-1)

nuclear family/familia nuclear Un grupo
familiar que incluye madre, padre y por
lo menos un hijo. (2-1)

nurse-midwife/enfermera comadrona Una
enfermera titulada que ha cursado estudios avanzados en el embarazo normal y
el parto. (6-3)

nurturing/educar y animar Alentar y estim-
ular a un niño y mostrarle cariño, apoyo e
interés. (3-1)

O

objective/objetivo Que se basa en los
hechos y no en los sentimientos propios o
en prejuicios para describir las cosas.
Véase **subjective/subjetivo.** (1-3)

object permanence/constancia perceptiva
La idea que un objeto sigue existiendo
cuando está fuera de vista. (10-1)

obstetrician/obstetra Médico que se especializa en el embarazo y parto. (6-1)

open adoption/adopción abierta Un tipo de
adopción (adoption) en que los padres
de nacimiento están informados acerca
de los padres adoptivos y hasta los
pueden conocer. *Véase* **closed adop-
tion/adopción cerrada.** (4-1)

orthodontist/ortodoncista Un especialista
dental que determina si un niño necesita
frenos dentales. (17-1)

ovum/óvulo La célula femenina necesaria
para la reproducción. (5-1)

P

pacifier/chupete Un pezón de goma asegu-
rado a un anillo plástico. (9-2)

parallel play/juego paralelo La situación en
que un niño juega independientemente
cerca de otro niño pero no junto con él.
Véase **cooperative play/juego cooperativo.** (12-2)

paraprofessional/ayudante de profesional
Un trabajador que ha cursado estudios
después de la escuela secundaria que lo
preparan para trabajar en un campo particular. (1-4)

parent coopertive/cooperativa de padres
Una guardería infantil donde los mismos
padres participan en el cuidado de los
niños. (3-3)

parenthood/paternidad y maternidad El
estado de ser padre o madre, que comien-
za con el nacimiento o adopción de un
niño. (2-2)

parenting/criar Cuidar a los hijos y ayudar-
los a que se desarrollen. (3-1)

paternity/paternidad La identificación legal
de un hombre como el padre de un niño.
(4-1)

pediatrician/pediatra Un médico que se
especializa en el tratamiento de niños.
(6-2)

peer pressure/presión de contemporáneos
La influencia de personas de la misma
edad. (4-1)

peers/contemporáneos Personas de la
misma edad. (15-2)

perception/percepción la habilidad de
aprender por medio de los sentidos. (10-1)

permanent teeth/dientes permanentes Los
32 dientes que reemplazan los **dientes de
leche (primary teeth)** y no pueden ser

reemplazados naturalmente, que comienzan a salir alrededor de los seis años. (14-1)

permissive style/estilo permisivo Una manera de criar a los hijos en que los padres les dan gran libertad, incluyendo el derecho de establecer sus propias reglas. *Véase* **authoritarian style/estilo autoritario, democratic style/estilo democrático.** (3-1)

phonemes/fonemas Los sonidos individuales que tienen las palabras. (16-1)

placenta/placenta Un tejido en el útero de la mujer embarazada con muchos vasos sanguíneos, que ayuda a llevar alimentos y oxígeno del cuerpo de la madre al del feto. (5-1)

play group/círculo de juego Un acuerdo entre varios padres de turnarse para cuidar en sus casas a los hijos de los demás. (3-3)

poison control center/centro para el control de venenos Unidad especial que aconseja y trata a las víctimas de envenenamiento. (18-1)

positive reinforcement/refuerzo positivo Una reacción que estimula una conducta particular para que se repita. *Véase* **negative reinforcement/refuerzo negativo** (3-2)

postnatal/posnatal El período después del nacimiento. (7-2)

postpartum/posparto El período después del parto. (6-3)

premature/prematuro Niños que nacen antes de las 37 semanas de desarrollo y pesan menos de 5 libras, 8 onzas (2.5 kg). (7-2)

prenatal development/desarrollo prenatal Cambios físicos que ocurren antes de que nazca el niño. (5-1)

preoperational period/período preoperacional La segunda etapa de aprendizaje de Piaget, durante la cual los niños piensan sobre todas las cosas en términos de sus propias actividades y de lo que perciben en ese momento. *Véase* **concrete operations/operaciones concretas, formal operations/operaciones formales, sensorimotor period/período sensoriomotriz.** (10-1)

prepared childbirth/parto preparado Un método de dar a luz en que se reduce el dolor por medio de la eliminación del miedo y del uso de ejercicios de acondicionamiento especiales. (6-3)

preschool/escuela preprimaria Un establecimiento que proporciona programas de enseñanza para niños de tres a cinco años. (3-3)

primary teeth/dientes de leche Los primeros dientes que le salen a un niño y comienzan a parecer a los seis o siete meses de edad. *Véase* **permanent teeth/dientes permanentes.** (8-1)

professional/profesional Un trabajador que tiene por lo menos un título de cuatro años de estudio en un campo especializado en una universidad o escuela politécnica. (1-4)

proportion/proporción La relación en el tamaño de distintas partes del cuerpo. (8-1)

puberty/pubertad Los cambios que producen en un niño la madurez física que le permiten reproducir. (17-1)

R

recall/retirada Una orden de la Consumer Protection Agency (Agencia para la Protección del Consumidor) de quitar un producto del mercado o de devolvérselo al fabricante para que lo arregle porque es peligroso. (10-2)

recessive/recesivo El gen que expresa una característica solamente si es emparejado con otro gen que es igual. *Véase* **dominant gene/gen dominante, gene/gen.** (5-2)

reflex/reflejo Una reacción instintiva y automática, como estornudar o bostezar. (7-3)

Rh factor/factor Rh Una característica de la sangre que indica la presencia o falta de una proteína en particular. (6-1)

role model/modelo de conducta Una persona que alguien admira y cuya conducta quiere copiar. (17-2)

rooming-in/compartir el cuarto La estancia del recién nacido en el cuarto de la madre día y noche en el hospital. (7-2)

rooting reflex/reflejo de succión La reacción automática de un recién nacido de virarse y comenzar a chupar cuando le tocan los labios o la mejilla. (7-3)

running record/expediente continuo Un método de anotar observaciones en que el observador escribe todo lo que ve acerca de un niño, grupo o maestro en particular durante un período de tiempo determinado. *Véase* **anecdotal record/ expediente anecdótico, developmental checklist/lista de control del desarrollo infantil, frequency count/recuento de frecuencia.** (1-3)

S

saturated fat/grasa saturada Grasa animal que se mantiene sólida a la temperatura del medio ambiente. (17-1)

sealant/sellador Una capa de plástico fina que se aplica sobre los dientes para prevenir la placa dental. (14-2)

self-centered/egocéntricos Personas que sólo piensan en sus propias necesidades y deseos. (12-1)

self-concept/concepto propio Cómo uno se ve a sí mismo. (12-1)

self-discipline/autodisciplina La habilidad de los niños de controlar su propia conducta que se aprende por medio de la **orientación (guidance).** (3-2)

self-esteem/autoestima Cómo uno se valora a sí mismo. (1-2)

sensorimotor period/período sensoriomotriz La primera etapa de aprendizaje de Piaget, en que los bebés aprenden principalmente a través de sus sentidos y acciones. *Véase* **concrete operations/operaciones concretas, formal operations/operaciones formales, preoperational period/período preoperacional.** (10-1)

separation anxiety/ansiedad causada por separación El temor de un niño de estar separado de sus padres, cuidadores familiares o ambiente normal. (12-1)

sequence/secuencia Orden en que suceden los pasos. (1-2)

service learning/aprendizaje a través del servicio Un programa que combina algún tipo de servicio a la comunidad con el trabajo escolar. (1-4)

sexuality/sexualidad La idea que una persona tiene de sí misma como varón o hembra. (4-1)

sexually transmitted disease (STD)/enfermedad transmitida sexualmente Una enfermedad que se pasa de una persona a otra por medio del contacto sexual. (4-1)

shaken baby syndrome/síndrome del lactante sacudido Una condición causada cuando los padres agitan a un bebé violentamente, lo cual puede dañarle el cerebro y resultar en otros problemas. (8-3)

sibling rivalry/rivalidad entre hermanos Competencia entre hermanos por el afecto y atención de los padres. (12-1)

single-parent family/familia monoparental Un grupo familiar que incluye un padre y por lo menos un hijo. (2-1)

sleeper/mameluco Traje de dormir de una sola pieza que cubre los pies, para los niños pequeños. (8-3)

small motor skill/capacidad motora de músculos menores Una destreza que depende del uso y control de los músculos pequeños de las muñecas, dedos y tobillos. *Véase* **large motor skill/capacidad motora de músculos mayores.** (11-1)

social development/desarrollo social El proceso de relacionarse con otros y de comunicarles lo que uno piensa. (9-1)

socialization/socialización el proceso mediante el cual los niños pequeños gradualmente aprenden a llevarse con las demás personas, primero en sus propias familias y después en grupos. (12-2)

speech-language pathologist/patólogo del habla y lenguaje Un especialista preparado para detectar y corregir problemas del habla. (13-2)

sperm/espermatozoide Célula masculina necesaria para la reproducción. (5-1)

sphincter muscles/músculos del esfínter Los músculos que controlan la eliminación. (11-2)

sprain/torcedura Herida causada por un estirón imprevisto y violento de una articulación o músculo. (18-1)

startle reflex/reflejo de Moro La reacción automática de un recién nacido a un sonido alto o al roce de su barriga, en que extiende las piernas hacia arriba, estira los dedos y abre los brazos y después los contrae todos rápidamente y hace un puño. (7-3)

stillbirth/aborto espontáneo La muerte del feto después de las 20 semanas de embarazo. *Véase* **miscarriage/aborto espontáneo.** (5-3)

stranger anxiety/ansiedad causada por extraños El miedo que les tienen los niños pequeños a las personas desconocidas, que usualmente demuestran llorando. (9-2)

subjective/subjetivo Que se basa en los prejuicios o sentimientos propios y no en los datos al juzgar o describir las cosas. *Véase* **objective/objetivo.** (1-3)

support group/grupo de apoyo Un grupo que les da a las personas con problemas la oportunidad de explorar y aceptar sus sentimientos. (19-1)

surrogate/suplente Una sustituta. (5-2)

symbolic thinking/pensamiento simbólico El uso de palabras y números para representar ideas. (10-1)

synapses/sinapsis Espacios entre las neuronas a través de los cuales se transmiten mensajes de una neurona a otra. (8-2)

synthetic fiber/fibra sintética Hilo hecho de sustancias químicas en vez de materiales naturales. (11-2)

systems/sistemas Redes complejas de personas u objetos que actúan en conjunto. (1-4)

T

temperament/temperamento La manera en que una persona reacciona hacia el mundo y se relaciona con los demás. (7-3)

temper tantrums/rabietas Ocasiones en que un niño desata su enojo o frustración gritando, llorando, pateando, golpeando y hasta aguantando la respiración. (12-1)

time-out/tiempo muerto Un período corto de tiempo en que un niño se sienta aparte de los demás o del centro de actividades por haberse portado mal. (3-2)

toddlers/tambaleantes Niños entre uno y tres años, llamados así por la manera insegura en que andan cuando empiezan a caminar. (11-1)

training pants/calzones de entrenamiento Pantalones cortos gruesos y absorbentes que se usan en lugar de pañales. (11-2)

transition/transición Período durante el cual los niños pasan de una actividad a la próxima. (20-2)

transitivity/transitividad La idea que una relación relativa entre dos objetos se puede extender a un tercer objeto. (17-4)

trial-and-error learning/aprendizaje por ensayo y error Aprendizaje que ocurre cuando un niño prueba distintas maneras de solucionar un problema antes de encontrar la que da resultado. (13-1)

U

ultrasound/ultrasonido Una prueba prenatal que utiliza ondas de sonido para crear una imagen de vídeo de un feto para determinar si tiene problemas de salud específicos. (5-3)

umbilical cord/cordón umbilical Un tubo largo que conecta la **placenta (placenta)** con el feto durante el embarazo; le lleva alimentos y oxígeno al bebé. (5-1)

uterus/útero El órgano en el cuerpo de una mujer en que el feto se desarrolla durante el embarazo. (5-1)

V

vaccine/vacuna Una pequeña cantidad de gérmenes de una enfermedad particular que se introduce en el cuerpo para que crea resistencia a esa enfermedad. (18-2)

values/valores Lo que le es importante a una persona. (2-1)

W

weaning/destete El proceso de dejar de mamar el pecho o el biberón y comenzar a beber de un vaso. (8-3)

work-based learning/aprendizaje basado en el trabajo Un programa en que los estudiantes combinan estudio en la escuela con preparacion en el trabajo. (1-4)

work environment/entorno laboral El ambiente físico y social en el trabajo. (1-4)

Z

zygote/cigoto El óvulo fertilizado. *Véase* **embryo/embrión, fetus/feto.** (5-1)

Credits

INDEX